Lecture Notes in Computer Science   1789
Edited by G. Goos, J. Hartmanis and J. van Leeuwen

T0216629

Springer
Berlin
Heidelberg
New York
Barcelona
Hong Kong
London
Milan
Paris
Singapore
Tokyo

Benkt Wangler   Lars Bergman (Eds.)

Advanced Information Systems Engineering

12th International Conference, CAiSE 2000
Stockholm, Sweden, June 5-9, 2000
Proceedings

 Springer

Series Editors

Gerhard Goos, Karlsruhe University, Germany
Juris Hartmanis, Cornell University, NY, USA
Jan van Leeuwen, Utrecht University, The Netherlands

Volume Editors

Benkt Wangler
University of Skövde
Box 408, 541 28 Skövde, Sweden
E-mail: benkt@ida.his.se

Lars Bergman
Framkom AB
Box 1243, 164 28 Kista
E-mail: lars@framkom.se

Cataloging-in-Publication Data applied for

Die Deutsche Bibliothek - CIP-Einheitsaufnahme

Advanced information systems engineering : 12th international
conference ; proceedings / CAiSE 2000, Stockholm, Sweden, June 5 - 9,
2000. Benkt Wangler ; Lars Bergmann (ed.). - Berlin ; Heidelberg ; New
York ; Barcelona ; Hong Kong ; London ; Milan ; Paris ; Singapore ;
Tokyo : Springer, 2000
    (Lecture notes in computer science ; Vol. 1789)
    ISBN 3-540-67630-9

CR Subject Classification (1998): H.2, H.4-5, J.1, K.4.3, K.6, D.2

ISSN 0302-9743
ISBN 3-540-67630-9 Springer-Verlag Berlin Heidelberg New York

Springer-Verlag is a company in the BertelsmannSpringer publishing group.
© Springer-Verlag Berlin Heidelberg 2000
Printed in Germany

Typesetting: Camera-ready by author, data conversion by Steingraeber Satztechnik GmbH, Heidelberg
Printed on acid-free paper   SPIN: 10720034   06/3142   5 4 3 2 1 0

Preface

CAiSE 2000 was the 12th in the series of International Conferences on Advanced Information Systems Engineering. In the year 2000 the conference returned to Stockholm where it was organized the very first time. Since that year, 1989, the CAiSE conferences have developed into an important forum for the presentation and exchange of research results and practical experiences within the field of Information Systems Engineering. The objective of the CAiSE conference series is to bring together researchers and practitioners in the field of information systems engineering to meet annually in order to discuss evolving research issues and applications in this field. The CAiSE conference series also aims to provide an opportunity for young scientists to establish relationships with senior scientists in their areas of interest.

Stockholm is an important center of research and development for some of the leading IT and communications companies in Europe and indeed, in the world. In tune with this environment, a major theme of CAiSE 2000 was "information systems and services in a digitized world". This theme reflects the vast improvements in communication technology, including the increasing use of Internet and WWW, that has taken place over the last years, and that has led to better communication and easier information access in general. In addition, this development has initiated changes in the way organizations cooperate and trade. Hence, we see the formation of virtual enterprises where smaller companies collaborate to solve tasks they cannot cope with alone. It also leads to improvements in information services to people as consumers and as citizens.

For such information services in a digitized world to become really useful it is necessary that they add value to the workings of businesses and people in their daily lives. This calls for enhancements of methods and tools in order better to understand organizations and the way they interact among themselves and with people. Also, there is a need for enhanced design methods and for services that are truly value adding and that function well together with the organizations' legacy systems. As a consequence, the conference featured paper presentations, panels, and tutorials that addressed these issues from a wide range of perspectives but with a common goal. That goal was to advance the theory and practice of analyzing and designing individual but integrated information services in an organizational context.

Of the 126 papers that were received 32 papers of high academic quality were selected for presentation at the conference. The papers covered topics such as web-based information systems, workflow models and systems, analysis patterns, component-based development, enterprise application integration, data warehousing and many others. In conjunction with the conference, tutorials were given by well-known experts on topics such as component-based development, data mining, business modeling, modeling for ERP systems, and requirements engineering. A special one-day industrial track was organized with experts from industry reporting on the implementation of novel information systems architectures.

The conference was preceded by a large number of scientific workshops covering topics such as modeling methods, requirements engineering, data warehousing, agent-oriented information systems, and business process modeling. A special symposium on information systems engineering was organized in honor of Janis Bubenko Jr., on his retirement.

CAiSE 2000 was organized jointly by the Department of Computer and Systems Sciences at Stockholm University and KTH, and the Swedish Institute for Systems Development (SISU). We would like to thank all those institutions and individuals who made this conference possible: the Swedish Research Institute for Information Technology (SITI), the University of Skövde, the Electrum Foundation, the sponsors and, of course, all the participants.

March 2000   Benkt Wangler
                                                                Lars Bergman

CAiSE 2000 Conference Organization

Advisory Committee

Janis Bubenko Jr.
Kungl. Tekniska Högskolan
Stockholm
Sweden

Arne Sölvberg
The Norwegian University of Science
and Technology, Trondheim
Norway

General Chair

Eva Lindencrona
Swedish Institute for
Systems Development
Stockholm, Sweden

Programe Chair

Benkt Wangler
University of Skövde
Sweden

Organizing Chair

Lars Bergman
Swedish IT Institute
Stockholm
Sweden

Tutorials Chair

Anders G. Nilsson
Karlstad University
Sweden

Workshop and Poster Chair

Anne Persson
University of Skövde
Sweden

Organizing Committee

Birgitta Olsson
Eriks Sneiders
Janis Stirna

Programe Committee

Alex Borgida	USA	Keith G Jeffery	United Kingdom
Sjaak Brinkkemper	The Netherlands	Paul Johannesson	Sweden
Panos Constantopoulos	Greece	Hannu Kangassalo	Finland
Jan Dietz	The Netherlands	Gerti Kappel	Austria
Marcello Finger	Brazil	Karlheinz Kautz	Denmark
Marcel Franckson	France	Pasi Kuvaja	Finland
Maria Grazia Fugini	Italy	Michel Léonard	Switzerland
Janis Grundspenkis	Latvia	Frederick Lochovsky	China
Remigijus Gustas	Sweden	Peri Loucopoulos	United Kingdom
Hele-Mai Haav	Estonia	Kalle Lyytinen	Finland
Yannis Ioannidis	Greece	Neil Maiden	United Kingdom
Juhani Iivari	Finland	Salvatore March	USA
Matthias Jarke	Germany	Peter McBrien	United Kingdom

John Mylopoulos	Canada
Moira Norrie	Switzerland
Antoni Olivé	Spain
Andreas Opdahl	Norway
Maria Orlowska	Australia
Michael Papazoglou	The Netherlands
Barbara Pernici	Italy
Naveen Prakash	India
Colette Rolland	France
Matti Rossi	The Netherlands
Michael Schrefl	Australia
Timos Sellis	Greece
Amilcar Sernadas	Portugal
Keng Siau	USA
Stefano Spaccapietra	Switzerland
Alistair Sutcliffe	United Kingdom
Bernhard Thalheim	Germany
Constantinos Thanos	Italy
Yannis Vassiliou	Greece
Yair Wand	Canada
Benkt Wangler (chair)	Sweden
Tony Wasserman	USA
Roel Wieringa	The Netherlands
Jian Yang	Australia
Naoki Yonezaki	Japan
Eric Yu	Canada
Roberto Zicari	Germany

Additional Referees

Giuseppe Amato	Italy
Per Backlund	Sweden
Joseph Barjis	The Netherlands
Alistair Barros	Australia
Danny Brash	Sweden
Janis Bubenko Jr.	Sweden
Carlos Caleiro	Portugal
Fabio Casati	Italy
Donatella Castelli	Italy
Rik Eshuis	The Netherlands
L. Feng	The Netherlands
Paula Gouveia	Portugal
Shigegi Hagihara	Japan
Wilhelm Hasselbring	The Netherlands
Bart-Jan Hommes	The Netherlands
Marius Janson	USA
Prasad Jayaweera	Sri Lanka
Ingi Jonasson	Iceland
Mira K-Matsson	Sweden
Steven Kelly	Finland
Sven-Eric Lautemann	Germany
Jianguo Lu	Canada
Paul Mallens	The Netherlands
Olivera Marjanovic	Australia
Kenji Masui	Japan
Paulo Mateus	Portugal
Yoshiaki Minamisawa	Japan
Werner Obermair	Australia
S.J. Paheerathan	Sri Lanka
Anne Persson	Sweden
Guenter Preuner	Australia
Claus Priese	Germany
Jaime Ramos	Portugal
João Rasga	Portugal
Wasim Sadiq	Australia
Shazia Sadiq	Australia
Han Schouten	The Netherlands
Klaas Sikkel	The Netherlands
Cristina Sernadas	Portugal
Eriks Sneiders	Latvia
Yannis Stavrakas	Greece
Janis Stirna	Latvia
Mattias Strand	Sweden
Masato Suzuki	Japan
Eva Söderström	Sweden
Arne Sölvberg	Norway
T. Thalhammer	Australia
Dimitri Theodoratos	Greece
Juha-Pekka Tolvanen	Finland
Panos Vassiliadis	Greece
Hans Weigand	The Netherlands
Peter Werner	Germany
Maria A. Wimmer	Austria
Kenji Yamashita	Japan
Noriaki Yoshiura	Japan

Table of Contents

---

* BIO stands for Biology, Biochemistry, Biotechnology, etc.
  COM stands for Computer, Communication, Computability, Complexity, etc.

[1] Requirements Engineering

Workflow Models and Systems

Patterns and Components

Enterprise Application Integration

The Information Systems Development Process

Reuse in Information Systems Engineering

Information Systems Reengineering

Modeling Languages

Databases and Data Warehousing

Investigations into Industrial Processes

BIO / COM*: Mixing Water with Fire

Dennis Tsichritzis

GMD-German National Research Center for Information Technology
Schloss Birlinghoven, D-53754 Sankt Augustin

1. Introduction

As we have reached a new century and a new millenium it is appropriate to comment on the past and predict the future. Undoubtedly the past century was shaped by material products and industrialization. Physics and Chemistry gave the foundation for new products that changed completely the economic activity and our lives. The scientific results of the nineteenth century were expanded and applied through engineering to create an industrial society. We influenced our environment at an unprecedented scale both for the good by providing technological wonders and the bad by creating pollution and using technology for war. Will the new century be just a continuation? There are already many signs pointing to a new direction. Material goods consumption is reaching its limits. In addition, it is debatable if the world can go on indefinitely consuming as it does today. Economic expansion needs, however, new products and new markets. Sustainable development points in that direction. What will be the basis in the future for scientific and economic development? In the next sections we will argue that BIO (Biology, Biotechnology) and COM (Computer, Communication) will provide that basis not only in isolation but in combination.

It is already widely accepted that the future economic development will be based on services and not so much on material products. Terms such as Information Society and Knowledge Society point in that direction. Computers and Communications have become indispensable in our daily lives. Finally, the expansion of the Internet and the stock market valuation of its related companies show that at least the investors are betting heavily on such a future. COM related services, companies and jobs are expanding like fire.

At the same time our lives are subject to another revolution. Biology is making tremendous progress. It is chartering new territory at an unprecedented scale. Biotechnology is already delivering economically significant results. Pharmacology and medicine are already beginning to reap the benefits of our increasing ability to understand life itself. BIO is the essence, the water, of this knowledge. As the application of science and technology increasingly changes our environment it is vital to our survival and well-being for us to understand how we function ourselves.

It is perhaps controversial but not so surprising to claim that the future will be shaped by these two areas, BIO and COM. Many scientific and general articles have already discussed these issues. The discussions, however, run in parallel as if these two areas are not only independent but are somehow competing in claiming the

---

* BIO stands for Biology, Biochemistry, Biotechnology, etc.
  COM stands for Computer, Communication, Computability, Complexity, etc.

B. Wangler, L. Bergman (Eds.): CAiSE 2000, LNCS 1789, pp. 1-6, 2000
© Springer-Verlag Berlin Heidelberg 2000

future. We believe that on the contrary many future developments will be based on their combination.

At first glance everything separates these areas. Biology studies life, its diversity of material and organizational forms, their natural evolution and interdependencies. Computers and Communications are based on abstractions, completely virtual and rationally optimized to function in the artificial world of our information problems. Whereas Biology is predominantly experimental, Computer Science is more mathematical and abstract. The favorite support for materialization of information abstractions is crystalline silicon, a very dead substance known for its stability, whereas biological organisms continually reconstruct themselves from unstable molecules based on carbon. Biotechnology is using fluids, catalysts and processes. Computer Engineering is using the solid state, electronics and programming. Even in their applications they differ. The BIO economic sector and the COM sector seem to be disjoint, at least so far. Needless to say, university departments and research projects are also usually far apart. We claim that they should get close very quickly because they need each other.

2. Computational Biology (COM-BIO)

We first look at what COM can do for BIO. The customers are in Biology and Biotechnology. The methods and the tools come from computers and communications. Biology in the past, in particular molecular and developmental biology, has had to focus on unraveling specific mechanisms, small pieces from complex biological organisms and ecosystems. How the whole process was happening, and why, were problems too difficult to attack. Lately, however, a wealth of knowledge on entire organisms and processes down to the molecular level is becoming available which enable us to address the questions of how and why. There is an avalanche of facts, of structures, of models which have to be studied, organized and disseminated. In short, there is an emergence of extreme complexity which needs to be mastered. If we view computer science not in terms of technology but in terms of substance everything we do serves to master complexity. Because our computer systems have become extremely complex we introduced tools to deal with complexity. Similar tools can be used to deal with the complexity of Biological systems.

- Algorithms of different sorts can be combined to approximate and simulate complex biological phenomena.
- Data Bases of different kinds are needed to organize rapidly accumulated knowledge and to make this knowledge readily available.
- Data mining techniques can be very important.
- Visualization tools can be used to explain structures and grasp behavior.
- Modeling concepts can be applied to abstract from known facts and produce general theories.
- Communication Networks and Digital Libraries can be introduced to support the wild expansion of scientific activity and economic development.

Take as an example bioinformatics which develops algorithms for the structural analysis of proteins and molecular complexes involving proteins. These methods can be applied to two very important problems in the pharmaceutical industry. The first problem is finding appropriate target proteins for the design of new drugs. These proteins have to be selected from a large set of hundreds or thousands of proteins turned up by high-tech genomics currently being developed. The second is to find the right drug binding to a given target protein. The key to solving both problems are pattern matching methods coming from computer science and statistics and being carefully taylored to this challenging application.

Information Technology and methodology can also help to develop a Theory of Biology. If the structure of proteins are known, their interaction is explained and their cycles of metabolism understood we still need to combine all of these in some sort of abstract framework. We claim that many areas of Computer Science from Algorithms, to knowledge modeling to AI can be very useful to underpin such a theory. We hope that Computer Science can play a similar role for Biology as Mathematics plays in Physics. In return, the challenge of both new paradigms and enormous complexity will force us to develop even more and better theoretical tools. Both computer science and biology are grappling for a theory of complex design processes, and this will be essential both for future computer engineering and biotechnology.

Computer science is playing a significant role in our attempts to understand the cognitive processes of our minds. The major activity of the field of Artificial Intelligence is not to build an artificial brain but to understand the workings of intelligence and learning through the analysis of model constructs within the context of the conceivable. Computer science is also already playing a significant role in understanding the abstract self-reproducing and self-organizing nature of biological organisms. The field of Artificial Life deals with the analysis of model constructs to understand life. This approach has a tradition dating back to von Neumann. We don't strive to produce artificial life. We only hope to produce model artifacts which behave as life and which can be used to explain and predict life.

The overall hope and promise to bring biologists together with computer scientists is that using analytical and synthetical means in an interleaving, coordinated, and systematic way we may be able to sort out basic principles in the organization of living systems and the processes of life such that it covers more than one level of description. This certainly will rise the quality of theories about living systems.

If we had a Theory of Biological systems we can predict behavior. For example, from a protein solution, we can obtain its structure. From its structure we can make hypotheses about behavior. Going backward from abnormal behavior we could suggest causes and remedies.

3. Biological Computing (BIO-COM)

We turn our attention on what BIO can do for COM. The customers and the applications are in Computing and Communications. The tools and the methods come from Biology and Biotechnology. Computers and Communications evolved over the years and are currently mainly based on digital electronic technology. In the future we may need to exploit novel ways of computing using perhaps quantum, optical or biological computing. In this paper we will concentrate on biological computing which has already been demonstrated in principle.

Beginning in the early '80s, physical molecular biologists began to build machines to deal with natural information processing in biological organisms. DNA sequencing machines, DNA synthesis machines and DNA amplification machines have become widespread. Even evolution machines were constructed. In the '90s, in the quest for ever higher levels of integration and following a market pressure, such machines have migrated to a silicon technology with extensive overlaps with the electronics industry. DNA Chips with arrays of different sequences bound to the surface of wafers are an example of such an approach

Biological communicators have also been studied. Directed diffusion and signal amplification is the usual mode of biological communication at the molecular level. The directionality is achieved mainly by selective transport across membranes or selective attachment to static or dynamic structures. The global signaling starting with antibodies in the clonal response of the immune system to foreign substances provides an impressive communication network, components of which are already finding application in biotechnology (e.g. antibody chips). The role of transport proteins in cells is getting increasing attention. Cell receptors, phosphorylation cascades, electron transfer reactions and intracellular calcium waves provide further examples of complex biomolecular signaling.

If we achieve substantial progress in biological computing and communication it does not necessarily imply that we will use these technologies in the same way as modern Computers and Communications are used. We do not expect that biological computers will control elevators or that we will base Internet on biological sea communications. There are many applications in controlling biological phenomena where we see tremendous possibilities. There we can directly interface real life biological processes with artificial biological computers and communications. The applications can be endless from medicine to pollution control. We need to concentrate on the applications that nature does better and avoid those that we already know how to do well with electronic computers. It is probably a mistake to try to prove the superiority of biological computers by using them to solve complex mathematical problems. Maybe they will never be as good as their electronic counterparts.

The most interesting, influence of biological computing and communication is potentially in the areas of Theory and Programming of computers.

The Theory of Computation evolved this century in a couple of phases before settling down to its current stable version. In the beginning there was an attempt to define computability in a constructive manner. Starting with computations we know (like arithmetic) and using composition and iteration we obtained some notion of computability (primitive recursive functions). It proved to be too narrow of a scope although much of what is computed is of that kind. The widely accepted notion of computability was obtained in a different way. Models of different kinds were defined (Church, Turing, Post) and then proved to be of equal power. Church then declared in his thesis that the informal notion of computability corresponds to the formal notion defined by any of these models. Many problems were proved to be not computable in their general from. In restricted form they are computed every day. The study of algorithms gave rise to different notions of complexity in time and space. A wide class of difficult problems were defined as NP complete, that is we can compute them in reasonable time (polynomial) if we could deal with non determinism (a form of uncontrolled parallelism). Specific constrained NP complete problems are of course computed often but we still cannot handle the non determinism in general (i.e. for large problems).

Biological computing can provide other paradigms which could unsettle the current state of computability and complexity theory. First, the constructive approach did not go far enough because only limited forms of combinations were used. Biological computing offers naturally, evolution, replication, even mutation which could prove very successful. The constructive way of defining computability will get a new boost. Second, the interaction between models was strictly controlled. A Turing Machine could only work on what was on its tape. A Turing machine with so called "oracles" could do more. Biological computing offers a paradigm of a variety of unrestricted interactions which may expand the scope of what is effectively computable. The so called Heuristics which were always used to solve real problems in practice could possibly be inside the model. Third, non determinism in the form of uncontrolled parallelism is built-in in biological computing. This implies that non-determinism is not simulated but it is effectively computed. The implications can be that a host of very hard problems could be effectively computable.

The biomolecular paradigm will also influence programming. Internet programming is already far removed from early programming techniques. It is component based, running in a distributed fashion on an architecture which is not even known a priori. Biological computing programming will be even more flexible. In what ways will we be able to influence and externally control Biological Computing? We are still in the initial phases.

We can provide input (for instance in the form of biomolecular sequence libraries) in a known environment and we can read the corresponding output or send it as input to a further such processor. A stored program approach can be designed using a dataflow-like hardware architecture, produced using microstructured silicon, with the program specified by a sequence of photomasks which determine the spatial location of specific biomolecules in the dataflow architecture. Aspects of message passing and interprocess communication can also be realized in this approach but clearly we are at a very early stage in this development. The programming languages in Biological computing may be similar or very different from what we have today. Biological computing will force us to redefine our notions of programming or reactivate old ones which are not in wide use.

In these new programming paradigms replication and evolution will play a very significant role. Biomolecular systems process enormous amounts of information in parallel while mutually constructing themselves. When specific subsequences on RNA are translated to make components of the translation apparatus or polymerases which can copy RNA, we perceive a partly programmed and partly autonomous processing of sequence information to make self-assembling construction components. This is a bootstrapping process involving both hardware (molecules and reactions) and software (specific sequences and folding algorithms). A tight coupling of information processing and construction was foreseen as a vital aspect of computer science by John von Neumann. Up until recently however, the technology has caused computers to be built with a complete temporal and spatial separation of hardware construction and information processing. Now self-reproducing biomolecular systems are revealing exciting new paradigms for massively parallel, self-repairing, robust, adaptive and constructive computation which break down this distinction between hardware and software and between a computer and its execution.

Biological organisms are so perfectly adapted to their environment as a result of an iterative optimization process, rather than of directly programmed design. Evolutionary optimization is a key feature of such biomolecular information processing. Molecular evolution can be harnessed to solve large difficult problems where physical simulation in software is intractable. Biomolecular systems occuring in biological organisms have evolved sophisticated ways of selecting fleeting structural patterns, to be converted into permanent structures which themselves become triggers for further structural pattern selection. Recently this basic mechanism has been harnessed to allow artificial *in vitro* self-replicating systems to be constructed. Adleman's demonstration that externally specified optimization problems could also be programmed and solved has now encouraged an exchange of ideas between computer scientists and molecular biologists working on molecular selection systems.

4. Concluding Remarks

We claimed that not only BIO and COM will shape the next century but their mutual support and cooperation will open new perspectives for both areas. We see already a flurry of activity but we also notice many barriers.

First, Biology and Computer Science are very far apart and there are too few scientists grasping both. Second, most Research organizations are concentrating on one or the other but seldom mix both. Third, Research Budgets are usually separate and combination projects are looked with suspicion in both areas. Fourth, each area has a wild expansion and it is natural for each one to be self centered. Fifth, senior persons in both areas may recognize the tremendous possibilities but there is massive inertia in their Institutions and Societies. Finally, companies and economic sectors are far apart. Biotechnology is being pushed by the Chemical and Pharmaceutical sector while Computers and Communications have their own sector, the Information Technology economic sector.

The most severe difficulties are in terms of scientific language. The two communities talk different languages. They initially don't understand each other. It is worthwhile to overcome all these barriers, Science seems to develop faster at the boundaries of areas rather than at their core. We expect BIO / COM to expand like fire and be as essential as water. The expected results can have major economic and societal implications. Mixing water with fire will be difficult. It is, however, worthwhile.

Why Is It So Difficult to Introduce RE Research Results into Mainstream RE Practice?

Hermann Kaindl [1] and John Mylopoulos [2]

[1] Siemens AG Österreich, Geusaugasse 17
A-1030 Vienna, Austria
hermann.kaindl@siemens.at
[2] Department of Computer Science, University of Toronto, 6 King's College Road
Toronto, Ontario, Canada M5S 1A4
jm@cs.toronto.edu

1 Motivation

For quite a long time research results in requirements engineering (RE) were developed without much interaction with, or impact on, practice. In 1993 Hsia *et al.* [2] made an honest evaluation of the requirements engineering practice. Since then, some improvements have been achieved, e.g., by some applications of *usage scenarios*. Nevertheless, mainstream practice is still to use one's favourite word processor to write down mostly unstructured text in natural language, even though there exists some influential work and good experience with approaches that have used RE results in real projects (see, e.g., [1, 3]). In fact, mainstream practice deals only rudimentarily with requirements, and what is done might not even deserve to be called "engineering".

2 Goal Statement

The goal of this panel is to really understand the issue of *why* it is so difficult to introduce research results from requirements engineering into mainstream practice. The result should be a (research) agenda that helps us to bridge the gap between theory and practice and, finally, to reach the people in the trenches so that they improve the way they deal with requirements.

3 Questions Addressed

In order to achieve the stated goal, the following questions (among others) will be addressed in the panel:

B. Wangler, L. Bergman (Eds.): CAiSE 2000, LNCS 1789, pp. 7-12, 2000
© Springer-Verlag Berlin Heidelberg 2000

- What are the obstacles to applying RE research results in practice?
- Does schedule pressure in real-world industrial projects have an influence?
- Is it the fault of customers and users that they do not know (much) about RE?
- Are the people working on requirements from the software perspective aware of RE research results?
- Does installing and enforcing rigorous software-development processes help?
- How can we (as the requirements engineering community) reach people in the trenches?
- Does RE research address the real issues arising in practice?
- Are more practical methods needed?
- Is better tool support needed?
- What are the social problems involved in changing practice?
- Are practitioners satisfied with their current requirements process?
- Are practitioners searching for better ways to do requirements?
- How do the practitioners view academic research and its results?

4   Position Statements of Panel Members

Sjaak Brinkkemper (sbrinkkemper@baan.nl) Baan Company R&D

The title of this panel seems to assume that there exists an abundance of research results of the RE research community being worthwhile to be considered for implementation in the RE practice. Speaking in the position of being responsible for the world-wide implementation of requirements engineering in one of the larger packaged software companies, I have to admit that there are few results that really make a difference and should be considered. Most RE research focuses on Yet Another Specification Technique, or contains the traces of simple desktop research with toy examples and invented problems.

This leads me to rephrase of the title: "Why is it so difficult to have critical issues of the RE practice investigated in mainstream RE research?". Any requirements listing of an arbitrary IT project will contain a complex myriad of statements expressing wishes of users/customers on a hardware/software artefact to be engineered by a team. Hence structuring, understandability, and formulation to name a few, are far more important to be improved. Engineering requirements is relatively simple, their management is considerably more difficult. As high level critical issues that deserve research projects right away I mention:

- Composition and communication of large volumes of requirements,
- Base-lining and scoping for release based software development,
- Empirical investigation of real-life projects,
- Tracking and tracing from requirements to designs and code.

Janis A. Bubenko Jr (janis@dsv.su.se) Royal Institute of Technology and Stockholm University

Problems encountered in transferring academic research results in Requirements Engineering (RE) to practical applications and "colleagues in the trenches" are similar to those in transferring research results from most Informatics disciplines, such as Information Systems Development Methodologies, CASE Technologies, and Software Engineering. All these areas experience difficulties in adopting research from academia. The case for RE is perhaps even a bit harder as RE is performed not only by systems analysts and engineers, but also, increasingly, by different "stakeholders" without a professional background in Informatics.

There are, in my opinion, two basic issues:

1. We are not in agreement regarding what requirements, or approaches to requirements specifications really stand for. Some of us are heavily engaged in development of more or less formal models and languages for representing requirements. We believe that there is only one way of specifying requirements: they should be formal, consistent, and complete. Others are more engaged in developing conceptual frameworks for functional as well as non-functional requirements. Still others are more concerned with the "process" of acquiring requirements and how to guide it. In Scandinavia some researchers are interested in participatory aspects of requirements development – how to get most out of the stakeholders in the process of acquiring requirements. Business oriented requirements engineering, on the other hand, focuses on achieving a best possible fit between business goals and processes and the supporting information system.

2. We cannot tell the people in the trenches what the benefit is of applying research results (whatever they are) to practical cases. We know from literature that 50% or more of all errors are made in the requirements stage, and that it costs many times more to correct these errors in later stages of systems development. We also know that many software projects never lead to systems that are applied as originally designed. Some are even never used (but paid for). We try to tell our practitioner colleagues these figures, but it does not seem to give any effect. If we want so "sell" something to practitioners then we must be able to tell them what they will *gain* by making heavy investments in skill development and in spending more resources in the requirements phase of systems development. And we must be able to illustrate this in monetary terms.

Issue one illustrates my opinion that there is no "standard model" for requirements specifications and requirements work. However, to some extent, all aspects, formal/technical, economical, conceptual, organisational, and social must always be considered. But the degree to which specifications should be developed may vary considerably depending on a number of situational factors. We can, for instance, imagine two extreme cases, one where there is no software development support in the company (all software development is out-sourced) and one where there is a "receptive and competent" software unit next door in the corridor. In case one, if the user company wants bids for tender from alternative suppliers then this calls for detailed and complete requirements specifications. If, on the other hand, the company has a good in-house software developer, then a realistic alternative is to have an iterative process and incrementally develop requirements and a working system. Perhaps we can, in this case, even do without formal models of requirements. Clearly, there are many additional alternative combinations of situational factors such as stakeholder maturity and skills, type of system to be built, maximum cost permitted, maximum time given, etc. Each combination will give more or less different guidelines how to develop requirements.

Issue two really says that we should do more research on the "economics of requirements specification". To my knowledge no directly useful research is reported on this issue, but I may be wrong. In conclusion, our lack of concrete knowledge of what organisations can gain from applying skill and time consuming requirements approaches is one of the major obstacles of getting research results adopted by practitioners. The only way to gain more knowledge about the economics of RE is to go out in the trenches and work together with the professionals.

Barbara Farbey[1] (b.farbey@cs.ucl.ac.uk) University College London

The position adopted is that a) RE research results will only be introduced into practice if they are shown to be aligned with, and sympathetic to, the goals of the business and b) the introduction of new thinking should be seen as an organisational innovation and managed as an exercise in change management.

The problem

Organisations face a highly competitive environment with intense pressure on costs, time to market and flexibility in the face of rapidly changing requirements. The range of development choices has opened up a brave new world of kernels, components and COTS as well as outsourcing. Contemporary sourcing policy demands new skills – commercial and process management, including requirements management – but RE and requirements management are not usually institutionalised.

Software providers are under the same pressures as their customers. Incorporating new methods into a contract means justifying the extra cost and time to their customers. And to their hard-pressed staff.

Universities could form a spearhead. But they do not have the resources to tackle large systems, nor do they necessarily have the domain expertise which companies see as essential. So they lack credibility.

A way forward

... is to treat the introduction of new results as a problem in innovation and strategic change and manage the change.

To do that we need to marshal the strategic as well as the operational arguments. And we need to:

---

[1] This statement is based on experience as the industrial liaison co-ordinator of RENOIR, an EU Research Network of Excellence, Project no. 20.800.

- get senior management commitment [4],
- identify and justify costs and risks, as well as promote benefits,
- design effective reward structures for good practice,
- advertise success [4],
- leverage and optimise skills across the supply network,
- make better use of universities' core competencies – teaching and the critical imagination,
- use universities for projects that are high-risk, high-gain problems, two to five years away.

Ivar Jacobsson (ivar@rational.com) Rational Software Corp.

Requirements engineering is really not a discipline in its own but part of something larger - that larger being software engineering or systems engineering. Finding the right requirements is just one set of activities in the whole chain of activities that need to work seamlessly together: initiated by business design, and followed by design, implementation, test, etc. And all these activities need to be integrated in an iterative development process that focuses at first creating the architecture in parallel with finding most of the requirements. This is why use cases have been so successful and so universally adopted. Use cases model the business to be designed, they capture the requirements on the software (for e-business that software is the business), they drive the design of architecture and components, and they drive the testing of the developed system. They bind together the whole development work in each iteration and in the whole development project.

5 Panel Format

In order to leave sufficient time for discussions, each panel member is limited to a short position statement presentation. The written statements above already show a diversity of views, so that the panel format should enable spontaneous, interactive discussion, involving both the panel members and the audience.

Acknowledgment

We would like to thank Pei Hsia for email discussions about the topic of the proposed panel.

References

1. S. Greenspan, J. Mylopoulos, and A. Borgida. Capturing more world knowledge in the requirements specification. In *Proceedings of the Sixth International Conference on Soft-*

ware Engineering (ICSE'82), 1982, also published in Freeman and Wasserman (eds.) *Software Design Techniques*, IEEE Computer Society Press, 1983.

2. P. Hsia, A. Davis, and D. Kung. Status report: Requirements engineering. *IEEE Software*, 10(6):75–79, 1993.

3. H. Kaindl. A practical approach to combining requirements definition and object-oriented analysis. *Annals of Software Engineering*, 3:319–343, 1997.

4. Pugh, D., (1993), Understanding and Managing Organisational Change, in Maby, C. and Mayon-White, W. (eds.), *Managing Change* (2nd Edition), Paul Chapman, London.

Information about the Moderators

Hermann Kaindl is a senior consultant at Siemens AG Österreich. His research interests include software engineering, with a focus on requirements engineering; human-computer interaction as it relates to scenario-based design and hypertext; and artificial intelligence, including heuristic search and knowledge-based systems.

Dr. Kaindl received the Dipl.-Ing. in computer science in 1979 and his doctoral degree in technical science in 1981, both from the Technical University of Vienna, where he has given lecture courses since 1984 and served as an adjunct professor since 1989. He is a senior member of the IEEE, a member of AAAI, the ACM, and the International Computer Chess Association, and is on the executive board of the Austrian Society for Artificial Intelligence.

John Mylopoulos is professor of Computer Science at the University of Toronto. His research interests include conceptual modelling, requirements engineering and knowledge management.

Prof. Mylopoulos has published more than 160 refereed journal and conference proceedings papers and five edited books. He is the recipient of the first ever Outstanding Services Award given out by the Canadian AI Society (CSCSI), a co-recipient of the most influential paper award of the 1994 International Conference on Software Engineering, a fellow of the American Association for AI (AAAI) and is currently serving as elected president of the VLDB Endowment Board. The most influential paper award was earned for the paper of reference [1]. The award is given out by the ICSE PC to the paper judged ten ICSE conferences later "... to be the most outstanding and influential on subsequent work ...".

Adaptive and Dynamic Service Composition in *eFlow*

Fabio Casati, Ski Ilnicki, LiJie Jin, Vasudev Krishnamoorthy[1],
and Ming-Chien Shan

Software Technology Lab
Hewlett-Packard Laboratories, 1U-4A
1501 Page Mill Road
Palo Alto, CA, 94304
{casati,ilnicki,ljjin,shan}@hpl.hp.com

Abstract. E-Services are typically delivered point-to-point. However, the e-service environment creates the opportunity for providing *value-added, integrated services,* which are delivered by composing existing e-services. In order to enable organizations to pursue this business opportunity we have developed *eFlow*, a system that supports the specification, enactment, and management of *composite* e-services, modeled as processes that are enacted by a service process engine. Composite e-services have to cope with a highly dynamic business environment in terms of services and service providers. In addition, the increased competition forces companies to provide customized services to better satisfy the needs of every individual customer. Ideally, service processes should be able to transparently adapt to changes in the environment and to the needs of different customers with minimal or no user intervention. In addition, it should be possible to dynamically modify service process definitions in a simple and effective way to manage cases where user intervention is indeed required. In this paper we show how *eFlow* achieves these goals.

1   Introduction and Motivations

In recent years the Web has become the platform through which many companies communicate with their partners, interact with their back-end systems, and perform electronic commerce transactions. Today, organizations use the Web not only as an efficient and cost-effective way to sell products and deliver information, but also as a platform for providing *services* to businesses and individual customers. Examples of e-services include bill payment, customized on-line newspapers, or stock trading services. As Web technologies continue to improve, allowing for smaller and more powerful web servers, and as more and more appliances become web-enabled, the number and type of services that can be made available through the Internet is likely to increase at an exponential rate.

---

[1] Now with Rightworks corp., 31 N. Second St., suite 400, San Jose, CA, USA. email: vasu@rightworks.com

B. Wangler, L. Bergman (Eds.): CAiSE 2000, LNCS 1789, pp. 13-31, 2000

Today, services are typically delivered point-to-point. However, the e-service environment creates the business opportunity for providing *value-added, integrated services,* which are delivered by composing existing e-services, possibly offered by different companies. For instance, an *eMove* composite service could support customers that need to relocate, by composing truck rental, furniture shipments, address change, and airline reservation services, according to the customer's requirements.

In order to support organizations in pursuing this business opportunity we have developed *eFlow*, a platform for specifying, enacting, and monitoring composite e-services. Composite services are modeled as business processes, enacted by a service process engine. *eFlow* provides a number of features that support service process specification and management, including a powerful yet simple service composition language, events and exception handling, ACID service-level transactions, security management, and monitoring tools.

Unlike "traditional" business processes, which are mostly executed in a predictable and repetitive way, composite services delivered through the Internet have to cope with a highly dynamic environment, where new services become available on a daily basis and the number of service providers is constantly growing. In addition, the availability of many service providers from different countries increases the competition and forces companies to provide customized services to better satisfy the need of every individual customer. These two characteristics of the e-service environment impose demanding requirements on a system that supports the development and delivery of composite services.

In order to stay competitive, service providers should offer the best available service in every given moment to every specific customer. Clearly, it is unfeasible to continuously change the process to reflect changes in the business environment, since these occur too frequently and modifying a process definition is a delicate and time-consuming activity. Ideally, service processes should be able to transparently adapt to changes in the environment and to the needs of different customers with minimal or no user intervention. Furthermore, it should be possible to dynamically modify service process definition in a simple and effective way to manage cases where user intervention is required, for instance to handle major changes in the environment or to cope with unexpected exceptional situations.

This paper shows how *eFlow* supports the definition and enactment of *adaptive* and *dynamic* service processes. We illustrate how the *eFlow* model enables the specification of processes that can automatically configure themselves at run-time according to the nature and type of services available on the Internet and to the requests and needs of each individual customer. We then present the dynamic change features provided by *eFlow*, that allow a great flexibility in modifying service process instances and service process definitions, enabling changes to every aspect of a process. Since dynamic process modification is a very powerful but delicate operation, one of our main goal has been to define very simple modification semantics, so that users can have a clear understanding of the effects of a modification. Prior to applying the changes, *eFlow* will enforce *consistency rules*, to avoid run-time errors resulting from the modifications, as well as *authorization rules*, to guarantee that only authorized users perform the modifications.

2   Overview of *eFlow*

This section presents an overview of the *eFlow* process model. We only present basic concepts that are needed in order to illustrate its adaptive and dynamic features. The interested reader is referred to [5] for details about the model and the implementation.

In *eFlow*, a composite service is described as a process schema that composes other basic or composite services. A composite service is modeled by a graph (the flow structure), which defines the order of execution among the nodes in the process. The graph may include *service, decision,* and *event* nodes. Service nodes represent the invocation of a basic or composite service; decision nodes specify the alternatives and rules controlling the execution flow, while event nodes enable service processes to send and receive several types of events. Arcs in the graph may be labeled with transition predicates defined over process data, meaning that as a node is completed, nodes connected to outgoing arcs are executed only if the corresponding transition predicate evaluates to true. A *service process instance* is an enactment of a process schema. The same service process may be instantiated several times, and several instances may be concurrently running.

Fig. 1 shows a simple graph describing a composite service that helps customers in organizing an award ceremony. In the figures, rounded boxes represent invocations of basic or composite services, filled-in circles represent the starting and ending point of the process, while horizontal bars are one of *eFlow* decision node types, and are used to specify parallel invocation of services and synchronization after parallel service executions.

The semantics of the schema is the following: when a new instance is started, service node *Data Collection* gathers information regarding the customer and his/her preferences and needs. Then, the *Restaurant Reservation* service is invoked, in order to book the restaurant and select the meals for the banquet. This node is executed first, since the characteristics of the selected restaurant (e.g., its location and the number of seats) affect the remainder of the service execution, i.e., the organization of the ceremony. Then, several services are invoked in parallel: the A*dvertisement* service prepares a marketing campaign to advertise the ceremony, the *Invitation* service proposes a choice of several types of invitation cards and delivers them to the specified special guests, while the *Registration* service handles guest registrations and payments. Finally, the *Billing* service is invoked in order to present a unified bill to the organizing customer. All services can be either basic services (possibly provided by different organizations) or composite services, specified by *eFlow* processes.

Service nodes can access and modify data included in a *case packet*. Each process instance has a local copy of the case packet, and the *eFlow* engine controls access to these data. The specification of each service node includes the definition of which data the node is authorized to read or to modify.

The *eFlow* model also includes the notion of *transactional regions*. A transactional region identifies a portion of the process graph that should be executed in an atomic fashion. If for any reason the part of the process identified by the transactional region cannot be successfully completed, then all running services in the region are aborted and completed ones are compensated, by executing a service-specific compensating action. Compensating actions may be defined for each service or may be defined at the region level. For instance, by enclosing the Advertisement, Registration, and Invitation services in a transactional region, and by providing compensating actions for each of these services (or one compensating action at the region level), we are guaranteed that either all of the services are executed, or none is.

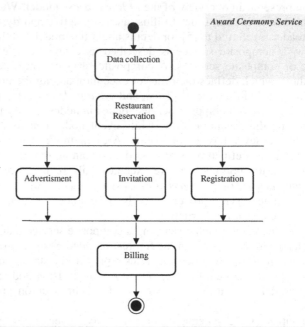

Fig. 1. Ceremony service process definition

Transactional regions may also include the specification of different isolation modes, that prevent data read or modified by nodes in the regions to be accessed by services that are outside the transactional region.

Process instances are enacted by the *eFlow engine*. The main function of the engine is to process messages notifying completion status of service nodes, by updating the value of case packet variables accessed by the service node and by subsequently scheduling the next node to be activated in the instance, according to the process definition. The engine then contacts the service broker in order to discover the actual service (and service provider) that can fulfill the requests specified in the service node definition, and eventually contacts the provider in order to execute the service.

The engine also processes *events* (either detected by the *eFlow* event monitor or notified by external event managers), by delivering them to the requesting event nodes. Notifications of occurred events and of service node completions are inserted into two separate transactional, First-in-First-Out queues (see Fig. 2). The engine extracts elements from the queues and processes them one by one. *eFlow* does not specifies any priority between the queues, but it does guarantee that every element in the queues is eventually processed. Finally, the engine logs every event related to process instance executions (to enable process monitoring, compensation, and to support dynamic process modifications) and ensures process integrity by enforcing transactional semantics and by compensating nodes executed within transactional regions in case of failures.

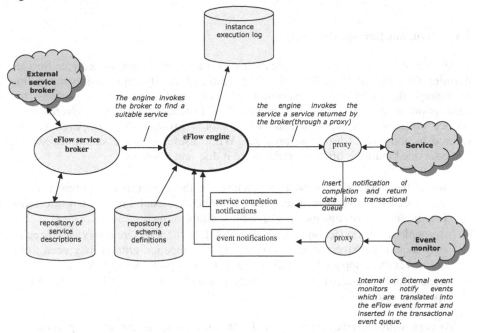

Fig. 2. The eFlow engine processes events and notifications of service completions in order to schedule service node executions

Like most Internet-based services, the *Award Ceremony* service provided by the *OneStopShop* company is executed in a highly dynamic environment. For instance, providers will continue to improve their e-services, and new providers may enter the market while some of the existing ones may cease their business. In addition, new types of e-services that can support the organization of an award ceremony may become available, such as renting of mega-screens and cameras, live broadcast of the ceremony over the Internet, or selection of trained personnel such as an anchorman. In the remainder of the paper we will show how *eFlow* addresses these challenges in order to allow service designer to provide composite services that naturally adapt to changes in the environment with minimal user intervention, that can be customized to fit the needs of every customer, and that are able to cope with unexpected exceptional situations.

3   Adaptive Service Processes

In order to manage and even take advantage of the frequent changes in the environment, service processes need to be *adaptive*, i.e., capable of adjusting themselves to changes in the environmental conditions with minimal or no manual intervention. *eFlow* provides several features and constructs to achieve this goal.

These include *dynamic service discovery*, *multiservice nodes*, and *generic nodes*. In the following we present an overview of these features.

3.1   Dynamic Service Discovery

A service node represents the invocation of a basic or composite service. Besides defining the data that the node is allowed to read and modify, and possibly a deadline to manage delays in service execution, a service node specification includes the description of the service to be invoked. For instance, within the *Advertisement* service node, we may specify that *eFlow* should invoke the *e-campaign* service offered by the *GreatAdvert.com* provider. While useful in some situations, such a static service binding is often too rigid, since it does not allow to:

–   select the appropriate service depending on the customer's requirements: for instance, some customers may prefer a low-cost e-mail campaign, while other may prefer advertisements via TV, radio stations, or web sites;
–   decouple service selection from the process definition: different service processes may require an advertisement service, and the selection criteria may need to be defined at the company level rather than at the composite service level;
–   dynamically discover the best currently available service that fits the need of a specific customer.

To cope with the characteristics of the Internet environment, *eFlow* provides an open and dynamic approach to service selection. The service node includes the specification of a *service selection rule*, which can have several input parameters (defined by references to workflow variables). When a service node is started, the *eFlow* engine invokes a *service broker* that will execute the specified rule and return the appropriate service. Service selection rules are defined in a service broker-specific language, such as XQL if e"speak [4] is used as the service broker.

eFlow only requires that the rule returns an XML document which includes the definition of input and output data, the URI used to contact the service, billing and payment information, and a priority value used to select a specific service when several services are returned by the rule (choice among services with the same priority is non deterministic). Mapping between service node input/output data and the parameters of the invoked service is performed by a *mapping function*, specified as a set of string pairs `<case packet variable name, service variable name>`. A mapping function must be defined for a <service node, service description> pair before the service can be invoked in the context of the service node.

eFlow users can replace the default broker and plug-in the service broker that best fits their needs. Plugged-in brokers are not even required to access the service repository: they can dynamically discover services by contacting other external brokers or service advertisement facility, in order to get the most up to date information about available services and their characteristics.

Service selection rules will be then defined in the language supported by that broker, and can include arbitrary service selection policies. Plugged-in brokers must either present to the engine the same (simple) interface of the default one, or an adapter must be interposed between the engine and the broker to map requests and responses. In addition, if service brokers dynamically discover services not stored in the service description repository, they must also return a mapping function that allows the mapping of service node input/output data to service parameters.

3.2 Multiservice Nodes

In some composite service processes there is the need of invoking multiple, parallel instances of the same type of service. For instance, a restaurant reservation brokering service may request rates and availability to several restaurants that provide on-line access to these information.

In order to allow the specification of these kinds of process semantics, *eFlow* includes the notion of *multiservice* node. The multiservice node is a particular kind of node that allows for multiple, parallel activation of the same service node.

The number of service nodes to be activated is determined at run time in one of the following ways:

1. It can be determined by the number of service providers able to provide a given service. For instance, for the award ceremony service, we may want to contact all restaurant in the San Francisco Bay Area that can host a specified number of guests.
2. It can be equal to the number of elements in a case packet variable of type list. In this case each service node instance receives one and only one of the list items as input parameter. The value of such item will affect service selection and execution. For instance, a list may include a set of customers of different nationalities for which we want to check their credit history. The number of service nodes that will be instantiated within the multiservice node will be equal to the number of customers, and each node will focus on one customer. A service selection rule will be executed for each service node to be activated; the rule can have the customer's data as input parameter, in order to select the appropriate credit check service for each customer, for instance depending on the customer's nationality.

An important part of a multiservice is the specification of when the multiservice can be considered completed and the flow can proceed with the successor service node. In most cases, the flow can proceed only when all invoked services have been completed. However, in other cases, there is no need to wait for all service instances to be completed, since the multiservice goal may have already been achieved before. For instance, suppose that we want to verify a customer's credit with several agencies: if our acceptance criteria is that all agencies must give a positive judgment for the customer to be accepted, then as soon as one agency gives a negative opinion we can proceed with service execution, without waiting for the completion of the other services, which may be canceled. The multiservice termination is specified by a condition, checked every time one of its service nodes terminate. If the condition holds, then the successor of the multiservice is activated and services in execution are canceled. An example of termination condition for the credit check example could be `Rejections.length>0`, where Rejections is a variable of type `ListOf (String)`, and length is an attribute common to every list variable that contains the number of elements in the list. Fig. 3 shows a sample specification of a multiservice node in *eFlow*. The specification includes the reference to the service node to be instantiated (multiple times) as part of the multiservice node, as well as the activation and termination conditions.

```
<MULTISERVICE_NODE id="check_customers_credit">
      <NAME> Check Customers' credit </NAME>
      <SERVICE_NODE id="check_single_customer_credit" />
      <DESCRIPTION>  Multiservice node that checks the credit
                     history of several customers in parallel
      </DESCRIPTION>
      <ACTIVATION mode="by_variable" varref="customers_list" />
      <TERMINATION> rejections.length>0 </TERMINATION>
</MULTISERVICE_NODE>
```

Fig. 3. Specification of a multiservice node in *eFlow*

3.3   Dynamic Service Node Creation

An important requirement for providers of Internet-based services is the ability of providing personalized services, to better satisfy the needs of every individual customer.

While the service process depicted in Fig. 1 may be suited for some customer, other customers might need additional services, such as rental of video/audio equipment or the hiring of trained personnel to work with such equipment. At the same time, some customers may not need the services offered by the *Award Ceremony* service process. For instance, they may not need an advertisement service or they may provide for it by themselves. Clearly, it is practically unfeasible to foresee all possible combinations of services which may be needed by each customer and to define a process for each potential type of customer. Besides, this would imply a very high maintenance cost, especially in the e-service environment where new types of services become available on a daily basis.

To cope with these demanding needs, *eFlow* supports the dynamic creation of service process definitions by including in its model the notion of *generic service node*. Unlike ordinary service nodes, generic nodes are not statically bound or limited to a specific set of services. Instead, they include a configuration parameter that can be set with a list of actual service nodes either at process instantiation time (through the process instance input parameters) or at runtime. The parameter is a variable of type ListOf(Service_Node). The specified services will be executed in parallel or sequentially depending on an *executionMode* attribute of the generic service node.

Generic nodes are resolved each time they are activated, in order to allow maximum flexibility and to cope with processes executed in highly dynamic environments. For instance, if the generic node is within a loop, then its configuration parameters can be modified within the loop, and the node can be resolved into different ordinary service nodes for each loop of the execution. Notice that generic nodes are different from multiservice nodes: multiservice nodes model the activation of a dynamically determined number of instances of the *same* service node, while generic nodes allow the dynamic selection of different service nodes.

```
<GENERIC_NODE id="award_ceremony_services">
  <NAME> Award Ceremony Services </NAME>
  <SERVICE_NODE_POOL> Ceremony Service Pool </SERVICE_NODE_POOL>
  <DESCRIPTION> Placeholder for service nodes related
                to a ceremony service,to be executed in parallel
  </DESCRIPTION>
  <SERVICE_SELECTION_VAR> SelectedServices</SERVICE_SELECTION_VAR>
  <EXECUTION_MODE mode="parallel" />
</GENERIC NODE>
```

Fig. 4. Sample XML description of a generic service node in *eFlow*

4   Dynamic Service Process Modifications

While adaptive processes considerably reduce the need for human intervention in managing and maintaining process definitions, there may still be cases in which process schemas need to be modified, or in which actions need to be taken on running process instances to modify their course. Process modifications may be needed to handle unexpected exceptional situations, to incorporate new laws or new business policies, to improve the process, or to correct errors or deficiencies in the current definition. We distinguish between two types of service process modifications:

– *Ad-hoc changes* are modifications applied to a single running service process instance. They are typically needed to manage exceptional situations that are not expected to occur again, such as the unavailability of a restaurant that had been booked for a ceremony.

– *Bulk changes* refer to modifications collectively applied to a subset (or to all) the running instances of a service process. For instance, suppose that an advertisement company on which many ceremony advertisement campaigns relied upon goes out of business. This situation can affect many instances, and it is practically unfeasible to separately modify each single instance. Bulk changes may also be needed when a new, improved version of a process is defined. If, for instance, a new law forces a modification of a process, then running instances will need to respect the new constraints as well.

4.1   Ad-hoc Changes

Ad-hoc changes are modifications applied to a single, running process instance. *eFlow* allows two types of ad-hoc changes: modifications of the process schema and modifications of the process instance *state*. In the remainder of this section we show how *eFlow* supports both type of changes.

Ad-hoc Changes to the Process Schema
eFlow allows authorized users to modify the schema followed by a given service process instance. The modifications are applied by first defining a new schema (usually by modifying the current one) and by then *migrating* the instance from its current schema (called *source* schema) to the newly defined one (called *destination*

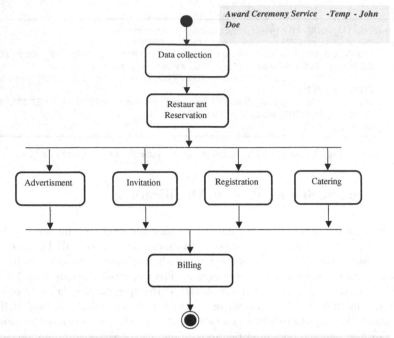

Fig. 5. Ad-hoc process definition to handle the request by customer John Doe

schema). For instance, suppose that a customer of *OneStopShop*, John Doe, is accessing a restaurant reservation service within an Award Ceremony process; John found a restaurant, *Chez Jaques,* that fully satisfies his needs in terms of number of seats, location, and atmosphere, but that does not serve food of satisfactory quality. John then asks *OneStopShop* to provide him a catering service, so that he can rent only the place and separately arrange for the food. Since John is a good customer and the company wants to keep his business, the process responsible decides to satisfy his request and modify the process definition (for this particular instance only) by adding a catering service, as depicted in Fig. 5.

Authorized users can modify every aspect of a schema, including the flow structure, the definition of service, decision, and event nodes, process data, and even transactional regions. *eFlow* only verifies that *behavioral consistency* is respected when migrating an instance to a destination schema (i.e., that instance migration does not generate run-time errors and that transactional semantics can be enforced).

Case migration is a very delicate operation, since it allows changing the rules of the game while it is in progress. Hence, our main design goal has been to define a very simple migration semantics, so that users can easily and clearly understand the behavior of the instance after the modifications have been applied, and avoid the risk of unexpected and undesired effects. In the following we describe how *eFlow* manages and performs instance migrations.

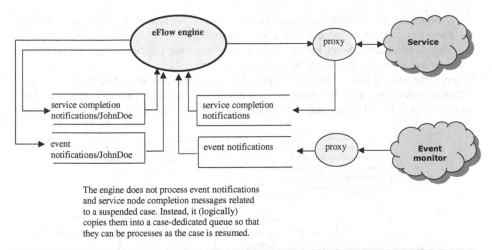

The engine does not process event notifications
and service node completion messages related
to a suspended case. Instead, it (logically)
copies them into a case-dedicated queue so that
they can be processes as the case is resumed.

Fig. 6. Events and notifications related to suspended instances are not processed, but are placed in a separate queue

Case migration operations

Case migrations are performed by a suitable *eFlow* module, called *migration manager*. The following operations are performed in order to migrate an instance from a schema to another:

1. An authorized user accesses the migration manager and identifies the instance to be migrated as well as the destination schema (details on user authorizations are provided in section 4.3). The destination schema must have been previously defined, either from scratch or by modifying the one being followed by the instance to be migrated.

2. The migration manager notifies to the *eFlow* engine that instance execution (for the process instance to be migrated) should be suspended. When a process instance is suspended, running services are allowed to complete. However, the engine does not schedule any new service and does not deliver events. When the engine processes a service completion notification related to a service node of the suspended instance, it puts this notification into an ad-hoc, temporary queue maintained for the suspended instance. The notification will be processed when instance execution is resumed. Similarly, events to be delivered to the suspended instance are also placed in a different logical queue (see Fig. 6), and will be delivered as instance execution is resumed. An instance can only be suspended when the engine is not processing messages related to it: in fact, the sequence of operations performed by the engine to process events or service node completion messages and to activate subsequent nodes is atomic.

3. The migration manager verifies that the migration preserves behavioral consistency.

4a. If behavioral consistency is preserved, then the migration manager builds an execution state for the instance in the new schema (details are provided below).

4b. If the instance cannot be migrated, the user is notified of the reason that does not allow the migration and is asked to modify the destination schema (or to indicate a different destination schema). Steps 1 to 4 will then be repeated. In the meantime, instance execution remains suspended.

5. The migration manager informs *eFlow* that instance execution can be resumed, now according to the destination schema.

At any time during this sequence of operations the user can abort the migration, and instance execution will be resumed according to the old process schema. The operations performed by the migration manager are summarized in Fig. 7.

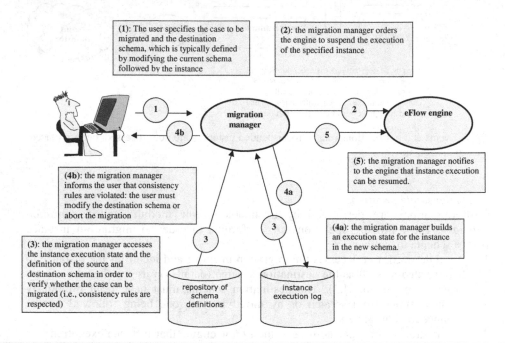

Fig. 7. Sequence of operations performed by the migration manager when migrating an instance

Consistency rules

An instance can be migrated from a version to another only if *behavioral consistency* is preserved. Behavioral consistency implies that the migration does not result in run-time errors or non-deterministic behaviors. In order to guarantee behavioral consistency, *eFlow* enforces the following rules:

1. Each service or event node that is active when the instance is suspended must be present in the destination schema. This rule is necessary since it allows the definition of an execution state for the instance in the new schema, and in particular the definition of which nodes should be set to the *active* state when execution is resumed, as explained below. In addition, it allows the engine to know how to correctly process completion messages related to those running services that will eventually be received. While the definition of active service nodes can differ from the one in the source schema (e.g., they may have different input data or different deadlines), their *write list* must be the same, since it is

expected that the running nodes will actually try to modify the value of those variables.

2. If a variable in the destination schema is also present in the source schema, then it must be of the same type. This rule is needed since variables will keep their current value after migration, and therefore the types in the source and destination schema must be the same.

3. Transactional regions not present in the source schema must not include any node which is part of the source schema and which is active or completed.

4. If a transactional region with the same identifier is present both in the source and destination schema, and the region was active at migration time, then:

    a. The isolation properties of these transactional regions must be the same.

    b. No node in the region of the destination schema should read (write) variables which are not also read (written) by at least one node of the same transactional region in the source schema. The only allowed exception is when the newly introduced variable is only used within the region.

    c. The region should not be extended "in the past", i.e., it should not include nodes that are also in the source schema, that have already been executed, and that are not part of the region in the source schema.

    Rules related to transactional regions are necessary since *eFlow* acquires the read and write locks necessary for enforcing the specified isolation mode at the start of the transactional region.

Migration semantics

The essence of the migration process consists in building an *execution state* for the instance in the new schema, and then in resuming instance execution. An execution state is formed by the value of the case packet variables and by the execution state of all service and event nodes in the instance. The values of case packet variables are set as follows:

- Variables in the destination schema that are also present in the source schema keep the value they had in the case packet of the migrated instance.

- Variables in the destination schema that are not present in the source schema are initialized with their default value (or are left undefined if no default value was provided).

The execution state of service and event nodes is defined as follows:

- Nodes of the destination schema that are also present in the source schema are initialized with the same execution state they had in the migrated instance (e.g., not started, active, completed, failed, canceled, timed out).

- Nodes of the destination schema that are not present in the source schema are initialized to the *not started* state.

After the instance state has been reconstructed, the migration is completed. The migration manager will then inform the engine that instance execution can be resumed. The *eFlow* engine then processes all events and all service completion messages included in the event and service completion queues that were created to manage instance suspension. Elements in these queues are processed with the same semantics used to process elements in the standard queues. After all elements included in both queues have been processed, the engine discards these queues and resume normal operations, that is, it resumes processing of the standard queues.

Modifications to the Process State

Besides changes to the process schema, authorized users can perform the following operations on an instance in execution:

- Change the value of case packet variables.
- Initiate the rollback of a process region or of the entire process.
- Terminate the process.
- Reassign a node to a different service: the running service is canceled, and the one specified by the user is invoked.

These actions are performed through the *service operation monitor* component of *eFlow*, and do not require instance suspension.

4.2   Bulk Changes

Bulk changes handle exceptional situations that affect many instances of the same process. Instead of handling running instances on a case-by-case basis, *eFlow* allows authorized users to apply changes to sets of instances that have common properties. Modifications are introduced by specifying one or more destination schemas and by defining which set of instances should be migrated to each schema. For instance, suppose that *OneStopShop* decides to provide, as a bonus, a security service for all ceremonies that involve more than 100 guests. To perform this, a new service process is defined, by modifying the *Award Ceremony* one, in order to include a security personnel service, as shown in Fig. 8.

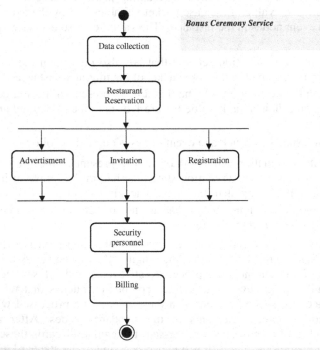

Fig. 8. Modified Award Ceremony service, now including a security service

Next, the service process responsible can migrate all running instances (related to a Ceremony service that involves more than 100 guests) to the newly defined one. Migrations are defined by means of a simple, rule-based language. A migration rule identifies a subset of the running instances of a given process and specifies the schema to which instances in this subset should be migrated. Rules have the form `IF <condition> THEN MIGRATE TO <schema>`. The condition is a predicate over service process data and service process execution state that identifies a subset of the running instances, while `<schema>` denotes the destination schema. Instances whose state does not fulfill the migration condition will proceed with the same schema. An example of migration rule is: `IF (guests>100) THEN MIGRATE TO "Bonus_Ceremony_Service"`.

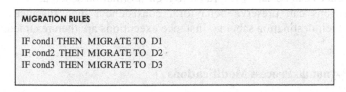

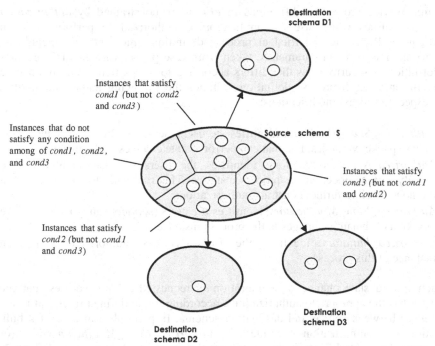

Fig. 9. Bulk migration: instances are migrated to different destination schemas depending on migration rules

The set of rules must define a partitioning over the set of active instances, so that each instance is migrated to one schema at most. Instances that do not satisfy any rule condition are not migrated. Fig. 9 exemplifies bulk migration. The sequence of operations performed in bulk migration is as follows:

1. The user defines, compiles, and checks in the migration rules. All destination schemas referred to by migration rules must have been previously defined.
2. *eFlow* suspends *all* running instances of the process.
3. *eFlow* verifies that the migration rules actually define a partition over the set of running instances. If the state of an instance satisfies more that one migration condition, the user is asked to revise the rules or abort the migration.
4. *eFlow* verifies that each instance can be migrated to the specified destination version of the process schema, i.e., it checks that behavioral consistency is preserved. In addition, it checks that the user who started the migration has the required authorizations to migrate each of the selected instances. Due to the delicacy of a bulk migration operation, *eFlow* does not perform any migration until all instances can be safely migrated to their destination schema.
5. If all migrations can preserve behavioral consistency, then instances are migrated to their destination schema. Instance executions are then resumed.

4.3   Security in Dynamic Process Modifications

Dynamic service process modifications in *eFlow* are constrained by *authorization rules* that defines which user or application is authorized to perform a given modification. Rules are specified at process definition time, and can include an arbitrary number of input parameters, taken from case packet variable. This enables the definition of security rules that differs according to the particular execution state of the instance. Each process definition includes the following authorization rules with respect to process modifications:

- *Authorized_State_Modifiers*: identifies the users (services) that have write access to case packet variables, i.e., that can perform state changes to the instance.
- *Authorized_Node_Modificators*: identifies the users (services) authorized to modify service nodes in the process instance. This rule can also be specified at the node level, to further constrain authorizations.
- *Authorized_Flow_Modificators*: identifies the users (services) authorized to make any kind of dynamic changes to the process instance.
- *Authorized_Initiators*: identifies the users (services) authorized to start an instance of this process

Each time a state change or a migration is requested, *eFlow* verifies that the requestor has the appropriate authorizations, according to the defined rules and to the differences between source and destination schema. In particular, in case of a bulk migration, authorization rule *Authorized_Node_Modificators* (or *Authorized_Flow_Modificators*, depending on the extent of the changes) defined in the *source* schema are executed for each instance to be migrated, and the migration is performed only if the user has the privileges to migrate *all* of these instances. In addition, since the migration will result in executions of the destination schema, rule *Authorized_Initiators* of the defined *destination* schema will be executed, to verify that the user is authorized to create instance of that schema.

5   Related Work

To the best of our knowledge, there is no commercial process management system that supports adaptive and dynamic features such as those of *eFlow*, neither among traditional workflow management systems (such as *MQ Workflow* [11] or *InConcert* [10]), nor among newly developed, open, XML- and web-based systems such as *Forte' Fusion* [9] and *KeyFlow* [6].

A few of these systems, such as InConcert and KeyFlow, provide some support for ad-hoc changes, by allowing simple modifications to the schema followed by a given instance as well as execution state modifications. Recently, some approaches to handle dynamic changes have been presented in the literature by the workflow research community.

One of the first contributions come from [2], that defines a correctness criterion for instance migration, based on the definition of the set of all valid node sequences: a change is correct if the execution sequence could have been obtained with the new schema. The paper, however, introduces a simple workflow model and restricts to a limited set of modifications.

Ad-hoc and bulk changes are discussed in [7]. Workflow changes are specified by *transformation rules* composed of a *source schema fragment*, a *destination schema fragment*, and of a *condition*. The system checks for parts of the process that are isomorphic with the source schema and replaces them with the destination schema for all instances for which the condition is verified. The paper also proposes a migration language for managing instance-specific migrations, conceptually similar to our migration language.

Other contributions to the area of workflow evolution come from [8,12]. In [12], a complete and minimal set of workflow modification operations is presented. Correctness properties are defined in order to determine whether a specific change can be applied to a given instance. If these constraints are violated, the change is either rejected or the correctness must be explicitly restored with exception handling techniques. Liu et al [8] focus instead on a language for workflow evolution, by which the designer can specify which instances should be migrated to which versions, depending on conditions over workflow data. The language is conceptually similar to that of [7] and to ours.

In designing *eFlow*, we took advantage of all these research contributions and extended them as follows:

- We designed a model and system that provides all the flexibility features required for a dynamic environment such as that of the Internet, including a wide range of possible ad-hoc and bulk changes;
- we designed a very simple, yet powerful migration language and a very simple migration semantics, to enable an easy understanding of the instance behavior after migration. This is a fundamental requirement in operational environments;
- we discussed migration in the context of a rich process model, which includes events and transactions. These model features posed us additional challenges in managing migrations;
- we introduced authorization constraints that allows the definition who is authorized to perform a given type of change;

- we defined the process followed by the system when the changes are made, focusing in particular on the delicate issue of instance suspension;
- finally, in addition to dynamic change support, *eFlow* also provides a set of adaptive features in order to strongly reduce the need for dynamic changes.

Adaptive process management is also recently gaining attention. The workflow model proposed in [1] includes a "shoot tip" activity: when a shoot tip activity is executed, the control is transferred to a process modeler that can extend the flow structure with one additional activity, which is inserted before the shoot tip activity. Next, instance execution will proceed by activating the newly inserted task and subsequently another "shoot tip" activity to determine the next step. Another interesting approach, which also allows for automatic adaptation, is proposed in [3]. The presented workflow model includes a *placeholder* activity, which is an abstract activity replaced at runtime with a concrete activity type, which must have the same input and output data of those defined as part of the placeholder. A selection policy can be specified to indicate the activity that should be executed. The model has an expressive power similar to the one allowed by *eFlow* dynamic service discovery mechanism. However, we do not restrict the input and output parameters of the selected activity to be the same of those of the node. In addition, we also provide the notion of generic and multiservice node for further achieving additional flexibility and we provide a set of dynamic modification features to cope with situations in which changes in the flow are needed.

6   Conclusions

In this paper we have shown how *eFlow* supports the dynamic composition, enactment, and management of *composite* e-services, i.e., of e-services built on top of other basic or composite services. In particular, we focused on the adaptive and dynamic features of *eFlow*, which are essential characteristics in order to cope with dynamic environments such as that of e-services. Our future research will be focused on providing effective means for monitoring and analyzing instances that have been modified one or more times during their executions.

In summary, we believe that the *eFlow* platform has the required characteristics and functionality to satisfy the need of Internet-based service providers. *eFlow* is integrated with the Hewlett-Packard e-service strategy; however, it is an open technology: it is based on Java and it is compliant with the workflow and Internet standards, such as XML and the Workflow Management Coalition Interface standards. Hence, it can be integrated and used in virtually any IT environment.

References

1. T. Dirk Meijler, H. Kessels, C. Vuijst and R. le Comte. Realising Run-time Adaptable Workflow by means of Reflection in the Baan Workflow Engine. Proceedings of the CSCW Workshop on Adaptive Workflow Management, Seattle, WA, 1998.

2. S. Ellis, K. Keddara and G. Rozenberg, Dynamic Change within Workflow Systems, Proceedings of (COOCS '95), Milpitas, California, 1995.
3. D. Georgakopoulos, H. Schuster, D. Baker, and A. Cichocki. Managing Escalation of Collaboration Processes in Crisis Mitigation Situations. Proceedings of ICDE 2000, San Diego, CA, USA, 2000.
4. Hewlett-Packard. e"speak Architectural Specifications. 2000.
5. Hewlett-Packard. *eFlow* model and architecture, version 1.0. 2000.
6. Keyflow Corp. Workflow Server and Workflow designer. 1999.
7. G. Joeris and O. Herzog. Managing Evolving Workflow Specifications with Schema Versioning and Migration Rules. TZI Technical Report 15, University of Bremen, 1999.
8. C. Liu, M. Orlowska and H. Li. Automating Handover in Dynamic Workflow Environments. Proceedings of CAiSE '98, Pisa, Italy, 1998.
9. J. Mann. Forte' Fusion. Patricia Seybold Group report, 1999.
10. R. Marshak. InConcert Workflow. Workgroup Computing report, Vol 20, No. 3, Patricia Seybold Group, 1997.
11. IBM. MQ Series Workflow - Concepts and Architectures. 1998.
12. M. Reichert, P. Dadam. ADEPTflex - Supporting Dynamic Changes of Workflows Without Loosing Control. Technical report 97-07, DBIS, University of Ulm, 1997.

Towards Extensible Information Brokers Based on XML

Jianguo Lu, John Mylopoulos, Jamie Ho

Department of Computer Science, University of Toronto
{jglu, jm, jamie}@cs.toronto.edu

Abstract. The exponential growth in the number and size of information services available on the internet has created an urgent need for information agents which act as brokers in that they can autonomously search, gather and integrate information on behalf of a user. Moreover, the inherent volatility of the internet and the wide range of information processing tasks to be carried out, calls for a framework that facilitates both the construction and evolution of such information brokers. This paper proposes such a framework named XIB (eXtensible Information Brokers).

Based on descriptions of relevant information services, XIB supports the interactive generation of an integrated query interface, generates wrappers for each information service dynamically, and returns to the user the composed result to a query. XIB depends heavily on XML-related techniques. More specifically, we will use DTDs to model the input and output of the service, use XML elements to denote the input and output values. By using this representation, service integration is investigated in the form of DTD integration, and query decomposition is studied in the form of XML element decomposition. Within the proposed framework, it is easy to add or remove information services on the internet to a broker, thereby facilitating maintenance, evolution and customization.

Keywords: XML, data integration, interoperability, wrapper, multi-agent system, mediator, web-based information system.

1 Introduction

The availability of information sources, services and deployed software agents on the internet is literally exploding. To find relevant information, users often have to manually browse or query various information services, extract relevant data, and fuse them into an usable form. To ease this kind of tedious work, various types of information agents have been proposed, including meta-searchers [28], mediators [11][4], and information brokers [9]. These provide a virtual integrated view of heterogeneous information services, and perform a variety of tasks autonomously on behalf of their users.

Two issues are critical in building such software agents: extensibility and flexibility. The internet is an open and fast changing environment. Information

B. Wangler, L. Bergman (Eds.): CAiSE 2000, LNCS 1789, pp. 32-46, 2000.
© Springer-Verlag Berlin Heidelberg 2000

sources, internet connections, and the information agents themselves may appear and disappear unpredictably, or simply change with no warning. Any software agent that operates within such an environment needs to be easily adaptable to the volatile internet environment. Likewise, in such an open environment there will always be new users who have different requirements for their information processing tasks. To meet such demands, the technology we use to build information agents needs to support customizability and evolution.

The XIB (eXtensible Information Broker) is a framework intended to facilitate the construction of information brokers that meet such extensibility and flexibility requirements. The basic idea is to make the web services currently only available to users also accessible from within other applications. To enable this, we define a service description language, called XIBL, intended to be used as the common language for various services. XIBL is based on XML. More specifically, the input and output descriptions are represented as DTDs, and input and output data are denoted as XML elements. Due to the wide adoption of XML notation, and the extensibility of the XML itself, XIBL is flexible enough to describe various services ranging from web services, database, and even Java remote objects.

There are three groups of users inside this framework, i.e., wrapper engineers, broker engineers, and end users. Wrapper engineers are responsible for wrapping up a particular service in terms of XIBL, and registering the service in a service server. Broker engineers select services from the service server, and build brokers where they define how to integrate the services. End users use the brokers.

Correspondingly, we provide *WrapperBuilder* and *BrokerBuilder* tools. *WrapperBuilder* is a visual tool that helps a user wrap up a service interactively. Through an interactive session, *WrapperBuilder* produces a service description written in XIBL and gets it registered in a service server. *BrokerBuilder* is a visual tool that interact with users to define a broker. The tool allows allow broker engineers to select from the service server the services they want to integrate, and to define the logic of the integration. Again, through an interactive session, a broker is generated automatically, without writing program code. Brokers will typically accept more complicated queries then any individual services, decompose the query into sub-queries, and compose the results from sub-queries into a coherent response to the user query. As well, facilities are provided so that brokers can replace a source that is out-of-service with the help of matchmaking capability of the service server. More details of the system can be found at www.cs.toronto.edu/km/xib.

In the following we first introduce the information service description language XIBL, which allows the description of websites or databases. Next we describe how a broker engineer defines or customizes an information broker, based on a set of such information service descriptions. Wrapper generation is described next, while section 5 discusses result composition. The paper concludes with a review of the literature and a summary of the key issues addressed.

2   Information Service Description Language XIBL

We classify web services into three categories, i.e., static, dynamic, and interactive. Static web services are those static HTML web pages. Dynamic services typically allow users to provide input on a HTML form and get a dynamically generated webpage. One example of such web services is a generic search engine. Interactive web services are a special class of dynamic web services that allow for the change of the state on the web server side and accomplish the service through multiple layers of interaction. E-commerce websites usually provide interactive services.

This paper focuses mainly on dynamic web services. This kind of service could be modeled

```
<XIB>
  <SERVICE NAME="AmazonSearch"/>
  <INPUT>
      <elementType id="query"> <string/> </elementType>
  </INPUT>
  <OUTPUT>
      <elementType id="author"> <string/> </elementType>
      <elementType id="title"> <string/> </elementType>
      <elementType id="publisher"> <string/> </elementType>
      <elementType id="year"> <string/> </elementType>
      <elementType id="price"> <string/> </elementType>
      <elementType id="book">
        <element type="$author" />
        <element type="$title" />
        <element type="$publisher" />
        <element type="$year" />
        <element type="$price" />
      </elementType>
      <elementType id="books">
        <element type="$book" occurs="ZEROORMORE" />
      </elementType>
  </OUTPUT>
  <INPUTBINDING>
      <BASE method="POST" action="cgi-bin">
          http://www.amazon.com</BASE>
      <BINDING variable = "query" mapsTo="keyword-query" />
  </INPUTBINDING>
  <OUTPUTBINDING>
      <script>
      titles = Elem(P, "a") inside Elem(P,"dt");
      dd     = Elem(P,"dd");
      title  = Text(titles[i]);
      ... ...

      </script>
  </OUTPUTBINDING>
  <DESCRIPTION> search for book information from Amazon.
  </DESCRIPTION>
</XIB>
```

Fig. 1. Amazon description

as a function. There are four layers of description for such services:

1. Where is the service. For our purposes, this may be the URL of a cgi script for a website, or the URL address of a database server.
2. What queries can it answer. For a database, this would usually be determined by the database query language (SQL or other). However, the queries that can be answered by a particular website are usually very limited. The XIB needs to provide a grammatical notation for specifying the set of queries that can be submitted.
3. What information can it provide. This is the output data we expect from the service, specified in a XML DTD.
4. Where is the data exactly located. For a database, this is specified in the database schema. For a website, on the other hand, pertinent data is usually hidden inside an HTML document, so we need to specify the exact location of those data.

We shall call these four components of a service description as `INPUT BINDING` `INPUT`, `OUTPUT`, and `OUTPUT BINDING`, respectively. Figure 1 is an example of an Amazon search service description.

2.1 Input and Output Descriptions

Information sources usually allow only a limited number of query forms to be submitted. The input description defines the set of queries acceptable to a particular service. It consists of a set of variables that a user can associate values with, and their corresponding range specification. One design goal of the description is to model the HTML form, so that a description can be generated from an HTML form or vice versa.

The input description takes the form of an XML schema expressed in XML-data [15], an extension of the XML DTD that can be embedded in an XML document. Figure 2 shows an example of a more complicated input/output description. The input part here means that the input variable `model` can be any string (which corresponds to the *text input* control in an HTML form), `cpu` can take values `PII350` or `PII400` (which correspond to the *menus* control in the HTML form), and `memories` can take values `32M`, `64M`, or both (which corresponds to the *menus* control with multiple selections in an HTML form).

```
<SERVICE NAME="computerSearch1">
<INPUT>
    <elementType id="model"> <string/> </elementType>
    <elementType id="cpu">
        <attribute name="cpuValue" atttype="ENUMERATION"
                   values="PII350 PII400" /
    </elementType>
    <elementType id="memory">
        <attribute name="memoryValue" atttype="ENUMERATION"
                   values="32M, 64M" />
    </elementType>
    <elementType id="memories">
        <element type="$memory" occurs="ONEORMORE"/>
    </elementType>
</INPUT>
<OUTPUT>
    <elementType id="computers">
      <element type="$computer" occurs="ZEROORMORE" />
    <elementType id="computer"/>
        <element type="$cpu"/>
        <element type="$memories"/>
        <element type="$hardDisk"/>
        <element type="$price"/>
        <element type="$address"/>
    </elementType>
    <elementType id="hardDisk">
        <attribute name="hardDiskValue" atttype="ENUMERATION"
                   values="6G 8G" />
    </elementType>
    <elementType id="price"> <string/> </elementType>
    <elementType id="address"/>
        <element type="$mail"/>
        <element type="$email"/>
    </elementType>
</OUTPUT>
```

Fig. 2. computerSearch1 input/output description

For the output descriptions, it is not adequate to use a variation of the relational data model as in [26]. Instead, we also use a syntax similar to DTD to allow for the description of a tree-like data structure.

In the example shown in figure 2, the output consists of zero or more `computer` elements, each consisting of `cpu`, `memory`, `hardDisk`, `price`, and `address` elements. The **address** element, in turn, consists of two other elements, **mail address** and **email address**.

In figure 1, the **INPUT** component is simply a **query** that can take arbitrary strings as its value. The **OUTPUT** component, on the other hand, declares that the result is **books**, and that **books** consists of zero or a more **book**. Each **book** consists of elements **author**, **title**, **publisher**, **year**, and **price**.

2.2 Input and Output Bindings

An input binding provides necessary information for the dynamic construction of an URL. For our example of figure 1, the input binding consists of the URL of the website in question, the cgi script name, and the mappings between the name used in the description and the attribute name used in the HTML form (the mapping from **query** to **keyword-query**).

```
<SERVICE NAME="computerSearch2">
<INPUT>
    <elementType id="cpu">
        <attribute name="cpuValue" atttype="ENUMERATION"
                   values="PII266 PII350" />
    </elementType>
    <elementType id="hardDisk">
        <attribute name="hdValue"
                   atttype="ENUMERATION" values="4G 8G"/>
    </elementType>
</INPUT>
<OUTPUT>
    <elementType id="computers">
        <element type="$computer" occurs="ZEROORMORE" />
    </elementType>
    <elementType id="computer"/>
        <element type="$model"/>
        <element type="$cpu"/>
        <element type="$memories"/>
        <element type="$hardDisk"/>
        <element type="$price"/>
    </elementType>
    <elementType id="memory">
        <attribute name="memoryValue" atttype="ENUMERATION"
                   values="32M 64M 128M" />
    </elementType>
    <elementType id="price"> <string/> </elementType>
    <elementType id="model"> <string/> </elementType>
</OUTPUT>
```

Fig. 3. ComputerSearch2 input/output description

The **OUTPUT BINDING** uses the markup algebra introduced in [17] to define the location of the data inside a HTML documents.

3   Broker Synthesis

Once web descriptions are available, a broker engineer can interact with the XIB to synthesize a broker as needed. First of all, the broker engineer needs to select a set of services to be integrated. The publication and selection of relevant services can be handled by a matchmaking agent [24].

To synthesize the broker with selected services, there are three things to be defined by the broker engineer. First, the user interface through which a query is submitted. Second, the output of the query, which consists of both the output format and the means to compose the results from each information source. Third, the mappings between the names in the broker and the names in each service. The following two subsections describe how the broker interface is defined and how the results are composed, while name mapping issues are discussed throughout these two subsections.

3.1   Definition of the Broker Query Interface

The broker query interface is an HTML form through which a user can submit queries. To derive the broker interface, first we must derive a broker XML schema from a set of input XML schemata, one for each service. Then we can generate an HTML form from the broker schema via XSL.

There are several requirements for the broker schema:

Generality The broker XML schema(DTD) should be capable of accepting queries(XML instances of the DTD) for every service. That is, every instance of each source XML schema should also be an instance of the broker schema.

Decomposability Every query acceptable by the broker schema (XML instance of the schema) should be decomposable to sub-queries that are acceptable to the services. In general, it is not desirable for the interface to let users submit queries that always fail to produce answers.

Normal Form The schema should be normalized so that the same element type or attribute name and value will not be defined twice. Since each schema element type or attribute will be transformed into an HTML form control, multiple definitions of an element or an attribute will require a user to duplicate the action to set a value in several places. Besides, to ensure the validity of the schema, multiple definition of element types should be removed.

The steps required to construct the broker input schema are as follows. Given two service input descriptions A and B, first construct the integrated schema (DTD) as

`<!ELEMENT X ((A|B)|(A,B))>`

which means that the broker input schema could be either A, B, or the sequential composition of A and B. Obviously, this schema satisfies condition one. The next step is to apply a set of schema transformation rules to simplify the schema so that element types,

```
<elementType id="model"> <string/> </elementType>
<elementType id="cpu">
    <attribute name="cpuValue" atttype="ENUMERATION"
              values="PII266 PII350 PII400" />
</elementType>
<elementType id="hardDisk">
    <attribute name="hdValue" atttype="ENUMERATION"
              values="4G 8G"/>
</elementType>
<elementType id="memories">
    <element type="#memory" occurs="ONEORMORE"/>
</elementType>
<elementType id="memory">
    <attribute name="memoryValue" atttype="ENUMERATION"
              values="32M 64M" />
</elementType>
```

Fig. 4. Computer search broker input XML schema

attributes, or values inside the integrated schema are not defined in multiple places. Each transformation rule will preserve the equality of the schemas. The process continues until no transformation rule is applicable.

Let's look at the example of generating a computer search interface from the descriptions in figures 2 and 3. To keep things simple, we suppose that the same entities in the two descriptions are denoted by the same name. When they are denoted by different names, the broker engineer needs to construct a mapping between those names.

By integrating the XML schemata in `computerSearch1` and `computerSearch2`, we have produced the `INPUT` description as in figure 4. We notice that in the broker schema the valid values of the `cpuValue` is obtained by combining the corresponding valid values from `computerSearch1` and `computerSearch2`. The correspondence between this XML schema and an HTML form is as follows. Element type `model` will produce an HTML *text input* control, element types `cpu` and `hardDisk` will produce *menus* controls, and `memories` will produce *menus* control that allows for multiple selection.

3.2   Definition of the Output XML Template

When the services are selected, there are numerous ways to integrate them. Given the two services `GlobeChaptersSearch` and `AmazonSearch`, we can use them to search for books that appear in both places, for books that can be shipped within 24 hours, etc. Here we are concerned with the comparison of the prices of the books in these two places. Hence the broker engineer needs to interact with the XIB to define the output XML template.

Given the output XML schemata for `AmazonSearch` and `GlobeChaptersSearch`, the broker engineer can define the output XML template as in figure 5.

This kind of template uses a simplified form of the XML query language XML-

```
CONSTRUCT
    <newbook>
        <author>$a </author>
        <title> $t </title>
        <AmazonPrice> $p3 </AmazonPrice>
        <GCPrice> $p2 </GCPrice>
    </newbook>
WHERE  <book>
        <author>$a </author>
        <title> $t </title>
        <price> $p1 </price>
    </book> IN "http://cs.toronto.edu/XIB/amazonSearch"
        CONDITION "amazonSearch.INPUT.query
                       =newSearch.INPUT.queryString"
AND
    <chapterBook>
        <authors>$a </authors>
        <bookName> $t </bookName>
        <ourPrice> $p2 </ourPrice>
    </chapterBook> IN
        "http://cs.toronto.edu/XIB/globeChaptersSearch"
        CONDITION "globeChaptersSearch.INPUT.query
                       =newSearch.INPUT.queryString"
AND
    <Converter>
        <amount> $p1 </amount>
        <result> $p3 </result>
    </Converter> IN
        "http://cs.toronto.edu/XIB/ConverterService"
        CONDITION "ConverterServive.INPUT.from=USD;
                     ConverterService.INPUT.to=CND;
                     ConverterSerivce.INPUT.amount=$p1"
```

Fig. 5. XML template

QL [10]. The major difference in the syntax of XIB templates is that the `IN` clause contains wrapper information, instead of an URL that points to an XML file. The `Construct` component of the template defines the intended output, i.e., a list of `<newbook>` elements which consist of elements `<author>`, `<title>`, `<AmazonPrice>`, and `<GCPrice>`. The `WHERE` part defines how to compose results from different information services. Note that the strings preceded by the sign $ denote variables. In this example, the `AmazonSearch` and `globeChaptersSearch` are joined on the `author` and `title`, and the `AmazonSearch` and `ConverterService` are joined on the price (amount) in USD. To do the currency conversion between US dollars and Canadian dollars, we need to use another information service `ConverterService` whose input and output definitions are as in figure 6.

4   Wrapper Generation

Wrapping a system is the process of defining and restricting access to a system through an abstract interface. A wrapper for information services accepts queries in a given format, converts them into one or more commands or sub-queries understandable by the underlying information service and transforms the native results into a format understood by the application. In the following we discuss wrapper generation for websites and relational databases.

```
<SERVICE Name="ConverterService"/>
<INPUT>
   <elementType id="amnt">  <string/>  </elementType>
   <elementType id="frm">   <string/>  </elementType>
   <elementType id="to">    <string/>  </elementType>
</INPUT>
<OUTPUT>
   <elementType id="conversion">
      <element type="$amount"/>
      <element type="$result"/>
      <element type="$from"/>
      <element type="$into"/>
   </elementType>
</OUTPUT>
```

Fig. 6. Currency Converter

4.1   Wrappers for Dynamic Web Services

A wrapper for a web-based information source is a special kind of wrapper in that the source involves websites and applications, while the native results are usually in the form of HTML documents. The basic functionality of such wrappers includes accepting a query and constructing the corresponding URL; also accessing a webpage given a URL, extracting the relevant information and returning the resulting XML DOM object to the broker.

When the output XML template is defined, the wrappers for each service will be generated dynamically. Wrappers are not developed a priori due to the fact that each information source has a vast array of services, while different broker or mediator will only use some of these service. For example, the `AmazonSearch` service also provides information on **publisher**, **publish year** etc. However, since the broker will not need this information, there is no need for the wrapper to produce it.

The process of generating XML wrappers for websites is described in figure 7.

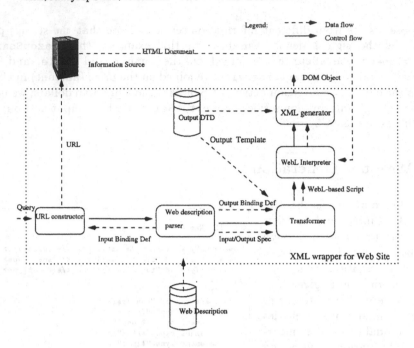

Fig. 7. XML Wrapper generation

The description parser parses the web description. From the input binding, the *URL constructor* is able to generate the URL to get the corresponding web-page in HTML format. In the `AmazonSearch` example, suppose the query string to the user interface is "`XML`", to search for books about XML, the generated URL is `http://www.amazon.com/cgi-bin?keyword-query="XML"`.

At the same time, given the output template, the output bindings, and the input/output descriptions, the *Transformer* will generate the *WebL* [17] scripts that can extract the relevant data. In our example, according to the `AmazonSearch` description, we can get information about publisher and publish year. However, since this information is not needed according to the output template, the generated *WebL* scripts won't extract it. The *WebL interpreter* will interpret the *WebL* scripts and extract the pertinent data. Finally, the *XML generator* transforms the output of the WebL interpreter to the XML format according to the output XML schema.

4.2   From Databases to XML

To allow for data exchange between databases and websites we need to be able to build XML wrappers for database systems. For our book comparison example, suppose there is another converter service provided by a relational database system and its description is as in figure 8. In this description the `INPUT` and `OUTPUT` specifications are the same as in figure 6. Inside the binding part, there are definitions for the database URL, the database driver, user account, password, and the database query.

5   Query Planning and Result Composition

Given a query from the broker interface, the broker needs to decompose the query and form a plan to execute the query.

Let's look at an example in the computer search case. Suppose that the following query is submitted through the broker input interface specified in figure 4:

Q=<cpu>PII350</cpu> <hardDisk>4G</hardDisk><memory>32M</memory>,

This asks for the selection of computer information satisfying the constraints that cpu is PII350, hardDisk is 4G, and memory is 32M.

First, the broker needs to decide which service is capable of accepting this query.

Suppose I and O are the input and output schemata of service S. A query Q is acceptable to a service $S(I, O)$, if either Q is an instance of I, or there is a decomposition of $Q = (Q_1, Q_2)$, such that Q_1 is an instance of I, and Q_2 is an instance of part of O.

In our example, since Q is not an instance of

```
<SERVICE NAME="ConverterDBService">
<INPUT>
   <elementType id="amnt"> <string/> </elementType>
   <elementType id="frm">  <string/> </elementType>
   <elementType id="to">   <string/> </elementType>
</INPUT>
<OUTPUT>
   <elementType id="conversion">
      <element type="#amount"/>
      <element type="#result"/>
      <element type="#from"/>
      <element type="#into"/>
   </elementType>
</OUTPUT>
<INPUTBINDING>
   <BASE> jdbc:msql://mika.ai.toronto.edu:1114
                   /converterDB </BASE>
   <DRIVER> com.imginary.sql.msql.MsqlDriver </DRIVER>
   <USER> guest </USER>
   <PASSWORD> 12345 </PASSWORD>
   <DBQUERY>
      SELECT amount, result, from, into
      FROM   ConversionTable
      WHERE amount=amnt AND from=frm AND into=to
   </DBQUERY>
</INPUTBINDING>
```

Fig. 8. Database description

the input schema of computerSearch2, it is decomposed into

Q_1= <cpu> PII350 </cpu> <hardDisk> 4G </hardDisk>
and
Q_2= <memory>32M</memory>,

which are instances of the input and output schemata of computerSearch2, respectively. Hence this query is acceptable to computerSearch2.

Once such decomposition is obtained, Q_1 is sent to the computerSearch2 and Q_2 is used as a filter condition inside the broker.

With the XML documents produced from the wrapper and the output template provided by the broker engineer, the task of result composition becomes easier. In our implementation, we transform the output template to the XML-QL query with some variables instantiated and the service name replaced by a concrete XML document. Then using the XML-QL engine, we can get the result XML document.

One complication that can arise here is that some input variables may not be instantiated beforehand. In our book search example, the converter can only be activated after the `AmazonSearch` is completed, i.e, when the value for the variable $P1 is available from the `AmazonSearch`. Thus the result composer needs to wait for that value, assign that value to the input variable of the `ConverterService`, generate a new query, and send it to the wrapper.

6   Related Work

6.1   Information Integration

Much work has been done on query planning and rewriting for information mediators[16]. Recently, XML-related issues have also been studied in this area. For example, MIX[4] is an XML-based DTD driven mediator prototype. In MIX, data exchange and integration relies on XML. The XML query language XMAS is used to define the integration view, and the graphical user interface BBQ (Blended Browsing and Querying) is used to generate complex queries driven by the mediator view DTD. The view DTD is derived from the view definition and source DTDs. MIX is not comparable with XIB in that MIX mediates between static web pagesm, while XIB is intended to integrate dynamic services that are modeled as functions.

Metawrappers [26] are components within a mediator architecture which decompose user queries and compose wrapper responses. The assumption here is that there are hundreds of information sources in a dynamic WWW environment, so there is a need to group similar information sources, and generate a non-redundant, least-cost plan for a given query. An extension of the relational data model is used to describe the source and metawrapper schemata. An input/output relation is used to describe the limited capability of a web source. Unlike the XIB, where the input and output could be XML schemata, the input and output in a metawrapper are sets of attributes. Moreover, the metawrapper assumes the existence of wrappers which are responsible for the direct access to information sources and the translation from different data model to a uniform data model, the source description in a metawrapper does not include the `BINDING` part in XIB.

WebSemantics[18] proposes an architecture to describe, publish, register, discover, and access relevant data over the internet using XML and XML-data. The focus is on data instead of the services available on the internet.

WIDL [27] is an XML application that tries to describe web sources so that they can interoperate. In WIDL, the input and output are simply described as a set of variables that have no structure, hence WIDL is unable to support the integration of new query interface and the result composition based on certain data schema.

6.2   Wrapper Construction

Wrapper construction or generation is the task of producing wrappers from source descriptions. The approaches to wrapper construction vary with respect to the level of abstraction of the input/output descriptions, the expressiveness of the descriptions, also the degree of tool support for the acquisition of the input/output descriptions and the transformation from the descriptions to executable code.

Input/output descriptions could be represented in a declarative language, e.g., [27][22]. They could also be represented as executable scripts [17]. The input/output descriptions may be provided manually[27], or obtained with the help of tools [22]. Alternatively, they may be induced automatically using machine learning techniques [20][13]. Our work has not addressed yet the important issue of acquiring automatically or semi-automatically such descriptions.

Compared to other wrapper construction proposals, our description language is very expressive. By using XML schemata to describe inputs

```
CONSTRUCT
  <newComputer>
      <cpu> $cpu </cpu>
      <memory> $mm </memory>
      <hardDisk> $hd </hardDisk>
      <price> $cndPrice </price>
      <address> $addr </address>
  </newComputer>
WHERE
(
  <computer1>
  <cpu> $cpu </cpu>
  <memory> $mm </memory>
  <hardDisk> $hd </hardDisk>
  <price> $cndPrice </price>
  <address> $addr </address>
  </computer1> IN
      "http://www.toronto.edu/XIB/computerSearch1"
      CONDITION "computerSearch1.INPUT.cpu=
          newComputer.INPUT.cpu;
      computerSearch1.INPUT.mm =newComputer.INPUT.mm;
      $hd=newComputer.INPUT.hd"
OR
  <computer2>
      <cpu> $cpu </cpu>
      <memory> $mm </memory>
      <price> $usdPrice </price>
      <address> $addr </address>
  </computer2> IN
      "http://www.toronto.edu/XIB/computerSearch2"
      CONDITION "computerSearch2.INPUT.cpu
          =newComputer.INPUT.cpu;
      computerSearch2.INPUT.hd
          =newComputerSearch.INPUT.hd;
      $mm = newComputerSearch.INPUT.mm"
)
AND
  <converter>
      <amount> $usdPrice </amount>
      <result> $cndPrice </result>
  </converter> IN
      "http://www.toronto.edu/XIB/converterService"
      CONDITION "converterService.INPUT.frm=USD;
          converterService.INPUT.to=CND;
          converterService.INPUT.amnt=$usdPrice"
```

Fig. 9. Computer search template

and outputs, we allow for the description of complicated queries and richly structured outputs. This is particularly important in view of the increasing complexity of HTML forms.

7   Conclusions

The key design features of the proposed eXtensible Information Broker (XIB) is its extensibility and flexibility. Given information source descriptions, broker engineers can build and maintain reliable information brokers with ease. Building a new information broker only involves several steps of interaction with the XIB. Moreover, the evolution and maintenance of such brokers is simple, since one can easily add or remove sources or services without consulting the code. Finally, information brokers built through the XIB can be built for reliability by including several redundant sources and services. For example, the broker engineer can prepare several currency conversion services in case one of them breaks due to a bad internet connection.

The main contributions of this work are as follows. Firstly, it provides a language and a tool to model dynamic web services in terms of XML. Secondly, it provides a platform for making web services accessible not only to users, but also to applications. Thirdly, as an example of such an application, we provide the *BrokerBuilder* that can integrate such services.

A prototype of XIB has been implemented and can be accessed at www.cs.toronto.edu/km/xib. The implementation adopted the XML parser XML4J developed by IBM. XSL is used to transform XML documents to HTML presentation, and the XML-data to HTML forms. Also, XML-QL is used to compose results. To construct wrappers for web sources, we used WebL to extract relevant information from an HTML document. For database wrappers, currently we are wrapping the miniSQL database and use JDBC to make the connection. Finally, the service server is implemented using Java RMI, while brokers are served using servlets.

We have experimented with the implemented XIB framework through four groups of examples. One group is concerned with the integration of book store information from sources such as *amazon*, *globalChapters*, along with currency converter services. The second group of services includes generic search engines like *altaVista*, *hotBot*, etc. By integrating this group of services, we provide new services similar to the popular metasearcher like *metacrawler*. The third group is to integrate movie review and local theater information services. This experiment is intended to try out the XIB with complementary, rather than similar, services. The fourth group concerns the integration of information from a set of computer stores. This group of services requires more complicated input and output format, and has allowed us to experiment with sophisticated input DTD integration and query decomposition.

Several issues need further investigation for this framework to scale up:

The vocabulary problem Although XML provides certain semantics for the data and hence facilitates the integration of services, given the assumption that service descriptions may be provided by different people, there may be different DTDs for the same task. In our current implementation, broker engineers have to specify the mappings between the DTD tag names. This is one of the bottleneck for the automatic generation of brokers. The problem will be tackled in two directions. One is to follow industry standards that are emerging, like RosettaNet and BizTalk. Another is to compute the distance between tag names based on statistic methods like co-occurrence and trigger pairs.

Interactive web services Our current framework can only model and integrate dynamic web services. There are many web services that need several layers of interaction, and require the modification of the state on the web server side. XIB is not able to cope with this kind of service.

Acknowledgments

The project was funded by the Government of Canada through the Networks of Centers of Excellence and the Institute of Robotics and Intelligent Systems. We would like to thank Kenneth Sinn for his contribution in the implementation of the system.

References

1. Vidur Apparao et al, Document Object Model (DOM) Level 1, W3C recommendation, http://www.w3.org/TR/REC-DOM-Level-1/.
2. Naveen Ashish, Craig Knoblock, Semi-automatic Wrapper Generation for Internet Information Sources, Second IFCIS Conference on Cooperative Information Systems (CoopIS), Charleston, South Carolina, 1997.
3. P. Atzeni, G. Mecca, P. Merialdo, Semistructured and Structured Data in the Web: Going Back and Forth, In SIGMOD Record, Special Issue on the Workshop on the Management of Semistructured Data, 1997.
4. C. Baru, A. Gupta, B. Ludaescher, R. Marciano, Y. Papakonstantinou, P. Velikhov, XML-Based Information Mediation with MIX, In Exhibitions Program of ACM SIGMOD 99.
5. Tim Bray, Jean Paoli, C. M. Sperberg-McQueen, Extensible Markup Language(XML) 1.0, W3C recommendation, http://wwww.w3.org/TR/REC-xml, 1998.
6. Chen-Chuan K. Chang, Hector Garcia-Molina, Andreas Paepcke, Predicate Rewriting for Translating Boolean Queries in a Heterogeneous Information System, ACM Transactions on Information Systems, vol. 17, no. 1, Jan. 1999.
7. Chen-Chuan K. Chang, Hector Garcia-Molina, Mind Your Vocabulary: Query Mapping Across Heterogeneous Information Sources, Proc. of the 1999 ACM SIGMOD International Conference On Management of Data, Jun. 1999.
8. James Clark, Stephen Deach, Extensible Stylesheet Language(XSL), W3C working draft, http://www/w3/org/TR/WD-xsl, 1998.
9. K. Decker, K. Sycara, M. Williamson. Matchmaking and Brokering. Proceedings of the Second International Conference on Multi-Agent Systems (ICMAS-96), Dec-96.
10. Alin Deutsch, Mary Fernandez, Daniela Florescu, Alon Levy,Dan Suciu , XML-QL: A Query Language for XML, W3C note, http://www.w3.org/TR/NOTE-xml-ql, 1998.
11. Craig A. Knoblock, Steven Minton, Jose Luis Ambite, Naveen Ashish, Pragnesh Jay Modi, Ion Muslea, Andrew G., Philpot, and Sheila Tejada. Modeling web sources for information integration, Proceedings of the Fifteenth National Conference on Artificial Intelligence, Madison, WI, 1998.
12. David Konopnicki, Oded Shmuedi, A comprehensive framework for querying and integrating WWW Data and services, Fourth IFCIS International Conference on Cooperative Information Systems, Edinburgh, 1999.

13. Bruce Krulwich, Automating the Internet Agents as User Surrogates, IEEE Internet computing, Vol. 1, No. 4, July/August 1997.
14. Nicholas Kushmerick, Daniel Weld, Robert Doorenbos, Wrapper induction for information extraction, IJCAI'97.
15. Andrew Layman,   et   al,   XML   Data,   W3C   note, http://www.w3.org/TR/1998/NOTE-XML-data-0105.
16. Alon Y. Levy, Anand Rajaraman and Joann J. Ordille, Querying Heterogeneous Information Sources Using Source Descriptions, Proceedings of the 22nd International Conference on Very Large Databases, VLDB-96, Bombay, India, September, 1996.
17. Hannes Marais and Tom Rodeheffer. Automating the Web with WebL. In Dr. Dobb's Journal, January 1999.
18. Mihaila, George and Raschid, Louiqa, Locating Data Repositories using XML, W3C Workshop on XML and Querying the Web, 1998.
19. Makoto Murata, Automatically Constructing the Intersection/Union/Difference of Two Schemas, XTech'99, march 7-11, 1999.
20. I. Muslea and S. Minton and C. Knoblock, STALKER: Learning Extraction Rules for Semistructured, Web-based Information Sources, AAAI-98 Workshop on AI and Information Integration, 1998, 74-81.
21. Y. Papakonstantinou, A. Gupta, L. Haas, Capabilities-Based Query Rewriting in Mediator Systems (Extended Version), in DAPD.
22. Raschid, Louiqa and Vidal, Maria Esther and Gruser, Jean-Robert. A Flexible Meta-Wrapper Interface for Autonomous Distributed Information Sources, Under Review. http://www.umiacs.umd.edu/users/mvidal/
23. Arnaud Sahuguet, Fabien Azavant, Wysiwyg Web Wrapper Factory (W4F), 1999.
24. K. Sycara, J. Lu, M. Klusch, S. Widoff, Matchmaking among Heterogeneous Agents on the Internet, in Proceedings of the 1999 AAAI Spring Symposium on Intelligent Agents in Cyberspace, Stanford University, USA 22-24 March 1999.
25. Vasilis Vassalos, Y. Papakonstantinou, Expressive Capabilities Description Languages and Query Rewriting Algorithms, http://www-cse.ucsd.edu/ yannis/papers/vpcap2.ps
26. Maria Esther Vidal, Louiqa Raschid, Jean Robert Gruser, A Meta-Wrapper for Scaling up to Multiple Autonomous Distributed Information Sources, In Proceedings CoopIS'98.
27. WIDL: Application Integration with XML, in "XML: Principles, Tools, and Techniques", the October print issue of O'Reilly's World Wide Web Journal, fall 1997.
28. http://www.metacrawler.com

Advertising Database Capabilities
for Information Sharing

Suzanne M. Embury[1], Jianhua Shao[1], W. Alex Gray[1], and Nigel Fishlock[2]

[1] Department of Computer Science, Cardiff University,
P.O. Box 916, The Parade, Cardiff, CF24 3XF, Wales, U.K.
{S.M.Embury|J.Shao|W.A.Gray}@cs.cf.ac.uk
[2] Pirelli Cables Limited Communication Cables,
Wednesbury Street, Newport NP9 0WS, Wales, U.K.
fishlocn@pirellicables.co.uk

Abstract. The development of networking technology has resulted in a computing environment which is highly distributed, heterogeneous and dynamic. In order for the autonomous software components in such an environment to share their information, and hence to collaborate with each other, they must be able to advertise their capabilities — that is, to express what they have got to offer — in a form that can be understood by other resources.

In this paper, we study the problem of advertising the capabilities of an important class of resources within distributed information systems: namely, databases. We argue that current advertising mechanisms have limitations when applied to database systems, and propose an approach which overcomes these limitations. The resulting advertisement language is flexible and allows database components to advertise their capabilities in both a general and a specific way. We have demonstrated its utility by using it to advertise capabilities within a network of product databases created for Pirelli Cables Ltd.

1 Introduction

The development of networking technology has resulted in a computing environment which is highly distributed, heterogeneous and dynamic. Users of this environment, and developers of software components for use within it, increasingly expect to be able to make use of the facilities provided by other software components *without prior agreement*. In other words, if a component A needs the results of some computation or query which can already be performed by component B, then A should be able to request that the service be performed on its behalf by B. Moreover, A should be able to make the decision to exploit B's services at the point at which the need for them arises — this decision should not be hard-coded in at the time that component A was created. If, at some later date, a faster, more reliable and more accurate component C comes on-line, A should have the option of making use of the higher quality services this new agent offers, even though the original developer of A had no idea that C would ever exist.

B. Wangler, L. Bergman (Eds.): CAiSE 2000, LNCS 1789, pp. 47–63, 2000.

In order to achieve this sort of flexibility, some mechanism is needed by which the various software components in a distributed information system (DIS) can publish details of their capabilities, and by which components that require some functionality can discover which other systems might be able to provide it. In response to the same need within multi-agent systems, some authors have proposed the use of a special kind of software agent which can perform resource discovery tasks of this sort on behalf of other agents. This type of agent is called variously a *match-maker agent* [7], a *middle agent* [4] and a *facilitator* [9]. Typically, a match-maker agent will receive *advertisements* from agents, describing the services they are willing to perform. When an agent wishes to discover who is capable of undertaking some particular task, it sends a description of that task to the match-maker, which compares the agent's requirements against the advertisements stored in its local database. The advertisements that match indicate the set of agents which can perform the task. Details of these are then returned to the requesting agent.

Components performing match-maker functions can offer similar advantages for distributed information systems (DISs): they can provide some degree of protection against change in the availability or capabilities of components, and they can ease the design of new components by acting as a machine-manipulable representation of the existing capabilities of the network. However, current advertising mechanisms have limitations when applied to a class of components that are of particular importance in DISs — database systems.

In this paper, we present an approach to match-making in DISs that takes into account the special requirements of database components, while retaining the flexibility to advertise the capabilities of other kinds of software component. In particular, we suggest that an accurate representation of the capabilities of a database system must include both *domain-specific* aspects (e.g. the classes and relationships stored by the database) and *operational* elements (e.g. the general capabilities of the query language supported by the DBMS). The proposed approach allows database components to advertise their capabilities in both a general and a specific way. We have tested it in the context of a small prototype network of information sources developed for Pirelli Cables Ltd.

The remainder of the paper is organised as follows. We begin, in Sect. 2, by considering the particular problems posed by the need to advertise database capabilities. We then summarise previous approaches to match-making in Sect. 3. Section 4 outlines our proposed advertisement format, and Sect. 5 presents the process by which advertisements in this format are matched to requests. Finally, conclusions are given in Sect. 6.

2   Advertising Database Capabilities

In order to illustrate the problems involved in advertising database capabilities, we will present some examples based on KQML [5], a standard framework for agent communication. The issues raised, however, are not specific to KQML, which is used here simply as a convenient notation for the purposes of illustration.

In a KQML-compliant system, agents communicate by exchanging messages. Each message is a list of components. The first component, known as the *performative*, indicates the type of communication (e.g. `tell` for passing information to an agent, and `ask-one` or `ask-all` for requesting information from an agent). The subsequent components, known as *arguments*, indicate the content of communication. For example, the following KQML message illustrates the performative by which an agent informs another agent (usually a match-maker) of its capabilities:

```
(advertise,
      :sender    testManager
      :receiver  matchMakerAgent
      :language  KQML
      :content   (ask-one,
                      :sender    <anyone>
                      :receiver  testManager
                      :language  Prolog
                      :ontology  Cables
                      :content   ''stress_test_result($date,
                                 $engineer, $specNo, $result)''))
```

Here, the :`sender` and :`receiver` arguments specify the agent which sent the message and the agent to which it is sent, respectively. The :`language` argument indicates the language in which the :`content` is expressed and :`ontology` defines the terms used in the content. The message in the above example states that the `testManager` agent is able to respond to `ask-one` messages whose arguments match with those given. That is, if the content of an `ask-one` message is expressed in Prolog and in terms of the `Cables` ontology, and if it matches the pattern given in the innermost :`content` slot, then the `testManager` agent can handle this message.[1]

When a request for some capability is received, the match-maker tries to match the content portion of the request against the content patterns in the advertisements. The success of this process depends on the following factors:

- *The precision of the advertisement.* The pattern given in an advertisement acts as a general description of a set of similar requests, any of which can be serviced by the adverting component. If a component over-advertises its capabilities (i.e. uses too general a pattern) then it may be asked to serve requests that it is not capable of handling. On the other hand, if a component under-advertises its capability (by using too strict a pattern) then it may not be asked to serve requests that it is quite capable of serving. In either case, matching performance is degraded.
- *The intelligence of the match-maker.* It is possible that the same capability may be specified in a number of ways. This means that the match-maker must

---

[1] The pattern takes the same form as a Prolog request, except that variables (specified here with the $ prefix) are used wherever we don't care about the form of the request.

be intelligent enough to recognise, for instance, equivalence or subsumption relationships between advertised capabilities, and between the capabilities and the request.

These two factors are inter-dependent. For example, if the match-maker is capable of learning from its experience, then over-advertisement may not be a serious problem. In this paper, however, we do not consider the issue of match-maker intelligence but focus instead on the problem of how database components can advertise their capabilities both precisely and at a sufficient level of generality.

To appreciate the problems associated with advertising database capabilities, consider the following example. Suppose that a database has the schema:

```
opticalCable(specNo, cableType)
stressTest(testDate, testEngineer, specNo, result)
```

and it wishes to advertise that it can answer all SQL queries expressible against this schema. Under the standard KQML advertisement scheme, the database component would be forced to advertise its capabilities by generating one advertisement for each form of query it can answer. For example:

```
(advertise,
      :sender    dbAgent
      :receiver  matchMakerAgent
      :language  KQML
      :content   (ask-one,
                       :sender    <anyone>
                       :receiver  dbAgent
                       :language  SQL
                       :ontology  Cables
                       :content   ''SELECT count(specNo)
                                    FROM opticalCable''))

(advertise,
      :sender    dbAgent
      :receiver  matchMakerAgent
      :language  KQML
      :content   (ask-one,
                       :sender    <anyone>
                       :receiver  dbAgent
                       :language  SQL
                       :ontology  Cables
                       :content   ''SELECT testEngineer, cableType
                                    FROM opticalCable c, stressTest t
                                    WHERE c.specNo = t.specNo''))
      :
and many more
      :
```

This need to anticipate all the query forms that might be sent to the database is unsatisfactory for the following reasons:

- For any realistic database system, trying to advertise *all* the queries that it can handle in this way is almost impossible. As a result, some queries will be left out, resulting in an inevitable under-advertisement of its capabilities.
- Even if we can tolerate a degree of under-advertisement, the match-maker will be loaded with a large number of highly-specific advertisements. This will degrade matching performance.
- Such specific advertisements are difficult to analyse intelligently. The best a match-maker can do is to match incoming requests syntactically and exactly.

All these points suggest that an approach to advertising database capabilities based purely on pattern-matching is unworkable. We require a more general and more expressive advertisement language in which a range of functionalities, rather than just service signatures, can be described. Indeed, the limitations of the pattern-based approach have been recognised by other researchers, and in the next section we examine the suitability of more advanced forms of agent-based match-making for advertising database capabilities.

3   Current Approaches to Advertising

The approach to advertisement discussed above is based on that proposed for facilitator agents, within the Knowledge Sharing Effort [9]. The role of a facilitator is to present the appearance of an agent which has the combined capabilities of all the other agents in the distributed system. Individual agents need communicate with just this single facilitator agent, rather than having to know the addresses and capabilities of all other agents on the network. In order to present this illusion, each facilitator maintains a database of advertisements, given in KQML, which are matched against incoming requests. However, the KSE researchers recognised the limitations of a purely pattern-based approach and allowed constraints to be placed on the values of pattern variables. When a request is matched against an advertisement, these variables are instantiated with values from the request and the constraints are checked against them.

This pattern matching style is most suitable when the capabilities of the advertising agent can be described as a small number of named services. It is much less practical for advertising very broad and generic services, such as database query answering, which may require the creation of a large (possibly infinite) number of advertisements. Later authors (e.g. [7]) have tried to redress this balance by extending the richness of the facilitator's pattern matching capabilities.

More recent work has generalised the concept of pattern-based content languages for advertisements to allow the description of many database queries in a single advertisement. Vassalos and Papakonstantinou, for example, have proposed a language called p-Datalog [13] for advertising database queries. This language generalises Datalog programs by introducing a distinguished form of variable that can be used in place of constants within rule definitions. In itself,

this is no more useful than the KQML patterns introduced in Sect. 2. However, a
further development of p-Datalog, called the Relational Query Description Language (RQDL) [12], allows pattern variables to be used in place of the functors
of terms, as well as their parameters. This allows a wider set of queries to be
described by a single specification. In particular, query types can now be specified independently of any domain facts (e.g. "fetch the <A> of all <B> whose
<C> attribute is greater than <D>"). This language allows many different
query forms to be described using a single advertisement, and so contributes to
solving the problems of database advertising. However, many kinds of agent can
only handle requests which are relevant to a particular domain. This is certainly
true of database components, which can only answer queries that are expressed
in terms of their own particular schema. Rich pattern matching capabilities, if
used without any regard to the domain of interest of the query, will result in
over-advertisement for database systems, with a corresponding degradation in
the performance of the network as a whole.

Other authors have focussed trying to provide richer constructs for modelling the domain-specific aspects of agent capabilities, rather than on extending
pattern matching. DISs such as SIMS [1] and TAMBIS [2] make no use of pattern matching and instead use only domain information to carry out resource
discovery tasks. For example, in both SIMS and TAMBIS a common domain
model expressed using a description logic is used to describe the combined domain models of all resources in the network. Relevant resources are identified
by classifying the incoming request against the common model, and identifying
those resources which commit to the concepts occurring within the request. This
form of advertisement, while appropriate in relatively homogeneous agent networks, can also result in over-advertisement, since it assumes that every agent
which commits to the concepts occurring within a request is able to answer that
request, regardless of whether its querying capabilities are up to the task.

In a variant on this domain-centred approach, Decker *et al.* have proposed an
advertising format for database agents based on KQML advertisements, in which
the advertisement language includes a specification of the schema over which
queries can be evaluated [3]. Under this approach, a resource is considered to be
a suitable recipient of a request if it involves no schema elements which are not
also recorded within the advertisement. While the recognition of the importance
of the schema in advertising database capabilities is a distinct step forward, we
believe that it is not appropriate to embed details of a database component's
schema explicitly within advertisements in this way. Firstly, the schemas of many
real database systems (particularly legacy database applications) are very large,
containing hundreds of tables and thousands of attributes. Duplication of all
this information within an advertisement results in highly complex capability
descriptions, which are difficult to reason with efficiently. Secondly, this approach
commits the database system to advertising requests relating to its schema *at
the time of the advertisement* and not as it may be at the time a request is to be
serviced. Over time, use of an advertising scheme that is intolerant of updates

to source schemas will mean that advertisements become out-of-date, resulting in both under- and over-advertisement.

More recently, the LARKS language for the advertisement of agent services [11] has been proposed, which combines a variety of different types of matching. LARKS assumes the availability of an ontology of terms, which is used to compute similarity measures between the terms used within a request and an advertisement. It also uses ideas from component-based development to determine whether the parameters of the advertised service are compatible with those in the request, and whether pre- and post-constraints on the parameters in the advertisement are compatible with those in the request. LARKS represents the most sophisticated approach to the advertisements of general agent services proposed to date. However, the use of "plug-in" matching to determine compatibility of parameters is not relevant to matching of database queries, which can have very similar parameters but very different semantics. Moreover, LARKS takes the unusual approach of requiring users to convert their requests into the same format used for advertisements before matching. Effectively, the user is forced to guess what the advertisement for the service they require might contain. While this is reasonable for named agent services, where very little semantics is available from analysis of the bare procedure call, it is less appropriate for database queries, where much of the semantics is present in the request itself.

If a capability is to be precisely defined, then both its *operational* aspects (i.e. "what the agent can do") and its *domain-specific* aspects (i.e. "what it can do it to") must be specified. Recognising this point, researchers on the InfoSleuth project have made some preliminary steps towards combining both elements in a single advertisement format [8]. Following the approach described above, InfoSleuth advertisements contain information on the subset of the common ontology that a particular resource can handle embedded within the advertisement. This allows consideration of domain-specific aspects. For the operational aspects, InfoSleuth advertisements may also contain terms ¿From a special *service ontology*, which defines different typ of operational capability (e.g. relational algebra). It is not yet clear what role these service terms will play in matching requests in the Infosleuth system. However, what is clear from our own investigations so far is that a *combined* approach to advertising both domain and operational elements is required if capabilities from a wide variety of agents and resource types are to be advertised. This is particularly true when attempting to advertise the potentially infinite capabilities of database systems in a precise, yet flexible manner. In the next section, we present our own approach to this problem.

4 An Advertisement Language for Database Capabilities

How does one describe the "domain aspects" and "operational aspects" of a component's capabilities? The domain of a database is defined by the entity types and the relationships (or other data model constructs) that appear in the database's schema. The operational aspect is defined by the underlying DBMS. Different DBMSs (particularly legacy systems) will offer different functionalities, and it is this that determines how the available data may be manipulated. Both aspects must be known to the match-maker if incoming requests are to be matched accurately. To accommodate this, we propose the following basic framework for advertisements:

```
(advertise,
    :sender       <component>
    :receiver     match-maker
    :language     Advertise
    :content      (ask-*,
                      :sender      <anyone>
                      :receiver    <component>
                      :language    <language>
                      :ontology    <ontology>
                      :domain      d-constraint(<expr>)
                      :operation   o-constraint(<expr>)
                      :content     <expr> ))
```

As in KQML advertisements, the outermost :content slot contains a specification of a collection of requests the advertising component is willing to service.[2] The innermost :content slot contains a pattern expression which describes the syntactic structures the advertising component is willing to handle.

Unlike KQML, however, there is also a :domain slot and an :operation slot, each of which specifies additional constraints on the pattern expression. The constraints given in the **domain** slot describe the characteristics of requests whose domain of interest matches that of the advertising component. The :operation slot, on the other hand, indicates that the component can only serve requests whose semantics satisfy the conditions it specifies. Thus, even if a request r matches a pattern expression e, it may still not be servable by the advertising agent if r fails on either the operational or domain constraints. Match-making is therefore based on semantic as well as syntactic considerations.

4.1   Simple Pattern Expressions

Before describing the form that the domain and operational constraints may take, we present the format of the pattern expressions that may be specified in the :content slot. We first define the concept of "capability" formally and then discuss how a capability may be described using simple expressions.

Definition 1. *A request is a recursive structure of the following form:*

$$\alpha(\tau_1, \tau_2, \dots, \tau_m)$$

where α is a constant term and each $\tau_i, i = 1, \dots, m$ is either a constant or a structure of this same form.

---

[2] ask-* matches with any of the range of ask performatives (ask-one, ask-all, etc.).

This definition approximates a syntax tree for the request language, and is intended to model the internal representation of the request within the match-maker agent. For example, the following SQL query:

```
SELECT specNo FROM opticalCable WHERE cableType = 'Unitube'
```

can be expressed as:

```
select(tables([opticalCable]), attrs([specNo]),
                    op(=, attr(cableType), 'Unitube'))
```

A *well-formed request* is a request whose structure represents a legal expression in the content language.[3] It is trivial to define this notion of legality of expression formally, and we do not define it here. However, we note that the arguments in the request structure are "positional", i.e. different permutations of arguments results in different requests. For example, the following:

```
select(tables([opticalCable]), attrs([specNo]),
                    op(=, attr(cableType), 'Unitube'))
```

```
select(tables([opticalCable]), attrs([specNo]),
                    op(=, 'Unitube', attr(cableType)))
```

are considered to be distinct requests.[4]

We define a component's capability in terms of the set of requests that it claims to be able to serve.

Definition 2. *Let $\mathcal{R} = \{r_1, r_2, \ldots, r_n\}$ be the set of all well-formed requests. A capability $\mathcal{C}$ is a set of such requests; that is, $\mathcal{C} \subset \mathcal{R}$. Each $c_i \in \mathcal{C}$ is referred to as a* capability element *(or* element *when the context is clear).*

Advertisement of a capability is therefore specification of the set $\mathcal{C}$. A naive approach is to enumerate all the elements as a disjunction. That is, the component anticipates all possible requests that it can answer and specifies each of them in detail. However, as we have argued, this approach is unworkable for database resources (or any component where $\mathcal{C}$ is large). To advertise a capability more concisely, we require a means of advertising several capability elements in one expression, and hence introduce the use of simple pattern expressions.

Definition 3. *A* simple pattern expression *takes one of the following forms:*

---

[3] In order to simplify the presentation, we assume a reduced dialect of SQL that can be represented by syntax trees of the form given. However, the issues discussed are largely independent of the choice of content language.

[4] This assumption is not a serious limitation. If, for example, our match-maker is intelligent enough to recognise the commutative property of the = operator, then it could treat both requests as equivalent. In this paper, however, we focus on the specification of capabilities, rather than the intelligence of the match-maker.

1. *a constant pattern $\alpha(\tau_1, \tau_2, \ldots, \tau_m)$, where each α, τ_1, $\ldots$, τ_m is a constant,*
2. *a variable pattern $\alpha(\tau_1, \tau_2, \ldots, \tau_m)$, where at least one $\alpha, \tau_1, \ldots, \tau_m$ is a pattern variable, or*
3. *a single pattern variable v.*

Note that if any τ_i, $1 \leq i \leq m$, is a recursive structure, then rules 1) and 2) apply recursively.

We denote a pattern variable in an advertisment by a literal with a $ prefix. For example, the following are all valid pattern expressions:

```
select(tables([opticalCable]), attrs([specNo]),
                    op(=, attr(cableType), 'Unitube'))
```

```
$opn(tables([opticalCable]), attrs([specNo]),
                    op(=, attr(cableType), $value))
```

```
$expr
```

The use of pattern variables in this way allows agents to abstract their capabilities (i.e. describe them more concisely). To capture this notion of abstraction formally, we give the following definition.

Definition 4. *Let c_1 and c_2 be two simple pattern expressions. We say that c_1 abstracts c_2 in the following mutually exclusive cases:*

1. *if c_1 is a single pattern variable v*
2. *if c_1 is a constant pattern $\alpha(\tau_1, \ldots, \tau_n)$ and c_1 lexically matches c_2*
3. *if $c_1 = \alpha(\tau_1, \ldots, \tau_n)$, $c_2 = \alpha'(\tau_1', \ldots, \tau_n')$ where α is a variable or $\alpha = \alpha'$, and for each $\tau_i, i = 1, \ldots, m$, τ_i is a variable or $\tau_i = \tau_i'$*

Again, if any τ_i is a recursive structure, then rules 2) and 3) apply recursively.

Definition 5. *Let C_1 and C_2 be two capabilities. C_1 subsumes C_2, denoted by $C_1 \succ C_2$, if for every $c_2 \in C_2$, there exists a $c_1 \in C_1$ such that c_1 abstracts c_2.*

Obviously, an ideal capability advertisement is a pattern expression that subsumes the intended set of requests both concisely and precisely. The use of pattern variables in expressions allows us to achieve this at various levels. At the lowest level, we have *domain abstraction*. That is, we allow pattern variables to be used wherever domain values are used. For example, the following is an abstraction of a class of capability elements that all have the same structure, but use different domain values:

```
select(tables([opticalCable]), attrs([specNo]),
                    op(=, attr(cableType), $value))
```

Here, `$value` is a pattern variable which can be instantiated with any constant value. As this example shows, the abstraction achieved at this level is fairly limited. The next level of abstraction, *argument-level abstraction*, overcomes this limitation to an extent. With this form of abstraction, we allow pattern variables to be used for the arguments of a capability element, e.g.

```
select(tables([opticalCable]), attrs([specNo]), $cond)
```

Here, a pattern variable (`$cond`) is used to abstract the class of SQL selection conditions. Thus, the above expression subsumes both:

```
select(tables([opticalCable]), attrs([specNo]),
                        op(=, attr(cableType), 'Unitube')))
```

and

```
select(tables([opticalCable]), attrs([specNo]),
                        op(<>, attr(cableType), 'Unitube')))
```

Note that as the capability elements become more abstract, the likelihood of over-advertisement increases and the accuracy of the advertisement becomes more dependent on the constraints given in the :operation and :domain slots.

As Vassalos and Papakonstantinou [13] have pointed out, it is also possible to use pattern variables to generalise operations. For example, the following expression illustrates this *operation-level* abstraction:

```
$db-op(tables([opticalCable]), $attrs, $cond)
```

The element in this example advertises that it is willing to serve any operation involving only the table `opticalCable`. This expression abstracts both of the following requests:

```
select(tables([opticalCable]), attrs([specNo]),
                        op(=, attr(cableType), 'Unitube')))
```

```
delete(tables([opticalCable]), (),
                        op(<>, attr(cableType), 'Unitube))
```

Operation-level abstraction is very general. Careful specification of constraints on such abstractions is therefore important if software components are not to be flooded with requests that they cannot answer.

All the abstractions we have introduced so far are limited in that they specify a fixed structure. In cases where a software component wishes to advertise a capability that is made of capability elements with different structures (e.g some with three arguments and some with two), we allow *structure abstraction* — the highest level of abstraction in our language. Consider the following example,

```
$any-req
```

Here the expression is a single pattern variable $any-req which abstracts, and hence can match, any request. Without appropriate constraints, this form of pattern leads to an extreme form of over-advertisement in which the agent claims to be able to serve any request whatever.

4.2   Composite Pattern Expressions

If we view matching as evaluation of a truth-valued function that returns true if the request matches the pattern and false otherwise, we can combine simple pattern expressions using the standard logical operators AND, OR and NOT. For example, the following composite pattern expression shows how two simple expressions may be combined using the OR operator:

```
select($tables, $attrs, op(=, $attr, $value)) OR
select($tables, $attrs, op(<>, $attr, $value))
```

This pattern expression matches a request if either of the two simple expressions match it. In other words, the set of requests that the component is willing to handle is the union of the request sets specified by the two simple expressions.

We can also use the AND and NOT operators to combine patterns. For example, a component C1 may advertise that it can handle the retrieval of any attributes from opticalCable relation, except the cableType attribute alone:

```
select(tables([opticalCable]), $attrs, $cond) AND NOT
select(tables([opticalCable]), attrs(cableType), $cond)
```

Of course, a similar effect could be achieved by adding a constraint to the :domain slot. We will now describe how such constraints can be used to limit the over-advertising tendencies of patterns.

4.3   Constraining Pattern Variables

The pattern variables introduced in the previous section are useful in that they allow database resources to specify a superset of the requests they are willing to handle very concisely. While, in general, over-advertisement is to be preferred to under-advertisement, it is clearly beneficial for all parties if advertisements can be specified as accurately as possible. Pattern variables must therefore be further constrained so that the match-maker agent is aware of any additional restrictions on the domain of interest or the semantics that can be handled by the advertising component. For example, a database component that stores details of optical cables cannot answer queries which relate to copper cables, even if some aspects of the query also relate to optical cables. Similarly, consider a wrapped component that is capable of evaluating certain SQL queries against a flat file, by converting them into instructions to the Unix Grep program. This component will only be capable of answering a restricted set of SQL queries; namely, those consisting of a series of simple projections and selections on the structure of the file.

Definition 6. *A domain constraint in an advertisement relating to a compo-nent* c *is a truth-valued expression, parameterised by the pattern variables ap-pearing in the advertisement. The constraint determines the subset of requests that match with the pattern expression that are concerned wholly with domain elements known to the component.*

Definition 7. *An operational constraint in an advertisement relating to a com-ponent* c *is a truth-valued expression, parameterised by the pattern variables ap-pearing in the advertisement. The constraint determines the subset of requests that match with the pattern expression that the component has the operational capacity to evaluate.*

For the purpose of this paper, we assume that both domain and operational constraints (as stated in the :**domain** and :**operation** slots of the advertisement format respectively) are first order logic expressions over pattern variables.[5] Consider the following fragment of an advertisement sent by component C1:

```
:operation   (simple_query $e)
:domain      (subset (domain $e) (commits_to C1))
:content     $e
```

Here, (simple_query $e) is a predicate which is true if the value of $e is equiv-alent to a request fragment with the semantics of a "simple" relational algebra query. We define a "simple" query to be one in which the condition of the query is a simple conjunction of comparison operators on attributes.

The domain constraint states that the domain elements occurring in the request must be a subset of the domain elements to which the advertising com-ponent commits. In other words, the component cannot answer queries asking about domain elements which are not contained within its schema. Notice that we have *not* embedded any details of the actual schema within the advertisement itself. Instead, we assume that the match-maker component has the responsibil-ity of discovering what the current set of commitments of component C1 are — perhaps by interrogating some ontological knowledge agent or data dictionary.

Operational and domain constraints like those given in the example are speci-fied by building expressions using the usual logical connectives (**and**, **or** and **not**) and a number of pre-defined predicates and functions, such as simple_query and commits, stored in a special purpose *task ontology*. If a predicate such as simple_query is not defined by a formula (i.e. it is a ground definition), then we assume that it is a Boolean valued function stored in the task ontology that returns true if its arguments have the required properties and false otherwise. In our prototype, for example, we have used the "grammar" shown below to recognise the subset of legal syntax tree forms that correspond to the class of simple queries.

---

[5] It is, of course, possible to use various other formalisms to specify the constraints, such as a description logic.

```
<simple_query>      ::= select(<tables>, <attributes>) |
                        select(<tables>, <attributes>), <condition>)
<tables>            ::= tables(<table names>)
<table names>       ::= <table name> | <table names>,<table name>
<attributes>        ::= attrs(<attribute names>)
<attribute names>   ::= <attribute name> |
                        <attribute names>,<attribute name>
<condition>         ::= op(=, <attribute name>, <attribute name>) |
                        op(=, <attribute name>, <constant>) |
                        op(=, <constant>, <attribute name>)
<attribute name>    ::= <name> | <table name>.<name>
<table name>        ::= <name>
<name>              ::= <identifier>
```

5 Matching Process

We now consider how a request from a user agent is matched with an advertisement by the match-maker. A request is first matched syntactically with the
pattern expression and then semantically with the constraints. The process of
syntactical matching is straightforward. An advertisement a matches a request
r if it can be made identical with r by substituting the pattern variables in a
with the corresponding values in r. In other words, a matches r if a abstracts r.
For example, the advertised pattern:

```
select(tables([opticalCable]), attrs([specNo]), $cond))
```

can be made to match the following request:

```
select(tables([opticalCable]), attrs([specNo]),
                    op(=, attr(cableType), 'Unitube'))
```

by substituting the variable $cond by op(=, attr(cableType), 'Unitube).
Our match-maker therefore performs a simple pre-order matching process, recursively matching the request with a simple pattern expression, argument by
argument from left to right. The complexity of the matching process is therefore
linear in the size of the advertisement base (the number of advertisements). The
matching of a request with a composite expression is a trivial extension to this
process.

Once the request has been matched with the pattern expression, the match-
maker will proceed to attempt a semantic match against the domain and operational constraints. The semantic matching process can potentially be very
complex, depending on the form of the constraints and the reasoning power of
the matchmaker. As our focus in this paper is the specification of advertisement,
we have used standard first order logic specification and inference for domain
and operation constraints, as discussed in the previous section. However, there
are clearly opportunities for improving the efficiency of matching by using more

advanced algorithms (based on constraint logic programming, for example). A simple match-maker based on the proposal presented in this paper has been implemented within the context of a case study of a distributed information system at Pirelli Cables Ltd Newport factory [6]. The matching process is implemented in Prolog, with a Java front-end. The JATlite toolkit was used to provide KQML-based communication between software components.

6   Conclusions

The ability to advertise database capabilities concisely yet precisely is an important pre-requisite for the development of flexible DIS architectures, based on "location-independent" cooperation between components. A DIS based on match-making is more resilient to both short- and long-term change in its constituent components, as existing components can automatically make the decision to use services offered by new components. We have described an approach to advertisement that overcomes the limitations of previous proposals for describing database capabilities. The result is a capability description language that combines the following advantages:

- Pattern variables may be used at all levels to allow many different request forms to be advertised using a single pattern expression.
- Further flexibility in describing capabilities is provided by the ability to combine patterns using the OR, AND and NOT operators.
- Additional constraints can be placed on the semantics of the capabilities which are advertised, over and above the syntactic constraints given by pattern expressions. This allows agents to characterise their capabilities much more precisely than would be possible using pattern matching alone.
- Despite our focus on pattern matching as the basis of our advertisement format, the importance of matching on domain concepts as a means of reducing over-advertisement is not neglected. Additional constraints can be specified to ensure that incoming requests are matched only with resources which share their domain of interest.
- Our approach does not require that the entire schema of the resource be embedded explicitly within the advertisement. Thus, we do not place unreasonable demands on the match-maker's ability to cope with very large advertisements, nor do advertisements grow out of date as resources evolve.

Our proposal thus combines the flexibility of pattern expressions of RQDL (albeit without the rigorous formal underpinnings of that proposal) with the realistic approaches to matching large domains in DIS systems and the ontological approach to operational constraints hinted at within the InfoSleuth proposal [8].

A number of open questions regarding the advertisement of capabilities for database agents still remain. There is as yet very little understanding of the trade-off between advertisement complexity (to reduce over-advertising) and the time required to match requests with such complex advertisements. It may be that a certain amount of over-advertisement is beneficial to the agent system as a whole if this means that the match-maker agent is able to operate efficiently. Further investigation is also required into the level of intelligence to be provided by the match-maker agent. For example, it may be useful to endow the match-maker with incremental learning capabilities to allow it to refine its database of advertisements based on experience. The match-maker can monitor the results of the requests it matches, to build up a knowledge base of the successful and unsuccessful cases. Initially, the system's performance would be relatively poor, as the match-maker would have very little knowledge of the participating resources, but it would improve over time as its experience grew. A facility for adaptive match-making of this kind could remove the responsibility for monitoring the capabilities of the network from individual components, and optimise the connections between consumer and provider components to improve overall performance of the DIS.

Acknowledgements

We are grateful to Martin Karlsson for the implementation, to Alun Preece for his helpful comments on a draft of this paper, and to the members of the OKS group at Cardiff University for their feedback on our advertisement format.

References

1. Y. Arens, C.-N. Hsu, and C.A. Knoblock. Query Processing in the SIMS Information Mediator. In Austin Tate, editor, *Advanced Planning Technology*, pages 61–69. AAAI Press, 1996.
2. P.G. Baker, A. Brass, S. Bechhfer, C. Goble, N.W. Paton, and R. Stevens. TAMBIS - Transparent Access to Multiple Biological Information Sources. In J. Glasgow *et al.*, editor, *Proc. of 6th Int. Conf. on Intelligent Systems for Molecular Biology*, pages 25–34, Montréal. AAAI Press, 1998.
3. K. Decker *et al.* Matchmaking and Brokering. In M. Tokoro, editor, *Proc. of 2nd Int. Conf. on Multiagent Sytems*, Kyoto. AAAI Press, 1996.
4. K. Decker, K. Sycara, and M. Williamson. Middle-Agents for the Internet. In *Proc. of 15th Int. Joint Conf. on Artificial Intelligence (IJCAI'97)*, pages 578–583, Nagoya, Japan. Morgan Kaufmann, 1997.
5. T. Finin, R. Fritzson, D. McKay, and R. McEntire. KQML as an Agent Communication Language. In *Proc. of 3rd Int. Conf. on Information and Knowledge Management (CIKM'94)*, pages 456–463, Gaithersburg, USA, 1994. ACM Press.
6. M. Karlsson. A Matchmaker Agent for Database Applications. Master's thesis, Cardiff University, September 1999.
7. D. Kuokka and L. Harada. Supporting Information Retrieval via Matchmaking. In C. Knoblock and A. Levy, editors, *Proc. of AAAI Spring Symp. on Information Gathering from Heterogeneous, Distributed Envs.*, pages 111–115. AAAI, 1995.
8. M. Nodine, W. Bohrer, and A.H.H. Ngu. Semantic Brokering over Dynamic Heterogeneous Data Sources in InfoSleuth. In M. Papazoglou, C. Pu, and M. Kitsuregawa, editors, *Proc. of 15th Int. Conf. on Data Engineering (ICDE'99)*, pages 358–365, Sydney. IEEE Computer Society Press, 1999.

9. N. Singh, M. Genesereth, and M.A. Syed. A Distributed and Anonymous Knowledge Sharing Approach to Software Interoperation. *International Journal of Cooperative Information Systems*, 4(4):339–367, 1995.
10. K. Sycara, J. Lu, and M. Klusch. Interoperability among Heterogeneous Software Agents on the Internet. Technical Report CMU-RI-TR-98-22, Robotics Institute, Carnegie Mellon University, October 1998.
11. K. Sycara, J. Lu, M. Klusch, and S. Widoff. Matchmaking among Heterogeneous Agents in the Internet. In S. Murugesan and D.E. O'Leary, editors, *Proc. of AAAI Spring Symp. on Intelligent Agents in Cyberspace*, Stanford, USA, 1999.
12. V. Vassalos and Y. Papakonstantinou. Describing and Using Query Capabilities of Heterogeneous Sources. In M. Jarke *et al.*, editor, *Proc. of 23rd Int. Conf. on Very Large Data Bases*, pages 256–265, Athens, 1997. Morgan Kaufmann, Inc.
13. V. Vassalos and Y. Papkonstantinou. Expressive Capabilities Description Languages and Query Rewriting Algorithms. *Journal of Logic Programming*, 43(1):75–122, 2000. Special Issue on Logic-Based Heterogeneous Information Systems.

A Personal Assistant for Web Database Caching

Beat Signer, Antonia Erni, and Moira C. Norrie

Institute for Information Systems
ETH Zurich, CH-8092 Zurich, Switzerland
{signer, erni, norrie}@inf.ethz.ch

Abstract. To improve the performance of web database access for regular users, we have developed a client caching agent, referred to as a personal assistant. In addition to caching strategies based on data characteristics and user specification, the personal assistant dynamically prefetches information based on previously monitored user access patterns. It is part of an overall multi-layered caching scheme where cache coherency is ensured through cooperation with a server-side database caching agent. The personal assistant has been implemented in Java and integrated into the web architecture for the OMS Pro database management system.

1 Introduction

Significant gains in performance for web access to databases can be achieved with a shift away from server-side access architectures towards web-based client-server database architectures. By moving components of the database system to the web client, user access times can be improved by reducing both server load and communication costs. Communication costs can be decreased through a combination of using socket-based communication instead of the slower Hypertext Transfer Protocol (HTTP) and eliminating some of the communication through client-side caching mechanisms and processing. In addition, further reductions in user response times can be achieved by predictive prefetching of data into an active cache based on observed user access patterns.

We have implemented such a web-based architecture for the object-oriented database management system OMS Pro [NW99,KNW98] in which client-side DBMS components include a generic object browser, schema editor, presentation editor and also caching agents [ENK98,EN98]. The client-side caching framework may optionally contain a *personal assistant* which provides registered users with an adaptive, persistent cache on their local machine. The personal assistant monitors a user's access behaviour in order to dynamically prefetch data in accordance with predicted access patterns. Cache coherency is ensured in cooperation with the server-side database agent where communication is established through the use of persistent socket connections between the client-side agents and the database agent. Changes to the database can therefore be propagated to all client-side agents ensuring that only current information is stored in the client agent's caches. The resulting multi-level caching scheme, together with its

B. Wangler, L. Bergman (Eds.): CAiSE 2000, LNCS 1789, pp. 64–78, 2000.

prefetching strategies, has enabled us to significantly improve performance while keeping the caching overhead small.

The personal assistant's cache provides benefits not only in terms of performance, but also in terms of mobile computing in that it allows objects of interest to be explicitly cached and then accessed without an active connection to the server side. We note however that this is not the main purpose of the cache and full, disconnected operation of OMS Pro databases with bi-directional, synchronised updates is supported through a general database connectivity mechanism, OMS Connect [NPW98].

Our architecture is specifically designed to cater for the requirements of web databases and the access patterns of their users in contrast to other proposals for advanced web caching schemes [Wes95,CDF+98,CZB98,BBM+97]. General web caching strategies typically do not cache dynamically generated documents, nor do they deal with the case of client-side applications retrieving query results from a database on the server side. In contrast, we recognise the browsing-style access patterns of many web-based information systems where users navigate from single entry points and frequently issue the same or similar requests to a database as is reflected by the heavy use of the "back"-button in web browsers.

Clearly, building client-server database systems on the web is similar in concept to any form of client-server database architecture. However, the fact that we access the database via a web browser with the client components implemented as Java applets presents some special technical challenges including problems of security restrictions, the general dynamic and temporary nature of the client-server relationship, interaction with browsers and non-uniformity across different browsers.

In Sect. 2, we present our general web-based client-server architecture in terms of the various caches and the agents managing them. Section 3 goes on to detail the functionality of the personal assistant and the active cache it maintains. The personal assistant's user interface is outlined in Sect. 4 and some implementation details are given in Sect. 5. Performance issues and preliminary measurement results are presented in Sect. 6, while concluding remarks are given in Sect. 7.

2   Web Client-Server Database Architecture

Currently, most architectures for web access to databases are server-based in that the whole database functionality resides on the server side [ACPT99]. To avoid the processing overheads associated with CGI architectures and provide support for interactive user sessions, Java servlets provide a general means of improving the efficiency and ease of development of server-based application systems [HCF98]. In the case of database systems, several general and DBMS-specific web servers tailored for database system access have been developed. However, with all of these solutions, processing tends to remain on the server side and communication is via the HTTP protocol with results presented as Hypertext Markup Language (HTML) documents.

While Java applets are being used increasingly to move processing to web clients, it tends to be the case in web information systems that there is a separation of application and database logic and all components of the DBMS remain on the server side. For example, an application applet may use a JDBC database server to retrieve information from a database [Ree97]. There are however disadvantages of this approach resulting from the fact that the applet and the database are only loosely-coupled, meaning that the applet cannot exploit the full functionality of the database system and has to do all the work of interpreting and assembling query results and then generating their presentation.

We are instead interested in making a DBMS web-capable in the sense that components of the DBMS can execute on the client side. Thus, it is not the case of client applications connecting via the web to server database systems, but rather adapting the DBMS to a dynamic client-server architecture in which the clients run through a web browser. The client-server architecture is dynamically generated when downloading the client as an applet over the Internet.

A major advantage of this approach is that database-specific caching strategies can be implemented on the client machine. Other advantages come in terms of the ease of providing clients with extended database functionality, eliminating unnecessary mappings through intermediate standard interfaces and generally providing the look and feel of a DBMS through the web for both developers and end-users. To this end, we have developed web components for OMS Pro.

In addition to client-side components for browsing and caching, we also have schema and object presentation editors which execute on the client side and enable databases to be designed and prototyped over the web. The general browser and developer components are heavily used in teaching since they enable students to browse, query, update and create databases via the web. Furthermore, they are valuable in providing on-line demonstrations of our OMS Pro system. The caching components with their own presentation layer are part of the Internet OMS framework which can be used by any web application system based on OMS Pro.

In Fig. 1, we show the web architecture of the resulting Internet OMS system [EN98], with respect to the general querying and browsing interface and cache management.

OMS Pro has an integrated server and we can therefore assume that the database on the server side is ready to accept requests. We show that, although the database is on the server side, it may be located on a machine other than that of the web server.

Initial access to the system is through a normal web browser using the HTTP protocol as indicated by step 1. An applet is returned and a front-end agent started on the client side. This front-end agent is responsible for communication with the server side, presentation of objects and the maintenance of a short-term session cache. Thus, when query requests are issued, the front-end agent checks whether they were previously requested in which case the results are already stored in the local session cache. Therefore, if users browse a database, going "back" to previous objects, no communication with the server is required.

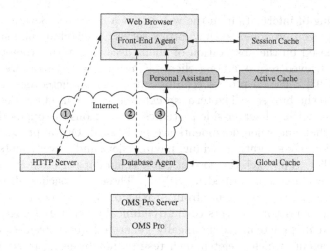

Fig. 1. Architecture overview of Internet OMS

A query result contains the required database data with additional metadata information such that the front-end agent can generate the appropriate view of the object and present it to the user.

The front-end agent sends requests to a database agent on the server side as shown in step 2. The database agent manages a global cache and notifies client-side caching agents of database updates that invalidate data objects in their caches. This is possible since we use two-way communication over persistent connections instead of HTTP. The global cache is beneficial across the user community in caching query results already requested by other users or by the same user in previous sessions. This proves to be extremely advantageous since web information systems usually have only a few entry points and the queries corresponding to points at the beginning of navigation paths tend to be repeated frequently and are relatively stable in terms of their results.

To further improve the performance for regular users, it is possible to locally install an adaptive caching agent, referred to as a *personal assistant*, which manages a client-side persistent cache. The personal assistant registers with the database agent on the server side and its cache is maintained in cooperation with the database agent. It manages a short-term session cache and long-term personal and prefetching caches. Separate caches are provided for image files. The personal assistant maintains a user access profile which is used to dynamically prefetch data during user sessions based on access predictions. In addition, users can explicitly specify data of interest and the personal assistant ensures that this data is always stored in the local cache and is current. The caches managed by the personal assistant are persistent in that they are written to disk every time the personal assistant is shut down (for security aspects see Sect. 5). In the case that a personal assistant is running on a client machine, the database agent informs the front-end agent and all communication is redirected through the personal assistant as indicated by step 3 in Fig. 1.

Prefetching of information on the web is not a new idea. Several approaches have already been proposed, such as proxy servers prefetching and storing popular pages based on the observation of client access patterns, thereby allowing sharing of retrieved results among clients [CY97]. A proxy-side pre-push technique by [JC98] relies on proxies sending (pushing) predicted documents from the proxies to the browsers. The term *speculative service* used by [Bes95] defines prefetching in terms of server-side statistics and actions, as opposed to clients controlling what and when documents are prefetched. Our approach goes more in the direction of cooperative caching, having client and server agents cooperate with each other to prefetch the correct data. A similar prefetching approach for general web caching is described in [SW97]. These approaches all concentrate on prefetching HTML documents from proxies or web servers to web browsers and neither proxies nor browsers cache dynamically generated pages. Since we are interested in prefetching dynamically generated query results, we provide cooperating agents which prefetch such results, not by using proxy or browser caches, but rather by providing our own caching hierarchy as shown in the dynamic client-server architecture in Fig. 1.

The partitioning of the local active cache and combination of various caching and prefetching mechanisms has enabled us to significantly improve performance while keeping the caching overhead in terms of space, processing and communication costs to an acceptable level. In the following sections, we describe the operation of these various cooperative agents and their caches in detail.

3   Personal Assistant and Its Active Cache

There are three different "subcaches" building up the active cache managed by the personal assistant: The *session cache*, the *personal cache* and a *prefetching cache* (see Fig. 2). These three caches are disjoint, i.e. the same information will be cached in at most one of the caches. They differ from the front-end agent's session cache in that their content is made persistent and is available in future sessions.

In recognition that multimedia files, especially images, form a vital part of most web-based information systems, we provide special support for the caching of images. Each of the three subcaches is divided into a part for caching query results and a part for caching images. We have chosen this approach because the image sizes are large relative to the query results and often the same image

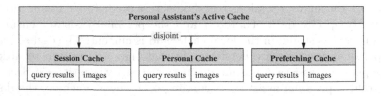

Fig. 2. Personal assistant's caching framework

is required by different queries. Due to this separation, an image will always be cached at most once, even if it is needed by more than one query. The caching space saved by this strategy, i.e. by eliminating image redundancy, is used to cache additional query results. Every time a query result is removed from a cache, we check if an associated image is still required by any other queries before removing it from the cache. This was done by introducing a reference counter indicating the number of queries using the image and implementing a *garbage collector*.

Note that the personal assistant will not cache any referenced HTML documents or multimedia files other than images, e.g. sound and movies.

3.1   Session Cache

The session cache, as its name suggests, acts as a short-term cache and will only cache query results recently used. Therefore the caching strategy used by the session cache is a simple least recently used (LRU) strategy (for further information about caching strategies see [Tan92,SG94,Fra96]). By using an LRU replacement strategy, the session cache will profit from the locality of a single session.

3.2   Personal Cache

A user may explicitly specify data of interest by defining query results to be permanently cached. These query results are then managed by the personal cache. To ensure that the data in the personal cache is always up to date, every time a new entry is added to the cache, the personal assistant registers it with the database agent on the server side. Whenever data changes in the database, the database agent checks whether registered queries are affected. If so, the database agent sends a cache invalidation message to the corresponding personal assistants, forcing them to update their caches to maintain cache consistency. Removal of a query result from the personal cache will cause the query to be unregistered with the database agent. Further, every time a personal assistant is started, the entire contents of its persistent caches are registered with the database agent.

The personal cache does not have a caching strategy, i.e. if there is no more place in the cache, the cache manager will not select a victim and replace it by the new entry to be added. If a user tries to add a new query result to the personal cache and there is no more space, the caching agent informs him that he either has to manually remove some entries from the cache or to increase the personal cache size at runtime. This "caching strategy" makes sense because the user wants to be sure that all the query results added to the personal cache will be present in the future and not be deleted by the cache manager without his knowledge.

Of the three subcaches, the personal cache has the highest priority since the user explicitly defined the query results to be permanently cached. Therefore, if an entry is added to the personal cache and is already part of either the session or prefetching cache, it will be removed from these caches to avoid cache redundancy. Further, a query result will not be added to the session or the prefetching cache if it is already present in the personal cache.

3.3   Prefetching Cache

In addition to the short-time session cache and the user defined personal cache, the prefetching cache will analyse user behaviour and try to predict the information the user will need in the near future. It dynamically adapts to a user's preferences without any interaction.

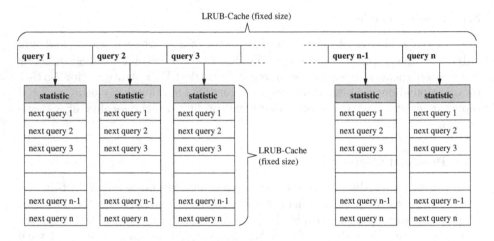

Fig. 3. Structure of the prefetching statistic

For each query requested by the user (*query 1* to *query n* in Fig. 3), the prefetching cache maintains a statistic of the succeeding queries and the number of times they were requested immediately after the current query (*next query 1* to *next query n* in Fig. 3). The statistic is in turn represented by a cache of limited size. So for each query, only a limited amount of possible succeeding queries – the queries which will most likely follow the current query – are considered in the statistic. The simplest replacement strategy for these statistic caches would be an LRU strategy. The problem is that these caches should act as long-term caches, i.e. the statistic will grow over a long period. Therefore we also have to consider the number of accesses for each cache entry when selecting a victim for removal. As a result, the LRU strategy is extended by the number of times a cache entry was requested resulting in an LRUB caching strategy where the number of cache hits acts as a *bonus* for entries which where often used in the past but have not been accessed recently. Considering these facts, we use the following weighting formula for cache entry i

$$weight_i = \frac{\alpha + (1 - \alpha)\, H_i}{T_i} \qquad 0 \le \alpha \le 1 \tag{1}$$

where H_i is the number of hits for entry i and T_i is the time since the last access of entry i. Each time an element has to be added to a full cache, the cache entry with the smallest weight will be removed from the cache. The influence of earlier cache hits can be adjusted by changing the value of α in (1). The smaller the value of α, the greater the weighting given to the number of cache hits (by setting $\alpha = 1$ we have a simple LRU cache).

The queries with their statistic are themselves maintained in a cache of limited size using the same LRUB caching strategy. Therefore, only for the queries most likely to be requested in the future will a statistic of the succeeding queries be present in the prefetching statistic. Each time a user requests a new query, the personal assistant checks whether there exists a statistic for it. If a corresponding statistic is present, the queries with the highest weights (the queries which will most likely succeed the current query) are selected. The corresponding query results will then be prefetched into the prefetching cache. The maximal number of query results to be prefetched is defined by the prefetching width. By increasing the prefetching width, the cache hit rate can be slightly improved but, as a negative effect, the database agent will have to handle an additional amount of queries.

The prefetching cache will profit from the fact that, in web interfaces to databases, users often browse in a similar way, i.e. as users navigate through the database, there exist "chains of queries" often requested in the same order. While a user analyses the result of one query, the personal assistant prefetches the predicted next query results. Over slower network connections, this active prefetching leads to better usage of the available bandwidth and may employ otherwise paid for, but idle, modem connection time.

The great advantage of the proposed dynamic prefetching mechanism over a "static" strategy of globally caching the most frequently used query results is that the prefetching cache, like a sliding window, always focuses on the current query. As a result, it only contains the data most likely required in the near future and therefore needs much less memory than a global strategy trying to achieve the same hit rate.

4   Agent User Interfaces

As can be seen from the description of the active cache in the previous section and the general client-server architecture in section 2, the overall system comprises many levels of caches and associated agents. It is therefore essential that tools be provided to facilitate system installation, administration and tuning. For each agent – database, front-end and personal assistant – a graphical user interface is provided that enables both the agent and associated cache parameters to be set and the operation of both the agent and the cache to be monitored. An example of such an interface is given in Fig. 4 which shows the graphical user interface of the personal assistant.

The parameters option enables the agent's associated properties, such as server host name and port numbers for communication with other agents, to be

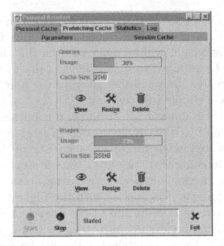

Fig. 4. Personal assistant's prefetching cache

specified. It also provides methods to start and stop the agent. The log option enables a log of agent activities to be inspected. Further it shows additional information about processed queries, clients connecting to the agent and other network specific details. All information presented in the log view is stored in a log file and therefore also can be inspected by means of a standard text editor after the agent has been terminated. The statistics option displays information such as the number of queries processed, their execution time (with or without images), the average execution time and the percentage cache hit rate.

Options are also available for each of the caches managed by the agent – in the case of the personal assistant these are the personal, prefetching and session caches. The graphical user interface shows information about the usage and size of both query and image caches. As shown in Fig. 4, it is possible to view, resize or delete the contents of the different caches.

In Fig. 5, a view of the query part of the prefetching cache is presented. As presented, the cache consists of a number of query results with the associated number of hits shown on the right hand side.

The personal cache is the only cache the content of which can be directly manipulated by the user. To make it easy for a user to specify query results

Prefetching Cache

Key	Processing Time	Last Hit	Hits
aql o388 place_of_interest	Feb 17, 2000 3:19:56 PM	Feb 17, 2000 3:20:01 PM	1
aql o364 place_of_interest	Feb 17, 2000 3:17:58 PM	Feb 17, 2000 3:17:58 PM	0
aql o328 place_of_interest	Feb 17, 2000 3:16:55 PM	Feb 17, 2000 3:16:55 PM	0
aql Eating_and_Drinking	Feb 17, 2000 3:20:01 PM	Feb 17, 2000 3:20:01 PM	0
aql Buildings	Feb 17, 2000 3:16:55 PM	Feb 17, 2000 3:19:39 PM	1
aql o382 place_of_interest	Feb 17, 2000 3:19:39 PM	Feb 17, 2000 3:19:39 PM	0
aql o365 place_of_interest	Feb 17, 2000 3:18:36 PM	Feb 17, 2000 3:18:36 PM	0
aql o374 place_of_interest	Feb 17, 2000 3:17:20 PM	Feb 17, 2000 3:17:20 PM	0
aql Museums	Feb 17, 2000 3:19:21 PM	Feb 17, 2000 3:19:21 PM	0

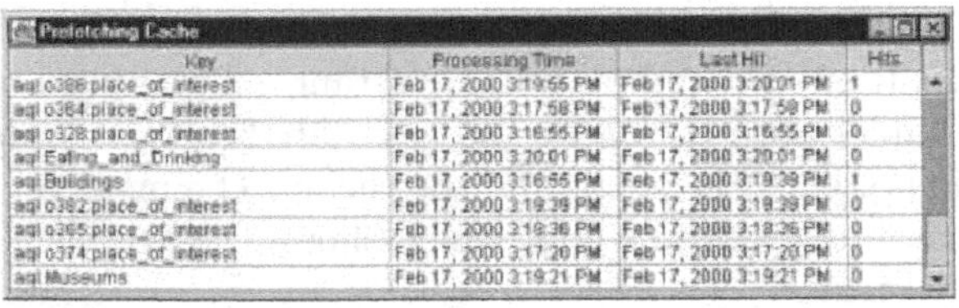

Fig. 5. Prefetching query cache content

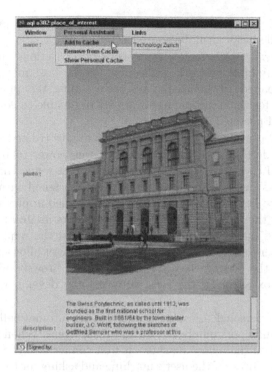

Fig. 6. Personal cache menu

to be permanently cached, the general object browser of Internet OMS was extended by the facility to add a query result to the personal cache by simple menu selection as shown in Fig. 6. To remove a query result from the personal cache, the user may either browse the currently cached query result and select the corresponding menu entry or directly view the personal cache and delete the query entry through the personal assistant's graphical user interface.

When resizing the personal cache, there is a different behaviour than with the other caches. If the user tries to resize either the personal query or image cache to a size smaller than the total size of all entries currently in the cache, he will be informed that the new size is too small. Query results would have to be manually removed from the cache until the space used is less than the desired new cache size.

Note that, in the case of the prefetching cache, deletion of either the prefetching query or image cache causes only the cache entries to be deleted and not the statistics on which the actual prefetching is based.

5   Implementation

All web client components of Internet OMS and also the server-side database agent are implemented in Java. The front-end agent is implemented as a Java applet accessed via a web browser. Optionally a personal assistant may be downloaded and installed as a local Java application.

By default, Java applets have several security restrictions including the fact that they can only open network connections to the host machine from which they were downloaded. In the case of our architecture, this presents a problem as it is necessary for the front-end agent applet to be able to communicate with a locally installed personal assistant.

Fortunately, recent browsers have provisions to give trusted applets the ability to work outside the usual restrictions. For this power to be granted to an applet, additional code has to be added to the applet requesting permission to do any "dangerous" actions and it has to be digitally signed with an unforgeable digital ID (private key). Each time a user runs a signed applet requesting some form of access to the local system, the browser checks its granted privileges for the corresponding signer. If the user already granted the requested additional power to the signer during an earlier session, the browser allows the access without interrupting the user's activities; otherwise the browser will show a Java security dialog box asking if the user will trust the developer the applet was signed by.

Every time a personal assistant is started, it automatically sends its IP-address and listening port number to the database agent. When a new front-end agent is executed on that client machine, it first connects to the database agent, sending it the IP-address of the user's machine and asking for the IP-address and port to which it should connect. The database agent will check if there exists a registered personal assistant with the same IP-address as the address received from the front-end agent. If a personal assistant is registered on the client, the database agent will send the IP-address and port of the personal assistant to the front-end agent. Otherwise the database agent will send its own IP-address and port so that the front-end agent connects directly to the database agent. For a user starting the front-end applet, the process will be the same whether he has installed a personal assistant or not.

6   Performance

To prove the efficiency of our agent architecture, we have built performance predictive models for the caching hierarchies of our system as described in [MA98]. We provide a formal way of dealing with performance problems of our architecture based on the theory of queuing networks. Performance models have been developed for the case where no caches are used at all, where only a global cache on the server side is used and also for the system taking advantage of the personal assistant's and front-end agent's caches [Ern00]. In this paper, we present first measurement results showing the advantages of using our personal assistant to reduce user response times over the case of accessing the database directly.

For the measurements, we queried the *City Database* which was developed to teach object-oriented database concepts in various lecture courses using the

OMS Pro system. The database contains information about cities and their places of interest such as hotels, museums, sightseeing tours etc.

The public web-interface for the City Database allowed us to collect query traces from a large amount of users. Since we are interested in testing performance improvements while using a personal assistant on the client side, we were in need of user traces of single persons to simulate their browsing behaviour. To build a realistic test environment for our simulations, we stressed the server and the network with a moderate workload consisting of our own collected traces.

We tested the system for a number of individual user traces. It is obvious that the personal assistant will achieve the best results when the browsing style of a specific user has been studied over a long period. We refer to this as the *best case*. If the personal assistant instead does not know anything about the browsing behaviour of a user, it is likely that the predicted queries will not be the next ones requested by the user and therefore the wrong data is prefetched into the personal assistant's cache. This is the *worst case* that can occur. The querying behaviour of every user lies somewhere between these two boundaries.

How can these two cases be analysed? For the best case, we provide the personal assistant with history data of user behaviour studied in previous sessions. In addition, we run the simulation feeding the system with one query after the other as provided by the query trace reproducing exactly the browsing behaviour of an individual user. The worst case can be simulated by providing no history data to the personal assistant and selecting queries from the query trace file at random. By randomly selecting the queries, the prefetching of the personal assistant is of little or no benefit. The two scenarios were simulated for several users without and with a personal assistant installed. The average response times are shown in Fig. 7.

The left bar chart shows the results for the worst case where no history data is delivered to the personal assistant and the queries are randomly selected from the query trace. The *total time* represents the average time to query the database, receiving not only the data but also all images a query result contains. The *query time* is the average time required to retrieve data only (without any

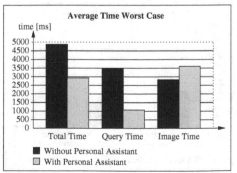 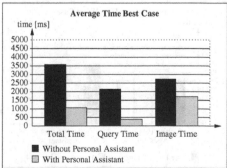

Fig. 7. Average response times

images). Finally, the *image time* represents the mean time necessary to fetch images. As shown, the total response time is reduced by the personal assistant even in the worst case scenario where absolutely no information about the user's browsing behaviour is available. The reduced response times result from the fact that the front-end agent's session cache size is increased by the overall cache size of the personal assistant.

The right part of Fig. 7 shows the results for the best case where the personal assistant's prefetching cache reduces user response times significantly. These results were achieved with a relatively small caching overhead in terms of space. For the database agent, a global cache of 20 kBytes is used while no image cache is necessary, since all images are already stored on the web server. The personal assistant has an image cache of 512 kBytes and a data cache of 40 kBytes counting the personal, prefetching and session cache together. In addition, we also have the session cache of the front-end agent, storing 20 kBytes of data and 512 kBytes of images. The query caches can be kept so small since the results contain data as well as metadata only in textual form. For images, only the references are listed within the query results, whereas the related pictures are stored in the image cache. The number of query results to be prefetched (prefetching width) is set to three, i.e. for each query at most three queries will be executed and the results prefetched. Of course, using larger caches would provide additional advantages in performance since more objects and pictures could be stored, but already with relatively small caches significant performance gains were achieved.

An interesting phenomenon occurs with the average image response times in the worst case scenario (left bar chart of Fig. 7). A more detailed version of the image response times with four different user sessions is shown in the left part of Fig. 8.

For all four users more time is required to download the images with a personal assistant installed. If the front-end agent requests an image and the image is not in the personal assistant's cache, it first has to be downloaded into the personal assistant's image cache and then forwarded to the front-end agent. This

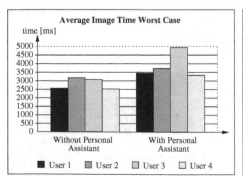
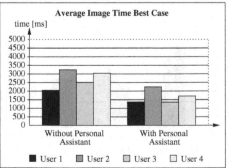

Fig. 8. Image response times

overhead becomes significant if the personal assistant's image hit rate is low (the average cache hit rates are shown in Table 1). Otherwise when correct data is prefetched as shown in the right part of Fig. 8, time for accessing images is drastically reduced.

Table 1. Average cache hit rates

	Worst Case		Best Case	
	queries	images	queries	images
Front-End Agent	13%	4%	33%	29%
Personal Assistant	29%	28%	75%	68%

The results shown by these preliminary experiments are promising. Additional future simulations are planned for heavy workloads and larger data and query sets. For the basis of these experiments, we first want to record typical querying patterns for other operational web-based application systems based on the OMS Pro database.

7 Concluding Remarks

In this paper, we presented our web-based agent architecture for accessing databases over the Internet. Cooperating agents on the client and server sides are responsible for managing local and global caches and ensuring cache coherency. In addition, a personal assistant can be installed on the client side to further improve user response times. The personal assistant monitors user behaviour and assists the user by prefetching the most frequently requested data into a local prefetching cache. Users may further explicitly declare data of interest to ensure that this data is permanently stored in the personal assistant's local cache.

Our architecture has been tested by simulating user sessions and comparing the results achieved with and without a personal assistant. First results show that significant gains in performance are achieved through the installation of a personal assistant on the client side. Even in the worst case scenario where the personal assistant cannot take advantage of learnt query access patterns for predictive prefetching of data, faster access to the data was achieved resulting from the increased overall cache size. Further, the multi-level caching scheme, together with its prefetching strategies, has enabled us to achieve significant performance improvements while keeping caching space to an acceptable level.

References

ACPT99. P. Atzeni, S. Ceri, S. Paraboschi, and R. Torlone. *Database Systems: Concepts, Languages and Architectures*. McGraw-Hill, 1999.

BBM+97. M. Baentsch, L. Baum, G. Molter, S. Rothkugel, and P. Sturm. Enhancing the web infrastructure — from caching to replication. *IEEE Internet Computing*, 1(2):18–27, March/April 1997.

Bes95.   A. Bestavros. Using speculation to reduce server load and service time on the www. In *Proceedings of the International Conference on Information and Knowledge Management, CIKM'95*, Baltimore, MD, November 1995.

CDF+98.   R. Cáceres, F. Douglis, A. Feldmann, G. Glass, and M. Rabinovich. Web proxy caching: the devil is in the details. In *Proceedings of Workshop on Internet Server Performance (WISP'98)*, Madison, WI, June 1998.

CY97.   K. Chinen and S. Yamaguchi. An interactive prefetching proxy server for improvement of WWW latency. In *Proceedings of the Seventh Annual Conference of the Internet Society (INET'97)*, Kuala Lumpur, June 1997.

CZB98.   P. Cao, J. Zhang, and K. Beach. Active cache: Caching dynamic contents on the web. In *Proceedings of IFIP International Conference on Distributed Systems Platforms and Open Distributed Processing (Middleware '98)*, 1998.

EN98.   A. Erni and M. C. Norrie. Approaches to Accessing Databases through Web Browsers. *INFORMATIK, Journal of the Swiss Informaticians Society*, October 1998.

ENK98.   A. Erni, M. C. Norrie, and A. Kobler. Generic Agent Framework for Internet Information Systems. In *Proceedings of IFIP WG 8.1 Conference on Information Systems in the WWW Environment*, Beijing, China, July 1998.

Ern00.   A. Erni. *A Generic Agent Framework for Internet Information Systems*. PhD thesis, ETH Zurich, to be published 2000.

Fra96.   M. J. Franklin. *Client Data Caching: A Foundation for High Performance Object Database Systems*. Kluwer Academic Publishers, 1996.

HCF98.   J. Hunter, W. Crawford, and P. Ferguson. *Java Servlet Programming*. O'Reilly & Associates, 1998.

JC98.   Q. Jacobson and P. Cao. Potential and limits of web prefetching between low-bandwidth clients and proxies. In *Proceedings of the 3rd International WWW Caching Workshop*, Manchester, England, June 1998.

KNW98.   A. Kobler, M. C. Norrie, and A. Würgler. OMS Approach to Database Development through Rapid Prototyping. In *Proceedings of the 8th Workshop on Information Technologies and Systems (WITS'98)*, Helsinki, Finland, December 1998.

MA98.   D. A. Menascé and V. A. F. Almeida. *Capacity Planing for Web Performance: Metrics, Models and Methods*. Prentice Hall, 1998.

NPW98.   M. C. Norrie, A. Palinginis, and A. Würgler. OMS Connect: Supporting Multidatabase and Mobile Working through Database Connectivity. In *Proceedings of Conference on Cooperative Information Systems*, New York, USA, 1998.

NW99.   M. C. Norrie and A. Würgler. OMS Pro: Introductory Tutorial. Technical report, Institute for Information Systems, ETH Zurich, CH-8092 Zurich, Switzerland, March 1999.

Ree97.   G. Reese. *Database Programming with JDBC and Java*. O'Reilly & Associates, 1997.

SG94.   A. Silberschatz and P. Galvin. *Operating System Concepts*. Addison-Wesley, 1994.

SW97.   J. Sommers and C. E. Wills. Prefetching on the web using client and server profiles. Technical report, Worcester Polytechnic Institute, June 1997.

Tan92.   A. S. Tanenbaum. *Modern Operating Systems*. Prentice-Hall, 1992.

Wes95.   D. Wessels. Intelligent caching for world-wide web objects. In *Proceedings of INET'95*, Hawaii, 1995.

Extending a Conceptual Modelling Approach to Web Application Design

Jaime Gómez[1], Cristina Cachero[1,*], and Oscar Pastor[2]

[1] Departamento de Lenguajes y Sistemas Informáticos
Universidad de Alicante. SPAIN
{jgomez,ccachero}@dlsi.ua.es
[2] Departamento de Sistemas Informáticos y Computación
Universidad Politécnica de Valencia. SPAIN
opastor@dsic.upv.es

Abstract. This article presents OO-$\mathcal{H}$Method, an extension of the OO-Method conceptual modelling approach to address the particulars associated with the design of web interfaces. It is based on the OO-Method class diagram, which captures the statics of the system. The design of the interface appearance and the navigation paths are driven by the user navigation requirements. To achieve its goal, OO-$\mathcal{H}$Method adds several navigation and interface constructs to the OO-Method conceptual model, which define the semantics suitable for capturing the specific functionality of web application interfaces. A new kind of diagram, the 'Navigation Access Diagram' (NAD) is introduced. All the concepts represented in the NAD are stored in a repository, and from there a functional interface is generated in an automated way. One of the main contributions of this paper is not the proposal of yet another method for web modelling but the extension of an existing conceptual modelling approach.

1 Introduction

In the last few years the scientific community has conducted major research both on the desirable characteristics of hypermedia applications and on the concepts and processes that make up an effective environment for the structured development of such applications. Many of these concepts have been proven useful and therefore applied to a number of design methods, such as HDM [9], HDM-lite [7], OOHDM [19], RMM [11], ADM [1,12] or Strudel [6]. This article presents OO-$\mathcal{H}$Method, an extension of a conceptual modelling approach known as OO-Method that supports the conceptual design of web applications. This method [14,15] is a powerful proposal for software production from conceptual models. OO-Method is based on a formal object-oriented model OASIS [13] and its main feature is that developers' efforts are focused on the conceptual modelling phase. In this phase, system requirements are captured according to a predefined, finite set of conceptual modelling patterns (representation of relevant concepts at

---

* This article has been written with the sponsorship of the Conselleria de Cultura, Educació i Ciència de la Comunitat Valenciana

B. Wangler, L. Bergman (Eds.): CAiSE 2000, LNCS 1789, pp. 79–93, 2000.

the problem space level). The full OO-implementation is obtained in an automated way following an execution model (including structure and behaviour). This execution model establishes the corresponding mappings between conceptual model constructs and their representation in a particular software development environment. Due to the lack of space, a formal description of OO-Method is not included. Interested readers are referred to [14]. OO-$\mathcal{H}$Method extends OO-Method, which implies that it relies on the information and functionality already provided by OO-Method, e.g. the control over pre and postconditions or the mandatory/optional nature of the value of the attributes. OO-$\mathcal{H}$Method allows the designer to center on the concepts needed to define a web user interface compatible with previously generated OO-Method applications. A new diagram is defined at the conceptual level. This diagram has specific semantics and notational characteristics to cover the observation, navigation and presentation aspects proven useful in the design of web applications. Following the philosophy of OO-Method, OO-$\mathcal{H}$Method applies two concepts: that of filters, based on the dynamic logic [10], and that of navigation patterns. Both the conversion of those patterns to their corresponding default presentation structure and the subsequent mapping of this structure into a set of default interface implementation constructs make possible the generation of the web architecture in an automated way. The code generated constitutes a true web interface to execute existing OO-Method applications over internet/intranet environments. The remainder of the article is structured as follows: section 2 provides a brief description of OO-$\mathcal{H}$Method in the context of the OO-Method approach. Section 3 presents the OO-$\mathcal{H}$Method conceptual model and describes in detail, by means of an example, the navigation access diagram that is used to capture user requirements semantics. Section 4 introduces the OO-$\mathcal{H}$Method execution model and shows the web interface that is generated out of the information captured in the navigation access diagram. A comparison with other related work is presented in section 5. Section 6 presents the conclusions and further work.

2   OO-$\mathcal{H}$Method

OO-$\mathcal{H}$Method is a generic model for the semantic structure of web interfaces, and so it is centered in global activities (authoring in the large) [9], that is, in classes and structures, and not in the content of the information nodes (authoring in the small). It is integrated in OO-Method, and extends the set of graphical elements necessary to get the abstract interaction model of the user interface. It also captures the information which each type of user (agent) can access and the navigation paths from one information view to another. An interface execution model is also provided in order to determine the way the conceptual model is implemented in a given developmental environment. It defines how interface and application modules are to communicate with each other. The navigation model is captured by means of the Navigation Access Diagram (NAD). Each piece of information introduced in the NAD has a corresponding formal counterpart, and is stored in a system repository. From there a functional interface can be generated in an automated way. The interface is coded according to the software environment chosen by the designer both on the client and on the server side.

The rest of the paper discusses both the conceptual and execution models.

3   Conceptual Model: The Navigation Access Diagram

As stated above, the navigation model is captured by means of one or more NAD's. It is necessary to have at least one NAD for each user-type (agent-type) who is allowed to navigate through the system. The first step in the construction of a NAD is the filtering and enriching of the information (classes, services and attributes) provided by the class diagram that was previously captured in OO-Method during the conceptual modelling phase. Conceptual modelling in OO-Method collects the system properties using three complementary models: the object model, the dynamic model and the functional model. For the purpose of this paper we are interested in the object model. The object model is a graphical model where system classes, including attributes, services and relationships (aggregation and inheritance), are defined. Additionally, agent relationships are introduced to specify who can activate each class service (client/server relationship). As each type of agent has a different view of the system and can activate different services, each one needs their own NAD. The filtering of the information is based both on the agent relationships from the object model and on a previous analysis of the navigation requirements, which sets boundaries to the information views required for each agent. This filtering process additionally allows the designer to create simplified prototypes and versions of the system. Furthermore, NAD's belonging to different OO-Method models could be combined under a common interface, which gives the method the capability to construct the system as a collection of collaborating web sites. For a complete perspective of the approach presented here, a small example is going to be employed: the library system. As a basic explanation (for reasons of brevity), it is assumed that, as is usual in such a system, there are readers, books and loans relating a book to the reader who orders it. There is a restriction that forbids a reader to have at any time more than three books on loan. If a book is not available, or the reader has already reached his three book limit, the book can be reserved. The librarian can search for books both by title and by author. Readers might play the role of unreliable readers in the system if one or more of their return dates had expired. If a reader is considered unreliable s/he cannot borrow any book. The class diagram of this example is shown in Fig. 1.

Classes are represented as rectangles with three areas: the class name, the attributes and the services. Inheritance relationships are represented by using arrows to link classes. For instance, the arrow between 'reader' and 'unreliable reader' denotes that 'unreliable reader' is a specialization of 'reader'. Aggregation relationships are represented by using a diamond from a given component class to its composite class. The aggregation determines how many components

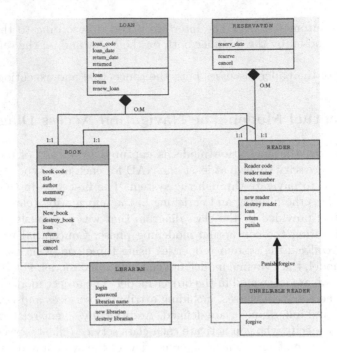

Fig. 1. *Class diagram of a library system*

can be attached to a given container and how many containers a component class can be associated with. For instance, the 'loan' composite class represents an aggregation between the component classes 'book' and 'reader'. Agent relationships are represented by using dotted lines that connect the associated client and server classes. In the example, the objects of the 'librarian' class can activate the services 'loan', 'return', 'reserve' and 'cancel' of the 'book' class. In order to design the NAD, the designer should know the navigation requirements of each type of user of the system. In the example it is assumed that the navigation requirements for the librarian user are as follows:

1. Lend a book. The librarian, acting on behalf of a reader, can search for a certain book either by author or by title. If the book is not available, or the reader already has three books on loan, a reservation on this book can be made for a future loan.
2. List active loans. For a given reader, the librarian can see at any moment the list of books s/he has borrowed from the library, and register the return of any of those books. Also, the librarian might want to look for extended information about each book (title, author, summary).
3. List out-of-date loans. The librarian can see the readers that have books with expired return dates, together with the date and the title of the books that should have already been returned. From this listing the librarian can decide whether to penalize them or not.

The main components of the NAD are navigation classes, navigation targets, navigation links and collections. Each of these constructs addresses the navigation model from a different dimension. We are going to further develop these concepts following the example presented above.

3.1   Navigation Classes

Navigation Classes (NC) have their grounding in the classes identified during the conceptual modelling phase, and are represented by means of a rectangle with three areas:

1. Head: it contains the name of the class
2. Attribute area: it contains the names and the scope of the attributes relevant to the considered agent and view.
3. Service area: it gathers the services available to the actual agent of the NAD.

All the attributes shown as part of a NC are accessible by the related agent, but the importance of each of these attributes may vary. OO-$\mathcal{H}$Method introduces the concept of attribute visibility in order to group the attributes depending on their relevance for the agent. This grouping will determine the way in which the user is able to access a given attribute. There are three types of attribute visibility:

1. Always Visible (V): their value is shown in every view of the object.
2. Referenced (R): their value is only referenced and so their consulting requires another step in the navigation path. The way of accessing this kind of attribute may vary depending on the implementation environment. In the case of working with HTML, for example, one possible way would be to show an anchor labelled as 'More Information'.
3. Hidden (H): Their value is neither referenced nor shown. The only way of accessing them is thus by means of a detailed view of the system.

This further differentiation of attributes reduces the possibility of the user feeling overwhelmed by the information shown on the views s/he has of the system.

Another relevant concept is that of Perspectives (P) [9,19]. The perspectives are defined on a set of edges, each one representing a relevant way of presenting the information. The perspectives types defined so far in OO-$\mathcal{H}$Method are:

1. Language: English, Spanish, German, French, Italian.
2. Rhetorical Styles: abbreviated, simplified, expert.
3. Medium: animation, image, text.

The best way of capturing perspectives in the NC is to define multivalued attributes, which are specified by means of a name and a set of values in brackets. Among the different perspectives, one of them must be declared as 'default', by means of a + sign. The perspectives have two possible scopes: global to the attribute type or local to each attribute. A global perspective is inherited by all the attributes of the type specified in the perspective. Global perspectives can be seen as 'visualization modes' [8], because they provide the application with different views of the same type of information to the same type of user. On the other hand, a local perspective adds possible visualization ways to local attributes. After deciding which information to show (navigation classes), the following phase is to define how to navigate through this information. When defining the navigation the designer must take into account many different aspects such as the order of objects, the filtering process or the cardinality of the access. These features are captured by means of different constructs associated with links, navigation targets and collections, which will be presented in the following sections.

3.2   Navigation Targets

The NC are grouped into Navigation Targets (NT). A NT is a set of NC which together provide the agent with a coherent view of the system. The general rule is to associate a NT to each user's navigation requirement. The NT has an associated scope: local to the actual type of agent (and so to the actual NAD) or global to the system. The graphical representation of an NT (see Fig. 2) is a rectangle that gathers all the classes involved in that view. An NT is defined by its name, which is located at a lapel in the upper-left corner of the rectangle. The concept underlying the NT is not new. Many authors have identified variants of such a concept: nodes [19], derived entities [9], hyperviews [7], macroentities [1] or targets[4]. Nevertheless, OO-$\mathcal{H}$Method uses a different approach, and bases its NT on user requirements, instead of on the physical presentation of the information (pages) as others do. For OO-$\mathcal{H}$Method, whether that information is presented in a single web page or divided among several pages is not important at this level of abstraction. In fact, the same NT could have several different materializations (pages), in a way similar to the 'targets' defined in [4].

The definition of the NT implicitly captures the 'navigation context pattern' [17]: the same nodes might appear in several NT as long as they do not represent the same information requirement, and in each NT its layout and navigation mode might be different. Note in Fig. 2 how, in the definition of 'book' provided in the 'loan book' NT, the principal attributes have been marked as 'always visible (V)' and two local perspectives have been added to the title of the book: text (default) and image (corresponding to a photo of the book cover).

3.3   Navigation Links

A Navigation Link (NL) is defined by:

1. Name.
2. Source navigation class.
3. Target navigation class.

4. Associated navigation patterns.
5. Associated navigation filters.

In OO-$\mathcal{H}$Method there are four types of NL:

1. Lr (requirement link): it shows the entry point to the NT. Every NT has a requirement link, which is drawn as a black circle with an arrow pointing at either the root navigation class or a collection inside that NT.
2. Ls (service link): it points at a service of a navigation class, and is drawn as a ray-arrow. It might have values of parameters associated.
3. Li (internal link): both its source and target NC remain inside a given NT. Its main characteristic is that its activation does not change the user context and, usually, it does not produce user disorientation.
4. Lt (traversal link): it is defined between navigation classes belonging to different navigation targets, and thus defines alternative visualization paths to the objects of the target classes.

The navigation links are always directed. This means that, if there is a need to navigate in both senses, two links must be explicitly or implicitly specified. The link label will be used as its identifier (for example, as the anchor text of the generated web page) so it should have a semantic meaning.

Furthermore, as shown in Fig. 2, all link types have both 'navigation patterns' and 'navigation filters' associated. Next both concepts will be developed.

Navigation patterns A navigation pattern is defined as a mechanism that allows a web user interface to share its knowledge about the way of showing the information objects to the user. Some authors [2] call them 'linking patterns'. OO-$\mathcal{H}$Method defines four navigation patterns, which can be associated both with navigation links and collections (see below). These are:

1. Index: access to a list of links to the different objects that form the population of the visualized class. In the view of each object there is always, added to the links derived from the semantic relationships among the classes being visualized (and captured in a navigation pattern), a link to the index page.
2. Guided Tour: it provides access to an object of the target population (depending on the associated filters) and a set of four operations: next, previous, first and last, in order to navigate through this target population.
3. Indexed Guided Tour: it combines the index with the guided tour mode.
4. Showall: It shows all the target objects together. It has an added attribute called 'cardinality' which allows the pagination of the answer and thus the limitation of the size of the pages and the load time for the user.

These patterns have been inherited from other well-known models such as HDM-lite [7], and enriched by adding a set of attributes that complete the navigation mode they represent. An example of this enrichment is the pattern attribute 'show in origin/show in destination'. The 'show in destination' attribute means that the information in the target objects will be shown in a different page, while 'show in origin' will present all the information about the target objects together with that of the source object. The selection of the most suitable navigation pattern depends on two variables:

1. Semantic relationships remaining under the link.
2. Granularity of the link: how many target objects are likely to be related to each object of the origin class.

Navigation Filters Associated to links and collections, a set of Navigation Filters (NF) can also be defined. A navigation filter restricts the order, the quantity (number) or the quality (characteristics) of the target objects. Formally, a navigation filter is a well formed formula (expressed in a subset of the dynamic logic [10]) that establishes a restriction on the attributes of the target class.

There are three types of filters:

1. Attribute filters: they specify values that must be conformed by the corresponding attribute values of the target population.
2. Condition filters: they can represent either method parameters (if associated to a service link) or additional rules and restrictions on the target population. A $ sign as the value of the filter means that such value has to be given by the user before traversing the corresponding link. This mechanism provides a means to define user-dependent target populations.
3. Order filters: they specify the order in which the target population will be accessed.

3.4   Collections

Another important decision about the user interface is how the information should be grouped in order to make it more accessible to the final user. In this context, another concept is introduced: the collection (see Fig. 2). A collection, represented by means of an inverted triangle, is a structure, hierarchical or not, which abstracts some concepts regarding both external and internal navigation. Collections have an associated scope (global, local to a NT or local to a NC), a set of filters and a set of navigation patterns associated and are a useful mechanism for limiting the interaction options between user and application, thus improving the usability of the system. A similar concept appears in different articles [6,4]. The collections can be nested but, as a rule of thumb, more than two nesting levels should be avoided, as they might disorient the user.

OO-$\mathcal{H}$Method defines four basic types of collections:

1. Classifiers: they define structures, hierarchical or not, for grouping information or service links which are to appear together.
2. Transactions: they group navigation services that are to work together. They should correspond with a transaction as defined in OO-Method.

3. Selectors: they group the objects that conform to the values gathered from the user. They usually have a condition filter associated.
4. History collections: OO-$\mathcal{H}$Method defines a history list [20] as a set of the last x links the user has traversed, where x is a parameter of this kind of collection and where the activation of one of these links will drive the user to the actual state of the required information, and not to the previous state, that is, the state it was in when it was visited for the first time.

Figure 2 shows a sample NAD of the librarian agent for the user navigation requirements specified above. Note that the access to the punish function is permitted inside the navigation target 'view out of date loans' which means that the librarian must check in this context the state of the reader's loans before punishing a reader.

4   Execution Model

The execution model provides the method with the representation details of the interface conceptual model for a target development environment. As the execution strategy is already defined in OO-Method, OO-$\mathcal{H}$Method is centered on defining how to implement the interface level information associated to web environments. All the concepts represented in the NAD are stored in an object repository and from there a default presentation diagram can be generated. Anyway, had the interface designer the need to refine such presentation and add some advanced features (e.g. multiple active views of the system), s/he could still edit this diagram (which will not be discussed here) and change it as needed. The subsequent mapping of this structure into a set of default interface implementation constructs provides the means to automatically generate the functional interface. The definition of the default navigation semantics (dependent on the semantic relationships existing in the conceptual schema) and that of a default interface layout (application of interface patterns to the elements of the conceptual schema) allow a CASE tool to suggest and/or derive certain application links and generate functional prototypes in an automated way. In Fig. 3 to 6 the prototype generated for the 'loan book' user navigation requirement is illustrated. The process is as follows: first, the generator tool looks for the entry point of the application. As nothing is stated in the diagram, it is assumed the entries to the different NT have an 'index' navigation pattern (see Fig. 3). Next, it generates a guided tour for the selected books. As the access to this class is made through a selector, the generator tool inserts a previous form where it asks for any of the fields (author or title) by which the search can be performed (see Fig. 4). The different screens of the guided tour (see Fig. 5) show all the information labelled as 'visible'. For each attribute perspective (expert summary, book cover image) a link is added to the form. In addition, the operations that can be performed on each object are also shown next to the book defining attribute (title). For each book there are two possibilities, depending on the state of the

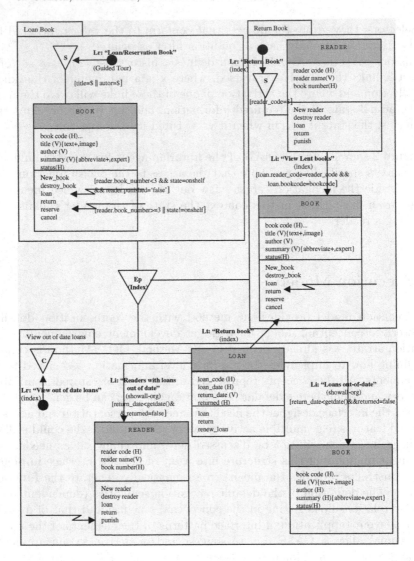

Fig. 2. *Simplified NAD of the Librarian Agent*

book and the number of books the reader has on loan. When the reader already has three books on loan or the book has been previously lent to another reader, then the service 'Make Reservation' is made available. On the contrary, when none of these conditions occur, then the available service is 'Lend Book'. As the value of the only parameter of the method 'Lend Book' (id-reader) must be introduced by the librarian, a form appears asking for its value. In Fig. 6 both this form and the system response is shown.

Fig. 3. Library entry point

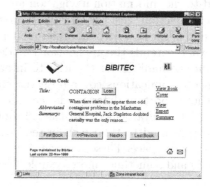

Fig. 4. Book search

Fig. 5. Guided tour applied to the search result

Fig. 6. Loan *service parameters request and result page*

5   Comparison with Related Work

All the methods studied so far share many of the concepts proven useful in the design of hypermedia applications. As an example, it could be cited the concept of 'collection', whose basic meaning is captured in HDM by means of the outlines, in RMM by means of the grouping mechanism, in NCM by union nodes and aggregations, in OOHDM by context classes and in HDM-lite by collections. Another example is that of perspectives, which appear with the same name and meaning in models such as HDM, HDM-lite and OOHDM. OO-$\mathcal{H}$Method captures these and other concepts gathered in the classical hypertext theory, but has a number of features that makes it overall different from other models. From the OO-$\mathcal{H}$Method point of view, one of the main drawbacks of some of these models is that they are focused on the modelling of hypermedia systems, oriented to the information navigation and visualization [3]. In such systems there is no interaction with the user apart from their navigation decisions (or at least it is not taken into account when modelling the system). On the contrary, OO-$\mathcal{H}$Method extends the applications modelled with OO-Method, and so provides specific mechanisms for the user to interact with the system. The resulting hypermedia applications cover both the static structure and dynamic behaviour. Another important difference is that these models from the very beginning focus on the structural aspects in the solution space (the data and how it is going to be presented to the user), instead of centering on the structural aspects in the problem space. These solution-driven approaches lead to longer development periods and sometimes more complex design processes.

OO-$\mathcal{H}$Method aims at being simple: it tries to define intuitive diagrams instead of declarative or query languages, which are more likely to overwhelm designers without a strong computer science background. We also try to avoid restructuring information already captured in other models specially suitable for this purpose. That is the case of derived entities in HDM, nodes in OOHDM or macroentities in ADM. We believe that this information rearrangement mixes together the information and the navigation perspectives, which we try to keep as independent as possible. In our approach, navigation is captured by means of links and structures associated to them (patterns, filters and collections), while the relevant information is captured in the classes inherited from the conceptual level. OO-$\mathcal{H}$Method is explicitly a user-driven approach. By introducing the concept of 'navigation target' we are grouping the functionality of the interface in separate modules, possibly designed by different people, that aim at meeting a user requirement, in the sense of a specific functionality asked for by the client. OO-$\mathcal{H}$Method shares some apparent similarities with the OOHDM model [18]. This fact is partly due to the OO-approach both methods take. The advantages of the OO-approach are discussed in [19]. Both of them derive from a similar class-schema that models the problem domain. Also, both methods clearly separate conceptual design, navigation design, presentation design and implementation. However, OO-$\mathcal{H}$Method simplifies the process of defining each phase by a mapping mechanism that can be directly applied to the class diagram. In OOHDM attributes with multiple perspectives become different attributes of the 'node class'. In our OO-Model, we exploit the existence of multi-valued attributes, and so maintain the concept of 'one attribute for each concept' independently of how they are stored in the database. Also, determining that the links (that is, the way a user is going to navigate through the classes) are attributes of the nodes again is closer, from our point of view, to the database storage structure than to a navigation requirement. In the last months the use of UML for the modelling of web applications [5] has also been proposed. We believe that this extension is particularly useful once you already have both a conceptual design and a specific implementation platform. The reason is that, rather than abstract implementation constructs, the UML web extension introduces concepts such as ActiveX controls, components or forms as classes of the model.

6   Conclusions

Conventional object-oriented methods have to provide a well-defined software development process by which the community of software engineers can properly design web-based applications from requirements in a systematic way. Our purpose has been to address these problems in the context of a conceptual modelling approach that has been proven successful for software production from conceptual models. The OO-$\mathcal{H}$Method can be seen as an extension of OO-Method to face the whole software production process. We focus on how to properly capture the particulars associated to the design of web interfaces. In order to achieve this goal, OO-$\mathcal{H}$Method adds several navigation and interface constructs to the OO-Method conceptual model, which define the semantics suitable for capturing the specific functionality of web application interfaces. A new kind of diagram, the navigation access diagram, has been introduced. Each piece of information introduced in the NAD is stored in a system repository. From there a functional interface can be generated in an automated way. As oppose to other existing web methods, the approach presented in this paper does not intend to be 'yet another method' for web modelling but to extend a consolidated conceptual modelling approach.

Summarizing, the most relevant contributions of this paper are the following:

1. The detailed presentation of the OO-$\mathcal{H}$Method approach as a successful attempt to cover the entire web-based software production process from an OO point of view in order to get the best from conventional and formal methods.
2. The description of the NAD that has been added to the OO-Method conceptual model to specify the navigation user requirements.

OO-$\mathcal{H}$Method is still defining and cataloguing a set of both navigation and interface patterns general enough as to guarantee the code reusability. Navigation patterns also aim at providing the user with a higher level of usability, and the designer with a repository of well known and useful navigation techniques. The identification of interface patterns is a much more open process, as the new technologies will certainly add more effective ways of displaying the information in a given environment. The usability of the different patterns once implemented will be tested and will become a critical factor for its final incorporation in OO-$\mathcal{H}$Method. Once completely categorized, a formal specification of user interfaces [16] will follow directly from these interface patterns.

Acknowledgments

We would like to thank the anonymous referees for their valuable comments to this work

References

1. P. Atzeni, G. Mecca, and P. Merialdo. Design and Maintenance of Data-Intensive Web Sites. In *Advances in Database Technology - EDTB'98*, pages 436–449, 03 1998.
2. M. Bernstein. Patterns of Hypertext. In *HYPERTEXT '98. Proceedings of the ninth ACM conference on Hypertext and hypermedia: links, objects, time and space. Structure in hypermedia systems*, pages 21–29, 1998.
3. M. Bieber and C. Kacmar. Designing Hypertext Support for Computational Applications. *CACM: Communications of the ACM*, 38(8):99 – 107, 1998.
4. S. Ceri, P. Fraternali, and S. Paraboschi. Design Principles for Data-Intensive Web Sites. *SIGMOD Record*, 28:84–89, 03 1999.
5. J. Conallen. Modeling Web Application Architectures with UML. *CACM: Communications of the ACM.*, 42(10):63–70, 10 1999.
6. F. M. Fern ndez, D. Florescu, J. Kang, A. Levy, and D. Suciu. Catching the Boat with Strudel: Experiences with a Web-Site Management System. In *Proceedings of ACM SIGMOD International conference on Management of data*, pages 414–425, 10 1998.
7. P. Fraternali and P. Paolini. A Conceptual Model and a Tool Environment for Developing more Scalable, Dynamic, and Customizable Web Applications. In *Advances in Database Technology - EDBT'98*, pages 421–435, 1998.
8. F. Garzotto, L. Mainetti, and P. Paolini. Designing Modal Hypermedia Applications. In *Proceedings of the eight ACM conference on HYPERTEXT '97*, 1997.
9. F. Garzotto and P. Paolini. HDM A Model-Based Approach to Hypertext Application Design. *ACM Transactions on Information Systems (TOIS)*, 11(1):1–26, 01 1993.
10. D. Harel. Dynamic logic. In D. Gabbay and F. Guenthner, editors, *Handbook of Philosophical Logic, Volume II: Extensions of Classical Logic*, volume 165 of *Synthese Library*, chapter II.10, pages 497–604. D. Reidel Publishing Co., Dordrecht, 1984.
11. T. Isakowitz, E. A. Stohr, and V. Balasubramanian. RMM: A Methodology for Structured Hypermedia Design. *CACM: Communications of the ACM.*, pages 34–44, 08 1995.
12. G. Mecca, P. Merialdo, P. Atzeni, and V. Crescenzi. The ARANEUS Guide to Web-Site Development. Technical report, Universidad de Roma, 03 1999.

13. O. Pastor, F. Hayes, and S. Bear. OASIS: An Object-Oriented Specification Language. In P. Loucopoulos, editor, *Proceedings of CAiSE'92 International Conference*, volume 593 of *LNCS*, pages 348–363. Springer-Verlag, 1992.
14. O. Pastor, E. Insfr n, V. Pelechano, J. Romero, and J. Merseguer. OO-METHOD: An OO Software Production Environment Combining Conventional and Formal Methods. In *CAiSE '97. International Conference on Advanced Information Systems*, pages 145–158, 1997.
15. O. Pastor, V. Pelechano, E. Insfr n, and J. G mez. From Object Oriented Conceptual Modeling to Automated Programming in Java. In *ER '98. International Conference on the Entity Relationship Approach*, pages 183–196, 1998.
16. S. R. Robinson and S. A. Roberts. Formalizing the Informational Content of Database User Interfaces. In *ER '98. International Conference on Conceptual Modeling*, volume 1507, pages 65–77. Springer, 11 1998.
17. G. Rossi, D. Schwabe, and A. Garrido. Design Reuse in Hypermedia Applications Development. In *Proceedings of the eight ACM conference on HYPERTEXT '97*, pages 57–66, 1997.
18. D. Schwabe and R. Almeida Pontes. A Method-based Web Application Development Environment. In *Position Paper, Web Engineering Workshop, WWW8*, 1999.
19. D. Schwabe, G. Rossi, and D. J. Barbosa. Systematic Hypermedia Application Design with OOHDM. In *Proceedings of the the seventh ACM conference on HYPERTEXT '96*, page 166, 1996.
20. L. Tauscher and S. Greenberg. Revisitation patterns in World Wide Web navigation. In *CHI '97. Proceeding of the CHI 97 conference on Human factors in computing systems*, pages 399–406, 1997.

Efficient Distributed Workflow Management Based on Variable Server Assignments

Thomas Bauer and Peter Dadam

University of Ulm, Dept. of Databases and Information Systems
{bauer,dadam}@informatik.uni-ulm.de
http://www.informatik.uni-ulm.de/dbis

Abstract. For enterprise-wide and cross-enterprise workflow (WF) applications, the load of the WF servers and the amount of communication in the subnets may become a bottleneck. This paper shows how a distributed WF control can be realized in a way that the load of the components at run time is minimized. For that purpose, the control of a WF instance may migrate from one WF server to another. The WF servers are assigned to the WF activities in a way that minimizes the communication load. The server assignments are determined at build time by analyzing the WF model with respect to the actor assignments. As these actor assignments may depend on preceding activities, static server assignments are not always reasonable. Hence, so-called variable server assignment expressions are introduced, which allow dynamic server assignment without expensive run time analyses.

1 Introduction

Workflow Management Systems (WfMSs) offer a promising technology for the implementation of process-oriented information and application systems. A significant limitation of current WfMSs, however, is their insufficient scalability, which is caused by the use of one central WF server. Already the processing of a single WF activity may require the transfer of multiple messages between the WF server and its clients; e.g., to transmit input and output data of the activity, to update worklists, or to invoke activity programs. As soon as the number of users increases, e.g., when the WF-based application may be accessed via the Internet, such a central WF server may become overloaded. For this reason, several multi-server approaches have been proposed in WF literature [1, 9, 16, 21].

1.1 Motivation

Having a closer look at enterprise-wide and cross-enterprise WF applications, it becomes obvious that not only a central WF server, but also the corresponding subnet may become a bottleneck. As an example consider a (simplified) loan request WF as shown in Fig. 1. Let us assume that the input and output data of the activities 1, 3, 4,

B. Wangler, L. Bergman (Eds.): CAiSE 2000, LNCS 1789, pp. 94-109, 2000

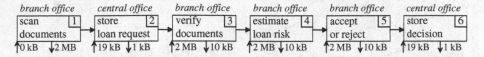

Fig. 1. Loan request WF (↑/↓: average size of the input / output parameter data of the activity)

and 5 contain scanned documents with a total average size of 2 MB[1]. Let us further assume that a bank has 30 branch offices, which are connected with the central office by a wide area network (WAN). Each branch office shall have 10 clerks; i.e., there are 300 clerks in the branch offices altogether. If we assume that a clerk requires 5 min = 300 sec for the execution of one activity instance, then one activity per second is executed on the average, each of them requiring 2 MB of parameter data. Hence, a central WF server has to transmit 2 MB/sec = 16 Mbit/sec of parameter data. Obviously, this would overload an Ethernet-based local area network (LAN). In order to get further insights, a simulation (c.f. section 5) of the scenario described was performed. It leads to the following results: The load[2] of the subnet of the central WF server is 15.7 Mbit/sec. In this context, it is very attractive to control each WF by the WF server of the corresponding branch office. In this case, no subnet has a load higher than 0.5 Mbit/sec. Another very important aspect in distributed systems (especially in widely distributed systems) is the data volume transferred by the gateways. If a central WF server is used in the sketched scenario, the gateways have to transmit 15.6 Mbit/sec. This corresponds to 243.8 permanently used ISDN channels (each with a capacity of 64 kbit/sec). If distributed WF control is used, instead, the gateways have only to transmit 80.6 kbit/sec; i.e., only 1.3 ISDN channels are required! This example shows, in a very impressive way, that an appropriate distributed WF control is not only important to avoid an overloading of the WF servers, but it is also essential to avoid bottlenecks in the communication network.

1.2 Distributed WF Execution in the ADEPT-WfMS

Before we explain the basic ideas of this paper, we shortly summarize our previous work on distributed WfMSs. Performance and scalability, especially in the context of enterprise-wide and cross-enterprise WF applications, belong to the central research issues of the ADEPT research project[3] [19]. An important goal of the ADEPT approach is the reduction of the total communication load caused by the WfMS. In order to achieve this, a WF instance may be controlled "piecewise" by different WF servers (see Fig. 2). Consequently, the control of a particular WF instance migrates from one WF server to another, if this helps to avoid communication across subnet boundaries

---

[1] Even much larger data volumes are possible in such enterprise-wide application scenarios; e.g., if multimedia data have to be transferred between different activities.

[2] This load is lower than 16 Mbit/sec because it is not possible to use the whole capacity of the clerks since this would cause their worklists to overflow. Therefore, a clerk of a branch office performs less than 1 activity/sec.

[3] ADEPT stands for Application Development Based on Encapsulated Pre-Modeled Process Templates.

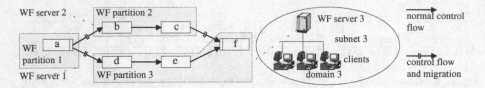

Fig. 2. Partitioning of a WF graph and distributed WF execution

when executing WF activities [3]. The concrete server assignments of the activities are completely computed at build time. They are based on probability distributions (PD) of activity executions within the individual subnets (which, in turn, are derived from the distribution of users and their roles; see [3] for details). That is, before creating a WF instance, the WF servers of the partitions are completely predetermined. Such static server assignments for activities show good results, if actor assignments (*ActorAss*) are of the kind "role = physician" or "role = nurse ∧ department = surgery". In these cases, the set of possible actors performing an activity (as precondition for the calculation of the PDs) can be determined already at build time.[4]

1.3   Problem Statement and Contribution of the Paper

Unfortunately, in practice, there are many cases in which concrete actor assignments depend on preceding activities (called "dependent actor assignments" for short). For example, it may be required that the same physician who examines a patient (activity *x*) must also write the corresponding medical report (subsequent activity *k'* in Fig. 3). As another example take a patient who must be cared by a nurse from the same department (activity *k*) in which he or she was previously examined. In the context of such dependent actor assignments, the following important problem occurs: The organizational unit (in the following called unit for short) to which the actors performing the activities *k* and *k'* belong, is not fixed until activity *x* is executed. What does this mean for the assignment of appropriate WF servers to the activities? If dependent actor assignments occur, it would be possible to calculate the best static server assignments by using conditional probabilities. Since static server assignments can not respect the dependencies, in too many cases the dependent activities would be controlled by the "wrong" WF server.

The main contribution of this paper is to develop a multi-server WfMS, which is based on the concept of *variable server assignments*. Instead of using only static server assignments, like "activity *x* is controlled by server S_s", in this approach logical server assignment expressions can be used as well. Such an expression may determine, for example, that "activity *k* is controlled by the server, which is located in the subnet of the actor performing the preceding activity *x*". These expressions allow to take run time data of the WF instance into account, when determining the concrete WF server controlling the activity instance. And, best of all, they create almost no additional overhead at run time when compared with the static case. In this paper, we

---

[4] The calculation relies on the assumption that no massive changes take place between build time and the execution of instances of this WF type.

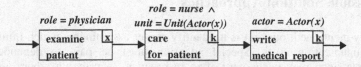

Fig. 3. Examples for dependent actor assignments

present the cost model and the distribution algorithm used to calculate appropriate variable server assignment expressions at build time. In addition, we present some simulation results which show that the communication load can be reduced significantly by using variable server assignments. Despite it is commonly accepted that distributed WF execution is essential – to our knowledge – ADEPT$_{distribution}$ is the only approach that treats the problem of dependent actor assignments in a distributed WfMS.

In the next section the conditions for the applicability of our approach are summarized. Section 3 describes possible solutions of the problem. The nucleus of this paper is presented in Section 4. It describes the algorithms for determining the server assignment expressions at build time. The efficiency of our approach is shown in Section 5 by means of simulations. In Section 6 related approaches are discussed. The paper concludes with a summary and an outlook in Section 7.

2   Assumptions and Preconditions

The approach introduced in this paper describes how load distribution is realized by the use of variable server assignments in ADEPT$_{distribution}$, the distributed variant of the ADEPT-WfMS. It is only based on the following realistic assumptions:

1. The WfMS uses an organizational model in which actors can be associated with organizational units as well as with roles.
2. The actors are assigned to an activity at run time by means of a selection predicate like "role = physician ∧ unit = radiology". This predicate may also reference preceding activities (dependent actor assignments, cf. Fig. 3). Otherwise, it is assumed that the actor of an activity is determined independently from other activities.
3. The WfMS uses several subnets as well as several WF servers. To simplify the following discussion, it is assumed that each subnet is equipped with one (and only one) WF server. Each of these WF servers may control each WF type and its partitions, respectively. A user may be permanently assigned to one or several subnets.
4. Each WF server can serve all WF clients registered in the WfMS, not only those of its domain (a subnet together with the corresponding WF server and clients is called *domain*).
5. The actors who may potentially execute a certain activity are not necessarily located in the same subnet.
6. The number of persons within a subnet who qualify to perform a certain activity does not change significantly between build time and run time.
7. The topology of the communication network does also not change significantly.

3   Possible Solution Approaches

As already mentioned, our aim is to identify server assignments which minimize the total communication costs. Special attention must be paid to dependent actor assignments since they occur very often in practice. In principle, there are several possible approaches for the assignment of WF servers to activities: The simplest and most frequently applied method is to assign a fixed server (statically) to each activity at build time or at the time the WF instance is started. This solution is not satisfactory for WFs for which dependent actor assignments have to be supported as well (see Section 1.3). Obviously, the best server assignments can be achieved if the WF server for the activity to be executed is determined after the preceding activity has finished. At this point in time, complete and current run time data of the WF instance is available. Thus the most suitable WF server can be determined. Unfortunately, this solution is not applicable in practice due to its high costs, in general. The execution of the necessary analyses would heavily burden the WF servers and thus negatively affect the performance of the WfMS. This is not acceptable for production WfMSs that have to cope with a high load.

Therefore, $ADEPT_{distribution}$ follows a strategy which combines a static pre-calculation (at build time) with dynamic aspects (i.e., evaluation of run time data) and, by doing so, combining the advantages of both approaches. Instead of a static WF server assignment, logical expressions for server assignments are created at build time, if this is reasonable. They reference run time data of the WF instance, thus making it possible to simply and efficiently determine the appropriate WF server at run time.

The main challenge of this approach is how to get suitable variable server assignments for the activities. One possibility would be to let the WF designer specify them explicitly at build time (analogous to the actor assignments). Unfortunately, the WF designer, without further support or information, will hardly be in the position to estimate the load in the subnets for a particular distribution. Therefore, it is essential to support him actively by means of a sophisticated WfMS modeling tool, which estimates the load of each system component (server, subnet, gateway) for the server assignments taken under consideration. This, in turn, requires an appropriate cost model. This cost model and the calculation of appropriate server assignments are described in the next section.

4   Determination of Optimal Server Assignments

In this section we describe how appropriate server assignments for WF activities can be calculated already at build time.

4.1   Cost Model

A cost model for determining the load of the system components which are critical under performance aspects (servers, subnets, gateways), has to consider at least the following costs:

- Costs for the transfer of parameter data (between a WF server and a WF client) when starting and finishing activity programs
- Costs for refreshing worklists at the client site
- Costs for data transfer between activity programs and external data sources
- Costs for migrating the control of a WF instance to another WF server (migration costs for short)

In addition to the information available from the WF template and from the organizational model, the estimated execution frequency and the average amount of data to be communicated (e.g., the size of the parameter data) have to be determined for each activity of the WF template. For already released WF templates, these data may be obtained by analyzing the audit trails of executed WF instances. Otherwise, they have to be estimated.

In the sequel we develop formulas which describe the data volume to be transported for a single system action (e.g., "start activity" or "migrate WF") and an individual system component. Subsequently, these simple formulas are used to construct a comprehensive formula, which describe the total load of the components. Thereby, $ExProb_k(i, j)$ denotes the probability that activity k is controlled by the WF server in subnet i and is processed by a user in subnet j (Table 1 summarizes the expressions which are used in this chapter). $MigrProb_{k,l}(i, j)$ denotes the probability that, when moving from activity k to activity l, the control migrates from the WF server i to the server j. These probabilities depend on the server assignments selected. We will show in Section 4.4 and 4.5 how they can be determined. For the moment, we consider them as given.

The expected value for the data volume (abbreviated by *data volume* in the following) for the *execution of an activity* (transport of input and output parameter data between WF server and client) is calculated as follows: The data volume emerging at server i for the execution of activity k results as the probability that server i controls activity k, multiplied by the average amount of data to be transported:

$$Vol_{Server,i}^{Act}(k) = \left(\sum_j ExProb_k(i, j) \right) \cdot (in\_parameter\_size_k + out\_parameter\_size_k) \qquad (1)$$

Table 1. Abbreviations used in this paper

Name	Meaning
$ActorAss_k$	actor assignment of activity k
$ActorProb_k(D|S)$	portion of the actors in the domain (subnet) D, given that activity k is controlled by server S
$DepMigrProb_{x,k}(j|i)$	probability of a migration to the WF server in subnet j (when moving from activity x to activity k), given that activity x was controlled by the server in subnet i
$DepServProb_k(S|u)$	probability that activity k is controlled by server S, given that actor u performs this activity
$ExProb_k(i,j)$	probability that activity k is controlled by the WF server of subnet i and processed by an actor of subnet j
$MigrProb_{x,k}(i,j)$	probability of a migration from the WF server in subnet i to the WF server in subnet j (when moving from activity x to activity k)
$ServAss_k$	server assignment of activity k
$ServProb_k(S)$	probability that activity k is controlled by the WF server S (in subnet S)

The *load of the subnets* is estimated as follows: In subnet i communication with respect to the execution of activity k takes place, either when the server is located in i or when a user of subnet i executes the activity. If both is valid, the communication must be counted only once (therefore $j \neq i$):

$$Vol_{Subnet,i}^{Act}(k) = \left(\sum_{j} ExProb_k(i,j) + \sum_{j \neq i} ExProb_k(j,i) \right) \cdot (in\_parameter\_size_k + out\_parameter\_size_k) \qquad (2)$$

The expected *data volume at the gateway* from subnet i to j ($i \neq j$) is calculated as follows:

$$Vol_{GW,i,j}^{Act}(k) = ExProb_k(i,j) \cdot in\_parameter\_size_k + ExProb_k(j,i) \cdot out\_parameter\_size_k \qquad (3)$$

The expected data volumes for refreshing the worklists ($Vol^{WL}(k)$) as well as for the communication of activity programs with external data sources ($Vol^{Ext}(k)$) can be calculated in a similar way (a detailed description can be found in [7]). The latter cost factor can be used to calculate a suitable allocation of externally stored application data (which is only referenced by the WF instances), in case this distribution is not predetermined already.

The migration costs at the transition from activity k to activity l are, of course, of special interest in the context of this paper. Incoming as well as outgoing migrations have to be considered. To calculate the expected data volume for server i, the average data volume communicated for this migration is multiplied by the probability that server i is involved in the migration. Here, it has to be noted that no communication takes place if the servers of the activities k and l are identical (therefore $j \neq i$).

$$Vol_{Server,i}^{Migr}(k,l) = \sum_{j \neq i} \left(MigrProb_{k,l}(i,j) + MigrProb_{k,l}(j,i) \right) \cdot migration\_size_{k,l} \qquad (4)$$

The data volume caused by the migration in the subnets affected is the same as for the WF servers:

$$Vol_{Subnet,i}^{Migr}(k,l) = Vol_{Server,i}^{Migr}(k,l) \qquad (5)$$

The gateways have to transport the following amounts of data:

$$Vol_{GW,i,j}^{Migr}(k,l) = MigrProb_{k,l}(i,j) \cdot migration\_size_{k,l} \qquad (6)$$

For each system component, these amounts of data have to be multiplied by the execution frequencies $ExFreq(k)$ of the activities (k) or of the migrations $MigrFreq(k, l)$, respectively. Then they have to be added up for all activities of all WF types ($WFTypes$) in order to determine the corresponding load of this component. For the servers the load is calculated as follows ($Load_{Subnet,i}$ and $Load_{GW,i,j}$ are determined analogously):

$$Load_{Server,i} = \sum_{wf \in WFTypes} \sum_{k \in wf} ExFreq(k) \cdot Vol_{Server,i}^{Act}(k) + ExFreq(k) \cdot Vol_{Server,i}^{WL}(k) \qquad (7)$$

$$+ ExFreq(k) \cdot Vol_{Server,i}^{Ext}(k) + \sum_{l \in wf \wedge l \neq k} MigrFreq(k,l) \cdot Vol_{Server,i}^{Migr}(k,l)$$

These loads are weighted with the component specific cost factors $C_{Server,i}$, $C_{Subnet,i}$, and $C_{GW,i,j}$ and they are added up in order to get the total costs. These cost factors specify the costs for transferring one byte over the server, the subnet, and the gateway. Thus, the WF designer can influence the load of each component. A high value of $C_{GW,i,j}$ has the effect that, for example, the WAN-connection (gateway) is used little. Hence, the target function to be minimized is as follows:

$$T = \sum_i C_{Server,i} \cdot Load_{Server,i} + \sum_i C_{Subnet,i} \cdot Load_{Subnet,i} + \sum_i \sum_{j \neq i} C_{GW,i,j} \cdot Load_{GW,i,j} \qquad (8)$$

The following section describes which server assignment expressions are possible for the activities. Section 4.3 shows how the server assignments can be selected in a way that minimizes T.

4.2   Server Assignment Expressions

For static server assignments, the identifiers of the WF servers are directly used as expressions. For variable server assignments, however, expressions may reference run time data of the WF instance. For most of the practically relevant scenarios, the location of the WF server or the actor of a preceding activity is referenced. In special cases the usage of additional WF control data (e.g., the start time of an activity), the inclusion of WfMS-external data (e.g., parameter data of activities), or the evaluation of mathematical functions or logical expressions may be reasonable as well. While server assignments of the first kind (see 1 - 4 below) can automatically be deduced from the WF model, the assignment expressions for the special cases (5.) must be explicitly specified by the WF designer. The server assignment expressions which are supported by ADEPT$_{distribution}$ are as follows:

1. $ServAss_k = S_i$
   Server S_i is statically assigned to activity k.
2. $ServAss_k = Server(x)$
   Activity k shall be controlled by the same server as activity x.
3. $ServAss_k = Domain(Actor(x))$
   Activity k shall be assigned to the server that is located in the domain of the user who has executed activity x.
4. $ServAss_k = f(Server(x))$ or $ServAss_k = f(Domain(Actor(x)))$
   A function f can be applied to all server assignments of type 2 and 3. Assume, e.g., that activity k is assigned to the manager of the actor who works on activity x. This manager may belong to a different domain than the actor of activity x (e.g., if he is assigned to a different department). In such cases, a simple mapping function can be used to perform the desired transformation. In [7] we describe how a suitable function f can be deduced automatically.
5. $ServAss_k = $ any given expression
   The WF designer may specify own server assignment expressions, which do not correspond to any of the expressions of type 1 - 4. Since they cannot be analyzed by the WfMS, the PDs cannot be calculated automatically. Therefore, the designer has to provide this information as well. The PDs are required by the algorithms of Section 4.4 in order to perform the calculations.

4.3   Determination of Optimal Server Assignments

In order to determine an optimal distribution of the activities of a WF template, in principle, the costs of all possible server assignments for all activities have to be computed and, by doing so, the server assignments with the minimal costs can be selected. Since a WF template may easily comprise more than 100 activities and each server assignment may reference any predecessor, this approach is not feasible, in general, due to its complexity $O(\#Act^{\#Act})$, where $\#Act$ denotes the number of activities of the WF template. Therefore, we suggest an algorithm (see Algorithm 1) which performs this task with polynomial run time complexity. It is based on a greedy approach and calculates the optimal result or a result that is close to this optimum for the practically relevant cases. It consists of two phases, which work as follows:

In Phase 1 a legal initial solution is determined. This is achieved by computing the optimal server assignment for each activity under the assumption (for the moment) that migration does not cause any costs. For each activity k all possible server assignments $PotServAss_k$ (using all possible expressions of type 1 - 4, c.f. Section 4.2) are tested. The cost calculation is performed by the function $calculate\_costs()$, which uses the cost model described in Section 4.1.

As only single activities are analyzed in Phase 1, the result vector $ServAss$ may contain unprofitable migrations as well. In Phase 2, Algorithm 1 examines which of these migrations are really reasonable. In order to eliminate undesirable migrations, the partitions P are inspected (all activities of a partition are controlled by the same WF server). It is analyzed, whether it is advantageous to combine such a partition P with a direct predecessor partition or a direct successor partition, in order to eliminate the migration between them. The motivation for this analysis is that it may be not worth migrating the (complete) WF instance from one server to another and back for only a few activities. Firstly, the algorithm considers small partitions P. By combining them with adjacent partitions they, step by step, form larger groups of activities among which no migrations take place. This integration process is continued until there are no more unprofitable migrations.

Algorithm 1: Calculation of the Server Assignments for a WF Type (Process Template)
Phase 1:
for each activity $k \in ProcessTemplate$ (in partial order corresponding to the control flow) **do**
    $MinCost = \infty$;
    for each $ServAss_k \in PotServAss_k$ **do**
        $Cost = calculate\_costs(ServAss, k)$;   // costs only of the activity k
        if $Cost < MinCost$ **then** $OptServAss = ServAss_k$; $MinCost = Cost$;
    $ServAss_k = OptServAss$;
Phase 2:
$MinCost = calculate\_costs(ServAss, all)$;   // costs of the whole WF (incl. migrations)
for $PartSize = 1$ **to** $\#activities(ProcessTemplate)$ **do**
    for each $P: |P|=PartSize$, P is a maximal subgraph with $\forall l_1, l_2 \in P: Server(l_1) = Server(l_2)$ **do**
        $OptServAss = NULL$;
        for each $a \notin P: \exists l \in P: a = predecessor(l) \lor a = successor(l)$ **do**
            for each $l \notin P$ **do** $TestServAss_l = ServAss_l$;
            for each $l \in P$ **do** $TestServAss_l = ServAss_a$;
            $TestCost = calculate\_costs(TestServAss, all)$;
            if $TestCost < MinCost$ **then** $OptServAss = ServAss_a$; $MinCost = TestCost$;
        if $OptServAss \neq NULL$ **then**
            for each $l \in P$ **do** $ServAss_l = OptServAss$;

4.4   Calculation of the Probability Distributions

After having explained which server assignments are suitable for an activity and how the corresponding costs can be calculated, the question remains, how the PDs $ExProb_k(i,j)$ and $MigrProb_{x,k}(i,j)$ can be determined.

As server assignments depend on run time data of the WF instance, different instances of a particular WF activity may be controlled by different WF servers. The probability that activity k is controlled by server S is denominated with $\mathbf{ServProb_k(S)}$. As different instances of k can be located in different units (and therefore may be controlled by different servers), the actor PD of k may be different for each server S. The portion of the actors of activity k that are located in domain D is called $\mathbf{ActorProb_k(D|S)}$, for the case that server S controls activity k. In the sequel we describe how $ServProb_k(S)$ and $ActorProb_k(D|S)$ can be determined. Once they are known, the probability that activity k is controlled by server S and that is executed by a user in domain D is given by: $ExProb_k(S, D) = ServProb_k(S) \cdot ActorProb_k(D|S)$.

4.4.1   Calculation of the Server Probability Distribution $ServProb_k(S)$

$ServProb_k(S)$ denotes the probability that server S controls activity k. It results from the server assignment $ServAss_k$ and the PDs of the activity x, that is referenced in $ServAss_k$. In Algorithm 2, the activities of the WF template are analyzed in the (partial) order defined by the control flow. Since activity x must be a predecessor of k, these PDs are, therefore, already known when analyzing activity k. In the following we describe how the server PD $ServProb_k(S)$ is calculated, if the server assignments as defined in Section 4.2 are considered. Case 5 is not considered here (and further on), as for this server assignment the PD has to be provided by the WF designer.

Algorithm 2: Calculation of the Server Probability Distribution $ServProb_k(S)$

case $ServAss_k = S_i$: $ServProb_k(S) = \delta_{S,S_i}$ [5]   (1)

case $ServAss_k = Server(x)$: $ServProb_k(S) = ServProb_x(S)$ (2)

case $ServAss_k = Domain(Actor(x))$: $ServProb_k(S) = ActorProb_x(S)$ with   (3)
$ActorProb_x(D) = \Sigma_S ActorProb_x(D|S) \cdot ServProb_x(S)$

case $ServAss_k = f(Server(x))$: $ServProb_k(S) = f(ServProb_x(S))$ (4a)

case $ServAss_k = f(Domain(Actor(x)))$: $ServProb_k(S) = f(ActorProb_x(S))$ with   (4b)
$ActorProb_x(D) = \Sigma_S ActorProb_x(D|S) \cdot ServProb_x(S)$

Explanations:

(1)   Since activity k is always controlled by the server S_i, it follows $ServProb_k(S) = 1$ for $S = S_i$ and $ServProb_k(S) = 0$ otherwise.

(2)   The same server is used for activity k as for activity x. Therefore the server PDs are identical.[6]

---

[5] Kronecker symbol: $\delta_{i,j} = 1$, if $i = j$ and $\delta_{i,j} = 0$, if $i \neq j$.

[6] Assuming that there are no branches between the activities x and k, which depend on the choice of the server of activity x. Such facts are difficult to detect because they concern data elements. Therefore, for branch and loop conditions, we have generally assumed that their result is independent of the current server.

(3)   The server of activity k is located in the domain of the actor of activity x. Therefore the server PD of activity k results from the actor PD of activity x. It does not matter which server has controlled activity x. Hence a server independent actor PD $ActorProb_x(D)$ is created by the weighted sum of the actor PDs for the different servers.

(4a) $ServProb_k(S)$ is calculated as described for case 2. Afterwards the function f is applied to the result (cf. [7] for details).

(4b)   The same as case 3, but in addition f is applied to the result.

4.4.2   Calculation of the Actor Probability Distribution $ActorProb_k(D|S)$

$ActorProb_k(D|S)$ describes the probability that the actor of activity k is located in domain D, if the activity is controlled by server S. As an example take a hospital with 3 wards, each of which owning its own server. Assuming that only nurses of ward 1 (domain 1) are in charge of the patients of ward 1, it is reasonable that server 1 controls this activity. Hence, an actor PD $ActorProb_k(D|1) = (1,0,0)$ results. Analogously, for server 2 we obtain $ActorProb_k(D|2) = (0,1,0)$ and for server 3 $ActorProb_k(D|3) = (0,0,1)$.

In the following, we present Algorithm 3, which calculates the actor PD $ActorProb_k(D|S)$. It considers all possible actors of activity k and determines for each of them the corresponding domain D (from the organizational model). Furthermore, it determines the server S that controls the activity k if it is performed by user u. The user is reflected in the actor PD $ActorProb_k(D|S)$ for the corresponding server S and the domain D. Thus, the calculation of $ActorProb_k(D|S)$ is performed according to the definition of the actor PD (see Section 4.4). Different servers may qualify – each with a certain probability – for the control of activity k if it is performed by user u. These probabilities are calculated by the function $DepServ(k, "Actor=u")$ (see below) and are stored in the vector $DepServProb_k(S|u)$. $DepServProb_k(S|u)$ determines the weight, with which the user u is reflected in $ActorProb_k(D|S)$.

Algorithm 3: Calculation of the Actor Probability Distribution $ActorProb_k(D|S)$
$Actors = \{u \mid$ user u qualifies as actor of activity $k\}$;
for each $u \in Actors$ **do**
    $D = Domain(u)$;
    $DepServProb_k(S|u) = DepServ(k, "Actor = u")$;
    for each S **do** $ActorProb_k(D|S) = ActorProb_k(D|S) + DepServProb_k(S|u)$;
normalize each line of $ActorProb_k(D|S)$ such that $\forall S: \Sigma_D ActorProb_k(D|S) = 1$;

The calculation of the *server PD* $DepServProb_k(S|u)$ for a certain user u is performed similar to the calculation of the user-independent server PD $ServProb_k(S)$ (c.f. Section 4.4.1). $DepServProb_k(S|u)$ does not only depend on the server assignment of activity k, however, but also on its actor assignment. In the following, due to lack of space, only some selected examples are presented. A comprehensive discussion of all possible cases of server and actor assignments can be found in [7].

- If the server assignment is static ($ServAss_k = S_i$) the calculation is trivial as the server is always the same: $DepServProb_k(S|u) = \delta_{S,S_i}$.

- If the actor assignment is independent from other activities (e.g., "*role = physician*") the server PD is independent from user u. Thus, the user-independent server PD can be adopted: $DepServProb_k(S|u) = ServProb_k(S)$.

- In Fig. 4a, the same physician, who works on activity x also performs activity k. Assume that $DepServProb_k(S|u)$ for user $u =$ "Dr. Smith" from domain 3 shall be calculated. Because of $ActorAss_k = Actor(x)$, Dr. Smith must have performed activity x as well. Since the server of activity k is allocated in the domain of the actor of activity x, it is allocated in the domain of Dr. Smith. As this is domain 3, the result is $DepServProb_k(S|u) = (0,0,1)$.
- In Fig. 4b, activity k is performed by another actor than activity x, but the actors belong to the same unit. Assume that $DepServProb_k(S|u)$ for the nurse Jane from the unit ward 2 shall be calculated. In this case, all users with the role physician who belong to the unit ward 2 have to be considered. These are exactly those users who could have executed activity x if activity k is performed by Jane. For each of these physicians the domain D is calculated because it determines − if this physician has performed activity x − the location of the server of activity k. This domain D is reflected in $DepServProb_k(D|u)$. Finally, $DepServProb_k(S|u)$ is normalized such that $\Sigma_S DepServProb_k(S|u) = 1$ holds.

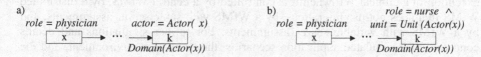

a)

role = physician   actor = Actor(x)

$\boxed{x} \longrightarrow \cdots \longrightarrow \boxed{k}$

Domain(Actor(x))

b)   role = nurse ∧

role = physician   unit = Unit (Actor(x))

$\boxed{x} \longrightarrow \cdots \longrightarrow \boxed{k}$

Domain(Actor(x))

Fig. 4. Examples for the calculation of the server probability distribution $DepServProb_k(S|u)$

Additionally to these aspects, it has to be noted that there are users who work part-time, or who work only part of the working day with the WfMS, or who may work in several domains. These users must not be treated in the same way as users working "full-time" only in one domain, because they produce less load in the single domain. In ADEPT$_{distribution}$, this circumstance can be modeled by assigning a weight $Weight(u)$ to each user u. This weight is used in Algorithm 3 to add $DepServProb_k(S|u)$ proportionally. Further possible weights are discussed in [7].

4.5   Migration Costs

In Phase 1 of Algorithm 1, the migration costs are ignored. In Phase 2, these costs are included. In order to calculate the migration costs, the migration probability $MigrProb_{x,k}(S_1, S_2)$ − with which the WF is migrated from server S_1 to server S_2 − has to be determined.

The probabilities for migrations from activity x to activity k can be described by a *migration matrix*. An entry $DepMigrProb_{x,k}(S_2|S_1)$ of this matrix describes the conditional probability that the WF migrates to server S_2, if the preceding activity x was controlled by server S_1 ($DepMigrProb_{x,k}(S_2|S_1)$ is defined as $P(server\ S_2\ controls\ activity\ k\ |\ server\ S_1\ controls\ activity\ x)$). Hence the migration probability results as: $MigrProb_{x,k}(S_1,\ S_2) = ServProb_x(S_1) \cdot DepMigrProb_{x,k}(S_2|S_1)$. In the following we describe how the matrix $DepMigrProb$ can be determined.

By analyzing the server assignments, it can be deduced which sets of activities of a WF instance are always controlled by the same server. At the transition between two

106   T. Bauer and P. Dadam

activities x and k belonging to the same set, the WF never migrates. This results in:
$\forall S_1, S_2: DepMigrProb_{x,k}(S_2|S_1) = \delta_{S_1,S_2}$

If the activities x and k are controlled by different WF servers, the usage of the server PD offers a simple method for the estimation of $DepMigrProb_{x,k}(S_2|S_1)$. The server PD $ServProb_k(S)$ describes the probability that the WF instance is located at the server S_2 after the migration. So the resulting migration probabilities may be approximated as: $\forall S_1, S_2: DepMigrProb_{x,k}(S_2|S_1) = ServProb_k(S_2)$

More sophisticated algorithms for calculating $DepMigrProb_{x,k}(S_2|S_1)$, which consider dependencies between the actors resp. the servers of the activities x and k, are presented in [7].

5   Efficiency of the ADEPT$_{distribution}$ Approach

In this section we demonstrate that the overall network load can be significantly reduced by the use of variable server assignments. For this purpose, we simulated the execution of a clinical WF when it is controlled by a central WfMS, by a distributed WfMS that does not use migrations, by a WfMS with static server assignments, and by a WfMS with variable server assignments. For further simulations and details concerning the simulated application scenarios, the simulation environment, and the interpretation of the results we refer to [5, 6].

Since the effects of variable server assignments shall be examined, the simulated WF contains dependent actor assignments. The simulation component simulates in a lifelike fashion the execution of many instances of this WF. At the same time it memorizes all occurring communications. This information is used to compute the total load of all WF servers, the average load per WF server, the load per subnet, and the load of the gateways. For each case considered, the load of the central WF server is used as reference basis. It is defined as 100. Fig. 5 shows the result of the simulation. To avoid confusion: We have been interested to show the (positive and negative) aspects of distribution and server migration with respect to server load and network load. To provide a reasonable reference basis for comparing the loads, we selected a scenario where a central WF server was not overloaded. It, therefore, could

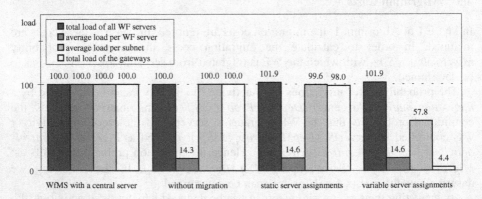

Fig. 5. Result of the simulation of a clinical WF

serve as reference point (100). This value (server load) cannot be improved in the distributed case because the synchronization overhead and the migration costs increase it. The simulation shows that variable server assignments significantly reduce the load per subnet and the data volume that has to be transferred by the gateways: The average load per subnet is 57.8% of the central case and the data volume transferred by the gateways results as only 4.4%.

6   Discussion

This section summarizes important concepts for scalable WfMSs and outlines some concrete approaches. For a more detailed discussion we refer to [4, 5, 6].

One extreme for the distribution model of a WfMS is a central server, which controls all activities. As it has to manage the whole system load, obviously, it represents a potential bottleneck. Some research prototypes which do not primarily deal with scalability issues (e.g., Panta Rhei [13], WASA [22], [10]) and most of the commercial systems belong to this category. The other extreme is a completely distributed system, which does not use any WF servers at all (e.g., Exotica/FMQM [2], INCAS [8]). In such a system, a WF migrates to the machine of the user who wants to perform an activity. With this approach, no server assignments are necessary as well.

Many approaches use multiple WF servers. As these systems require a strategy for the assignment of the servers to the activities, they are classified according to this criterion. In [1] identical replicates (clusters) of the WF engine are used. Whole WF instances are controlled by a randomly selected cluster. Therefore, no server assignments are necessary. In [20] the systems CodAlf and BPAFrame are described, which allocate an activity's WF server on the machine of the corresponding application (e.g., a DBMS). A similar approach has been suggested by $METEOR_2$ [11] and by METUFlow [12].

Like $ADEPT_{distribution}$, several approaches try to allocate the servers close to the actors of the activities. MENTOR [16] partitions state/activity charts in a way that allows to formally verify the equivalence of the distributed executions to the central case. All users of one activity have to belong to the same "processing entity". The server of this processing entity is selected for that activity. The same distribution strategy is followed by WIDE [9] using CORBA remote object access instead of migrations. In MOBILE [15] the different aspects of a WF are treated by different servers but there is no migration. This approach was extended in [21] by selecting the server for each (sub) WF at run time. The TEAM model [17] considers cooperating organizations. In this scenario, the locations of the WF servers are predetermined.

In $ADEPT_{distribution}$, the communication costs are considered by the distribution algorithm. That is, it takes into account (and tries to avoid the case) that the communication system can become a bottleneck. To our knowledge, it is the only approach that analyzes the load in order to minimize the communication costs by means of a suitable distribution. The other systems do not offer variable server assignments; the influence of dependent actor assignments on the distribution is not considered.

7   Conclusion and Outlook

WfMSs that allow the explicit modeling of the flow of control, the flow of data, and the dynamic assignment of actors to the activities offer a promising technology for the realization of enterprise-wide, process-oriented application systems. The flexibility achievable with these systems, however, is reflected in a relatively high communication load between the control components (the WF servers) and the application components (the WF clients). In WfMSs with hundreds of WF clients and thousands of active WF instances, the resulting load of the WF servers as well as of the communication network plays an essential role for the response times and also for the usability of the WfMS in total.

A possibility to reduce the network load is to keep, if possible, the communication between WF servers and their WF clients local within one subnet; i.e., to avoid subset-spanning communications. This can be achieved, if a WF instance is not necessarily completely controlled by the initiating WF server. Instead, its control may "migrate" to other WF servers, if necessary. In [3] we have presented an approach using static server assignments. In this paper, we have significantly extended this approach and examined how dependent actor assignments can be supported adequately by a WfMS. With dependent actor assignments, the possible actors of an activity depend on previous activities. This is a practically very relevant case, which has not been considered in the WF literature so far. We have shown how suitable load estimations can be already performed at build time. Additionally, we have shown how the WF control can be realized in a way that the WF server of an activity can be chosen dynamically at run time. For this purpose, we have introduced variable server assignment expressions as well as models for probability and cost estimations. The cost model and the distribution algorithms were implemented and measurements were performed in order to show their correctness [14]. In addition, the effectiveness of the techniques presented was confirmed by simulations. Distributed WF execution (inclusive variable server assignments) was realized in the ADEPT-WfMS. Since the whole system is implemented in Java, it can be used in the Internet.

To get a complete picture, several additional aspects have to be considered as well (c.f. [18]). Transactional aspects, for example, may influence the communication load. Due to lack of space we could not discuss that in this paper. Our analysis performed so far make us confident that our approach suffers not much more (if at all) than most of the other distributed approaches.

Acknowledgements: We would like to thank our colleagues Manfred Reichert and Clemens Hensinger for their valuable suggestions.

References

1. G. Alonso, M. Kamath, D. Agrawal, A. El Abbadi, R. Günthör, and C. Mohan: *Failure Handling in Large Scale Workflow Management Systems*. Technical Report RJ9913, IBM Almaden Research Center, 1994.
2. G. Alonso, C. Mohan, R. Günthör, D. Agrawal, A. El Abbadi, and M. Kamath: *Exotica/FMQM: A Persistent Message-Based Architecture for Distributed Workflow Management*. Proc. IFIP Working Conf. on Information Systems for Decentralized Organisations, Trondheim, 1995.
3. T. Bauer and P. Dadam: *A Distributed Execution Environment for Large-Scale Workflow Mana-*

gement Systems with Subnets and Server Migration. Proc. 2nd IFCIS Conf. on Cooperative Information Systems, pages 99-108, Kiawah Island, SC, 1997.

4. T. Bauer and P. Dadam: *Architectures for Scalable Workflow Management Systems – Classification and Analysis.* Technical Report UIB 98-02, Universität Ulm, Fakultät für Informatik, 1998 (in German).
5. T. Bauer and P. Dadam: *Distribution Models for Workflow Management Systems – Classification and Simulation.* Informatik Forschung und Entwicklung, 14(4):203-217, 1999 (in German).
6. T. Bauer and P. Dadam: *Efficient Distributed Control of Enterprise-Wide and Cross-Enterprise Workflows.* In: Proc. Workshop Enterprise-wide and Cross-enterprise Workflow Management: Concepts, Systems, Applications, 29. Jahrestagung der GI, pages 25-32, Paderborn, 1999.
7. T. Bauer and P. Dadam: *Variable Server Assignments and Complex Actor Assignments in the ADEPT Workflow Management System.* Technical Report UIB 2000-02, Universität Ulm, Fakultät für Informatik, 2000 (in German).
8. D. Barbará, S. Mehrotra, and M. Rusinkiewicz: *INCAs: Managing Dynamic Workflows in Distributed Environments.* Journal of Database Management, Special Issue on Multidatabases, 7(1):5-15, 1996.
9. S. Ceri, P. Grefen, and G. Sánchez: *WIDE – A Distributed Architecture for Workflow Management.* 7th Int. Workshop on Research Issues in Data Engineering, Birmingham, 1997.
10. U. Dayal, M. Hsu, and R. Ladin: *A Transactional Model for Long-Running Activities.* Proc. 17th VLDB, pages 113-122, Barcelona, 1991.
11. S. Das, K. Kochut, J. Miller, A. Sheth, and D. Worah: *ORBWork: A Reliable Distributed CORBA-based Workflow Enactment System for METEOR₂.* Technical Report #UGA-CS-TR-97-001, Department of Computer Science, University of Georgia, 1997.
12. A. Dogac et al: *Design and Implementation of a Distributed Workflow Management System: METUFlow.* Proc. NATO Advanced Study Institute on Workflow Management Systems and Interoperability, pages 61-91, Istanbul, 1997.
13. J. Eder, H. Groiss, and W. Liebhart: *Workflow Management and Databases.* Proc. 2ème Forum Int. d´Informatique Appliquée, Tunis, 1996.
14. H. Enderlin: *Realization of a Distributed Workflow Execution Component on Basis of IBM FlowMark.* Master's thesis, Universität Ulm, Fakultät für Informatik, 1998 (in German).
15. P. Heinl and H. Schuster: *Towards a Highly Scaleable Architecture for Workflow Management Systems.* Proc. 7th Int. Workshop on Database and Expert Systems Applications, pages 439-444, Zürich, 1996.
16. P. Muth, D. Wodtke, J. Weißenfels, A. Kotz-Dittrich, and G. Weikum: *From Centralized Workflow Specification to Distributed Workflow Execution.* Journal of Intelligent Information Systems, 10(2):159-184, 1998.
17. G. Piccinelli: *Distributed Workflow Management: The TEAM Model.* Proc. 3nd IFCIS Conf. on Cooperative Information Systems, pages 292-299, New York, 1998.
18. M. Reichert, T. Bauer and P. Dadam: *Enterprise-Wide and Cross-Enterprise Workflow-Management: Challenges and Research Issues for Adaptive Workflows.* In: Proc. Workshop Enterprise-wide and Cross-enterprise Workflow Management: Concepts, Systems, Applications, 29. Jahrestagung der GI, pages 56-64, Paderborn, 1999.
19. M. Reichert and P. Dadam: *ADEPT_flex – Supporting Dynamic Changes of Workflows Without Losing Control.* Journal of Intelligent Information Systems, 10(2):93-129, 1998.
20. A. Schill and C. Mittasch: *Workflow Management Systems on Top of OSF DCE and OMG CORBA.* Distributed Systems Engineering, 3(4):250-262, 1996.
21. H. Schuster, J. Neeb, and R. Schamburger: *A Configuration Management Approach for Large Workflow Management Systems.* Proc. Joint Conf. on Work Activities Coordination and Collaboration, San Francisco, 1999.
22. G. Vossen, M. Weske, and G. Wittowski: *Dynamic Workflow Management on the Web.* Technical Report 24/96-I, Lehrstuhl für Informatik, Universität Münster, 1996.

A Logical Framework for Exception Handling in ADOME Workflow Management System[*]

Dickson Chiu[1], Qing Li[2], and Kamalakar Karlapalem[1]

[1]Department of Computer Science, University of Science and Technology,

Clear Water Bay, Kowloon, Hong Kong

{kwchiu,kamal}@cs.ust.hk

[2]Department of Computer Science, City University of Hong Kong,

Tat Chee Avenue, Kowloon, Hong Kong

csqli@cs.cityu.edu.hk

Abstract. We have been developing ADOME-WFMS as a comprehensive framework in which the problem of workflow exception handling can be adequately addressed. In this paper, we present detailed design for ADOME-WFMS with procedures for supporting the following: an integrated approach starting from exception detection to exception resolution, reuse of exception handlers, and automated resolution of expected exceptions.

1 Introduction

Exception handling in workflow management systems (WFMSs) is a very important problem since it is not possible to specify all possible outcomes and alternatives. Effective reuse of existing exception handlers can greatly help in dealing with workflow exceptions. On the other hand, support for workflow evolution at run-time is vital for an adaptive WFMS. Any WFMS that provides a comprehensive solution for exception handling needs to provide a framework for the specification and support for generic exception handlers that can be fine-tuned to handle different run-time exceptions. Reuse of workflow definitions and exception handlers are very important in the smooth operation of a flexible WFMS.

In this paper, we model a business process as a workflow (an activity) executed by a set of problem solving agents. We use the terms *activity* and *workflow* interchangeably. A *Problem Solving Agent* (PSA) is a hardware/software system or a human being, with an ability to execute a finite set of tasks in an application domain. Typically an activity is recursively decomposed into *sub-activities* and eventually down to the unit level called *tasks* (as illustrated by the example in Fig. 3). A task is usually handled by a *single* PSA. The WFMS schedules and selects the PSAs for executing the tasks. We match the tasks with PSAs by using a capability-based *token/role*

---

[*] This research has been partly funded by HKSAR RGC Grant HKUST 747/96E.

B. Wangler, L. Bergman (Eds.): CAiSE 2000, LNCS 1789, pp. 110-125, 2000
© Springer-Verlag Berlin Heidelberg 2000

approach [19], where the main criterion is that the set of capability tokens of a chosen PSA should be matched to the requirement of the task. A *token* embodies certain capabilities of a PSA to execute certain functions / procedures /tasks, e.g., programming, database-administration, Japanese-speaking, while a *role* represents a set of responsibilities, which usually correspond to a job-function in an organization, e.g., project-leader, project-member, programmer, analyst, etc. Each PSA can play a set of PSA-roles and hold a set of extra capabilities. For example, John is a Japanese analyst-programmer who is leading a small project; thus, he may play all the above-mentioned roles (project-leader, project-member, programmer, analyst, etc.), and in addition holds an extra capability (token) of Japanese-speaking.

In this context, we employ an Advanced Object Modeling Environment (ADOME [23]) to not only specify generic exception handlers but also facilitate the reuse and adaptation to handle specific instances of exception that occur at run time. In particular, our ADOME exception handling environment facility provides the following features:

- Dynamic binding of exception handlers to classes, objects and roles, and to activities with scoping.
- Addition, deletion and modification of handlers at run-time through workflow evolution support.
- Specifying and reusing exception handlers upon unexpected exceptions with the Human Intervention Manager.

In contrast with traditional software systems, workflows usually evolve more frequently, making reuse a vital issue. On the other hand, workflow evolution often takes place at execution time, making it much more difficult to handle. There have been few WFMSs designed to address these two problems (viz. reusing exception handlers and workflow evolution) effectively and adequately. In this regard, we have been developing ADOME-WFMS as a comprehensive framework in which the problem of workflow exception handling can be adequately addressed.

We use an integrated, event-driven approach for execution, coordination, and exception handling in our WFMS. Events (such as database events / exceptions, or external inputs) trigger the WFMS *Activity Executor* to start an activity. The WFMS *Activity Executor* uses events to trigger execution of tasks, while finished tasks will inform the *Activity Executor* with events. Upon an exception, exception events will trigger the WFMS *Exception Manager* to take control of resolutions.

In this paper, we present a logical framework of exception handling (with detailed design and main algorithms) for ADOME-WFMS, covering reuse issues in specifying exceptions and their handlers and a novel solution based on workflow evolution. More details regarding classification of exceptions and handlers, and modeling aspects for ADOME-WFMS are given in [8] while ADOME-WFMS exception driven workflow recovery are presented in [9]. The objectives and contribution of this paper include: (i) the mechanism of the ADOME-WFMS and resolution of expected exceptions, (ii) support of reuse for workflow definitions, constraints, exception types and handlers in ADOME-WFMS, and, (iii) demonstration of the feasibility of ADOME-WFMS for effective support of exception handling through effective reuse.

The rest of our paper is organized as follows. Section 2 describes the architecture and basic execution mechanisms of ADOME-WFMS. Section 3 presents how

ADOME-WFMS resolves for expected exceptions. Section 4 explains how reuse can be facilitated. Section 5 compares related work. Finally, we conclude the paper with our plans for further research in Section 6.

2 Architecture of ADOME-WFMS

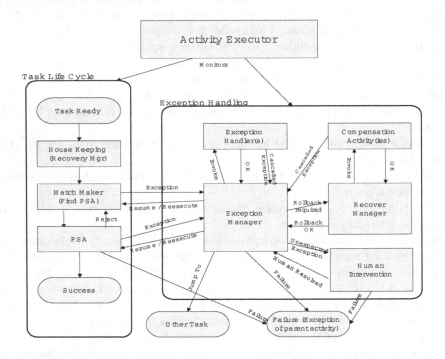

Fig. 1. ADOME-WFMS Task Execution, Exception and Recovery

The ADOME system was developed to enhance the knowledge-level modeling capabilities of OODBMS models [23], so as to allow them to more adequately deal with data and knowledge management requirements of advanced information management applications, especially WFMSs. The architecture of ADOME is characterized by the seamless integration of a rule base, an OODBMS and a procedure base. Role extension to the OO model has been employed for accommodating dynamic nature of object states and for capturing more application semantics at the knowledge level. Roles also act as "mediators" for bridging the gap between database, knowledge base and procedure base semantics, and facilitating dynamic binding of data object with rules and procedures [22]. Advanced ECA rules are also supported [5,6]. The following components / enabling technologies of ADOME are useful for various aspects of a WFMS, especially facilitating reuse:

- *Object-oriented database (OODB)* – Using OODB for the modeling and processing of complex objects and their relationships is almost a consensus for building an advanced WFMS and other next generation information systems. For example, the composition hierarchy for modeling activities, sub-activities down to tasks and isa hierarchy for PSAs not only captures more semantics than traditional relational models, but also helps in reuse of their definitions in the WFMS. It also enables easier maintenance, understandability and extensibility than the large number of inter-related tables [19]. Moreover, the OO paradigm enables flexible passing of different forms of data among agents and tasks, with the OODB providing for a convenient general persistent storage for almost everything in the WFMS that requires to be recorded.

- *Roles* – Roles enables PSA objects to be dynamically associated with one or more different functions, responsibility and authority. It also captures attributes, states, methods and knowledge specific to individual positions/agents rather than the PSA player objects. With roles extended with multiple-inheritance, capabilities and roles for PSAs can be much better represented in a hierarchy (c.f. [7]).
- *Rules* – Declarative exception handlers in the form of Event-Condition-Action (ECA) rules enables automatic execution and exception handling based on events, where the *exceptions* correspond to the event part, while the *handlers* correspond to the condition-action parts. Rules can also be used for processing declarative knowledge such as organization policies, agent selection criteria, exception handling criteria, etc.
- *Flexibility of objects and schema* – This facilitates exception handling since real-time modification to objects, roles, rules and even workflow evolution are required during execution of workflow.

One of the main objectives of ADOME-WFMS is to provide extensive possibilities for reuse. In addition to the reuse of workflow definitions [7,8], we present in this section the modeling for exceptions, handlers and constraints that facilitate reuse. The ADOME prototype has been built by integrating an OODBMS (ITASCA [16]) and production inference engine (CLIPS [12]). Therefore, a WFMS can be implemented on top of it with relative ease. The architecture and functional aspects of the resultant ADOME-WFMS are as follows (cf. Fig. 1):

- *ADOME active expert OODBMS* (not shown in figure) provides a unified enabling technology for the WFMS, viz., object and role database, event specification and execution, rule / constraint specification and processing.
- *Activity Decomposer* facilitates the decomposition of activities into tasks. The user provides the knowledge and related data to decompose activities into tasks by a user interface.
- *Organizational Database* manages data objects for the organization, as well as PSA classes, instances and their capability token (role) specifications. Besides maintaining user-specified extensional tokens / roles systematically, intensional token/role derivation for a PSA is also supported.
- *Activity Executor* coordinates execution by user-raised and database generated events.

- *Match Maker* selects PSAs for executing tasks of an activity according to some selection criteria. ([8] describes the details in capability modeling and the mechanisms of the match maker of ADOME-WFMS.)
- *Exception Manager* handles various exceptions by re-executing failed tasks or their alternatives (either resolved by the WFMS or determined by the user) while maintaining forward progress.
- *Recovery Manager* performs various housekeeping functions, including rollback to maintain the WFMS in consistent states. (Details can be found in [9])

2.1   Exception Handling Mechanisms of ADOME-WFMS

In this paper, we shall concentrate on using a centralized control and coordination execution model centered on the *Activity Executor* of the WFMS. The *Activity Executor* monitor task execution status and enforces deadlines. For the normal task life cycle, it initiates the PSAs to be selected by the *Match Maker* to carry out their assigned task and get the response (if any) from the PSA upon task completion. On the other hand, if a task raises exception events or does not respond within the deadline (i.e., *time out*), the *Exception Manager* will respond and handle it.

2.1.1   Normal Workflow Execution

An event driven activity execution model with meta-ECA-rules can be found in [8]. Moreover, this provides a unified approach for normal activity execution and exception handling [8,19]. The mechanisms of ADOME-WFMS activity execution (cf. Fig. 1) are explained as follows:

- There is an *Activity Decomposer* module, which generates ECA rules for automatic coordination during the execution of workflow and stores them in the database [8,19].
- Users and external applications can trigger the corresponding start-events to start work.
- Upon a start-event, if the activity is a composite one, the activity executor will raise a start-event for the first sub-activity. This process will continue recursively downward the composition hierarchy until a leaf task is reached.[1] The activity executor invokes the *Match Maker* to select the appropriate PSA(s) for the task and then initiates the task. (Algorithm of the *Match Maker* is detailed in [8])
- The selected PSA will acknowledge or reject the assignment by raising a corresponding reply event.
- After finishing, the assigned task successfully, the PSA replies to the activity executor by raising a finish-event. The *Activity Executor* then carries on with the next step according to the result passed back.
- Upon failures or time out, the PSA or the system will raise an appropriate exception event to invoke the *Exception Manager*.

---

[1] This approach can handle dynamic resource allocation, online modification of workflow and exceptions in a rather flexible manner.

2.1.2   Detection of Events and Exceptions

The data dependency, temporal dependency and external input dependency, can be expressed by means of a uniform framework of events, such as *Data operations, Workflow, Clock Time, External Notification, Abstract Events*. Besides primitive events, any (recursive) combination of conjunction, disjunction, or sequence of other events can define a composite event. These events are all detected by the underlining ADOME event facilities as described in [5,6]. Since exceptions are ADOME events, detection of exceptions for ADOME-WFMS is well supported at run-time:

- External exceptions – events raised by external entities can be intercepted by the WFMS. These external events must be *apriori* characterized as events generated due to exceptions.
- Workflow exceptions raised by WFMS components, e.g.:
  Match Maker – cannot find PSA
  Activity Executor - PSA reject assignment, not enough resources
  Organization Database – data constraint violations upon update
  Exception Manager – (ignored) failure of task / sub-activity will cause exception
     to its parent
- Workflow exceptions detected by automatic ADOME ECA rules and/or constraints, e.g.:
  Activities cannot meet deadline
  Activities constraint violation (e.g. budget exceeded)

2.1.3   Handling Exceptions

As supported by the underlying ADOME facilities, the following information will be passed to the *Exception Manager* during the exception:

- source and type of exception,
- for workflow exceptions, state information of the task / activity [8],
- any extra parameters defined by the exception type (e.g., budget value).

The *Exception Manager* then takes control and carries out the following:

1. Perform notification if necessary.
2. Identify the appropriate exception handler(s) and execute them. Handles are modeled as sub-activities in ADOME-WFMS. One or more handlers will be executed until the problem is solved (c.f. Section 3).
3. If no appropriate exception handlers are found (i.e., an unexpected exception), or human intervention is specified, the *Human Intervention Manager* (c.f. Section 4) will be invoked. The human can then select the appropriate handler and/or perform workflow evolution (c.f. [10]).
4. If rollback is required, the *Recovery Manager* will be invoked for compensating activities (c.f. [9]).
5. Resume / redo execution, jump to the appropriate step as decided by step 2. or 3., or abort the current task / sub-activity so that the exception propagate to its parent for further handling. Though failure may propagate up the activity composition hierarchy, this approach localizes exception and thus reduces loss of work done.

3   Handling Expected Exceptions in ADOME-WFMS

In this section, we first discuss how exception handlers are identified and executed in ADOME-WFMS with the example in Fig 2. Then we discuss in depth how reuse is facilitated with advanced exception modeling based on the ADOME mechanisms.

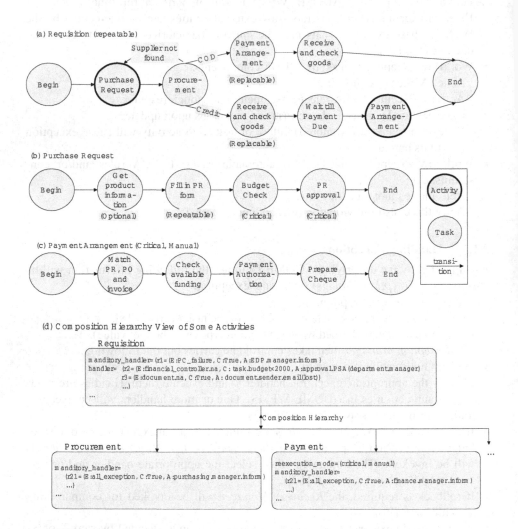

Fig. 2. Example Workflow of Requisition Procedures

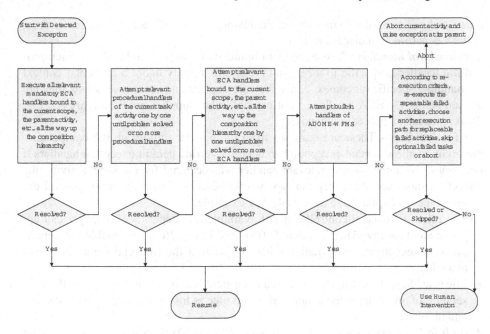

Fig. 3. Flowchart for identifying and Executing Exception Handlers

3.1   Identifying and Executing Exception Handlers

One or more exception handlers may be qualified to handle an exception that occurs. As illustrated in Fig. 3, the ADOME-WFMS Exception Manager employs the following priority order for selecting the appropriate exception handler:

1. Mandatory ECA handlers - Since the users specify these as mandatory, all relevant handlers (with event matched and condition fulfilled) bounded to the current scope are executed in the order of the task / sub-activity, its parent and all the way up to the *global* activity. For example, a mandatory ECA rule specifies that all exceptions should notify the purchasing manager in the procurement activity (*r21* in Fig. 2(d)) while a global mandatory ECA rule specifies all PC failures should be reported to the EDP manager (*r1* in Fig. 2(d)). In this case, the failure of a PC in the purchasing department causing an exception will trigger both rules and inform the purchasing manager and the EDP department.

These mandatory actions may or may not solve the problem causing the exception, such as, logging and notification. If they cannot solve the problem, other categories of exception handlers will be executed. For example, all exceptions in the 'Payment arrangement' activity (cf. Fig. 2(c)) are regarded as having severe consequences, so the financial manager will be informed (*r31* in Fig. 2(d)) and manual handling of exception is required.

Furthermore, the organization manager may later find that it is useful for all exception in a department be reported to its manager. So rules *r21* and *r31* are combined and generalized as a new global mandatory rule *r4*=(E: all_exception, C: True, A: task.department.manager.inform).

2. *Procedural handlers* - These are extra branches for exception handling. Each procedural handler is specific to a certain task or sub-activity under a particular context for handling specific outcomes. Since they are explicit and context sensitive, they are chosen before (3) ECA handlers. For example, the 'supplier not found' arc (cf. Fig. 2(a)) represents a procedural handler.

3. *ECA handlers* - These are searched from the current activity up the composition hierarchy to allow special exception handlers to override default exception handlers if necessary. If more than one relevant handler was declared for the same activity, the one(s) for more specific exception type would be chosen over the more general exception type (as explained in Section 4). For example,

- The rule "If financial controller is not available, the department manager can approve any task involving less than $2000" (*r2* in Fig 2(d)) will enable the department manger to approve small purchase requests if the financial controller is not available.
- The rule "Send Email to the issuer if a document is lost" (*r3* in Fig 2(d)) will cause sending of an email to the supplier if an invoice is lost in the step 'Match PR, PO and invoice'.

4. *Built-in handlers* - For generic exceptions, ADOME-WFMS has built-in exception handlers, such as:

- If a PSA rejects a task assignment or the best candidate PSA is not available, the WFMS will find the next available PSA.
- If all PSAs capable of executing the task are busy or the required resources are occupied, the WFMS will either wait or choose alternate execution paths.

ADOME-WFMS supports a lot of exception handling resolutions relating to PSA assignment based on capability matching, such as amending the capabilities of PSAs and changing capability requirements for a task instance [8]. This is important because significant portions of internal (workflow) exceptions are due to failures in finding (suitable) PSA(s) for the execution of tasks. Moreover, ADOME supports advanced analysis for PSA capabilities termed as "capability role/token multiple inheritance hierarchy" and "token derivation network theory"[8]. This increases the chance of finding suitable PSA(s) automatically (thus avoiding PSA not available exception), and finding alternate PSAs for repeating a task upon exception. For automatic switching of PSA assignment among tasks, the above-mentioned capability processing features are vital to the success of this resolution scheme. It should be noted that quite a number of traditional WFMSs like Flowmark [1] and OASIS [24], do not readily support or employ the notion of *capability matching* for PSA assignment to tasks.

5. *Re-execution criteria* - ADOME-WFMS can resolve and decide for the correct alternative PSAs or alternate execution branch automatically if the re-execution pattern for a task has been specified. This feature can save many tedious explicit jumps and aborts, especially with scoping in ADOME-WFMS (cf. Section 4). Moreover, this way one can resolve many unexpected exceptions if re-execution helps.

The WFMS will automatically re-execute the *repeatable* failed activities; choose another execution path for *replaceable* failed activities; skip *optional* failed tasks, if none of the above handlers is specified. However, *critical* failed tasks without explicit handlers are unexpected exceptions. (Section 3.2 discusses prevention of cascaded exceptions and loops.) Therefore, it will result in human intervention. Upon re-execution, in order to maintain work continuity and save starting up overhead, the same agent is preferred unless otherwise specified. The next candidate would be the nearest capable sibling or ancestor according to the organization structure (i.e., most probably a member of the team or the supervisor). For example:

- The 'Requisition' activity specified in Fig. 2(a) is repeatable and thus 'purchase request', 'procurement' etc. are all *repeatable* unless otherwise stated.
- As funding may not be available for cash on delivery (COD) or the supplier may not be willing to deliver the ordered goods if the new company's credit limit is exceeded, the two branches following 'Procurement' (cf. Fig. 2(a)) are *replaceable*.
- Upon 'Purchase Request', the user may not need to 'get product information' because he may know that very well or he does not even know how to get such information. (E.g., the user may just specify that he wants a chair costing around $500 and let the procurement department take care of the rest.) Hence, this task is optional (cf. Fig. 2(b)).
- As illustrated in Fig. 2(b), tasks 'Budget check' and 'PR approval' are flagged critical so that the sub-activity 'Purchase Request' will fail immediately if these tasks are not executed. However, 'Purchase Request' is repeatable so that the user can also revise the budget and /or product specification to retry for approval.

3.2   Handling Cascaded Exceptions and Loops

In order to handle cascaded exceptions effectively and avoid infinite generation of cascaded exceptions, the following *safety* measures are employed in ADOME-WFMS:

- Notification within the exception handling activity to the human deciding on the handler for an unexpected exception (e.g. to report even expected exceptions).
- If cascaded exceptions occur, the same human should be notified for better management and decisions.
- Tighter constraints, such as deadline and budget, can be introduced to avoid the exception handling activity to run indefinitely and let the control pass back for human decisions.
- When a human decides a jump back to a previously executed step as exception handler (including simple redoing of the currently failed task), there may be a potential danger of looping and the human will thus be warned.
- The *Activity Executor* will keep track of the sequence of executed tasks. If the same task in the same context is executed for over a certain number of times (or a specified iteration count), a warning or exception will be raised for human intervention or alternative actions.

- Backtracking so that the human can undo some of the decisions taken (if possible) and finalize on the resolution once all different aspects of exception handling are taken care of.

4   Exception Modeling for Reuse in ADOME-WFMS

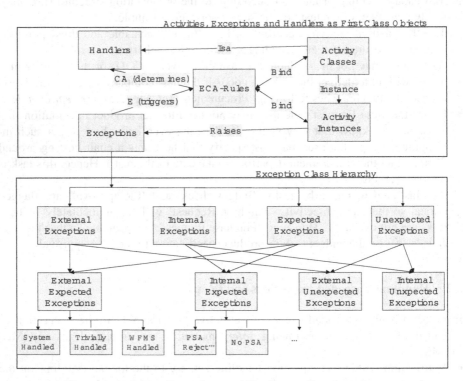

Figure 4. Activities, Exceptions, and Handlers as first-class objects

Figure 4 illustrates the main entities and relationships in ADOME-WFMS regarding to exception handling. These entities are all modeled as first-class objects. In particular, the class *exceptions* is a subclass of class *events*. Taxonomy of exceptions and handlers can be found in [8]. Handlers are modeled as sub-activities so that they can carry out any complicated actions; and nested exceptions are supported by recursive invoking of the *Exception Manager*.

In ADOME-WFMS, declarative exception handlers in the form of ECA rules can be bound to selected classes, objects and roles. Furthermore, handlers can be specified within the scope of different activity and sub-activity levels, i.e., the handler applies not only to the body of the target activity but also to all its sub-activities and tasks.

Similarly, human intervention requirements of exception handling (automatic, warning, cooperative and manual) and re-execution patterns (optional, critical, repeatable and replaceable) for sub-activities and tasks are specified within the scope of this composition hierarchy, with the lowest level taking priority in specification and thus overriding those of higher levels.

The ADOME-WFMS *Human Intervention Manager* supports the user to modify all the above declarations and associations at run-time as described in [8,10]. The power of ADOME-WFMS in reuse over other systems (such as [3,4,11,19,20]) is mainly due ADOME's ability in dynamic binding of rules to different dimensions (objects, roles, sub-activities, etc.) at run-time as explained below. However, a methodology in workflow design to facilitate reuse of exception handlers is beyond the scope of this paper.

4.1   Reusing Exception Handlers

Since exceptions can be common in a WFMS, reusing exception handlers is vital to the effectiveness, user-friendliness and efficiency of the WFMS. In ADOME-WFMS, mechanisms for reuse of exception handlers follow from its structure:

* For procedural exception handlers, arcs from more than one peer tasks / sub-activities at the same level (siblings inside the same parent activity) can lead to the same exception handler for some degree of sharing.
* Because of scoping, only one declarative exception handler is required for each exception type for each activity composition hierarchy (as explained in the previous section).
* Declarative exception handlers are first-class ECA rule objects. A rule object r is declared and defined once and then can be associated with more than one scope by repeated binding. (E.g., Bind $r9$ to *payment*, *requisition*).
* Since exceptions are events (which are first-class objects in ADOME), exception classes are also arranged into an 'isa' hierarchy. Thus, an exception handler for a super-class will also handle an exception of a sub-class. (E.g., an exception handler for program_error will handle subscript_out_of_range also.)
* Extending the event-part with 'or' event composition can generalize exception handlers (e.g., E: program_error ∨ PC_failure, A: EDP.manager.inform), and increase the applicability of the exception handlers.
* Meta-level rules can be instantiated through parameters and supplied methods to specify rules, such as budget rules instantiated with actual budget figure.

4.2   Reusing Constraint Definitions

In order for modification of task instances and workflow evolution to be in accordance with users' requirement, we employ a strategy of associating consistency constraints with appropriate entities of different levels and dimensions as explained below. When constraints are violated at run-time, appropriate exceptions will be raised for handling. Since constraints are also implemented as ECA rules in ADOME-

WFMS, reuse and evolution of consistency constraints are both possible and similar to those of exceptions and exception handlers in general. Associating constraints to different levels and dimensions can be naturally specified with ADOME's facilities:

- Organization Composition Hierarchy - organization, units, sub-units and groups. Reuse is supported through inheritance down the composition hierarchy. The objective of the organization is also that of its units, sub-units and groups, while individual units can only have their more specific objectives not violating that of the organization.
- Activity Composition Hierarchy – projects (any collection of activities), activities, sub-activities, tasks. Reuse is supported through inheritance down the composition hierarchy. Deadlines and budgets are typical examples. Furthermore, scoping produces further flexibility for handling violation of constraints so that failed sub-activities (ignored exceptions) can be remedied by a higher-level activity.
- Role/Token Hierarchy – Positions and capability. Reuse is supported through multiple-inheritance down the hierarchy. For example, programmers (and hence senior programmers) are allowed to log on to the development computer account; however, the minimum productivity index of a senior programmer can be specified to be higher than that of a junior programmer by overriding rules as supported by ADOME [5,6].
- Any class and sub-classes of objects in ADOME-WFMS (such as PSA and resources).
- Combination of above levels and dimensions. As supported by ADOME [5,6], constraints and rules are first class objects and can be bound to objects, classes, and roles repeatedly. These can also be generalized or specialized by the 'or' and 'and' connectors. For example, programmers, engineers and managers should be university graduates.

4.3   Reusing Compensation Transactions for Workflow Recovery

Compensation transactions are considered as part of the exception handling procedure and are modeled as sub-activities of the exception handlers in ADOME-WFMS. In fact, the execution and definition of compensation transaction are implemented as ECA rules, which corresponds to the integrated framework of event-driven activity execution in ADOME-WFMS. This allows different compensation transactions to be executed according to the exception type and general conditions under execution [9]. The reuse of definitions of compensation transactions follows from its rich set of features in reuse of exception handlers:

- Once a compensation transaction is defined, they can be used in different contexts.
- "*Simple rollback*" (restoring the previous value or state of the object like handling traditional database update in workflow) and "*mark void*" (keeping useful documents or partial work done for reference) are implemented as pre-defined compensation transaction.
- The activity decomposition hierarchy also provides scoping for associating compensation transaction with a sub-activity tree.

- A compensation transaction can be bound to each rollback class and sub-class of objects (also for roles and sub-roles).
- Dynamic use of compensation transactions according to different exception events can be facilitated with the flexibility in event definition: event isa-hierarchy and event 'or' composition.

5   Related Work

A classical article on exception handling is [2], which focused on database aspects of exception and handling techniques instead of workflow systems. On the other hand, notable advanced WFMSs have been developed in the past years [1, 4, 13, 18, 19, 21, 24, 25]. Among them, TriGSflow [16] and the work of Kumar et al [18], perhaps have the closest basic design with ours in that it adopts an OO design, and utilizes rules and roles. However, they did not address a variety of exception conditions or use capability matching for tasks and agents.

Ellis, et al [14] is among the earlier work in workflow evolution. WIDE [4] used object and rule modeling techniques and suggested some measures in handling exceptions. Exceptions were classified but not handling approaches. They also addressed reuse and management of exception handlers with implementation details, but not adequately considered high level semantics, especially inter-relationship among entities in a WFMS. Their workflow evolution primitives were not at a semantic level. PROSYT [11] addressed inconsistencies and deviations in general process support systems (where WFMS is considered as a kind of process support systems), but the contribution was more on the formal modeling than semantic modeling. [3] presented a framework for tolerating exceptions in WFMS close to ours [8], but without details in logical and implementation levels.   [20] adopted a knowledge-base approach to handling exceptions in WFMS, with strong emphasis on agent management. [26] studied the categories of exceptions in WFMS but did not involve workflow evolution.

Flowmark uses Sagas and flexible transactions for modeling workflow exception handling; and its extension, Exotica/FMDC [1], handles disconnected agents. Since Flowmark only finds out all possible candidates for task execution and then lets them volunteer for the execution instead of using capability matching, effectiveness and fairness may be impaired. WAMO [13] also uses Sagas and flexible transactions for supporting workflow exception handling. It also offers a preliminary classification of exceptions in which we have made some extensions in our taxonomy of exception categories (cf. [8]). Similarly, other works like [15], ConTract [25] and OPERA [17] focus on transactional aspects and thus on lower level issues.

In summary, other workflow systems either do not address exception-handling problems comprehensively or concentrate only on extended transaction models. Furthermore, few systems have advocated (let alone supported) an extensive meta-modeling approach (based on PSAs, match-making, exception handling, etc.). Compared with the systems close to us, ADOME-WFMS has the most features to facilitate reuse.

6   Conclusion

This paper has presented adaptive exception handling in ADOME-WFMS, a flexible WFMS based on ADOME; an active OODBMS extended with role and rule facilities. Compared with other research on this topic, ADOME provides an improved environment for developing a WFMS, which can adapt to changing requirements, with extensive support for reuse. In particular, the resultant system (i.e., ADOME-WFMS) supports a rich taxonomy of exception types and their handling approaches, and a novel augmented solution for exception handling based on workflow evolution. Effective reuse of workflow definitions, exceptions, handlers and constraints in ADOME-WFMS has also been presented. This paper has also described in detail, how expected exceptions are actually resolved with the ADOME-WFMS Exception Manager. It should be noted that, though exception handling is highly automated in ADOME-WFMS by scoping, binding and reuse, human intervention management must be provided to support for (totally) unexpected exceptions and drastic workflow evolutions. ADOME-WFMS is currently being built on top of the ADOME prototype system, with a web-based user interface [10] to accommodate the whole range of activities.

References

1. G. Alonso, et al. Exotica/FMDC: a workflow management system for mobile and disconnected clients. *Distributed & Parallel Databases*, **4**(3):229-247 (1996).
2. A. Boridga, Language Features for Flexible Handling of Exceptions, *ACM Trans. on Database Systems* (1985).
3. A. Borgida and T. Murata, A Unified Framework for Tolerating Exceptions in Workflow/Process Models - A Persistent Object Approach, *International Joint Conference on Work Activities Coordination and Collaboration (WACC '99)*, San Francisco (1999).
4. F. Casati, G. Pozzi. Modeling and Managing Exceptional Behaviors in Workflow management Systems, Proceedings of CoopIS'99, Edinburgh, Scotland, September 1999
5. L. C. Chan and Q. Li. Devising a Flexible Event Model on top of a Common Data / Knowledge Storage Manager. In *Proceedings of 6th Intl. Workshop on Information Technologies and Systems (WITS '96)*, Cleveland, Ohio, pp.182-191 (1996).
6. L. C. Chan and Q. Li. An Extensible Approach to Reactive Processing in an Advanced Object Modeling Environment. In *Proceedings of 8th Intl. Conf. on Database and Expert Systems Applications (DEXA '97)*, LNCS(1308), pp.38-47, Toulouse, France (1997).
7. D. K. W. Chiu, K. Karlapalem and Q. Li. Developing a Workflow Management System in an Integrated Object-Oriented Modeling Environment. In *Proceedings of 6th Int'l Conf. on Sofware Engineering and Knowledge Engineering (SEKE'98)*, pp.71-78, San Francisco (1998).
8. D.K.W. Chiu, Q. Li and K. Karlapalem, "A Meta Modeling Approach for Workflow Management Systems Supporting Exception Handling", Special Issue on Method Engineering and Metamodeling, *Information Systems*, Elsevier Science, 24(2):159-184 (1999).
9. D.K.W. Chiu, Q. Li and K. Karlapalem, Facilitating Exception Handling with Recovery Techniques in ADOME Workflow Management System, *Journal of Applied Systems*

Studies, Cambridge International Science Publishing, Cambridge, England (2000 to appear).

10. D.K.W. Chiu, Q. Li and K. Karlapalem, A Web-based Interface for ADOME Workflow Management System Facilitating Exception Handling, submitted to WISE'2000.

11. G. Cugola, Inconsistencies and Deviations in Process Support Systems, *PhD Thesis, Politecnico di Milano* (1998)

12. http://www.ghg.net/clips/CLIPS.html

13. J. Eder and W. Liebhart. The Workflow Activity Model WAMO. In *Proceeding of CoopIS-95*, pp 97-98. (1995).

14. S. Ellis et al , Dynamic Change within Workflow Systems, *Proceedings of the Conference on Organizational Computing Systems* (1995).

15. D. Georgakopoulos, M. F. Hornich and F. Manola. Customizing Transaction Models and Mechanisms in a Programmable Envioronment Supporting Reliable Workflow Automation. *IEEE Transactions on Knowledge and Data Engineering.* 8(4):630-649 (1996).

16. Ibex Corporation. *http://www.ibex.ch/*

17. C. Hagen and G. Alonso, Flexible Exception Handling in the OPERA Process Support System, *18th International Conference on Distributed Computing Systems* (ICDCS 98), Amsterdam, The Netherlands (1998).

18. G. Kappel, et.al. Workflow Management Based on Objects, Rules, and Roles. *IEEE Bulletin of the Technical Committee on Data Engineering* 18(1)11-18 (1995).

19. K. Karlapalem, H. P. Yeung and P. C. K. Hung. CapBaseED-AMS - A Framework for Capability-Based and Event-Driven Activity Management System. In *Proceeding of COOPIS '95*, pp. 205-219 (1995).

20. Mark Klein and Chrysanthos Dellarocas, A Knowledge-Based Approach to Handling Exceptions in Workflow Systems, Proceedings of the Third International Conference on Autonomous Agents, Seattle, Washington (1999).

21. A. Kumar, et.al. A framework for dynamic routing and operational integrity controls in a workflow management system. In *Proceedings of the Twenty-Ninth Hawaii International Conference on System Sciences* 3:492-501 (1996).

22. Q. Li and F. H. Lochovsky. Roles: Extending Object Behaviour to Support Knowledge Semantics. In *Proceeding of Int'l. Symposium on Advanced Database Technologies and Their Integration*, Nara, Japan, pp. 314-322 (1994).

23. Q. Li and F. H. Lochovsky. ADOME: an Advanced Object Modeling Environment. *IEEE Transactions on Knowledge and Data Engineering*, 10(2):255-276 (1998).

24. C. Martens and C.C. Woo. OASIS: An Integrative Toolkit for Developing Autonomous Applications in Decentralized Environments. *Journal of Organizational Computing*, New Jersey: Ablex Publishing Corporation, 7(2&3):227-251 (1997).

25. A. Reuter and F. Schwenkreis. ConTacts - A Low-Level Mechanism for Building General-Purpose Workflow Management Systems. *IEEE Bulletin of the Technical Committee on Data Engineering* 18(1)4-10 (1995).

26. Saastamoinen, H. T., On the Handling of Exceptions in Information Systems, Ph.D. Thesis, University of Jyväskylä (1995).

Controlled Flexibility in Workflow Management*

Justus Klingemann

German National Research Center for Information Technology (GMD)
Integrated Publication and Information Systems Institute (GMD-IPSI)
Dolivostraße 15, D-64293 Darmstadt, Germany
klingem@darmstadt.gmd.de

Abstract. Traditional workflow models are centered around the structure of a workflow. Other requirements and goals like time and cost can be represented only indirectly. As a result, when the workflow is executed, the WfMS can only enforce the structural constraints. This becomes a problem when the workflow deviates from its normal execution, e.g., due to errors or delays.

In this paper we propose an approach to extend the definition of workflows which allows to make the underlying goals explicit. In addition, we introduce flexible elements into the workflow specification. We make use of these flexible elements in a controlled way to achieve a balanced fulfillment of all goals – structural as well as non-structural – under various runtime conditions.

1 Introduction

Workflow management is a fast evolving technology which is increasingly being exploited by businesses in a variety of industries [1,2,3,4]. Its primary mission is to handle business processes. A *workflow* is the automation of a business process. Such a business process has certain goals. These are often multidimensional: Certain tasks have to be performed, a certain quality has to be achieved, the business process or at least certain activities have to be performed in a certain timeframe and the process shall not exceed a certain cost. To allow the system to support the goal fulfillment, these goals have to be made explicit. In addition, a sufficient degree of freedom is necessary to actively control the workflow execution towards an optimized goal fulfillment. To create this freedom, we integrate execution alternatives in form of flexible elements into the workflow structure. This approach to flexibility is especially useful for production workflows as well as cross-organizational workflows in which manual ad hoc interventions are undesirable as they raise additional organizational problems like who is responsible for a new activity or how they affect the autonomy of the involved organizations. System support for the adaptation at runtime is also beneficial when the effects of possible execution alternatives on the goals are too complex to allow a user to perform these adaptations interactively.

* This work has been partially supported by the ESPRIT project CROSSFLOW (www.crossflow.org). However, it represents the view of the author.

B. Wangler, L. Bergman (Eds.): CAiSE 2000, LNCS 1789, pp. 126–141, 2000.
© Springer-Verlag Berlin Heidelberg 2000

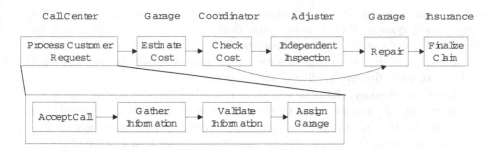

Fig. 1. A cross-organizational workflow to process a motor damage claim

To motivate our approach we will use an example from the insurance domain. This application has been analyzed in the CROSSFLOW project [5]. Figure 1 shows a simplified workflow used to process a motor damage claim. The workflow is started with the processing of the customer request which is performed by a call center. Like each activity in this cross-organizational workflow, this is a subworkflow on its own. The processing of the customer request for example consists of four activities. In the first activity the call is accepted. Then, the call center gathers information about the accident, the customer and other involved persons. In the next activity, this information is validated. For example, it is checked, whether the customer is properly insured to use this service. In the final activity, the customer is advised about garages which are located nearby. After the processing of the customer request, the garage which has been chosen by the customer becomes active. It has to assess the estimated repair costs. This cost estimate is then checked by an organization which is specialized in the coordination of the processing of motor damage claims. If the estimated costs are above a certain threshold, an independent adjuster is appointed to inspect the damaged car and to re-assess the repair costs. When the independent inspection is finished or it needs not be performed, the garage repairs the car. As a last step in the workflow, the insurance performs some administrative tasks and thus finalizes the claim.

The business goals are not exclusively captured by the sequence of steps represented in Figure 1. In the case of an insurance company an important business goal is to keep the customer satisfied. The processing of an insurance claim is one of the rare occasions where customers are able to judge the performance of their insurance. Therefore, the insurance has to demonstrate that it handles the claim of the customer efficiently. With respect to the workflow execution, this translates to the requirement that the claim processing has to be finished within five days.

Statically, this requirement can be taken into account by estimating the execution times of all activities and making sure that on all execution paths the sum of the estimated execution times is less than five days. However, in this approach the deadline is only represented implicitly. As a result, when unexpected events occur only the structural constraints can be enforced, i.e., a workflow management system (WfMS) makes sure that all activities are executed in the prescribed order even though the deadline may be violated. Therefore, we call a workflow *multidimensional* if it allows to represent explicitly non-structural goals along other dimensions like time or costs.

The motor damage claim process is a typical example. On the one hand, the processing of the claim should be cost efficient. On the other hand, it is important for the insurance to execute the process within five days to keep the customer satisfied. A cost efficient execution implies that in case of a more expensive damage an adjuster is brought into play who inspects the car. Under normal conditions enough time is available for this activity within the desired timeframe of five days. However, if a delay occurs, e.g., due to communication errors among the call center, the insurance and the coordinator, this might not be the case. As a consequence, the runtime priorities can change. To maintain the customer's satisfaction, the insurance might be willing to drop activities like the inspection of the car by an adjuster and instead make sure that the car is repaired in time.

This decision also depends on the parameters. For example, it might be desirable to adapt the workflow if the estimated repair cost is only a little bit in excess of the threshold and on the other hand the risk of failing to repair the car in time is high if the repair is delayed until the inspection is finished. However, if the repair cost is very high and the delay only moderate so that there is a good chance to finish the repair in time, it might be preferable to execute the workflow as planned.

To increase the flexibility and allow an adaptation of the workflow to the conditions at runtime the specification of different execution options is necessary. This includes different aspects. First, alternative execution structures have to be specified. Our approach to do this is described in Section 2. As a second part, the desired quality of service (QoS) goals have to be provided. They allow to compare the utility of the different execution options. The specification of QoS goals and their relationship to QoS parameters is described in Section 3. In Section 4 we give a complete example how our approach is applied to enhance a workflow specification and adapt its execution. Afterwards, we give an overview of the related work and finally some conclusions.

2   Making the Workflow Structure Flexible

To enable different execution options we have to relax the workflow structure. We consider the workflow structure as consisting of two parts. The first part is mandatory. It consists of activities which have to be executed (if the respective enabling conditions evaluate to true) for the workflow to be successful, as well as ordering relationships which have to be obeyed. A second part consists of execution alternatives which can be selected depending on requirements at runtime.

To specify the structure of a workflow, a set of constructors like sequence, or-split, or-join, and-split and and-join has emerged which forms the basis of most workflow models [6]. We use these constructors to specify the overall structure of the workflow and its mandatory parts. To specify execution alternatives, we use so called *flexible elements*. A flexible element (FE) is a construct that represents different execution alternatives, i.e., it is a set of different subworkflows. We identify three kinds of flexible elements namely alternative activities, non-vital activities, and optional execution orders.

Alternative Activities This flexible element allows to represent different tra-de-offs with respect to the goals of the workflow, e.g., a high-quality option which requires a considerable execution time versus a quicker option which produces results with a lower quality. This provides a way to switch among these alternatives depending on the priorities at runtime. It is represented by a list of activities in square brackets. At runtime exactly one of them will be chosen for execution.

Non-vital Activity This flexible element specifies that an activity can either be executed or omitted, i.e., it is non-vital. Activities are non-vital if they are beneficial under certain conditions but should better be omitted in other situations. Non-vital activities are represented by adding the tag *nv* to the activity. Non-vital activities can be considered as a special case of alternative activities, if they are modelled as the alternative between the activity itself and an empty activity $\emptyset$.

Optional Execution Order This flexible element can be used if activities should be re-ordered to expedite the execution of urgent activities. It allows to specify a sequence of activities in a specific order which can be considered as a preferred or default order. However, this order is not mandatory and the activities can alternatively be executed without any restriction on their order, i.e., in parallel. This flexible element is specified by a list of activities in braces.

We call a traditional activity, i.e., a unit of work, an *elementary activity*. A *flexible workflow (FWF)* is a workflow in which each activity is either an elementary activity or a flexible element. If no ambiguity occurs, we will use the terms activity and elementary activity interchangeably.

Note, that execution alternatives in flexible elements are different from or-split/join structures. The decision which successor of an or-split is executed is made based on the evaluation of a predicate and cannot be influenced. In contrast to this, each choice among the alternatives of a flexible element is considered as correct and the decision can be made based on global goals of the workflow.

To relate a flexible workflow to the possible traditional workflows that can be derived from it, we define some additional terms. For a flexible element *fe* a *resolution* is a function that maps *fe* to one specific alternative. For a flexible workflow a resolution r maps each flexible element to a specific alternative, i.e., each flexible element *fe* is replaced by $r(fe)$. Let *fwf* be a FWF and r a resolution function for *fwf* then we call $rfwf = r(fwf)$ a *resolved flexible workflow (RFWF)* of *fwf*. With $R(fwf)$ we denote the set of all RFWF of *fwf*.

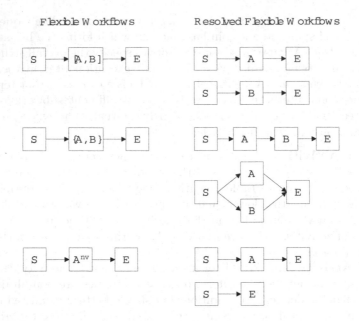

Fig. 2. Examples for flexible workflows and their resolved flexible workflows

Figure 2 shows examples of different flexible workflows and their corresponding RFWFs. In this figure S, E, A, B are elementary activities. The first FWF specifies that all RFWF have to start with S and end with E and in between either A or B is executed. The second example shows an optional execution order, i.e., either A is executed before B or both activities can be executed in parallel. The last example contains the non-vital activity A.

3   Enhancing a Flexible Workflow with QoS Goals

In this section we will explain our approach to model QoS goals and how they are used to enhance a workflow specification. The basic building block of a QoS goal is a QoS parameter. A dimension on which QoS parameters can be defined is called *QoS dimension*. Examples are time, cost or application specific dimensions like the accuracy of a specific result. A *QoS parameter* is a specific quantity defined on a QoS dimension. Examples for QoS parameters on the dimension time are the duration of an activity or the duration of the overall workflow. As QoS parameters we consider any property that can be assigned to or derived from a partial or complete workflow instance. A *QoS goal* is an optimization criterion that is assigned to a QoS parameter. To allow the formulation of QoS goals we will in the following give a classification of QoS parameters.

3.1 Classification of QoS Parameters

Depending on how they are obtained we distinguish three kinds of QoS parameters.

Elementary QoS Parameters As elementary QoS parameters we define parameters which can be directly observed, i.e., monitored, from a running workflow instance. Examples are the output parameters of activities, the current time, and the execution time or cost of terminated activities. Elementary QoS parameters form the basis for the measurement of QoS goals.

Derived QoS Parameters Derived QoS parameters are functions of other QoS parameters, i.e., if qos_0 is a derived QoS parameter, then there exists a user-defined function f and a set of QoS parameters $qos_1, \ldots, qos_n$ with $qos_0 = f(qos_1, \ldots, qos_n)$. An example for a derived QoS parameter in the insurance scenario is the expected cost saving by appointing an assessor depending on the repair cost estimated by the garage. A special case of derived QoS parameters are 0-ary functions, i.e., constants. Constants can be considered as external parameters. An example are the costs of the assessor which are needed to determine the total cost savings by appointing an assessor.

Predicted QoS Parameters Predicted QoS parameters are quantities which make assertions about the future behavior of a workflow. Predicted QoS parameters require a prediction function. Each prediction is related to a resolved flexible workflow, i.e., a workflow for which decisions for each flexible element have been made.

The dependency relationship among QoS parameters can be described as a graph. We require that this graph does not contain any cycles. For example, there must not be the dependency $qos_1 = f_1(qos_2)$ and at the same time $qos_2 = f_2(qos_1)$. Each of the nodes in this graph can be assigned a QoS goal. Usually, a QoS goal will be assigned to the root of a subgraph that forms a tree.

3.2 Specification of QoS Parameters

The necessary specifications depend on the respective class of QoS parameters. For elementary QoS parameters we have to make sure that the relevant parameters are monitored. This is specified by means of a *monitoring condition* that defines the parameter that has to be monitored as well as the activity to which it belongs.

For the specification of derived QoS parameters we have to provide the necessary function as well as the list of parameters.

To allow for predictions, we have to specify a prediction function. The structure, complexity, and specification effort for a prediction function heavily depends on the QoS parameter to be predicted, the complexity of the used prediction model and the available information about the behavior of the workflow. If we want to predict the execution time of a workflow or a part of it, we can model the statistical behavior of the workflow, i.e., the activities and the control flow conditions. This means that we have to provide probabilities for the activation of control flow edges originating from an OR-split and information about the duration of activities. Depending on the desired accuracy, we can model the duration of activities just by means of the expected duration or provide a complete distribution function.

Instead of explicitly specifying the prediction function, we can alternatively derive a prediction function from the observed behavior of earlier workflow executions. In this case, we assume that the future behavior will be similar to the observed behavior in the past. We call the use of existing workflow logs to derive a prediction function *offline monitoring*. An approach for offline monitoring based on continuous-time Markov chains has been described in [7].

3.3   Specification of QoS Goals

We define a QoS goal as a triple $g = (q, f, w)$ where

1. q is a QoS parameter as defined in the previous section,
2. f is a fulfillment function,
3. w is a weight.

The fulfillment of a goal is specified by means of a function f : QoS parameter $\to [0, 1]$. The fulfillment describes whether the goal is satisfied or not. For a continuous function it describes the expected degree of fulfillment.

In the following we focus on two classes of QoS goals called *extremity goals* and *range constraints*. A range constraint aims at keeping a QoS parameter within a boundary. For notational simplicity we will interpret a boolean condition containing a QoS parameter as a function of this QoS parameter. In the deterministic case the boolean value *true* is mapped to 1 whereas the boolean value *false* is mapped to 0. Thus, an example of a fulfillment function for the QoS parameter *total execution time* is

$$\text{total execution time} < \text{deadline.}$$

This boolean condition is a shorthand for the function

$$f(\text{total execution time}) = \begin{cases} 1 & \text{if total execution time} < \text{deadline} \\ 0 & \text{else.} \end{cases}$$

In the stochastic case the boolean condition represents the expected value of this function. This is equivalent to the probability that the boolean condition is evaluated to *true*.

An extremity goal aims at maximizing or minimizing the QoS parameter. Usually the fulfillment function will be a linear mapping from the range of values which are expected in real-world applications into the interval $[0, 1]$. For example consider the minimization of the *total execution cost*. If we expect that the costs are always positive and can never exceed 100, then a fulfillment function f could be

$$f(\text{total execution cost}) = 1 - \frac{\text{total execution cost}}{100}.$$

Note, that values closer to 1 always indicate a higher fulfillment of the goal.

The weight of a goal is used to indicate the relative importance of the goals. It can be an arbitrary positive number.

3.4 Specification and Optimization of Multidimensional Workflows

We now have the ingredients to define a multidimensional workflow as a flexible workflow which is enhanced with a set of QoS goals. We formally define a *multidimensional workflow (MDWF)* as an ordered pair (fwf, g) where *fwf* is a flexible workflow and $g = \{g_1, \ldots, g_n\}$ is a set of QoS goals. We extend definitions for FWFs in a straightforward way to MDWF by applying them to the FWF part of a MDWF.

The relevant *runtime conditions* of a workflow execution are represented in our model by the values of monitored elementary QoS parameters and the values of predicted QoS parameters. For each runtime condition and each choice for the different structural alternatives, i.e., each resolved MDWF *rwf* we can calculate the fulfillment of each goal. Using this information we can define the *total utility* as the weighted sum of the goal fulfillment:

$$\text{total utility}(rwf) := \sum_{g_i \in g} \text{weight}(g_i) * \text{fulfillment}(g_i)$$

The total utility is calculated for a resolved MDWF, i.e., a workflow for which decisions for each flexible element have been made. To execute a workflow with the maximal total utility possible for specific runtime conditions, we therefore have to make the appropriate choice among the alternatives of the flexible elements. Thus, to optimize the execution of a MDWF *mdwf* we have to find a resolved MDWF *rwf* with

$$\forall rwf_i \in R(mdwf) : \text{total utility}(rwf_i) \leq \text{total utility}(rwf).$$

A straight forward optimization algorithm is therefore to enumerate all possible resolved FWFs which result from a flexible workflow specification, calculate their total utilities and choose the flexibility alternatives according to the resolved flexible workflow with the highest utility. To adapt to possible changes during the workflow execution, this algorithm is executed each time the execution thread encounters a flexible element. More efficient optimization strategies have to depend on the QoS parameters subject to goals and the structure of the workflows. One example for such an optimization algorithm which is used to optimize a temporal and a utility goal is described in [8].

4 An Example for the Specification and Enforcement of Multidimensional Workflows

In the following, we consider the simplified workflow for the motor damage claim scenario described in Section 1. Using the primitives presented in Section 2, the flexible workflow structure can be specified as shown in Figure 3.

Fig. 3. The motor damage claim process as a flexible workflow

This workflow has exactly one flexible element, namely the non-vital activity Independent Inspection. Therefore, we have to execute the decision algorithm exactly once, namely immediately after the activity Check Cost has terminated. In the remainder of this section we will describe how the goals of this workflow can be modelled and how these goals influence the execution of the workflow.

4.1 Use of Deterministic Predictions

Informally, the first goal of the workflow is to minimize the cost. For the motor damage claim, this translates to the requirement to appoint an assessor to perform an independent inspection if this activity can save cost. The overall cost savings of the independent inspection again depend on the expected reduction of the repair cost as a result of the inspection, and the cost of the inspection itself. The calculation of the total savings is therefore performed as follows. As elementary QoS parameter we need the estimated repair cost provided by the garage as a result of the activity Check Cost. Hence, we have to define an appropriate monitoring condition:

$$\text{Monitor}(\text{Check Cost}, \text{estimated repair cost})$$

To derive the reduction of the repair cost due to the inspection, we specify an appropriate function. In our example we use

$$\text{repair savings}(\text{estimated repair cost}) := \frac{\text{estimated repair cost}}{10}.$$

To calculate the total savings we again specify a derivation function and in addition to this provide an external parameter which describes the cost of the assessment itself:

$$\text{cost assessment} := 50$$

total savings(estimated repair cost) :=

$$
\begin{cases}
\text{repair savings(estimated repair cost)} & \text{if Independent Inspection executed} \\
-\text{cost assessment} & \\
0 & \text{else}
\end{cases}
$$

Since we want to specify a goal on the parameter total savings, we have to define an appropriate fulfillment function. Assume that all repair costs are in [0, 10000]. Then we can define

$$
\text{fulfillment}_1(\text{total savings}) := \frac{\text{total savings} + \text{cost assessment}}{1000}.
$$

Note, that total savings could be negative, if the cost of the assessment exceeds the savings in repair cost. To map the fulfillment into the interval [0, 1], we therefore add the cost assessment. We further would like to give this goal a weight of 10. This allows us to define the first goal as

$$
\text{goal}_1 := (\text{total savings}, \text{fulfillment}_1, 10).
$$

Our second goal is to execute the workflow within five days. To check this range constraint we need information about the execution time that has already been elapsed since the start of the workflow. To obtain this information we specify the following monitoring condition:

$$
\text{Monitor}(\text{Check Cost}, \text{time until end of})
$$

To get information about the remaining time until the end of the workflow, we need a prediction function. The signature of such a function for the prediction of the length of the time interval between the end of the activity Check Cost and the end of the workflow would look as follows:

$$
\text{remaining time} := \text{Predict}(\text{resolved workflow}, \text{end}, \text{Check Cost}, \text{end}, \text{workflow})
$$

Assume that we have provided a prediction function which uses a deterministic model for the activity duration. For this example we further specify the execution time of activities used by the prediction function as duration(Independent Inspection) = 1 day, duration(Repair) = 2 days, and duration(Finalize Claim) = 0.2 days. As a result, the prediction function would return a duration of 1 + 2 + 0.2 days = 3.2 days for the execution option including the inspection activity and 2 + 0.2 days = 2.2 days for the execution option without the inspection activity.

The monitored information about the elapsed execution time together with the predicted information about the remaining execution time allows us to specify the derived QoS parameter total execution time as the sum of remaining time and the time until end of the activity Check Cost. We can now specify the fulfillment function as

$$
\text{fulfillment}_2(\text{total execution time}) := \text{total execution time} < 5 \text{ days}
$$

and the second goal (using a weight of 2) as

$$goal_2 := (\text{total execution time}, \text{fulfillment}_2, 2).$$

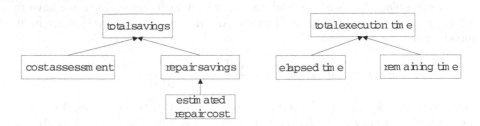

Fig. 4. The relationship of QoS parameters

Figure 4 shows the two trees that result from the dependency relationship of the QoS parameters.

Now we will consider the different decisions depending on the parameters. First, consider the total savings. For a workflow without an inspection, the fulfillment of this QoS parameter always has the value of 0.05. For a workflow which performs an independent inspection, the value of this QoS parameter linearly increases with the repair cost. For a repair cost below 500, its fulfillment value is below 0.05. In this case, the inspection will always be omitted as its contribution to the total utility is inferior to the option to omit it. For repair costs above 500, we have to make a trade-off with the second goal.

Considering the second goal, we see that the goal is always fulfilled, if the elapsed execution time at the end of the activity Check Cost is less than 1.8 days. In this case, both execution options make sure that the workflow is finished in time. On the other hand, if the elapsed time is more than 2.8 days, none of the execution options will allow the workflow to be finished in time. As a result, for these two cases, the fulfillment of the second goal is independent from the chosen structural alternative. The interesting case occurs if the elapsed time is between 1.8 and 2.8 days. In this case, the execution of the inspection results in missing the deadline whereas omitting the inspection allows to keep the deadline and thus, increases the total utility by 2. Therefore, the decision depends on the estimated repair cost. From the calculation of $goal_1$ we see that the increase of the contribution to the total utility resulting from the execution of the inspection is equal to 2 for an estimated repair cost of 2500. Hence, if the elapsed time is between 1.8 and 2.8 we will execute the inspection if the estimated repair cost is above 2500. If it is below, we will skip the inspection. In case the estimated repair cost is exactly 2500, both options have the same utility and a random choice can be made.

4.2 Use of Stochastic Predictions

Let us now consider a slightly modified example. The modification consists of the statistical model for the prediction function. In the following, we will examine the case where the prediction function provides us with a probability distribution for the remaining execution time. Therefore, if the elapsed time when the activity Check Cost is terminated is x, the prediction function provides us with the conditional probabilities

$$p_1 = P(\text{remaining time} < 5 - x \mid \text{Independent Inspection executed}),$$
$$p_2 = P(\text{remaining time} < 5 - x \mid \text{Independent Inspection skipped}).$$

These probabilities constitute the fulfillment values of the second goal for the different execution options depending on the time x at the point of decision. As a result, the decision procedure has to be generalized. Due to the use of probabilities, the expected increase in the utility of the second goal by means of skipping the inspection is $(p_2 - p_1) * 2$, where $(p_2 - p_1)$ is the increase in fulfillment and 2 the weight-factor. Note, that the technique described in Section 4.1 can be considered as a special case. If we have the same fixed execution times for activities as in Section 4.1, we would have $p_2 = p_1 = 0$ for $x > 2.8$ and $p_2 = p_1 = 1$ for $x < 1.8$ and thus, a utility of 0. For $1.8 \leq x \leq 2.8$ we have $p_2 = 1$ and $p_1 = 0$ and thus, a utility of 2. However, this generalization allows us to get more precise results in case of non-deterministic activity durations.

To make a decision, we have to compare the gain in utility of the second goal with a possible reduction in utility of the first goal if we skip the inspection. As discussed in Section 4.1, the fulfillment value of the first goal is 0.05 if the inspection is skipped and $\frac{\text{estimated repair cost}}{10000}$ if the inspection is performed. Therefore, the decrease in utility resulting from skipping the inspection is $\left(\frac{\text{estimated repair cost}}{10000} - 0.05 \right) * 10$. If we combine these two results, we see that it is beneficial to skip the inspection if

$$(p_2 - p_1) * 2 > \left(\frac{\text{estimated repair cost}}{10000} - 0.05 \right) * 10. \tag{1}$$

To make the example more concrete let us assume that the durations of the activities a_i follow a normal distribution $N(\mu_i, \sigma_i^2)$ with mean μ_i and variance σ_i^2. We still use the same expected values for the duration as in Section 4.1 but we a add a positive variance. For this example we specify the execution times as duration(Independent Inspection) $= N(1, 0.25)$, duration(Repair) $= N(2, 0.25)$, and duration(Finalize Claim) $= N(0.2, 0.01)$, e.g., the duration of the Independent Inspection has as normal distribution with mean 1 and variance 0.25 and thus, a standard deviation of 0.5.

Since the remaining workflow is a sequence, we know that the duration of the remaining workflow is the sum of the individual durations of the activities. Therefore, we can make use of the summation property of normal distributions (see for example [9]):

Theorem 1. *Let $X_1, X_2, \ldots, X_n$ be n independent random variables having normal $N(\mu_1, \sigma_1^2)$, $N(\mu_2, \sigma_2^2), \ldots, N(\mu_n, \sigma_n^2)$ distributions, respectively. Then $Y = X_1 + X_2 + \cdots + X_n$ is normally distributed with mean $\mu_1 + \mu_2 + \cdots + \mu_n$ and variance $\sigma_1^2 + \sigma_2^2 + \cdots + \sigma_n^2$.*

Therefore, we know that the remaining execution time of the workflow after the activity Check Cost has terminated is distributed $N(3.2, 0.51)$ if the inspection is performed and distributed $N(2.2, 0.26)$ if the inspection is omitted.

In the following, we will determine the advantageous execution structure for the situation that exactly two days have elapsed when we have to make the decision whether to execute the activity Independent Inspection or not. By using the cumulative distribution function for normally distributed random variables we can calculate that

$$p_1 = P(\text{remaining time} < 5 - 2 \mid \text{Independent Inspection executed}) = 0.390,$$

$$p_2 = P(\text{remaining time} < 5 - 2 \mid \text{Independent Inspection skipped}) = 0.942.$$

This means that we will keep the deadline with a probability of 39.0% if we perform the inspection and with a probability of 94.2% if we skip the inspection. Therefore, the expected increase in the utility of the second goal by means of skipping the inspection is $(0.942 - 0.390) * 2 = 1.104$. From (1) we can calculate that in this case it is beneficial to skip the activity Independent Inspection exactly if the estimated repair costs are below 1604.

5   Related Work

The idea to incorporate additional constraints into workflow specifications has especially drawn attention with respect to temporal goals. However, a common feature of all these approaches is that they mainly check whether a temporal constraint is fulfilled or not but do not actively apply this knowledge to adapt the workflow. In addition to this, all deadlines are considered as hard, i.e., there is no possibility violate them in certain situations.

Closest to our approach is the work of Panagos and Rabinovich [10,11,12]. They impose a deadline on a workflow execution and check at runtime, whether the deadline will be kept or not. They transform the overall deadline into individual deadlines for each activity and propose different criteria to decide when a workflow is considered as late. Depending on the delay of a workflow and the cost to abort the workflow at different stages, the workflow instance is either allowed to continue or aborted. The approach is similar to our work in the sense that they check the expected goal fulfillment at runtime and react on this. However, the only reaction policy in case of a late workflow is to abort the execution, whereas we aim at a graceful service degradation by adapting the workflow.

Marjanovic and Orlowska [13,14] propose an algorithm which is a generalization of a shortest path algorithm and the critical path method to calculate the maximal and minimal duration of a workflow. This algorithm is applied for verification purposes to find out whether deadlines are kept for all possible workflow instances, which can occur for different decisions in or-splits. They further extend this approach to check whether different temporal constraints are inconsistent.

Other approaches for calculating temporal properties and specifying temporal constraints of workflows can be found in [15,16]. In [15] a strategy is proposed to ensure at runtime that a specific kind of temporal constraint, namely upper and lower bounds on the temporal distance of two activities, is fulfilled. In case of an upper bound, the first activity involved in the constraint is delayed and in case of a lower bound, the second activity is delayed. However, this approach does not help in situations where it is necessary to accelerate the execution instead of delaying it.

Flexible workflows are a very active research area and since the seminal work of Ellis et al. [17] numerous approaches have been developed. See for example [18,19] for an overview. However, the goal of these approaches is to allow manual changes to the workflow structure. These can be either ad hoc changes to react to problems at runtime or evolutionary changes which are usually the result of a business process reengineering effort. Problems considered in this research area are for example the transition of running workflow instances to the new structure [17] and techniques to ensure the consistency of the resulting workflow, especially with respect to dataflow dependencies [20]. The only other approach known to the author that automatically derives the necessary changes from the runtime conditions is the work of Müller and Rahm [21]. They describe an approach using logic-based rules. These rules decide when an adaptation to running workflow instances is necessary and how the workflow structure has to be adapted. Hence, the resulting specification can be viewed as a rule-based workflow specification in which the possible execution paths and the conditions under which they are taken are represented as rules. In contrast to this, in our approach the workflow is adapted to a set of goals.

An approach to optimize and speed up the execution of workflows is described in [22]. The idea of this approach is to separate the preconditions for the start of an activity into data flow and control flow parts. Whereas an activity is *enabled* to start when the corresponding control flow condition is fulfilled, it is *ready* to start when the necessary input data is available. This makes it possible to start activities that have no side effects immediately after all input data is available. This can be the case before the control flow condition can be evaluated. If the control flow condition eventually turns out to be false, the activity is simply aborted. Although this is an interesting approach to speed up a workflow execution, it is limited to special cases and in many situations more severe modifications are necessary to ensure that a deadline is kept.

Other optimization techniques are more oriented towards the appropriate assignment of resources and tuning the underlying system components to the application requirements. An example can be found in [23].

6 Conclusion

In this paper we have developed an approach towards multidimensional workflows. This approach makes the workflow structure flexible in a controlled way. It further allows to model the underlying goals of a workflow and provides a way to systematically make use of the flexibility to adapt the workflow execution for an optimized goal fulfillment. As an initial step towards optimized decision making we have presented an optimization algorithm which compares all possible execution alternatives. We are currently working on more efficient optimization strategies. These depend on the QoS parameters subject to goals and the structure of the workflows. One example for such an optimization algorithm which is used to optimize a temporal and a utility goal is described in [8]. In addition, we have started to implement our approach for controlled flexibility within the CROSSFLOW demonstrator. The demonstrator system uses MQSeries Workflow from IBM [24] (the former FlowMark) as its underlying Workflow Management System. An overview about the components necessary to realize multidimensional workflows as well as how flexible elements are mapped to the process model offered by MQSeries Workflow can be found in [8].

Acknowledgements

The author would like to thank Karl Aberer, Thomas Tesch, Ralph Busse, Yigal Hoffner and Paul Grefen for their helpful comments.

References

1. D. Georgakopoulos, M. Hornick, and A. Sheth. An overview of workflow management: From process modeling to workflow automation infrastructure. *Distributed and Parallel Databases*, 3(2), April 1995.
2. A. Sheth, D. Georgakopoulos, S. Joosten, M. Rusinkiewicz, W. Scacchi, J. Wileden, and A. Wolf. Report from the NSF workshop on workflow and process automation in information systems. *ACM SIGMOD Record*, 25(4):55–67, 1996.
3. A. Cichocki, S. Helal, M. Rusinkiewicz, and D. Woelk. *Workflow and Process Automation – Concepts and Technology*. Kluwer Academic Publishers, 1998.
4. F. Leymann and D. Roller. *Production Workflow – Concepts and Techniques*. Prentice-Hall, 2000.
5. S. Browne and M. Kellet. CrossFlow Deliverable D1a: Insurance (Motor Damage Claims) Scenario. Report, Esprit Project No. 28635, January 1999.
6. WfMC. Workflow standard – Interface 1: Process definition interchange process model. Technical Report WFMC-TC-1016-P, Workflow Management Coalition, November 1998. Version 7.04.
7. J. Klingemann, J. Wäsch, and K. Aberer. Deriving service models in cross-organizational workflows. In *Proc. of RIDE – Information Technology for Virtual Enterprises*, pages 100–107, Sydney, Australia, March 1999.
8. J. Klingemann. CrossFlow Deliverable D8a: Flexible Change Control. Report, Esprit Project No. 28635, January 2000.

9. A. O. Allen. *Probability, Statistics and Queueing Theory.* Academic Press Inc., second edition, 1990.

10. E. Panagos and M. Rabinovich. Reducing escalation-related costs in WFMSs. In Dogac et al. [25].

11. E. Panagos and M. Rabinovich. Predictive workflow management. In *Proc. of the third Int. Workshop on Next Generation Information Technologies and Systems (NGITS)*, Neve Ilan, Israel, June 1997.

12. E. Panagos and M. Rabinovich. Escalations in workflow management systems. In *Proc. of the Workshop on Databases: Active and Real-Time (DART)*, Rockville, Maryland, November 1996.

13. O. Marjanovic and M. E. Orlowska. On modeling and verification of temporal constraints in production workflows. *Knowledge and Information Systems*, 1(2):157–192, May 1999.

14. O. Marjanovic and M. E. Orlowska. Time management in dynamic workflows. In *Proc. of the second Int. Symposium on Cooperative Databases and Applications (CODAS'99)*, Wollongong, Australia, March 1999.

15. J. Eder, E. Panagos, and M. Rabinovich. Time constraints in workflow systems. In *Proc. of the 11th Int. Conference on Advanced Information Systems Engineering*, pages 286–300, Heidelberg, Germany, June 1999.

16. H. Pozewaunig, J. Eder, and W. Liebhart. ePERT: Extending PERT for workflow management systems. In *Proc. of the first East-European Symposium on Advances in Database and Information Systems (ADBIS)*, pages 217–224, St. Petersburg, Russia, 1997.

17. C. Ellis, K. Keddara, and G. Rozenberg. Dynamic change within workflow systems. In *Proc. of the Conf. on Organizational Computing Systems*, pages 10–21, Milpitas, California, August 1995.

18. M. Klein, C. Dellarocas, and A. Bernstein, editors. *Proceedings of the CSCW-98 Workshop Towards Adaptive Workflow Systems*, Seattle, Washington, November 1998. http://ccs.mit.edu/klein/cscw98.

19. A. Sheth. From contemporary workflow process automation to adaptive and dynamic work activity coordination and collaboration. In *Proc. of the DEXA Workshop on Workflow Management in Scientific and Engineering Applications*, pages 24–27, Toulouse, France, September 1997.

20. M. Reichert and P. Dadam. ADEPT$_{flex}$ – supporting dynamic changes in workflows without loosing control. *Journal of Intelligent Information Systems*, 10(2):93–129, 1998.

21. R. Müller and E. Rahm. Rule-based dynamic modification of workflows in a medical domain. In *Proc. of the GI-Fachtagung Datenbanksysteme in Büro, Technik und Wissenschaft*, pages 429–448, Freiburg, Germany, March 1999.

22. R. Hull, F. Llirbat, J. Su, G. Dong, B. Kumar, and G. Zhou. Adaptive execution of workflow: Analysis and optimization. Working paper, Bell Labs, 1999.

23. D. Roller. Performance prediction and optimization in workflow-based applications. In *Proc. of the sixth Int. Workshop on High Performance Transaction Systems*, Asilomar, California, September 1995.

24. IBM. *MQSeries Workflow: Concepts and Architecture*, 1999. Version 3.2, GH12-6285.

25. A. Dogac, L. Kalinichenko, T. Özsu, and A. Sheth, editors. *Workflow Management Systems and Interoperability.* NATO-ASI Series. Springer Verlag, 1998.

A Formal Model
for Business Process Modeling and Design

Manolis Koubarakis[1] and Dimitris Plexousakis[2]

[1] Dept. of Electronic and Computer Engineering
Technical University of Crete
73100 Chania, Crete, Greece
manolis@ced.tuc.gr
[2] Dept. of Computer Science
University of Crete
71305 Heraklion, Crete, Greece
dp@csd.uch.gr

Abstract. We present a formal framework for representing enterprise knowledge. The concepts of our framework (objectives and goals, roles and actors, actions and processes, responsibilities and constraints) allow business analysts to capture enterprise knowledge in a way that is both intuitive and mathematically formal. We also outline the basic steps of a methodology that allows business analysts to produce detailed, formal specifications of business processes from high-level enterprise objectives. The use of a formal language permits us to verify that the specifications possess certain correctness properties, namely that the responsibilities assigned to roles are fulfilled and that the constraints are maintained.

1 Introduction

The problem of *representing, analysing* and *managing* knowledge about an organisation and its processes has always been very important. Recently, management and computer science researchers have debated the use of information technology for tackling this complex problem [10,22,9,11,33]. Ultimately this community is interested in improving the understanding of organisations and their processes, facilitating process design and analysis and supporting process management. The topic is also of great practical importance to industry as an aid to designing organisational structures, processes and IT infrastructure that achieve business goals in an efficient and flexible way. A specific area of interest is in deriving, checking and improving business process definitions used as input to wrokflow systems.

In this paper we present a formalism that can be used to represent knowledge about organisations and their business processes. Motivated by F³ [19] and EKD [12,2] we develop an *enterprise model* which consists of five inter-connected submodels (organisational submodel, objectives and goals submodel, process submodel, concepts submodel and constraints submodel) that can be used to describe *formally* different aspects of an organisation. However, unlike

B. Wangler, L. Bergman (Eds.): CAiSE 2000, LNCS 1789, pp. 142–156, 2000.
© Springer-Verlag Berlin Heidelberg 2000

these projects, our framework emphasises formality and advocates the use of situation calculus [20,27] and the concurrent logic programming language Con-Golog [5] for representing knowledge about organisations and their processes. In this respect, we continue the work of one of us [24,25] (but also [33,15]) who suggested to use these formal tools to model organisations. Early steps towards the development of our model were presented in [13].

Creating an enterprise model can be instructive in itself, revealing anomalies, inconsistencies, inefficiencies and opportunities for improvement. Once it exists it is a valuable means for sharing knowledge within the enterprise. It can also be used to formulate and evaluate changes. The knowledge sharing role also extends to the enterprise's IT infrastructure. It is in principle possible, for example, to extract process definitions to be input to a workflow management system. Furthermore, it would be possible for business process support software to query the enterprise model to find out who is fulfilling a given role in a given process. Formal enterprise models, such as ours, are ones in which concepts are defined rigorously and precisely, so that mathematics can be used to analyze extract knowledge from and reason about them. An advantage of formal models is that they are self-consistent and have certain properties. For instance, one can prove formally that responsibilities assigned to roles are fulfilled, and constraints are maintained as a result of process execution. A few words about our representational framework are in order here. We will represent enterprise knowledge using an extension of the formalism of *situation calculus* [20,27]. This formalism has been designed especially for knowledge representation and reasoning in dynamically evolving domains. Technically, our basic tool will be a *many-sorted first-order language* $\mathcal{L}$ which is defined in the following way. The logical symbols of $\mathcal{L}$ include parentheses, a countably infinite set of variables, the equality symbol = and the standard sentential connectives. The remaining machinery of $\mathcal{L}$ (sort, predicate and function symbols) will be defined in Sections 2, 3 and 4 where intuitive modeling concepts will need to be formalised.

The rest of this paper is structured as follows. Sections 2, 3 and 4 present our enterprise model. We then sketch a methodology that enables business analysts to go from high-level enterprise-objectives, to detailed formal specifications of business processes for realizing these objectives. Finally, section 6 discusses related work and presents our conclusions.

2   Organisational and Goal Modeling

In this section we initiate the presentation of the five submodels making up our enterprise modeling framework. Throughout the paper we will demonstrate the features of our proposal by considering an imaginary Computer Science department DEPT as our enterprise. We assume that this department has so far no postgraduate program, and it is now considering the development of processes for the admission and education of postgraduate students.

The first submodel is the organisational submodel with main concepts *actor* and *role*. An *actor* is a person or a software/hardware system in the context of the organisation we are modeling (e.g., an employee, a customer, a printer etc.).

Actors are distinguished into *human* and *automated* ones. Actors are capable of executing certain activities, but they might not be capable of executing others.

An *organisational role* involves a set of *responsibilities* and *actions* carried out by an actor or a group of actors within an organisation [23,6]Organisational roles can take many forms [23]: a unique functional group (e.g., Systems Department), a unique functional position (e.g., Managing Director), a rank or job title (e.g., Lecturer Grade A), a replicated functional group (e.g., Department), a replicated functional position (e.g., Director), a class of persons (e.g., Customer) or an abstraction (e.g., Progress Chasing).

Role instances are acted out by actors. Different actors can play different roles at different moments of time (e.g., today the Managing Director can be John Smith, tomorrow it can be Tony Bates). Many instances of the same role can be active at any moment in time.

The concepts introduced above can be defined formally by introducing appropriate constructs of $\mathcal{L}$ (e.g., unary predicates *Actor*, *HumanActor*, *AutomatedActor* and *Role*, and binary predicate *PlaysRole*) and writing axioms that capture their semantics.

The second component of our enterprise model is the objectives and goals submodel. The central concept in this submodel is an enterprise goal. An *enterprise goal* is a desired state of affairs [19,14,22,33,12]. Examples of enterprise goals are the following: "all customers enquiries are answered within one day", "profits are maximised" and so on. In our framework goals are associated with the following components of other submodels:

– *Roles and actors* (organisational submodel). Goals are assigned to roles as a matter of policy by the organisation. Organisational goals become responsibilities of roles and the actors playing these roles.
– *Processes* (process submodel). The *purpose* of a process is the achievement of one or more goals. For example, the process of managing project X might have the purpose of achieving the goal "project X is completed successfully".
– *Entities* (concepts submodel). Every goal refers to certain enterprise entities. For example, the goal "two C++ programmers should be hired by the Systems Department" refers to entities "Systems Department" and "C++ programmer".

Explicit capturing of enterprise goals is important because it allows us to study organisations and their processes from an *intentional* point of view [32]. For example, this enables us to represent not only "what" information (e.g., what sub-processes form a process) as in standard process representations, but also "why" information (e.g., why a specific activity is done). When goals are combined with other intentional concepts like actors and roles, we are also enabled to represent "who" information (e.g., "who is responsible for bringing about a state of affairs").

2.1   Enterprise Goals

Organisational goals can be *reduced* into alternative combinations of subgoals [4,31,14,19,12,2] by using *AND/OR goal graphs* originally introduced in the area of problem solving [7]. For example, the goal "our sales targets are achieved" can be AND-reduced to two goals "our sales targets for product A are achieved" and "our sales targets for product B are achieved".

We utilise the notion of goal reduction to define the concept of objective. An *organisational objective* is a goal that does not present itself through goal reduction. In other words, an objective is a top-level goal; it is an *end* desired in itself, not a *means* serving some higher level end [18].

Goals can *conflict* with each other [4,31,19,29]. In our framework goals $G_1, \ldots, G_n$ conflict if they cannot be *satisfied* simultaneously given our knowledge about the enterprise [29]. Goals can also *influence* positively or negatively other goals [21,31,19]. Such interactions between goals must be noted explicitly to facilitate goal-based reasoning (see Section 5).

2.2 Defining Goals Formally

Organizational goals can be described formally or informally. Organisational objectives and other high-level goals are usually difficult to formalise. These goals should be described only informally, and reduced step by step to more concrete and formal goals. Appropriate formal concepts and tools for assisting goal reduction (in the context of requirements modeling) are discussed in [4].

Because a goal is a desired state of affairs many concrete and formal goals can be formalised as *sentences* of $\mathcal{L}$ as demonstrated by the following example.

Example 1. The operational goal "enquiries are answered by a member of staff as soon as they are received" can be formalised by the following sentence of $\mathcal{L}$:

$$(\forall a)(\forall e)(\forall x)(\forall s)(\forall s')$$
$$(Staff(a) \wedge Enquiry(e) \wedge Action(x) \wedge Situation(s) \wedge Situation(s') \wedge$$
$$Received(e, a, s) \wedge s' = Do(x, s) \supset Answered(a, e, s'))$$

In the above sentence predicates have the obvious meaning and $s' = Do(x, s)$ means that s' is the situation (i.e., state) resulting from the execution of action x in situation s. The sentence can be read as "any situation in which a member of staff receives an enquiry gives rise to an action that causes the enquiry to be answered by that member of staff". Note also that the use of a formal language forces one to be very precise and dispense with informal concepts such as "as soon as".

3 The Process Submodel

A complete process model should allow representation of "*what* is going to be done, *who* is going to do it, *when* and *where* it will be done, *how* and *why* it will be done, and *who is dependent* on its being done" [3]. Our process model allows one to answer five of these seven questions. We do not include a spatial attribute for processes and we do not consider dependencies explicitly [32].

The main concepts of the process submodel are: *action, process, role, actor* and *goal*. The process submodel is connected to the organisational submodel through the concepts of *actor* and *role*. All actions carried out as part of a process are executed in the context of an organisational role by an actor playing that role. In this respect we have been inspired by the Role-Activity diagrams of [23]. The process submodel is also closely related with the objectives and goals submodel: processes are operationalisations of organisational goals [1].

3.1   Primitive and Complex Actions

Our process submodel is built around the concepts of situation calculus [20,27] and the concurrent logic programming language ConGolog [5]. The situation calculus is a first-order language for representing dynamically evolving domains. A *situation* is a state of affairs in the world we are modeling. Changes are brought to being in situations as results of actions performed by actors. Actions are distinguished into *primitive* and *complex*. Usually an action is considered to be primitive if no decomposition will reveal any further information which is of interest. To deal with these new concepts, we enrich our language $\mathcal{L}$ with a sort *Action* for actions and a sort *Situation* for situations. Actions are denoted by first-order terms e.g., $SendOfferLetter(act, app)$. For an action α and a situation s, the term $Do(\alpha, s)$ denotes the situation that results from the execution of action α in situation s. Relations whose truth values may differ from one situation to another are called *fluents*. They are denoted by predicate symbols having a situation term as their last argument. Primitive actions are introduced formally by expressions of the following form:

> **action** α
>   **precondition** ϕ_1
>   **effect** ϕ_2
> **endAction**

where α is an action, and ϕ_1, ϕ_2 are formulas of $\mathcal{L}$.

Example 2. The following expression defines the action of forwarding an application *app* by actor *act1* to actor *act2*:

> **action** $ForwardApp(act1, act2, app)$
>   **precondition** $Has(act1, app)$
>   **effect** $Has(act2, app) \land \neg Has(act1, app)$
> **endAction**

Our framework permits the recursive definition of *complex actions* (simply actions from now on) by adopting the syntax and semantics of ConGolog [5]:

- *Primitive actions* are actions.
- The special action of *doing nothing* is an action and is denoted by **noOp**.
- *Sequencing*. If α_1, α_2 are actions, then $\alpha_1; \alpha_2$ is the action that consists of α_1 followed by α_2.
- *Waiting for a condition*. If ϕ is a formula of $\mathcal{L}$ then $\phi?$ is the action of waiting until condition ϕ becomes true.

- *Non-deterministic choice of actions.* If α_1, α_2 are actions, then $\alpha_1 | \alpha_2$ is the action consisting of non-deterministically choosing between α_1 and α_2.
- *Non-deterministic choice of action parameters.* If α_1, α_2 are actions, then $\Pi_x(\alpha_1)$ denotes the non-deterministic choice of parameter x for α_1.
- *Non-deterministic iteration.* If α is an action, then α^* denotes performing α sequentially zero or more times.
- *Conditionals and iteration.* If α_1, α_2 are actions, then **if** ϕ **then** α_1 **else** α_2 defines a conditional and **while** ϕ **do** α_1 defines iteration.
- *Concurrency.* If α_1, α_2 are actions, then $\alpha_1 \parallel \alpha_2$ is the action of executing α_1 and α_2 concurrently.
- *Concurrency with different priorities.* If α_1, α_2 are actions, then $\alpha_1 \gg \alpha_2$ denotes that α_1 has higher priority than α_2, and α_2 may only execute when α_1 is done or blocked.
- *Non-deterministic concurrent iteration.* If α is an action, then $\alpha^{\parallel}$ denotes performing α concurrently zero or more times.
- *Interrupts.* If $\overline{x}$ is a list of variables, ϕ is a formula of $\mathcal{L}$ and α is an action then $\langle \overline{x} : \phi \to \alpha \rangle$ is an interrupt. If the control arrives at an interrupt and the condition ϕ is true for some binding of the variables then the interrupt triggers and α is executed for this binding of the variables. Interrupts are very useful for writing *reactive* processes.
- *Procedures.* Procedures are introduced with the construct **proc** $\beta(\overline{x})$ **endProc**. A *call* to this procedure is denoted by $\beta(\overline{x})$.

Examples of complex actions are given in Figures 1 and 2 (see Section 5).

3.2   Categories of Actions

We distinguish actions into *causal* and *knowledge-producing*. Causal actions change the state of affairs in the enterprise we are modeling (e.g., the action of forwarding an application form). Knowledge-producing actions do not change the state of the enterprise but rather the mental state of the enterprise actors (e.g., a perceptual or a communicative action) [28,16]. It is known that knowledge-producing actions can be defined in the situation calculus formalism [28,16].

Finally, actions can be *exogenous*. This concept corresponds to the notion of external event in other process frameworks. Exogenous actions are necessary in an enterprise modeling framework since they allow us to "scope" our modeling and consider certain parts of the enterprise (or its environment) as being outside of the area we are modeling. Exogenous actions can also be handled by the situation calculus formalism [5].

3.3   Business Processes

A *business process* can now be informally defined as a network of actions performed in the context of one or more organisational roles in pursuit of some goal. Formally, a business process is defined by an expression of the following form:

> **process** *id*
> > **purpose** *goals*
> > *RoleDefs*
> **endProcess**

where *id* is a process identifier, *goals* is a list of goals (separated by commas) and *RoleDefs* is a sequence of statements defining roles and their local ConGolog procedures. The purpose statement in a process definition introduces the purpose of a process i.e., the organisational goals *achieved* by the process. The concept of purpose captures *why* a process is done [3].

Processes are distributed among organisational roles and ConGolog procedures are used to capture the details of a process. Roles and their procedures are defined by expressions of the following form:

> **role** *id*
> > **responsibility** *resps*
> > *ProcedureDefs*
> **endRole**

where *id* is a role identifier, *resps* is a list of goals (separated by commas) and *ProcedureDefs* is a set of ConGolog procedures. The responsibility statement declares that role *id* is responsible for achieving the goals in list *resps*. Examples of role definitions are given in Figures 1 and 2 (see Section 5).

Our formal framework permits the detection of conflicts that may arise due to the presence of multiple roles or the association of multiple procedures with a single role. This and other cases of incomplete or incorrect process specifications can be detected using the machinery presented in section 5.3.

4 The Concepts and Constraints Submodels

The *concepts* submodel contains information about enterprise entities, their relationships and attributes. Information in this submodel is formally expressed by sentences of $\mathcal{L}$ using appropriate predicate and function symbols (e.g., for our DEPT enterprise a predicate $Has(act, app)$ might be used to denote that actor *act* has application *app*). Enterprise data are part of this submodel.

The *constraints* submodel is used to encode restrictions imposed on the enterprise. Constraints can be formally expressed by sentences of $\mathcal{L}$ using the machinery of the situation calculus and the symbols defined in the rest of the submodels. Constraints can be static (i.e., referring to a single situation) or dynamic (i.e., referring to more than one situation) [25]. An example of a static constraint is given in Example 3 (Section 5.3).

5 A Goal-Oriented Methodology
for Business Process Design

This section outlines a methodology which can be used by an enterprise that wishes to develop a *new* business process. The methodology starts with the objectives of the enterprise concerning this new development and produces a detailed formal specification of a business process which achieves these objectives. The formal specification is developed as a set of submodels (based on the concepts discussed in previous sections) that capture the new process from various viewpoints. The steps of the proposed methodology are the following:

- Identify the organisational objectives and goals. Initiate goal reduction.
- Identify roles and their responsibilities. Match goals with role responsibilities.
- For each role specify its primitive actions, the conditions to be noticed and its interaction with other roles.
- Develop ConGolog procedures local to each role for discharging each role's responsibilities.
- Verify formally that the ConGolog procedures local to each role are sufficient for discharging its responsibilities.

The steps of the methodology are presented above as if strictly ordered, but some of them will in practice need to run concurrently. Also, backtracking to a previous step will often be useful in practice. The final product of an application of the methodology is a complete enterprise model that can be used to *study* and *analyse* the proposed business process. The specification can also serve as a guide for the development of an information system implementing the process.

This section does not intend to present the methodology and its application in detail (for this the interested reader should go to [13]. We will only discuss some of the issues involved in Steps 1 and 2, and then concetrate our attention to Steps 4 and 5, where our approach significantly improves on related methodologies (e.g., EKD [2,12] or GEM [26]).

5.1   Goal Reduction and Responsibility Assignment

The first step of the proposed methodology is the elicitation of an *initial statement* of the enterprise objectives and goals concerning the new process. This will involve brainstorming sessions with the enterprise stakeholders, studying documents (e.g., mission statement) outlining the strategy of the enterprise to be modelled (and possibly other enterprises in the same industry sector), and so on [2]. During this activity the analyst using our methodology must try to uncover not only prescriptive goals, but also descriptive ones [1].

After we have a preliminary statement in natural language of the enterprise objectives and goals, then the process of constructing a corresponding AND/OR goal graph by asking "why" and "how" questions can begin [4]. This process involves reducing goals, identifying conflicts and detecting positive and negative interactions between goals. The process of goal reduction will lead to a better understanding of the organisational goals, and very often to a reformulation of their informal definition. This step of our methodology is identical with goal reduction steps in goal-oriented requirements modeling frameworks [31,21,4,30] and related goal-oriented enterprise modeling frameworks [19,12,2].

An important issue that needs to be addressed at this stage is the distinction between *achievable* and *unachievable* (or *ideal*) goals. Ideal goals need to be considered, but in the process of AND/OR-reduction they need to be substituted by weaker goals that are actually achievable [30].

After the AND/OR graph corresponding to informal goals is sufficiently developed and stable, the process of *goal formalisation* can start. For example, one of the goals in our postgraduate program example can be the follwoing goal G_1: "enquiries are answered by a member of staff as soon as they are received". This goal can be formalized as has already been shown in example 1.

In parallel with the process of goal reduction, the business analyst should engage in the identification of roles and their responsibilities (Step 2 of the methodology). Role identification is achieved by interacting with the enterprise stakeholders and by considering goals at the lowest level of the developed goal hierarchy. Given one of these goals and the the roles currently existing in the organization, the analyst should then decide whether one of these roles (or a new one) can be designated as responsible for achieving the goal. If this is possible then the goal becomes a role responsibility, otherwise it needs to be refined further. This might sound simple, but role identification and responsibility assignment is a rather difficult task and business analysts could benefit from the provision of guidelines for dealing with it. Such guidelines are discussed in [22].

In our example we assume that the following roles are introduced: Postgraduate Tutor (notation: *Tutor*), Postgraduate Secretary (notation: *Secretary*) and Member of Academic Staff (notation: *Staff*). For the purposes of our discussion it is not necessary to consider a role for students enquiring about or applying to the prostgraduate program. Students are considered to be outside of the process and interaction with them is captured through the concept of exogenous actions.

Let us also assume that the following responsibility assignments are made. The Postgraduate Secretary will be responsible for hadling all correspondence with applicants but also for forwarding applications to the Postgraduate Tutor, who will be responsible for doing an initial evaluation of applications and forwarding applications to appropriate members of academic staff. The latter will be responible for evaluating promptly all applications they receive. Once roles have been identified and responsibilites assigned, the goal hierarchy should be revisited. Now goal statements can be made more precise by taking into account the introduced roles, and formal definitions of goals can be rewritten. For example, goal G_1 can be rephrased as "enquiries are answered by the Postgraduate Secretary as soon as they are received". This is formalized as follows:

$$(\forall a)(\forall e)(\forall x)(\forall s)(\forall s')$$
$$(Actor(a) \wedge Enquiry(e) \wedge Action(x) \wedge Situation(s) \wedge Situation(s') \wedge$$
$$PlaysRole(a, Secretary) \wedge Received(e, a, s) \wedge s' = Do(x, s) \supset$$
$$Answered(a, e, s'))$$

5.2   Defining Roles Using ConGolog

The first step in specifying a role is to identify the *primitive actions* that are available to each role, the *conditions* to be monitored and the *interactions* with other roles. Then the detailed specification of the dynamics of each role is given using the syntax of Section 3. For each role, the business analyst has to specify a ConGolog procedure called *main*, which gives the details of the behaviour of the role. Of course, *main* can invoke other local procedures.

In the process we have modelled so far, we have found ConGolog very natural and easy to use. In most cases it was straightforward to write a piece of ConGolog code for each responsibility of a role, and then combine those pieces to form a complete specification of the dynamics of the role. We expect to come up with more precise guidelines for using the language as our experience with it increases.

For our example let us first consider the role *Tutor*. This role can perform the causal action *ForwardApp* (defined in Example 2) and the knowledge producing action *SendMsg(sender, recipient, msg)* which means that actor *sender* sends message *msg* to actor *recipient*. A precise specification of *SendMsg* and other useful communicative actions in situation calculus can be found in [17]. Role *Tutor* also needs to watch for condition *Has(actor, app)* where *actor* is the actor playing the role *Tutor* and *app* is an application. The complete specification of roles *Tutor*, *Secretary* and *Faculty* are shown in Figures 1 and 2 respectively.

The ConGolog code should be easy to understand but the follwoing comments are in order. First, notice that in the interest of brevity we have omitted unary predicates like *Actor, Application* etc. that are used to type variables. We have also omitted specifying explicitly the responibilities assigned to each role; only G_1 is specified as a responibility got role *Tutor*. Symbol *self* is a pseudo-variable denoting the actor playing the role inside which the variable appears. The reader should notice how natural it is to specify in ConGolog reactive processes using interrupts and concurrency. The specification of the role *Secretary* is perhaps more involved because a message queue (in the spirit of [17]) is used. The case where more than one members of academic staff want to supervise the same applicant is omitted. We also omit the specification of exogenous actions that capture the interaction between the role *Secretary* and the applicants (that

role *Tutor*
responsibility G_{132}

proc *main*
$\langle app: Has(self, app) \rightarrow$
   if $AvgMark(app) < 70$ **then**
      for *act*: *PlaysRole(act, Secretary)* **do**
         $SendMsg(self, act, \ulcorner INFORM(Unacceptable(app)) \urcorner)$
      endFor
   else for *act*: *PlaysRole(act, Lecturer)* **do**
      $ForwardApp(self, act, app)$
      endFor
   endIf $\rangle$
endProc
endRole

Fig. 1. Role Postgraduate Tutor

role *Secretary*
responsibility G_{12}, G_{131}, G_{134}

proc *main*
$\langle infoReq :\ Received(self, infoReq) \rightarrow ReplyTo(infoReq)\rangle$
$\gg$
$\langle app :\ Has(self, app) \rightarrow$
   for *act* : *PlaysRole(act, Tutor)* **do**
      Forward(self, act, app)
   endFor$\rangle \gg$
while True do
   SenseMsg;
   if $\neg Empty(MsgQ(self))$ **then**
      if $First(MsgQ(self)) = (lect, \ulcorner INFORM(WantsToSupervise(lect, app))\urcorner)$
      then *SendOfferLetter(self, app)*
      else if $First(MsgQ(self)) = (tut, \ulcorner INFORM(Unacceptable(app))\urcorner)$ **then**
         SendRejectionLetter(self, app)
      endIf
   endIf
endWhile
endProc
endRole

role *Faculty*
responsibility G_{133}

proc *Eval(self, app)*
if $GoodUniv(Univ(app)) \wedge AvgMark(app) > MinMark(self) \wedge NoOfStud(self) <$
$MaxNoOfStud(self)$ **then**
   for *act* : *PlaysRole(act, Secretary)* **do**
      SendMsg(self, act, $\ulcorner INFORM(WantsToSupervise(self, app))\urcorner$)
   endFor
endIf
endProc

proc *main*
$\langle app :\ Has(self, app) \rightarrow Eval(self, app)\rangle$
endProc
endRole

Fig. 2. Roles Post Graduate Secretary and Faculty

are part of the outside environment). Given the above specifications for roles *Secretary, Tutor* and *Faculty*, the specification of the complete business process is straightforward using the syntax of Section 3.

5.3   Formal Verification

In this step we *verify formally* that each role responsibility is fulfilled and each constraint is maintained by the ConGolog procedures defined for each role. To perform verification we utilize the techniques reported in [24,25], which are based on a systematic solution to the frame and ramification problems [27]. Specifically, we are interested in determining whether: (i) responsibilities of roles can be fulfilled, and (ii) constraints are preserved or violated as a result of process execution. In case where such a proof or disproof is not possible at process specification time, strengthenings to the specifications of actions that are relevant to the responsibilities/constraints are proposed, so that any process implementation meeting the strengthened specifications provably guarantees that the responsibilities/constraints will be satisfied in the state resulting from action execution. The method derives ramifications of constraints and action preconditions and effects, and uses them to strengthen the action specifications [24,25].

Example 3. Consider the specification of the action $SendOfferLetter$ shown below. The predicate $Accepted(app)$ denotes that application app has been accepted by DEPT. Similarly, $WantsToSupervise(lect, app)$ means that academic $lect$ would like to supervise the student of application app.

> **action** $SendOfferLetter(app)$
>   **precondition** $(\exists\ lect)\ WantsToSupervise(lect, app)$
>   **effect** $Accepted(app)$
> **endAction**

Assume that we wish to enforce the policy that no applicant can be both accepted and rejected. This constraint may be expressed by the following sentence of $\mathcal{L}$ (and belongs to the constraints submodel):

$$(\forall p)(Accepted(p) \supset \neg Rejected(p))$$

It is evident that the action specification given above does not exclude a situation in which both $Accepted(app)$ and $Rejected(app)$ are satisfied. We can easily see that if the constraint is to be preserved in the situation resulting from performing action $SendOfferLetter$ then $\neg Rejected(p)$ is a logical implication of the constraint, i.e., a ramification of the constraint and the action specification. Our ramification generator proposes that the term $\neg Rejected(p)$ be used to strengthen the action specification (by conjoining the term with the action precondition or effect). The strengthened specification is now guaranteed not to violate the constraint in any possible execution of the action $SendOfferLetter$.

Albeit short[1] and simple, the above example conveys the idea behind the derivation of ramifications for strengthening action specifications. More complex examples and details can be found in [24,25]. The same ideas can be used to verify formally that roles fulfill their assigned responsibilities.

The aforementioned work provides results for verifying properties of primitive actions and of processes including sequencing of actions, when the constraints

---

[1] We have intentionally omitted presenting all the steps in the generation process due to lack of space.

refer to at most two distinct states. The derivation of similar results for processes synthesized using any of the remaining ConGolog constructs - including concurrency and non-determinism - and for general dynamic constraints is a topic of current research. Our previous work can also accommodate knowledge-producing actions in a single-agent environment. The theoretical basis of ConGolog has been extended to include exogenous and knowledge-producing actions in a multi-agent environment [16]. The adaptation of these ideas in our analysis and verification techniques is an ongoing effort.

We argue that the ability to verify properties of processes is essential for business process design and re-engineering. The process specifier realizes the implications of actions as far as goal achievement is concerned and the implementor is saved the burden of having to find ways to meet postconditions and maintain invariants. Furthermore, optimized forms of conditions to be verified can be incorporated into process specifications and consistency is guaranteed by the soundness of the verification process [25].

6 Discussion

The first paper to propose situation calculus and ConGolog (more precisely its earlier version Golog) for business process modeling was [24]. Since then similar ideas have appeared in [25,33,15]. But so far, ConGolog has not been used in conjunction with a more general framework like ours that offers intentional concepts like actors, roles and goals. Situation calculus is also the formalism of choice for the TOVE enterprise modeling project [8]. However, TOVE concentrates mostly on enterprise ontologies rather than process design and verification.

The concepts of goals, actors and roles also appear prominently in the i^* framework [32,33] where the need for *intentional concepts* in enterprise modeling is emphasized. There is also clear connection of our work to goal-oriented methodologies for requirements engineering especially KAOS [4]. This connection has been explained in detail in previous sections of this paper so we will not elaborate on it here.

Our work is also related to (and has been inspired by) the enterprise modeling frameworks of F^3 [19] and its successor EKD [2]. Lee's Goal-based Process Analysis (GPA) is also related to our research [14]. GPA is a goal-oriented method and can be used to analyse existing processes in order to identify missing goals, ensure implementation of all goals, identify non-functional parts of a process, and explore alternatives to a given process. Finally, our work has many common ideas with the GEM models and methodology [26]. Detailed comparisons of our work with these related efforts appears in the extended version of this paper (available from the authors).

The vast majority of business process modeling efforts lack formal methods for verifying properties of processes. Exceptions to this rule is the efforts in [15] where the use of ConGolog is advocated as well. We share similar long term research goals with these researchers, and would like to demonstrate that formal languages and methods can offer significant advantages in the design and analysis of business processes.

References

1. A.I. Anton, M.W. McCracken, and C. Potts. Goal decomposition and scenario analysis in business process reengineering. In *Proceedings of CAISE'94*, pages 94–104, 1994.
2. J. Bubenko, D. Brash, and J. Stirna. EKD user guide, 1998. Available from ftp://ftp.dsv.su.se/users/js/ekd_user_guide.pdf.
3. B. Curtis, M. Kellner, and J. Over. Process Modelling. *Communications of ACM*, 35(9):75–90, 1992.
4. A. Dardenne, A. van Lamsweerde, and S. Fickas. Goal-Directed Requirements Acquisition. *Science of Computer Programming*, 20:3–50, 1993.
5. G. De Giacomo, Y. Lesperance, and H. Levesque. Reasoning About Concurrent Execution, Prioritised Interrupts and Exogenous Actions in the Situation Calculus. In *Proceedings of IJCAI'97*, pages 1221–1226, August 1997.
6. J.E. Dobson, A.J.C. Blyth, J. Chudge, and R. Strens. The ORDIT Approach to organisational requirements. In M. Jirotka and J. Goguen, editors, *Requirements Engineering: Social and Technical Issues*, pages 87–106. Academic Press, 1994.
7. R. Fikes and N. Nilsson. STRIPS: A new approach to the application of theorem proving to problem solving. *Artificial Intelligence*, 2:189–208, 1971.
8. M.S. Fox and M. Gruninger. Enterprise Modelling. *The AI Magazine*, pages 109–121, Fall 1998.
9. D. Georgakopoulos, M. Hornick, and A. Sheth. An Overview of Worklfow Management: From Process Modelling to Workflow Automation Infrastructure. *Distributed and Parallel Databases*, 3:119–153, 1995.
10. M. Hammer and J. Champy. *Reengineering the Corporation: A Manifesto for Business Revolution*. Harper Collins, 1993.
11. N. R. Jennings, P. Faratin, M.J. Johnson, P. O'Brien, and M.E. Wiegand. Using Intelligent Agents to Manage Business Processes. In *Proceedings of the First International Conference on The Practical Application of Intelligent Agents and Multi-Agent Technology (PAAM96)*, 1996.
12. V. Kavakli and P. Loucopoulos. Goal-Driven Business Process Analysis - Application in Electricity Deregulation. In *Proceedings of CAISE'98*, 1998.
13. M. Koubarakis and D. Plexousakis. Business Process Modeling and Design: AI Models and Methodology. In *Proceedings of IJCAI-99 Workshop on Intelligent Workflow and Process Management: the New Frontier for AI in Business*, 1999.
14. J. Lee. Goal-Based Process Analysis: A Method for Systematic Process Redesign. In *Proceedings of the Conference on Organizational Computing Systems (COOCS'94)*, 1994.
15. Y. Lesperance, T.G. Kelley, J. Mylopoulos, and E. Yu. Modeling dynamic domains with congolog. In *Proceedings of CAISE'99*, 1999.
16. Y. Lesperance, H. Levesque, and R. Reiter. A situation calculus approach to modeling and programming agents, 1999. Available from http://www.cs.toronto.edu/~cogrobo/.
17. Y. Lesperance, H.J. Levesque, F. Lin, D. Marcu, R. Reiter, and R.B. Scherl. Foundations of a Logical Approach to Agent Programming. In M. Wooldridge, J.P. Muller, and M. Tambe, editors, *Intelligent Agents Volume II – Proceedings of ATAL-95*, Lecture Notes in Artificial Intelligence. Springer Verlag, 1995.
18. P. Loucopoulos and V. Karakostas. *System Requirements Engineering*. McGraw Hill, 1995.

19. P. Loucopoulos and V. Kavakli. Enterprise Modelling and the Teleological Approach to Requirements Engineering. *International Journal of Intelligent and Cooperative Information Systems*, 4(1):45–79, 1995.

20. John McCarthy and Patrick J. Hayes. Some Philosophical Problems From the Standpoint of Artificial Intelligence. In B. Meltzer and D. Mitchie, editors, *Machine Intelligence*, pages 463–502. Edinburg University Press, 1969.

21. J. Mylopoulos, L. Chung, and Nixon B.A. Representing and Using Non-Functional Requirements: A Process-Oriented Approach. *IEEE Transactions on Software Engineering*, 18(6):483–497, 1992.

22. M. Ould. Modelling Business Processes for Understanding, Improvement and Enactment. Tutorial Notes, 13th International Conference on the Entity Relationship Approach (ER' 94), Manchester, U.K., 1994.

23. M. A. Ould. *Business Processes: Modeling and Analysis for Re-engineering and Improvement*. Wiley, 1995.

24. D. Plexousakis. Simulation and Analysis of Business Processes Using GOLOG. In *Proceedings of the Conference on Organizational Computing Systems (COOCS'95)*, pages 311–323, 1995.

25. D. Plexousakis. *On the efficient maintenance of temporal integrity in knowledge bases*. PhD thesis, Dept. of Computer Science, University of Toronto, 1996.

26. A. Rao. Modeling the service assurance process for Optus using GEM. Technical Report Technical Note 69, Australian Artificial Intelligence Institute, 1996.

27. R. Reiter. The Frame Problem in the Situation Calculus: A Simple Solution (Sometimes) and a Completeness Result for Goal Regression. In *Artificial Intelligence and Mathematical Theory of Computation: Papers in Honor of John McCarthy*, pages 359–380. Academic Press, 1991.

28. R. Scherl and H. Levesque. The frame problem and knowledge producing actions. In *Proceedings of AAAI-93*, 1993.

29. A. van Lamsweerde, R. Darimont, and E. Letier. Managing Conflicts in Goal-Driven Requirements Engineering. *IEEE Transactions on Software Engineering*, November 1998. Special Issue on Managing Inconsistency in Software Development.

30. A. van Lamsweerde, R. Darimont, and Massonet P. Goal-Directed Elaboration of Requirements for a Meeting Scheduler: Problems and Lessons Learned. In *Proceedings of RE'95*, 1995.

31. E. Yu and J. Mylopoulos. Understanding "Why" in Software Process Modelling. In *Proceedings of the 16th International Conference on Software Engineering*, pages 135–147, Sorrento, Italy, 1994.

32. E. Yu and J. Mylopoulos. Using Goals, Rules and Methods to Support Reasoning in Business Process Reengineering. In *Proceedings of the 27th Annual Hawaii International Conference on Systems Sciences*, pages 234–243, Hawaii, 1994.

33. E. Yu, J. Mylopoulos, and Y. Lesperance. AI Models for Business Process Reengineering. *IEEE Expert*, 11(4):16–23, 1996.

Conceptual Patterns
for Reuse in Information Systems Analysis

Petia Wohed

Department of Information and Systems Sciences
Stockholm University/Royal Institute of Technology
Electrum 230, 164 40 Kista, Sweden
petia@dsv.su.se

Abstract: Reuse of already existing resources and solutions has always been a strategy for reducing the costs in the information systems development process. Construction and organization of small pieces of reusable solutions, also called patterns, in libraries for reuse support, has taken a central place within research during the last years. In this paper, a methodology for collecting conceptual patterns and a navigation structure for suggesting the most suitable one during the information systems analysis process are suggested. The study has, so far, been carried out on one domain only, but it provides a theoretical background for research on other domains as well.

1 Introduction

The concept of patterns is increasingly used in the context of information systems development. A pattern is a piece of a solution for a problem reusable in different situations. The main purpose of the use and reuse of patterns is to reduce the costs for the design and implementation of information systems. The idea of reuse of different parts of a solution is also at the heart of the approaches of object orientation and component-based development. These paradigms become more and more commonly used and are widely spread in the sphere of implementation, a line of development clearly distinguished by the character of the current environments for standard programming languages providing large libraries of reusable objects.

However, the concept of pattern is still not widely used within the initial phases of information systems development, i.e. analysis and design. One of the problems may lie in the lack of standardised patterns collected in libraries and supported by development tools. Another problem may lie in the lack of suitable patterns. In order to make a pattern applicable in several different situations it often tends to result in a too general pattern to be easily applicable, and such a general pattern is sometimes even difficult to understand.

In this paper, both these problems are addressed for the area of information systems analysis. It provides a theoretical foundation for a modelling wizard tool, which collects a number of conceptual patterns as well as navigates the designers to the most suitable one for a particular situation. Such a tool, supporting the initial phases of the database design process, is an attempt to complement database management systems like Microsoft Access, or as a part of a visual modelling tool

B. Wangler, L. Bergman (Eds.): CAiSE 2000, LNCS 1789, pp. 157-175, 2000

supporting an OO-development process of information systems like Rational Rose. A prototype for such a wizard collecting more than 360 patterns has been developed.

The difference from earlier approaches is the idea of preserving a number of different patterns within the same domain, in order to keep them concrete and easy to use. In order to identify the necessary pattern, a navigation structure consisting of a number of queries, to be answered by the designer, is suggested. This navigation structure may also be considered as a method for modelling support and is the main contribution of this work.

The paper is organised as follows. The next section surveys related research in the area. In Section 3, the modelling formalism is defined. In Section 4, a number of patterns within the same domain are analysed and a number of questions are distinguished outlining the differences between the patterns. Section 5 gives an example of the behaviour for a domain dependent modelling wizard tool built by the questions received from Section 4. Section 6 gives a theoretical background for the identified questions. Finally, Section 7 concludes the paper and gives directions for further work.

2   Related Research

The identification, naming, and classification of different phenomena in a Universe of Discourse (UoD) have long been incorporated in the discipline of taxonomy. One of the oldest and most well known taxonomy is Linné's taxonomy for species. However, when dealing with information systems it is not sufficient to only identify and classify the relevant phenomena in the UoD for which an information system has to be built, but it is also necessary to specify their properties and relations, something characterising the discipline of ontology. Slightly simplified and inspired by [10] and [4] we consider an ontology as a conceptualisation of the UoD in a certain language (see [10] for a complete definition of the concept). One of the main reasons for building ontologies is the reuse capability they provide. Some examples of ontologies are CYC [6] developed by Cycorp, The Enterprise Ontology [19] developed at the University of Edinburg, and TOVE (Toronto Virtual Enterprise) [21] developed by the University of Toronto. Common for all of these three ontologies is that they conceptualise the organisational structure of enterprises and are meant to be used for support in the information systems design process. To position our work in the context of the work provided by the ontology engineers, we will refer back to Guarino's framework for ontology driven information systems design [10], where two dimensions are identified. The first one is the temporal dimension distinguishing between the development-time and run-time for a system, and the second one is the structural dimension consisting of the three components of an IS namely application programs, information resources (i.e. databases and knowledge bases), and user interfaces. Hence, the focus of this paper is on the development-time for databases, and the work reported here may be considered as an application of ontology for the purpose of reuse.

Parallel whit the work of ontology, work in the field of reusable patterns has been carried out. Some of the works relevant here is the one provided by Maiden in his doctoral thesis [16], concerning the question of specification reuse. His paradigm builds on reuse by analogies. A number of domain abstractions are identified and formalised using a structure called meta-schema that defines seven knowledge types as necessary for a requirement specification. The source domain is also specified using this meta-schema. A comparison of the knowledge types of the source domain model with those of the domain abstraction is then possible and provides an analogy analysis, meant to identify possibilities for reuse. Even if Maiden does not call his domain abstractions 'patterns', the idea is still reuse of already constructed specifications. However, the work presented in this paper differs from the work provided by Maiden by concentrating only on the conceptual patterns and not on the whole requirement specification. It also differs by suggesting a navigation structure for identifying the most suitable pattern.

Two other works on patterns, during recent years, have been provided by Fowler [8] and Hay [12], who, after analysing a number of domains, suggest conceptual patterns meant to guide inexperienced systems developers or simply as starting points for those more experienced. However, no navigation support has been discussed by them, so the work reported here may be considered as a continuation of the work done by Fowler and Hay, through the investigation on navigation support.

When talking about patterns, two more works have to be mentioned: the work provided by Coad et al [5] and the work provided by Gamma et al [9]. Each of these works provides a library of patterns that are usually referred to. Goad's library consists of analysis patterns, whereas Gamma's library consists of design patterns. Coad's patterns are quite general, often consisting of no more than two, three classes, and they are meant to be varying consolidated into different object models. Furthermore Coad selects a number of strategies that are aimed to guide a designer in the analysis process. However these strategies are not formalized in the sense that they easily can be implemented in a computer, which is also the difference from our approach. Furthermore, the patterns suggested by Gamma are design patterns and they are meat to support the design process, whereas the patterns analyzed in our work are analysis patterns. The difference between analysis contra design patterns is the perspective from which the patterns are build; analysis: specifying the requirements for a system; and design: specifying the solutions for a system.

An alternative work on creating libraries of reusable objects also partly inspired by Fowler [8] and Coad [5] is the work provided by Han, Purao and Storey [11]. The point of departure in their work is so called design fragments - reusable solutions with a lower granularity than domain models, but higher granularity and specificity than analysis patterns. The main results are (a) a methodology for building such design fragments collected in a repository, and (b) two clustering algorithms for identifying common pattern set starting from a natural language requirements specification, which may be used as a navigation structure for identifying possible starting points for a designer. The work reported here may be considered as a complement to the work provided by Han et al. The main differences are, however, that: (a) the navigation structure by Han et al starts with a requirement, something not required in our work; and (b) the navigation structure may suggest more than one design fragment as a relevant starting point for a designer, whereas in our approach only one pattern is suggested.

Finally, viewed from a traditional knowledge engineering perspective, this work builds on the work provided by Moulin and Creasy [18] who integrates the earlier work of Chen [3] and Sowa [20] by adding linguistic elements from Fillmore's case grammar [7]. Moulin and Creasy present a simplified picture of the design process retyped in Figure 1, where the dotted rectangle encircles the phases being subject for

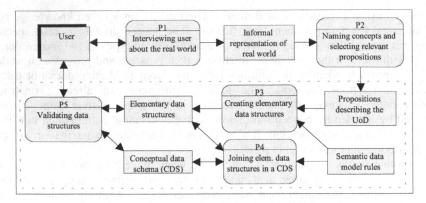

Fig. 1. Modelling the designer's behaviour (retyped from [18])

automation in modern modelling tools. Our approach builds partly on Moulin's and Creasy's ideas for using linguistic elements on conceptual modelling. The difference, however, is that we investigate how to automate the processes that have not been automated earlier, i.e. the processes outside the dotted rectangle. Consequently, we focus on the process P1 'Interviewing user about the real word' (from Figure 1) in order to support the users in building conceptual schemas, or, as it also can be considered, in order to guide the users to find the most suitable pattern. This shift of focus changes slightly the design process as represented in Figure 2 where the modelling process is simplified by the use of patterns. A modelling wizard tool is intended to support the interviewing process P1 and build a conceptual schema gradually, by using a pattern library. During this process the user shall be able to rename and complete the proposed solution, i.e. process P2. Furthermore, an integration module (supporting the processes P3 and P4 in Figure 2) has to be incorporated with the modelling wizard tool in order to offer integration facilities and make it possible to consolidate local schemas into a global one.

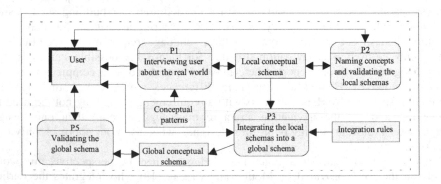

Fig. 2. The process model for our approach

3   Conceptual Schemas

In this section we briefly introduce the modelling language which is used. A formal definition of it, based on the definitions represented in [14] and [15] may be found in the first part of the Appendix.

The basic construct in conceptual modelling approaches is the object. Objects that are similar to each other are grouped together into object types, such as Person and Country. Objects have different properties, which are modelled by attributes, and they can be related to each other, which is represented by relationships. In our graphical notation (see Figure 3) object types are represented by rectangles, attributes by bulleted lists inside the object types, and relationships by labelled arrows. The object type initiating a relationship is called the domain of that relationship and the object type in its end is called the range. Generalisation constraints are shown by dotted arrows where the head of an arrow points to the super-type. For each relationship, the mapping constraints specify whether it is single-valued, injective, total or surjective. A relationship is single-valued when each instance of its domain is connected to at most one instance of its range. A relationship that is not single-valued is multi-valued. A relationship is total when each instance of its domain is connected to at least one instance in its range. A relationship that is not total is partial. A relationship is injective (surjective) when its inverse is single valued (total). Since most of the relationships in our schemas are single valued, not injective, total and not surjective, only the cardinality constraints that differ from this uniformity will be specified explicitly.

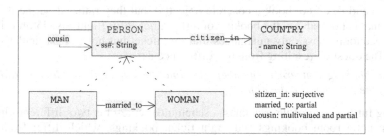

Fig. 3. Example of a conceptual schema

The description of the domain represented by the model in Figure 3 is as follows: a PERSON is a citizen_in a COUNTRY and (s)he may have several cousins. The distinction between MAN and WOMAN is kept. A person may only marry_to someone with the opposite sex, and polygamy is only allowed for women.

4   The Booking Domain

In this section a number of different patterns in the booking domain are considered. The similarities and differences between them are analysed and a number of questions are constructed for gathering information about the specific features within the domain.

The analysed patterns are shown in Figure 4 and most of them may even be considered as special cases of Fowler's 'Resource Allocation' pattern [8] pp. 168-172. The conceptual schemas may be used within the corresponding enterprises: a) a dentist cabinet; b) a university; c) a chain of movie theatres; and d) a travel agency. Even if all these examples are taken from the same domain the only common thing in their conceptual schemas, at a first glance at least, seems to be the BOOKING object type, which occurs all over. The rest of the schemas differ from each other considerably.

One main difference is that in schema a) a booking may concern only one object, whereas in schema b) and d) a booking may concern several different objects, which the object type BOOKING_LINE_ITEM with its relationship to BOOKING shows. With respect to this difference, the following question may be placed in order to identify which of those two alternatives pertains in a particular situation.

Does a booking consist of one object, or may it consist of several objects?

Notable is that even if several tickets may be booked within the same booking in schema c) the construction is more similar to the one in schema a) where only one object is booked at a time, but not to those in b) and d) where several objects are booked. Hence, the construction of schema c) also depends on the fact that exactly the same kind of objects are booked which leads further to the next identified difference, namely the difference between the booked object. Schema a) and b) represent the booking of a dentist and a room, correspondingly. In both these cases the booked thing is a concrete object, the dentist Peter or the room 605 at DSV. In contrast the schemas c) and d) do not book a concrete object(s), but they rather describe the kind of object that is booked. I.e. the booking of a flight ticket for flight SA345 on Friday 7 May 99, economy class only guarantees that one ticket but not any particular one is booked. The question resulting from this difference is:

Does a booking concern a (number of) concrete object(s), or does it rather specify the character of the object(s)?

Analysing further, one of the schemas – schema d) represents two different kinds of bookings: hotel room bookings and flight ticket bookings, which differ from each other by their properties. This is shown by specialising the object type BOOKING_LINE_ITEM into HOTEL_BOOKING and FLIGHT_BOOKING. In the rest of the schemas the bookings belong to the same category. In order to identify whether the bookings objects are from the same category or not, the following question may be placed:

Do all the bookings have the same character or may they be divided into several categories?

Continuing the observations, it also can be noted that in schema b) information about the booking orders is kept by the object types BOOKING_ORDER and ORDER_LINE_ITEM. This distinguishes b) from the rest of the schemas and gives rise to the next question:

Is it necessary to keep information about the request for a booking, before making the booking?

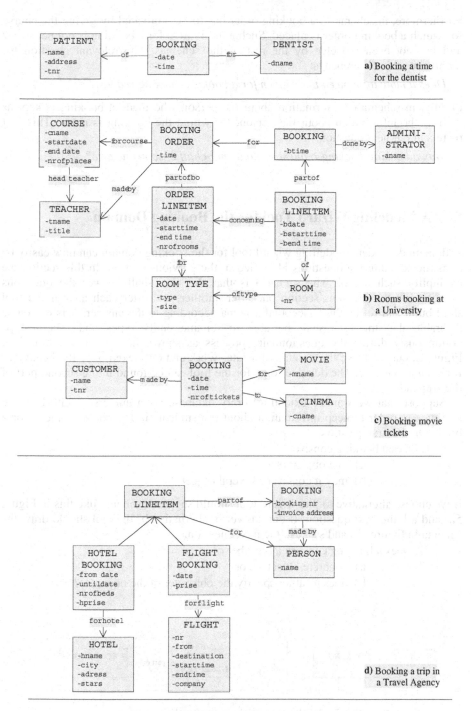

a) Booking a time for the dentist

b) Rooms booking at a University

c) Booking movie tickets

d) Booking a trip in a Travel Agency

Fig. 4. A number of booking patterns

Furthermore, in schema b) a booking order has to be motivated by giving the course for which a booking order is placed. Such a motivation for a booking is not necessary and has not been modeled by the rest of the schemas. The relevant question for identifying this difference is:

Does a motivation need to be given for a booking/booking request?

Finally, in schema d) information about the person who made a booking is kept as well as the information about the person, for whom the booking is made. This fact results in our next question.

May a booking/booking request be done on behalf of someone else?

5   A Modeling Wizard Tool for the Booking Domain

A domain dependent modelling wizard tool for the booking domain can now easily be constructed using the questions identified in the previous section. In this section we exemplify such a tool. The scenario is that the user shall answer the questions identified in the previous section one after another, and after each answer the tool shall build and refine the conceptual schema according to the answer. It is of course desirable that the user shall be able to rename entity types and relationships continuously during the questionnaire process as shown in the process model in Figure 2, but we leave these details for later work and only exemplify the behaviour for such a tool here. The detailed logic for the tool can be found in the second part of the Appendix.

Suppose that we want to extend a library database for a university with booking facilities in order to keep information about the students in the booking queue for a book. On the first question:

    1. Does a booking consist

        a) one object, or

        b) may it consist of several objects?

if we choose alternative a), the wizard tool should suggest a schema like this in Figure 5a) and ask the next question. If our answer is alternative b) the tool should draw the schema in Figure 5b) and still ask the next question.

    2. Does a booking concern a (number of)

        a) concrete object(s), or

        b) does it rather specify the character of the object(s)?

Fig. 5. The alternative solutions after the first question

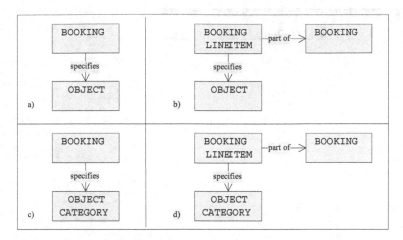

Fig. 6. The alternative solutions after the second question

An answer a) should result in expanding the schema into the one shown in 6a) or b), depending on the point of the departure, which is the result from our previous answer. The answer b) should result in the schema from 6c) or d).

In this way, the wizard tool should interview the user and piece by piece should build a schema depending on the answers. So, if the answers give the information that a booking consists of several objects, that the bookings have two different characters, that both order and motivation for a booking are necessarily to keep information about, and that a booking can not be done on behalf of someone else (se the right part of Figure 7), the resulting schema suggested by the wizard should be the one shown in Figure 7. (When implementing the prototype, the UML notation was used for object types, relationships, and generalization constraints for practical reasons. For the mapping constraints the notation used by Johannesson and explained in the appendix was kept.)

6   Completeness of the Questions

In the previous two sections, we analysed one domain and showed how a tool may support the modelling process within this domain. An important issue is to investigate the completeness of the questions, i.e. whether they can be used for gathering all information for the analysed domain, necessary for the construction of a satisfactory conceptual schema.

To reason about the completeness of the questions we divide them into different categories and analyse whether each category is covered by the questions belonging to it and whether the categories are suitable for discussing the completeness of the analysis. The following four categories are identified:

- questions with case grammar character;
- questions for cardinality identification;
- questions for power types identification;
- questions for generalisation/specification constraints.

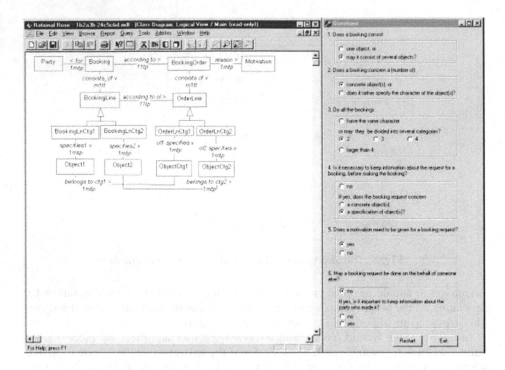

Fig. 7. A screen shot of the modelling wizard

Questions with case grammar character: The concept of case here refers to what usually has been called a deep case, i.e. the categorisation of noun phrases to the conceptual role they play in an action described by a sentence. Some examples of cases are agent: one who performs the action; recipient: one for whom the action is performed; object: one who suffers the action; instrument: an object used to perform the action; location: the place where the action is performed. The set of the cases is obviously discussible, which has resulted in a number of case systems, se [2] for a survey. However, the choice of a case system is not critical in this phase, as the focus here is to show how a case system may be used and also further tailored in order to make it suitable for modelling purposes.

Turning now to the way cases are used in conceptual modelling, it may generally be said that they are used for semantically enrichment of the schemas. (See [18] for a discussion about the advantages of using case grammar within conceptual modelling and [13] for a concrete application based on this semantically enrichment of conceptual schemas.) Briefly, applying case grammar to conceptual modelling implies that the object types in a schema represent the verb and noun phrases, and the relationships between the object types represent the cases. One restriction is that the domains for the relationships are only object types representing the verb phrases. The semantically enrichment results from the categorisation of the noun phrases into cases. It also should be noted that such a categorisation of noun phrases requires that an action have been described in some way. Hence, the case grammar is only suitable for schemas describing actions and not for schemas describing, for instance, product structures. With this limitation in mind we are going back to one of our conceptual schemas in Figure 4 and applying case grammar theory to it.

Figure 4c) describes that: "A number of tickets for a movie to a cinema may be booked by a person". Example of information stored in an information base for this schema (see Figure 8) is: "Peter has booked two tickets for the movie 'Lecture on Conceptual Modelling' to the cinema Sergel for the 2 of June '99 six o'clock" i.e. {booking(b1),date(b1,990602),time(b1,'18.00'),nr_of_tickets(b1,2),custom er(c1),name(c1,'Peter'),movie(m1),mname(m1,'Lecture on conceptual model- ling'),cinema(cn1),cname(c1,'Sergel'),made_by(b1,c1),for(b1,m1), to(b1, cn1)}. Analysing now the sentence describing the schema and the schema itself, we note that: the action 'tickets may be booked' is represented by the object type BOOKING; and that the rest of the noun phrases i.e. person, movie, and cinema are represented by the object types CUSTOMER, MOVIE and CINEMA, correspondingly. The cases for the noun phrases 'person', 'movie', and 'cinema' are 'agent', 'object', and 'location', correspondingly, and they are captured by the relationships made_by, for and to, correspondingly. In Moulin and Creasy's notation the cases are explicitly showed in a schema, something we have not used in our modelling language. However, the cases may be used as automatically generated names for the relation- ships suggested by a tool, which the users shall be able to change afterwards.

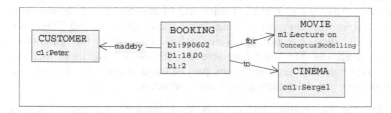

Fig. 8. Instance example for the schema from 4c)

The question is then which of the cases are relevant for a domain. The only way to give an answer to this question is to analyse a number of different patterns within a domain, and investigate the cases that have been used in those patterns, similarly to the analysis we provided for the booking domain. The booking schemas in Figure 4 ware selected to represent some (as much as possible) distinct booking situations we have encountered. Concluding the analysis for this domain, we can point out that the cases occurring in all schemas are 'object', 'agent' and the 'time for which a booking is made'. The 'recipient' is not explicitly modelled since it represents the system, for which the analysis is provided. Neither seems the 'instrument' be a relevant case for this domain. Instead cases for 'order' and 'motivation' for a booking may be of importance as well as cases for 'location where the booking is valid' and the 'time when a booking is made'. Since these cases occur in some of the schemas only, we will call them for *optional cases* for the booking domain. Looking back at our questions, we identify the last three questions as questions for identifying whether an optional case shall be included in a particular schema or not. We also note that the set of questions is not complete since it does not cover all optional cases. In order to get a complete set of questions for a domain, questions for all identified optional cases have to be included.

Questions for cardinality identification: Going the other way around and analysing the first question, we can se that it does not belong to the previous category. It does not address the conceptual role of the noun phrases, but is rather meant to bring information about the cardinality for the modelled object. Hence we classify this question as a question for cardinality identification.

Questions for power types identification: Into this category we classify the second question. The terminology of power types within conceptual modelling was introduced by Martin and Odell [17]. One example of a power type is the object types BOOK with the properties author and copyright_owner representing the general existence of an object. In contrast the object type COPY, related to BOOK, with the property exemplar_number, contains the physical objects and represents the materialisation of the BOOK. The distinction of power types has also explicitly been done by Fowler [8], who even divides his schemas into two levels: operational and knowledge level, in order to sort each object type to the correct level.

Questions for generalistion/specification constraints: Since the third question is placed in order to identify whether a specialisation hierarchy shall be introduced to the schema or not, we classify it into this category. Historically, the first formalisms for conceptual modelling (called entity relationship languages) did not had any generalisation/specification facilities. However, the formalisms were soon extended to even capture possibilities to represent this kind of constraints which was considered as a comfortable way for representing some parts of the UoD. The modelling languages with such capabilities were called languages for extended entity relationships diagrams. Since the language we are using have these facilities, it is natural to investigate whether there is any part of our domain that with advantage can be modelled using generalisation/specialisation structures.

Summarising the discussion, the first question category i.e. questions with case grammar character comes from the ideas for using linguistic instruments for enriching conceptual schemas. We have also pointed out how the completeness of the questions within this category can be improved by taking into account the relevant cases. The three other categories are closely related to the specific features of conceptual modelling. A review of five object structures that frequently occur within conceptual modelling is given in [1] (pp 125-131). Our last three aspects cover three of the reviewed in [1] object structures. The other two reviewed structures in [1] are not relevant for this work due to the limitation done on domains including actions by introducing the case grammar.

7   Conclusions and Further Research

In this paper, we have investigated and proposed a method for supporting the process of conceptual modelling. The ambition has been that this support shall be automated, i.e. a modelling wizard tool built for asking a number of questions and suggesting conceptual schema patterns, shall implement the results from this work.

As a first step, an analysis on an example domain is provided. A number of different conceptual patterns, for the booking domain, are considered in order to identify the similarities and differences between them. The differences are used for constructing a number of questions intended to support the modelling process within this domain. The logic for a domain dependent wizard tool is proposed in order to verify the possibility for automating such support. We also reason about the nature of the proposed questions, and whether they are complete and suitable for the purpose they were created for. The main idea has been the usage of case grammar in questions construction, but question covering some other conceptual modelling features have also been necessarily. In order to verify the results from this work a prototype for a modelling wizard based on the results from it has been developed. The prototype implements the booking domain only, but it is considered as a necessary step before continuing the work on a domain independent wizard.

Beside the work with the evaluation of the prototype, more theoretical work needs to be done in order to be able to build a domain independent wizard, namely an investigation on the cases occurring in different domains. Domain specific questions, as well as domain independent questions, have to be identified and constructed. Also, the different solutions or patterns, which shall be proposed by a tool, have to be specified, similarly to those proposed here for the booking domain wizard tool.

Furthermore, it is also necessary to provide research on how a general tool shall be constructed in order to support the modelling of complex UoD ranging over, not only one but, several different domains. One possibility should be to equip the modelling wizard with schema integration facilities. Still a number of questions should need to be considered in order to co-ordinate the behaviour of the tool with the behaviour of a user. One such question is to investigate the human's techniques when modelling complex domains and her way of dividing complex problems into smaller parts, either to make them easily to grasp and solve, or to distribute the responsibilities between different parties.

Another direction for further research is work on attributes that are not cases. For instance, name and address for a person are usually not considered as cases, but rather as simply properties. Then the case grammar should not help us identifying these attributes, but it still should be useful if a modelling wizard tool is able to suggest the most commonly such properties for an object type.

Finally, work for eliminating the limitation, resulting from the use of case grammar, needs to be provided. As we already pointed out earlier the case grammar may only be used for domains where an action is involved. Therefore, it is important to investigate how the modelling process within domains excluded from this study may be supported.

Acknowledgements

I would like to thank my advisor Docent Paul Johannesson for his valuable comments on earlier drafts of this paper.

References

[1]   M. Boman, J.A.Bubenko jr, P. Johannesson and B. Wangler, *Conceptual Modelling*, Prentice Hall Series in Computer Science, 1997.

[2]   B. Bruce, "Case Systems for Natural Language", *Artificial Intelligence*, vol. 6, pp. 327-360, 1975.

[3]   P.P. Chen, "The Entity-Relationship Model – Toward a Unified View of Data", *ACM Transactions on Database Systems*, vol. 1, no. 1, pp. 9-36, 1976.

[4]   R.M. Colomb, "Completeness and Quality of an Ontology for an Information System", in N. Guarino (ed.) *Formal Ontology in Information Systems*, Frontiers in Artificial Intelligence and Applications, IOS Press, pp. 207-217, 1998.

[5]   P. Coad, D. North, M. Mayfield, *Object Models: Strategies, Patterns, and Applications*, Prentice Hall, 1995.

[6]   CYC® Ontology Guide: Table of Contents, url: http://www.cyc.com/cyc-2-1/toc.html, June 10 1999.

[7]   C.H. Fillmore, The case for case, in Bach and Harms, eds. *Universals in Linguistic Theory*, Holt, Rinehart and Winston, New York, 1968.

[8]   M. Fowler, Analysis Patterns: Reusable Object Models, Addison-Wesley, 1997.

[9]   E. Gamma, R. Helm, R. Johnson, J. Vlissides, *Design Patterns: Elements of Reusable Object-Oriented Software*, Addison-Wesley, 1995.

[10] N. Guarino, "Formal Ontology and Information Systems", in N. Guarino (ed.) *Formal Ontology in Information Systems*, Frontiers in Artificial Intelligence and Applications, IOS Press, pp. 3-15, 1998.

[11] T.-D. Han, S. Purao, V.C. Storey, "A Method for Building a Repository of Object-Oriented Design Fragments", in J. Akoka, M. Bouzeghoub, I. Comyn-Wattiau, E. Métas (eds.) *Conceptual Modeling – ER'99*, Lecture Notes in Computer Science, Springer, pp. 203-217, 1999.

[12] D.C. Hay, Data Model Patterns: Conventions of Thought, Dorset House Publishing, 1996.

[13] P. Johannesson, "Using Conceptual Graph Theory to Support Schema Integration", in *12th International Conference on Entity-Relationship Approach*, Ed. R. Elmasri, pp. 280 - 289, Dallas, Omnipress, 1993.

[14] P. Johannesson, "Schema Transformations as an Aid in View Integration", in Fifth International Conference on Systems Engineering, Ed. C. Rolland, pp. 144 - 251, Paris, Springer, 1993.

[15] P. Johannesson, *Schema Integration, Schema Translation, and Interoperability in Federated Information Systems*, Dissertation at Department of Computer and Systems Sciences, Stockholm University and Royal Institute of Technology, Sweden, 1993.

[16] N.A. Maiden, *Analogical Specification Reuse During Requirements Engineering*, Dissertation at Department of Business Computing, Scholl of Informatics, City University, London, 1992.

[17] J. Martin and J. Odell, *Object-Oriented Methods: A Foundation*, Prentice Hall, 1994.

[18] B. Moulin and P Creasy, "Extending the Conceptual Graph Approach for Data Conceptual Modelling", *Data and Knowledge Engineering*, vol. 8, no. 3, pp. 223-248, 1992.

[19] Ontology ENTERPRISE-ONTOLOGY, url: http://www-ksl-

svc.stanford.edu:5915/FRAME-EDITOR/UID-21&sid=ANONYMOUS&user-id=ALIEN, June 10 1999.

[20] J.F. Sowa, *Conceptual Structures: Information Processing in Mind and Machine*, Addison-Wesley, 1984.

[21] TOVE Manual, url: http://www.ie.utoronto.ca/EIL/tove/ontoTOC.html, June 10 1999.

Appendix

Formal Definition of a Conceptual Schema

The formalism presented here is based on those proposed by Johanesson in [14] and [15].

Let P and C be two sets of symbols. A (first order) *language* based on <P,C> written L(P:C) is defined on an alphabet consisting of connectives, quantifiers, punctual symbols, variables, constants C, and predicate symbols P, where each predicate symbol has an arity. A *formula* in a language L is defined as usual. A *term* is a constant or a variable. An *atom* is a formula of the type $p(t1,...,tn)$, where p is a predicate symbol from P and $t1, ..., tn$ are terms and we say that p has arity n.. A *ground formula* is a formula without variables.

An *integrity constraint* is any closed first order formula. Certain special cases of constraint in conceptual modelling are *typing constraints*, *cardinality constraints* and *generalisation constraints*, which we are defining below.

- A *typing constraint* is either of the form
  - $\forall x \forall y (A(x,y) \rightarrow D(x))$; or of the form
  - $\forall x \forall y (A(x,y) \rightarrow R(y))$:
  where the first one is read "the domain for A is D" abbreviated "domain(A) = D" and the second one "the range for A is R" abbreviated "range(A) = D".
- *Cardinality constraints* concern the cardinality of a conceptual relation. The following four type of cardinality constraints are necessary to define a relationship.
  - The relationship A is single valued iff $\forall x \forall y \forall z (A(x,y) \wedge A(x,z) \rightarrow y=z)$
  - The relationship is A injective iff $\forall x \forall y \forall z (A(y,x) \wedge A(z,x) \rightarrow y=z)$
  - The relationship is A total iff $\forall x (P(x) \rightarrow \exists y A(x,y))$, where P is the domain of A
  - The relationship is A surjective iff $\forall x (P(x) \rightarrow \exists y A(x,y))$, where P is the range of A
- A *generalisation constraint* is a formula of the form $\forall x (P(x) \rightarrow Q(x))$ abbreviated "P $\subset$ Q"

A *conceptual schema* CS is a pair <L,IC>, where L is a language and IC is a set of integrity constraint as defined above. L is restricted to only contain unary and binary predicate symbols. The unary predicate symbols are called object types and the binary predicate symbols are called relationships. Furthermore, we distinguish a subset LP of the set P of predicate symbols i.e. LP $\subset$ P, and call the elements of LP for lexical predicates symbols. This distinction is necessary in order to keep away data values from object identifiers. We restrict the domain for a relationship to only belong to P-LP. Relationships whose range is from LP are called attributes. In Figure 9 a graphical representation of a schema is shown using a UML similar notation. The graph shows that the schema contains five predicate symbols {PERSON, MAN, WOMAN, COUNTRY, String} where String is a lexical predicate symbol i.e. String $\subset$ LP. The schema contains, further, five binary predicate symbols, three of which are relationships, namely {cousin, citizen_in, married_to}, and the other two, {ss#, name}, are attributes. The figure also shows a number of typing constraints i.e. 'domain(citizen_in) = PERSON' and 'range(citizen_in) = COUNTRY'. The generalisation constraints 'MAN $\subset$ PERSON' and 'WOMAN $\subset$ PERSON' are showed by dotted arrows. Furthermore the quadruples next to the relationships shows the mapping constraints in the order they are presented above i.e 'single valued, injective, totality, surectivity'. '1' stands for single valued/ingective, 'm' otherwise, and 't' stands for total/surjective, 'p' otherwise.

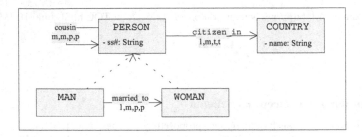

Fig. 9. Example of a conceptual schema

We finally give a definition for an information base. An *information base* for a conceptual schema CS = <L(P,C), IC> is a set IBcs of ground atoms whose predicate symbols belong to P. An example of an information base for the schema in Figure 9 is {man(p1), person(p1), woman(p2), person(p2), ss#(p1,'Peter'), ss#(p2,'Mary'), married_to(p1,p2)}

Formal Definition for a Domain Dependent Modelling Wizard Tool for the Booking Domain

In this part of the appendix the questions identified in Section 4 are reformulated in order to be suitable for a user dialog implemented in a modelling wizard tool. Each question is followed by a formal definition for the logic of the tool i.e. the schema it will build and suggest to the user.

1. **Does a booking consist**
    - **a)   one object, or**
    - **b)   may it consist of several objects?**

    ```
    a) CS:= {BOOKING}
    ```

    ```
    b) CS:= {BOOKING,BOOKING_LINE,consists_of,
             domain(consists_of)=BOOKING,
             range(consists_of)=BOOKING_LINE}
    ```

2. **Does a booking concern a (number of)**
    - **a)   concrete object(s), or**
    - **b)   does it rather specify the character of the object(s)**

    ```
    a) CS:= CS ∪ {OBJECT,specifies,range(specifies)=OBJECT}
            ∪ {domain(specifies)=BOOKING_LINE|BOOKING_LINE exists}
            ∪ {domain(specifies)=BOOKING|BOOKING_LINE does not exist}
    ```

    ```
    b) CS:= CS ∪ {OBJECT_CATEGORY,specifies,
                      range(specifies)=OBJECT_CATEGORY}
            ∪ {domain(specifies)=BOOKING_LINE|BOOKING_LINE exists}
            ∪ {domain(specifies)=BOOKING|BOOKING_LINE does not exist}
    ```

3. **Do all the bookings**
   a) **have the same character,**
   or may they be divided into several categories? If yes, is the number of categories
   b) **smaller than, or equal to four (give the number X of categories), or**
   c) **larger than four.**

a) CS does not change

```
b) CS:= CS ∪ {OBJECT1,…,OBJECTX,specifies1,…,specifiesX,
                 range(specifies1)=OBJECT1,…,
                 range(specifiesX)=OBECTX|OBJECT exists}
          ∪ {OBECT_CATEGORY1,…,OBECT_CATEGORYX,
                 specifies1,…,specifesX,
                 range(specifies1)=OBJECT_CATEGORY1,…,
                 range(specifiesX)=OBECT_CATEGORYX|
                                             OBECT_CATEGORY exists}
          - {OBJECT,OBJECT_CATEGORY,specifies,domain(specifies),
                                             range(specifies)}
          ∪ {BOOKING_LN_CATEGORY1,…,BOOKING_LN_CATEGORYX,
                 BOOKING_LN_CATEGORY1 isa BOOKING_LINE,…,
                 BOOKING_LN_CATEGORYX isa BOOKING_LINE,
                 domain(specifies1)=BOOKING_LN_CATEGORY1,…,
                 domain(specifiesX)=BOOKING_LN_CATEGORYX|
                                             BOOKING_LINE exists}
          ∪ {BOOKING_CATEGORY1,…,BOOKING_CATEGORYX,
                 BOOKING_CATEGORY1 isa BOOKING,…,
                 BOOKING_CATEGORYX isa BOOKING,
                 domain(specifies1)=BOOKING_CATEGORY1,…,
                 domain(specifiesX)=BOOKING_CATEGORYX|
                                 BOOKING_LINE does not exist}
```

c) CS does not change

4. **Is it necessary to keep information about the request for a booking?**
   a) **No.**
   If yes, does the request concern
   b) **a concrete object(s), or**
   c) **a specification of object(s).**

a) CS does not change

```
b) CS:= CS ∪ {BOOKING_ORDER,according_to,
                 domain(according_to)=BOOKING,
                 range(according_to)=BOOKING_ORDER}
          ∪ {ORDER_LINE,consists_of_ln,according_to_ln,
                 domain(consists_of_ln)=BOOKING_ORDER,
                 range(constist_of_ln)=ORDER_LINE,
                 domain(according_to_ln)=BOOKING_LINE,
                 range(according_to_ln)=ORDER_LINE|BOOKING_LINE exists}
          ∪ {ORDER_CATEGORY1,…,ORDER_CATEGORYX,
                 ORDER_CATEGORY1 isa BOOKING_ORDER,…,
                 ORDER_CATEGORYX isa BOOKING_ORDER|
                         BOOKING_CATEGORY1,…,BOOKING_CATEGORYX exist}
          ∪ {ORDER_LN_CATEGORY1,…,ORDER_LN_CATEGORYX,
                 ORDER_LN_CATEGORY1 isa ORDER_LINE,…,
                 ORDER_LN_CATEGORYX isa ORDER_LINE|
                     BOOKING_LN_CATEGORY1,…,BOOKING_LN_CATEGORYX exist}
```

```
CS:= CS ∪ {OBJECT1,…,OBJECTX,o_specifies1,…,o_specifiesX,
             range(o_specifies1)=OBJECT1,…,
             range(o_specifiesX)=OBJECTX,
             domain(o_specifies1)=ORDER_CATEGORY1,…,
             domain(o_specifiesX)=ORDER_CATEGORYX|
                      ORDER_CATEGORY1,…,ORDER_CATEGORYX exist}
       ∪ {OBJECT1,…,OBJECTX,o_specifies1,…,o_specifiesX,
             range(o_specifies1)=OBJECT1,…,
             range(o_specifiesX)=OBJECTX,
             domain(o_specifies1)=ORDER_LN_CATEGORY1,
             domain(o_specifiesX)=ORDER_LN_CATEGORYX|
                      ORDER_LN_CATEGORY1,…,ORDER_LN_CATEGORYX exist}
       ∪ {OBJECT,o_specifies, range(o_specifies)=OBJECT,
             domain(o_specifies)=BOOKING_ORDER|ORDER_LINEv
                   ORDER_CATEGORY1v…vORDER_CATEGORYX do not exist}
       ∪ {OBJECT,o_specifies,range(o_specifies)=OBJECT,
             domain(o_specifies)=ORDER_LN_CATEGORY|
                            ORDER_LINE exist, ORDER_LN_CATEGORY1v…v
                              ORDER_LN_CATEGORYX do not exist}


CS:= CS ∪ {belongs_to1,…,belongs_toX,
             domain(belongs_to1)=OBJECT1,…,
             domain(belongs_toX)=OBJECTX,
             range(belongs_to1)=OBJECT_CATEGORY1,…,
             range(belongs_toX)=OBJECT_CATEGORYX|
                      OBJECT_CATEGORY1,…,OBJECT_CATEGORYX exist}
       ∪ {belongs_to,domain(belongs_to)=OBJECT,
             range(belongs_to)=OBJECT_CATEGORY|
                                OBJECT_CATEGORY exists}
```

c) like b) and exchanging OBJECT and OBJECT_CATEGORY

5. Does a motivation need to be given for
- **a booking?** (Relevant only if the information about a booking order is not necessary, since the booking order is concerned as a motivation itself)
  - **a) yes**
  - **b) no**
- **a booking order?** (Relevant when it is necessary to keep information about the booking orders)
  - **c) yes**
  - **d) no**

```
a) CS:= CS ∪ {MOTIVATION,motivated_by,domain(motivated_by)=BOOKING,
                range(motivated_by)=MOTIVATION}
```

b) CS does not change

```
c) CS:= CS ∪ {MOTIVATION,motivated_by,range(motivated_by)=MOTIVATION,
                domain(motivated_by)=BOOKING_ORDER}
```

d) CS does not change

6. May a booking be done on behalf of someone else? (relevant only when a booking requirement is not necessary to keep information about)
  - **a) no**

If yes, is it important to keep information about the party who made the booking?
  - **b) no**
  - **c) yes**

May a booking request be done on behalf of someone else? (Relevant only when it is necessary to keep information about the booking requirement)

    d)   **no**

If yes, is it important to keep information about the party who placed the request?

    e)   **no**

    f)   **yes**

```
a) CS:= CS ∪ {PARTY,booking_for,domain(booking_for)=BOOKING,
                range(booking_for)=PARTY}


b) like a)


c) CS:= CS ∪ {PARTY,booking_for,booked_by,
                domain(booking_for)=BOOKING,range(booking_for)=PARTY,
                domain(booked_by)=BOOKING,range(booked_by)=PARTY}


d) CS:= CS ∪ {PARTY,booking_for,domain(booking_for)=BOOKING_ORDER,
                range(booking_for)=PARTY}


e) like d)


f) CS:= CS ∪ {PARTY,booking_for,ordered_by,
                domain(booking_for)=BOOKING_ORDER,
                range(booking_for)=PARTY,
                domain(ordered_by)=BOOKING_ORDER,
                range(ordered_by)=PARTY}
```

Evaluating a Pattern Approach as an Aid for the Development of Organisational Knowledge: An Empirical Study

Colette Rolland[1], Janis Stirna[3], Nikos Prekas[2],
Peri Loucopoulos[2], Anne Persson[4], and Georges Grosz[1]

[1]Centre de Recherche en Informatique
Université Paris 1 – Sorbonne
90, rue de Tolbiac
75013 Paris – France
{rolland, grosz}@univ-paris1.fr

[2]Department of Computation
University of Manchester Institute of
Science and Technology (UMIST)
P.O. Box 88
Manchester M60 1QD, UK
{N.Prekas, pl}@co.umist.ac.uk

[3]Dpt. of Computer and Systems
Sciences
Royal Institute of Technology and SU
Electrum 230, S-16440, Kista, Sweden
js@dsv.su.se

[4]Department of Computer Science
University of Skövde
P.O. Box 408, S-541 28 Skövde, Sweden
anne.persson@ida.his.se

Abstract. Patterns are a powerful paradigm that has emerged in recent years as a mechanism that can help towards the consolidation and dissemination of design experiences. In the context of the European research project ELEKTRA we developed a pattern approach for capturing best business practices of change management in the electricity sector. In this paper we briefly present this approach and concentrate on the issue of validating the pattern approach through evaluation of its different features. In particular, we define three constituent features, namely the *knowledge* contained in patterns, the *language* used to construct patterns and the *method* for developing the patterns. For each of these features we define an evaluation hypothesis and then test this hypothesis against a set of criteria and metrics. The experiments conducted and the results are presented in summary.

1   Introduction

This paper presents the results of the European research project ELEKTRA (ELectrical Enterprise Knowledge for TRansforming Applications [1]) with respect to the creation of a knowledge base for change management in the electricity sector. In particular, one of the objectives of the project was to "*create and capture best business practices of change management for re-using them in similar situations in other Electricity Supply Industry (ESI) companies*". To accomplish this task, we used an approach for disseminating best business practices based on the pattern concept [2, 3]. In this paper we present an overview of the pattern development approach, and we then focus on its validation. In the context of ELEKTRA, patterns are viewed as *generic and abstract organisational design proposals*. Patterns encapsulate organisational knowledge in a way that facilitates its reuse [4]. The main emphasis is

B. Wangler, L. Bergman (Eds.): CAiSE 2000, LNCS 1789, pp. 176-191, 2000
© Springer-Verlag Berlin Heidelberg 2000

on providing solutions to important and recurring problems within the context of an organisation. The ELEKTRA project has produced a knowledge base that contains patterns of change management for the electricity sector from knowledge mainly developed during the project. The main goal was to produce generic and reusable organisational solutions in the areas of Electricity Distribution and Human Resource Management. The results are extensively presented in [5]. In order to reach the project goal, we developed a pattern development approach that mainly consists of:

- a *language* for describing the knowledge embedded in patterns as well as meta-knowledge to facilitate the reuse of patterns,
- a *method* for supporting the discovery of potentially re-usable business practices and solutions, and their generalisation in a way they can be applicable in more than one organisation.

This paper mainly addresses the *validation* of the pattern approach. The validation process consists of an *evaluation* of the three features of the pattern approach, namely (a) the ESI knowledge base, (b) the language used to describe the patterns and (c) the method followed to develop them. This evaluation was performed through *empirical studies*. The evaluators were mainly domain experts from the two electricity supply companies participating in the project. For each feature we defined hypotheses and then, tested the hypotheses against a set of criteria using metrics.

The paper is organised as follows. Section 2 outlines the pattern concept and its use in the area of business and organisational development. Section 3 presents the ELEKTRA pattern approach, i.e. the pattern language, the method for pattern development and the pattern repository. Section 4 then presents the methodology for pattern evaluation including hypothesis and experiments, while section 5 discusses the actual evaluation results. Finally, section 6 presents our conclusions and discusses future work.

2   Patterns as Organisational Solutions

Recent years have witnessed an increasing interest in the use of patterns within the software development community and in particular by those advocating and practising object-oriented approaches and re-use. In [6], Alexander defines a pattern as describing *"a problem which occurs over and over again in our environment and then describes the core of the solution to that problem, in such a way that you can use this solution a million times over, without ever doing it the same way twice"*.

A good number of similar definitions of the term "pattern" exist today [7; 8; 9]. All these definitions share two main ideas. First, a pattern relates a recurring problem to its solution. Second, each problem has its unique characteristics that distinguish it from other problems. The ELEKTRA project has further elaborated the pattern concept and applied patterns towards documenting best business practices in organisations. The patterns that we defined and used in ELEKTRA are *generic and abstract organisational design proposals* that can be easily adapted and reused in different organisational situations.

ELEKTRA patterns represent solutions to specific problems within the context of an organisation, problems that are important and recurring in a variety of cases. The emphasis, therefore, has been on the fact that patterns address important and repeatable problems within the sector of interest. Each pattern couples a problem with a solution and reflects the context of its applicability, as well as the way in which it can be reused. Patterns address both the description of the enterprise in terms of business processes (and the strategic goals that these processes realise) and the description of the way in which organisations evolve by performing change. This led to the definition of two types of patterns:

- *Product Patterns,* dedicated to representing and modelling the different situations in the area of interest.
- *Change Process Patterns,* dedicated to modelling the change process in the area of interest.

This typology of patterns was devised with the purpose of ensuring the repeatability of the change process. The roles that process patterns and product patterns play in the task of managing organisational change are shown in Figure 1.

Fig. 1. The role of patterns in managing the change process [2].

A change process pattern constitutes a proposed solution to the problem of designing a new situation by describing the steps necessary for the implementation of the new situation, i.e. by offering a way of achieving the future state of affairs. A product pattern on the other hand describes the situation itself by detailing individual aspects of the business involved. Product patterns and change process patterns can then be viewed as complementary elements, in that they both contribute towards solving the greater design problem.

3   Pattern Development

This section presents the main features of the ELEKTRA pattern approach – the pattern language, the method used for developing the patterns, and the pattern repository, also called the ESI knowledge base.

3.1   The Pattern Language

In ELEKTRA, we placed emphasis both on developing patterns and on providing enough information about these patterns so as to make them effectively reusable. Thus we made the distinction between the *knowledge perspective* of the pattern and its *usage perspective*, captured in the *body* of the pattern and its *descriptor*, respectively. The former is the part of the knowledge that is effectively reused whereas the latter aims to provide sufficient information on the pattern and to describe the context in which the body of the pattern can be reused. ELEKTRA patterns therefore consist of four main elements, each is now detailed in turn.

The *body* presents an overview of the proposed solution. In most cases this type of knowledge was represented using a diagrammatic form, i.e. conceptual models, or natural language. The typology of models used is that proposed by the Enterprise Knowledge Development methodology (EKD). More about EKD can be found in [10] and [11].

The *formal signature* describes the pattern in such a way as to facilitate its indexing and retrieval. The formal signature consists of the pattern *type*, the *domain* of its applicability, and the *usage intention* according to which it can be used. Formalised natural language was used to represent this part of pattern knowledge.

The *informal signature* gives a complete description of the pattern. This description consists of the *problem* that the pattern intends to solve, the *context* of its applicability, the prevailing *forces* that influence the situation, and the proposed *solution* to the problem. The solution field offers a description of the proposed approach to tackling the problem complementary to the one given in the body of the pattern. Additional elements of the informal signature (e.g. the *rationale* behind the solution, the *consequences* etc.) complete the pattern description. Natural language was used to represent the informal signature.

The *guidelines* give advice as to how the pattern is to be reused and applied in a real enterprise context. For representing the guidelines, we used natural language.

An example of change process pattern is given in Figure 2. The pattern concerns the problem of introducing the buying and selling of electricity. In the goal graph of Figure 2, the proposed solution suggests different alternatives to organise the market in an AND/OR graph, these concern the introduction of a Pool, of bilateral contracts or of a Central Buying Authority.

The ELEKTRA pattern language was organised using a hierarchical indexing mechanism presented in [2]. The hierarchy of patterns was built using the formal signature of the patterns, and specifically by associating usage intentions of patterns. The pattern hierarchy was therefore organised in an intentional manner. This solution permits us to keep atomic patterns in the thesaurus while expressing their possible composition through a hierarchy that can be used for indexing and retrieval purposes.

3.2   The Pattern Development Method

In order to tackle the increased demands of developing patterns that encapsulate knowledge about change management, we defined a method that involves domain experts and method experts (analysts) in close co-operation. The process is iterative, it consists of the following four steps (see [2 ; 3] for details) :

   (a) *Elicitation of Candidates* aims at identifying potential change process patterns and product patterns. The output of the elicitation process is a list of candidate patterns described at a sufficient level of detail in order to proceed to their evaluations.
   (b) *Suitability Evaluation* aims to determine the suitability of a candidate pattern. Domain experts grade the candidate patterns obtained as a result of the previous step so that their further development can be decided upon.

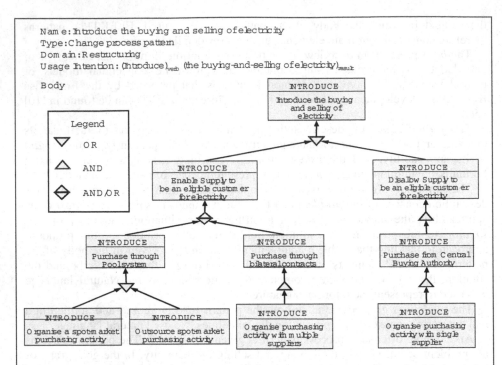

Name: Introduce the buying and selling of electricity
Type: Change process pattern
Domain: Restructuring
Usage Intention: (Introduce)$_{verb}$ (the buying-and-selling of electricity)$_{result}$

Body

Problem : In an environment with many electricity producers and many suppliers, electricity has to be bought by Supply from the producers and sold to the final customers.

Context: The deregulation directives of the EC set a framework for the trading of electricity, where a number of alternatives are available.

Forces: The way in which Supply trades electricity is defined by the overall legal and institutional framework in which all participants of the electricity market have to operate.

Solution: Depending on the framework chosen for the entire ESI sector, a Supply company will have some options for trading electricity. If a Pool system is adopted, Supply must participate in a spot market for electricity; this can be done directly through a respective department activity or it can be outsourced to an external agency. If a system of bilateral contracts is adopted (e.g. minimum ISO), then an activity of negotiating and establishing contracts with electricity producers must be organised. Finally, if a single buyer system is adopted, Supply will be purchasing electricity from the Central Buying Authority.

Consequences: According to the selected framework, Supply will behave either as a captive customer (in the case of CBA) or as an eligible customer (in the cases of Pool and trading through contracts). This means an entirely different internal structuring and operation. In the latter case the competition in the electricity market is more intense and therefore Supply will also need to behave in a more flexible and adaptive way.

Related patterns: Trading of electricity through CBA system, Trading of electricity through bilateral contracts, Trading of electricity through Pool, Outsourced trading of electricity through Pool

Guidelines: Selecting one of the modes for trading electricity depends on the direction into which the entire ESI sector will be heading. If an increased degree of competitiveness is desired, then the options of trading through a Pool or through bilateral contracts will be selected. The option of bilateral contracts in particular offers maximum freedom with respect to negotiation of quantities and prices of power with the producers. If, on the other hand, slower steps towards deregulation are desired, the CBA option offers more centralised control of the market and thus fewer possibilities for autonomous behaviour by Supply.

Fig. 2. An example of change process pattern

(c) Documenting aims at describing the reusable knowledge in the format of the Pattern Template. The domain experts, in co-operation with the analysts, provide the remaining elements pattern.

(d) Verification aims at determining adequacy of the knowledge embedded in the pattern. The wording of all elements in the pattern template is carefully studied and modified if necessary, as are interconnections between related patterns.

3.3   The Resulting Knowledge Base

By applying the aforementioned method, we produced the *ESI knowledge base*. It consists of two sets of patterns: one for the case of Distribution and one for the case of Human Resource Management (HRM). The total number of patterns developed is 31 for Distribution (12 change process patterns, 19 product patterns) and 31 for HRM (14 change process patterns, 17 product patterns). These patterns represent a number of important and recurring problems that arise when managing change in these two areas of the ESI sector. They are available in [2]. In addition the ELEKTRA patterns are accessible via the Internet on the following addresses:

Distribution patterns: http://www.co.umist.ac.uk/~prekas/DistributionPatterns/Pattern_Index.html
HRM patterns: http://www.dsv.su.se/~danny/patternlibrary/main.html

4   Experimental Method

The method to evaluate the ELEKTRA pattern approach is structured around the three following questions:

- *WHAT should be evaluated?* We answered this question by identifying the main *features* of the ELEKTRA pattern approach and by defining *hypotheses* associated to each feature that were considered important to evaluate. We identified *three features*, which we believe fully cover the approach. We identified 21 hypotheses, each of them representing an aspect of pattern design that we expect the ELEKTRA pattern approach to improve. It is by evaluating these hypotheses that we can test whether or not the expected improvements have, in fact, been realised.

- *WHEN should the evaluation be performed?* The evaluation can be performed only after a fairly complete and coherent set of patterns has been developed. We performed the evaluation of ELEKTRA patterns after we had worked for more than one year within the project to define the overall framework and populate the ESI knowledge base.

- *HOW should the evaluation be performed?* To perform the evaluation we conducted *experiments* in the form of *workshops*. We conducted a number of workshops with the participation of 26 ESI experts. In order to determine whether a hypothesis could be validated or not, we adopted the use of *evaluation criteria* and *metrics* [12, 13, 14]. We identified evaluation criteria and defined metrics in order to measure each hypothesis in a given experiment against a given criterion. This means that the evaluation frame is a 5-tuple of the form:

$$< experiment, feature, hypothesis, criterion, metric>.$$

There is one *result* for each 5-tuple that represents an atomic evaluation. These atomic results form the basis of more global evaluations and measurements. A detailed presentation of the evaluation process and results is available in [5]. We limit ourselves here to a summary of both, the evaluation process and obtained results.

Feature 1: ESI knowledge Embedded in Patterns	
Global hypothesis : *"The ESI knowledge base is potentially useful for solving organisational problems within the Distribution and HRM domain in the context of deregulation".*	
CRITERIA	HYPOTHESIS
Usefulness	H1: Usage of the pattern provides a substantial contribution in the context of a real problem-solving application.
Relevance	H2: The pattern addresses a significant problem in the ESI sector.
Usability	H3: The pattern can be used in the context of a real application.
Adaptability	H4: The solution advocated by the pattern can be modified to reflect a particular situation.
Adoptability	H5: Domain experts are likely to use the pattern for resolving a particular problem of interest.
Completeness	H6: The pattern offers a comprehensive and complete view of the problem under consideration and of the proposed solution.
Coherence	H7: The pattern constitutes a coherent unit including correct relationships with other patterns.
Consistency	H8: The pattern conforms to existing knowledge and vocabulary used in the ESI sector.
Prescriptiveness	H9: The pattern offers a concrete and tangible proposal for solving a problem, in particular with respect to the steps necessary for its implementation as described in the guideline.
Granularity	H10: The pattern addresses the given problem at an appropriate level of detail.
Feature 2: The Pattern Language	
Global hypothesis: *"The pattern language permits an effective knowledge capture and transfer".*	
CRITERIA	HYPOTHESIS
Usefulness	H11: The language captures and conveys the relevant knowledge for describing patterns.
Comprehensiveness	H12: The different elements of the pattern (formal signature, informal signature and body) are adequate for understanding its purpose.
Richness	H13: The language is able to describe the different aspects of a pattern one is expecting in such a description.
Ease of use	H14: The language eases knowledge capture in patterns.
Relevance	H15: The conceptual primitives chosen are appropriate for expressing the respective parts of pattern knowledge.
Feature 3: The Method to Develop Patterns	
Global hypothesis: *"The method is an adequate means for guiding the development of the ELEKTRA patterns".*	
CRITERIA	HYPOTHESIS
Completeness	H16: The method offers a comprehensive and complete view of the activities to be performed for developing patterns.
Coherence	H17: The method is described in a coherent way.
Prescriptiveness	H18: The method offers a concrete and tangible proposal for developing patterns, in particular with respect to the steps necessary for its implementation.
Relevance	H19: The method helps in organising and guiding pattern development.
Usability	H20: The method can be used in the context of a real application.
Usefulness	H21: The method offers an adequate means for understanding how patterns shall be developed.

4.1   Hypotheses

The three features of the ELEKTRA pattern approach that were selected for the evaluation process are as follows:
1.   The ESI *knowledge* embedded in the patterns
2.   The pattern *language* used to express the knowledge
3.   The *method* used to develop patterns

For each of these features, we defined a global hypothesis. Each global hypothesis is further refined into a number of more precise hypotheses that constitute to the evaluation criteria shown in the table below.

4.2   Experiments

The evaluation was conducted in the form of workshops. Each workshop was devoted to evaluation of one feature. Workshops for evaluation of feature 1: "ESI knowledge embedded in patterns" were separated for Distribution patterns and for HRM patterns.

Participants
In total 26 evaluators were involved in the evaluation task. They were equally assigned for each of the Distribution and HRM cases – 13 for each case. The evaluators were experienced professionals with an extensive amount of knowledge in their respective areas of expertise. In their majority (24 out of 26), they represented the two electricity companies of the ELEKTRA project; two evaluators were independent consultants in the Distribution area. Some of them had some general knowledge about the ELEKTRA project and had been involved in pattern development within the project; no other specific preparations were carried out prior to the evaluation workshops.

Procedure
The evaluation workshops were conducted according to an agenda comprising a common part for all workshops and a specific part for each individual feature evaluated.

The common part included the following items:
- presentation of the objectives of the evaluation
- presentation of the ELEKTRA evaluation approach
- background to the patterns work and EKD notation used for documenting patterns
- presentation of the questionnaire(s)
- tutored completion of the questionnaire(s)
- general discussion about the possible use of the ESI knowledge base

The specific part for workshops devoted to evaluation of the knowledge embedded in patterns included:
- presentation of the pattern language
- short presentation of pattern clusters and of each pattern of each cluster

The specific part for workshop devoted to evaluation of the method used pattern development included the:

- presentation of the pattern development method

The evaluators were asked to respond to questions in a questionnaire. Questions cover all the hypotheses to be tested against the set of criteria for each. The response was a grading from 1 to 5 for each criterion. Thus, each atomic evaluation is a value from 1 to 5 associated to a 5-tuple

< *experiment, feature, hypothesis, criterion, metric*>.

For example, the average value of the 5-tuple <Workshop 1, Knowledge embedded in patterns, The knowledge embedded in patterns provides a substantial contribution for an ESI company to resolve an existing problem, Usefulness, 1 to 5> was 4.3.

Evaluators were also given an opportunity to give additional comments when they felt that these were necessary. Workshops ended with an open discussion about the overall usability of the ESI knowledge base and possible ways how it could be improved.

5   Evaluation Results

This section presents the results of the evaluation process. We divided the discussion in three parts according to the features of the knowledge base we have evaluated.

5.1   Evaluation Results of the Knowledge Embedded in Patterns

As both parts of the ESI knowledge base – Distribution patterns and HRM patterns - constituted coherent parts, the evaluation of these hypotheses was accordingly divided into two parts. The evaluation process for both parts was similar, but the evaluators were different. For each case, a cluster of patterns from the entire pattern hierarchy was selected for evaluation. The selection of pattern clusters for validation was made with the following goals in mind:

- The selected patterns should contain a representative sample of information from the pattern library;
- they should form coherent clusters addressing the most important problems among those included in the knowledge base;
- they should include both change process patterns and product patterns.

We will briefly outline these two pattern clusters along with the respective evaluation results.

Evaluation Results for Distribution patterns

Two clusters of patterns were selected from the original hierarchy of Distribution patterns, as illustrated in 3:

- One cluster addressing *the problem of performing structural change in the Distribution business area*. The cluster consists of the change process patterns "Introduce structural unbundling", "Introduce new services based on network assets", and "Introduce the buying and selling of electricity". These three patterns address to a great extent the problem of dealing with structural change in the transition from a monopolistic environment to an unbundled, competitive market.

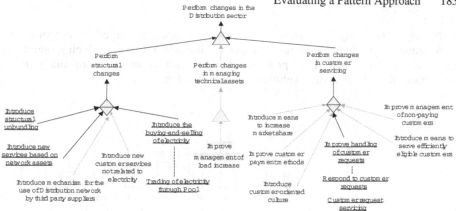

Fig. 3. Distribution patterns selected for validation as part of the original Distribution pattern hierarchy. Patterns chosen are underlined.

Related to the last of these three change process patterns is the one product pattern of this cluster, namely "Trading of electricity through Pool". This pattern complements the solution to the problem of introducing the trading of electricity, by describing one of the possible ways of organising an electricity market.

- One cluster addressing *the problem of performing changes in customer servicing in the Distribution business area.* This cluster includes the change process pattern "Improve handling of customer requests", and the product patterns "Respond to customer requests" and "Customer request servicing" (as well as its refinement through the associated pattern "Customer request servicing by phone"). This group of patterns addresses the problem of handling customer requests and possible ways of improving the services already offered.

The full description of the Distribution patterns that were evaluated during the validation process can be found in [2] and [3]. As shown in Figure 4, the average markings achieved by the Distribution patterns in both clusters are encouraging. All patterns achieved an average above 3.50, most of them standing close to or above 4 (see Fig. 4). Change process patterns achieved higher overall averages than product patterns.

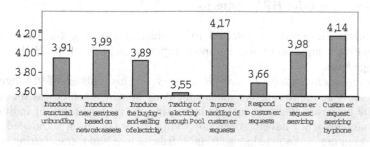

Fig. 4. Average values scored by Distribution patterns.

Figure 5 sums up the average marks to test each of the 10 hypotheses for this feature. Overall, the Distribution patterns achieved their highest markings in the questions related to usefulness and relevance, achieving an average of 4.34 for H1 and H2 respectively (see Fig. 5). This is, to some degree, an expected outcome: the understanding of what constitutes an important issue in a domain (which produces the candidate patterns and their problem descriptions) is much more likely to be unanimous than the proposed solutions to each problem.

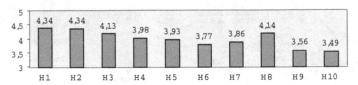

Fig. 5. Average values per hypothesis scored by all Distribution patterns.

The Distribution patterns were also rated well for their consistency with knowledge and vocabulary used in the ESI sector (average 4.14 for H8). This result is encouraging with respect to the process followed to develop the patterns, as it was the involvement of the domain experts in all steps of the process that assured this consistency. A further high average mark was achieved for usability of patterns in real applications (average 4.1 for H3). The patterns received their lowest markings for granularity (average 3.49 for H10), prescriptiveness (average 3.56 for H9) and completeness (average 3.77 for H7). This reflects the evaluators' view that some patterns did not tackle the respective problems in enough depth. In particular, the evaluators noted a need for more detailed solution descriptions as well as a more complete coverage of the options available for solving each problem. Therefore, we can assume that hypotheses H7, H9 and H10 are only partially verified and that improvements have to be done with regard to them before the Distribution patterns can be effectively used.

Overall we concluded that the Hypothesis: *"the Distribution part of the ESI knowledge base is useful for solving organisational problems within the Distribution domain"* is verified.

Evaluation Results for HRM Patterns

Three pattern clusters were selected for evaluation (see Fig. 6). They serve as a representative sample and cover the most important aspects of the HRM part of the knowledge base.

C5: Managing Individual Human Resources – This cluster of Change Process Patterns aims at improving the management of human resources at the individual level. The proposed solutions include increasing the responsibility of individuals for their own competency development, improving the organisation's knowledge sharing culture, creating a knowledge sharing infrastructure, and transferring individual competence to organisational competence.

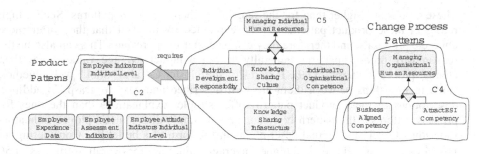

Fig. 6. HRM patterns selected for evaluation are grey-shaded.

C2: Employee Indicators Individual Level – This cluster of Product patterns provides a proposal how to measure employee related Human Resource properties. The pattern cluster selects types of data (measurable variables) that can be used to formulate goals for individuals. Three types of data are distinguished. Each of them is presented in a separate sub-pattern: Employee attitude indicators, Employee assessment indicators with regard to knowledge, and Employee experience data.

Clusters C5 and C2 are related in the sense that intentions expressed in C5 require certain ways of measuring HR related properties of employees, expressed in C2.

C4: Managing Organisational Human Resources – This cluster of Change Process Patterns aims at improving the management of human resources at the organisational level. The proposed solutions include increasing alignment of competency management with business strategy (further refined in a number of sub-patterns) and improving the attractiveness as an employer in the ESI sector. Due to the limited time for evaluation only the two top-level patterns in cluster C4 were evaluated. These patterns are "Business Aligned Competency" and "Attract ESI Competency".

As shown in Figure 7, the average values of HRM patterns are reasonably high: the average marking for all HRM patterns is above 3. Two thirds of them are above 4 (see Fig. 7).

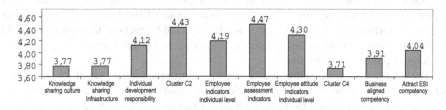

Fig. 7. Average marks scored by HRM patterns.

The highest scoring HRM patterns based on the average values are product patterns in the cluster C4. The average value of the entire cluster is 4.43 while patterns in this cluster scored the following values:

Employee indicators individual level	4,19
Employee assessment indicators	4,47
Employee attitude indicators individual level	4,30

These values are higher than for the remaining change process patterns. Such a high rating of these product patterns can be explained by the fact that they offer more concrete proposals, and therefore they can be easier to appreciate. This can also be the reason why product patterns generally scored a higher average value (4.35) than change process patterns (3.89). Patterns of the cluster C4 also "stick" well together, since relationships between them are well described and easy to grasp. In addition descriptions of these product patterns offer simpler explanations than the ones for process patterns – the pattern body contains a simple diagram (Employee Indicators Individual Level) and textual descriptions in the form of a bullet list. Considering all HRM patterns and clusters the highest average values are for overall usefulness (4.56 for H1), relevance to the ESI sector (4.43 for H2) and consistency with domain knowledge (4.28 for H3) – see Figure 8.

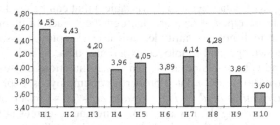

Fig. 8. Average values per hypothesis scored by the HRM patterns.

The lowest average values are for completeness of the knowledge embedded in patterns (3.89 for H6), for prescriptiveness of the proposed solution (3.86 for H9), and for granularity or appropriateness of the level of detail (3.60 for H10). Many evaluators suggested that the level of abstraction is too high and the suggested solutions are not operational enough in order to be easy to implement. Such a rating also influenced the overall rating of some patterns.

Some hypotheses were refined into a number of more precise hypotheses. For example, the hypothesis regarding the completeness of the knowledge embedded in patterns addressed the following three aspects – completeness of the description of the problem, completeness of the proposed solution, and completeness of relationships with other patterns (see Figure 9).

The evaluators also expressed a need to introduce more detailed and precise solutions to the problems addressed. Another contribution towards achieving more complete solutions would be to add specific examples of known cases where similar solutions have been applied. Such patterns would then serve as proposals for organisational designs. It is not surprising, that for these criteria product patterns (cluster C2) scored higher marks than change process patterns since they by nature address more concrete and complete solutions. In particular cluster C4, containing two change process patterns at high abstraction level, received the most of critique to this respect.

From these markings we can conclude that hypotheses regarding completeness of the knowledge (H6), prescriptiveness (H9), and granularity (H10) are only partially verified. The comments received give excellent guidelines towards improving the knowledge base. This leads us to conclude that the overall hypothesis: *"the HRM part of the ESI knowledge base is potentially useful for solving organisational problems within the HRM domain"* is verified.

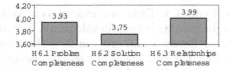

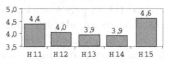

Fig. 9. Average values of hypotheses regarding completeness

Fig. 10. Average marks per criterion scored by the Pattern Language.

5.2   Evaluation Results of the Pattern Language

Figure 10 presents the overall results of the evaluation of the pattern language per hypothesis. The pattern language achieved its highest results in the hypotheses concerning the "Relevance" (H15) and "Usefulness" (H11). This high rating for these two hypotheses indicates that the evaluators believe the structure of a pattern is adequate for conveying the knowledge one can expect from it. The comprehensiveness and the clarity of the language need some improvements.

A study of the evaluation results focused on the different elements of the pattern template indicates that on average, the *guidelines* received the highest marking (4.7). The *informal signature* received the second highest marking which is not surprising since this element gives a complete description of both the problem that the pattern is trying to solve, its context of applicability, its forces and the solution proposed to the problem. Despite its formality the *formal signature* gets a reasonably high marking. Considering that its usefulness can only be appreciated through the retrieval process, one can conclude that the language is rather right in providing a formal signature. The considerably lower average value (3.5) scored by the pattern *body* shows that a formal conceptual modelling notation is presumably not clear enough to be easily understood by the large majority of pattern users.

On the basis of this data we conclude that the hypothesis *"the pattern language permits an effective knowledge capture and transfer"* is verified.

5.3   Evaluation Results of Pattern Development Method

The average value for the evaluation of the method used to develop patterns is 3.8 out of 5 (see Figure 11). This is an encouraging result since not all evaluators were familiar with the problem of pattern development at the beginning of the evaluation process. The method has been well perceived and well understood with regard to its objectives.

All criteria have an average above 3.50, most of them close to 4. Fig. 11 gives the average marking per criterion.

Fig. 11. Average values scored by the pattern development method.

"Usefulness" (H21) gets a marking of 4 out of 5. Therefore, evaluators consider that the method offers an adequate means for guiding pattern development. The average marking of "Completeness" (H16) is the lowest of all criteria: 2.6. The evaluators consider that a step is missing to determine the initial pool of candidate patterns. The average marking for the criteria "Coherence" (H17), "Prescriptiveness" (H18), "Relevance" (H19) and "Usability" (H20) is between 4 and 4.2. This means that evaluators found *the method consistent (the ordering of the steps as advocated by the method was found correct), relevant and useful*. Thus, this hypothesis is partially verified.

6   Conclusion and Discussion

The ELEKTRA pattern evaluation case study was a valuable source for drawing important conclusions about organisational patterns. Below we summarise the most important of them:

- A too high level of abstraction should be avoided when describing the solution to an organisational problem. The evaluators frequently expressed an opinion that the abstraction level is inappropriate for the kind of problem that is solved, and most often is too high. The links between patterns should also be made more visible. This would create a clearer picture of the context in which a pattern is to be used.
- Patterns in clusters are easier to understand and are therefore more appreciated than isolated patterns. The pattern clusters present broader and therefore more complete solutions. Thus the pattern users can faster grasp the overall idea of how the proposed solutions can be applied in their situation.
- Patterns should describe concrete solutions instead of guidelines and suggestions on how to tackle the problem in general. The proposed solutions should be illustrated by "best practices" and references to similar cases in real life.
- Patterns describing alternative solutions should have guidelines for choosing an appropriate solution depending on a particular situation in organisation. The evaluation confirms that the ESI knowledge base is on average *useful for solving organisational problems in the context of a deregulated electricity market*. It is also most likely that HRM patterns, due to their relative independence from the particular domain, can be re-used in different organisational contexts, even outside the ESI sector. The evaluation process also gave us a stimulus for further improvements and refinements of the knowledge contained within patterns, the format used to present patterns to potential users, the coverage of the patterns base, and the method used for developing patterns.

The next step will be to broaden the evaluation process and set up a Grand Jury approach like it has been successfully tested in the context of design patterns (see [15] and http://www.cs.clemson.edu/~tmiller/jury/jurorinfo.html).

References

1. Elektra Consortium, *ELEKTRA – Electrical Enterprise Knowledge for TRansforming Applications*, Project Proposal, ESPRIT Project No. 22927, 1996
2. ELEKTRA Consortium, *Molière: The ESI Knowledge Base Specification*, ELEKTRA Project Deliverable Document, ESPRIT Project No. 22927, 1999
3. Prekas N., Loucopoulos P., Rolland C., Grosz G., Semmak F., Brash D., *Developing patterns as a mechanism for assisting the management of knowledge in the context of conducting organisational change*, 10th International Conference and Workshop on Database and Expert Systems Applications (DEXA'99), Florence, Italy, 1999.
4. Rolland C., Grosz G., Loucopoulos P., Nurcan S., *A Framework for Encapsulating Best Business Practices for the Electricity Supply Industry into Generic Patterns*, 2nd IMACS Int. Conf. on Circuits, Systems and Computers - IMACS-CSC '98, Athens, Greece, 1998.
5. ELEKTRA Consortium, *Newton: Validated ESI Knowledge Base*, ELEKTRA Project Deliverable Document, ESPRIT Project No. 22927, 1999
6. Alexander C., S. Ishikawa, M. Silverstein, M. Jacobson, I. Fiksdahl-King, S. Angel, *A Pattern Language*, Oxford University Press, New York, 1977.
7. Coplien J., D. Schmidt (eds.), *Pattern Languages of Program Design*, Addison Wesley, Reading, MA, 1995.
8. Gamma E., R. Helm, R. Johnson, J. Vlissides, *Design Patterns: Elements of Reusable Object-Oriented Software*, Addison Wesley, Reading, MA, 1995.
9. Fowler M., *Analysis Patterns: Reusable Object Models*, Addison-Wesley, 1997.
10. Bubenko J.A.jr, Stirna J., Brash D., *EKD User Guide*, Dpt. Of Computer and Systems Sciences, Royal Institute of Technology, Stockholm, Sweden, 1997 available on http://www.dsv.su.se/~js/ekd_user_guide.html
11. Loucopoulos P., Kavakli V., Prekas N., Rolland C., Grosz G., Nurcan S., *Using the EKD Approach: The Modelling Component*, UMIST, Manchester, UK, 1997
12. Fenton N., *Software metrics: A Rigorous approach*, Chapman and Hall, NY, 1991
13. P. Oman and J. Hagemeister, *Metrics for Assessing Software, System Maintainability*, 1992 IEEE Conference on Software Maintenance (Orlando, FL, Nov. 1992), IEEE Computer Society Press.
14. Fonash, P., *Metrics for Reusable Code Components*, Ph.D. Dissertation, George Mason University, 1993.
15. [Mc Gregor 97] : J.D. Mc Gregor, "Using A Juried Approach for Design Pattern Validation", Proc. Of the 7th International Conference on Software Quality (7ICSQ), Montgomery, Alabama USA, October 6-8, 1997.

Specifying Processes with Dynamic Life Cycles

Rick van Rein

University of Twente, Dept INF
PO Box 217, NL-7500 AE Enschede, the Netherlands
vanrein@cs.utwente.nl

Abstract. We propose an alternative notation and semantics for process models in object analysis, to resolve problems with current diagram languages. Our dynamic life cycles are communicating state diagrams. Our life cycles support polymorphic creation, and they are straightforwardly composed. We provide an operational semantics, and demonstrate how to interact with a system of life cycles.

Keywords. object orientation, polymorphic creation and deletion, conceptual modelling, communication, state diagrams, life cycles, process algebra, component composition.

Introduction

Modern systems analysis and conceptual modelling is performed with object oriented methods, which offer rich notation to capture the constraints on implementations. An often-used notation is OMT, increasingly replaced with UML. The most-used models in these languages are *class diagrams* (which express classes with associations between them) and *state diagrams* (which express dynamic aspects of classes).

An example of a class diagram in OMT notation is found in figure 1, which shows a library (example taken from the analysis course on Catalysis [5]; Catalysis is an analysis and design method exploiting the notation of UML). This library registers *books*, which may be lent by *members*. A *book* has a *title*, against which *reservations* can be made.

Class diagrams have evolved from entity relationship diagrams [7], which explains why they represent data aspects but no process aspects. A result of the emphasis on data aspects in object oriented analysis is that associations lack a deeper meaning than "two connected classes." Many designs do not even name associations!

In the design in figure 1, the *lentby* association optionally refers to a *member*, but no knowledge is added on when a *member* is found over that association. Furthermore, the meaning of the association can only be found by interpreting the word 'lentby' — a common source of misunderstanding. Similarly, the class diagram does not reveal whether the *lentby* and *heldby* links can lead to an object at the same time.

B. Wangler, L. Bergman (Eds.): CAiSE 2000, LNCS 1789, pp. 192–211, 2000.

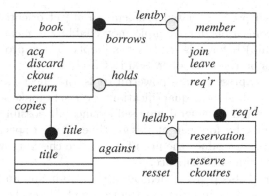

Fig. 1. Class diagram for a library system.

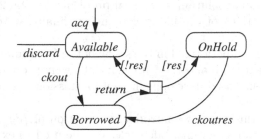

Fig. 2. State chart for a book in the library.

To express such dynamic aspects of the design in an object oriented way, a state diagram is usually drawn, like the one in figure 2, and some methods (like Catalysis) add mutually exclusive predicate expressions to the states, to hold for all *b:book*:

$$b.Available = (b.lentby = nil) \wedge (b.heldby = nil)$$
$$b.Borrowed = (b.lentby \neq nil) \wedge (b.heldby = nil)$$
$$b.Onhold \ = (b.lentby = nil) \wedge (b.heldby \neq nil)$$

This *does* answer our previous questions. A caveat here is the use of the value *nil*, which always introduces danger of loss of referential integrity; luckily, the relation between *nil* values and states makes it possible to check the models for *nil* dereferencing.

The state diagram in figure 2 demonstrates another place where a predicate expression can be of use, namely when the *return* operation is applied to a *book;* in this case, some condition (mentioned as *res* here) specifies whether or not the *book* is put on hold for some *reservation*. The disadvantage of this approach is that the *book* must be aware of the existence of *reservations*. It would be better for extensible designs when *books* are just entities with an *Available* and a *Borrowed* state, processing *ckout* and *return* operations, and not minding about *reservations*. Unfortunately this is not possible because a *ckout* for a reservation (distinguished here by naming it *ckoutres)* poses additional constraints and also terminates the resolved *reservation*.

Another class of process related problems in object oriented models is how to express synchronisation; for example, not enabling a *member* to *leave* the library (membership) before his *lends* set is empty. These problems are solved with preconditions on the *leave* operation in Catalysis.

Predicate logic expressions are powerful tools for object modelling, but not without a downside; free-form quantifications over sets make automatic model checking very hard and in general impossible since all possible runtime occurrences of sets cannot be foreseen at design time. Design specific ('free form') predicate expressions introduce the need for runtime checking, which has a negative impact on runtime performance.

The remainder of this paper is dedicated to introducing an (object) process model that contains more information than current life cycle models; the presentation is structured as follows: section 1 introduces and defines the concepts of life cycles by showing solutions to typical problems; section 2 shows a number of practical applications of the life cycle concept; finally, we draw conclusions and look forward to future research.

This work has been performed in the scope of the Quantum project, in which Compuware's UNIFACE lab and the University of Twente cooperate. UNIFACE is a leading component-based development tool for mission-critical applications.

Our approach. In this paper we introduce our notion of *(dynamic) life cycles*, as a variation on state diagrams. Life cycles can be used to express the process view on a class or component. They are capable of communicating with each other, and to create and destruct themselves on the fly. Life cycles pass around identities of life cycle instances (called *lifes*, the process view on objects). We choose not to model nesting, direction, or fixate the number of participants for operations; instead, we model an event-like scheme with the possibility to extend the set of event participants in several ways. Our events interact synchronously, so that lifes have the capability to block events.

We define the operational semantics for our life cyclesin the functional programming language Miranda[1] [3]; it is a precise, high-level language that hardly forces us to over-specify, it is executable and relatively easy to read.

1   The Concept of Life Cycles

This section introduces the concept of (dynamic) life cycles, by showing which problems exist, and how they are solved by life cycles. Each problem is introduced with an example, and guides the definition of the graphical syntax and an operational semantics for life cycles.

1.1   Undirected Events

Problem. Events mentioned in state diagrams can be related to 'the real world' in a number of ways. State charts by Harel [9] and in UML [16] usually have a

---

[1] Miranda is a trademark of Research Software Ltd.

notion of events coming from outside the state charts' domain. To provide state charts with the ability of initiating further actions, they can send out events. This approach is also taken in ROOM [19] and in our own protocol checking work [17].

This approach is not free of problems. Firstly, it is often debatable [12] [2] what the semantics are if a multitude of events arrives at the same time, and whether a nesting of events is allowed. It seems that no reasonable choice covers all cases of practical interest. We believe that the problem is that the event-sends-event structure reveals too many details of implementation in programming languages, notably C++.

Discussion. We believe that this problem is caused by the imperative idea of events calling each other. To model all aspects of these calls well, the models either contain a lot of complicating detail, or fail to be sufficiently precise for verification by automatic tools. In contrast, process-algebras [1] are simpler and express similar information. In these models however, events are just atomic actions that communicate, with no distinction between caller and callee.

Solution. Our choice is to simplify the semantics of events in state charts, by removing knowledge of the direction of event communication. Instead, we observe something happening in the 'real world' (what we will henceforth call an *event occurrence*), and our life cycles define *events*, which are system-perspectives of event occurrences.

We define an *event* as a name plus a list of parameters (introduced in subsection 1.4). We define event occurrences *evocc* as a set[2] of events. This makes it possible to model complicated event occurrences that can be matched by different events in different places:

$$event \equiv (name, [param])$$
$$evocc \equiv [event]$$

Based on these definitions, we define a *lifecycle* as a triple containing a name, a set of states (which we define as simple names, unique within a *lifecycle*), and a set of *transitions* (which we introduce in subsection 1.6):

$$lifecycle \equiv (name, [state], [transition])$$

Where we leave the types *name* and *state* unspecified, and defer the definition of *transition* to later.

Example. In figure 3, we show a simple system comprising of two life cycles. An event occurrence in this system is [*acq*], which matches the event *acq* in *book* but is ignored in *members*. Another event occurrence is [*ckout*], which is matched by an event *ckout* in both *member* and *book* life cycles and which therefore is a

---

[2] Miranda does not support sets as language primitives; we will therefore use lists without taking order or multiplicity of elements into account.

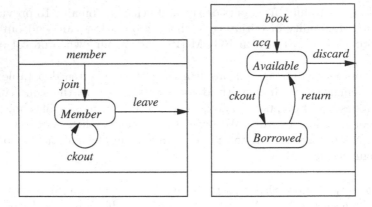

Fig. 3. Library in normal state diagram notation.

step that the two life cycles make at the same time. Though not useful in this application, it would be correct to consider [*acq, leave*] as an event occurrence, which is matched by *acq* in *book* and by *leave* in *member*. Instead of a nested calling structure between events, the events communicate by observing the same event occurrences at the same time.

1.2   Dynamic Communication Structures

Problem. Modern software development aims for modular (or 'component-based') development, in the hope that modules can be composed after they have been separately built. This makes it necessary to construct modules that can dynamically modify their patterns of interaction with the environment.

A problem encountered in implementing this wish is the strict pairing of caller to callee in most implementation languages. This style of specification makes it hard to add or remove a party without adding or removing its communication partners at the same time.

Discussion. An elegant and general scheme for communication is one where *any number* of parties may participate in an event. When a party wants to participate in an event, it cannot be ignored just because it currently is in a wrong state for participation. So, when a life cycle (like *book* in figure 3) contains the operation *return*, it can block that operation on other life cycles if it is not yet ready to participate in it. However, if a life cycle (like *member*) does not contain the *return* event, it simply ignores occurrences of that event.

The ideas of synchronisation (or 'blocking') described here are well known in concurrency theory. It is found in LOTOS [6] [4] as ||, and in ACP [1, §4.2], CSP [10] and CCS [14] as ||. Collaborative processing of events is known in programming languages as *rendez-vous synchronisation*. It is found in the languages Ada [11] and in Occam [3] [13]. Furthermore, there seems to be a correspondence between event occurrences and distributed transactions [21].

---

[3] Occam is a registered trademark of INMOS Limited.

Solution. To be able to talk about acceptance or blocking of event occurrences, we introduce a small algebra in which the interesting values are:

- *Ignore* to denote that an event (occurrence) is ignored;
- *Match xs* to denote that an event (occurrence) is accepted provided that the unifications in *xs* are established;
- *Block* to denote that an event (occurrence) is blocked and therefore may not take place.

The algebra provides a type *acceptance* with these values and a *compose* operation to compose lists of such values:

$$acceptance ::= \; Ignore \mid Match \; [(arg, arg)] \mid Block$$

$$isIgnore = (= \; Ignore)$$

$$isMatch(Match \; b) = True$$

$$isMatch \; x = False$$

$$isBlock = (= \; Block)$$

$$compose :: [acceptance] \rightarrow acceptance$$

$$
\begin{aligned}
compose \; xs \; &= \; Block, && \text{if } \exists x \in xs@isBlock \; x \\
&= \; Match \; [v \mid (Match \; vs) \leftarrow xs; v \leftarrow vs], && \text{if } \exists x \in xs@isMatch \; x \\
&= \; Ignore, && \text{otherwise}
\end{aligned}
$$

Using this *acceptance* algebra, we can define a function that indicates how two events match. This function uses the notion of parameters in events, which are introduced in subsection 1.4; in short, a parameter can either be an *In* or *Out* value with the usual meaning, or it can be a *Force* value which means that an event with a different value for that parameter *Block*s if it matches on the non-*Force*d parameters.

The *eventmatch* function returns *Ignore* if there is a discrepancy between the types of the two events. Note that *Out* parameters are treated as part of the event name. If the events do not *Ignore* each other, they should *Match* or *Block*; the latter case occurs when a *Force* parameter (introduced in subsection 1.4) has a wrong value. When *Match* is returned, variable bindings due to parameters are returned as well. So:

$$eventmatch :: event \rightarrow event \rightarrow acceptance$$

$$
\begin{aligned}
eventmatch \; (n, p) \; (n', p') \; &= \; Ignore, && \text{if } n \neq n' \vee \#p \neq \#p' \\
&= \; Ignore, && \text{if } \exists x \in matchers@mismatch \; x \\
&= \; Block, && \text{if } \exists x \in unification@blocking \; x \\
&= \; Match \; unification, && \text{otherwise}
\end{aligned}
$$

    where

$$matchers = zip(p, p')$$

$$mismatch((Out, Bound \; v), (Out, Bound \; v')) = v \neq v'$$

$$mismatch((d, w), (d', w')) = False$$

$$unification = [(w, w') \mid ((d, w), (d', w')) \leftarrow matchers]$$

$$blocking((Bound \; v), (Bound \; v')) = v \neq v'$$

$$blocking(w, w') = False$$

Example. With the above definition of *eventmatch*, it is possible to verify the examples in the previous subsection. Since we have not yet considered parameters, we will set the lists of parameters to [], the empty list. The event *acq* is modelled formally as ("acq", []) and we find that *eventmatch* ("acq", []) ("acq", []) = *Match* [] and *eventmatch* ("acq", []) ("ckout", []) = *Ignore*. We generalise this notion to the matching with event occurrences in subsection 1.6.

The problem of allowing dynamically changing numbers of collaborators on an event occurrence can be solved with the *eventmatch* definition: Those events that *Ignore* an occurring event will not take part in it; those that *Block* cause the whole event occurrence to *Block* (thanks to the *compose* operator) and if this does not happen, all events that *Match* take part in the occurring events.

1.3   Creation and Destruction of Lifes

Problem. A running life cycle system must support instances, which we call *lifes*: some *books* in our library will be *Borrowed*, while others are *Available*. To keep track of different books, life cycles must be instantiated to *lifes*. Only for a life is it sensible to speak of its current state, and a life is what responds to event occurrences, or blocks them.

Some common problems related to creation and destruction of lifes or objects are polymorphic creation of a new instance (often solved with factories [8]) and when to destruct a life or object (often solved with garbage collection [22]).

Discussion. We prefer to solve creation and deletion of lifes without explicit operations. We prefer creation and destruction to be a response of a life cycle system to a plain event occurrence, because this hardly requires additional life cycle concepts.

Process algebras such as ACP [1, table 35], which model concurrent processes, silently remove a finished process; this is part of the design of the concurrency operators. There is also a process algebra, namely the π-calculus [15], which introduces a similarly elegant creation construct: a process P may be prefixed with a replication operator, with the interesting property that $!P = P||!P$, which is any number of P processes interleaved. This appears like an infinite-sized pool of instances of P being ready to get created at the first communication with one of the Ps.

The π-calculus approach to process creation is generally considered elegant because it eliminates the requirement of explicit creating operations. Creation is just an effect of normal communication in the π-calculus.

Solution. To handle instances of life cycles, which we call *lifes*, we define a *life* to be a quadruple with its *lifecycle*, an identity that is unique for that life cycle, a current *state* taken from the life cycle, and a binding relation for currently known variables (treated in subsection 1.4):

$$life \equiv (lifecycle, lifeID, state, binding)$$

The type *lifeID* is only required to support an equivalence relation; in our examples, we assume that *lifeID* is represented as *num*. This paper works only with life cycles with one creating transition, and these are mutually exclusive, so that for each life cycle, at most one instance is created during any event occurrence.

We define a global system state *sys* as a set of life cycles and a set of lifes that instantiate those life cycles:

$$sys \equiv ([lifecycle], [life])$$

We define creation and deletion as actions on such a *sys*. Later restrictions will ensure that only one instance at a time can be created for each life cycle. We already exploit this knowledge here and create one *life* for every *lifecycle* in a system, exploiting a special state *nirwana* that we reserve to represent the state of a life before its creating transition(s) or after its destroying transition(s):

> $nirwana :: state$
>
> $nirwana =$ "Nirwana"
>
> $inNirwana :: life \rightarrow bool$
>
> $inNirwana(lc, lid, st, b) = (st = nirwana)$

The *nirwana* state is useful, because it enables the creation of non-existent lifes in a pre-natal state in the following *birth* function, and destroys outlived and never-used lifes in the *death* function:

> $birth, death :: sys \rightarrow sys$
>
> $birth(lcs, ls) = (lcs, ls +\!\!+ [(lc, nid\ lc, nirwana, [(this, nid\ lc)]) \mid lc \leftarrow lcs])$
>> where
>> $nid\ lc = id\_not\_in\ [lid \mid (lc', lid, y, z) \leftarrow ls; lc' = lc]$
>
> $death(lcs, ls) = (lcs, ls -\!\!- [l \mid l \leftarrow ls; inNirwana\ l])$

We do not specify id_not_in, except that for all xs it holds that $(id\_not\_in\ xs) \notin xs$.

Example. The *birth* and *death* functions are applied just before and after a basic step of a life cycle system. This means that for every lifecycle, there is always a life ready to be instantiated in response to an event occurrence. Similarly, a life can engage in an event occurrence which terminates its life, and it would be implicitly cleaned up by the *death* function.

To demonstrate the conceptual simplicity of our approach to creation, imagine adding a (redundant) constraint to our library, to express that every *ckout* of a *book* must be followed by a *return* of that *book*. This can be done by adding the life cycle in figure 4. This creates a new life on the fly, as a side-effect of the occurrence of a plain *ckout* event. The *ckout* event receives no special treatment anywhere else than on the creating arrow in this new life cycle; deletion is similar.

1.4   Parameters and Variables

Problem. If we instantiate numerous lifes from the *book* life cycle, we do not wish them to jointly transit from the *Available* state to the *Borrowed* state, but

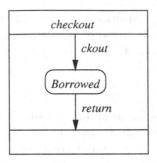

Fig. 4. The checkout life cycle.

rather one at a time. However, it is at the same time useful to let events be globally visible, to enable any life to participate in any event occurrence.

Discussion. We need to give every life its own identity, with a *this* notation, just like the keyword representing the 'current object' in object-oriented programming languages. The *this* keyword makes it possible to distinguish lifes from each other; but the events should also distinguish between different lifes involved, rather than life cycles. Therefore, we introduce parameters on events.

Normal object-oriented programming languages often support *overloading* of operations, where two operation names are only equivalent when the number and types of parameters somehow match. We take this same approach, and go one step further, by not only looking at the types of parameters, but also at the identities of the parameters. This is like multi-methods, defined from a process perspective.

To make it possible to give out parameters other than *this*, a life cycle can define variables to hold references to (other) lifes. These variables can be read or written as event parameters.

Solution. Every life can define a set of variables, which hold references to (other) lifes. These values are passed around in parameters to events and event occurrences. Two important properties of parameters are their direction and whether or not they are (already) bound to a value.

The direction of parameters may be:

- *In*, denoted with *?* graphically, for variables whose value is read from the parameter. The value for these parameters is not constrained by this parameter.
- *Out*, the graphical default, for variables that are exposed to a match along with the name of the event. The third clause of *eventmatch* exists because of this matching on *Out* parameters.
- *Force*, denoted with *!* graphically, to enforce that an event's parameter matches a variable's value. An example of this will be introduced in subsection 1.5. If the rest of an event *e* matches but this parameter does not, then *e* is *Blocked*.

The parameter may either be an *Unbound* reference to a variable (mentioning that variable by name) or it may be *Bound* to some *lifeID* value:

$$param \equiv (dir, arg)$$
$$dir ::= \ In \mid Out \mid Force$$
$$arg ::= \ Unbound \ var \mid Bound \ lifeID$$
$$var \equiv name$$

Variable names are unique within a life cycle. Furthermore, every life cycle defines a variable named "this", that already holds the *lifeID* of a life on creating transitions; all other variables can only get values by obtaining them as *In* parameters from some event occurrence:

$$this :: var$$
$$this = \text{"this"}$$

A life cycle definition only contains *Unbound* parameters, but after a life is instantiated, variables are filled in. We define a *binding* to be a mapping from *Unbound* to *Bound* parameters; this is the way variable values are represented in a *life*. The *bind* function applies a *binding* by mapping it over a *transition*, whose introduction we defer to subsection 1.6:

$$binding \equiv [(var, lifeID)]$$
$$bind :: binding \rightarrow transition \rightarrow transition$$
$$bind \ bnd \ (f, t, eves) = (f, t, map \ (eventbind \ bnd) \ eves)$$

> where
> $eventbind \ bnd \ (nm, parms) = (nm, map \ (parmbind \ bnd) \ parms)$
> $parmbind \ ((nm, val) : nms) \ (d, Unbound \ nm) = (d, Bound \ val)$
> $parmbind \ (nv : nms) \ x = parmbind \ nms \ x$
> $parmbind \ y \ x = x$

A variable v may only be used as an *Out* or *Force* parameter in transitions leaving a state s if either v is *this* or v is mentioned at least once as an *In* parameter on each possible path leading to state s. This is a syntactical constraint on life cycles.

Example. Figure 5 presents a redesign of the library of figure 3, where the events have parameters. For example, the event occurrence *ckout(b,m)* communicates with *book b* and *member m*; therefore, a single *book b* is checked out, and other books remain in the state in which they were; also, if some *book b'* is in *Borrowed* state, then it does not block the *ckout(b,m)* event occurrence, provided that b' differs from b.

1.5 Enforcing Synchronisation

Problem. Imagine extending the library in figure 5 with reservations (on *books* rather than *titles* for simplicity). Then, whenever a reserved *book* is returned,

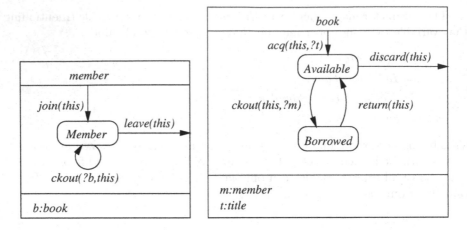

Fig. 5. Two library life cycles with parameters.

it must be put on hold. In many object methods, this is done by splitting the *return* transition like in figure 2. In our life cycle approach, we prefer to exploit communication to add a constraint, stating that the next *member* to check out the *book b* must be the *member* for whom *b* was put on hold.

Discussion. With only *In* and *Out* parameters, life cycles could not express this kind of 'identity enforcement.' An *In* parameter matches with anything, and an *Out* parameter simply *Ignores* event occurrences that have different identities for that variable. Therefore, we need to introduce another kind of parameter, which disallows (or *Blocks*) event occurrences with non-matching parameters.

Solution. We will graphically annotate such parameters with a *!* which is pronounced '(en)force.' In our formal models, we use the direction *Force* for these parameters. If an event occurrence *eo* matches an event on name, parameter count and all *Out* parameters, then there still is the question whether *eo* should be *Matched* or *Blocked*; the latter is chosen in case a *Force* parameter has different value from the value in *eo*. This is what has been formalised in clause 5 of the definition of *eventmatch*.

Example. Figure 6 defines the *reservation* life cycle. This life cycle is created when a *reserve(?b, ?m)* event occurs, and awaits the *return* of *book b*. Wen this book is returned, the *reservation* life claims it, and adds a constraint on the next *ckout* of *b*, stating that it may *only* be checked out by *member m* who made the *reservation* initially. The result is a dynamic extension to the communication structure which deals with the added constraint due to the *reservation*; the *book* need not be aware of this additional constraint.

    Note how the asymmetry between the book and the member in *ckout* corresponds to a conceptual asymmetry: *member m* should be able to check out other *books* than *b*, but *book b* may not be checked out by another *member* than *m*.

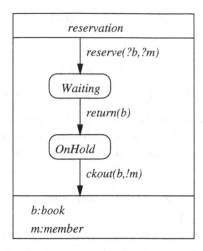

Fig. 6. Enforcing a certain *member* parameter value.

1.6 Multiple Perspectives on Event Occurrences

Problem. In the previous solution, we introduced a *reservation* on *books*. It is better to reserve *titles* than *books,* to support the situation where two copies (*books*) of the same *title* are owned by the library. Such a *reservation* life cycle that awaits a *title* cannot be made without requiring the title in the parameter list of the events that make a book available, thus also on *return*. The *title* has thus far not been a parameter to the *return* event, and it would be a demonstration of bad extensibility of life cycles if we would add it now.

Discussion. This is a common problem; from one perspective, there should be certain parameters to an event occurrence, and from another perspective there should be other parameters. This is caused by different perspectives on the same event occurrence. From the perspective of a *book,* only the *book* returned is of interest. From the perspective of a *reservation,* the *title* is also of interest.

We want to support observing event occurrences from different perspectives, much like in step failures semantics [20]. We therefore allow *multiple events per transition.* Each of these events can represent a different perspective on the transition. To ensure that all perspectives occur at the same time, the events on a transition must all occur together.

Note how this approach replaces that of nested states, as used in state charts. Nested states have a hierarchical ordering, and that hierarchy is for one perspective only. Another perspective usually shows up as a cross-level transition, which indeed is part of the syntax of state charts. We therefore believe that an extension of life cycles with hierarchical states would *weaken* the concept of life cycles rather than improve it.

Solution. A transition in a life cycle is annotated with any number of events:

$transition \equiv (state, state, [event])$

$transfrom :: lifecycle \rightarrow state \rightarrow [transition]$

$transfrom \ (n, x, ts) \ from = [(f, t, es) \mid (f, t, es) \leftarrow ts; f = from]$

Now that we have seen that event occurrences as well as transitions are represented with sets of events, it is possible to define when they match; informally, this is true when for every event in the transition, there is a matching event in the event occurrence:

$evoccmatch :: evocc \rightarrow transition \rightarrow acceptance$

$evoccmatch \ eo \ (f, t, es) \ = Block,$ if *blocked*

                $= compose \ [eventmatch \ e' \ e \mid e' \leftarrow eo; e \leftarrow es],$

   where   otherwise

   $matchdom = [e \mid e \leftarrow es; \exists x \in eo@(isMatch \circ eventmatch \ e) \ x]$

   $blocked = [] \neq matchdom \neq es$

In general, a *match* is found if no inconsistencies exist in the required *Match* unifications:

$match :: evocc \rightarrow transition \rightarrow acceptance$

$match \ eo \ tr = consistent(evoccmatch \ eo \ tr)$

   where

   $consistent \ Ignore = Ignore$

   $consistent(Match \ xs) \ = Matchxs,$

                        $if \ and \ [a = a' \mid (x, a) \leftarrow xs; (x', a') \leftarrow xs; x = x']$

   $consistent \ x = Block$

Example. To notate multiple events on one transition, we intersect the transitions with a comma, pronounced 'and.' For example, in the life cycle for a *book*, it is sensible to introduce an event *avail(this,t)* along the transition that now holds the event *return(this)* only. The *avail* event can be caught in the *reservation* life cycle. Moreover, from the perspective of books becoming available, we can see the acquisition of a new *book* as an *avail(this,t)* event too. The resulting life cycles for *book* and *reservation* are therefore as given in figure 7. It is sufficient to *mention* the existence of a *title*, we need not define its life cycle.

1.7 Step Semantics

This subsection is dedicated to describing precisely what the semantics of a step of a complete life cycle system are. The general approach is to first find out what transitions a single life can make given some event occurrence, then what happens if these are applied to a single life, and then map this approach over all life cycles in the system.

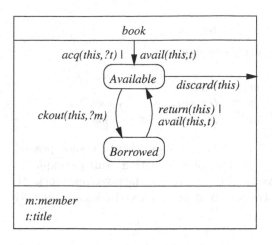 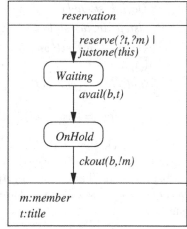

Fig. 7. The use of multiple events per transition.

The *lifesteps* function lists every possible *transition* that a life can engage into, given its current state and an event occurrence. The result lists the *acceptance* for every possible *transition*. The result is a set (implemented here as a list); an empty set means that no non-blocking transitions are possible; one result means that a unique transition can be made; multiple results means that a non-deteministic choice can be made between the outcomes.

$$lifesteps :: evocc \rightarrow life \rightarrow [(transition, acceptance)]$$
$$lifesteps\ eo\ (lc, lid, st, b) = matched\ \underline{else}\ ignored$$
   where
   $transitions = [(tr, match\ eo\ tr) \mid tr \leftarrow map\ (bind\ b)\ (transfrom\ lc\ st)]$
   $nonblocked = [(tr, acc) \mid (tr, acc) \leftarrow transitions; \neg isBlock\ acc]$
   $matched = [(tr, acc) \mid (tr, acc) \leftarrow nonblocked; isMatch\ acc]$
   $ignored = [(tr, acc) \mid (tr, acc) \leftarrow nonblocked; isIgnore\ acc]$
   $[]\ \underline{else}\ ys = ys$
   $xs\ \underline{else}\ ys = xs$

This makes it possible to construct a function *steplife* that constructs a list of possible future *lifes* from a current *life* and an *evocc* happening to it:

$$steplife :: evocc \rightarrow life \rightarrow [life]$$
$$steplife\ eo\ l = map\ (actualstep\ l)\ (lifesteps\ eo\ l)$$

With the *actualstep* function, a transition is applied to a life; this influences the state in which the life resides. Furthermore, old bindings *bnd_old* are removed as far as they are read by this step, and new bindings *bnd_new* are added instead for read-in variables:

$$actualstep :: life \rightarrow (transition, acceptance) \rightarrow life$$
$$actualstep\ (lc, lid, st, bnd)\ (tr, Ignore)$$

$$= (lc, lid, st, bnd)$$

$$actualstep \ (lc, lid, st, bnd) \ ((f, t, es), Match \ ms)$$

$$= (lc, lid, t, mkset((bnd \ — \ bnd\_old) \ +\!\!+ \ bnd\_new))$$

where

$$bnd\_old = [(var, val) \ | \ (var, val) \leftarrow bnd;$$
$$\exists x \in ms@((Unbound \ var \ =) \circ snd) \ x]$$
$$bnd\_new = [(var, val) \ | \ (Bound \ val, Unbound \ var) \leftarrow ms]$$

A life can block the execution of an *evocc* that it can accept in some possible future; this is a consequence of the dynamic communication principle explained in subsection 1.2. The function *futureblock* determines if the given *sys* blocks the given *evocc* because of some future transition of which all variables are currently bound:

$$futureblock :: evocc \rightarrow sys \rightarrow bool$$

$$futureblock \ eo \ (lcs, ls) = \exists x \in ls@futureblockinglife \ x$$

where

$$futureblockinglife \ l = \exists x \in futurematches \ l@((\neg) \circ isIgnore) \ x$$
$$futurematches \ l = [acc \ | \ (tr, acc) \leftarrow futurelifesteps \ [nirwana] \ eo \ l;$$
$$allbound \ tr]$$
$$allbound(f, t, es) = [var \ | \ (nm, parms) \leftarrow es;$$
$$(d, Unbound \ var) \leftarrow parms; d \neq In] = []$$

This uses a function *futurelifesteps*, which lists, once again for each possible *transition*, the possible *acceptance* value, only this time taking the future after that step into account in the *acceptance* value. This blocks on events that are *Ignore*d or *Match*ed in the current state, but that *Block* in some future state.

$$futurelifesteps :: [state] \rightarrow evocc \rightarrow life \rightarrow [(transition, acceptance)]$$

$$futurelifesteps \ states \ eo \ l = [(tr, compose(acc(tr, a) : accs(tr, a))) \ |$$
$$(tr, a) \leftarrow stepstodo]$$

where

$$stepstodo = lifesteps \ eo \ l$$
$$stepsdone((f, t, es), a) =$$
$$filter \ otherstate \ [actualstep \ l \ ((f, t, es), Match \ [])]$$
$$otherstate(lc, lid, s, b) = s \notin states$$
$$acc = compose \circ map \ snd \circ concat \circ map(futurelifesteps \ (states' \ l) \ eo)$$
$$\circ stepsdone$$
$$accs(tr, a) \ = [], \quad if \ \# \ states = 1$$
$$= [a], \quad otherwise$$
$$states'(lc, lid, s, b) = s : states$$

When a *sys* makes a step, every *life* decides independently which of its possible futures to select; therefore, the whole *sys* has as its possible futures the cartesian product of the possible futures of all its *lifes*. Note how we apply the functions *birth* and *death* to obtain the desired effect of creation and destruction as side-effects of communication:

$$step :: evocc \rightarrow sys \rightarrow [sys]$$
$$step\ eo\ sys\ = [],\ \text{if } futureblock\ eo\ (birth\ sys)$$
$$= ((map\ death) \circ sysstep \circ birth)\ sys,\ \ \text{otherwise}$$
where
$$sysstep(lcs, ls) = [(lcs, ls')\ |$$
$$ls' \leftarrow cartesian(map\ (mkset \circ steplife\ eo)\ ls)]$$

The *step* function is the interface through which users of a life cycle system can make the system perform steps.

2 Interacting with a Life Cycle System

The previous section introduced our life cycle concept. In this section we demonstrate how commonly requested information is available in a life cycle system. We describe the demonstrations in this example in our semantics language Miranda, to achieve sufficient precision, also outside the boundaries of our life cycles.

2.1 A Component with a Book LifeCycle

The *book* life cycle in figure 7 is translated into the formal notation by introducing a number of transitions with sets of events on them, and building the *book* life cycle from it:

$$book :: lifecycle$$
$$book = (\text{``book''}, [nirwana, \text{``Available''}, \text{``Borrowed''}],$$
$$[bookT1, bookT2, bookT3, bookT4])$$

where
$$bookT1 = (nirwana, \text{``Available''}, [(\text{``acq''}, [(Out, Unbound\ this),$$
$$(In, Unbound\ \text{``t''})]), (\text{``avail''}, [(Out, Unbound\ this),$$
$$(Out, Unbound\ \text{``t''})])])$$
$$bookT2 = \ldots$$

It is possible to apply event occurrences, including things like members joining the library, to this system (or component) of one life cycle; it simply ignores such event occurrences because no (future) transition of the *book* communicates with a *join* event. This is useful, since it means that an additional life cycle (or component) that does take the *join* event occurrence into account can process it. The *book* does not care about *joins*, but is not blocking them either; this is the idea of compositionality behind life cycles.

Assuming a library with a *book* life cycle present (and no *reservation* life cycle), it is possible to acquire a new book with event occurrences like *acq*:

$$acq, ckout, return :: lifeID \rightarrow lifeID \rightarrow sys \rightarrow [sys]$$

$$discard :: lifeID \rightarrow sys \rightarrow [sys]$$

$$acq\ b\ t = step\ [(\text{``acq''}, [(Out, Bound\ b), (Out, Bound\ t)]),$$
$$(\text{``avail''}, [(Out, Bound\ b), (Out, Bound\ t)])]$$

$$ckout\ b\ m = \ldots$$

$$return\ b\ t = \ldots$$

$$discard\ b = \ldots$$

The *acq* event occurrence matches the *bookT2* transition in the *book* life cycle when the right values for b and m are filled in. Assume a library system with no instances: $([book], [])$. Applying *acq* 1 3 to this system returns a list with one future library system, in which a book with *lifeID* 1 and title 3 is registered in state *In*. Applying *ckout* 1 7 to this result leads to a library system with that same book in *Borrowed* state.

$$exlib_0 = ([book], [])$$

$$[exlib_1] = acq\ 1\ 3\ exlib_0$$

$$[exlib_2] = ckout\ 1\ 7\ exlib_1$$

$$nolibs = discard\ 1\ exlib_2$$

$$[exlib_3] = return\ 1\ 3\ exlib_2$$

$$[exlib_4] = discard\ 1\ exlib_3$$

It is impossible to *discard* that book from the resulting library $exlib_2$; it should first be returned. This is the kind of synchronisation constraints that we strive for with life cycles, and which is inspired on the communication primitives in process algebras.

Note how the *step* function for the *ckout* and *acq* functions is used in the same way; the fact that *acq* constructs a new object is not visible here, meaning that we succeeded in hiding the creation (and destruction) of objects entirely.

2.2   Deriving Association Information

In the introduction of this paper, we argued that associations contain too little temporal information, and often require further constraints. In this subsection, we demonstrate how association information can be obtained from a life cycle system.

The vagueness of associations means that several definitions are thinkable; for example, in which states of the 'from' object (or life) the association is defined. We introduce the following helper function to define such associations:

$$assoc :: lifecycle \rightarrow [state] \rightarrow var \rightarrow sys \rightarrow [(lifeID, lifeID)]$$

$$assoc\ lc\ ss\ v\ (lcs, ls) = [(f, t)\ |\ (lc', f, s, b) \leftarrow ls; lc = lc';$$
$$s \in ss; (v', t) \leftarrow b; v = v']$$

Given a life cycle *lc* and the states *ss* in which the association should hold, and a variable *v* in *lc* (which must be defined in all the states *ss*) points to the 'to' object (or life), this function returns a list of links (association instances) between 'from' and 'to.'

An example application of this function is the *lentby* association from the introduction:

$$lentby :: sys \rightarrow [(lifeID, lifeID)]$$

$$lentby = assoc \ book \ [\text{“Borrowed”}] \ \text{“m”}$$

For example, $lentby \ exlib_1 = lentby \ exlib_3 = []$ but $lentby \ exlib_2 = [(1, 7)]$, denoting that in $exlib_2$ a book 1 is *Borrowed* by member 7.

Note how life cycle models need no *nil* values to model absense of links; instead, process state information is used to say which variables are defined.

2.3   Global Process Analysis

Unlike UML state charts, our life cycles communicate in a precisely defined way. The semantics of life cycles thus expresses sufficient information to infer global system behaviour. Consequently, we see possibilities to perform a number of interesting global process checks on a system of life cycles. We intend to perform research on these process checks [18], in spite of the unbounded number of lifes that can be created.

Deadlock avoidance. One way to avoid deadlock is to ensure the following: *Given that the life cycle system $s \in S$, there must be a trace of event occurrences that leads from s to a system without lifes.* The smallest set S to avoid deadlock contains precisely those states that are reachable from a life cycle system without lifes. If a deadlock avoiding checker accepts a life cycle system, an important class of problems has been avoided; furthermore, in the attempts to come to such a system design, the checker can provide valuable feedback to the designer.

Referential integrity. In systems that deal with pointers (like variables in our life cycles), it is important to ensure referential integrity. In systems that use *nil* pointer values, it is desirable to avoid the possibility of runtime exceptions caused by *nil* dereferences. In general, these problems are hard to solve before runtime. For life cycles, this is simpler, since they specify global process knowledge more directly.

We intend to make a checker that ensures the following: *If a life l is in Nirwana state, it is not referenced anywhere.* In other words, in Nirwana state it is safe to delete a life. This resolves the debate [22] on whether to garbage collect or to explicitly delete, since the moment of deletion is precisely known.

Non-determinism. We explicitly allow non-determinism caused by more than one transition from the same life cycle state matching the same event occurrence. This is because non-determinism has a useful interpretation: something outside the current scope of reference (e.g. some data-related issue) decides on the transition to follow. Checker tools must treat non-determinism as a choice that they cannot influence or count on. In our previous work on protocol checking [17], we used non-determinism in a similar way, namely to model choices made during the execution of an atomic action.

3 Conclusions and Future Work

This paper introduced a variation on state diagrams called (dynamic) life cycles. We presented a graphical notation and a precise semantics.

Our life cycles present some features that we did not find in comparable work: life cycles support polymorphic creation and deletion of new instances as a side-effect of normal steps. Life cycles systems are straightforwardly composed to larger systems. Life cycles can express dynamically changing synchronisation constraints. Life cycles allow redundancy and non-determinism in models.

Life cycles can express multiple perspectives on events as a means of dynamic binding; we expect this to be a good replacement for hierarchical state charts, whose precise meaning is not trivial.

Life cycles contain more information than traditional models. Associations can be inferred from life cycles. Information on which steps can be performed next, and which instances can act as parameters to those steps, can be inferred from life cycles. Finally, life cycles describe how the process aspects of a total system behave, which makes us believe that several global correctness properties become testable; think of deadlock avoidance and referential integrity.

In our future work, we hope to perform such global correctness checks in spite of the unbounded number of lifes in a life cycle system. We intend to gain better understanding on how processes in workflow and implementation objects cooperate. We also wish to investigate the use of refinement in workflow models. We are also interested in relating this work to models like CSP and LOTOS to see if life cycles introduce new formal aspects (possibly, dynamically evolving communication alphabets). Our eventual goal with this work is to come to a simple yet powerful process notion and accompanying verification tools for object oriented models.

Acknowledgements. I wish to thank Maarten Fokkinga for providing constant feedback and input on the ideas behind life cycles. I wish to thank Compuware, in particular Wim Bast, Tom Brus and Edwin Hautus, for providing the challenging practical environment in which this work evolved.

References

1. J.C.M. Baeten and W.P. Weijland. *Process Algebra.* Cambridge University Press, 1990.
2. M. von der Beeck. A comparison of Statecharts variants. In H. Langmaack, W.P. de Roever, and J. Vytopil, editors, *Formal Techniques in Real-Time and Fault-Tolerant Systems*, pages 128–148. Springer, 1994. Lecture Notes in Computer Science 863.

3. R. Bird and P. Wadler. *Introduction to functional programming*. Prentice Hall, 1988.
4. T. Bolognesi and E. Brinksma. Introduction to the ISO specification language LOTOS. *Computer Networks and ISDN Systems*, 14(1):25–29, 1988.
5. D. D'Souza and A. Wills. *Catalysis: Practical Rigor and Refinement*. Addison-Wesley, 1998.
6. P.H.J. van Eijk, C.A. Vissers, and M. Diaz, editors. *The formal description technique LOTOS*. Elsevier Science Publishers B.V., 1989.
7. S.B. Elmasri, R. Navathe. *Fundamentals of database systems*. Benjamin/Cummings, 1994.
8. E. Gamma, R. Helm, R. Johnson, and J. Vlissides. *Design Patterns: Elements of Reusable Object-oriented Software*. Addison Wesley, Reading, 1996.
9. D. Harel. Statecharts: A visual formalism for complex systems. *Science of Computer Programming*, 8:231–274, 1987.
10. C.A.R. Hoare. *Communicating Sequential Processes*. Prentice Hall, 1985.
11. ISO, editor. *Ada 95 Reference Manual, Language and Standard Libraries*. 1994. ISO/IEC 8652:1995(E).
12. D. Latella, I. Majzik, and M. Massink. Towards a formal operational semantics of UML statechart diagrams. *Formal Methods for Open Object-Based Distributed Systems*, pages 331–347, 1999.
13. Inmos Ltd. *Occam 2 Reference Manual*. Prentice-Hall, 1988.
14. R. Milner. *A calculus of communicating systems*. LNCS. Springer-Verlag, 1980.
15. R. Milner. The polyadic π-calculus: a tutorial. Springer-Verlag, Aug 1991.
16. Rational Software Corporation. *UML Semantics*. Rational Software Corporation, 1997.
17. R. van Rein and M. Fokkinga. Protocol assuring universal language. *Formal Methods for Open Object-Based Distributed Systems*, pages 241–258, 1999.
18. R. van Rein and M.M. Fokkinga. Static checking of dynamic protocols. 1999. submitted to CONCUR'99.
19. B. Selic, G. Geullekson, and P.T. Ward. *Real-time Object-Oriented Modeling*. John Wiley & Sons, Inc., 1994.
20. D. Taubner and W. Vogler. Step failures semantics and a complete proof system. *Acta Informatica*, 27:125–156, 1989.
21. X/Open, editor. *Distributed Transaction Processing: Reference Model, Version 3*. Feb 1996.
22. B. Zorn. The measured cost of conservative garbage collection. *Software, Practice and Experience*, 23(7):733–756, July 1993.

Design Principles for Application Integration

Paul Johannesson and Erik Perjons

Department of Information and Systems Sciences,
Stockholm University/Royal Institute of Technology,
Electrum 230, 164 40 Kista, Sweden
{pajo, perjons}@dsv.su.se

Abstract. Application integration is a major trend in information technology today. In this paper we present a number of principles for the design, validation and presentation of process models which align the applications of an organisation to its business processes. The design principles are divided into two groups. The first group consists of guidelines that obtain different views of the models and thereby facilitate for different stakeholders, e. g. business managers, designers and operators, to use common models and process languages. The second group of principles consists of guidelines to check the completeness of the process models. The paper also presents a process description language, BML (Business Model Language), which is tailored for modelling application integration.

1 Background

Three of the major trends in information technology today are the Web, enterprise software packages, and application integration. The Web provides an environment that can link a company's customers, suppliers, partners, and its internal users. Enterprise software packages offer an integrated environment to support business processes across the functional divisions in organisations. Some packages, like enterprise resource planning (ERP), for example SAP R/3 and BaanERP, manage back-office requirements, while other packages provide front-office capabilities, e.g. customer services. Common to Web applications as well as enterprise software packages is the need for application integration. Application integration is required to connect front office systems with back office systems, to transfer business processes to the Web, and to create extended supply chains involving customers, partners, and suppliers. Application integration is also needed for wrapping legacy systems and for migrating to new environments.

The demand for application integration is also fuelled by the move to process orientation in many organisations. Traditionally, organisations have been functionally divided, i.e. companies have been separated into departments such as market, production, and service. However, the functional organisation has been shown to have a number of weaknesses. In particular, it requires a huge administration to handle issues crossing functional borders, and considerable resources are allocated to tasks that do not create value. In order to overcome the problems of a functional organisation, companies have been concentrating on business processes, i. e. the set of related activities that create value for the customers. These processes cross the

B. Wangler, L. Bergman (Eds.): CAiSE 2000, LNCS 1789, pp. 212-231, 2000
© Springer-Verlag Berlin Heidelberg 2000

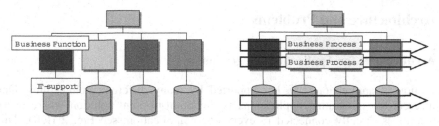

Fig. 0. The traditional function oriented structure, to the left, with the "stovepipe" like relation between business functions and IT systems. To the right the process oriented organisation which requires an integration of the IT systems.

internal borders of an organisation and also sometimes the external borders to other organisations, [6], [22], [27].

Supporting cross-functional processes raises new demands on the IT systems or applications. Traditionally, the applications have been built around departments or functions in the companies. The result has been a "stovepipe" like relation between the functions and the applications, where every function in the company is supported by its own IT-system or applications. This architecture is not satisfactory for process oriented organisations; to support the business processes in full the applications must be integrated, [18], see Fig. 1.

To handle this integration of applications in an efficient way, technologies, tools, and methodologies are required. One main technology is the Process Brokers, also called Process Management Systems, which aim at aligning the applications of an organisation to its business processes. A Process Broker provides an integrated, graphical environment in which all process logic for connecting applications can be encapsulated. The Process Broker enables users to visualise, construct, analyse, simulate and execute processes for application integration. Utilising the Process Broker technology for application integration is a complex design activity. Therefore, it requires adequate methodological support so that well-structured and easily understandable models can be produced. The purpose of this paper is to contribute to such methodological support by introducing a number of principles for the design, validation, and presentation of process models aligning the applications of an organisation to its business processes. The paper is a result of a joint project between the Royal Institute of Technology and Viewlocity, which aims at further developing technology, methods and Viewlocity's modelling language BML for application and process integration, [20], [27].

The remainder of the paper is organised as follows. Section 2 provides a brief overview of different architectures for application integration, in particular the Process Broker architecture. The section also discusses characteristics and problems of application integration. Section 3 describes related research about process modelling languages, and in Section 4 we describe a process modelling language BML (Business Model Language) which is used in the remainder of the paper. A classification of messages and processes, which is the base of the proposed design principles, is described in Section 5. In Section 6, we present our design principles with modelling examples. Finally, in Section 7, we summarise the paper and give suggestions for further research.

2 Architecture and Problems

2.1 Architectures for Application Integration

Integration of applications can be supported by many different architectures. One architecture for integrating applications is the point-to-point solution where every application is directly connected to every other application, see Fig. 2 (left). This solution could work for a small number of applications, but as the number of applications increases, the number of connections quickly becomes overwhelming. The Message Broker architecture reduces this complexity, see Fig. 2 (middle). The main idea is to reduce the number of interfaces by introducing a central Message Broker and thereby make it easier to support the interfaces. If one of the applications changes format, only one connection has to be changed: the one to the Message Broker, [26].

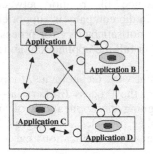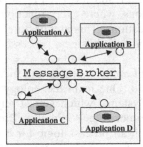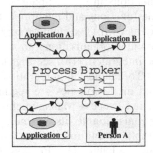

Fig. 1. The point-to-point strategy to integrate applications, to the left. In the middle the Message Broker architecture, which reduces the number of interfaces. To the right the Process Broker, which collect all process logic in the Broker.

The Process Broker, see Fig. 2 (right), is an extension of the Message Broker. In addition to handling format conversions, the Process Broker also encapsulates the process logic for connecting applications. When all process logic resides in one place, it becomes possible to study, analyse, and change the processes using a graphical interface, [5], [15], [27]. This visualisation reduces the complexity and enables different categories of people to take part in the process design.

2.2. Problems in Application Integration

The Process Broker technology requires methodological support so that designers can construct models that align the applications to the business processes. Experiences of a real world modelling study at a European telecommunication company demonstrate several problems when modelling application integration. The telecom company intended to handle an integration of applications by means of a Process Broker, which aimed at facilitating the complex interaction between administrative and technical applications. The problems we noticed can be summarised as follows:

Unstructured and complex models. Application integration often results in highly unstructured and complex models. One reason for this is that exception handling, which describes what to do when applications and human users do not respond in an expected way, makes up a large part of an application integration specification and thereby easily obscures the main business logic. Furthermore, there is often extensive communication between the Process Broker and different applications, which also tends to conceal the essential business logic.

Redundancy. The Process Broker does not maintain control over external applications, which means that these applications can be updated without the Broker being notified. As a consequence, it is often desirable to maintain redundant information that duplicates parts of the information in the external applications. This redundant information enables the Process Broker to maintain a complete, correct, and easily available record of its interactions with customers. However, this duplication of information requires mechanisms for handling possible inconsistencies.

Incomplete models. Since models for application integration tend to become large and complex, there is a risk that designers overlook parts of the models that are needed to maintain completeness and consistency.

Communication among stakeholders. It is possible to distinguish among four kinds of stakeholders: domain experts such as business managers, owners of external applications, business and technical designers, and operators that handle the day-to-day operations. Different stakeholders require different views of the system, while at the same time they need to be able to communicate with each other using common models and languages.

In the rest of the paper, we try to address these problems by proposing a set of design principles for application integration. We also introduce a process language called BML and argue that it facilitates communication between stakeholders. Table 1 summarises how the problems identified are addressed.

Table 1. The table shows in which section of the paper the identified problems are attended.

Problems:	Section 4: Choice of language: BML	Section 5.2: Process Classification	Section 6.1: View guidelines	Section 6.2: Completeness Guidelines
Unstructured and complex models		X	X	
Redundancy		X		
Incomplete models				X
Communication among stakeholders	X		X	

3 Related Work

In the beginning of the 90's process orientation became one of the most important trends in management practice as well as research. Authors such as Hammer and Davenport, [6], [14], advocated a radical change from a functional perspective to a process focussed perspective in order to improve customer satisfaction, shorten lead times, increase productivity, and handle technological development. Initially, process orientation achieved most attention in the manufacturing discipline, but in recent years it has also gained prominence in the information systems community, [12].

A number of languages and methodologies for process specification and design have been proposed. Many of these languages are based on Petri nets, [21], e.g. UML activity diagrams. A distinction can be drawn between *activity oriented* and *communication oriented* process languages. An activity oriented process language, e.g. UML activity diagrams or EPC, [23], is intended for handling arbitrary processes including material processes involving physical actions. Therefore, the activity oriented language diagrams usually represent a mix of automated and manual actions. A communication oriented language, on the other hand, focuses on communicative processes describing the interaction between people and systems in terms of sending and receiving messages, which provides an opportunity to support the communication by means of information technology. Communication oriented languages have been heavily influenced by speech act theory, [24]. One of the first systems based on a communication and speech act oriented approach was the Coordinator, developed by Winograd and Flores, [25], which supported the communication process in the work place. The idea of applying a speech act based approach to information systems analysis and design was also employed by the SAMPO (Speech-Act-based office Modelling aPprOach) project in the middle of the eighties, [3]. These ideas were further developed in recent work on Business Action Theory, [13], [17], and in the DEMO (Dynamic Essential Modelling of Organisations) approach, [7], [8]. We believe that a communication oriented approach is particularly suitable for application integration and Process Brokers, as application integration basically consists of the interchange of messages between systems and people.

A technology related to the Process Broker is the Workflow Management System, [16]. The first generation of Workflow systems, during the 80's and the early 90's, was supporting communication between people, concentrating on document routing. The next generation of Workflow technologies put the business processes in focus. By also involving automatic actors, the automation of the processes could be facilitated further, [18]. The next step for the Workflow systems should be to implement enterprise wide workflow solutions and provide tools for managing the processes themselves. This process management includes process modelling, process reengineering as well as process implementation and automation, [11], [27]. The Process Broker can be seen as this next step to process management, by providing modelling and simulation capabilities, but the Process Broker also enables rapid modifications of the business processes thanks to its flexible way of handling application integration.

In the marketplace, a new breed of middleware technologies focused on enterprise application integration has emerged. Message Broker vendors provide functionality that enable applications to interoperate with a minimum of custom coding. Some of the major products here are Viewlocity's AMTrix and SmartSync, [1], IBM's MQSeries Integrator, [19], and Entire Broker from Software AG, [9]. Several of the Message Broker vendors are adding process modelling and simulation capabilities to their products, thereby moving into the Process Broker market. Some of the major products in this market are: Viewlocity's SmartSync Model Manager [27], Extricity Software's AllianceSeries [10], Vitria Technology's BusinessWare [2], and HP's Changeengine [15].

4   BML – A Language for Application Integration

To visualise the application integration there is a need for a process description language. This section briefly introduces such a language, BML (Business Model Language), which is developed by Viewlocity, [27]. The language has similarities to SDL (Specification and Description Language), [4], but is more adapted to application integration. BML is a communication oriented process language, see Section 3, which means that it focuses on describing interaction between systems through the sending and receiving of messages. This makes the language suitable for application integration and Process Brokers. Another important advantage of BML is that the language can be used for the business specification and design as well as operation of systems. This means that the same language can be used in different phases of a system's life cycle: in feasibility analysis, in requirements specification, in the design and implementation phases, and even in the operation phase. This enables different categories of stakeholders to use the same language for different purposes. The language can also be used directly as an implementation language and to some extent replace ordinary programming language. Further advantages with BML are its capability to describe and partition the interaction and interfaces between processes that work concurrently. Concurrency is common in application integration, when for example several applications are to be updated in parallel. The possibility of partitioning in BML reduces the complexity of handling large systems, through creating manageable and understandable parts with limited dependencies.

BML can describe the structure as well as the behaviour of a system by using two kinds of graphical diagrams. The structure of the system is visualised by a static diagram, see Fig. 3, which describes the processes in a static mode. The static diagram describes the messages sent between the processes and between the processes and the environment, i. e. the external applications and people.

The dynamic behaviour of a system is described by using process diagrams, see Fig. 4. These diagrams can be seen as templates, visualising the order in which the messages shall be sent and received. For each process diagram there is a number of process instances, that are created during runtime. The process instances execute independently of each other, but can communicate by sending and receiving messages asynchronously. Each instance has an input queue, see down to the left in Fig. 4, where received messages are stored. A process instance can either be waiting in a stable state or perform a transition from one state to another. A transition is initiated when a message in the input queue is chosen and consumed.

Following the example in Fig. 4, the process instance starts in a Start state (circle without a name). Only the messages *m1* from *process a* and *m2* from *process c* can initiate a transition. The message *m1* is first in the queue and is therefore consumed, and the process instance performs a transition to the state *Wait for Event 1*. During the transition a message *m3* is sent to *process c*. Thereafter the message *m9* is first in the queue. Since only message *m5* can initiate a further transition from *Wait for Event 1*, the message *m9* is discarded. The next message in the queue is then *m5*, which can initiate a transition from *Wait for Event 1* to some other Wait for Event state (not specified in the example). During the transition data can be manipulated, decisions can be made, new process instances can be created and messages can be sent to other process instances or to the process instance itself.

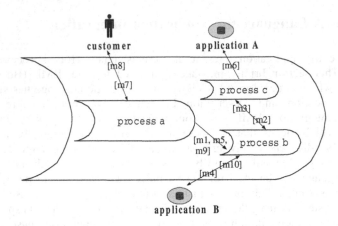

Fig. 2. The static diagram in BML visualises the structure of the processes in a system.

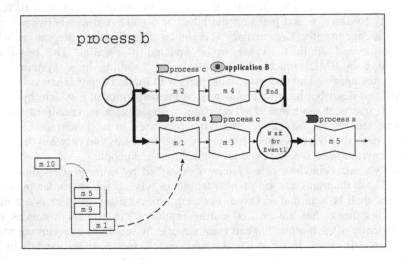

Fig. 3. A process instance with the input queue.

An important feature of BML is also the data model, which is not used in the examples of this paper. Each process diagram has a data model that describes the structure, type and meaning of the data that is handled in the diagram. The data model also describes the structure of the data in the different messages.

The main BML symbols are the following, see also Fig. 5:

Wait for Event and **Start.** The process instance is waiting in the Wait for Event state until a message is received or a timer has expired. A Wait for Event symbol without a name is the starting state.

End. Describes the end of the flow of the process instance.

Receive Message. Describes the consumption of a message from the input queue.

Send Message. Describes the sending of a message.

Automated Business Activity. Describes operations that will be performed on the process instance.

Automated Business Decision. The control flow is dynamically changed depending on different business rules.

Start Timer and **Expire Timer**. In application integration, the notion of time is important and timers occur frequently to obtain delays and supervision. When a timer is started it will be provided with a timeout value. The starting is represented by an hourglass "full of time", and the timeouts by an hourglass "out of time".

Application and **Human actor**. Both are symbols of external actors.

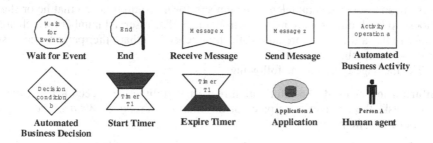

Fig. 4. Symbols used in BML

5 Classifications of Messages and Processes

5.1 A Classification of Messages

In this section, we introduce a classification of messages as a basis for formulating the design principles in Section 6. The classification is based on speech act theory. However, it is our experience that users often find it difficult to classify messages directly according to the basic speech act types. Therefore, we introduce a set of message types which are more closely related to the messages typically found in application integration.

The study of speech acts has been an active research area in analytical philosophy since World War II, and the most influential approach to date is speech act theory as developed by John Searle, [24]. Searle proposes a taxonomy for speech acts consisting of five classes: assertives, commissives, directives, declaratives, and expressives. These are also called the illocutionary points of a speech act. An assertive is a speech act, the purpose of which is to convey information about some state of affairs of the world from one agent, the speaker, to another, the hearer. An example is "It is raining". A commissive is a speech act, the purpose of which is to commit the speaker to carry out some action or to bring about some state of affairs. An example is "I promise to be at home before nine o'clock". A directive is a speech act, where the speaker requests the hearer to carry out some action or to bring about some state of affairs. An example is "Please bring me the salt". A declarative is a speech act, where the speaker brings about some state of affairs by the mere performance of the speech act. An example is "I hereby pronounce you husband and wife". An expressive is a speech act, the purpose of which is to express the speaker's attitude about some state of affairs. An example is "I like coffee".

Based on Searle's classification of speech acts, we give a list of message types below which frequently occur in application integration. The message types are requests for information and services and the responses to these requests. We also identify messages for reserving, booking, and releasing resources. The difference between reserving and booking is that reserving is a preliminary stage to booking. A reservation could either be followed by a booking or a cancelation of the reserved resource. The distinction is important if the system automatically should cancel reserved resources that not have been booked after a certain time. For example, a person can reserve several telephone numbers for a certain time, so that he or she can choose to book one or more numbers from them. The reserved numbers which are not booked after a time limit are automatically released so that other persons can reserve or book the numbers.

The message types are the following:

Information request. An information request is a directive speech act in which the sender asks the receiver for a piece of information. *Example: What is the telephone number to the help desk?*

Service request. A service request is a directive speech act in which the sender asks the receiver to carry out a service. Typical examples of services are to deliver a product, get an authorisation, and booking a resource. In contrast to an information request, a service request does not ask for information about a state of affairs – it requires a state of affairs to be changed. *Example: Provide me with a new telephone subscription.*

Reservation request. A reservation request is a special service request in which the sender asks the receiver to reserve a resource for a period of time, meaning that the resource cannot be reserved or booked by anyone else during this period of time. *Example: Reserve five different telephone numbers (which the customer can choose from).*

Booking request. A booking request is a special service request in which the sender asks the receiver to make a resource available for the sender. *Example: Book the telephone number that the customer has chosen.*

Information confirmation. An information confirmation is an assertive speech act in which the sender, in response to an information request, provides the receiver with a piece of information. *Example: The telephone number to the help desk is 07-70 70 70.*

Service confirmation. A service confirmation is an assertive speech act in which the sender, in response to a service request, informs the receiver that the required service has been carried out. *Example: You have been provided with a new telephone subscription.*

Reservation confirmation. A reservation confirmation is a special service confirmation in which the sender, in response to a reservation request, informs the receiver that the required reservation has been made. *Example: The telephone number is reserved (until the customer has chosen to book the number or a certain time limit has passed).*

Booking confirmation. A booking confirmation is a special service confirmation in which the sender, in response to a booking request, informs the receiver that the required booking has been made. *Example: The telephone number is booked.*

Service promise. A service promise is a commissive speech act in which the sender, in response to a service request, commits itself to carry out the required service. *Example: The delivery department promises to send the ordered telephone.*

Notification. A notification is an assertive speech act in which the sender informs the receiver about the changes of some state of affairs. *Example: The customer has started to use the subscription.*

Cancel reservation. A cancel reservation is a directive speech act in which the sender asks the receiver to cancel a previous reservation. *Example: Release a reserved number.*

Cancel booking. A cancel booking is a directive speech act in which the sender asks the receiver to cancel a previous booking. *Example: Release a booked number.*

5.2 A Classification of Processes

In this section, we introduce a classification of processes. The purpose is to support the designer in building well-structured and easily understandable application integration models. The classification identifies types of processes which are largely independent of each other and which can be combined with clear and simple interfaces. This makes it possible to partition a system of processes into manageable and understandable parts.

A starting point of the classification is the customer, an actor for whom a process is to create value. By emphasising the customer, we can distinguish between customer oriented processes that directly interact with the customer, processes that support the customer oriented processes in various ways, and processes that manage more technical and informational aspects.

The classification identifies the following types of processes:

Customer process. A customer process focuses on the interaction with the customer. A customer process may contain messages to or from a customer or another process types, but not to and from external actors, i.e. applications or people (except the customer). The purpose of a customer process is to show the business logic from the customer's point of view.

Interface process. An interface process handles the interaction with the external applications or people (except the customer). An interface process may contain messages to and from all other types of processes as well as to and from external applications and people. An interface process interacts with exactly one external application or person. The purpose of the interface processes is to insulate the interfaces of external applications from the main business logic. For example, when the format of messages sent from an external application changes, only the data model in the interface process has to be modified while the customer processes can be left untouched. There are two subtypes of interface processes:

Request process. A request process handles information or service requests from other processes.

Release process. A release process handles cancel reservations or cancel bookings from other processes.

Synchronisation process. A synchronisation process synchronises a number of interface processes. It may contain messages to and from different types of processes, but not from external applications and people. The purpose of a synchronisation process is to encapsulate a piece of business logic – typically a synchronisation process takes care of a request from a customer process by invoking and synchronising a number of interface processes.

Maintenance process. A maintenance process handles the internal storage of information that duplicates the information in external applications, see Redundancy in Section 2.2. There are two subtypes of maintenance processes:

Update process. An update process takes care of a notification from a customer or synchronisation process and stores the information carried by the notification.

Consistency process. A consistency process is a process that checks whether there is any inconsistency between internally stored information and information in external applications. A consistency process also takes appropriate action when an inconsistency is detected.

A typical structure of a model using the process classification is shown in Fig. 11. The customer process contains the main business logic with respect to the customer. It interacts with synchronisation processes and interface processes in order to take care of the customer's requests. It also sends notifications about the customer interaction to maintenance processes, not shown in Fig. 11. We believe that this structure supports flexibility, stability, and understandability by separating main business logic from more technical and informational aspects. By using the design principles of Section 6, designer will automatically arrive at an application integration model with the proposed structure.

6 Design Principles

In this section, we introduce a number of design principles in the form of guidelines for the design, validation, and presentation of application integration models. These guidelines are divided into two groups. The first group consists of guidelines to obtain different views of process models, while the second group consists of guidelines to check the completeness of process diagrams.

The main idea behind the guidelines in the first group, the view guidelines, is to obtain a series of views of processes starting with a customer oriented view on the business level. This first view means that the Process Broker can be seen as a mediator between the customer, i.e. the one for whom value is to be created, and a set of applications and people, see Fig. 6. Note that the customer does not communicate directly with the applications and other people, but only through the Process Broker.

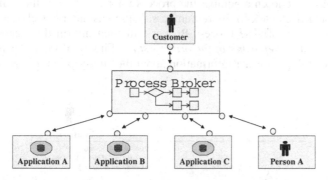

Fig. 5. The customer does not communicate directly with the applications and other people, but only through the Process Broker.

The succeeding views add more and more details moving from a business perspective to a more technical perspective. Each view is an extension of the previous one, either through adding subprocesses or through introducing new components into the existing diagrams. Note that the Process Broker contains all the modelled processes in the example, i. e. the Process Broker is the internal system, while the external system is the one represented by applications and people.

The purpose of the guidelines in the second group, the completeness guidelines, is to support the designer in creating processes that include complete discourse structures and not only fragments. In particular, the completeness guidelines can be used to ensure that requests are always handled in an appropriate way, and that outstanding bookings and reservations are taken care of in cases of exception.

6.1 View Guidelines

In this section, we present a number of views supporting a top-down approach. Each view is illustrated by means of a telephony case, in which a customer wants to order a subscription.

View 1. Customer interaction. This view models the interactions between the Process Broker and the customer, i.e. the messages exchanged by the customer and the Broker as well as the flow of control. In this view, there is only one process diagram.

The first tasks of the designer in this view are to clarify how the process is initiated, what messages the customer sends to the Process Broker, and what messages the Process Broker sends to the customer. Based on this information, the designer constructs a static diagram, see Fig. 7. The corresponding process diagram is shown in Fig. 8. The *Order subscription process* is initiated when it receives a message called *Order initiated* from the customer. Furthermore, the customer asks for a number of telephone number suggestions, *Request number proposals*. The answer from the Process Broker, is the message *Number proposals*. The customer can now choose one of the numbers or ask for further telephone number suggestions if he or she is not satisfied by those suggested. The receiving message from the customer, *Customer response,* is therefore evaluated in a decision point, *Nr chosen.* If the customer has not chosen a number the process instance follows the "false" path back and the customer can ask for more numbers. If the customer has chosen a number the order is taken care of. The Process Broker will then inform the customer about the status of the order, *Reporting of the order's state.* Finally, if the order is approved of, the customer will get further information about the subscription, *Information delivery.*

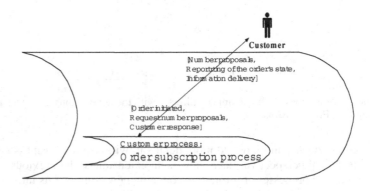

Fig. 6. The static diagram in view 1

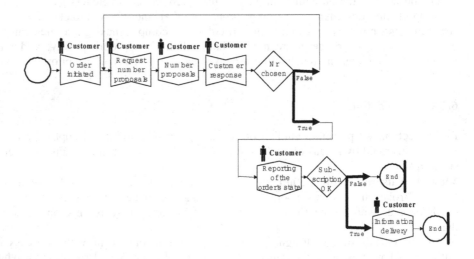

Fig. 7. The Order subscription process (view 1).

View 2. Broker requests. This view is an extension of view 1, which describes how the Process Broker produces the messages it sends to the customer. For each Send Message symbol from the Broker in view 1, a pair of one Send Message symbol and one Receive Message symbol is added.

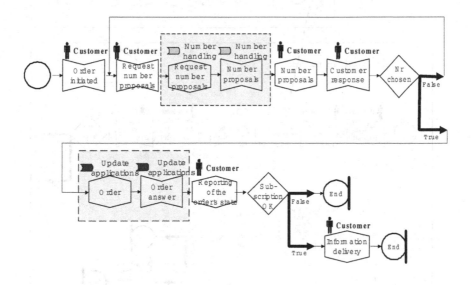

Fig. 8. The Order subscription process (view 2).

The first thing the designer must do when creating this view is to determine how the messages sent by the Process Broker are to be produced, which means that Send Message symbols in view 1 should be identified and analysed. Before the Send Message symbol *Number proposals* in Fig. 9, one Send Message symbol, *Request number proposals*, and one Receive Message symbol, *Number proposals*, are added, see symbols surrounded by the upper dotted box in Fig. 9. (Note that the dotted boxes are not part of the BML notation; they are used in the examples to help the reader identify the extensions for every new view introduced.) The Send Message and Receive Message symbols in the upper dotted box represent the messages sent to and received from a new subprocess, *Number handling process*. In view 2, the applications to be integrated are still not visible. They will become visible in the next view, where the introduced subprocesses are modelled.

View 3. External system interaction. Each subprocess introduced in view 2 is specified here. Only information and service requests and the responses to these are included in this view.

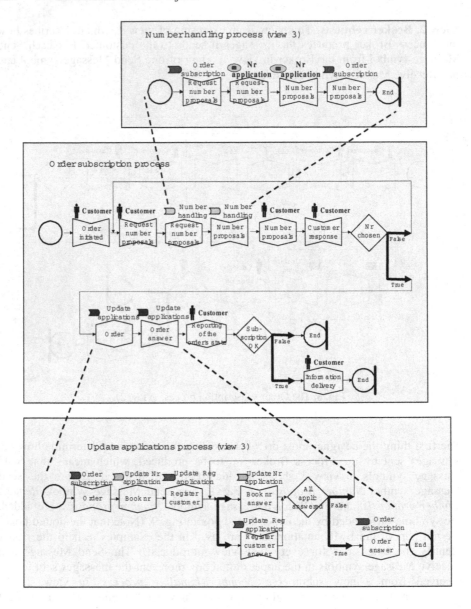

Fig. 9. Some of the process diagrams in view 3.

This view models the interaction with the applications to be integrated. In the simplest case, a subprocess is an interface process, i.e. it communicates with exactly one application, see Section 5.2. An example of an interface process is *Number handling process* at the top in Fig. 10, which makes a call to one application, *Nr application*, which returns an answer, *Number proposals*. The *Number handling process* finally forwards the answer to the process that invoked the subprocess, i.e. *Order subscription process*.

In some cases, it is convenient to introduce two or more levels of subprocesses. If the subprocess to be specified requires interaction with several applications, the designer should first construct a synchronisation process, see Section 5.2. The synchronisation process *Update applications process,* at the bottom in Fig. 10, invokes its own subprocesses and synchronises these. These subprocesses, *Update Nr application process* and *Update Reg application process,* and the relation to the synchronisation process, *Update application process*, are shown in the static diagram in Fig. 11. Each of the invoked subprocesses is an interface process and look like the interface process *Number handling process* in Fig. 10.

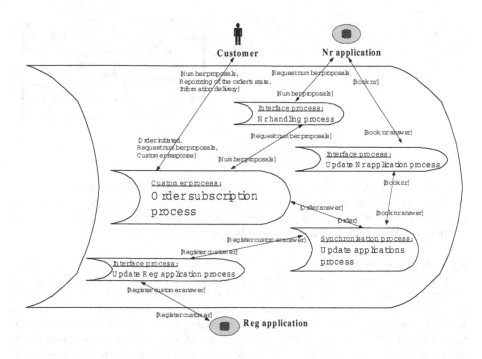

Fig. 10. The static diagram in view 3.

View 4. Exception handling. This view specifies the exception handling. For each Receive Message symbol, whose sender is an external application or a human actor, a Start timer and an Expire timer are added as well as the behaviour when the exception is raised, see dotted boxes a) and c) in Fig. 12.

Views 1 – 3 specify only the normal course of events. In view 4, the designer specifies how to handle exceptions, i.e. situations where an actor has not replied to a request within a pre-specified time limit. This means that the designer first has to extend all interface process diagrams by adding Start timers and Expire timers, as well as the behaviour after a timer has expired. Furthermore, the designer may have to extend the process diagrams at a higher level, i.e. the synchronisation or the customer processes, in order to describe how to handle error messages from the interface processes. An example of this is shown in Fig. 12, describing the interface process *Number handling process* which returns a message, *Number Proposals=*"*No answer in time*", to the *Order subscription process* when the timer has expired. The *Order subscription process* then has to handle the "No answer in time" message. Note that the timer symbols can only be found in the interface processes and sometimes in the customer process. The latter situation occurs if the designer wants the system to handle situations where the customer does not answer in time.

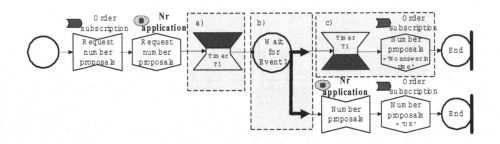

Fig. 11. The Number handling process (view 4).

In this view Wait for Event state symbols must also be added before every Receive Message symbol, see dotted box b) in Fig. 12. Note that before the first Receive Message symbol, *Request number proposal*, there is already a state symbol, the Start symbol. The Wait for Event and Start symbols are described in section 4.

View 5. Resource releasing. This view adds all messages of the type Cancel reservation and Cancel booking. When a process cannot be completed as intended, it becomes necessary to release the resources that have been reserved or booked during the process. This releasing of resources is handled in view 5 by extending the process diagrams accordingly by introducing certain release interface processes, see Section 5.2. In Fig. 13 the messages *Delete booking* and *Delete registration* are sent to the release interface processes *Delete Nr application process* and *Delete Reg application process,* see dotted box.

View 6. Notifications. This view adds all messages of the type Notification.

There are two main types of situations where notifications are required. First, when an exception has occurred, it is customary to inform an operator about this event so that he or she may take appropriate action. Secondly, a notification may be sent to a maintenance process, see Section 5.2, which redundantly stores information about essential states of affairs.

6.2 Completeness Guidelines

The completeness guidelines below exploit the fact that messages typically occur in certain dialogue structures. A very simple dialogue structure consists of a pair: a question followed by an answer. Another well-known dialogues structure is the conversation for basic action, introduced by Winograd and Flores in [25], which consists of the four steps: request, negotiation, fulfilment, and acknowledgement.

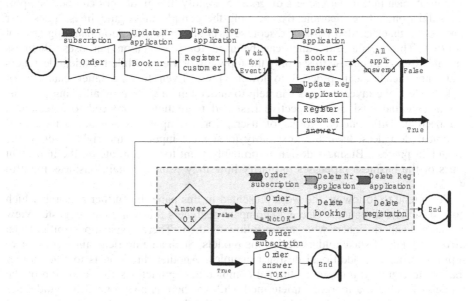

Fig. 12. The Update application process (view 5).

The following guidelines are a preliminary result of our research. Further research will produce additional guidelines.

1. In a process diagram, every information request and service request should be followed by a corresponding information confirmation or service confirmation, respectively. This pair of request and confirmation is optionally followed by a notification.
2. In a process diagram, every reservation request should be followed by a corresponding booking request by the same actor.
3. In a process diagram, every reservation request should be followed by a corresponding cancel reservation. A process instance typically takes this path when some intermediate request has not been satisfied.
4. In a process diagram, every booking request should be followed by a corresponding cancel booking. A process instance typically takes this path when some intermediate request has not been satisfied.

7 Concluding Remarks and Further Research

In this paper we have addressed methodological support for modelling the aligning of application integration to business processes. The main contribution is the guidelines introduced above which can be used in several ways. First, they can be used in design.

A designer could utilise the view guidelines by first constructing a process diagram according to view 1 and then gradually refine it until a set of diagrams in view 6 is obtained. Furthermore, the designer can use the completeness guidelines to guide the design of each individual process diagram. Secondly, the guidelines can be a support for validation and verification. By checking the completeness guidelines, a designer can ensure that essential parts of discourse structures and exception handling are not omitted. Thirdly, the guidelines can be used for presentation purposes. Business oriented users can choose to see only the top view or views, while technical designers and implementers can proceed to lower views. Even for the latter category of stakeholders, the layered views can help to understand a system by allowing to focus on an essential business perspective first and thereafter to proceed to a technical perspective. Different categories of users, for example customers, business and technical designers, have the possibility to suggest input on the right level in the modeling process. Business designers probably want to concentrate on the important parts of the business processes to clarify how they want the main business logic to work.

We intend to follow up the work presented in this paper by further research which goes in several directions. One is to compare designers following the suggested view guidelines with designers who are not following them. There is also a possibility to let different kinds of stakeholders design the models. Such an empirical study could give input to refined or additional design principles. Another direction is to find further dialog structures to produce additional completeness guidelines for validation of the models. To obtain a more complete methodology there is also a need for guidelines helping to design the data models, which describe the structure, type and meaning of the data beeing handled in the process.

Acknowledgements

This work was performed as part of the NUTEK (Swedish National Board for Industrial and Technical Development) sponsored project Process Broker [20]. The authors are grateful to Jan-Owe Halldén, Mikael Nilsson and Christer Wåhlander at Viewlocity for their valuable suggestions and knowledge. We also tank our colleagues at the Royal Institute of Technology, especially Birger Andersson, S.J. Paheerathan, Prasad Jayaweera, Nasrin Shakeri and Benkt Wangler for commenting earlier versions of this paper.

References

1. AMTrix. Viewlocity. URL: http://www.viewlocity.com/solutions/, 1999-11-25
2. Atwood, R.: Bringing Process Automation to Bear on the Task of Business Integration. Vitria Technology (1999). URL:
   http://www.vitria.com/products/whitepapers/ seyboldwp.html, 1999-11-25
3. Auramäki, E., Lehtinen, E., Lyytinen, K.: A Speech Act Based Office Modelling Approach. In: ACM Transactions on Office Information systems. Vol. 6, no. 2 (1988) 126-152
4. Belina, F., Hogrefe, D., Amardeo, S.: SDL with Applications from Protocol Specification. Carl Hanser Verlag and Prentice Hall International, UK (1991)

5. Butterworth, P.: Automating the Business Processes of Mission-Critical Distributed Applications. Forté Software (1997). URL: http://www.forte.com/product/downloads.html, 1999-10-04
6. Davenport, T.: Process Innovation: Reengineering work through information technology. Business School Press, Boston (1993)
7. Dietz, J.: Modelling Communication in Organizations. In: Riet R. v. d. (ed): Linguistic Instruments in Knowledge Engineering. Elsevier Science Publishers (1992) 131 - 142
8. Dietz, J.: Business Modeling for Business Redesign. In: proceedings of the 27th Hawaii International Conference on System Sciences. IEE Computer Society Press (1994) 723-732
9. Entire Broker. Software AG. URL: http://www.softwareag.com/corporat/solutions/applintegr/default.htm#b1, 1999-11-25
10. Extricity AllianceSeries. Extricity Software. URL: http://www.extricity.com/products/alli_series_over.html, 2000-02-21
11. Georgakopoulos, D., Hornick, M.: An Overview of Workflow management: From Process Modeling to Workflow Automation Infrastructure. In: Distributed and Parallel Databases, 3 (1995) 119-153
12. Green, P., Rosemann, M.: An Ontological Analysis of Integrated Process Modelling. In: proceedings of the 11th International Conference, CaiSE'99. Springer-Verlag, Heidelberg (1999) 225-240
13. Goldkuhl, G.: Generic Business Frameworks and Action Modelling. In: proceedings of conference Language/Action Perspective'96. Springer-Verlag (1996)
14. Hammer, M., Champy, J.: Reengineering the Corporation. A manifesto for Business revolution. New York (1993)
15. HP Changengine Overview. Hewlett Packard Company (1998). URL: http://www.ice.hp.com/ cyc/af/00/101-0110.dir/aovm.pdf, 1999-10-04
16. Jablonski, S., Bussler, C.: Workflow Management. Thomson, London (1996)
17. Lind, M., Goldkuhl, G.: Reconstruction of different Business Processes – A Theory and Method Driven Analysis. In: proceedings of Conference on Language/Action Perspective '97. Veldhoven (1997).
18. Makey, P. (ed): Workflow: Integrating the Enterprise. Butler Group report. Hessle (1996)
19. MQSeries Integrator, IBM. URL: http://www-4.ibm.com/software/ts/mqseries/, 1999-11-25
20. Process Broker architecture for system integration, Homepage of the Process Broker Project (1999). URL: http://www.dsv.su.se/~pajo/arrange/index.html, 1999-11-25
21. Reisig, W.: Petri Nets: an introduction. Springer-Verlag, Berlin (1985)
22. Riempp, G.: Wide Area Workflow Management: Creating Partnership for the 21st Century. Springer-Verlag (1998)
23. Sheer, A.: ARIS-Business Process Modelling. Springer-Verlag, Berlin (1998)
24. Searle, J.R.: Speech Acts – An Essay in the Philosophy of Language. Cambridge University Press (1969)
25. Winograd, T., Flores, F.: Understanding Computers and Cognition: A New Foundation for Design. Ablex, Norwood, N.J. (1986)
26. Yeamans, L.: Enterprise Application Integration. NSAG Inc. URL: http://www.messageq.com/EAI_survival.html, 1999-10-04
27. Wåhlander, C., Nilsson, M., Skoog, A.: Introduction to Business Model Language & SmartSync Model Manager, Copyright Viewlocity (1998)

CHAOS: An Active Security Mediation System

David Liu[1], Kincho Law[2], and Gio Wiederhold[1]

[1] Electrical Engineering Department, Stanford University, Stanford, CA
davidliu@stanford.edu
[2] Civil and Environmental Engineering Department, Stanford University, Stanford, CA
law@cive.stanford.edu
[3] Computer Science Department, Stanford University, Stanford, CA
gio@db.stanford.edu

Abstract. With the emergence of the Internet, collaborative computing has become more feasible than ever. Organizations can share valuable information among each other. However, certain users should only access certain portions of source data. The CHAOS (Configurable Heterogeneous Active Object System) project addresses security issues that arise when information is shared among collaborating enterprises. It provides a framework for integrating security policy specification with source data maintenance. In CHAOS, security policies are incorporated into the data objects as active nodes to form active objects. When active objects are queried, their active nodes are dynamically loaded by the active security mediator and executed. The active nodes, based on the security policy incorporated, can locate and operate on all the elements within the active object, modifying the content as well as the structure of the object. A set of API's is provided to construct more complex security policies, which can be tailored for different enterprise settings. This model moves the responsibility of security to the source data provider, rather than through a central authority. The design provides enterprises with a flexible mechanism to protect sensitive information in a collaborative computing environment.

1 Introduction

1.1 Security in Collaborative Systems

The emergence of Internet has greatly extended the scope of collaborative computing. Businesses share information to shorten their product development time; hospitals share information to provide better care to their patients [Rin+97]. However, collaborations pose extensive security problems. In fact, protecting proprietary data from unauthorized access is recognized as one of the most significant barriers to collaborative computing [HSRM96].

Software engineers have attempted to apply traditional security approaches to their specific collaborative computing paradigm. Encryption, firewalls, and passwords are used for secure transmission and storage of information [Den83]. User access rights are used in file systems to protect directories and files from unauthorized accesses [GS91]. These systems rely on domain access control for the security of their data and

B. Wangler, L. Bergman (Eds.): CAiSE 2000, LNCS 1789, pp. 232–246, 2000 focus on protecting systems from adversaries. However, they do not properly address the security issues in collaborative computing environments, where information needs to be selectively shared among different domains [JST95]. The following characteristics can be observed in a collaborative computing environment:

1. There is no clear enemy. Users access parts of the information sources. Unless information sources can be broken into small autonomous units, firewalls and passwords cannot provide the functionality needed. If the data sources are finely partitioned, their management becomes complex and difficult.

2. Typically, the information stored in an organization is not organized according to the needs of external accesses. It is in rare cases that security requirements can be properly aligned with organizational needs. For example, medical records are created and organized according to the patients in a hospital rather than according to doctors and staff on whom security clearance needs to be placed.

3. It is impossible to rigorously classify the data by potential recipients. For instance, a medical record on a cardiac patient can include notations that would reveal a diagnosis of HIV, so that this record should be withheld from cardiology researchers. A product specification may include cost of the components provided by suppliers, a competitive advantage that should be withheld from customers.

Ideally, collaborating enterprises would integrate their multiple existing relevant data sources and access them for specific collaborations as a single system. Such seamless interoperation is inhibited today by different protection requirements of the participating systems. Different systems, autonomously developed and managed, implement different access control policies and will impose different constraints to be satisfied before allowing participants access to data.

1.2 Security Mediator

Previous proposals address the problem within a federated database context, where a global schema, possibly under control of a central authority, is defined on the local data sources [Bel95, JD94, ON95, VS97]. Moreover, access control is generally assumed to be regulated by discretionary policies, where access decisions are taken with respect to authorizations stated by users. Mandatory security policies in distributed systems have been investigated, and some interoperation aspects have been addressed [GQ96, TR92].

Unfortunately, protection capabilities of current systems provide limited and little, if any, support for security of dynamic information. First of all, current DBMS work under the assumption that data are classified upon insertion, by assigning them the security level of the inserted subject. They provide no support for the re-classification of existing databases, when a different classification lattice and different classification criteria need to be applied [CFM+95, Lun+93]. Most approaches to managing security are static, where data structures, as columns and rows in relational databases are pre-classified to have certain types of access privileges. These systems presuppose a central model, in the hands of a database administrator [JL90].

To cope with security issues in dynamic collaborative computing environments, security mediators are introduced. Mediators [WG97] are intelligent middleware that sit between information system clients and sources. They perform functions such as integrating domain-specific data from multiple sources, reducing data to an appropriate level and restructuring the results into object-oriented structures. The mediators that are applied to security management are called *security mediators* [WBSQ96b]. An example of a security mediation system is the TIHI project [WBSQ96a], in which a rule system is used to automate the process of controlling access and release of information. Applicable rules are combined to form security policies, which are enforced by the mediator for every user. Results are released only if their contents pass all tests. This model (**Fig. 1**) formalizes the role of a mediation layer, which has the responsibility and the authority to assure that no inappropriate information leaves an enterprise domain.

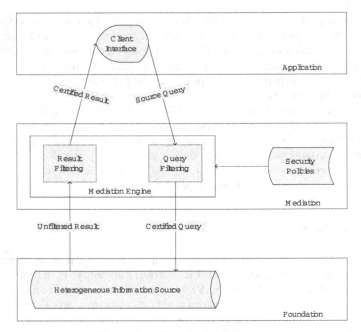

Fig. 1: Static Security Mediation

Security rules act like meta-data in a database. They are predefined by the security expert for the system and are applied to data items that are returned from the queries. Since all rules are statically specified and checked, we call this type of system *static security mediation* system. In such systems, there is a security officer whose responsibility is to implement and control the enterprise policies set for the security mediator. Databases and files within the domain provide services and meta-data to help the activities of the security mediator.

While static security mediation addresses a broad range of security issues in collaborative computing, it suffers certain shortcomings that motivate the proposed approach to move security policies from the mediation layer to the foundation layer and to give more flexibility in specifying security policies.

First of all, in many scenarios, it is natural to have the information source set and manage its own security policy. A heterogeneous information system may organize its source data as information islands, and each island is maintained distinctively from the others. This organization is becoming more pervasive for Internet services. We observe that source data maintenance and security policy specification are tightly related in these situations. When source data get updated, especially when their data structure changes, the related security policies may need to be modified accordingly.

Secondly, it is difficult to design a rule base security mediator that fits a broad range of heterogeneous information systems. Enterprise security policies are specified in terms of the primitive rules predefined for the static mediation system, making it difficult to develop a comprehensive set of rules that can be effectively combined to satisfy a very broad range of security needs.

Generally, rules are best applied to relational databases since they are defined on table schemas. In the case of unstructured data that lack a predefined schema, rules are difficult to apply. Furthermore, acting as meta-data in a database, rules act on tables. They are most suited to filter out rows of data entries, but lack the capability to prune the structure of the result entries to allow partial access to the data. Traditional view based access control system [GW76] could be used to amend this deficiency. Separate views can be constructed for each partial structure while appropriate access rights can be assigned to each view. However, this approach is similar to that of domain access control. Managing views and maintaining their secret labels become very complex as the system grows [WBSQ96b].

1.3 Active Security Mediation

We propose a solution to these problems in CHAOS. We define a special type of objects, *active objects*, which incorporate security policies into data objects as *active nodes*. Rather than treating rules as meta-data acting on tables, we enforce security by invoking functions contained in active nodes that act on data objects. The design of CHAOS is schematically shown in **Fig. 2**.

In CHAOS, each information source is treated as an information island that has its own access control policies. An incoming client query request is first checked by a Query Filtering module, where unauthorized request to the heterogeneous system are denied. The Query Planner and Query Dispatcher modules are in place to decompose a client query into source queries that individual heterogeneous sources can answer. The methods of query transformation belong to a different scope of schema integration, hence are not discussed in detail here. Upon receiving query requests from the mediation layer, the foundation layer sources fetch the query results, wrap them as active objects, and pass the active objects onto the mediation layer. The Result Filtering module will interpret encapsulated active nodes and translate active objects into regular data objects before passing them onto the client.

In the TIHI model [WBSQ96a], it is assumed that the people controlling the sources do not care much about security. That is true for many medical doctors, who willingly share data and do not realize how far the data might spread and embarrass the patients. When private information gets leaked, it is the institution, as the holder of the data, who assumes the responsibility. In the CHAOS model the assumption is that the owners of the data care about the security of the data, often for competitive business reasons, sometimes perhaps even being competitive within an institution. This model fits those institutions that delegate much authority to enterprise units.

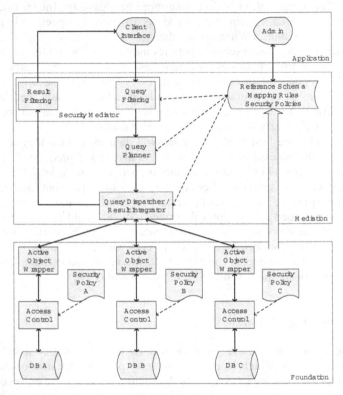

Fig. 2: CHAOS Active Security Mediation

By incorporating active nodes into data objects, we provide a tight integration between security policy specification and source data maintenance. Each data object has a clear view of all policies that are applicable to it. Furthermore, security policies can be applied to individual data objects, providing a fine grain of control. We use Java as the active node specification language, giving greater expressive power to the security system. For the ease of system configuration and maintenance, we provide an extendible set of API's that allow more complex policies to be composed. At the same time, unlike static security mediation system where policies are solely based on primitive rules, CHAOS does not place any restriction on whether active nodes use API's to manipulate their objects.

2   CHAOS System Design

2.1   Active Object

Objects are used as the basic data model to describe source data in the CHAOS. Most clients are best served by information in object-oriented form that may integrate multiple heterogeneous sources [PAGM96]. Specifically, in CHAOS, data are represented in XML[1]. Such choice is made because of XML's nature of extensibility, structure, and validation as a language. However, the concept and our system design can be easily extended to other data models. In subsequent section we show a sample application of the CHAOS system architecture that uses a relational database as the source data repository.

XML is a meta-markup language that consists of a set of rules for creating semantic tags used to describe data. An XML element is made up of a start tag, an end tag, and content in between. The start and end tags describe the content within the tags, which is considered the value of the element. In addition to tags and values, attributes are provided to annotate elements. In essence, XML provides the mechanism to describe a hierarchy of elements that forms the object.

Active object is a special type of XML object. In active objects, two types of elements are defined: data elements and *active elements*. A data element, like any regular XML elements, describes the content of an object; an active element, on the other hand, no longer describes the content of an object but rather contains the name of an *active node* that operates on the object and generates the content. We use attributes to identify active elements by setting their *active-node* attribute to *true*.

2.2   Active Element

Each active element contains one *active node*, a Java class that will be interpreted by the mediator runtime environment. Java[2] is chosen as the function description language because of Java's support for portability, its flexibility as a high-level language, and its support of dynamic linking/loading, multi-threading and standard libraries.

All active nodes are derived classes of *ActiveNode* (See Appendix A.1), and they overload the *execute* function to provide specific functionality. The *execute* function takes three parameters: the current active element handle, the root element handle, and the client environment information. The mediator runtime environment fills in these three parameters when the mediator loads the active nodes during the runtime.

Java Project X[3], a Java based XML service library package, is preloaded into the CHAOS security mediator runtime environment. The package provides core XML capabilities including a fast XML parser with optional validation and an in-memory object model tree that supports the W3C DOM Level 1 recommendation[4]. Using the

---

[1] For details about XML, go to http://www.w3.org/XML/.

[2] For details about Java, go to http://www.javasoft.com.

[3] For details about Java Project X, go to http://developer.java.sun.com/developer/products/xml.

[4] For details about document object model, go to http://www.w3.org/DOM.

API's provided by the package, we can parse XML documents, query elements in an XML object, and modify the content and structure of the object.

In order for active nodes to interact with data elements in an active object, a mechanism is needed to locate all elements. We employ the concept of label path [GW97] from the LORE [MAG+97] project and define *tag path*:

Definition: A tag path of an element e_0 is a sequence of one or more dot-separated tags, $t_1(s_1).t_2(s_2)...t_n(s_n)$, such that we can traverse a path of n elements $e_1, e_2, ..., e_n$ from e_0 where node e_i is the child of e_{i-1} and is the s_i-th child that has the tag t_i. In case where s_i is not specified, its default value is 1.

With the tag path definition, active nodes can uniquely locate an element *e* by specifying the root element of the object and a tag path that traverse from the root element to *e*. All elements within an active object can be reached and manipulated by the active nodes that are contained in the object. In the cases where multiple active objects are to be manipulated by a common active node, the active objects can be combined together to form a larger object such that a common root element can be provided to the *execute* function.

The CHAOS system provides a set of *ActiveNode* API's. Elements within an active object can be queried, structure of an active object can be altered, and statistical information about an active object or an element can be generated. Based on these API's, more complex functionality can be constructed. As opposed to static mediation system, where policies are constructed based on primitive rules, *ActiveNode* API's place no limitation on how the policies can be constructed. The API's are provided merely for convenience rather than for restriction.

With multiple active nodes in an active object, the order in which they are executed may affect the final mediated result. CHAOS adopts a depth first ordering approach in loading and interpreting active elements within an active object.

2.3 Security Mediator

Security mediator is the component in CHAOS where client source query is parsed and certified, active objects are queried and interpreted, and mediated results are returned. As shown in **Fig. 3**, a security mediator is composed of two main modules: Query Filtering and Result Filtering. In addition, an exception-handling module is inserted in case abnormal system behavior occurs.

Query Filtering Module
A Query Filtering module deals with parsing and certifying incoming query request to the heterogeneous source. The Client Environment Handling component customizes the active security runtime environment depending on specific client. Client environment information is put into a system defined *ClientEnv* object, which will be passed onto Query Certification and Active Node Invocation Components. Similar to the TIHI system, the mediator processes the incoming query and checks for its validity. The Query Certification components can look up a static table of rules. Based on the incoming query request and client environment information, it

restructures and forwards the query to the underlying heterogeneous information source.

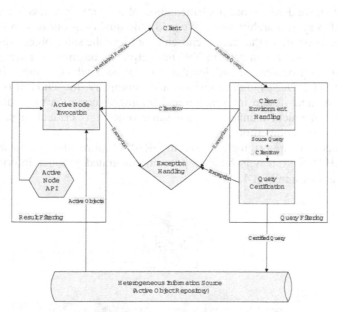

Fig. 3: Active Security Mediator Architecture

Result Filtering Module
The core of the Result Filtering module is the Active Node Invocation component. For all the incoming active objects, the component identifies the active nodes in an object and dynamically loads in the appropriate encapsulated active nodes. Active nodes are invoked by calling their *execute* function with parameters assembled by the mediator. Active nodes will operate on the active objects that contain them. The resulted objects will be forwarded to the client. An Active Node API library is provided to facilitate security policy construction. As indicated in the previous section, all active nodes are derived from *ActiveNode* class. Useful functions and class definitions are put in the *ActiveNode* class. They can be accessed as API's through *ActiveNode*'s method interface. The library is preloaded into the mediator for dynamic linking and invocation by active nodes.

Exception Handling
It is critical for the system to have a comprehensive exception handling policy. Our current implementation prohibits any results from getting through the mediator in the case of exception. In addition, the conditions are logged for future maintenance.

3 System Implementation

In this section, we describe our implementation of a sample business inventory system using CHAOS system architecture. We study the quality of our design by comparing it with other alternatives that can be chosen to achieve the same objectives.

In order to better compete in the marketplace, businesses have the need to streamline their procurement and distribution processes which requires integration of all relevant data. Our example considers a PC company, for whom it is important to deliver the product design information and pricing information to its distributor in a timely and convenient manner. At the same time, it is critical to protect its cost structure from the competitors.

The source data are originally stored in ORACLE, a relational database, on top of which a CHAOS system is built to provide integrated product information. The schemas are shown in **Fig. 4**.

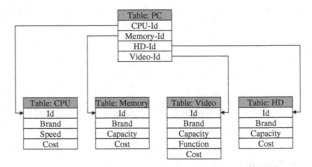

Fig. 4: Relational Schemas for an Inventory Database

In a heterogeneous information system, no particular data model can be assumed for the original information source. Using XML, however, we can pack heterogeneous data into uniform logical objects. Integrating heterogeneous information is a research issue that is addressed in [PAGM96, GW97]. Necessary mediators are added to perform the data conversion. Therefore, we treat the heterogeneous information source in CHAOS as an active object repository. All source data are converted into active objects before they are exchanged between the foundation layer and the mediation layer of the information system. Necessary mediators are added to perform the data conversion.

For our example, relational data stored in ORACLE database are converted into active objects. Together with regular data elements, active elements are assembled to form active objects. **Fig. 5** shows a sample active object that is assembled by a source mediator that queries the relational information source.

There are two active nodes contained in the active object: *price* and *security1*, which will be dynamically loaded and interpreted by the security mediator when the object is passed through the security mediator. The price information will be generated by the active node *price*, and security will be enforced by the active node *security1*. Both *price* and *security1* are written in Java (See Appendix A.2) and are based on the *ActiveNode* API's provided by the system.

```
- <PC>
  - <CPU>
      <Brand>P II</Brand>
      <Speed>400</Speed>
      <Cost>190</Cost>
    </CPU>
  - <Memory>
      <Brand>Micron</Brand>
      <Capacity>64MB</Capacity>
      <Cost>100</Cost>
    </Memory>
  - <HD>
      <Brand>Seagate</Brand>
      <Capacity>9.1GB</Capacity>
      <Cost>150</Cost>
    </HD>
  - <Video>
      <Brand>Diamond</Brand>
      <Capacity>32MB</Capacity>
      <Function>AGP 4x</Function>
      <Cost>190</Cost>
    </Video>
    <Price active-node="yes">price</Price>
    <Security active-node="yes">security1</Security>
  </PC>
```

Fig. 5: Sample Active Object

The active node *price* sums up the cost of all elements and then multiply the cost by a factor (here specified as *1.2*). Effectively, active nodes provide a simple mechanism to specify derived data, thereby maintaining data dependency among various components in an object. To achieve the same objective with traditional database system designs, few other alternatives can be considered, each with certain drawbacks. A database update program can be run on top of a relational database to maintain the data dependency. However it is extremely difficult if not impossible to determine the optimal update frequency. As an alternative, every client application can embed a procedure that updates the database on queries. Obviously, this approach is a software engineering nightmare. Active database systems [Day88] could also be considered to address this issue. These systems integrate production rules facility into the conventional database systems. Production rules can be considered as the bonding between the data and the functions in a database system. However, data are required to be migrated into a single active database, a very difficult process for heterogeneous data sources. With active objects, such migration is not needed.

The responsibility of the active node *security1* for the active object shown in **Fig. 5** is to filter the information and reshape the structure of the active object based on the client that makes the query. For different clients, certain information needs to be withheld. Only internal users are granted the access to the cost structure of any product. Specified in the active node *security1*, if the client is not an *internal* user, the *Cost* elements of all components will be trimmed, hence withholding the confidential information.

Comparing to a view based access control system, an alternative to address the partial data access issue, CHAOS is cleaner and more flexible. In a view based access control system, different views need to be specified, each with a different schema. For two different user groups, that may not seem to be a great challenge. However, maintenance of views and their secret labels can quickly become a significant management problem when the complexity of the security needs grows. For example, if we want to change the security policy to allow each procurement department access to the cost information of their own components but not the cost information of the other components, four more views need to be specified and maintained. Whereas in CHAOS, no separate views need to be constructed. The information source can specify the policy for partial access to its content by adding few more clauses in the active node *security1*.

The results for different client queries are shown in **Figure 6** and **Figure 7**. The internal result is generated by a query submitted by a client who belongs to the *internal* clique. All component information and pricing information are returned in the result object. In addition, the active node *security1* adds a time-stamp element to the object. The external result is generated for an *external* client. Comparing to the internal result, external result does not contain any component cost information, which is pruned by the active node.

Fig. 6: internal Result   Fig. 7: external Result

4 Conclusion

The CHAOS system provides a framework for integrating security policy maintenance with data source maintenance. Active nodes are incorporated into the data objects of which they control the security policy. They can locate and operate on all elements within the active object, modifying the data content and the structure of the object. This approach moves the responsibility for security to the source provider, rather than through a central authority.

We would like to emphasize that there are many fundamental differences between CHAOS and view-based access control approach:

1. View-based approach is mostly adopted in the presence of structured data sources, in particular relational data source. In the case of unstructured data that lack a predefined schema, view-based approach is not applicable. CHAOS, on the other hand, does not depend on a predefined schema. It is applicable to all types of data sources.

2. In view-based approach, policies are specified on table, defining the actions of columns of data. In CHAOS, policies are specified on individual data object level, providing a finer grain of control.

3. Views-based approach predefines the structure of a view. The structure of a view is not modifiable once it is defined. CHAOS allows ActiveNode to dynamically modify the structure of an active object.

4. By incorporating active nodes into data objects, CHAOS provides a tight integration between security policy specification and source data maintenance. Each data object has a clear view of all policies that are applicable to it.

Unlike rule based security systems, policies in CHAOS are specified in a general programming language. The system does not need to rely on an initial set of primitive rules to be functional. We provide a set of API's that can be used to construct more complex and powerful policies. These API's are provided for mere convenience and can be expanded. This approach offers much greater flexibility.

Similar to most security measures, the active security mediation does not offer 100% guarantee. It is restrained by the quality of the system design and the implementation of the policies. However, it provides a clear, simple and powerful mechanism to carry out enterprise policies effectively.

Acknowledgements

This work is partly supported by the Center for Integrated Facility Engineering at Stanford University, by the National Science Foundation under grant ECS-94-22688, and by DARPA/Rome Laboratory under contract F30602-96-C-0337. The authors would also like to acknowledge a "Technology for Education 2000" equipment grant from Intel Corporation in support of the research.

References

[Bel95]   Steven M. Bellovin. Security and Software Engineering. In *B.Krishnamurthy, editor: Practical Reusable UNIX Software*. John Wiley & Sons, 1995.

[CFM+95]   S. Castano, M.G. Fugini, G. Martella and P. Samarati. Database Security. Addison-Wesley, 1995.

[Day88]   U. Dayal. Active Database Management Systems. In *Proceedings of the Third International Conference on Data and Knowledge Bases*, 1988.

[Den83]   Dorothy E. R. Denning. Cryptography and Data Security. Addison-Wesley, Reading, MA, 1983.

[GS91]   Simson Garfinkel and Gene Spafford. Practical Unix Security. O'Reilly and Associates, Inc., 1991.

[GQ96]   L. Gong and X. Qian: Computational Issues in Secure Interoperation. *IEEE Transactions on Software Engineering*, IEEE, January 1996.

[GW76]   P. P. Griffiths and B. W. Wade. An Authorization Mechanism for a Relational Database System. *ACM Transactions on Database Systems*, 1(3):243-255, Sept. 1976.

[GW97]   Roy Goldman and Jennifer Widom. Dataguides: Enabling Query Formulation and Optimization in Semistructured Databases. *VLDB Conference*, 1997.

[HSRM96]   Martin Hardwick, David L. Spooner, Tom Rando, and K.C. Morris. Sharing Manufacturing Information in Virtual Enterprises. *Comm. ACM*, 39(2):46-54, Feb. 1996.

[JD94]   D. Jonscher and K.R. Dittrich. An Approach for Building Secure Database Federations. In *Proc. of the 20th VLDB Conference*, 1994.

[JL90]   Sushil Jajodia and Carl E. Landwehr: Database Security IV: Status and Prospects. North-Holland, 1990.

[JST95]   D. Randolph Johnson, Fay F. Sayjdari, and John P. Van Tassell. Missi Security Policy: A Formal Approach. Technical Report R2SPO-TR001-95, National Security Agency Central Service, July 1995.

[Lun+93]   Luniewski, A. et al. Information Organization Using Rufus. *ACM SIGMOD*, Washington DC, May 1993. pp. 560-561.

[MAG+97]   J. McHugh, S. Abiteboul, R. Goldman, D. Quass, and J. Widom. Lore: A Database Management System for Semistructured Data. *SIGMOD Record*, 26(3):54-66, Sept. 1997.

[ON95]   YongChul Oh and Shamkant Navathe. Seer: Security Enhanced Entity-Relationship Model for Secure Relational Databases. In *Papazoglou (ed.): OOER'95*, Springer LCNS 1021, 1995, pp.170-180.

[PAGM96]   Y. Papakonstantinou, S. Abiteboul, and H. Garcia-Molina. Object Fusion in Mediator Systems. *VLDB Conference*, 1996.

[Rin+97]   David M. Rind et al.: Maintaining the Confidentiality of Medical Records Shared over the Internet and the World Wide Web. *Annals of Internal Medicine*, Vol.15 No.127, July 1997, pp.138-141.

[TR92]   B. Thuraisingham and H.H. Rubinovitz. Multilevel Security Issues in Distributed DBMS III. *Computer & Security*, 11:661-674, 1992.

[WBSQ96a]   Gio Wiederhold, Michel Bilello, Vatsala Sarathy, and XiaoLei Qian. Protecting Collaboration. In *Proceedings of the NISSC'96 National Information Systems Security Conference*, pages 561-569, Oct. 1996.

[WBSQ96b]   Gio Wiederhold, Michel Bilello, Vatsala Sarathy, and XiaoLei Qian. A Security Mediator for Healthcare Information. In *Proceedings of the 1996 AMIA Conference*, pages 120-124, Oct. 1996.

[WG97]   Gio Wiederhold and Michael Genesereth. The Conceptual Basis for Mediation Services. *IEEE Expert, Intelligent Systems and their Applications*, 12(5), Oct. 1997.

[VS97]   S. De Capitani di Vimercati and P. Samarati. Authorization Specification and Enforcement in Federated Database Systems. *Journal of Computer Security*, 5(2):155-188, 1997.

Appendix

A.1 Sample ActiveNode API

```
public class ActiveNode
{
    /*
     * Entry point, needs to be overloaded
     */
    public String execute(Element current, Element root,
                          ClientEnv env);

    /*
     * Query elements within an active object
     */
    protected Node getNode(Element root, String path);
    protected String getString(Element root, String path);
    protected int getInt(Element root, String path);

    /*
     * Manipulate structure of an active object
     */
    protected Node removeNode(Element root, String path);
    protected void removeAllNode(Element root, String tag);
    protected void appendNode(Element root, String path,
                              Node child);
    protected void appendNode(Element root, String path,
                              Node child);

    /*
     * Miscellaneous statistical functions
     */
    protected int sumAllNodes(Element root, String tag);
    protected int getNumChildren(Element root, String tag);

    /*
     * Utility functions
     */
    protected void initLog(boolean onoff);
    protected void log(String msg);
}
```

A.2 Sample Active Nodes

Active Node *price*

```
public class price extends ActiveNode
{
    public String execute(Element current, Element root,
                          ClientEnv env)
    {
        int cost = sumAllNodes(root, "Cost");

        return String.valueOf(1.2 * cost);
    }
}
```

Active Node *security1*

```
public class security1 extends ActiveNode
{
    public String execute(Element current, Element root,
                          ClientEnv env)
    {
        /* Check the clearance of the client */
        if (!env.Clique().equals("internal")) {
            removeAllNodes(root, "Cost");
        }

        /* Add a time stamp to the object.  */
        createTextElement(root,
                          "",
                          "TimeStamp",
                          new Date().toString());

        return "checked for " + env.Clique();
    }
}
```

Modeling and Composing Service-Based and Reference Process-Based Multi-enterprise Processes

Hans Schuster, Dimitrios Georgakopoulos, Andrzej Cichocki, and Donald Baker

MCC, 3500 West Balcones Center Drive, Austin, Texas 78759
{schuster, dimitris, andrzej, dbaker}@mcc.com

Abstract. *Multi-enterprise processes* (MEPs) are workflows consisting of a set of activities that are implemented by different enterprises. Tightly coupled Virtual Enterprises (VEs) typically agree on abstract MEPs (*reference MEPs*), to which each enterprise contributes *single-enterprise processes* (SEPs) that implement and refine the activities in the reference MEP. On the other end of the spectrum, loosely coupled VEs use *service-based MEPs* that fuse together heterogeneous *services* implemented and provided by different enterprises. Existing process models usually couple activities with their implementation. Therefore, they cannot effectively support such MEPs. In this paper, we introduce a *Polymorphic Process Model* (PPM) that supports both reference process- and service-based MEPs. To accomplish this, PPM decouples *activity interface* from *activity implementation*, and provides process *polymorphism* to support their mapping. In particular, PPM determines activity types from the activity interfaces, permits activity interface subtyping, and provides for the mapping of MEP activity types to concrete implementations via interface matching. We illustrate that these key PPM capabilities permit the late binding and use of multiple activity implementations within a MEP without modifying the MEP at run time or enumerating the alternative implementation at specification time.

1 Introduction

A *Virtual Enterprise* (VE) appears like a traditional enterprise to its customers but provides services and products that rely on the core business processes and the resources of multiple constituent enterprises. The enterprises that comprise a VE may be participating in a long-term strategic alliance or collaborate only for the duration of one electronic commerce transaction. Just like traditional enterprises, VEs realize business objectives by defining and implementing (multi-enterprise) business processes. These are abstract process descriptions, consisting of a set of activities that must be performed by the members of the VE.

Multi-enterprise business processes are implemented by multi-enterprise workflow processes we refer to as *multi-enterprise processes* (MEPs). Unlike traditional workflow processes where all activities are implemented by the same enterprise, each enterprise in a VE implements only a subset of the MEP activities. Furthermore, the same MEP activity may be implemented by multiple enterprises, and the provider of the implementation of this MEP activity may vary in different instances of the same MEP. Finally, each participating enterprise may have multiple implementations of the same MEP activity. For example, a telecommunications service provider implements

B. Wangler, L. Bergman (Eds.): CAiSE 2000, LNCS 1789, pp. 247-263, 2000
© Springer-Verlag Berlin Heidelberg 2000

an activity informing the customer that the service has been established. The provider may have multiple implementation alternatives for this activity, including notify the customer by phone, mailing a letter, sending a fax or email.

Current workflow models [10, 13, 16] couple activities with their implementation. This is similar to a procedure call in a traditional programming language. Therefore, when designing a process consisting of activities that have multiple implementations, the process designer has to choose one of the alternative implementations. However, this precludes the use of any other implementation of the same activity that may be more appropriate in another processes instance or another part of the process that repeats this activity. For example, the method of notifying a client that the requested service has been performed may depend on the client's location, time of the day, cost, etc. To permit alternative implementations the designers of traditional workflow processes often expand each activity to a subprocess that captures all possible implementation alternatives as separate activities and allows choice of implementation via decision activities, normal control, and data flow. This solution introduces additional activities in the original process and the structure of the resulting process will differ significantly from the business process it implements. Therefore, this solution complicates the maintenance of the business process as it evolves and additional activity implementations become available.

These problems are alleviated in VEs that use *reference processes*. Such processes typically capture standard business activities within a certain industry, such as telecommunications [15]. A reference process is public and its purpose is to specify how multiple enterprises can work together. Therefore, reference processes provide activity decomposition and coordination "guidelines" that improve the ability of enterprises to form effective VEs. At the same time, each participating enterprise maintains considerable flexibility in determining how to implement activities in a reference process. The implementation of such a reference MEP must be able to hook up the various heterogeneous implementations of its activities as provided by the participating enterprises. In situations where the enterprises that participate in a VE maintain their autonomy to a level that reference MEPs cannot be used, the participating enterprises usually provide *services* that are not targeted to a specific MEP, i.e., they are implemented and maintained in isolation. In this case, service-based MEPs must integrate these heterogeneous services, e.g., as proposed in [4].

In this paper we introduce a *Polymorphic Process Model* (PPM) that generalizes the process model presented in [4]. PPM supports both service- and reference process-based MEPs. To accomplish this, PPM decouples *activity interface* from *activity implementation*. This permits PPM activity types to be determined by the activity interfaces. Activity interfaces are modeled as state machines that include application-specific operations and states, and have input/output parameters. Application-specific operations provide an abstraction of an activity's behavior, while application-specific states provide an abstraction of the activity state resulting from the execution of the activity operations or internal processing. In addition, activity interfaces allow (abstract) activity types to be mapped to concrete activity implementations by matching their interfaces. To support such mappings PPM introduces process *polymorphism*. This includes a mechanism for activity interface subtyping and a mechanism for late binding that enables the use of multiple implementations within a process without modifying this process at run time or enumerating the alternative implementation at specification time. These permit supporting MEPs in both reference process- and service-based VEs.

The rest of this paper is organized as follows: In the following section, we present examples of MEPs using a reference process and services and discuss key requirements for their modeling, implementation, and enactment. Section 3 introduces activity types and interfaces. The mapping of activity interfaces that provides the basis for developing interchangeable implementations of abstract activities is discussed in Section 4. Activity polymorphism is discussed in Section 5. Section 6 gives an overview on related work. Conclusions are presented in Section 7.

2   Multi-enterprise Processes

To illustrate key requirements in supporting *multi-enterprise processes* (MEPs), we describe two alternative MEPs for universal telecommunications service provisioning: *reference process-based MEPs* and *service-based MEPs*. We illustrate that these MEPs can satisfy the requirements of virtual telecommunications enterprises using contrasting business models. In particular, we first introduce a *reference process-based MEP*. Such MEPs are appropriate for tightly coupled VEs where participating enterprises internally employ business models and corresponding core processes (*single-enterprise processes*, or SEPs), that are designed to accommodate each other. This is accomplished by agreeing on abstract VE processes, or *reference MEPs*, to which each enterprise contributes SEPs that implement and refine its (abstract) activities. Reference process-based MEPs are appropriate for relatively long-lived VEs with cooperating partners that are willing to adapt their SEPs to implement the parts of the MEP reference processes they are supposed to perform. An example of reference process-based MEP is discussed in Section 2.1.

The contrasting solution to reference process-based MEPs are *service-based MEPs*. These are appropriate for loosely-coupled VEs, i.e., VEs consisting of enterprises that want to hide their internal SEPs from their partners in the VE and cannot (or choose not to) introduce changes to their SEPs. Therefore, service-based MEPs are appropriate for relatively short-lived VEs, such as those that last only for the duration of a single electronic commerce transaction, and VEs consisting of competitors that occasionally join forces. An example of service-based MEP is described in Section 2.2. In this paper we do not discuss VEs using MEPs that combine both reference processes and services. Such MEPS must address the combination of the problems described in this paper.

2.1   Reference Process-Based MEP

A reference MEP is a process that consists of abstract subprocesses, i.e., subprocesses that lack implementation. The abstract subprocesses and the MEP process itself are implemented by SEPs provided by the enterprises in the VE.

As an example of a reference MEP consider a universal telecommunications service provisioning process that allows clients to request local, long distance, wireless, and internet service from a *universal service provider*. This reference MEP is depicted in Figure 1. It specifies that the process starts when a customer of the universal service provider requests a universal telecommunications service. Subprocess *Exchange Info* involves an operator collecting information from the customer, or a customer directly providing the information via a web browser. When sufficient customer data are collected, subprocess *Order Service* is performed to (1) verify that the information provided by the customer is accurate, and (2) create a corresponding universal service order record. When *Order Service* is completed, the top process starts *Provide Local Exchange Service*, *Provide Long Distance Service*, *Provide Wireless Service*, and *Provide Internet Service*.

These abstract subprocesses are implemented by SEPs provided by different enterprises, i.e., the local, long distance, wireless, internet, and universal service providers. When all selected subprocesses are completed, subprocess *Bill* is preformed to create a single bill for all telecommunications services in the universal service. Finally, *Care for Customer* involves a human operator who verifies that the provided service meets the customer needs.

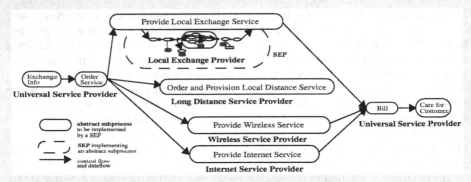

Fig. 1. Reference MEP for universal telecommunications service provisioning

The universal service provider in Figure 1 may be a distinct enterprise from the local, long distance, wireless, and internet providers. However, in our example VE the universal service provider may be any of the providers of the component services. In particular, the provider of the universal service is determined by the customer who decides which of enterprise to contact for universal service. All enterprises in our example VE have a top level SEP that implements the reference MEP in Figure 1, i.e., they can provision universal service. In addition, large VEs may have multiple enterprises that implement and provide the same component service.

Reference processes are emerging in both industry [15] and academia [9]. Industrial reference processes capture standard business processes within a certain industry branch, e.g., reference processes for the telecommunication industry are proposed by the TeleManagement Forum [15]. Reference processes developed by academic research, such as the process handbook project [9], also stay on a declarative business process level. Therefore, existing reference process concepts provide no solutions for implementation and enactment of reference process-based MEPs.

2.2   Service-Based MEP

A service-based MEP is a process that fuses together *services* provided by different enterprises. Such services may encapsulate SEPs implemented by commercial work-flow management systems (WfMSs), CORBA servers, basic programs, legacy information systems, etc. However, from the perspective of the MEP that integrates them, services are black boxes that provide only a set of service operations to control them and determine their state.

To integrate a service, a service-based MEP must use *service activities*. These are service proxies that convert the operations and/or states of each service to the behavior of an activity that is incorporated in the MEP. In VEs with multiple providers of the same service, service-based MEP must provide abstract activities that can have multiple implementations. The execution of an abstract activity involves selecting one particular implementation during run-time, binding it to the abstract activity, and running it. An example of a service-based MEP for a universal telecommunications service provisioning is depicted in Figure 2.

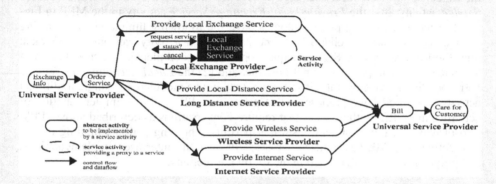

Fig. 2. Service-based MEP for universal telecommunications service provisioning

Service-based MEP must deal with service autonomy and heterogeneity. In reference-based MEPs, this problem is mitigated by the agreement of the participating enterprise to comply with reference MEPs. However, in service-based MEPs no such agreement exists. Furthermore, service designers typically have no direct knowledge of the service models and implementations used by other enterprises. Therefore, service-based MEP requirements include:

1. *service activities* that can effectively model and control heterogeneous services, and
2. activity *polymorphism*, i.e., ability to associate and bind service activities at various degrees of specialization to the MEP activities/processes they implement.

Modeling heterogeneous services involves enhancing traditional workflow activity types [16, 6] with *application-specific* operations and states. Controlling a service encapsulated in a service activity requires support for *conversations* between the activity that needs to control a service activity (the service *client*), and service activity itself. Such conversations involve multiple interactions where clients perform multiple invocations and receive intermediate results that may be used in further invocations. The *Local Exchange Service* illustrated in Figure 2 is a simplified service that provides operations to request local exchange service installation, determine its status, and cancel it. The service activity that serves as the proxy of the *Local Exchange Service* is a conversational activity. In particular, suppose that the *Order Service* in Figure 2 needs to query the *Local Exchange Service* to determine whether it failed to complete installing the service within the agreed time frame. In this case, the *Order Service* may cancel the *Local Exchange Service* or do necessary adjustments, e.g., notify the universal service customer. To support such conversation, the service activity for the *Provide Local Exchange Service* provides the following application-specific operations: *request service()*, *status()*, and *cancel()*. In addition, the service activity has application-specific activity states that indicate the progress, success, or failure of the service installation.

Conversational activities cannot be captured directly by existing service activities/ proxies [13, 10] and existing process models [16, 6] which assume that activities are invoked once, enter their running state, and produce no data until they are completed or terminated (stopped). For example, if we use an existing process model to capture the cancellation of the local exchange service we must add a *Cancel Local Exchange Service* activity after the *Provide Local Exchange Service* activity in the MEP in Figure 2. Therefore existing process models have the following limitations in capturing service request and cancellation: (1) the cancellation activity can only be invoked after the Local Exchange Service request operation is completed, i.e., cancellation of a service request in progress is not possible, and (2) the *Local Exchange Service* and corresponding service operations in Figure 2 cannot be modeled as a single traditional activity. The model we propose in this paper, i.e., PPM, allows implementation of activities in a MEP with services that require conversations as described above. PPM also provides activity polymorphism that permits subtyping and late binding of service activities to MEP activities/processes. PPM activity interfaces, implementations, and polymorphism are discussed in the following sections.

3   Activity Types and Interfaces

To allow application modeling, process models, e.g., [16], provide *types* for activities, resources, and dependencies. Activity types are either basic activity types or processes (composite activity) types. These types are used to develop application models that are instantiated during enactment.

To support the requirements of service- and reference process-based MEPs discussed in Section 2, we have developed a *Polymorphic Process Model* (PPM) that decouples activity types from activity implementations. Just like in CORBA™ [11] and Java™ [14], the type of an activity in PPM is determined by the activity interface. Therefore, to avoid confusion by using the term "activity" with different meanings, in the rest of this paper we distinguish the activity *type* (represented by an *activity interface*), the *activity implementation*, and the use of an activity within a process called *activity variable*. This is analogous to object oriented programming languages, e.g., Java™ [14], which also distinguish object interfaces and *abstract classes* (corresponding to activity types), concrete *classes* (corresponding to activity implementations), and typed variables (such as activity variables) that may hold

tions), and typed variables (such as activity variables) that may hold references to object (activity) instances.

In PPM a process activity type consists of an activity interface, activity variables, resource variables, and dependency variables. Activity variables represent the subactivities of a process. Resource variables describe the resources needed during process execution. Dependency variables define the data and control flow rules for the subactivities of the process. In contrast, basic activity types are restricted to an activity interface and resource variables.

PPM requires that both activity types and implementations have *activity interfaces*. In PPM, activity interfaces are used to map activity types to activity implementations The interface of an activity type captures its implementation requirements at an abstract level, while the interface of an implementation captures the capabilities of the implementation at a concrete level. In PPM, both abstract and concrete activity interfaces are state machines that capture:

- application-specific activity states and operations that cause activity state transitions
- input and output parameters

These are discussed in Sections 3.1 and 3.2.

3.1 Activity State Machine Types

In the initial paragraphs of Section 3, we noted that in PPM activity types are determined by their interfaces that consist of an *activity state machine type* (ASMT) and activity input/output. An ASMT determines the possible *activity states* for instances of the respective activity interface and corresponding *state transitions*. Formally, an ASMT is a tuple (S, T) whereby S is the set of states and T is the set of transitions $t = (s_1, s_2)$, where $s_1, s_2 \in S$ and $t \in T$. State transitions may be caused by invoking explicit *activity operations*. In the following sections we describe ASMTs in detail.

Activity Operations. Activity operations, such as start and terminate, drive the execution of activities and the corresponding state transitions in a process. Our PPM supports two types of explicit activity operations: *generic operations* and *application-specific operations*. *Generic operations* include the application-independent operations that are provided by the WfMC standard: *create(), start(), pause(), resume(), finish(),* and *terminate().* PPM complements these standard operations with a generic *state_change_of_subactivity()* operation. This operation is discussed further in Section 4.1.

In addition to generic operations, PPM permits *application-specific operations* that are defined by the process designer as needed to model a specific activity type. They represent control operations that are available on running activities. For example, an activity that implements ordering of local exchange service may offer application-specific operations to check the *status* of the order, *add* additional items to the order (e.g., call waiting, caller ID, etc.), and *remove* items from the order. Application-specific activity operations are supported only by few WfMSs, e.g., CMI [4] and the MOBILE WfMS [7].

Activity states. To enable interoperability with standard WfMC activities [16], PPM provides a set of generic activity states, i.e., *Uninitialized*, *Ready*, *Running*, *Suspended*, and *Closed* with *Completed* or *Terminated* substates. These generic activity states and state transitions constitute the *generic ASMT* depicted in Figure 3.

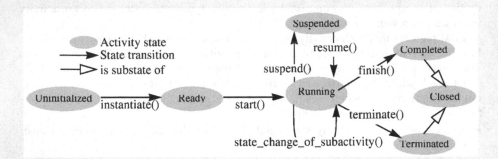

Fig. 3. Generic Activity State Type

In addition to generic states, PPM supports application-specific states. For example, consider the ASTM of the *Provide Local Exchange Service* activity in the telecommunications MEP in Figure 1. Suppose that this activity has two application-specific states, *Provisioning* and *Fulfilling*. Figure 4 shows the corresponding ASMT. The *Provide Local Exchange* service activity enters its *Provisioning* state when it starts running and the service provider starts allocating resources needed to provide the service, such as lines and slots in telecommunication switches. The activity state changes to *Fulfilling* when all necessary resources have been allocated and the activation of the service begins.

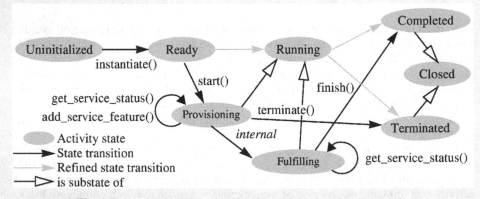

Fig. 4. Example: ASMT for Provide Local Exchange Service activity

The *Provisioning* and *Fulfilling* states in Figure 4 are a refinement of the *Running* state. The *Provisioning* to *Fulfilling* transition is labeled as *internal* in Figure 4. *Internal* is a special operation indicating that this state transition is not under the control of the process enactment system and it is caused solely by the activity implementation.

Internal state changes need special treatment in a process specification (this is discussed further in Section 4.2). After service installation has been confirmed, the activity enters its *Completed* state. An order can be canceled as long as it has not been fulfilled. Cancellation is represented by a transition from the *Provisioning* state to the *Terminated* state. To keep the example simple we omit activities necessary to cancel a service order.

Activity state machine subtyping. The ASMT shown in Figure 4 is a subtype of the generic ASMT in Figure 3. The refined ASMT is called a *subtype* of the original ASMT (referred to as the *father type*). When an activity state is refined, all state transitions of the refined activity state have to be replaced by transitions involving one or more of its substates. Such transitions are depicted as grey arcs in Figure 4. Suppose that C is a subtype of an ASMT F. C is a *valid* activity state machine subtype (ASMsubT) of F if and only if: either a transition happens between two substates of the same parent state, or there is a corresponding transition between the parent states in the father type.

Formally, the valid states and transitions of an activity state subtype can be defined by considering that for each subtype C of a ASMT father type F there is a function *refine_state*. This function defines how the states of the father type F are refined by the subtype C by mapping each state of F to the corresponding set of C's states. Thus, assuming that S_F is the set of F's states, S_F is the domain of *refine_state*. Similarly, if S_C is the set of C's states, S_C is the range of *refine_state*.

Condition for valid states: To enable an unambiguous state refinement, each state of C must be a refinement of exactly one state of F, i.e., $\forall s_1, s_2 \in S_F: (refine\_state(s_1) \cap refine\_state(s_2) \neq \emptyset \Leftrightarrow s_1 = s_2)$ AND $S_C = \bigcup_{s \in S_F} refine\_state(s)$

Conditions for valid transitions: Assuming that T_C and T_F are the sets of transitions in C and F, respectively, and C is a subtype of F, one of the following must hold for each transition $(s_1, s_2) \in T_C$:

- both s_1 and s_2 are refinements of the same state in F, i.e., $\exists s \in S_F: s_1 \in refine\_state(s)$ AND $s_2 \in refine\_state(s)$,
- or there is a corresponding transition (s_a, s_b) in the father type F, i.e., $\exists s_a, s_b \in S_F: (s_a, s_b) \in T_F$ AND $s_1 \in refine\_state(s_a)$ AND $s_2 \in refine\_state(sb)$.

These conditions on building activity types ensure that application-specific extensions can always be generalized in a meaningful way to a father type.

3.2   Input/Output Parameters

In addition to an ASMT, an activity interface includes the activity input and output parameters. The combination of ASMTs and parameters is required by PPM to define the activity type. PPM adopts the existing data types from standard workflow process models [16]. In particular, in PPM the *input (output) parameters* of an activity A are a set of typed data variables, denoted as I_A (O_A). When an activity is started its input parameters are assigned with values as specified by the dataflow dependencies of the enclosing process. In traditional workflow models, activity output is produced when the activity ends. PPM extends this by permitting output parameter values to be made available when the activity enters a specific state. As a consequence, activities can output data while they are still running.

Formally, the *output behavior* of an activity interface A can be defined as a function $ob_A: O_A \rightarrow S_A$ that maps each output parameter o of A to the state s of A that produces o (S_A is the set of states of A). Therefore, $ob_A(o) = s$ means that the value of the output parameter o is available after the activity has reached the state s for the first time. Therefore, if an activity writes to an output parameter after the activity has already reached the state in which this parameter becomes available, readers of the output parameter will read the result of the latest write. For example the invoice amount of an order is different after an additional item has been added to the order.

4   Activity Implementation and Control

Activity implementation in PPM mainly involves mapping abstract activities to SEPs and/or services that implement them. To map abstract activities (basic activities or subprocesses) to concrete processes and services, we introduce the notion of *concrete* and *abstract* activity types. An activity type is *concrete* if it has a corresponding implementation, and all state transitions in its ASMT are labeled with operations supported by this implementation. An *abstract* activity type does not have a corresponding implementation, and may contain one or more unlabeled state transitions in its ASMT. The distinction between abstract and concrete activity types is necessary to decouple the activity interface from the activity implementation. For example, consider the abstract *Provide Local Exchange Service* activity in both Figure 1 and Figure 2. Consider that this activity has the abstract ASMT illustrated in Figure 4. The abstract *Provide Local Exchange Service* may be implemented by a SEP (e.g., as in the reference MEP in Figure 1) or by a service activity (e.g., as in the service-based MEP in Figure 2). These alternative implementations of *Provide Local Exchange Service* are interchangeable at run-time.

In the following sections we discuss how abstract activity types are implemented by mapping them to concrete activity types. Section 4.1 discusses abstract activity implementation by a process (e.g., a SEP). Section 4.2 presents the implementation of an activity by a service activity and the implementation of service activities themselves.

4.1   Mapping Abstract Activities to Concrete Process Activities

The mapping of an abstract activity type to a concrete SEP depends on whether the SEP provides generic or application-specific operations in its concrete ASMT.

Mapping generic operations. In the following paragraphs we consider the mapping of an abstract MEP activity to a concrete SEP type that provides only generic operations. If an abstract MEP activity is implemented by a concrete SEP, each operation of the abstract activity is implemented by a concrete subactivity in the SEP. This is accomplished by mapping the operations and empty transition labels in the ASMT of the abstract activity to generic operations of the concrete ASMT.

For example, consider the abstract *Provide Local Exchange Service* activity whose ASMT is illustrated in Figure 4. This abstract MEP activity defines *get_service_status()* and *add_service_feature()* operations that query the service status and add additional service features, such as call waiting. Each of these operations is implemented by a subactivity in the concrete SEP whose ASMT depicted in Figure 5. This is accomplished by mapping the operations *get_service_status()* and *add_service_feature()* of the abstract ASMT to appropriate *state_change_of_subactivity()* (or shorter *sc_of_sub()*) operations. In particular, while the concrete process is in the *Provisioning* state, additional items may be added to an order by invoking *sc_of_sub (add_Item, any)*. The keyword *any* indicates that any state change of the *add_item* subactivity is permitted in this state of the concrete process. Assuming that the *add_Item* subactivity has been enabled by the normal control flow, *sc_of_sub (add_Item, any)* causes the start of the *add_Item* subactivity.

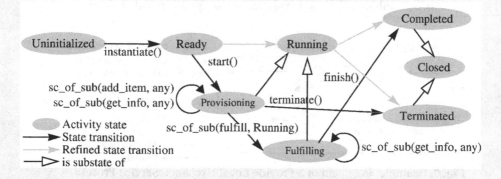

Fig. 5. Example: Generic ASMT type of Provide Local Exchange Service activity

Mapping application-specific operations. Unlike generic activity operations, such as *create()* and *start()*, application-specific operations must be specified by the process designer. In contrast to methods in object-oriented programming languages and distributed object systems, application-specific activity operations cannot be implemented by arbitrary code. In process models such as PPM the process subactivities and their dependency net, is a lower level specification that constitutes the process implementation. Since application-specific activity operations provide an abstraction of this implementation, each application-specific process activity operation is implemented by a *script* that invokes one or more activity operations on the subactivities of this process.

As an example, consider an abstract *Provide Local Exchange Service* activity with the ASMT illustrated in Figure 4. Suppose that this abstract activity is implemented by a concrete process that includes two application-specific operations: *info()* and *item()*. Assume that the ASTM of this concrete process is depicted in Figure 6.

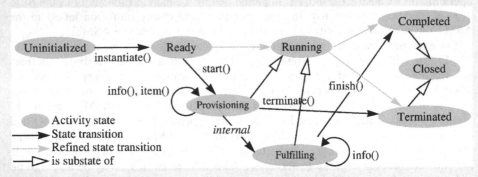

Fig. 6. Example: Application-specific ASMT of Provide Local Exchange Service activity

In this example, the application-specific operations *info()* and *item()* in Figure 6 are implemented by subactivities of the concrete *Provide Local Exchange Service* process. In particular, *info()* and *item()* are implemented by the *get_local_status* and *add_local_item* subactivities and the integration script illustrated in Figure 7.

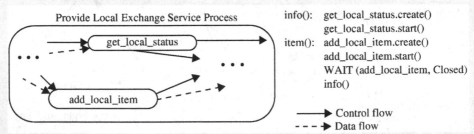

Fig. 7. Example: Fragment of a Provide Local Exchange Service Process

The *info()* and *item()* operations of the concrete ASMT are shown on the right side of Figure 7. *Info()* just creates and starts an instance of the *get_local_status* activity. *Item()* starts an instance of the *add_local_item* activity, waits for its termination, and then invokes the *info()* operation to inform the caller about the outcome. Note the scripts do not move data between the activities. Data flow is covered by the process net.

4.2   Mapping Abstract Activities to Concrete Service Activities

In the following paragraphs we present how an abstract activity is implemented by a concrete service activity, and then we discuss the implementation of the service activity itself.

Mapping abstract activities to concrete service activities. If the abstract *Provide Local Exchange Service* activity in Figure 4 is implemented by an external service, the abstract activity is implemented by a service activity that by definition has no subactivities. In this case, the *get_service_status()* and *add_service_feature()* operations of the abstract activity are implemented by service-provided operations, say *info()* and *item()*, that retrieve status information and add additional items, e.g., *item(CallWaiting)*. Figure 6 shows the concrete ASMT of such a service activity.

Implementing concrete service activities. As we discussed in Section 2.2, *service activities* are proxies that convert the operations and/or states of each service to the behavior of an activity that is incorporated in the MEP. The implementation of an activity interface by a service activity is conducted by implementing of a corresponding *service activity proxy program (SAPP)*. Note, that services that support only a single *start()* invocation degenerate to basic or program activities [6, 16].

In contrast to activity interfaces and process specifications, which are descriptive specifications, the SAPP is to be coded in a traditional programming language. The service activity program uses the process system's API to access its input and output, to trigger internal state transitions, and to publish its activity operations to the process system. Hence, the SAPP is also an advanced wrapper program [12] for integrating external software systems. The deployment of a real program for this purpose is necessary, because the SAPP has to deal with the (possibly proprietary) communication protocols and formats of the software system and translates them to the format used by the process management system. However, generic SAPPs are provided to deal with traditional basic activities that have only generic states and operations.

By permitting application-specific states and operations, the service activities are far more powerful than SWAP [13] and the Workflow Management Facility [10]. Both of these propose a variant of a proxy mechanism that permit only the generic states and operations defined by the WfMC standard [16]. Therefore, they are not capable of capturing application semantics of services.

4.3   State-Dependent Control and Data Flow

PPM provides control flow *dependencies/transitions* that are similar to those provided by traditional WfMSs, e.g., [6], and the WfMC standard [16]. PPM extends the traditional notion of control flow transitions to permit application-specific states to be used in control flow. Such control flow transitions are denoted as $(av_{source}, s_{source}) \rightarrow (av_{target}, s_{target})$. They indicate that a state transition of an activity av_{target} to the s_{target} state is permitted after activity av_{source} enters state s_{source}. To ensure that the PPM dependencies can be enforced, only application-specific extensions of the *Running* state may be enabled by PPM control flow transitions. Additionally, transitions to *Running* substates that may be entered by *internal* operations (state transitions) are not allowed, because such transitions cannot be controlled by the execution system.

Just like control flow, PPM extends the traditional data flow dependencies to consider the states of the involved activities. In particular, in a traditional dataflow dependency $(av_{source}, out_{source}) \rightarrow (av_{target}, in_{target})$ the value of the output parameter out_{source} of an activity av_{source} flows to the input parameter in_{target} of an activity av_{target} after av_{source} is closed (ends). PPM extends the semantics of a $(av_{source}, out_{source}) \rightarrow (av_{target}, in_{target})$ dataflow dependency by allowing the data to flow as soon as av_{source} has reached the $ob_{source}(out_{source})$ state (ob was defined in Section 3.2). To avoid inconsistencies in the dependency net, we adopt the strategy that dataflow has to follow control flow [8]. That is, for each dataflow dependency $(av_{source}, out_{source}) \rightarrow (av_{target}, in_{target})$ there must be a control flow path from av_{source} to av_{target} that starts at av_{source} from:

- state $ob_{source}(out_{source})$, or
- a state that is reached later than $ob_{source}(out_{source})$ in av_{source}'s state machine.

State-dependent control and dataflow are powerful primitives. In the activity scenario used in the previous sections, these dependencies enable the provisioning activity to output service activation information as soon as it has reached the *Fulfilling* state. A process that uses this activity can initiate further activities (using state-dependent control flow) as soon as this info becomes available.

5   Activity Polymorphism

Activity Polymorphism is permitting an activity variable to (1) use (i.e., hold references to) activity instances that have more specialized type than the type of the activity variable, and (2) use different implementations for the same activity variable at process execution time. Polymorphism allows flexibility in matching and using activity types and activity implementations provided by different enterprises.

In Section 5.1, we present the PPM solution for subtyping/specializing activity interfaces, by focusing on input/output subtyping and ASMT subtyping. In Section 5.2, we introduce activity placeholder. This primitive adds late binding that is needed to implement the selection of an activity implementation at runtime.

5.1   Activity Interface Subtyping

This extends activity state machine subtyping in Section 3.1 by considering activity inputs and outputs. Analogously to programming languages an activity type should be regarded as subtype A_C of a father activity type A_F if instances of A_C show at least all the behavioral characteristics that instances of A_F show. This ensures that wherever an instance of A_F is expected an instance of A_C can be used instead. However, A_C may show additional behavior that cannot be directly observed at A_F as long as this additional behavior can be generalized to a behavior of A_F. In terms of activity interfaces as defined in Section 3 this means that an activity interface A_C with activity operations aop_C, activity state type $asmt_C$, and input/output parameters (I_C, O_C, ob_C) is an activity interface subtype of A_F with activity operations aop_F, activity state type $asmt_F$, and in/output parameters (I_F, O_F, ob_F) if:

1. $asmt_C$ is an activity state subtype of $asmt_F$
2. $I_C \subseteq I_F$
3. $O_C \supseteq O_F$
4. $\forall v \in O_F$: $ob_F(v) = ob_C(v)$ or there is no path in the state machine of $asmt_C$ where $ob_F(v)$ or a substate of $ob_F(v)$ can be reached before $ob_C(v)$ is reached.

Condition (1) ensures that the observable states of the child type can be generalized to the states of the father type. This is guaranteed by the definition of activity state subtypes. Condition (2) prevents an interface subtype from expecting more input parameters than the father type. This way, a process expecting an instance of the father type provides also sufficient input for any subtype. Condition (3) states that a subtype has to provide at least the output expected to be produced by the father type. The subtype may have additional outputs that are discarded by someone expecting an instance of the father type. Condition (4) places an additional restriction on the output behavior of activity subtypes. Because a process can rely on an activity variable of type A_F to produce output in a particular state (this is needed by state dependent dataflow discussed in Section 4.1), an activity subtype must not produce its output later than the father type, i.e., in a state that can be reached after the output producing state of the father type.

Please note that there is no mandatory condition on A_C's and A_F's activity operation sets aop_C and aop_F. If we assume that the process enactment system provides a worklist that informs each client about the operations currently available on a specific work item, a human client and also a flexible software agent that acts as a client can perform the right operations on every activity. However, if static programs are used as clients that cannot analyze the operation information on a work item and rely on the father's operation set aop_F, $aop_C = aop_F$ must hold.

5.2   Activity Placeholders

Activity placeholders allow for runtime assignment (late binding) of an activity implementation to a given activity variable. The type of the placeholder is determined by its interface. The placeholder is used instead of a concrete activity implementation in the declaration of an activity variable within a process. An activity placeholder has a *selection policy* attached, which is used at runtime to select the actual activity type for the placeholder's activity variable. To ensure the consistency of the process, within which an activity placeholder is used, the set of possible activity types from which the selection policy chooses one is the set of subtypes of the placeholders activity interface type.

Activity placeholders and the corresponding selection policies can be used in many application scenarios. For example, a generic reference process can be configured to use the activity implementations available in a given enterprise by providing a selection policy that plugs in the enterprise's implementation for each activity interface. If multiple enterprises provide implementations for an activity interface, the selection policy may use a broker to choose the implementation that offers the best quality of service [4]. In application areas where the process designer does not have the expertise to chose a particular activity implementation, e.g., in crisis mitigation applications where only expert process participants know which concrete tests to perform, the selection policy may permit such a participant to select which implementation to use [5].

6   Related Work

Separation of interface and implementation as well as interface subtyping and polymorphism are well-known concepts in programming languages, e.g., Java™ [14], and distributed (object) systems, e.g., CORBA [11]. They are particularly useful in heterogeneous environments because they enable the client of an object to be implemented and maintained independently from the implementation(s) of an object. We have adopted these ideas into the process world. Although object-oriented programming languages provide useful abstractions, they are not suitable for process modeling, since they do not include types and classes for capturing and implementing processes. Implementing such types and classes requires considerable effort, as indicated by current WfMS.

To the best of our knowledge current work in workflow management and process models does not provide abstraction mechanisms as the ones presented in this paper. The process handbook project [9] has the notions of inheritance and specialization of processes. However, this approach stays on a declarative business process level, i.e., implementation and enactment of the proposed concepts stays open in [9]. Van der Aalst et al. [1, 2] propose an inheritance mechanisms for process implementations with the objective to deal with dynamic change and evolution in workflows. Both approaches do not separate activity interfaces and implementation, however it is essential to our approach.

7   Conclusion

In this paper we presented a novel model for multi-enterprise processes (MEPs), namely, the Polymorphic Process Model (PPM). The main advantage of this model lies in its ability to support both service-based MEPs and MEPs using a reference process specification. PPM accomplishes this task by separating the activity interfaces from activity implementations, and defining the activity interfaces in terms of activity state machines and its input/output parameters. That in turn leads to the ability of using multiple implementations for the same activity in MEPs without the need for modifications of the specification or the running process. Together with strict rules of activity type subclassing, these characteristics allow for seamless integration of services and processes provided by multiple independent enterprises.

A prototype of a process management system based on a subset of this model has been successfully implemented in MCC's Collaboration Management Infrastructure System [3]. A set of sample applications, including health care-related crisis management processes, military operation coordination, and telecommunication provisioning service, have been designed, implemented, and demonstrated, proving that the PPM fulfills its promise.

However, not all aspects of the PPM are fully developed yet. For example, the runtime choice of a particular service to be executed as the resolution of a placeholder is a demanding problem. We have done some initial work in this area, but many problems considered crucial for the success of Virtual Enterprises (whose core business is choosing and composing external services) are left to be solved. Key remaining problems include the semantic description of the services, the description of the quality of the services (necessary for a meaningful service comparison), and the development of service contracts beyond the activity types we discussed in this paper.

References

1. van der Aalst, W.M.P: Generic Workflow Models: How to handle dynamic change and capture management information. In: *Proc. of the Fourth IFCIS Conf. on Cooperative Information Systems (CoopIS'99)*, Edinburgh, Scotland, September 1999.
2. van der Aalst, W.M.P. ; Basten, T. ; Verbeek, H.M.W. ; Verkoulen, P.A.C. ; Voorhoeve, M.: Adaptive Workflow: An Approach Based on Inheritance. In: Ibrahim, M. ; Drabble, B. (Eds.): *Proc. Workshop Intelligent Workflow and Process Management: The New Frontier for AI in Business*, 16th. Int. Joint Conf. on Artificial Intelligence (IJCAI'99). Stockholm, Sweden, August 1999.
3. Collaboration Management Infrastructure, *http://www.mcc.com/projects/cmi*, 2000.
4. Georgakopoulos, D. ; Schuster, H. ; Baker, D. ; Cichocki, A.: Managing Process and Service Fusion in Virtual Enterprises. In: *Information Systems, Special Issue on Information Systems Support for Electronic Commerce*, **24**(6), 1999.
5. Georgakopoulos, D. ;Schuster, H. ; Cichocki, A.; Baker, D. : Collaboration Management Infrastructure in Crisis Response Situations. In: *Proc. 16th Int. Conference on Data Engineering (ICDE'2000)*, San Diego, March 2000.
6. *IBM FlowMark - Managing Your Workflow*. Version 2.3, IBM, 1996.
7. Jablonski, S. ; Bußler, C.: *Workflow Management - Modeling Concepts, Architecture and Implementation*. International Thomson Computer Press, 1996.
8. Leymann, F. ; Altenhuber, W.: Managing Business Processes as an Information Resource. In: *IBM Systems Journal*, 33(2), 1994.
9. Malone, T.W. ; Crowston, K. ; Lee, J. ; Pentland, B.: Tools for Inventing Organizations: Toward a Handbook of Organizational Processes. In: *Proc. of the 2nd IEEE Workshop on Enabling Technologies Infrastructure for Collaborative Enterprises*, Morgantown, WV, April 20-22, 1993.
10. Object Management Group: *Workflow Management Facility*. Revised Submission, OMG Document Number bom/98-06-07, July 1998.
11. Object Management Group: *The Common Object Request Broker: Architecture and Specification*. Revision 2.3.1, October 1999.
12. Schuster, H. ; Jablonski, S. ; Heinl, P. ; Bußler, C.: A General Framework for the Execution of Heterogeneous Programs in Workflow Management Systems. In: *Proc. First IFCS Int. Conf. on Cooperative Information Systems (CoopIS 96)*, Brussels, 1996.
13. *Simple Workflow Access Protocol (SWAP)*. *http://www.ics.uci.edu/~ietfswap/*, 1999.
14. Sun Microsystems: *Java™. http://java.sun.com/*, 2000.
15. TeleManagement Forum: *http://www.tmforum.org/*, 1999.
16. Workflow Management Coalition: Interface 1: Process Definition Interchange Process Model. Document Number TC-1016-P, Document Status – Version 1.1, October 1999.

Gossip: An Awareness Engine
for Increasing Product Awareness
in Distributed Development Projects

Babak A. Farshchian

Dept. of Computer and Information Science
Norwegian University of Science and Technology, Trondheim
http://www.idi.ntnu.no/~baf

Abstract. More and more product development projects involve geographically distributed groups of developers. One problem in such groups
is the long term lack of awareness of the activities in remote sites. In this
paper we discuss the importance of awareness in distributed product
development projects. We argue that generic services are needed in development environments for providing continuous awareness of remote
sites. We introduce a product awareness model that puts focus on a
shared composite product and the propagation of awareness in it. We
describe the design and implementation of this awareness model in form
of an awareness engine called Gossip.

1 Introduction

Information systems development is an area of intensive human collaboration
[BJ75]. A normal practice for managing collaboration in large scale IS development projects has been to divide the system into parts and have the parts be
developed separately by groups of developers, in this way reducing the amount
of ad hoc communication and dependencies [Par72,Con68]. However, many recent case studies of project groups have revealed that this is not an easy task.
No matter how rational the division of the system into parts is, each group will
still need a large amount of information about what is happening within and
across the groups in order to coordinate its work [HG99,Gri98,KS95]. Access to
this ad hoc information becomes particularly problematic when the developers
are geographically distributed. The effect of geographical distances on long term
collaboration has been well documented in the literature. Herbsleb and Grinter [HG99], Kraut and Streeter [KS95], and Krasner et al. [KCI87] document the
occurrences of communication breakdowns when there are organizational or geographical barriers among the group members.

In a study of researchers from 70 research labs, Kraut and Egido [KE88] found
that there was considerably higher collaboration frequency among researchers
having offices in the same corridor than among those who did not. The reason, according to the authors, is that physical proximity increases the *frequency*
and the *quality* of communication, and decreases the *cost of initiating* communication. As members of co–located groups, developers have the advantage of

B. Wangler, L. Bergman (Eds.): CAiSE 2000, LNCS 1789, pp. 264–278, 2000.

constantly being *aware* of the status of the product being developed by simply using their social abilities, such as "looking over the shoulder" of each other, being involved in chance encounters in the corridors, and having a much greater opportunity for "keeping in touch" with each other. In distributed cooperation, both the amount and the quality of this information decreases. In addition, providing and consuming this *awareness information* becomes an explicit burden on the co–workers simply because most of the natural social channels of communication are eliminated.

In the recent years there has been a large amount of research conducted with the aim of developing tools to support distributed development groups in performing specific and recurring types of tasks. Tools are developed for supporting collaborative modeling [DLN97], JAD sessions [CGN95], programming [HW98], and more. In addition to these specific tools and environments, we believe there is a need for more generic tools for simulating long–term physical proximity of the distributed project members, making it easy and less costly for the developers to initiate collaboration when they need it. In this way strict geographical divisions can be relaxed, and the collaboration can proceed in a more natural and flexible way. One essential step in doing this is to develop support systems that increase the amount of long term awareness provided to project members about the activities of remote co–workers.

As a part of our research on product development environments, we have been developing a framework for supporting collaboration in distributed product development projects. The framework consists of three parts (Fig. 1). An underlying *product layer* is in charge of providing awareness of a distributed virtual product consisting of parts. A *cluster layer* implements mechanisms for grouping product parts into collaboration aware clusters, such as diagrams. An *application layer* assists the integration and use of various development tools.

In this paper we describe *Gossip*. Gossip implements the product layer, and is in charge of keeping all the other parts of the framework constantly aware of user activities involving different parts of the product, in this way providing a shared collaboration space for distributed development groups. The structure of the paper is as follows: In Sect. 2 we will look at different approaches to awareness support. In Sect. 3 we introduce our product awareness model. Section 4 describes Gossip, which implements this awareness model in form of an awareness engine. Section 5 provides a discussion and directions for future work.

2   Approaches to Awareness Support

Awareness is the information that human beings exchange with their environment in order to coordinate their work with others. Providing computer–based mechanisms for supporting exchange of awareness information has shown to be of central importance to the design of collaboration support systems [GG98]. For the purpose of this paper, we will organize the research in awareness support along two dimensions (Fig. 2). The first dimension focuses on the *quantity* of the exchanged awareness information compared to the natural co–located situations.

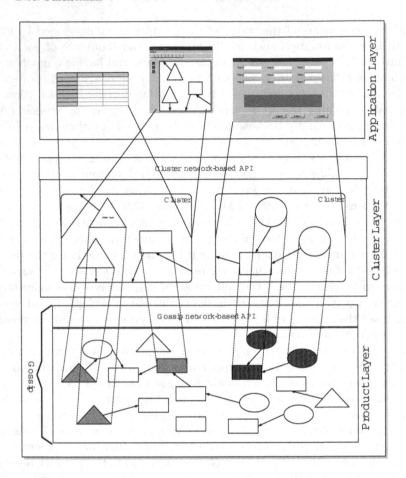

Fig. 1. A framework for supporting product awareness in distributed product development environments.

The second dimension is the level of *organizational awareness* provided by the awareness mechanism. By organizational awareness we mean awareness of the overall organization of the work. High quantities of awareness information are normally important in order to increase the "naturalness" of the collaboration, while access to proper organizational awareness facilitates collaboration in large groups.

The quantity of transmitted awareness information is largest in co–located situations, where all the available social channels are used to their full capacity. *Media spaces* are probably the closest imitations of co–located situations regarding the quantity of awareness information. A typical media space consists of permanent video and audio connections between geographically distributed sites. In addition to the large amount of awareness information, the permanence of the

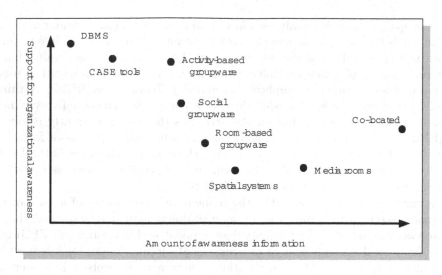

Fig. 2. A comparison of different awareness models.

connections reduces the cost of initiating collaboration, contributing further to the creation of a common social space in the long run [BHI93].

Smaller amounts of awareness information are typically transmitted through software based collaboration support systems. This is both because of the difficulty of collecting this information from the group's natural context, but also because of the difficulty of visualizing this information in a proper way. A challenging part of implementing awareness support is thus to find the proper *awareness model* for the domain to be supported. This model will decide what awareness information will be delivered to whom, in this way both making better use of the limited information bandwidth, and ensuring that those who need the awareness information will get it.

Several awareness models have been proposed in the literature. Normally, awareness models have a notion of *shared space, presence* and *focus*. Shared space is where collaboration objects have to reside in order to be able to produce and consume awareness information. An object makes its presence known to the shared space by registering itself with a set of parameters. Once present in the shared space, the objects commit to update their presence information regularly. Objects can in addition *focus on* other objects by providing to the shared space a set of parameters that defines their focus. The focus can also be updated regularly. In the *spatial model* of Benford and Fahlèn [BF93], for instance, each object declares its presence in the shared space by its coordinates according to some spatial measure (e.g. geographical location). By changing its coordinates, an object can "move" in the shared space. The focus of each object is defined in form of an "aura"; each object will be able to receive awareness about other objects that are inside its aura, e.g. are close to it. Moving in the space will also move the object's aura.

The spatial model is mainly used in virtual reality settings. A similar awareness model is the *room–based model*, where awareness of the activities in a virtual room is propagated to all the inhabitants of the room, while the "walls" limit the propagation of awareness information to the outside. This model is used in many shared workspace applications, notably TeamRooms [RG96]. A third model is the *activity–based model*. Here, awareness information delivery is not based on spatial relations, but on the activities the user is currently involved in [FPBP95]. *Social awareness models*, on the other hand, put more focus on human participants and interactions among these. One such model is the *locale* model used in Orbit [MKF+97]. The locale model provides awareness based on "social worlds," e.g. centers of social activities.

Awareness can be connected to the immediate surroundings of a user, or to a broader scope of happenings in an organizational context (the organizational awareness axis in Fig. 2). The activity–based model used in GroupDesk [FPBP95] provides a good example of high organizational support. GroupDesk is used in conjunction with a workflow application, where a user involved in a step in a workflow is made aware of the activities in other related steps. Spatial and room–based awareness models are more limited in the organizational support dimension since they strictly focus on the physical space surrounding a user. Social models support well the informal organizational structure, which may or may not mirror the formal structure.

Though CASE and similar product–based tools provide access to an organizational context in form of a large shared product, the degree of awareness information exchange is low [VS95]. Central repositories used in product–centered development tools provide a first technological step for supporting collaboration, but more is needed. These repositories are normally developed in form of time–sharing systems. In particular, they are based on the assumption that conflicts among developers should be delayed as long as possible [JMR92], with the consequence of isolating developers from each other. Despite this attempt to isolate, Vessey and Sravanapudi [VS95] found that having access to a shared product and being able to observe the changes done to it by others had an implicit coordinative role in CASE tools. In the next section we will introduce a new awareness model that tries to address this problem by supporting exchange of explicit product awareness among developers.

3   A Product Awareness Model
for Distributed Product Development

In this paper we introduce an awareness model that uses the product, in particular its structure, as a basis for providing awareness to the developers in a distributed project. Our assumption, as discussed in the introduction, is that a developer needs to have constant awareness of the activities related to a shared product. These activities are first and foremost related to the parts of the product that a developer is directly working on, but a developer may also need to be informed about the activities related to other parts of the product that are some-

how related to "his" parts. We believe this model can be useful in a distributed
product development context because the product is normally the main focus of
work for the developers, and the shared product is something the developers can
"talk about." Being kept updated about what is happening to the product will
reduce the risk for double–work and integration problems. In addition, since the
product is normally used throughout the project's life independent of the way
the developers work and the way they are combined in groups, the product can
be used as a permanent information basis for coordinating the work.

Our product awareness model will increase the quantity of product awareness,
and will make it easy for developers to exchange this awareness information.
Next section describes the details of the model. We emphasize that product
awareness is only one of several forms of awareness in a product development
environment [HG99]. Therefore the model introduced here should be used in
combination with other models in order to support true simulation of physical
proximity motivated in the introduction.

3.1 The Core Concepts of the Model

The product awareness model introduces a virtual space for exchanging awareness of activities involving a shared product. The model also supports *propagation*
of awareness; awareness information can propagate from one part of the product
to another, possibly through several intermediate parts. In this way, a group
of developers working on one part of the product can get the proper awareness
from any other part, in addition to the part they directly work with. This propagation property is important because of often large size and complex structure
of the products being developed. The core concepts of the model are product
model, product object, awareness relation, direct awareness, mediated
awareness, awareness producer, and awareness consumer. These concepts
and the associated relations are shown in the ER diagram in Fig. 3.

Product model is a representation of the shared product being developed by
a group of developers. Product model constitutes the *shared space* where different parts of a product can register their *presence* in form of product objects.
Product objects may represent documents, diagrams, source codes, etc. The
product parts may already be stored in a CASE repository, on the Internet,
or in a database elsewhere. For each such part, only one product object may
exist in the product model, but the granularity of the parts is not limited by
the awareness model. Each product object is capable of generating awareness
information as a result of being manipulated.

The model supports a notion of *focus* for product objects. Each product
object's focus is defined by creating awareness relations from those product
objects it focuses on, and to the product object itself. Each awareness relation has therefore a *source* and a *destination* product object, indicating the
direction of the flow of awareness information. Criteria for deciding what each
product object should focus on, i.e. how awareness relations should be created among product objects, is not defined by the model. Awareness relations may be defined based on product architecture, or other criteria such as the

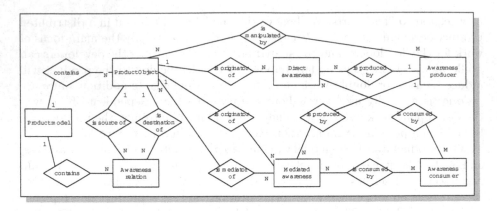

Fig. 3. The main concepts of the product–based awareness model and the relationships among them.

specific usage patterns of a project group. These criteria are mainly defined by the cluster and application layers in the framework shown in Fig. 1. The awareness model and its implementation only focus on providing easy mechanisms for creating **awareness relations** as needed.

A **product model** is in this way created in order to mirror the real product and the various relations among its parts. An example of a **product model** is shown in Fig. 4. It represents a product consisting of three main modules, *database, middleware* and *user interface*. In addition, each module consists of other sub–modules. In this example, **product objects** are created for each module or sub–module in the product. **Awareness relations** are created among the **product objects**, reflecting the paths through which one would like product awareness to be propagated. In this case an **awareness relation** exists from the database module to the middleware module, and one from the middleware module to the user interface module. For each of these modules, all the sub–modules are also connected to their parent module using awareness relations. This means, for instance, that if some object in the database module is modified, the middleware module will get awareness information about the modifications.

As the product development process proceeds, product parts may be manipulated in different ways. Manipulation activities include those that are normally supported by development tools, such as creating, accessing and deleting product parts. It is assumed that each manipulation of a product part is simulated in the **product model** by manipulating the part's corresponding **product object**. The various types of manipulation are not defined by the awareness model. Groups of developers can define and share their own manipulation types in the application layer of our framework (shown in Fig. 1). The awareness model represents developers and their tools as **awareness producers**. Each manipulation activity performed by an **awareness producer** will produce a unit of **direct awareness** in the **product model**. This information indicates a change in the

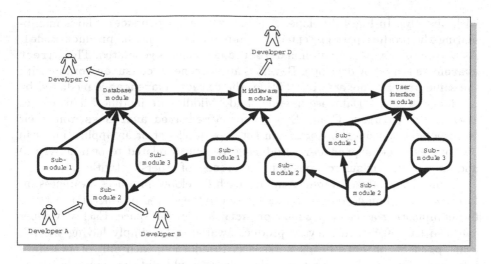

Fig. 4. An example Gossip product model. The rectangles are product objects and the arrows are awareness relations.

product object's presence in the shared space. Each **direct awareness** contains information about the **awareness producer** who did the manipulation, the **product object** that was manipulated, an identifier for the manipulation type, and other user–defined values depending on the type of the manipulation.

Developers sharing the same **product object** can exchange **direct awareness** related to these objects. Moreover, **direct awareness** can be propagated to other **product objects**.Propagation of awareness inside the **product model** happens through the *mediation* mechanism. Each **product object** broadcasts all its awareness to all the **product objects** in the **product model**. Each **product object** that is focusing on the broadcasting **product object** will generate a new **mediated awareness** based on the broadcasted awareness. This **mediated awareness** contains the same information as the original awareness, except that its originator **product object** is changed to the receiving **product object**. However, the **mediated awareness** also contains a pointer to the originally manipulated **product object** (the "is mediator of" relation in Fig. 3). Mediation from a **product object** X to a **product object** Y is thus possible only if a path consisting of (possibly several) **awareness relations** exists from X to Y.

Awareness consumers represent developers or other applications that make use of the awareness generated by the **product model** and its **product objects**. In the framework of Fig. 1 **awareness consumers** are the clusters in the cluster layer, but awareness may also be consumed directly by any application. **Awareness consumers** have access to both **direct awareness** (produced by the **product objects** they work with directly) and **mediated awareness** (produced by other **product objects**, related to the **product objects** they work with directly). In Fig. 4 developer A is an `awareness producer` who is manipulating the product part presented by "Sub–module 2" in the `product model`. As a result of his manipulation, a `direct awareness` is generated. This `direct awareness` is used by developer B, who is an `awareness consumer` working with the same `product object`. In addition, the `direct awareness` is mediated by `product objects` "Database module" and "Middleware module." This causes `awareness consumers` C and D to receive a `mediated awareness` from their corresponding `product objects`. An actor (a developer or an application) can be both `awareness producer` (producing awareness related to own activities) and `awareness consumer` (consuming awareness of others' activities).

Using this product awareness model, each developer produces awareness information based on his own activities related to the shared product, for instance by manipulating a set of `product objects` in his workspace. Each developer can also have access to relevant product awareness by simply having the relevant `product objects` in his workspace. In addition, each unit of awareness information is directly connected to the developer who did the manipulation, in this way opening for social interaction among developers with related interests in the shared product. Another advantage of the model is that each developer only needs to focus on those `product objects` that are of direct importance to his own work, disregarding the rest. The `product objects` he is working with will inform him about peripheral changes in the product that might be of interest to him, at the same time hiding the irrelevant part of the awareness information. This can greatly reduce the effort needed for keeping an eye on everything that might be important to the developer's work.

4   Gossip: An Awareness Engine for Supporting Product Awareness

In the recent years the need for having generic awareness services has increased. A generic awareness service typically provides an interface for different kinds of clients to produce and consume awareness information in an easy way. Notification servers have been used widely as a technical solution for providing awareness services [RDR98]. Using a notification server, a client can generate events, which are captured by the server and redistributed to other clients. In addition, a notification server also has to decide, based on an awareness model, which clients need to receive which notifications. A notification server that implements an awareness model may be called an *awareness engine*. We have developed an awareness engine called Gossip for implementing the product awareness model described in the previous section. The functionality and the internal architecture of Gossip are described in the next sections.

4.1   The Functionality of Gossip

Gossip provides a set of uniform network–based services for creating and maintaining a product model in an evolutionary manner, and for delivering notifications based on the clients' activities related to this model. The product model

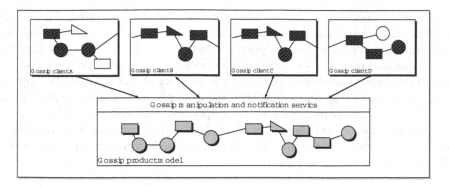

Fig. 5. Clients can use the services provided by Gossip to register their product objects and create awareness relations among them.

manipulation operations may be integrated into the various tools of the developers, making it possible to automatically maintain the product model while each developer is working with his local product part. In addition, a uniform notification delivery service makes it easy to recieve and consume notifications of other developers' manipulations.

Figure 5 shows a usage scenario for Gossip. Different clients communicate with Gossip in order to register a subset of their product parts (objects with black color) as product objects in Gossip (objects with gray color). In addition, awareness relations are created among the product objects registered in Gossip independently from which client owns which product objects. In this way, all the clients are integrated in a shared collaboration space based on a shared product model. Gossip enforces its own name space for the registered product objects, and implements mechanisms for keeping the product model consistent. The clients, on the other hand, are responsible for correct updates to the product model using Gossip's network protocol.

Manipulation mechanisms are accessible in form of *operations* on the shared product model. There are two groups of manipulation operations, *product object manipulation* and *awareness relation manipulation*. In addition, Gossip produces different *notification events* as result of product object manipulations. Query mechanisms are also provided to the clients in order to ask Gossip about various product model information. The following describes manipulation and notification functions provided by Gossip.

Product Object Manipulation. Clients can issue requests for product object manipulation. Besides product object registration and deletion, Gossip supports operations such as adding, changing, reading and deleting *attribute=value* pairs for each product object. The attribute sets for each product object type are defined by client groups, and will resemble the attributes of the real product parts that are to be shared within the client group. Note that product parts (e.g. the actual files, documents, diagrams, descriptive attributes, etc.) need not be stored in Gossip, but a pointer to each part can be registered. This policy requires that product manipulation operations precisely *simulate* the actual manipulations done on the product parts at each client site. This implies that the clients can still use their local repositories, and at the same time use Gossip to exchange product awareness. They will use product object manipulation operations to inform Gossip about how they manipulate their product parts. In this way Gossip will help its clients to keep updated about each other's activities related to a shared (distributed) product. Each client can choose to register in Gossip only a sub–set of its product parts (in Fig. 5, product parts with white color are not shared among clients).

Awareness Relation Manipulation. In addition to object manipulation, clients can also request awareness relation manipulation in order to create and manipulate awareness relations among existing product objects. Awareness relations are stored fully inside Gossip. Each awareness relation is represented in form of a set of *operation=strength* pairs, where *operation* decides what kind of awareness information the relation will mediate, and *strength* decides how many product objects each awareness information can be mediated through. For instance, if an awareness relation has an "updateAttribute" field with a strength of 2, the relation will mediate awareness related to all "updateAttribute" operations that have not already been mediated twice. Using operation=strength values for each awareness relation one can filter most of the information that is considered unnecessary. For instance, awareness of read operations on an attribute from a product object that is "three objects away" is normally considered not so important, while it would be interesting to get information about who is currently reading the objects in one's own workspace. Gossip supports operations for adding and deleting awareness relations, and adding, deleting, and updating operation=strength pairs on the existing awareness relations.

Notifications. Notifications are sent only for product object manipulations. There are two types of notifications, *direct* and *mediated*. Direct notifications have a pointer to the client who did the manipulation, and a pointer to the product object that was manipulated. Mediated notifications have in addition a list of pointers to all other product objects that the notification has passed through (recall that for mediated awareness, the manipulated product object is different from the product object that provides the awareness, as shown in Fig. 4). Additional information can be contained in each notification event for allowing the receiving client synchronize its own state. For instance, a "createNewObject" notification will contain the identifier of the new product object, and an "updateObject" notification will have the name and the new value of the updated attribute.

The set of available operations is extendable. In particular, there is no limit on which attributes can be manipulated for each product object, and the manipulation types that can be simulated are not predefined. All this can be decided among the clients sharing the product model. Gossip will only propagate the awareness and produce the proper notification events.

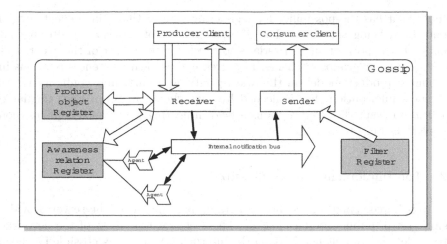

Fig. 6. The internal architecture of Gossip.

4.2   The Architecture of Gossip

Figure 6 shows the internal architecture of Gossip. There are two types of Gossip clients. *Producer clients* can send requests to Gossip for performing an operation on the product model (product object or awareness relation manipulation). The product model is stored in two registers, *product object register* and *awareness relation register*. Each product object manipulation operation may change the product object register, and will eventually generate one or more notification events (awareness relation manipulations do not produce notifications). *Consumer clients* can receive notification events from the server. A client can choose to be a producer, a consumer, or both. When a request is sent to Gossip by a producer client, *Receiver* receives the request and is responsible for performing the requested operation on the product model. After an operation is performed, the producer client will get an acknowledgement event, and a new direct notification event is created. This direct notification is then sent to an internal *notification bus.*

Each awareness relation is implemented in Gossip in form of an *awareness agent* with a source and a destination product object. Awareness agents are responsible for generating mediated notification events on behalf of their destination product objects, and therefore listen to the internal notification bus to monitor product object manipulations. Each awareness agent will check the notification bus for events that have originated from the agent's source product object. For each such event, the agent will generate a new mediated notification event on behalf of its destination product object. These mediated notification events are again sent to the notification bus, and other awareness agents may in turn generate new events based on them.

Sender receives all the notification events from the notification bus. It then checks each event against a *filter register* before sending them out. Each consumer client has the possibility for registering a filter that will prevent certain events from being sent to it. The filter uses a set of criteria for filtering out events. One important such criteria is to check for the owner of the event. Different clients, or groups of clients, may create their own awareness relations in the shared product model, in this way specifying a particular configuration of awareness information that is needed by that client or group. Each mediated notification event therefore contains a field indicating which such configuration the event belongs to.

4.3   The Implementation of Gossip

Gossip is implemented in the Java programming language. The server provides a small set of public interface classes. These classes hide most of the network–related details from clients. Making the interface as simple as possible has been one of our main goals in order to motivate developers to develop Gossip–enabled clients, or extend existing clients with Gossip–related functionality. Using the interface classes the clients can easily send requests to, and receive notifications from Gossip.

Network communication in Gossip, both towards clients and internally in the notification bus, is based on JSDT[1] (Java Shared Data Toolkit). JSDT is a flexible toolkit provided by Sun as an extension to the Java Development Toolkit. This toolkit implements useful groupware abstractions such as sessions and channels. The connection between the clients and Gossip is through a JSDT session. Inside this session, two channels are used for communication between Gossip and the producer and consumer clients.

The internal notification bus is implemented in form of a network channel that is accessible only by other Gossip servers. Several Gossip servers can share the same notification bus, in this way creating a Gossip network. This is useful for scalability and performance reasons. Our experience with using Gossip shows that inside a high–speed local network notifications are distributed in real time. We have in fact used Gossip in a synchronous graphical group editor where the notifications are used to synchronize the screens of the clients. The notifications are distributed in a much slower speed on the Internet. Having one local server for each local group can help to build a more optimized Gossip infrastructure.

5   Conclusions

In this paper we have discussed the importance of awareness in product development projects where the developers cooperate across geographical distances for long periods of time. We have discussed product awareness, and have introduced an awareness model that puts focus on the shared product and the propagation of awareness in large composite products. This awareness model is implemented

---

[1] http://java.sun.com/products/java-media/jsdt/

in form of an awareness engine called Gossip, which is used as a part of a framework for collaboration support in distributed product development. The design and implementation of Gossip are described.

In addition to Gossip, and as a part of the discussed framework, we have implemented two test applications. One is a graphical editor for creating simple Entity–Relation models. This editor is used to demonstrate the capability of Gossip to support synchronization of screens in real time. The editor also demonstrates how the various operations in a tool can be configured to automatically trigger operations in Gossip. The other application is a shared workspace application that demonstrates how different awareness models can be used in combination.

There are several issues that constitute our future research and development agenda. One important issue is privacy. The high specialization of labor among developers makes it unrealistic to expect that they will expose information about their activities without a second thought. The name "Gossip" is chosen deliberately to emphasize this. Gossip provides easy mechanisms for inserting and removing product parts from a shared space, but more advanced mechanisms, such as access control, are needed.

The current version of Gossip does not fully implement the filtering mechanisms discussed in the previous section. We need more usage data in order to find out what filter mechanisms and criteria are needed. With large scale deployment of Gossip, filter mechanisms will become a necessity not only for having higher degree of individual tailoring, but also because of technical issues involved regarding network bandwidth usage.

Acknowledgements

I thank Arne Sølvberg, Monica Divitini, and the anonymous reviewers for their comments on this paper. Part of this research is supported by a grant from Andersen Consulting Forskningsfond, Norway.

References

BF93.   Steve Benford and Lennart Fahlèn. A Spatial Model of Interaction in Large Virtual Environments. In *Proceedings of ECSCW, Milano, Italy*, pages 109–124, September 1993. Kluwer Academic Publishers.

BHI93.   Sara Bly, Steve R. Harrison, and Susan Irwin. Media Spaces: Video, Audio, and Computing. *Communications of the ACM*, 36(1):28–47, January 1993.

BJ75.   Frederick P. Brooks Jr. *The Mythical Man–Month – Essays on Software Engineering*. Addison–Wesley, Reading, MA, 1975.

CGN95.   Erran Carmel, Loey F. George, and Jay F. Nunamaker, Jr. Examining the Process of Electronic JAD. *End User Computing*, 7(1):13–22, 1995.

Con68.   Melvin E. Conway. How do committees invent? *Datamation*, 14(4):28–31, April 1968.

CSC98.   CSCW'98, editor. *Proceedings of the Conference on CSCW, Seattle, Washington, USA*, November 1998. ACM Press.

DB92.   Paul Dourish and Victoria Bellotti. Awareness and Coordination in Shared
             Workspaces. In *Proceedings of the Conference on CSCW, Toronto, Canada*,
             pages 107–114, October 1992. ACM Press.
DLN97.   Douglas L. Dean, James D. Lee, and Jay F. Nunamaker, Jr. Group Tools
             and Methods to Support Data Model Development, Standardization, and
             Review. In *Proceedings of the 30th Hawaii Int'l Conf. on System Sciences*.
             IEEE Computer Society Press, 1997.
FPBP95.   Ludwin Fuchs, Uta Pankoke-Babatz, and Wolfgang Prinz. Supporting
             Cooperative Awareness with Local Event Mechanisms. In *Proceedings of
             ECSCW, Stockholm, Sweden*, pages 247–262. Kluwer Academic Publisher,
             September 1995.
GG98.   Carl Gutwin and Saul Greenberg. Effects of Awareness Support on Group-
             ware Usability. In *Proceedings of CHI, Los Angeles, CA, USA*, pages 511–
             518, April 1998. ACM Press.
Gri98.   Rebecca E. Grinter. Recomposition: Putting It All Back Together Again.
             In CSCW'98 [CSC98], pages 393–402.
HG99.   James D. Herbsleb and Rebecca E. Grinter. Splitting the Organization and
             Integrating the Code: Conway's Law Revisited. In *Proceedings of ICSE'99,
             Los Angeles, California, USA*, May 1999. ACM Press.
HW98.   Chung-Hua Hu and Feng-Jian Wang. A Multi–User Visual Object–Oriented
             Programming Environment. In *Proceedings of COMPSAC'98, Vienna, Aus-
             tria*, pages 262–268, 1998. IEEE Computer Society Press.
JMR92.   Matthias Jarke, Carlos Maltzahn, and Thomas Rose. Sharing Processes:
             Team Coordination in Design Repositories. *Intelligent and Cooperative In-
             formation Systems*, 1(1):145–167, March 1992.
KCI87.   Herb Krasner, Bill Curtis, and Neil Iscoe. Communication Breakdowns
             and Boundary Spanning Activities on Large Programming Projects. In
             Proceedings of Empirical Studies of Programmers, Washington D.C., USA,
             pages 47–64. Ablex Publishing Corporation, December 1987.
KE88.   Robert Kraut and Carmen Egido. Patterns of Contact and Communication
             in Scientific Research Collaboration. In *Proceedings of the Conference on
             CSCW, Portland, OR, USA*, pages 1–12. ACM, September 1988.
KS95.   Robert E. Kraut and Lynn Streeter. Coordination in Software Development.
             Communications of the ACM, 38(3):69–81, March 1995.
MKF+97.   Tim Mansfield, Simon Kaplan, Geraldine Fitzpatrick, Ted Phelps, Mark
             Fitzpatrick, and Richard Taylor. Evolving Orbit: a progress report on
             building locales. In *Proceedings of Group'97, Pheonix, USA*, pages 241–
             250, November 1997. ACM Press.
Par72.   D. L. Parnas. On the Criteria To Be Used in Decomposing Systems into
             Modules. *Communications of the ACM*, 15(12):1053–1058, 1972.
RDR98.   Devina Ramduny, Alan Dix, and Tom Rodden. Exploring the design space
             for notification servers. In CSCW'98 [CSC98], pages 227–235.
RG96.   Mark Roseman and Saul Greenberg. TeamRooms: Network Places for Col-
             laboration. In Proceedings of the Conference on CSCW, Cambridge, Mass.,
             USA, pages 325–333, November 1996. ACM Press.
TW97.   Hilda Tellioğlu and Ina Wagner. Negotiating Boundaries – Configuration
             Management in Software Development Teams. *Computer Supported Coop-
             erative Work*, 6(4):251–274, 1997.
VS95.   Iris Vessey and Ajay Paul Sravanapudi. CASE Tools as Collaborative Sup-
             port Technologies. *Communications of the ACM*, 38(1):83–95, 1995.

How Culture Might Impact on the Implementation of Enterprise Resource Planning Packages

Marina Krumbholz and Neil Arthur McDougall Maiden

Centre for Human-Computer Interaction Design
City University
Northampton Square, London, EC1V OHB
Tel: +44-171-477-8412
Fax: +44-171-477-8859
M.Krumbholz@city.ac.uk

Abstract. ERP (Enterprise Resource Planning) packages provide generic off-the-shelf business and software solutions to customers. However, these are implemented in companies with different corporate and national cultures, and there is growing evidence that failure to adapt ERP packages to fit these cultures leads to projects which are expensive and overdue. This paper describes research which synthesises social science theories of culture to be able to model and predict the impact of culture on ERP package implementation. It describes a knowledge meta-schema for modelling the surface and the deeper manifestations of culture, and for integrating these models with more common business concepts such as processes, events and information flows. It reports data from an analysis of a recent ERP implementation in a higher education institution to validate the knowledge meta-schema. It concludes with an outline of a method for ERP implementation to ensure a fit with the customer's corporate and national culture.

1. The Impact of Culture on ERP Implementation

ERP (Enterprise Resource Planning) software packages are an essential part of enterprise-wide information systems. An ERP package, such as SAP's R/3, is a large off-the-shelf software solution which provides integrated business and software systems to a customer. Unlike the traditional software development approach, which promotes building systems from scratch, ERP packages encapsulate reusable best business processes and software. Customers purchase the package then configure its business processes and software systems to meet their requirements. At the end of 1997, Business Week estimated the value of the ERP market at $10 UK billion and growing. Indeed, ERP packages are a significant part of a total software package market set to surge ahead with total licence revenues growing from $8.5 UK bn worldwide in 1998 to $20.8 UK bn in 2003, and predictions that over 60% of Europe's business solutions will be developed from packages by 2003 (source: Forrester research).

B. Wangler, L. Bergman (Eds.): CAiSE 2000, LNCS 1789, pp. 279-293, 2000

However, a recent Standish Group report on ERP implementation projects reveals that these projects were, on average, 178% over budget, took 2.5 times as long as intended and delivered only 30% of promised benefit. A survey of 12 recent projects revealed that adapting the implementation to the prevailing cultural style was one important cause of this project under-performance [7]. This importance of culture is hardly surprising. A customer who implements an ERP package has to change its business processes to the ERP supplier's best-practice processes [4]. The change both impacts on the customer's corporate culture (i.e. the ways that things are done in the organisation) and is constrained by it. In Europe, the picture is even more complex because companies also have diverse national cultures which influence this corporate culture and make the successful implementation of multi-national ERP solutions difficult. A recent such ERP implementation encountered major problems due to differences between the different participating national partners [10]. Indeed, evidence suggests that ERP implementations in North America have been more effective because of the more complex European corporate and national cultures [22]. If more ERP implementations are to deliver their promised benefits within budget, we need to understand how corporate and national culture impact on ERP implementations, and how this understanding will deliver better methods for implementation partners and customers to use.

In contrast to the lack of research in computer science, social and system science has researched the influence of corporate and national culture on organisational behaviour. Unfortunately this research neither addresses issues which are specific to information systems development, nor does it have a tradition of model-theoretic approaches which are familiar in information systems research to describe and predict problems and their solutions. If we are to implement ERP solutions which recognise corporate and national cultures, we need at least to model culture to describe and to predict its impact on an ERP implementation. This is the focus of a current research programme based in the Centre for HCI Design and supported by the world's largest ERP vendor SAP. This paper reports first results from the programme.

The model of culture presented in this paper synthesises social and system science theories of corporate [e.g. 20] and national [e.g. 21] culture. A method then applies the resulting model to design and evaluate methods for adapting ERP implementations to fit the corporate culture. It assumes that the customer's national culture is manifest through the corporate culture. As shown in Figure 1, current ERP package implementations reveal 3 types of culture-related problem which impact on a successful implementation: (i) the current corporate culture clashes with the planned future culture; (ii) the supplier's culture, implicit in the ERP package, clashes with the customer's corporate culture, and; (iii) the new business processes (configured using the ERP solution) clashes with the existing corporate culture. All of these types of clash necessitate customisation of the business processes and software to resolve the clash. However, such customisation is expensive: on average 10-20% of an ERP implementation budget is spent on ERP customisation (source: Forrester Research).

Our research posits that to detect these 3 types of culture-related clash we need to be able to model: (i) the customer's business processes and solution systems; (ii) facets of the corporate and national culture which impact on the implementation of

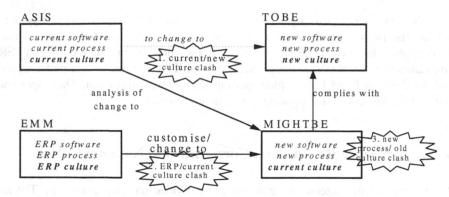

Fig. 1: How culture impacts on ERP implementation. During an ideal ERP implementation process there will be 4 different models of the organisation's culture, processes and software systems: (i) the ASIS model, which describes the organisation's current culture, processes and software; (ii) the TOBE model, which describes the required culture, processes and software; (iii) the ERP model, which describes the ERP supplier's processes, software and culture; (iv) the MIGHTBE model, which describes how future processes and software will operate in the current culture.

these business processes; (iii) how these facets of corporate and national culture impact on the business and software solutions. The research also posits a method to exploit these models during ERP implementation. The implementation team will use current ERP modelling approaches to model the current and future business processes. It will then extend these models with features of corporate and national culture. The team will discover potential problems by analysing the differences between the two business process models using predictions of possible problems using theories of corporate and national culture. The method will also deliver advice to the implementation team to resolve these problems through a set of Culture Impact Patterns. The outline method is shown in Figure 2. This paper reports research into the first stage of the method, to model the essential characteristics of corporate culture which impact on ERP package implementation.

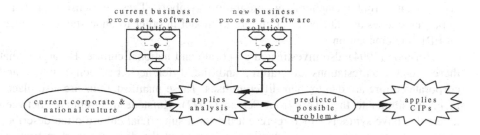

Fig. 2: An outline of the extended ERP implementation method for culture-sensitive ERP implementation.

The remainder of this paper is in 5 sections. Section 2 summarises existing social science theories of culture. Section 3 presents the first-draft model of culture. Section 4 describes the results from studies of the impact of culture of an ERP implementation on a UK customer. Section 5 outlines cultural impact patterns, their link to the model and how implementation teams might use them. The paper ends with a brief discussion and presentation of future research.

2. Social Science Research on Corporate and National Culture

Most social science research on culture can be divided into two camps [8]. The first camp claims that culture is something tacit which arises naturally. The other, more common view is that culture is something explicit, which arises from social interaction. Social science research also divides research into culture into research into national cultures, business cultures and corporate cultures. A good starting point is Schein (1992) who provides the following definition of corporate culture:

> "a pattern of basic assumptions – invented, discovered or developed by a given group as it learns to cope with its problems of external adaptation and internal integration – that has worked well enough to be considered valid and therefore to be taught to new members as the correct way to perceive, think and feel in relation to those problems".

He argues that corporate culture can be divided into three layers. In the outer layer there are values which are written down statements about the strategies, missions and objectives of the organisation. In the middle layer there are beliefs which are the issues that the employees of an organisation talk about. In the inner layer there are the "taken for granted" assumptions which are those aspects of the organisational life which people find it difficult to recall and explain. Schein also describes 10 dimensions that he uses to differentiate between corporate cultures in different organisations. These are the observed behavioural regularities of human interaction; the group norms; the espoused corporate values; the formal philosophy; the rules of the game; the climate; the habits of thinking; people's mental models and/or linguistic paradigms; their shared meanings; their embedded skills; and the organisation's root metaphors' or integration symbols. These dimensions indicate important classes and attributes of culture to model in order to understand its impact on ERP implementation.

Hofstede (1994) also investigated corporate and national culture. He argues that there are 4 manifestations of culture, and the differences between national and corporate culture are due to their different uses. These manifestations are also placed in layers similar to the layers from Schein (1992). Hofstede differentiates between layers that have symbols which represent the most superficial culture often described as practice, layers which have values which represent the deepest manifestations of culture, and intermediate layers which describe heroes and rituals indicative of the corporate culture. He claims that national culture differences reside more in values and less in practices, and organisational culture differences reside more in practices and less in values. Furthermore, he claims that we can detect national and corporate culture differences using a set of dimensions similar to those from Schein (1992). From extensive empirical studies Hofstede provides 4 dimensions, which differentiate between national cultures: power distance, individualism-collectivism, masculinity-femininity, and uncertainty avoidance [11]. Likewise, he detects 6 dimensions to differentiate between organisational cultures: process- versus results-oriented; employee- versus job-oriented; parochial- versus professional-dependent; open versus closed systems of communication; loose versus tight control; and normative versus pragmatic organisations [11]. As with Schein's findings, Hofstede's dimensions indicate important elements of culture which we need to model in order to understand the impact on ERP implementation.

Trompenaars (1994) argues that national culture can be described with 3 layers similar to those from Hofstede. A central theme of Trompenaar's argument is that people organise themselves in such a way so as to increase the effectiveness of their problem-solving processes, and so have formed different sets of implicit logical assumptions to enable this to happen. Each culture distinguishes itself from others in terms of its solutions to these problems. These problems can also be classified to differentiate between national cultures in a similar way to which Hofstede uses his 6 dimensions. These classes are how people relate to each other (sub-divided into universalism versus particularism, individualism versus collectivism, neutral versus emotional, specific versus diffuse, achievement versus ascription), people's attitudes to time, and people's attitudes to the environment [21]. Again, these classes provide a basis for modelling the critical determinants of corporate and national cultures.

Our extensive research of the key social sciences research into culture summarised here reveals 4 conclusions, which we might be able to exploit to improve ERP implementation:

• theories of corporate and national culture have similar definitions of culture and share important concepts which include values, beliefs and norms;
• these theories distinguish between the deep manifestations and the superficial features of corporate and of national culture;
• critical determinants of a corporate culture reside more in observable practices, whereas critical determinants of a national culture reside more in the nation's deeper set of values;
• corporate and national culture can be described using multiple dimensions which give us a set of overlapping facets with which to describe aspects of culture.

Our wider research programme uses these conclusions to posit 4 key research hypotheses which drive the programme. First, it posits that corporate and national culture has a direct impact on ERP implementation problems which customer organisations experience during implementation. Second, it posits that social science theories can describe the problems observed in current ERP implementations. Third, it posits that a synthesis of social science theories of culture can be applied to explain culture-related problems which arise during ERP implementations. Fourth, the programme posits that these theories can be applied to predict such problems in future ERP implementations. In the next section we report research which explores the first and second hypotheses. We apply social science research to develop a first-draft model of corporate and national culture which can be applied to describe culture-related problems during ERP implementations. It is the main focus of this paper.

3. A Model of Culture for ERP Implementation

The enhanced ERP implementation method outlined in section 1 integrates current business processes approaches with models of corporate and national culture to discover potential problems using predictions of possible problems using social science theories of corporate and national culture. The basis of the model is a knowledge meta-schema for modelling the critical elements of corporate and national culture. This, in itself, is an innovative advance. Social science does not have a tradition of conceptual modelling to describe and analyse systems. Indeed, non-computer science disciplines resist conceptual modelling because it is too difficult to capture and describe the knowledge without losing the essential context of the knowledge. However, the common definitions of culture from social science researchers offer exciting opportunities. We have synthesised and extended these social science theories to model the problems observed in current ERP implementations.

The first stage of the research was to design a knowledge meta-schema capable of representing both the deeper manifestations and the superficial attributes of corporate and national culture, and the critical causal associations between them. The knowledge meta-schema also integrates these attributes with standard business process models such as SAP's EPC models so that the knowledge meta-schema can be used in methods such as SAP's ASAP method. For readers unfamiliar with these models, a segment of an EPC model for invoice processing taken from version 4.5 of SAP's R/3 includes events, processes and event flows for business processes. The full first-draft knowledge meta-schema is shown in Figure 3 below.

Space does not allow us to give a full definition of the knowledge meta-schema. Instead we provide key definitions drawn first of all from software and business process models common in current ERP implementation methods such as ASAP. An **agent** is a type of object, which processes actions [18]. Agents perform actions to achieve goals. With respect to culture, agents have beliefs, values and norms that govern their actions. One instance of an agent can be one individual person, a collection of people, one machine or a collection of machines. An **action** is the process of doing something with the intention of achieving a desired goal [17]. Actions are constrained by pre-conditions and post-conditions. **Pre- & post-conditions** are conditions which must occur for an action to begin or end. An **event** is a moment in time when something happens. In the knowledge meta-schema events start and end actions. An **object** is something which is manipulated for the attainment of a goal. An object can be a physical object (e.g. a radio), an infological object (e.g. information about an incident) or an object with both physical and infological elements (e.g. an incident report). A **goal** is a high-level objective that the system should meet. Goals are achieved by actions performed by agents manipulating objects [5]. These concepts are common in most current ERP business modelling approaches

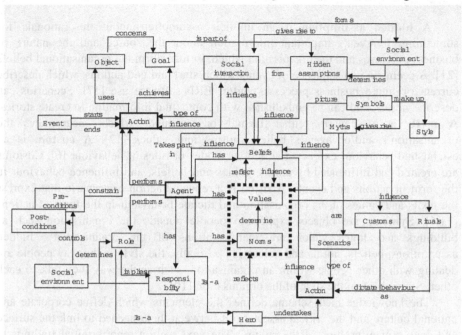

Fig. 3: The knowledge meta-schema that describes elements of corporate and culture, which impact on ERP implementation

and represent many of the more observable indicators of corporate culture according to Hofstede (1994).

The rest of the knowledge meta-schema is drawn from social science research into culture which is summarised in the previous section. All are critical determinants of corporate and national culture according to the theories reported in the previous section. A **role** defines the obligations of an agent. An agent can fulfil one or more role types. **Responsibilities** define the liabilities of the agents associated with the role they perform. Agents are responsible for fulfilling a role and initiating, controlling or undertaking actions related to their role [17]. A **hero** is a human agent admired by other agents in the organisation [6]. Heroes are agents that, through their role and responsibilities, undertake actions which reflect the organisational beliefs, norms and values. A **social interaction** describes an interaction between agents. It is a specialisation of an action. Social interaction can influence agents and their beliefs. A **belief** is an agent's feeling that something is true, or good or exists [11,20]. Beliefs influence agents and their actions, values and norms, and the customs and rituals adopted within an organisation [8]. Each belief is influenced and formed by hidden assumptions. A **value** is a standard, a principle or an ideal about the worth or importance of something. Each value can exist on spectrums such as good versus evil and normal versus abnormal [11,20]. Each value also reflects a belief and so influences agents and their actions. A **norm** is a standard expectation of what is normal and what is right or wrong [11,21]. A norm influences values which reflect beliefs and, in turn, influence agents and actions.

A **hidden assumption** is an implicit assumption about the rationale for something. It reveals important information about the source and the nature of business processes and the organisation which, in turn, form the organisational beliefs [21]. A **scenario** is a sequence of events which start and end actions, which describe current or future business processes and/or ERP software use [17]. Scenarios can describe norms, and can be embellished with contextual information to create stories. A **myth** is a scenario, either factual or invented, which encapsulates the organisation's and/or agent's beliefs, norms and values [12]. A **custom** is an established behaviour expressed as actions, codes or rules of behaviour [6]. Customs are created and influenced by norms, values and beliefs, and influence behaviour in the form of actions and events. A **ritual** is a repeated action or scenario that express the goals and values of the organisation and dictate behaviour in the form of actions [11,6]. **Symbols** are objects explicit to people outside the organisation such as buildings and logos which are manifestations of the organisation's hidden assumptions, beliefs, norms and values [11]. Finally, the **style** is the way people are dealing with other people within an organisation, such as the way they talk to each other. Symbols form the style of the organisation [19].

The knowledge meta-schema defines the elements which define corporate and national culture and the critical associations between them needed to link the surface and deeper manifestation of the culture. The next section reports initial findings to validate the knowledge meta-schema's effectiveness for describing these critical elements of culture which influence ERP implementations.

4. Validating the Knowledge Meta-schema: The Impact of Culture on an ERP Implementation

In order to validate whether the knowledge meta-schema can describe critical elements of culture, we undertook field studies in an UK higher education establishment whose finance department had recently implemented SAP's R/3. We undertook two interviews each with three different stakeholders of the implementation ERP package. In the first interview, each stakeholder was asked to describe his/her job, department, background information and problems which had arisen due to the implementation. In the second interview, the stakeholders were asked questions to elicit evidence about the corporate culture of the institution. A prepared set of questions were asked to elicit underlying causes, including possible cultural causes, for those problems mentioned in the first interview. The questioning method was derived from a synthesis of culture dimensions undertaken by the authors based on dimensions from Hofstede, Schein and Trompenaars reported in section 2. These dimensions enable us to describe and compare critical manifestations of corporate and national culture. The application of a "neutral" method from social science research counters claims that the studies "found what they were looking for" in terms of the posited knowledge meta-schema.

1. How long have you been working in the department?
2. What is your position in the organisation?
3. How well do you believe you understand the culture of the university and department?
4. Do you have any contact with other departments?
5. Do you believe that you fit to the university or the departmental culture?
6. If then how have your roles and responsibilities changed as a result of the new system?
7. Were partner consultants involved with you during the new system implementation?
8. How has your work changed as a result of the new system?
9. What problems have arisen as a result of the new system?
10. Have these problems impacted on how work is done? How?
11. Have there been any security implications from these problems?
12. Do you and your colleagues talk about these problems?
13. What do you see as the source of these problems and why?
14. Have problems arisen from poor implementation of the new system?
15. Have these problems been supported by high-level management?
16. Were you happier with the old system?
17. What was your first impression of the new system, and has it changed?
18. Have problems experienced by you and your colleagues led to stress?
19. How would you characterise the general climate prevailing in the department now after the ERP implementation?

Fig. 4: Questions asked during the first interview.

4.1. The First Interviews

The first interview elicited information about stakeholders, the corporate culture, the ERP implementation and the problems or issues that it created. The interviewer asked open-ended questions followed by more specific ones to elicit reasons and rationale about the culture and the ERP implementation-related problems. This provided data about how the current system, the ERP implementation, problems which arose during the implementation and the climate resulting from the implementation. A sample set of questions is shown in Figure 4. All interviewees responded to these questions.

4.2. The Second Interviews

The purpose of the second interview was to elicit surface manifestations of corporate culture, then use a variation of the laddering technique from knowledge engineering [16] to elicit deeper determinants of culture which were possible causes of these surface manifestations and problems reported in the first interview. The elements of culture found on outer layers of the social science models are the observable manifestations of culture. Elements of culture found in the inner layer are tacit, more important determinants of national and, to a lesser degree, corporate culture. Our questions were designed to elicit the observable manifestations of culture described on the outer layers then use precise verbal probes to elicit tacit rationale for these manifestations. This use of external manifestations of culture to elicit deeper underlying causes was the principal reason for two interviews rather than one. The

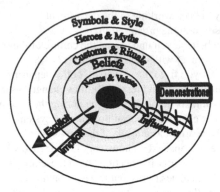

Fig. 5: a synthesis of the layers of the elements of culture taken from social science research to provide a basis for the questioning method.

specific questioning approach was based on a synthesis of these layers of culture from social science research which is shown in Figure 5. Questions asked to elicit the external manifestations of the culture included: Is management more concerned with getting work done than with the people who do the work, Is good work rewarded, and Are there "rules" that a newcomer must learn to be accepted in the department? The laddering technique was then applied to "drill down" through the layers of culture shown in Figure 5 through repeated asking of "why?" and "how?" questions.

All interview data was analysed to determine key culture-related phenomena relevant to the ERP implementation. Relevant segments were transcribed and analysed by the authors. Each of these segments was then analysed further to determine critical elements of culture and causal associations between them using the knowledge meta-schema definitions outlined in section 3 and detailed questions asked in the second interview.

4.3. Preliminary Results

Results from the first interview reveal that most ERP implementation problems were related to procedures, workloads and the lack of training made available to the end-users of the new system. The interviewees offered numerous opinions about why this was. Reasons included the lack of access to official training courses and the time to go on the training courses. This data provided the basis for the second interviews. The results from the second interviews were more complex. We are still completing a full analysis of the data to determine the degree of fit between the elicited data and the posited knowledge meta-schema. This paper samples this data, and presents 3 result segments which demonstrate the detected patterns of the results so far.

The first transcript segment reveals the problem of an uneven allocation of extra work resulting from the implementation of the ERP system. The accounts services manager believed that his work would be easier and more fun because of the implementation of R/3. He believed that he would learn a new system and make his work better and more efficient. However, after implementation, work such as

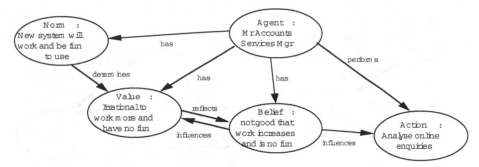

Fig. 6: a partial instantiation of the knowledge meta-schema using data from the second interview with the accounts services manager.

analysing online enquiries increased and became more complex, which he believed was irrational. The increased work had a direct effect on his satisfaction and motivation to complete the work, which led to more mistakes. The definitions of culture were applied to the transcript data to determine elements of culture, and then a simple model was developed. This instantiation of the knowledge meta-schema to model the elements of culture identifiable from the data is shown in Figure 6.

The application of the knowledge meta-schema identifies the importance of the agent's norms, values and beliefs on problems arising from a process (shown as an action in the meta-schema). The critical element of this model is the violation of the agent's expectation expressed as a norm, which in turn reflects the agent's beliefs which influences the agent's behaviour in the process. This model-driven analysis of the problem is a richer explanation of the observed problem than just saying that the agent's increased workload impacts on the analysis of online enquiries. Indeed, the identification of an important agent norm enables us to explain and predict other possible problems with other processes undertaken by the same agent or similar agents if the norm does not occur. In short, the use of the knowledge meta-schema enables us to identify, describe and model more fundamental drivers which influence ERP implementations.

In another transcript segment, the accounts assistant believed that the implementation and training on the new system that he would receive would enable him to do his work faster and more accurately. However, he believed that the training received on the new system was inadequate. This individual valued high-quality training to use such a new system successfully. Instead the lack of training increased the number of mistakes and he believed that he was unable to perform his roles and responsibilities effectively. This was also a view held by other colleagues in the department. Again the definitions of culture were applied to the transcript data to determine elements of culture, and a simple model which instantiates the knowledge meta-schema was developed. This model is shown in Figure 7.

Again the knowledge meta-schema highlights the influence of the agent's norms, values and beliefs on a process. The accounts assistant values training and expects training to be available for the new system, but he believes that the insufficient training influe nces performances of processes such as issuing invoices. Again the

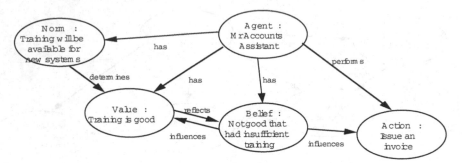

Fig. 7: a partial instantiation of the knowledge meta-schema using data from the second interview with the accounts assistant.

critical element of this model is the violation of the agent's expectation expressed as a norm (training will be available) which in turn reflects the agent's beliefs which influences the agent's behaviour in the process. As with the first model, this model-driven analysis provides us with a richer explanation of the observed problem than a simple statement of inadequate training. Indeed, the identification of an important agent norm again enables us to explain and predict other possible problems with other processes undertaken by the same agent or similar agents if the norm does not occur.

In a third transcript segment the accounts payable manager believed that staff levels should match the new work levels across the department. However, the introduction of the new system meant that he had to import information from the old system into the new system on top of his other work activities, whereas other sections in the department received extra staff to manage the implementation of the new system. The accounts payable manager felt that this was unfair. His increased workload led to less interest, less motivation and more mistakes. The model derived from this segment of transcript data is shown in Figure 8.

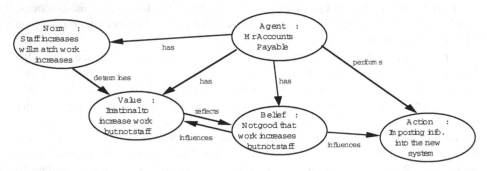

Fig. 8: a partial instantiation of the knowledge meta-schema using data from the second interview with the accounts payable manager.

This model reveals an emerging pattern in agent's norms, values and beliefs relevant to this ERP implementation. The accounts payable manager expected staff levels to match work levels resulting from the new system, and believes that it is not good if this does not happen which in turn influenced his performance on business processes. The critical element of the model is the violation of the agent's norm which determines values and beliefs which influence his actions. Again the model-driven analysis provides us with a richer explanation of the observed problem. The identification of another important agent norm again enables us to explain and predict other possible problems with other processes undertaken by the same agent or similar agents if the norm does not occur.

4.4. Preliminary Conclusions

Preliminary evidence from the studies reported here and elsewhere reveals 5 conclusions regarding the impact of the corporate culture on ERP implementation:

* social science techniques are effective for eliciting culture-related data about ERP implementations, albeit after the implementation has taken place;
* the posited knowledge meta-schema can be applied to model this data;
* the application of the knowledge meta-schema introduces more precision to the description of ERP implementation problems;
* the knowledge meta-schema can be applied to model critical elements of culture which influence implementation problems: in the 3 models shown the meta-schema was applied to link the violation of an agent's norm or expectation to observable problems linked to business processes;
* these implementation problems are modelled as complex patterns of knowledge about agents, norms, values, beliefs and actions, as shown in Figures 6, 7 and 8.

The posited ERP implementation method will only be effective it offers consultants and customers sufficient leverage over the implementation problems. The main benefit of the knowledge meta-schema shown in these preliminary results is that the meta-schema enables us to model more important but deeper influences which can influence all business processes which agents are involved in. The final section explores one solution for exploiting this leverage which builds on the fifth conclusion, that implementation problems are modelled as complex patterns of knowledge about agents, norms, values, beliefs and actions.

5. Delivering Benefits: Cultural Impact Patterns

One criticism of existing management science theories of culture is their lack of application to improve organisational change. We aim to deliver this application through patterns which describe culture-related impacts. A pattern is an abstraction of a problem, a solution to the problem AND the context(s) in which this solution is applicable [9]. Patterns have come to IT design from architectural design. Alexander (1977) posits that pattern languages are collections of patterns used by a process to generate artefacts that are complexes of patterns.

Pattern detection and application necessitates a more formal expression of the problem in context. This is where the knowledge meta-schema comes in. The models which instantiate the knowledge meta-schema, shown in Figures 6, 7 and 8, enable us to model this problem and context so that solutions to improve ERP implementations can be applied to the right problem at the right time. However, the successful identification and application of these patterns remains research conjecture which we will examine later in the research programme.

6. Conclusions and Future Work

This paper reports the results of preliminary research into the implementation of ERP packages in organisations with diverse corporate and national cultures. It exploits social science theories [11,21] to posit a model of corporate and national culture characteristics, which, we hypothesise, impact on ERP implementations. It describes a knowledge meta-schema with which to model these characteristics. Post-implementation studies of an ERP implementation in a higher education institution were undertaken to provide data to validate the knowledge meta-schema's power of description. Preliminary findings are positive: the knowledge meta-schema was applied to detect the importance of deviations from agent's expected norms which influence how the agent undertakes business processes. The elicitations of these cultural norms are an example of how the identification of the deeper cultural characteristics can offer greater leverage to customers and consultants during ERP implementation. The results provide the foundation for accepting the first and second research hypotheses of this research programme stated in the final paragraph of section 2.

However, the data reported here only provide weak validation of parts of the knowledge meta-schema and no validation at all of social science theories to explain and predict the impact of different corporate and national cultures on ERP implementations. Instead the reported scientific results raise our awareness of the potential importance of culture on ERP implementation only hinted at anecdotally so far in Gulla & Mollan (1999) and Densley (1999). The paper also advocates the possible use of patterns to detect and resolve common, recurring problems during ERP implementations. To provide more complete validation the authors are currently undertaking on-site studies of the implementation of several ERP packages in the same organisations across Europe. Data elicited from these studies will provide more extensive validation of the knowledge meta-schema and, more importantly, predictions from social science theories which will deliver real benefits to the proposed ERP implementation method. We look forward to reporting these more complete results when they are available.

References

1. Alexander C., 1977, 'A Pattern Language', Oxford University Press.
2. Anton A. & Potts C., 1998, 'The Use of Goals to Surface Requirements for Evolving Systems', Proceedings 19th IEEE International Conference on Software Engineering, IEEE Computer Society Press.
3. Cartwright S. & Cooper G.L., 1996, 'Managing Mergers, Acquisitions and Strategic Alliances: Integrating people and cultures', Butterworth-Heinemann Oxford.
4. Curran T.A. & Ladd A., 1999, 'SAP R/3 Business Blueprint', Prentice-Hall.
5. Darimont .R & Van Lamsweerde A., 199*, 'Formal Refinement Patterns for Goal-Driven Requirements Elaboration', Proceedings 4th ACM Symposium Foundations of Software Engineering, ACM Press, 179-190.
6. Deal T. & Kennedy A., 1982, 'Corporate Cultures: The Rites and Rituals of Corporate Life', Penguin Books, London.
7. Densley B., 1999, 'The Magnificent Seven: Getting the Biggest Bang from the ERP Buck', Proceedings 1st Intl Workshop EMRPS99, eds J. Eder, N. Maiden & M. Missikoff, Istituto de Analisi dei Sistemi ed Informatica, CNR Roma, 59-65.
8. Dobson P., Williams A., & Walters M., 1993, 'Changing Culture: New Organisational Approaches', Institute of Personnel Management, London, 2nd edition.
9. Gabriel R., 1995, 'Patterns of Software', Oxford University Press.
10. Gulla J.A. & Mollan R., 1999, 'Implementing SAP R/3 in a Multi-Cultural Organisation', Proceedings 1st Intl Workshop EMRPS99, eds J. Eder, N. Maiden & M. Missikoff, Istituto de Analisi dei Sistemi ed Informatica, CNR Roma, 127-134.
11. Hofstede G., 1990 & 1994, 'Cultures and Organisations', Intercultural Co-operation and Its Importance for Survival. Software of the Mind, Author of Culture's Consequences, Harper Collins, London.
12. Johnson G., 1992, 'Managing Strategic Change: Strategy, Culture and Action', Long Range Publishing 25(1), pp??
13. Johnson G. & Scholes K., 1997, 'Exploring Corporate Strategy: Text and Cases', Prentice Hall Europe.
14. Kotter J.P. & Heskett J.L., 1992, 'Corporate Culture and Performance', The Free Press, New York USA.
15. Maiden N. A. M., Minocha S. & Manning K., 1996, 'Socio-Technical System Scenarios: A Template based Approach', Technical Report, Centre for HCI Design, City University, London.
16. Maiden N.A.M. & Rugg G., 1996, 'ACRE: A Framework for Acquiring Requirements', Software Engineering Journal 11(1).
17. Maiden N.A.M, 1998, 'SAVRE: Scenarios for Acquiring & Validating Requirements', Journal of Automated software Engineering 5, 419-446
18. Ncube c. & Maiden N.A.M., 1999, 'Guidance for Parallel Requirements Acquisition and COTS Software Selection', Proceedings 4th IEEE Symposium on Requirements Engineering, IEEE Computer Society press, xx-xx
19. Peters & Waterman, 1982, 'In Search of Excellence'', Harper & Raw, New York.
20. Schein E. H., 1992, 'Organisational Culture and Leadership', Jossey-Bass Publishers, San Francisco.
21. Trompenaars F., 1994, 'Riding the Waves of Culture: Understanding Cultural Diversity in Business', Nicholas Brealey Publishing, London.
22. Vernon M., 1999, 'ERP endangered species?', Computer Weekly, 4/11/99 p.32

Capture and Dissemination of Experience about the Construction of Engineering Processes

Christian Rupprecht, Martin Fünffinger, Holger Knublauch, Thomas Rose

Research Institute for Applied Knowledge Processing (FAW)
Helmholtzstraße 16, D-89081 Ulm, Germany
{rupprech, fuenffin, knublauc, rose}@faw.uni-ulm.de

Abstract. Process know-how is instrumental to govern engineering processes in a network of engineering departments as well as migrate changes of processes due to emerging technological or other opportunities. In this paper we present a process construction kit for the capture and dissemination of process knowledge at the level of process structures as well as process construction experience. Our approach ranges from the formal capture and maintenance of know-how about processes to the implementation of process adaptations in terms of object-oriented concepts. Requirements are drawn from specific reference applications in the automotive engineering and the plant construction domain.

1 Introduction

For the past years, process management has been coined by terms such as business process re-engineering [10,13], workflow support [11], or even process innovation [3]. The prime focus has been the (re-) design of process flows with respect to efficiency, quality or customer satisfaction. That is, optimisation of enterprise resources has been the focal point. Only recently, the attention is shifting from an enterprise resource planning stance towards a business enabling stance to generate expertise. Rather than optimising processes, the prime goal is to generate business opportunities. Process knowledge, be it at the level of process structures or experience about process construction, emerges as critical factor for an enterprise's performance.

As a matter of fact, many aspects of process experience that used to be implicit in the organisational culture, need to be made explicit and even transferable. The prime objective of our research is to elevate the capability to capture and disseminate experience in the construction of engineering processes. The question arises of how to "construct" processes in light of best-practice and technological opportunities, e.g. employ simulation methods instead of crash tests with prototypes.

In our approach, the construction of a process refers to the intellectual task of specifying the activities and their relationships. This task is further compounded by the nature of engineering processes, which are prevailingly characterised by attributes such as innovative, individual, dynamic, interdisciplinary, strongly interrelated, strongly parallel, iterative, communication intensive, anticipatory, planning intensive, uncertain, risky, etc. [18]. Modelling such processes is necessary for reasons of transparency, documentation, execution, communication, co-ordination, co-operation, planning, what-if analysis, etc.

B. Wangler, L. Bergman (Eds.): CAiSE 2000, LNCS 1789, pp. 294-308, 2000
© Springer-Verlag Berlin Heidelberg 2000

Original services of a pro-active process construction approach should include:

- initial construction of processes based on best-practice, technological opportunities, and quality guidelines;
- on the fly adaptations along the dimensions of extension, refinement, individualisation, and configuration;
- online alarm amid execution.

Our approach is founded in a process construction kit. The process construction kit consists of a repository for managing basic building blocks and structures of processes, and an array of operators for adapting pieces of processes as well as orchestrating processes from smaller pieces.

Based on experiences in two large European companies in the automotive and utility plant construction sectors, we defined a process engineering environment for the construction, assessment, synchronisation, and individualisation of processes [21,22]. The specific intention is to provide dedicated support to process engineers who themselves are experts in the engineering domain, i.e. there are no third party champions involved that formally represent and adapt processes following a sequence of interviews. The process construction kit aims at the conceptual design of processes in terms of ontologies while at the same time offering automated support for individualising processes.

This paper is organised as follows. In section 2, we elaborate the essentials of processes, process models, and their use with regard to process construction. Section 3 presents our approach for managing process experience at a conceptual and system level. The main objective is to establish a comprehensive framework for coping with developing experience in process construction — ranging from a conceptual framework "down to" an ontology-based formal representation of process construction methods. Related approaches are discussed in section 4, while future extensions of the overall framework are discussed in section 5.

2   Processware

2.1   Processes

In the field of process management, many definitions carrying different foci on the term process can be found. In order to gain a common understanding for this paper on what a process is, we define a *process* as a set of temporally or logically ordered activities intended to reach a goal involving resources. In ordinary usage, a task is often synonymous with a process. In this paper, we understand a *task* as the definition of a goal together with the information about data, objects, resources, rules and other constraints needed for achieving this goal, whereas working on the task is called a process. *Activities* have no externally visible substructure and they are performed by *agents* that can be humans or machines (cf. [12]).

The order of activities can be derived either from their temporal constraints or logical relations among each other. Temporal constraints can be specified, e.g. by assigning starting and ending time to activities. In this case, a temporal order of activities in terms of a time schedule (e.g. gantt chart) can be derived without knowing anything about logical dependencies. Logical relations between activities capture knowledge about the sequence of activities on a more generic level independent of a specific time schedule. In both cases, the result is the ordered sequence of activities, which emphasises the dynamic character of processes.

2.2   Process Models

A process can be regarded as a system where the elements are activities and resources and the relations are the sequential or logical dependencies between those elements. The set of relations describes the *process structure*.

Unlike many other definitions, we understand the design of a process model as a *constructive process* rather than a mere mapping of a process structure given in reality. A process structure is not per se existent in reality and cannot be perceived as such; it is created by subjective interpretation of the real world and mental construction out of a world of experience and imaginations [23]. Regarding a process as a system means already creating a mental model of the original process. An original process does not necessarily have to be a "real" process that has occurred in the past or is observed in the present, but it can also be a potential solution of how things could be done in the future. Thus, we define a *process model* as a mental or explicit representation of original processes.

In general, directed graphs are used for the explicit representation of processes. When we speak of process models in this paper, we mean semi-formal, computational representations in symbolic notation, i.e. general process elements like activities and their relations are represented by formal symbols (boxes and vectors) and additional information are attached non-formally, e.g. naming the symbols in natural language.

Practically all process representation techniques use the notion of decomposition [16]: process models can be decomposed into different sub-processes, which again can be made up of other sub-processes. Sub-processes on the lowest level of decomposition are called activities. The decomposition of processes results in an aggregation hierarchy.

Every formal process representation technique (e.g. SADT-diagrams, Petri-nets, event driven process chains etc.) is based on a specific modelling method and a meta-model, which provides guidelines for the construction of process models. Depending on the intended goal of the representation form, other elements of interest besides activities and logical dependencies can be represented in a process model. Those most frequently mentioned are [2]:

- *Agent* – an actor (human or machine) who performs an activity;
- *Role* – a coherent set of activities assigned to an agent as a unit of functional responsibility
- *Artefact* – the output of an activity.

In complex system development processes, most of the output is manifested in documents. As a matter of fact, documents constitute processes. Therefore, in our approach, we take into account the representation of documents as an artefact created or modified by the enactment of activities.

2.3   Use of Process Models

Process models are created for a specific purpose. Essentially, process modelling is the first step to come up with a formalisation of processes, which serves as the basic platform to build upon [15]. FRICKE ET AL. put forward several aspects why modelling development processes is necessary and worth the effort [7]. Process modelling objectives can be classified into five basic categories [2]:

- *Facilitate human understanding and communication* – process transparency helps people (including the customer) to communicate on the work to be done and to understand what part they play in the game. Process models may serve as a prerequisite for audits and as an excellent learning aid for employees [18].
- *Support process improvement* – process improvements are based on process model assessments, be it in terms of formal reasoning (e.g. static or dynamic analyses) or visual assessment (cf. [19]).
- *Support process management* – a process model provides a sound basis for detailed planning and easier monitoring, measurement and co-ordination of an actual development project.
- *Automate process guidance* – The documentation of process structures enables the capturing and later reuse of process know-how. The objective is to provide "guidance, suggestions, and reference material to facilitate human performance of the intended process" [2].
- *Automate process execution support* – This aims at the derivation of data structures for the development or adaptation of information systems supporting the enactment of processes. Parts of the process can be automated, e.g. by distributing and supplying information and documents electronically with the help of a workflow management system [11].

In the following, we introduce an approach which basically goes along the line of automated process guidance.

3   Approach

Process management constitutes a prime competence to value generation. Process models capture know-how about ways of working in the past or intended in the future. However, a static process model contains no information about *why* work had or has to be done in a certain way. Prevailing process models and supporting tools lack in the adaptation of actual processes. That is, there are sophisticated design, analysis, and management methods and tools, but methods for customising processes in the design and even execution phase are sparse. With our approach, we aim at creating generic, reusable representations of process construction knowledge in terms of an ontology (cf. [6,8]) that can be applied across a variety of future process cases by means of a process construction kit.

3.1   Conceptual Framework

3.1.1   Process Individualisation

Due to the non-repetitive project character of complex system engineering processes process planning can be performed at the modelling level of process instances. These process instances must be individually tailored according to the current project-specific context (requirements and constraints), in order to serve as a useful basis for process execution and automation at an operational level [22]. We call the process of adapting a process model according to a specific context *process individualisation*. It is necessary when generating new process instances at the beginning of a project as well as during project run-time, when constraints and requirements change.

In general, instantiation and individualisation refer to two different dimensions of process modelling (figure 1). In the sense of object-oriented modelling, process models can be on different levels of information modelling, i.e. a meta model gives guidelines for creating a model on the type level, which can be instantiated for execution (cf. [12]). But this instantiation does not necessarily include the adaptation of the process model to a specific context. That is why the dimension of individualising process models can be regarded as orthogonal to the levels of information modelling. A meta model is always meant to give guidelines for many cases; thus, it does not make sense to develop a project-specific meta model.

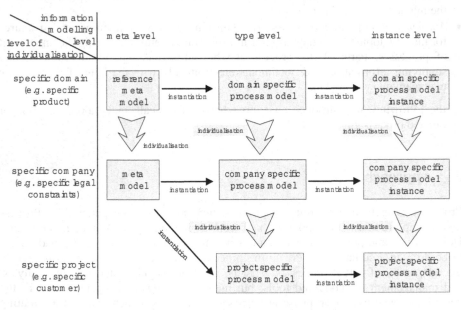

Fig. 1. Levels of modelling and individualisation

3.1.2   Process Construction Kit

In our approach, the specific *context* of a process model is described explicitly by a model of constraints and requirements. Together with the corresponding individual process instance, this model forms a *process case* (see figure 2). These process cases can be reused as best-practice patterns for other cases by copying them.

The likelihood of a process case "fitting" a hundred percent on another project-specific context without any manual adaptations is rather low. Therefore, *reference process models* are needed on a generic level, i. e. they are automatically adaptable to a specific context via defined operators. For example, reference process models (cf. [20]) can refer to a certain product type or a certain procedure (like ISO 9000 certification). New process instances can be generated by automated individualisation.

For complex and innovative engineering processes, it is not sufficient to document a best-practice process once and follow this pattern for ever in all future process cases. Just as little, an overall generic reference process can be modelled that can be adapted to all future process cases. For reasons of higher reusability and flexible connectivity, an extensive process model can be stripped down to temporally and logically isolated units called *process building blocks*. Such building blocks should have only few interfaces to other process models or building blocks, and they should "know" how they may be connected to other building blocks. Similar to reference process models, process building blocks should be generic, in order to allow an automated individualisation and configuration of a new project-specific process instance. Generic reference process models comprise generic building blocks and are augmented with additional, non-generic process structures.

Constraints and requirements have influence on the design of processes. They can be used to describe the context of a process. Values of such constraints and requirements come from a set of discrete values (e.g. a product type or boolean values) or from a continuous interval (e.g. numeric value for the project-specific order value). Constraints and requirements and their relationships are captured at a generic level in terms of an ontology, which provides guidance in modelling an actual context.

Experience in process construction is broken down into single design decisions that are captured in terms of *construction rules*. A construction rule consists of a condition part which refers to constraints and an execution part which triggers construction operators. Construction rules are represented as dependencies among constraints and process building blocks in the ontology. By applying these construction rules to a specific model of constraints and requirements, proposals for adaptations to the process model are generated.

Documents and other resources are connected to the process models in terms of informational dependencies.

The knowledge base of the process construction kit is extendable, that means, users can define new constraints, requirements, reference process models, process building blocks, and construction rules at any time on a generic level and add them to the ontology. By collecting and maintaining such knowledge from different engineers, process modelling experience (i.e. the reasons for process design decisions in a specific context) can be captured and reused for future process modelling cases.

3.1.3   Example for a Process Individualisation

This approach allows one to tailor process models in accordance with project-specific requirements, as it is particularly relevant for processes in the domain of complex system engineering [18]. Figure 3 demonstrates the basic principle of advisor-based guidance with an example for the project-specific adaptation of a plant construction process model. It shows how an advisor derives the suggestion to instantiate, individualise and insert a generic process building block (*"apply for export permission"*) before another process building block (*"decide: bid or no bid"*) due to a specific legal constraint (*"export certification: necessary"*). In figure 3, dashed arrows represent dependencies and solid arrows represent guided system operations.

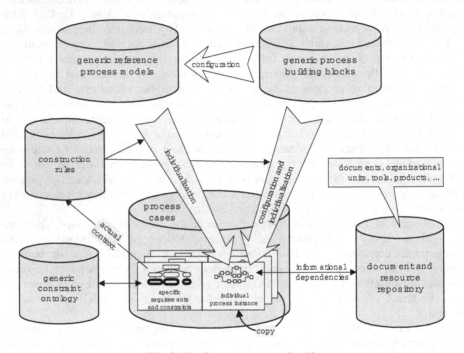

Fig. 2. The Process construction kit

Amid process modelling, an engineer selects constraints from the constraint ontology. Each selection or later change in a constraint may trigger an advisor, which highlights the parts of the process where potential alterations arise due to the change, generates advice on how to conduct the alterations, and provides a textual explanation.

3.2   Technical Approach

3.2.1 Basic Concepts
Technically, we understand the construction of processes as the application of specific operators on a process model to transform that model to an adequate representation of a specific process. From this point of view, processes and activities are objects with certain attributes (e.g. title, status and duration) [1] and associated operators. The set of operators includes operators for instantiation, adaptation and configuration. These operators are context-sensitive, i.e. an operator takes the specific constraints of a process case into account. Objects, operators and constraints together form a network of interrelated concepts.

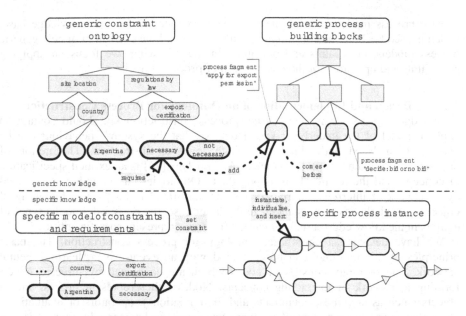

Fig. 3. Basic principle of a process model adaptation

Operators may either be triggered by user interaction (e.g. a user inserts an activity into a process by applying the AddActivityOperator) or by the system itself, responding to a change in the context of a process. In the latter case, the system acts as an agent by proposing an adaptation of the process model, which reflects the context altered. Some of the process adaptation steps may require additional input (e.g. users responsible for an activity), which cannot be solely provided by the system. In this case, the system provides assistance to gather the necessary data in a formalised dialog with the user.

By associating applied operator instances with affected object instance, it is possible to follow the history of changes carried out during the construction of a process case. Moreover, associating operator instances with constraint instances that lead to their application, it is also possible to record *why* a change has occurred. In this way, the process of constructing an explicit process model is recorded in the form of a history of changes made to a process instance and the reasons that lead to the change.

Thoroughly analysing the history of process cases – be it by human effort or computer support - may lead to the identification of new or more efficient construction rules. Dependencies between constraints, operators, and process objects are stored on a generic level in an ontology. The structure of generic reference process models and process building blocks is recorded in a construction plan, which is made up of a collection of operators. Operators in turn may also trigger other operators. By recursively traversing and applying the network of operators that describes generic process models one ends up at basic operators like createActivity or addActivityToProcess.

By these means, the system is capable of applying the explicit knowledge about process construction in terms of operators and to generate proposals for the adaptation of the process model, which are suitable for a current situation. Process cases, the generic process models, constraints and operators together form a knowledge base, which is used for both the construction of new cases and the derivation of new generic process models, constraints and operators. In the following, we focus on applying constraints and operators for the construction of process models.

3.2.2   Design and Implementation of an Ontology for Process Construction

Knowledge based systems, such as the process construction kit, should contain an explicit model of the underlying knowledge, so that the system's behaviour can be visualised, analysed and edited on a high level of abstraction. The notion of ontologies is fundamental in this context. An *ontology* [24] is an explicit specification of concepts and the relationships among them. Ontologies can be either represented by a network of interrelated terms, or - as demonstrated in [14] - as a hierarchy of object oriented classes and instances. In the latter case, the classes define the types of entities in the knowledge base, whereas the instances represent specific entities.

We have designed a class-based ontology for process construction. The basic principles of this ontology can be compared with an event-driven, learning neural network. The ontology consists of nodes which are connected by directed edges, forming a network of interacting concepts. Nodes either represent process model objects (such as activities, documents and their relations), operators or evaluations. Evaluable nodes have a state of a given type, such as boolean, discrete, string or numeric. Constraints are represented in the states of these nodes.

The state of the network is defined by the initial state of its nodes and the sequence of incoming events, such as user actions or state changes. Whenever a node changes, it notifies its predecessors which then in turn may change their state. Thus, events may propagate through the net, finally reaching condition and operator nodes. If an operator node is reached, the associated action is being applied in the given context. Operators might instantiate new processes or building blocks, update attributes of a given activity, or insert a building block into a process model instance.

An excerpt of the ontology's class hierarchy is presented in figure 4. All classes are derived from the abstract base class Node, which provides services for the event flow between adjacent nodes. The abstract class ProcessObject describes entities from the process model. Activities are basic ProcessObjects, representing executable real-world process steps. Processes can have a number of child ProcessObjects. Instances of the classes BooleanNode, DiscreteNode, StringNode and NumericNode can be evaluated to a value of their respective type. They either deliver constant values (as in the DiscreteValue class), variable values (as in the DiscreteVariable class) or derived values (as in the Equality class, which is linked to two EvaluableNodes and evaluates to true if the values of these adjacent nodes are equal). Boolean nodes, such as instances of the Equality class, can trigger Operator nodes, such as the AddActivityOperator, which constructs a new Activity with given properties. Operators can also be nested to complex operator sequences. Thus, complex process models can be generated and modified. The applied Operators are stored together with the ProcessObjects, serving as a backward reference, which can be used to analyse the development process leading to a process model.

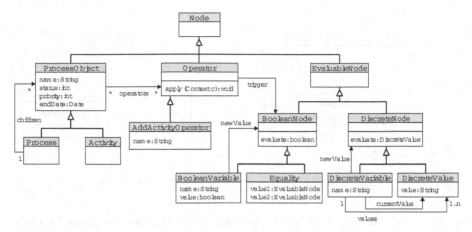

Fig. 4. A simplified excerpt of the classes implementing the ontology for process construction (in UML notation)

An ontology built from these simple types of nodes represents the generic process models, the knowledge about constructing a process, and the current process case. At the same time, the ontology is executable and can be used to create or modify an existing process model. To do so, the concepts (or classes) from the ontology are linked to object-oriented methods which can be applied to them. Using the framework for implementing ontologies presented in [14], it is possible to attach methods to ontologies without sacrificing the abstract high-level view of the ontology. This implementation technique is based on object-oriented *reflection*, i.e. the ability to analyse the structure of a class hierarchy and the state of an object network at run time. This allows one to display and modify the ontology with generic tools, e.g. to visualise the ontology's reasoning processes at run time.

The knowledge encoded in the ontology can also be used by various problem solving engines, such as the advisor that generates proposals for possible process adaptations. Such engines can traverse the network of adjacent concepts in order to identify related entities. Furthermore, the ontology implicitly contains the generic construction rules, which can be extracted and presented in a user-readable way. These construction rules can be generated automatically by learning from the operators applied in the given contexts.

3.2.3   Example Scenario

Figure 5 presents an excerpt of the ontology instances for the example presented in section 3.1.3. In this ontology, a given process has an attribute "DestinationCountry", which is modelled in a namesake `DiscreteVariable`. This variable can take one of its possible values, as shown below. From an abstract point of view, the knowledge encoded in this ontology specifies that the `AddActivityOperator` for the "Apply for export permission" activity shall be executed if the destination country variable is "Argentina".

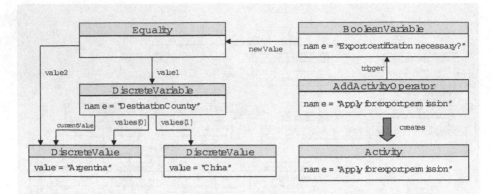

Fig. 5. A small ontology representing knowledge about when an application for export permission is necessary and what to do in this case

A sample use case of this ontology is shown in figure 6. The scenario starts with the user creating a new process on the GUI. The GUI creates a new `Process` instance, displays it on the screen and selects it. This will set the new `Process` to be the GUI's current editing context. Then the user specifies the destination country of the process to be "Argentina". The GUI assigns this new value to the DestinationCountry variable. This variable notifies its predecessors in the ontology network about its state change. Thus, the `Equality` is being evaluated and notifies in turn its predecessor node, i.e. the ExportPermission variable. This finally triggers the `AddActivity-Operator`, which creates a new `Activity` and uses the GUI context to add it to the selected process.

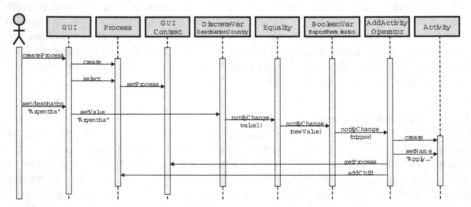

Fig. 6. A simple scenario based on the ontology from figure 5

4   Related Work

Most of the commercially available process modelling tools use non-generic methods for the process description. Non-generic reference process models can only serve as static templates that need to be adapted to specific requirements manually.

However, some approaches in research are related to our work:

With the *ARIS Process Generator*, an approach for automated customising of process models to a specific company has been developed and implemented in a prototype [9]. The context is described by answering pre-defined, semi-structured interviews. Such a tool is meant to be used by third party champions like organisation consultants for the configuration of standard software. However, there are no concepts for expanding and maintaining knowledge about process modelling, as it is necessary for capturing experience from the process participants.

ProTail is a tool-prototype for automated adaptation of the V-model, a standard for software development processes [17]. Here, a process model is individualised according to specific project constraints. However, the description of the process context is limited to the pre-defined constraints of the V-model. Mutual dependencies between the constraints are not considered.

The aim of *CoMo-Kit* is to capture and reuse knowledge about the execution of processes by recording the selection of process variants during run-time [4]. But the approach does not support the description of a project-specific context by constraints and the automated derivation of process model adaptations.

The *Handbook of Organisational Processes* is meant to serve as a handbook, which users can browse for alternative process models at various levels of specialisation and decomposition. The approach "allows people to explicitly represent the similarities (and differences) among related processes and to easily find or generate sensible alternatives for how a given process could be performed" [16]. Alternatives can be compared only within a bundle of related alternatives by trade-off matrices on multiple dimensions. The specialisation of a generic process model is performed according to defined goals and the type of organisation. This approach is not suitable for the automated adaptation of a process model to an individual, project-specific context.

With the approach of *WEGA*, process modelling know-how is captured in generic design patterns and reused for the construction of process models [5]. The approach is based on the notion of software reuse by design patterns. A pattern manager supports the retrieval and application of appropriate design patterns. The design patterns can be adapted to a specific situation, but the adaptation is limited to a manual selection of pre-defined parts.

5   Conclusion

We have presented an approach for project-specific individualisation of engineering processes. Know-how about engineering processes is a crucial ingredient for a successful operation of any virtual organisation. Large companies in fact already "live" the concept of virtual organisations in their internal operations. Our approach is founded in the assumption that engineering experts will capture and maintain their know-how about engineering processes. Initial pilot applications have proven this approach, i.e. to move process modelling tasks from consulting experts towards engineering experts and process engineers.

The process construction kit is operational in that it allows the formal representation of processes and operators at an abstract level while compiling modifications to the implementational level for execution. Knowledge about process design is represented in terms of operator sequences related to constraints. Each constraint is represented as a Boolean node.

We have developed a dedicated ontology editor that allows one to specify and modify process models at a generic as well as instance level [14]. Currently, we are designing an ontology for classifying engineering processes and refining operators for individualisation in project-specific contexts. Particular emphasis will be put on a domain-specific ontology for the support of simultaneous engineering teams in the automotive sector. Main intention is to support the co-ordination of process tasks in a network of engineers, the identification of critical process structures and states, and the advice about options for process amendments. In order to do so, the ontology will be founded upon basic patterns of construction processes derived from empirical studies of automotive development processes.

In general, the question arises of how to learn process knowledge, be it success stories or lessons learned in worst cases. Co-operation with engineering experts is one side of the coin for capturing experience about the construction of engineering processes. In an enterprise-wide perspective, communities of practice might even serve as organisational means to additionally extract and disseminate best practice and lessons learned from worst cases. Yet, automatic mining or case based reasoning might be another solution. We will explore metrics to assess processes based on various reference numbers for quality, goal compliance, etc.

So far, the process modelling component of our system has been tested at user sites for the capture of processes, in particular emphasising the notion of graphical process presentation for visual assessment [21]. The assessment of processes draws upon the duality of formal reasoning and mental perception [19]. Advisors care about specific features of processes that are based upon formal theories. Visualisation techniques are employed to support process engineers in cases where formal theory about process characteristics are missing. That is, automated layout algorithms are used to generate different perspectives on processes.

Moreover, we call for intuitive interaction means that organises processes in spatial regions and allows engineers to walk along process chains and navigate to neighbouring regions, be it a neighbourhood with regard to time, process or information dependencies.

Acknowledgements

Part of this work is being supported by the German Federal Ministry of Education and Research (BMB+F) as part of INVITE (Research Grant No. 01 IL 901 B 4). For further information on INVITE: http://www.invite.de.

References

1. Bider, I., Khomyakov, M.: Business Process Modeling: Motivation, Requirements, Implementation. In: Demeyer, S., Bosch, J. (eds.): Object-Oriented Technology: ECOOP'98 Workshop Reader, LNCS 1543, Springer (1997) 217-218
2. Curtis, B., Kellner, M.I., Over, J.: Process Modeling. In: Communications of the ACM 35 (1992) 9, 75-90
3. Davenport, T.H.: Process Innovation: Reengineering Work through Information Technology, Harvard Business School Press, Boston (1993)
4. Dellen, B., Maurer, F., Pews, G.: Knowledge Based Techniques to Increase the Flexibility of Workflow Management. In: Data & Knowledge Engineering Journal, North Holland (1997)
5. Ferstl, O.K., Hammel, C., Pfister, A., Popp, K., Schlitt, M., Sinz, E.J., Wolf, S.: Verbundprojekt WEGA: Wiederverwendbare und Erweiterbare Geschäftsprozess- und Anwendungssystem-Architekturen. In: Statusband des BMBF Softwaretechnologie, Berlin (1998) 3-21
6. Fox, M.S., Gruninger, M.: Ontologies for Enterprise Integration. In: Proc. 2nd Conf. on Cooperative Information Systems, Toronto, Ontario (1994)
7. Fricke, E., Negele, H., Schrepfer, L., Dick, A., Gebhard, B., Härtlein, N.: Modeling of Concurrent Engineering Processes for Integrated Systems Development. In: Proc. 17th Digital Avionics Systems Conf.: Electronic in Motion, Bellevue, WA (1998)
8. Gruninger, M., Fox, M.S.: The Role of Competency Questions in Enterprise Engineering. In: Proc. IFIP WG5.7 Workshop on Benchmarking - Theory and Practice, Trondheim, Norway (1994)
9. Hagemeyer, J., Rolles, R., Scheer, A.-W.: Der Schnelle Weg zum Sollkonzept: Modellgestützte Standardsoftwareeinführung mit dem ARIS Process Generator. In: Scheer, A.-W. (ed.): Publications of the Institut für Wirtschaftsinformatik at the University of Saarbrücken, Germany, Report No. 152, Saarbrücken (1999)
10. Hammer, M., Champy, J.: Reengineering the Corporation – a Manifesto for Business Revolution, Harper Collins Publishers, New York (1993)
11. Jablonski, S.: Process Modelling and Execution in Workflow Management Systems. In: Proc. Int. Working Conf. on Dynamic Modelling and Information Systems, Nordwijkerhout, Netherlands (1994)
12. Jennings, N.R., Norman, T.J., Faratin, P., O'Brian, P., Odgers, B.: Autonomous Agents for Business Process Management, Int. Journal of Applied Artificial Intelligence (to appear) (2000). http://www.elec.qmw.ac.uk/dai/pubs/
13. Johansson, H.J., McHugh, P., Pendlebury, A.J., Wheeler III, W.A.: Business Process Reengineering: Breakpoint Strategies for Market Dominance, Chichester (1993)
14. Knublauch, H., Rose, T.: Reflection-enabled Rapid Prototyping of Knowledge-based Systems. In: Proc. OOPSLA'99 Workshop on Object-oriented Reflection and Software Engineering, Denver, CO (1999)
15. Kratz, N., Rose, T.: Modelling and Analyzing Processes in Production and Administration. In: Tzafestas, S.G. (ed.): Management and Control in Manufacturing Systems, Springer, Berlin (1997) 118-142
16. Malone, T.W., Crowston, K., Lee, J., Pentland, B., Dellarocas, C., Wyner, G., Quimby, J., Osborne, C., Bernstein, A.: Tools for Inventing Organisations: Towards a Handbook of Organizational Processes. Technical Report of the Center for Coordination Science, Massachusetts Institute of Technology, Cambridge (1997)
17. Münch, J., Schmitz, M., Verlage, M.: Tailoring Großer Prozessmodelle auf der Basis von MVP-L. In: Montenegro, S., Kneuper, R., Müller-Luschnat, G. (eds.): Vorgehensmodelle – Einführung, Betrieblicher Einsatz, Werkzeug-Unterstützung und Migration: Papers of the 4th Workshop, GMD-Report No. 311, Berlin-Adlershof, Germany (1997) 63-72

18. Negele, H., Fricke, E., Schrepfer, L., Härtlein, N.: Modeling of Integrated Product Development Processes. In: Proc. 9th Annual Int. Symposium of INCOSE Systems Engineering: Sharing the Future, Brighton, UK (1999)
19. Peter, G., Rose, T., Rupprecht, C.: Towards Reducing the Complexity of Process Modeling by Advisors, Explicit Context Modeling, and Visualisation Techniques. In: Proc. 10th Mini EURO Conf. on Human Centered Processes (HCP '99), Brest, France (1999) 315-320
20. Remme, M., Allweyer T., Scheer A.-W.: Implementing Organizational Structures in Process Industry Supported by Tool-Based Reference Models. In: Proc. Conf. on Computer Integrated Manufacturing in Process Industries CIMPRO, East Brunswick, New Jersey, USA (1994) 233-247
21. Rose, T.: Visual Assessment of Engineering Processes in Virtual Enterprises. In: Communications of the ACM 41 (1999) 12 45-52
22. Rupprecht, C., Peter, G., Rose, T.: Ein Modellgestützter Ansatz zur kontext-spezifischen Individualisierung von Prozessmodellen. In: Wirtschaftsinformatik 41 (1999) 3 226-236. An earlier version of this article appeared in: Scheer, A.-W., Nüttgens, M. (eds.): Electronic Business Engineering – Proc. 4th Int. Conf. on Business Informatics in Saarbrücken, Germany, Physica, Heidelberg (1999) 353-373
23. Schütte, R.: Grundsätze Ordnungsmäßiger Referenzmodellierung: Konstruktion Konfigurations- und Anpassungsorientierter Modelle. Gabler, Wiesbaden (1998)
24. Studer, R., Fensel, D., Decker, S., Benjamins, V.R.: Knowledge Engineering: Survey and Future Directions. In: Proc. 5th German Conf. on Knowledge-based Systems, Würzburg, Germany (1999)

Practical Reuse Measurement in ERP Requirements Engineering

Maya Daneva

Clearnet Communications, 200 Consilium Place, Suite 1600
Toronto, Ontario M1H 3J3, Canada
mdaneva@clearnet.com

Abstract. Component-based, architecture-centric requirements engineering processes have been applied in Enterprise Resource Planning projects for a decade, but have only relatively recently achieved significant recognition in the broader software engineering research community. This sub-area is now entering a new level of maturity by beginning to address the reuse aspects in the ERP RE process. The present article makes a first contribution to applied ERP requirements reuse measurement by incorporating reuse metrics planning as part of the implementation of metrics on an ERP project. Relevant process integration issues are tackled in the context of SAP R/3 implementation projects.

1 Introduction

Requirements Engineering (RE) forms the major concern in the implementation of any Enterprise Resource Planning (ERP) software package. It is an expensive process referring to the creation, the analysis, the adaptation, and the management of a large number of artifacts, or descriptions. It begins with the identification and the documentation of the company's organizational units, their business processes and data needs and continues throughout the entire implementation cycle in the form of tracking of the life history of any particular requirement and business issue. The better the resulting business requirements are formulated, the faster the progress in subsequent phases, because the necessary decisions concerning the future ERP solution have been taken and agreed upon [19]. To make the RE process more efficient and to assure high quality results, the ERP community has adopted systematic requirements reuse approaches, developed an infrastructure of processes, people and tools for customers to reuse and, most recently, delivered component-based solutions to common business process and data requirements derived from numerous industry-specific business cases. These represent domain-specific frameworks with three major features [13]: an *architecture* defining the structure of integrated information systems within the business problem domain, a set of *business application components* engineered to fit the architecture, and a set of *tools* that assist the consultant in building component-based solutions using the domain knowledge within the architecture.

B. Wangler, L. Bergman (Eds.): CAiSE 2000, LNCS 1789, pp. 309-324, 2000
© Springer-Verlag Berlin Heidelberg 2000

Currently, in spite of the increased attention that ERP requirements reuse has attracted, the wide application of reuse process methods and techniques, and the awareness of the benefits they have brought to ERP-clients, very few approaches have emerged to quantitatively measure the results from requirement reuse the customers have achieved [2]. As Pfleeger points out, we 'can not do effective reuse without proper measurement and planning' [14].

The present paper tackles this issue from measurement planning perspective. We present a requirements reuse measurement plan that links the reuse measurement needs to the ERP reuse goals and action items to be taken in the RE process. Our objective is to provide a sound and consistent basis for incorporating reuse metrics planning as part of the implementation of metrics on an ERP project. For the purpose of this research, we place the requirements reuse measurement activities in the context of implementing the SAP R/3 System, a leading product in the ERP software market [19]. However, our approach is generic enough and could easily be applied to any other ERP project implementation. In what follows, we first explain the motivation for our research effort. Then, we discuss the components of our reuse measurement plan and provide some illustrative examples of how measurements are useful. Section 5 generalizes our experience and reports on early lessons learnt and critical success factors. Section 6 concludes the paper and suggests directions for future work.

2 Motivation

An ERP requirements reuse measurement process is a systematic method of adopting or adapting standard reuse counting practices in ERP RE, measuring the ERP reuse goals, and indicating reuse levels targeted at the beginning and achieved at the end of each stage of the ERP implementation cycle. The main purpose of this process for ERP customers is to learn about their own business, technological and environment opportunities by learning how much reuse their ERP-supported business processes could practice. The motivation behind the integration of the reuse measurement process in the RE process includes the following:

- Reuse measurement data available early in the project will enable the reuse process to be planned and reuse planning to be done as part of the RE process.
- Reuse metrics will provide a foundation for building and reinforcing partnerships, increasing customers' understanding of the ERP functionality, reprioritizing the business requirements, communicating the value of ERP-reuse.
- Reuse measurement will reduce the probability of errors and accidental omissions in the business process requirements.
- The reuse measurement process will serve as a vehicle for faster resolution of requirements problems and conflict. Metrics data will help focus requirements elicitation and negotiation meetings and resolve architectural problems.
- Reuse data will serve as an input to an effort estimation model.

3   Components of a Requirements Reuse Measurement Plan

The requirements reuse measurement process should be documented in the form of a reuse measurement plan [5]. Its purpose is to establish a reuse measurement practice as part of a larger organizational process, namely, the ERP RE process. Moreover, it represents a communication vehicle to ensure that all the team members agree with the approach as well as serves as the on-going reference model to manage the implementation of reuse metrics. The plan defines the measurement process with exact information on stakeholders involved, measurement frequency, sources of metrics data, counting rules, metrics data interpretation rules, tools support, reports to be produces, and action items that can be taken based on the metrics data (Fig.1.).

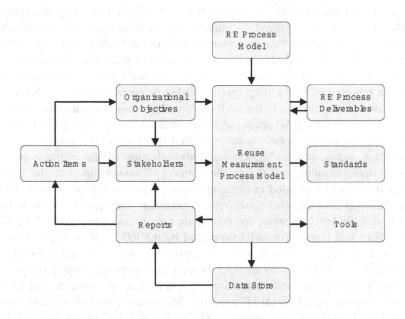

Fig.1. The components of the SAP reuse plan

Stakeholders and their objectives define what is to be achieved by running a reuse measurement process. Next, as per the recommendations provided by software metrics researchers and practitioners [14, 15], a model of the RE process is needed to capture the ERP reuse activities and to understand where measurements fit in. It should provide sufficient knowledge of (i) how to map reuse measures to RE activities, (ii) where and when in the RE process measurements could be taken, and (iii) how measurement activities could be integrated into the larger process. Given this context, a reuse measurement process model is required to specify what to count as requirements reuse, what units of measure to use, and how to count it. Furthermore, tools, data stores and standards for data collection, processing and packaging are to be selected to ensure the quality of the reuse metrics data. Finally, the plan concludes with strategies for using the reuse data. These are presented in terms of metrics data reports to be created and action items that can be formulated based on the reported data. The components of our ERP reuse measurement plan are discussed in great detail in the next sections.

3.1 Understanding Stakeholders and Their Roles

Adequate and timely consultation of the parties interested in ERP is of great importance to the planning of reuse metrics. It helps us (i) make sure that the definitions of our metrics are based on our SAP team members' goals, (ii) eliminate misunderstandings about how metrics data is expected to be used, and (iii) define relevant procedures for packaging, cataloguing, publishing and reporting reuse metrics data.

To identify the stakeholders, we applied the approach developed by Sharp et all in [17]. Based on early SAP project documentation, we developed stakeholder interaction diagrams that captured three important aspects of our team working environment: relationships between stakeholders, the relationships of each stakeholder to the system, and the priority to be given to each stakeholder's view. The organizational knowledge represented in the diagrams is needed to manage, interpret, balance and process stakeholders' input into the SAP requirements reuse measurement process. It was used to structure the SAP project team members in four groups: (i) *business decision makers*, who are corporate executives from the steering committee responsible for the optimization, standardization and harmonization of the business processes across multiple locations, and define the concept of ownership over the SAP R/3 system and are most interested in learning about the business benefits from SAP reuse, (ii) *business process owners*, who are department managers responsible for the project in specific business areas, and contribute the necessary line know-how, design new processes and procedures to be supported by the R/3 business application components and provide the project with the appropriate authority and resources, (iii) *technical decision makers*, who are SAP project managers responsible for planning, organizing, coordinating and controlling the implementation project, and (iv) *configurators*, who are both internal IT team members and external consultants involved in various work packages, e.g. process and data analysts, configuration specialists, ABAP programmers, system testers, documentation specialists. Each stakeholder has its own questions that should be answered by using the metrics data. Business decision makers would like to know:

- What level of standardization could be achieved by reusing ERP software assets?
- What competitive advantages does the team get from ERP reuse?
- What are the implications of reusing ERP processes in a constantly changing business environment?
- How to align business processes across locations so that ERP reuse can yield significant cost reductions and enterprise-wide benefits?
- What implementation strategy fits better with the project?

Business process owners might ask:

- How ERP reuse works with volatile process requirements?

- How much customization effort is required to implement minor/major changes in the business application components?
- What reuse expectations are realistic?
- What processes have the greatest potential for practicing reuse?
- What activities in our processes prevent us from reusing more?

Technical decision-makers need to know:

- How much effort is required to produce the user and training documentation associated to the customized components?
- How much reuse the team did?

Configurators might ask:

- Are there any rejected requirements that should be re-analyzed because of re-use concerns?
- What implementation alternative fits best?
- Which segments of the requirements are likely to cause difficulties later in the implementation process?

The questions relevant to each group have been documented and attached to the stakeholder interaction diagrams.

3.2 RE Process Model Outline

The standard methodology for rapid R/3 implementation, called AcceleratedSAP (ASAP), provides a disciplined reuse-driven, architecture-centric process for coordination, controlling, configuring and managing changes of the R/3 business application components [1,11]. To investigate the ASAP RE process, we modelled it as a spiral (Fig. 2.). Its the radial arms represent the increasing collection of information by three types of activities: (i) *requirements elicitation* activities which deliver the foundation for the business blueprint and are concerned with finding, communication and validation of facts and rules about the business, (ii) *enterprise modelling* activities which are concerned with the business processes and data analysis and representation, and (iii) *requirements negotiation* activities which are concerned with the resolution of business process and data issues, the validation of process and data architectures and the prioritization of the requirements. The ASAP methodology suggests four iterations of the spiral. Level 0 iteration aims at developing a clear picture of the company's organizational structure based on the pre-defined organization units in the R/3 System. Next, the main objective of level 1 iteration is to define aims and scope for business process standardization based on the R/3 application components. Level 2 iteration aims at deriving company-specific business process architecture based on scenarios from the standard SAP process and data architecture components. Finally, level 3 iteration refers to the specification of data conversion, reporting and interfaces requirements. The major actors in these activities are business process owners who are actively supported by the SAP consultants and the internal SAP process and data architects. Next, the ASAP RE process is supported by the following tools: (i) the *ASAP Implementation Assistant* [11] which provides reusable questionnaires, project plans, cost estimates, blueprint presentations, blueprint templates, project reports and checklists, as well as manages the documentation base; (ii) the *SAP Business*

Engineer, a platform including a wide range of business engineering tools fully integrated into the R/3 System [1]; (iii) *enterprise modelling tools* (ARIS-Toolset, Live-Model and Visio) which have rich model management capabilities and assist in analyzing, building and validating customer-specific process and data architectures based on the reusable reference process and data models.

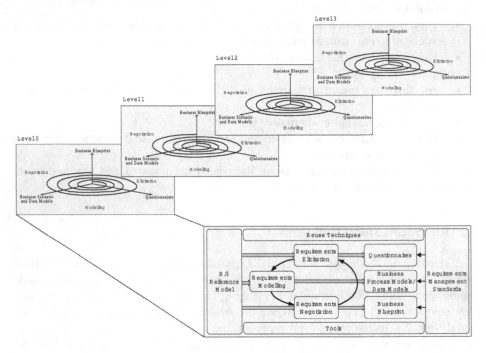

Fig.2. The SAP requirements engineering process

The ASAP RE begins with reuse, ends with reuse and includes reuse in all the tasks in-between. It is based on proven reuse practices and techniques and it ensures that the requirements are correct, consistent, complete, realistic, well prioritized, verifiable, traceable and testable. This is achieved by using the R/3 Reference Model, a comprehensive architectural description of the R/3 System including four views: *business process* view, *function* view, *data* view and *organizational* view. Specifically, the R/3 Reference Process Models represent integrated and function-spanning collections of business processes that occur often in practice and can be handled to the greatest extend possible automatically if a corporation implements the complete R/3 System [11]. Instead of building an integrated information system from scratch, with the R/3 Reference Model we build a solution from reusable process and data architectures based on SAP's business experience collected on a large scale. Our analysis indicates that the R/3 Reference Model supports the RE process in multiple ways: (i) in *requirements elicitation*, it provides a way for process owners and consultants to agree on what the SAP business application components are to do, (ii) in *requirements modelling*, it serves two separate but related purposes. It helps to quickly develop a requirement definition document that shows to the business owners the process flow the solution is expected to support. Beyond that, it can be seen as a design specification document that restates the business specification in terms of R/3 transactions to be implemented, and (iii) in *requirements negotiation*, the R/3 Reference Model serves as a validation tool. It makes sure that the solution will meet the owners' needs, it is technically implementable and it is maintainable in future releases.

Reusing architectural components in the RE process is saving both time and money. As the business process requirement analysis is the most expensive consulting service in a business engineering exercise, the reuse of the R/3 Reference Model definitely provides the greatest savings.

3.3 Process Integration Model

This section describes exactly how reuse measurement can be integrated with the RE activities and where in the RE process reuse measurement data will be taken (Fig. 3). It involves several assumptions:

- Reuse data are extracted by an SAP process analyst on the basis of two major RE deliverables: business scenario models and business object models;
- reuse metrics data analysis is based on quantitative indicators;
- reuse metrics data is used to support stakeholders' decision during the requirements negotiation and elicitation;
- reuse metrics data is reused at a later stage to support decision making in planning for future releases, upgrades and major enhancements.

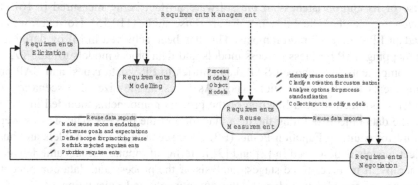

Fig. 3. Integration of requirements reuse measurement in RE

We suggest reuse measurement be applied once the modelling activities of level 2 iteration are completed and the customer-specific process and data architectures are built (Fig.3). Given the reuse metrics data, the SAP process analyst may decide what negotiation / elicitation activities to take place next. The use of the metrics data is discussed in more detail in Section 4.

Our integration model implies that reuse measurement activities support the RE process in five areas: (i) definition of measurable reuse goals and expectations, (ii) quantitative analysis of process and data architecture reuse prior to solution design; (iii) assessment of the requirements specification, (iv) better understanding of the technical risks early in the ERP implementation cycle, (v) definition of the scope of ERP reuse and how it fits into the business environment.

3.4 The Measurement Process

As Pfleeger [14] recommends, we have to choose reuse metrics based on what is visible for the SAP project team in the requirements modelling process of level 2 iteration. Our approach uses the results of our previous research on the derivation of reuse indicators from SAP scenario process models and business object models [2]. It is based on the notion of "reuse percents" [18] suggests a reuse indicator that includes reused requirements as a percentage of total requirements delivered [2]:

$$SAP\_Reuse = (RR / TR) * 100\%$$

where *RR* represents reused requirements, and *TR* represents total requirements delivered. In this paper, requirement borrowed from the R/3 Reference Model are classified as *reusable* if it does not require modification. If borrowed requirement does require minor or major enhancement before use, we term it *'customized requirement'*.

To build well-defined and valid metrics [7], we selected a consistent and reliable means for structuring and collecting data to make up metrics. A standard functional size measurement methodology, namely Function Point Analysis (FPA) [8] was applied to size the total and the reused requirements in the project. It was chosen because of its appropriateness to the software artifact being measured [8,16] and its proven usage and applicability in software reuse studies [10,15]. However, we needed to adapt FPA the SAP requirements. This has been achieved in [3] by defining rules for mapping SAP business process models and data object models to the FPA counting components: we mapped SAP data entities to FPA data types, and SAP process components to FPA transaction types. As a result, the size of a scenario process model is assumed to be a function of the process components included in the model and the data objects defining the data that support the process. The step-by-step procedure for counting Function Points (FP) from scenario process models and business object models is described in [2] and [3] in terms of inputs, outputs and deliverables. Generally, it involves three stages: analysis of the process and data components, assignment of complexity values to the components and calculation of the final FP value.

Based on the analysis of the changes [11] that could be applied to the R/3 Reference Model throughout the reuse-based process modelling exercise, the measurement data collected throughout the FP sizing procedure [3], and the modes of component reuse investigated by Karllson [10], we have defined three levels of requirements reuse [2]:

- *Level 3:* It refers to process and data components that were reused without any changes. This category of reuse would bring the greatest benefits to the

SAP customer's organization. Scenarios with higher reuse rate at this level have greater potential of practicing reuse.

- *Level 2:* It refers to *minor enhancements* applied to reference processes and data components. A minor enhancement is defined as a change of certain parameter of a business process or a data component that does not result in a change of the process logic. This category of reuse refers to those processes and data components of the R/3 Reference Model that logically match the business requirements but their parameters need to be changed at code level to achieve their business purpose. Level 2 reuse is as desirable as level 3 reuse.

- *Level 1:* It refers to *major enhancements* applied to reference processes and data components. A major enhancement is any considerable modification in the definition of a process or a data component that affects the process logic from business user's point of view. This category of reuse refers to those processes and data components that do not match the business requirements and require changes at conceptual level, as well as at design and code level to achieve their business purpose. Level 1 reuse is at least desirable.

In these definitions, the term *process (component)* refers to the functional units of any SAP scenario process models and the term *data component* means a data entity, a relationship or an attribute from the data model describing the SAP business data requirements. Furthermore, we introduce a level of new requirements, *No_Reuse,* to acknowledge the fact that reuse is not practiced at all. It refers to newly introduced processes and data components. This does not mean a reuse category; it just helps us to partition the overall requirements and to get understanding of how much requirements are not covered by the standard scenario processes and business objects.

Given our definition of what to count as reuse and how to count it, we have derived three reuse indicators [2]:

$$\text{Level}_i \text{SAP\_Reuse} = (\ RR_i\ /\ TR\ )*100\%$$

where $i = \{1, 2, 3\}$, RR_i represents reused requirements at Level $_i$, and TR represents total requirements delivered. The indicator

$$\text{No\_Reuse} = (\ NR\ /\ TR\ )*100\%\ ,$$

where NR represents the new requirements, and TR has the above meaning, reports the percentage of requirements that can not be met by the R/3 application package unless some customer-specific extensions are not developed.

Currently, case studies are being carried out to validate empirically our counting model and its application procedure [4]. This exercise is being done on the basis of Jauqet's and Abran's framework [9] for investigating measure validation issues.

3.5 Assembling a Toolset for Data Collection

Reuse measurements are only as good as the data that is collected and analyzed [7]. To assure the quality of the reuse data, at least three tools are needed: (i) a form for recording all the counting details; (ii) a reuse metrics database, and (iii) a process knowledge repository. We extended the FP counting form suggested in [8] by including information needed for calculating the reuse indicators. Based on our FP counting model [3], we devised a counting form usage procedure that indicates at exactly what point each piece of data should be collected. information has been stored and processed in Excel spreadsheet software. Summarized and detailed reports have been extracted from Excel tables. For example, Table 2 shows the size numbers for four SAP business scenarios and Table 3 presents the summarized results from measuring reuse. Since reuse metrics provide knowledge about the business processes, reports on metrics data should be considered as part of the SAP process documentation. It can be stored, packaged, catalogued and published by using a corporate intranet repository as well as standard process modelling tools and the ASAP Implementation Assistant. In this way, data is made available for review and analysis to all interested parties. Users of SAP documentation can easily navigate from scenario process models to functional size and reuse metrics data.

Table 2. Reuse levels for five SAP scenarios

Business Scenarios	$Level_3$	$Level_2$	$Level_1$	No
	FP	FP	FP	FP
Project-related Engineer-to-Order Production	141	57	68	128
Procurement of Stock Materials	74	198	32	127
Procurement of Consumable Materials	86	165	0	30
External Service Management	96	31	14	0

Table 3. Reuse levels for five SAP scenarios

Business Scenarios	$Level_3$	$Level_2$	$Level_1$	No
	Reuse	Reuse	Reuse	Reuse
Project-related Engineer-to-Order Production	36%	15%	17%	32%
Procurement of Stock Materials	19%	50%	8%	22%
Procurement of Consumable Materials	31%	59%	0%	10%
External Service Management	68%	22%	10%	0%

3.6 How to Link Reuse Data to Action Items

Measurements are considered useful if they help stakeholders (i) understand what is happening during the ERP RE process, and (ii) control what is happening on the ERP project [7]. Typically, two types of reuse profiles could be derived from a requirements reuse measurement table (Table 3): *scenario-specific* profiles which present the levels of reuse pertinent to a given scenario, and *level-specific* profiles which show how the requirements are reused at a specific level within a project. Business decision-makers can use both types of profiles in at least three ways: (i) multiple reuse profiles of two or more different ERP products (SAP, BAAN, PeopleSoft) can be compared to determine which package best serves the needs of the company and offers the greatest opportunity for reuse; (ii) multiple reuse profiles of different releases (SAP R/3 3.1, 4.0B, 4.5, 4.6) of one ERP package could be compared to determine which release brings biggest benefits to the company; (iii) multiple reuse profiles of a single ERP package (e.g. SAP R/3) can build an assessment of the overall level of standardization of the ERP solution in the organization. Reuse profiles of a single ERP package (e.g. SAP R/3) can be used by technical decision-makers to plan and control the reuse levels in the later phases of the ASAP implementation process. Business process owners and configurators can track requirements reuse levels over time to control the changes in overall reuse during the iterations of the RE process.

Furthermore, the specific use of each profile is systematically documented by using a Reuse Data Usage Table. It is built to characterize four aspects of a reuse profile: who needs to read the profile data, what the profile can help us understand, what the profile can help us control and what action items are likely to be taken based on the reuse profile. Tables 4 and Table 5 reports on the current usage of the scenario-specific and level-specific profiles, respectively. (BDM, PO, TDM and C stand for business decision-makers, process owners, technical decision-makers and configurators, respectively.)

4 Discussion on the Reuse Data Usage

The examples of Table 2 and 3 show scenarios referring to two SAP components: Project System and Materials Management. The *Project-related-Engineer-to-Order* scenario describes how to manage projects for building cell sites for a country-wide mobile telephone network. Its *Level , Reuse* and *No_Reuse* ratings are relatively high due to significant customization and numerous external interfaces required by the process owners. Next, the scenarios of *Procuring Stock Materials* and *Procuring Consumable Materials* refer to the business workflow in purchasing, inventory management, and warehouse operations. They cover the processes of material requirements planning, purchase requisition processing, purchase order processing and goods receipt processing. Furthermore, the *External Service Management* scenario documents the workflow for service provisioning and handling contractors in cell site construction. This scenario is the one, which practices most *Level 3* reuse.

Table 4. Reuse data usage table for scenario-specific profiles

Usage	BDM	PO	TDM	C	Action items
Understand the customization risk for upgrade projects.	x	x	x	x	1. Assess the difficulty in the migration of processes with low reuse rates. 2. Reengineer the business requirements. 3. Budget and plan resources for extra gap analysis for the processes with low reuse rates.
Understand how much reuse the team did.		x	x	x	1. Set reuse expectations for later stages. 2. Define scope for practicing reuse. 3. Make process reuse recommendations.
Understand reuse constraints / Assess the level of standardization.	x	x		x	1. Elaborate alternative process flows to eliminate the need for customization. 2. Re-assess reuse levels. 3. Compare processes to select the best alternative.

Table 5. Reuse data usage table for level-specific profiles

Usage	BDM	PO	TDM	C	Action items
Define focus for negotiation meetings.		x		x	1.Review scenarios on a function-by-function basis to justify why customization is necessary. 2.Structure requirements in three categories: must-to-have, nice-to-have and possible-but-could-be-eliminated.
Select an implementation strategy.	x	x	x		3.Consider a step-by-step approach to a sequenced implementation, if Level 1 reuse dominates. 4.Consider a big-bang approach, if Level 3 reuse dominates.

The scenario-specific data usage table suggests what benefits the reuse measurements bring to those team members who are responsible for planning for reuse and assigning target reuse levels to each scenario to be achieved throughout the R/3 implementation project. Some examples of how these profiles are helpful include the following:

- The data can be used in level 3 requirements elicitation to understand what prevents the team from reusing more. In the *Project-related-Engineer-to-Order* scenario, the low level of reuse is due to three reasons: (i) the standard R/3 functionality does not offer sufficient support to the business practices specific to a mobile telecommunication services provider, (ii) numerous external interfaces to legacy systems should be built, and (iii) business processes in cell site construction have not been standardized across the locations: different regional cell site groups wanted to use the SAP syetsm differently.

- The data are useful in planning for both new implementations and upgrades. In the first case, documentation development risks that were not foreseen may appear for processes with high *Level , Reuse* or *No_Reuse* rates. They are likely to need additional resources (e.g. business process owners, internal training specialists, and documentation analysts) to get documented. In case of upgrades, reuse profiles help the team assess the degree of difficulty involved in the migration to the new release. For example, Table 2 suggests that the process of *Project-related Engineering-to-Order Production* should be migrated with extra caution.

Next, the level-specific usage table is important to requirements negotiation activities. Two illustrative examples refer to the requirements prioritization activities and the implementation strategy selection activities:

- The reuse data help the team decide what to focus the negotiation efforts on.]. As the process owners get better understanding of the SAP reuse, and recognize the R/3 customization is one of the most risky matters to deal with in the package implementation, they become more conscious to the avoidance of unnecessary adaptation and are willing to re-prioretize the requirements
- The level-specific profiles can help both business and technical decision-makers determine what SAP implementation strategy fits best with the organizational objectives. If *Level 1* reuse dominates and much customization efforts are anticipated, the team is likely to adopt a step-by-step approach to a sequenced implementation of the SAP components. If *Level 3* reuse rates are the highest ones, the customization risks are reduced and a big-bang approach to implementing multiple components seems to be reasonable.

5   Packaging Experiences

SAP requirements sizing and reuse counting has been practiced in four SAP projects: three new implementations and one upgrade. While applying the process, we collected and documented some facts and observations about the context of reuse measurement. Thus, we obtained a set of experience packages that suggested explanations of how and why the measurement process worked as part of the RE cycle [1]. Each package consists of characteristics of the project context, a logical conclusion about specific aspects of the measurement process and a set of facts and observations that support this conclusion. The conclusions represent either early lessons learnt that tell us what and how worked in the process or critical success factors that suggest why it worked.

A summary of our early lessons learnt is given as follows:

- Requirements reuse measurement helps us understand in both qualitative and quantitative terms the role of the pre-defined process models in ERP RE.
- The measurement process must be focused on defining action items based on the reuse data metrics, not on collecting and reporting data.
- The process leads to consistent traceability information being maintained for all the business processes.

- It increases the probability of finding poorly prioritized requirements.
- Reuse data is a central record of all the process specific reuse information.
- Reuse data helps to focus the validation process.
- Reuse measurement should not be practiced as a short-term process that would be dropped at the end of the SAP implementation cycle. Measuring requirements reuse should not be considered as one-sided gathering of information. It is neither one-time process knowledge capture, nor a quick fix.

Moreover, 10 critical success factors have been identified:

- Apply a stakeholder identification method to the SAP project organization. This made sure that all important stakeholders have been captured, and yet that irrelevant actors have not been included.
- Use the ASAP standard processes, deliverables and tools. This significantly shortened the time needed to model the RE process and to spot where in this process measurements could be taken, analyzed and used.
- Adopt (if possible) or adapt a standard methodology for sizing the business requirements. FPA proved its usefulness and applicability in ERP RE.
- Integrate the reuse measurement process incrementally. Pilot it by applying it to the business scenarios pertinent to a selected ERP component.
- Consider the metrics data reports as a supplement to the business blueprint. The business process owners should review it as the other deliverables included in the business blueprint.
- Take extra efforts to experiment with the reuse measurement process and to collect and document the series of action items the team members suggest based on the metrics data.
- Understand the role of the reusable components and the reuse techniques in the ERP RE process.
- Maintain a limited number of requirements reuse measurement process documents: it is sufficient to start with a reuse measurement plan, a FP form and a customizable report template for presenting the results.
- Think out a strategy of how to maximize the benefits of the business engineering tools the team uses in the course of the ERP implementation. These can be of great support to the measurement process.
- Use the data for planning action items.

6   Conclusions

This paper has looked in depth at the most important planning aspects of requirements reuse measurement in ERP projects. We blended stakeholder interaction analysis with a process integration model that ensures the visibility of both reuse measurement and RE activities. This resulted in a practical requirements reuse measurement plan that could be applied incrementally to selected portion of the business requirements as well as to the entire project. The plan documents the components of a consistent measurement process: relevant stakeholders, a RE process model, a process integration model, counting rules, tools and reuse data usage tables. The process is kept reasonably simple so that team members can concentrate on their requirements elicitation and negotiation activities with functional size and reuse counting and data report generation playing a supporting role. Experiences of practicing the reuse measurement process have been packaged to derive early lesson learnt and critical success factors for an on-going ERP reuse measurement initiative.

It is the believe of the author, that the plan is applicable beyond the ERP RE context of SAP R/3 implementation projects. The reuse measurements work best where there exists reference process and data models of the business application components being implemented. Thus, the approach could find applicability in implementation projects based on other ERP packages, for example BAAN and Peoplesoft. In addition, it can be used in business applications where business process modelling captured the interactions in the business workflow and the data objects from the business area. Next, different company-specific or project-specific aspects, for example project communication [20], process maturity and stability, might lead to shortening or eliminating of some stages in reuse metrics planning. Basically, the decision for how to handle reuse at requirements level is a risk-based one and depends on the assessment of the risk of having the customization of a standard package out of control versus the costs and the residual risk of each possible reuse handling option.

We consider the work reported in this article as only the beginning of an ongoing effort to develop better requirements reuse measurement practices. Further work will take several directions. One is to build a lessons learnt architecture by using product/process dependency models [7]. Second, it would be interesting to investigate some ERP effort estimation models based on our measures. Lastly, we plan to develop an approach to evaluating the added value benefits from ERP requirements reuse.

The author would like to thank the anonymous reviewers whose comments led to the improvement of this paper.

References

1. Curran, T., A. Ladd, SAP R/3 Business Blueprint, Understanding Enterprise Supply Chain Management, 2nd. Edition, Prentice Hall, Upper Saddle River, NJ (1999)
2. Daneva M.: Mesuring Reuse of SAP Requirements: a Model-based Approach, Proc. Of 5th Symposium on Software Reuse, ACM Press, New York (1999)
3. Daneva, M., Deriving Function Points from SAP Business Processes and Business Objects, Journal of Information and Software Technologies (1999). Accepted for publication
4. Daneva M., Empirical Validation of Requirements Reuse Metrics. In preparation.
5. Desharnais, J.-M., A. Abran, How to Successfully Implement a Measurement Program: From Theory to Practice. In: Müllerburg, M., Abran A. (eds.): Metrics in Software Evolution, R. Oldenbourg Verlag, Oldenburg (1995), 11-38.
6. ESPRIT Project PROFES, URL: http://www.ele.vtt.fi/profes.
7. Fenton, N., Pfleeger, S.L.: Software Metrics: Rigorous and Practical Approach, PWS Publishing, Boston Massachusetts (1997)
8. Garmus D., D. Herron, Measuring the Software Process, Prentice Hall, Upper Saddle River, New Jersey (1996).

9. Jacquet, J.-P., Abran, A.: Metrics Validation Proposals: a Structured Analysis. In: Dumke, R., Abran, A. (eds.): Software Measurement, Gabler, Wiesbaden (1999), 43-60.
10. Karlsson, E.-A. (ed.): Software Reuse, John Wiley & Sons, Chichester (1998)
11. Keller, G., Teufel, T.: SAP R/3 Process Oriented Implementation, Addison-Wesley Longman, Harlow (1998)
12. Lozinsky, S.: Enterprise-wide Software Solutions, Addison-Wesley, Reading MA (1998)
13. McClure, C.: Reuse Engineering: Adding Reuse to the Software Development Process, Prentice-Hall, Upper Saddle River, NJ (1997)
14. Pfleeger, S.L.: Measuring Reuse: a Cautionary Tale, IEEE Software, June (1997)
15. Poulin, J. Measuring Software Reuse: Principles, Practices, and Economic Models, Addison-Wesley, Reading, MA (1997)
16. Robinson, S. , J. Robinson, Mastering the Requirements Process, Addison- Wesley, Readings, MA (1999)
17. Sharp, H., A. Finkelstein, G. Galal, Shakeholder Identification in the Requirements Engineering Process, Proceeding of the 1st Intl. Workshop on RE Processes/ 10th Intl Conf. on DEXA, 1-3 Sept., 1999, Florence, Italy.
18. Statz, J., Leverage Your Lessons, IEEE Software, March/April (1999), 30-33.
19. Welti, N., Sussessful R/3 Implementation, Practical Management of ERP Projects, Addison-Wesley, Harlow, England (1999).

Building Extensible Workflow Systems Using an Event-Based Infrastructure

Dimitrios Tombros and Andreas Geppert

Department of Information Technology, University of Zurich
{tombros, geppert}@ifi.unizh.ch

Abstract. This paper describes an approach towards the systematic composition of workflow systems using an event-based approach. The complex nature of workflow systems and the heterogeneity of the application systems which are integrated require powerful general purpose composition mechanisms. Furthermore, it is advantageous if the functionality of the underlying workflow management system can be adapted to the type of workflow applications for which a system is intended. We propose an extensible event-based architectural framework for workflow systems which allows the composition of workflow systems by reuse and customization of reactive components representing workflow system processing entities. We also consider the structure of a build-time repository to support this architectural framework.

1 Introduction

Traditional software development methods do not meet the evolving requirements of heterogeneous and process-oriented systems. A principal open problem remains the systematic development of workflow systems (WFS) based on appropriate abstractions. The current state of WFS technology has not yet reached consensus on the proper component abstractions for the workflow domain. Instead, there is a proliferation of research proposing the benefits of particular workflow management concepts. Some efforts, such as those of the Workflow Management Coalition and the OMG Workflow Workgroup [16], attempt to converge various ideas in the workflow management community. Still, however, WFS development remains a largely ad hoc effort done on a case-by-case basis.

A methodical approach to WFS development utilizes component-based engineering, in which new WFS are composed out of already existing, reusable artifacts. Component-based WFS development is however in a very early stage. This is not only an inherent problem of workflow management technology but can also be explained in the general context of system composition research. Based on general observations concerning software composition [12], we consider the following facts as especially relevant for WFS development:

- It is not clear how domain knowledge should be captured and formalized to support component-oriented development. Especially in the domain of workflow management, there has been little or no research in this issue. The definition of reuse-oriented domain-specific models is still an ongoing process.

B. Wangler, L. Bergman (Eds.): CAiSE 2000, LNCS 1789, pp. 325–339, 2000.

– There is no synergy between analysis and design. The relation between workflow specification and workflow implementation has not been considered under the perspective of reusability. For example, most workflow specification
languages provide reuse mechanisms for workflow artifacts, but do not consider the reuse of processing entity (PE) implementations. The mapping of
workflow specifications to WFS implementation is ad hoc.
– There are no generally accepted methods for the design of frameworks supporting component-based WFS development. In the domain of workflow
management an architectural perspective and the resulting framework-based
development approach is in a very early stage.
– There are no software tools which facilitate component-oriented WFS development. The support provided by workflow management systems (WFMS)
in this respect is limited to mere workflow specification.

We follow a composition-based approach for WFS built around an appropriate architectural framework. The approach supports the architecture-centric
development and extension of WFS. It consists of the following elements:

– a lightweight but extensible generic event-based workflow execution and application integration platform;
– an approach for the analysis of the WFS architecture and the classification
of WFS components. We consider components as self-contained units of abstraction, with defined connection interfaces, and an individual life cycle (see,
e.g., [12,19] for more elaborate discussions of the nature of components);
– a domain-specific metamodel for the description of the architecture and functionality of the intended WFS;
– a framework for the composition of WFS out of pre-existing parameterized
component templates; and
– support for the reuse-based composition of WFS through an architecture artifact repository and the event-based execution platform. This infrastructure
provides a workflow specification execution system.

In this paper, we concentrate on the domain-specific metamodel and the
compositional framework for WFS. Due to space considerations, we describe
only briefly the underlying analytical approach and the repository-based reuse
of WFS components.

The remainder of this paper is organized as follows. The next section introduces the WFS development life cycle. Sections 3 and 4 discuss PE as reusable
components. Section 5 presents repository support for WFS construction, section
6 discusses relevant related work, and section 7 concludes the paper.

2   Workflow System Development Life Cycle

In this section, we introduce a WFS development life cycle based on composition of reusable components. A WFS consists of heterogeneous real-world PE
each of which contributes to the tasks of the WFS in some way. Typical PE

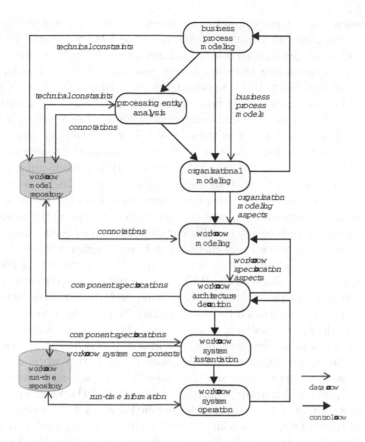

Fig. 1. Workflow system development lifecycle

include application software, WFS interface software (e.g., worklist interfaces, or administration tools such as a workflow execution monitor and visualization tool used as an example in this paper), and human entities. Depending on the specific workflow application, a different set of PE may be required. These are represented by appropriate WFS components as described below.

In a nutshell, the aim of the WFS construction process is to compose reusable representations of the PE together into a coherent system. Any WFS provides minimal functionality for workflow management. This core WFMS comprises an event composition, routing and notification subsystem (described in more detail in [8]), a subsystem for executing event-condition-action rules (ECA rules) [22], buildtime and runtime repositories, as well as a set of component design and instantiation tools. Additional components can be added to the WFS as required, organizational aspects of the PE can be defined, workflow specifications can be designed, and eventually, workflow instances can be created and enacted. The lifecycle consists of the following groups of activities (see Fig. 1).

We assume that a project initiation phase precedes the entire lifecycle. In this phase, the goals with respect to the developed WFS are set. The project management team determines which business processes will be automated by the WFS. An appropriate *business process modeling* (BPM) formalism should be selected at this point. It is important however, that a mapping is provided by the BPM environment to the target workflow specification language.

Processing Entity Analysis and Integration. PE are integrated in a WFS; they either extend the functionality of the core WFS or are the resources that carry out the business-related workflow tasks. For example, in the course of our work we were able to augment the core WFS with workflow monitoring and event auditing components. The analysis and integration of PE includes the composition of a reactive component template which represents the PE based on the analysis of its characteristics. These characteristics determine the properties of the component that represents the PE. For each PE it is defined which workflow tasks (services) it provides to its clients, which are in general other PE.

Organizational Modeling. Once new PE (i.e., their representing component templates) have been added to the WFS, organizational aspects such as specific attributes (e.g. costs per execution time unit) and relationships between PE (e.g. is-supervisor-of relationships among human PE) may have to be modeled to support the definition of task assignment rules refering to organizational aspects.

Workflow Modeling. New workflow specifications can be constructed by referencing and using information available about PE and other workflow specifications. The use of an appropriate workflow specification language which supports the reuse of process definition artifacts is required. For the monitoring component mentioned above, its behavior was specified such that it should be notified of the occurrence of the events which the WFS administrator wanted to monitor.

Workflow Architecture Definition. The next phase involves the development of a homogeneous event-based architecture model of the WFS. The architectural elements are summarized in Table 1, where the correspondence between relevant facts from the real world, their respective aspect in workflow specification, and finally the provided architectural abstraction is depicted.

Workflow System Instantiation and Enactment. New instances of the defined workflow component templates can be created. These create and enact the defined workflow models.

Multiple iterations of these above steps may be required to compose a WFS.

3   Analysis of Workflow System Architecture

Successful composition-based construction of WFS requires appropriate abstractions as well as the maintenance of sufficient information about their functionality and semantics To that end, we represent explicitly the integration-related properties characterizing a PE type with respect to the WFS under construction. These properties are termed *processing entity connotations* (see Fig. 2). Components and connectors [1] are implementation level constructs defining the structure and communication paths of a WFS. PE connotations associate the

Table 1. Workflow system architecture definition elements

Business process model aspect	Workflow modeling aspect	Architectural abstraction
information system components and connectors	workflow system architectural structure	reactive component templates, event type registrations
organizational constraints under which the workflow is executed	organizational model	organizational relations
PE functionality used in business process	workflow tasks	services
activity execution sequence	control flow	ECA-rules
activity data dependencies	data flow	event parameters
business rules	task assignment	suitability, dispatching
human role, application functionality	PE behavior	ECA-rules, rule packages

properties of the PE type with the characteristics of the components and connectors needed to adequately represent PE in the WFS.

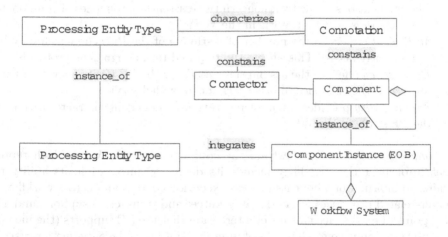

Fig. 2. Relationships between workflow system composition elements (in UML)

The definition of PE connotations is based on a faceted classification scheme [15] and consists of so-called *traits* (properties of PE). Unlike the pure faceted classification, leafs of the classification trait trees may be either *simple terms* or *expressions*. Simple terms are chosen from the standard vocabulary of the domain, while expressions describe a dependency to other elements of the WFS architecture—elements which are not necessarily components. Such elements may be defined outside the scope of the classification scheme (e.g., in the workflow model). The classification serves three main purposes: (i) determination of the required properties of the components used for PE representation, (ii) analysis of the integration issues facing the composer of a WFS, and (iii) architecture-centric based development and reuse [3].

Table 2. Connotation of the EVE monitoring interface component

Participation	Optionality	optional
	Multiplicity	max(num_of(EVE_server))
	Dependency	local_EVE_server, defined(MonitorWF)
	Functionality	user interaction, display, notification
Implementation	Automation	interactive
	State	yes
	Server type	concurrent
	Guarantee	none
	Access point	in, out: implicit-triggering (EVE messages)

Participation traits characterize a PE's role in a particular WFS. They define architectural constraints on the WFS:

- *Optionality* refers to the requirements concerning the existence of the PE. The implications of the trait concern the existential properties of component instances representing the PE in the WFS.
- *Multiplicity* refers to the number of instances of the PE type which may be concurrently active. This affects the required task assignment protocols.
- *Dependency* refers to the assumptions made by the PE for its operation with respect to the existence of other PE and provided services.
- *Functionality* provides an implementation-independent characterization of the PE's role in the WFS.

Implementation traits constrain the components of the WFS which represent/implement the PE. They include its degree of automation, its ability to maintain information about its process execution context and across workflows, server-related properties, execution guarantees and transaction support, and access points, i.e., the mechanisms of interaction that the PE supports (the incoming interface) and the mechanisms of interaction it uses (the outgoing interface).

Additional traits may be required and even within traits which seem complete, i.e., all except those concerning interface and service, additional terms may be required. Such modifications and additions are not excluded by the classification scheme. However, the implications and effects they have on the architectural framework will have to be considered.

An example of a connotation for a monitoring interface component is presented in Table 2. The participation traits define that the component is not required for system operation and may be instantiated at most once for each server in the system. Its operation depends on the operation of the server for which it is instantiated and on the definition of a monitoring workflow type defining monitoring services. The component provides user interaction, display, and notification functionality.

4   Reusable Workflow System Components

Processing entities are represented on the architectural level by instances of composite reactive components called *event occurrence brokers* (EOB). They execute workflow tasks as a reaction to workflow-relevant situations in their environment. The occurrence of these situations is manifested by events. EOB generate and react to WFS events, and map their meaning to concepts present in the vocabulary of the respective PE. In other words, they provide a homogeneous representation of heterogeneous real-world PE and provide the PE functionality to the WFS-internal miniworld.

4.1   Events and Services in Workflow Systems

The most flexible and loose model of integration is asynchronous interaction based on events. An event-based approach to data, control, and process integration in a WFS architecture has many advantages [2]. Hence, in our approach events are the sole component integration and interaction mechanism, i.e, they are the only available type of connectors between EOB in a WFS. Events are used for the following purposes:

- signaling of relevant workflow situations and definition of control flow,
- invocation of functionality provided by PE, and
- exchange of data between PE.

The event typology is a tree subdivided into primitive and composite events. Primitive events belong to the following types: *time events*, *interaction events*, and EOB *internal events*. EOB internal events are relevant only for the implementation of EOB-internal communication.

Time events can be absolute, relative, or periodic. Absolute time events express real-time points and are defined in terms of a time specification expressing a date and time recorded by a local clock site.

The exchange of coordination information between EOB takes place by the signaling and reaction to EOB interaction events. Thus the semantics of EOB interaction events are associated with execution states of workflows. The manifestation of these events are event messages which are forwarded by the underlying communication infrastructure to EOB which have a registered interest in these events, called the event listeners. Interaction events are service requests, confirmations, replies, and exceptions. These events contain system-provided (implicit) and user-provided parameters. Through the use of service request events the execution of services by EOB can be triggered. The initiation of service execution is signalled by request confirmation events. Finally, the results of service execution can be communicated to other EOB by service reply events.

The special meaning of exception event types with respect to the other event types consist in the fact that for each such type defined, a corresponding exception handling component must be defined, i.e., an EOB which has some predefined reaction on the event occurrence.

Composite events are used to express complex workflow situations. As with primitive events, we distinguish between event types and occurrences of these types. Composite event types are defined by applying unary and binary event operators to event types. The event operators include conjunction, sequence, exclusive-or and inclusive-or disjunction, repetition, iteration, and negation. The main extension is the concurrency operator which is meaningful only in the context of distributed systems. Composite events have formal semantics described in detail in [20]. It is important to mention that workflow execution based on events produces an *event history*.

Services are defined based on the function traits of PE. A service is provided by one or more EOB in the WFS called the server(s) in the context of a service execution. It can be requested by other EOB which are the clients in the context of that execution. Services define the PE capabilities assumed for a given WFS, independent of the EOB defined in the system. They represent the interface between workflow specification and WFS architecture and can be leveraged to workflow task types declared in a workflow schema. In other words, workflow specification makes use of the service abstraction in order to define the functionality of desired processing steps.

A service identifies an operational interface with a predefined set of parameters which are provided by the client EOB during service request. It also identifies a set of replies which express the possible outcomes of a service execution. These replies may have various parameters provided by the server EOB.

4.2   Event Occurrence Brokers

An EOB is an instance of a composite component template built from reusable subcomponents which implement parts of the EOB functionality and communicate through an internal message bus. The type of the EOB determines its subcomponents, their properties, and the events they understand. Every EOB includes at least the following subcomponents: an event delivery (EDI) and an event posting (EPI) interface, a persistent state management subcomponent, an ECA rule management subcomponent, and a PE management subcomponent. This structure is depicted in Fig. 3.

The component instances composing a WFS communicate by broadcasting event messages over a reliable shared message bus which provides a single message broadcast operation. Thus, all component instances connected to the message bus are notified of an event message and react accordingly. The set of messages each component understands is fixed for each subcomponent type. The general EOB-internal message structure is the following: *(message_name, message_origin, message_parameters)*. The message parameters are typed using the OMG Interface Definition Language [13]. Messages can be sent either in a synchronous or asynchronous mode; in the first case the message sender expects a response message with the output parameters, in the second case the message sender can continue processing.

An EOB contains a *state manager* (STATEMAN) implemented over some storage system not further specified. The STATEMAN is responsible for the

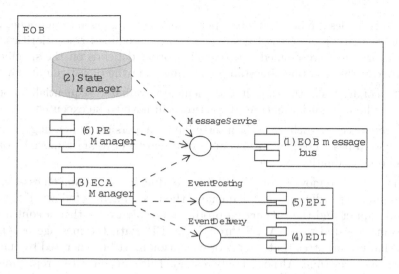

Fig. 3. General structure of an EOB and its subcomponents

persistent storage of the EOB state objects. Persistence is achieved by a system-provided persistent root whose constituents, i.e., composite objects declared in the EOB state persist automatically.

Every EOB contains a *rule management* (ECAMAN) subsystem responsible for management and execution of ECA rules expressing the behavior of EOB. ECA rules are used to implement the following functionality:

Initiation of service execution by PE. Workflow service specification does not always correspond directly to the operations or services provided by PE. For example, a workflow service may be implemented by a series of database queries and the subsequent evaluation of the results. This processing logic is described in ECA rules which bridge the semantic gap between application operations and services provided (by EOB) in the WFS.

Enforcement of task execution ordering and guarding of task execution conditions. The workflow schema expresses various dependencies among workflow tasks. These dependencies are expressed by composite events and by the rule actions which generate new events which eventually trigger the subsequent tasks. ECA rule conditions can be used to express task execution constraints which can be evaluated against task execution results available through event parameters.

Exception and failure handling. ECA rules are used to specify failure handling. They can also express recovery policies.

Rule execution by the ECAMAN is performed as follows:

1. An event arrives at the delivery interface of the ECAMAN.
2. At some point in time, the ECAMAN process examines the oldest event in the delivery queue by sending EDI the message *peek()*, and determines the set of active rules that are fired by this event.

3. All fired rules are inserted into a persistent pending evaluation queue, where the relative order of the rules depends on the defined rule priorities. If no rule priorities are defined, the queueing order depends on the specification order or rule creation timestamp (starting from the oldest rule first).

4. The conditions of the rules in the queue are evaluated sequentially. For each rule whose condition is true, the action will have to be executed.

5. A reference to such rules is inserted into a persistent pending execution queue. Rules whose conditions are evaluated to false are removed from the pending evaluation queue.

6. The event is removed from the EDI by sending it a *consume()* message. Each rule in the pending execution queue is then examined as follows: if the event is a request and the rule action produces a reply event, then a confirmation event is posted to the WFS through the EPI with the message *put()*. This actually guarantees that a reply or exception must be generated by the EOB at some later time. Although only a single rule can generate a reply, multiple rules may be triggered by the same request, without however producing a subsequent reply.

7. The rule actions in the pending execution queue are executed sequentially. After action execution is completed, each rule is removed from the pending execution queue. If an action produces a reply event, this is posted to the WFS through the EPI.

8. When the pending execution queue is empty, the next event can be examined from the delivery interface.

Interaction with PE is implemented by the *PE management* (PEMAN) subsystem. In general, the PEMAN implements the access to the functionality of PE by using some wrapping technique to access the external systems; it may alternatively implement the desired functionality itself in some programming language without accesing other software. The PEMAN however understands a set of operations which are called in ECA rule actions. It implements the automation and access point traits of the PE connotation (see above).

As already mentioned, the PEMAN may wrap an external system (e.g., a database application), implement system functionality (e.g., store an event log), or provide a user interface (e.g., the monitoring interface). When the PEMAN directly implements desired functionality, the WFS infrastructure plays the role of a white-box PE for a workflow task. The implementation of different wrapping techniques is a problem which has been addressed by a large body of research; in our work we concentrate on the issues relevant to the use of these wrapping techniques within a reactive component-based WFS architecture.

In the case of the monitoring EOB, the component has to be registered as a listener to all events which denote workflow situations to be monitored (e.g. all service request events). It reacts to occurrences of these events by changing its internal state to visualize the execution state in a defined way (e.g. change the color of a graphical screen element).

Table 3. The EOB typology based on the ECAMAN and PEMAN properties

EOB type	ECAMAN rule action execution	PEMAN functionality
caller	single-threaded	execution of envelope
uni-server	single-threaded	implementation of a wrapping method for an external server system
multi-server	multi-threaded	implementation of a wrapping method for an external server system
user	single-threaded	user worklist management and interaction
group	single-threaded	-
uni-extender	single-threaded	implementation
multi-extender	multi-threaded	implementation

Depending on the properties of EOB subcomponents, different types of EOB can be composed. The typology—as determined from the properties of participating ECAMAN and PEMAN—is presented in Table 3.

A complete WFS assumes the existence of a specialized EOB called an event engine (EVE). EVE is a distributed glue system which—among other functions—provides event composition and notification functionality to EOB according to the interest they have registered. EVE is described in more detail in [8] and enforces the semantics described in [20]. EOB in a WFS consume and produce events. The correctness of their behavior and thus the correctness of the operation of PE in the WFS can be examined over the resulting event history. An EOB has behaved correctly iff:

- it has reacted to all requests it is responsible for;
- it has reacted to all situations for which it defines workflow-specific rules and it is responsible for; and
- it has produced a reply or an exception for each request it has confirmed.

Finally, we note at this point that the correctness of the composed WFS depends on the maintenance of certain invariants which can be derived from participation traits of the involved PE. For example, dependency traits describe completeness constraints on the WFS architecture which can be examined at the EOB-implementation level. A detailed discussion of such invariants is omitted due to space considerations.

5 Repository-Based Composition

The abstractions previously described support the composition of WFS. The main abstractions—EOB types and their services—can be most closely compared to software schema abstractions [10]. Software schemas are formal extensions to reusable components which, however, emphasize the reuse of abstract algorithms and data structures. The abstraction specification of the software schema is the

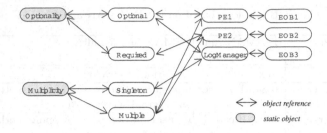

Fig. 4. Example of participation traits and PE in the buildtime repository

formal exposition of the algorithms and data structures, in service definitions, behavior and state of the EOB types. The abstraction realization corresponds to the source code produced when EOB types are instantiated.

The development of effective and usable repositories for software artifacts represent an active field of research (e.g., [5,9]). In our work we have attempted to utilize the experience and results gained from this research within the context of WFS composition. The object-oriented build-time repository schema represents a complete mapping of WFS artifacts as discussed next.

For each participation trait an object of type Participation_Trait exists in the build-time repository. Its attributes are the terms—which can be composite objects in themselves—defined for the trait. A term contains a collection of references to objects of the type Processing_Entity, each of which can be associated with an EOB object. This structure is exemplified for two traits in Fig. 4.

Organizational units defined in the organizational schema are represented by Organizational_Unit objects. Organizational relationship types are represented as OrgRel_Type interface types.

Each EOB is represented by a composite EOB object, whose structure and implementation depends on the EOB type. An appropriate interface type is defined for each EOB type. Subcomponents of an EOB are instances of STATEMAN, PE-MAN, and ECAMAN types. These are collections of references to State_Variable_Type objects, Operation_Type objects, and ECA_rule objects. Implementations of PE-MAN subcomponents are stored as symbolic links to object files.

Services are represented by Service_Interface objects. For each service definition a corresponding Request and Confirmation event type object is created. For each reply and exception event type a corresponding Reply and Exception event type object is created. Confirmation, reply, and exception event type objects have bi-directional references to their request event type object. Event type parameter objects are created for each parameter based on corresponding interface types.

An interface type ECA_Rule for ECA rules is defined. It contains references to the event type objects in its event clause. Composite event types implicitly defined in the rule event clause are represented by objects of the appropriate interface type. These are created when the rule object is stored in the repository. An ECA_Rule also contains references to conditions. Conditions are sequences of clauses containing object references of the form *({AND| OR|NOT}, name, type, logical_operator*) where name and type are references to corresponding objects defined in the repository, the logical operator must be defined for the type, and the boolean operators determine the relationship to the previous element. The precedence order of the expression determines the order of sequence elements. Actions are sequences of operation_name clauses where operation_name is a name of an operation type defined for the EOB, or a raise-operation for an event type. The corresponding objects can be retrieved through predefined queries. Additionally, actions of extender rules can contain symbolic links to source and object code files.

During the creation of objects in the build-time repository, some objects can be in the *in-development* state (e.g., because they reference names of as yet undefined objects). This is allowed during the composition phase of a new WFS. However, when the WFS is instantiated, every participating object must be in the *in-production* state. This is ensured by the transactions which create objects in the runtime system and ensure that the WFS invariants are respected. Additional states can be defined if required by the development process.

6 Related Work

The systematic development of workflow management applications has been recently identified as an important research issue. Consequently, some relevant publications have appeared which advance the issue beyond initial attempts focussing primarily on the expressiveness of workflow modeling.

In [14], an object-oriented environment for the development of transaction-based workflow applications is provided whose emphasis lies on the reuse of process objects with predefined scheduling and transactional behavior. The—rather strong—assumption of the existence of a mapping between external operations and native operations is made.

A stronger emphasis on application integration and the definition of a workflow application system architecture is presented in [17] where a type library for wrapping different applications is provided which are subsequently implemented by different execution objects. The provided support is focused on the implementation aspect and does not consider in depth the systematic reuse of software components. Similarly, in [21] a framework for the systematic integration of software tools in process-centered environments by using specialized wrappers is described. Although the authors only consider software development tools, their work is applicable to WFS. Compared to our work however, the emphasis lies on the implementation of the integration mechanisms and not on the definition of a reusable component-based system architecture.

APEL [7] is a platform-independent environment for the development of process-oriented systems. It provides modeling abstractions for various aspects of such systems and maps them to low-level executable formalisms. The initial emphasis has been in covering a large spectrum of design activities; the authors state that support for systematic reuse is part of their intended future work.

Event-based approaches have been advocated by several authors [4,6,11] for workflow execution and cooperative information systems. In contrast to these efforts, events in our approach are conceptual and architectural constructs (instead of execution level constructs). In contrast to CoopWARE [11] (which considers services as the major abstraction), PE and their representation as EOBs are the most important abstractions on which the composition of WFS is based.

Finally, we refer at this point to emerging component standards and especially to Enterprise JavaBeans [18] which proposes a generic component model for server-side components. This model is bound to a particular programming language and considers application-neutral implementation aspects. Our approach, in contrast, adresses domain-specific issues, attempts to provide support for the development of a specific class of applications, and is explicitly kept independent from a particular implementation language.

7   Conclusions and Evaluation

The systematic composition of WFS provides an efficient way to construct the large complex application systems that are typical in the workflow management domain. In this paper we described an approach for the reuse-based development of such applications:

 - we implement WFS by extending the functionality of a core event-based integration platform;
 - we provide mechanisms for the characterization and classification of PE;
 - we provide a component-based architectural framework for WFS; and
 - we support a repository-based development process which can benefit from extensive large-grain component reuse.

Despite the promising initial experiences we have made with our system, it still remains to be seen if a reuse-based WFS development approach can become part of an industrial environment. As the main problems during the introduction of the approach we anticipate the initial population of the repository with process entities which actually have a reuse potential and the implementation of PEMAN components for various applications. Especially the second task is complex and requires the use of developer resources without an immediately visible return-on-investment. Furthermore, in our future work we plan to extend the system to support WFS evolution through workflow component versioning and a set of well-defined modification operations on EOB. These operations should respect the invariants defined in the WFS framework.

References

1. R. Allen and D. Garlan. A Formal Basis for Architectural Connection. *ACM Trans. on Software Engineering and Methodology*, 6(3), July 1997.
2. D.J. Barrett, L.A. Clarke, P.L. Tarr, and A.E. Wise. A Framework for Event-based Software Integration. *ACM Trans. on Software Engineering and Methodology*, 5(4):378–421, October 1996.

3. B. Boehm and W. Sherlis. Megaprogramming. In *Proc. DARPA Software Technology Conference*, Arlington, VA, April 1992.
4. F. Casati, S. Ceri, B. Pernici, and G. Pozzi. Deriving Active Rules for Workflow Management. In *Proc. 7th DEXA*, Zurich, Switzerland, September 1996.
5. P. Constantopoulos, M. Jarke, J. Mylopoulos, and Y. Vassiliou. The Software Information Base: A Server for Reuse. *VLDB Journal*, 4(1):1–43, 1995.
6. G. Cugola, E. Di Nitto, and A. Fuggetta. The JEDI Event-based Infrastructure and its Application to the Development of the OPSS WFMS. Technical report, CEFRIEL, Politecnico di Milano, 1998.
7. S. Dami, J. Estublier, and M. Amiour. APEL: a Graphical yet Executable Formalism for Process Modeling. In E. Di Nitto and A. Fugetta, editors, *Process Technology*. Kluwer Academic Publishers, 1997.
8. A. Geppert and D. Tombros. Event-Based Distributed Workflow Execution with EVE. In *Proc. IFIP Int'l Conf. on Distributed Systems Platforms and Open Distributed Processing (Middleware '98)*, Lake District, England, September 1998.
9. S. Henninger. An Evolutionary Approach to Constructing Effective Software Reuse Repositories. *ACM Trans. on Software Engineering and Methodology*, 6(2), April 1997.
10. C.W. Krueger. Software Reuse. *ACM Computing Surveys*, 24(2):131–183, 1992.
11. J. Mylopoulos, A. Gal, K. Kontogiannis, and M. Stanley. A Generic Integration Architecture for Cooperative Information Systems. In *Proc. 1st CoopIS*, Brussels, Belgium, June 1996.
12. O. Nierstrasz and L. Dami. Component-Oriented Software Technology. In O. Nierstrasz and D. Tsichritzis, editors, *Object-Oriented Software Composition*, pages 3–28. Prentice Hall, London, 1995.
13. The Common Object Request Broker: Architecture and Specification. Revision 2.0. Object Management Group, July 1995.
14. M. Papazoglou, A. Delis, A. Bouguettaya, and M. Haghjoo. Class Library Support for Workflow Environments and Applications. *IEEE Transactions on Computers*, 46(6), June 1997.
15. R. Prieto-Diaz and P. Freeman. Classifying Software for Reusability. *IEEE Software*, 4(1), 1987.
16. M.T. Schmidt. The Evolution of Workflow Standards. *IEEE Concurrency*, June 1999.
17. H. Schuster, S. Jablonski, P. Heinl, and C. Bussler. A General Framework for the Execution of Heterogenous Programs in Workflow Management Systems. In *Proc. 1st CoopIS*, Brussels, Belgium, June 1996.
18. Sun Microsystems. *Enterprise JavaBeans Specification Version 1.0*, March 1998.
19. C. Szyperski. *Component Software: Beyond Object-Oriented Programming*. Addison-Wesley, 1997.
20. D. Tombros, A. Geppert, and K.R. Dittrich. Semantics of Reactive Components in Event-Driven Workflow Execution. In *Proc. CAiSE*, Barcelona, Spain, June 1997.
21. G. Valetto and G. Kaiser. Enveloping Sophisticated Tools into Computer Aided Software Engineering Environments. *Journal of Automated Software Engineering*, 3(3-4), 1996.
22. J. Widom and S. Ceri. *Active Database Systems*. Morgan Kaufmann, 1996.

Defining Components in a MetaCASE Environment

Zheying Zhang

Department of Computer Science and Information Systems
University of Jyväskylä, PL 35, FIN-40351 Jyväskylä, Finland
zhezhan@cc.jyu.fi

Abstract. In this paper we describe how to improve method reusability in a metaCASE environment called MetaEdit+. The suggested component based approach helps unify design artefacts into components with explicit interfaces and meaningful context descriptions. We describe a method artefact from three perspectives: concept, content, and context. We create a component concept by using a hierarchical facet-based schema, and represent contextual relationship types by using definitional and reuse dependency, usage context, and implementation context links. This is the first attempt to explicitly define components into a metaCASE environment.

1   Introduction

Manufacturing industries learnt long ago the benefits of moving from custom development to an assembly of pre-fabricated components to speed up time-to-market and reduce costs. In the same manner, information system development can be significantly improved if applications can be quickly assembled from pre-fabricated software components. This strategy, called component-based development (CBD), has been a goal for nearly two decades. The recent focus on component-based systems has shown that CBD allows better quality, faster development, and effective change management [1]. It represents a further step in the industrialisation of information system development, and will become the next wave in application development.

Introducing components in information system development offers potential to reuse code and other design artefacts, and will lead to an faster assembly of applications. Some component-based CASE tools, e.g. SoftModeler [2], ObjectiF [3], and Rational Rose 98 [4], provide support for component based analysis and design. These tools expand beyond the functionality of current metaCASE environments that were originally designed without component thinking. Because metaCASE environments can be used for both methodology specifications and methodology supported system design activities, they manipulate more diverse artefacts than CASE tools. Most of these artefacts are used as independent task units, and relate to the others by semantic definitions or dependencies. These artefacts and the "knowledge" embedded in form good sources for reuse, especially across projects. It is therefore feasible to introduce component thinking into a metaCASE environment. Based on our knowledge, there are no studies of how to introduce components in environments supporting method engineering. This is the first attempt to study component definition

B. Wangler, L. Bergman (Eds.): CAiSE 2000, LNCS 1789, pp. 340-354, 2000

for all design artefacts. It will bring benefits of CBD into the metaCASE environment. The most significant one is that the application development can be improved by using quickly assembled components [5]. Although some metaCASE environments, e.g. MetaEdit+ [6], provide limited facilities to support reuse activities in the method engineering and software design process, the application of component concept will further improve reuse. In this paper, we will take MetaEdit+ as a target environment of our study, but the same principles apply to other environments as well.

This paper describes a framework for scalable tools and techniques that increase artefact reusability. We study features of design artefacts, and the possibility of packaging them into "components". After that, these artefacts are further defined into components based on three perspectives: concept, content, and context. These perspectives are based on a 3C model [7]. In the process of defining components, possible solutions to component representations in MetaEdit+ are outlined.

2   Components

A component can be thought as a unit of independent deployment that can be reused by a third party. ECOOP'96 (the European Conference on Object-Oriented Programming) offers the following definition of a software component:

"A software component is *a unit of composition* with contractually specified *interfaces* and explicit *context dependencies* only. A software component can be deployed independently and is subject to composition by third parties."

A component thus has three basic features: explicit interfaces, a context of services, and the design for reuse. Among these basic features, explicit interfaces, the context of services, and the unit of composition form a complete component. The design for reuse is the purpose and the result of an application of a component. In industry, a component forms a coherent package of software that can be independently developed and delivered, while in a metaCASE environment, a component can be any design artefact, i.e. a metamodel, or a chunk of source code. The metamodel component is different from the method fragment as discussed in method engineering language (MEL) [8]. A method fragment can be used to describe every aspect of a method. It does not integrate the concept and the relationships among method fragments into a unified whole. Instead the metamodel component has an explicitly specified interface and relationships with the environment. Such a structure can ease the management of metamodels and improve reusability.

A good specification of a component helps users understand it and reuse it [9]. One of the attempts to characterise reusable software components is the 3C model [10]. It provides a metamodel to describe a software component using three distinct aspects of a reusable component: concept, content and context. A concept forms the abstraction captured in a component; a content is the implementation of the interface; and context describes the environment where a component interacts. The component includes the conceptual context, the operational context and the implementational context. We can see that these three aspects form the basic elements and features of software components currently used in industry, e.g. object components in CORBA.

3   Components in MetaEdit+

A metaCASE environment can be used to build system development tools. Instead of providing one fixed software engineering environment, as most traditional CASE (computer aided software engineering) tools do, a metaCASE environment provides also facilities for method engineering which involves design, construction and adaptation of methods, techniques and tools for various system development contingencies [11]. Therefore, a metaCASE tool can generate a variety of CASE tools, depending on the methodology used. Several metaCASE tools have been developed during the last decade, e.g. commercial products such as MetaEdit+ (MetaCASE Consulting), MethodMaker (Mark V), ToolBuilder (Sunderland/IPSYS /Lincoln); and research prototypes such as MetaView (Alberta) and MetaGen (Paris).

MetaEdit+ is a fully configurable metaCASE environment that provides functionality for dual processes: CASE and CAME (computer aided method engineering) [6, 12-15]. MetaEdit+ offers GOPRR [12] metamodelling language to implement the CAME functionality. It provides concepts, rules, and semantics to specify, generate, and customise methodologies as sets of metamodels that can be further instantiated to models that present solutions for an application domain. GOPRR stands for the acronym of Graph, Object, Property, Relationship, and Role. These types form the primary meta data types that can be used to model artefacts for methodologies. The conceptual GOPRR modelling constructs are shown in Table 1.

Table 1. GOPRR Metamodelling language

Meta Data Types	Description
Graph (G)	A graph is a specification of a method (technique). It is an aggregation concept that contains all other GOPRR meta types. E.g. the definition of State Transition Diagram is a graph.
Object (O)	An object is a conceptual thing in the universe around us. E.g. State, Start, and Stop are objects in the definition of a State Transition Diagram.
Property (P)	Properties describe/qualify characteristics associated with other meta types. E.g. State name is a property of State.
Relationship (R)	A relationship forms an association between two or more objects. It connects objects through roles. E.g. Transition is a relationship used to connect two States.
Role (R)	A role is a link between an object and a relationship to specify how an object participates in a relationship. E.g. From and To are two roles indicating that a Transition relationship is from one State to another State.

Based on GOPRR metamodelling language, MetaEdit+ accordingly involves diversity artefacts for methodology specification and information system design. For example, in the methodology specification process, the object *State*, the relationship *Transition*, and other types of data are artefacts that form a larger artefact in the UML methodology called a State Diagram. In the same manner, in the system design process, e.g. a *Phone call state diagram* has different states such as *Busy, Dialling, DialTone*, and so on, which are independent artefacts with their own features. These artefacts can be regarded as encapsulated units, but normally without complete interfaces and contextual relationship representations. They are some sorts of "semi-components". We temporarily call them components, although they are not themselves components. In MetaEdit+, what we call components are sets of design "models", represented in graphic "notations"; metamodel artefacts of methodology specifications; and chunks of code that represent services. Meanwhile, due to the symmetric processes supported in MetaEdit+, they differ in terms of information level, granularity, and representational features.

3.1 Information Levels

Artefacts in MetaEdit+ can be grouped into two levels: model level and metamodel level. The model level information covers a project development lifecycle. It consists of design artefacts with different forms of representation for different development stages, such as diagrams for system design and source code for final implementation. Some examples of design artefacts in MetaEdit+ are shown in Fig. 1. It represents a *Phone call state diagram* in the form of diagram, table, and matrix. Besides, State *DialTone* is represented as one composition artefact.

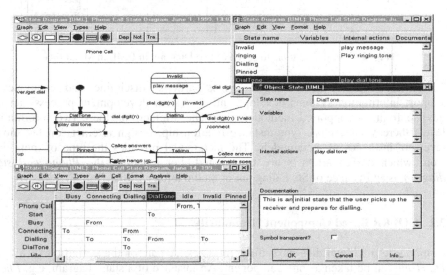

Fig. 1. Model level artefacts to specify a Phone Call State Diagram in MetaEdit+

The metamodel level information forms a semantic specification of system development methodologies by using GOPRR metamodelling language. These metamodels are specified in form-based tools and their graphic representations are specified in the Symbol Editor. As shown in Fig. 2, the Object *State* and its symbol definition, as well as other artefacts and semantics to construct the Graph *State Diagram*, such as binding definition, decomposition definition, and explosion definition, are specified in different windows. *State Diagram* is part of the specification of UML methodology. We can see from Graph Tool that *State Diagram* belongs to a project UML.

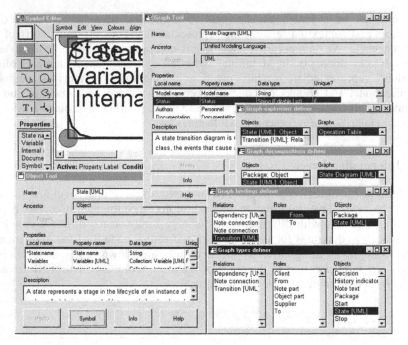

Fig. 2. Form-based tools to specify State Diagram in UML in MetaEdit+

It is known that a methodology provides particular disciplines and techniques to support information systems development. A system development process can not deviate from its supported methodologies. The artefacts on these two information levels thereby have close type-instance relationship: design artefacts on the model level are instances of metamodels. The metamodel provides the type of meta data from which design artefacts are instantiated. For example, the *Phone call state diagram* is an instance of State diagram of methodology UML.

3.2 GOPRR Based Component Granularity

Components in MetaEdit+ have different sizes. A part of the definition of a State *DialTone* can be taken as one component. An instance of a state diagram, e.g. *Phone call state diagram*, can be taken as a component as well. Accordingly, components can be grouped into different granularity levels.

Granularity specifies the size of the "manipulation" or "retrieval" units under consideration. It is derived from representational or operational semantics that is based on underlying modelling concepts and their representations. A fine-grained granularity level component includes a detailed and formal specification, such as a chunk of source code. A coarse-grained component includes more general information about a sub-system, or the whole of an application and hides away the detailed specification and implementation, such as a diagram. The coarse-grained component can be detailed into one or several fine-grained sub-components with a coherent syntax and semantics. Generally, the component granularity implies how effective CBD can be. As the components become coarser grained, the reuse opportunities decrease, while the productivity increases [5].

In MetaEdit+, the basic meta data types are applied to model various methodologies. These can be further instantiated to specify an information system development project either in part or as a whole. We thereby distinguish between a component unit, a graph, and a project.

- *Component* units are primary data types of MetaEdit+. They are non-property date types, like object, relationship, role, or their instances. For example, *State* in Fig. 2 is an object type component, and *DialTone* in Fig. 1 is an instance of *State* in the project *Phone call design*. Component units form the smallest atomic level component in MetaEdit+. Any further decomposition would not be worth the effort of storage, retrieval, and manipulation.
- A *graph* forms a collection of objects, relationships, roles and properties. It provides a representation of a technique on the metamodel level, and results in diagrams describing specific tasks within a specific application domain. For example, a specification of a state diagram is a graph level component.
- A *project* is a design product, or a plan to produce it. Like graph, it has a dual meaning. On the metamodel level, a project is a methodology including a set of techniques and rules that guide system development, such as UML methodology. On the model level, it is represented as a system development project consisting of design models and code.

4   Describing Components in MetaEdit+

To benefit from CBD, we should define a uniform interface to represent design artefacts in MetaEdit+ and find a reasonable way to display contexts among components, although the original design of MetaEdit+ does not include the component idea. Since 3C model [7] provides basic elements of components used in industry, we apply it to describe components. The model is represented in Fig. 3.

According to the 3C model, a component in MetaEdit+ can be described using three aspects: concept, content, and context.

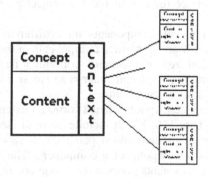

Fig. 3. Component model

The *concept* is realised by an interface specification. It provides abstract information about a component's functionality and associated semantics. Since a component interface defines its access point and indicates its further usage which are concerned by users, the way to specify the interface thereby has an important role in the component representation. *The content* forms an implementation of the concept. It is a substantial part of a component and outlines features and behaviours described in the interface. Following the specification on the concept and the content level, *the context* defines the contextual dependency among components and specifies the "domain of applicability". It is the most beneficial and complicated part of a component specification, since the context provides more detailed information from a wider perspective that helps users understand and reuse a component.

The three aspects represent a software component as an organic whole. Since components are not limited to source code, the representation of a concept, content, and context need to be adapted to the metaCASE environment and associated artefacts. In the following, we will discuss these three composition aspects in the context of MetaEdit+.

4.1 Concept

The component concept provides abstraction information of its functionality and associated semantics, like the pre- or post-conditions. In the same environment, components normally have the same concept schema. However, in MetaEdit+, since different granularity level components represent the information on different abstraction levels, it is difficult to outline a uniform interface. Generally, besides the general information such as the name, author, version and so on, a component unit has no explicit service to be represented in its interface. For example, *DialTone* is a state with information such as the name, the created date, or the version. It is difficult to describe its service although *DialTone* is a component in the *Phone call state diagram* that specialises a call session. On the other hand, the graph level components can express a concrete function and imply the semantics of its usability. Its interface thereby includes properties and explicit functionality specification, such as *Phone call state diagram* that specifies the state transition in a call process. The project level components represent the organisational information and application domain information. Their interface thereby includes a project purpose and its development strategies.

For each granularity level, components have different abstraction schemata to represent their interface. Moreover, since components in the same project have close dependencies, they can share some common conceptual descriptions in the interface. To effectively represent the component concept and to avoid the redundancy, we need a hierarchical concept description schema.

A hierarchical concept description schema forms an extension of a faceted schema, as proposed by Prieto-Díaz [16, 17]. It includes several faceted schemata. A faceted schema uses a number of predetermined perspectives called facets to represent the concept. A facet forms a viewpoint of a component. The viewpoint definition may include functions that components perform, their outputs, the application domain, and so on. A value for a facet is a facet value. The set of facet values for a component forms a fact descriptor, which represents the component concept. Generally, the facet-based schema works effectively in the repository when the collection of components is very large and growing continuously, and there are larger groups of similar components [18]. This is exactly the form that a MetaEdit+ repository has.

The hierarchical structure between the schemata derives from distinct component concept representations at different granularity levels. The same schema specifies the concept of the same granularity level components, but is distinguished from the schemata on other granularity level components. By using the hierarchical attribute description schema, the integration relationship between a fine-grained sub-component and its interrelated coarse-grained super-components becomes tractable. The hierarchical concept description schema is represented in Fig. 4. The faceted schema of components on both the graph level and the component unit level includes a facet "SuperComp" which is used to trace its coarse-grained super-components and thus to achieve the shared conceptual information.

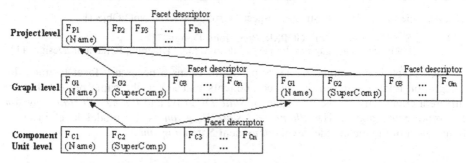

Fig. 4. The traceability in a hierarchical concept description schema

Such a hierarchical concept description schema not only represents the component concept, but also avoids information redundancy. The facet descriptor provides a possible schema to specify the component query criterion. In the following, we attempt to define facets that specify the concept of components on the project level, the graph level, and the component unit level.

Project Level. A project level component is coarse-grained. Like a framework, it helps organise a way to deliver a methodology specification, or a service in a specific application domain. Normally, the component forms an assembly of (the graph level) components with associated semantic definitions. The latter binds them together. The component interface includes a unique name and a general specification of its functionality and semantics. Facets of a project are defined as a set:

{Name, Application domain, Methodology, NoOfGraph}

    E.g.   {UML, method engineering, GOPRR, 9}
           {Phone call design, User interface, <UML, Methodology A>, _}

In the facet descriptor, the application domain illustrates the field(s) to which a project belongs, and implies its services; the methodology represent the disciplines and semantics applied in a project; and the NoOfGraphs indicates the scale and complexity of a project. Generally, the more graphs involved in one project, the more complicated the project will be. Following the facet descriptor, there are two examples: one describes an implementation of a UML methodology by using GOPRR metamodelling language, and the other describes a *phone call design* project, which uses both UML methodology and in-house methodology "A" for system design.

Graph Level. A graph is smaller in scope than a project, but a complete specification of services, such as the specification of static objects and their relationships, the input-output transformations, and the activities concerned with time and state changes. These specifications form three basic aspects of information modelling ontology: structure, function, and dynamic behaviour [19-21], and thus form an important facet to describe the abstraction dimensions. Meanwhile, since system development goes through several stages which may be supported by different techniques, the graph components must distinguish between different abstraction levels, e.g. analysis, design, and implementation. The abstraction level and techniques can be taken as facets as well. The facets of a graph level component can be defined as a set:

{Name, SuperComp, Type, Abstraction aspect, Abstraction level, NoOfObject}

> E.g.   {State Diagram, UML, GOPRR, Behaviour, Design, 7}
> {Phone call state diagram, Phone call design, State Diagram, Behaviour, Design, 11}

Each graph has a unique name. SuperComp forms a necessary facet to trace the integration relationship among the components that are in the same project, but on different granularity levels. Examples of *State Diagram* and *Phone call state diagram* are represented above. The *Phone call state diagram* is the model level instance component of the metamodel level component *Sate Diagram*.

Component Unit Level. A component unit is a definition of an object, a relationship, a role, or an instance of the meta data type. They are the primary data in the GOPRR specification. Their facets can thereby be defined using GOPRR properties, as show in the following set:

{Name, SuperComp, Type, Property, Behaviours}

> E.g.   {State(UML), State diagram, Object, <State name, Variables, Internal actions, Symbol transparent?>, _ }
> {DialTone, Phone call state diagram, State(UML), _, play dial tone}

As can be seen, *State(UML)* is an object type component having properties such as *State name*, *Variables*, and so on. *DialTone* is an instance of type component *State(UML)*, which is a composition of *Phone call state diagram*, and have behaviour of *playing dial tone*.

Summary. In the last three sub-sections, we have defined the facets. For a detailed explanation on the facets and their values, please refer to the appendix. We should notice that it is impossible to predefine all facets and values for components, since the number and type of components is extensible as more projects are specified in MetaEdit+. Therefore, the facets and their values are not exhaustive, and can be extended at any time. Meanwhile, we should notice that a common problem with the facet-based approach lies in mishandling synonyms and misinterpreting words that have some lexical ambiguity [22]. To solve the same problem in component interface representation in MetaEdit+, the facets can be specified using a limited vocabulary, and the specifications can be chosen from the controlled vocabulary list.

4.2 Content

The content is a substantial part of a component, e.g. a software component content includes an implementation of the functionality or service specified in its concept part. In MetaEdit+, the component content varies from one context to another. On the metamodel level, the component is a collection of GOPRR based concepts and syntax specified in a method. On the model level, a component can be represented in diagram, matrix, table, or source code.

4.3 Context

The context forms specific relationship types among components and the development environment in which the component is designed. It is more complicated than the concept and the content representation, but benefits largely component reuse. In [7], the context of a reusable software component is further defined as:

- Conceptual context – conceptual relationship between the component and other components,
- Operational context – the characteristics of the manipulated data, and
- Implementation context – implementation dependency relationship between the component and other components.

Each aspect of a component context in MetaEdit+ is a little different from a software component context. It can be represented as follows:

Conceptual Context. With the growing number of concepts and the increasing interdependency in an information system development methodology, models for system analysis and design become more and more complex. Conceptual dependencies between components exist. There are varied conceptual dependencies in different contexts, e.g. a definitional dependency in the component definition description, and the reuse dependency in the reuse context.

A *definitional dependency* from a concept CPx to a concept CPy is created if CPx is used in the definition of CPy [23]. In short, it represents integration relationships among components. MetaEdit+ uses Info Tools to represent such definitional dependencies between selected components or graphs (see Fig. 5). The left-side figure represents a definitional dependency of a metamodel level component *State*, which is a composition of the graph level component *State Diagram*. It includes property type component units, e.g. *State name*, and *internal action* for its definition. The right-side figure represents a definitional dependency of one instance of *State* on the model level, called *Dialling*. As shown in the list, *Dialling* is defined in Project *mcc* in three representations (a graph, a matrix, and a table) of the model *Phone call state diagram*.

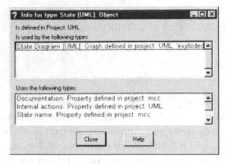
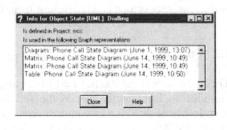

Fig. 5. Definitional dependency representation for the selected type/instance

Fig. 5 represents a definitional dependency of the graph level and the component unit level components. The same representation can be extended to project level components as well. It specifies a definitional relationship by relating a component's interdependent super- or sub-components. Such a relationship enhances users' understanding of a component on the whole, and thereby helps them select coherent sub-sets of a component and choose suitable ways (e.g. deep copy for components with significant changes or shallow copy for minor changes) for reuse.

When a component is built by reuse, *reuse dependency* specifies the reuse context between components. A reuse dependency relates a component with its original component(s) by specifying reuse associated information, such as the type of reuse, the way of reuse, modifications on the component concept and content, as well as the experiences collected in reuse processes. The contextual information effectively helps users study component features and outlines the possibility of reuse. For example, by inspecting the reuse dependency of an object component *State(UML)* in methodology UML, we learn that it is a shallow copy of the component *State* in OMT methodology. More properties such as *Internal actions* are added in *State(UML)*; and it is a horizontal reuse [24]. The reuse context implies that *State(UML)* refers to *State*, and any modifications on *State* will affect *State(UML)* as well.

Operational Context and Usage Context. An operational context defines characteristics of the manipulated data, such as types and operations available on the content of a component. It works on the code level component and organised to derive executable code. Since components in MetaEdit+ are mainly design artefacts, the operational context on source code limits the component information representation in MetaEdit+. We thereby define a usage context to specify the usage information among models.

Besides the concise functionality and the associated semantics abstracted in the component concept, a *usage context* records more detailed component usage information. It includes functional interdependencies among graph level components, suitable application domains and experiences accumulated, such as occurred problems and possible solutions. The usage context provides enriched information of using a component for user's reference.

Implementation Context. An implementation context describes how the component depends on other components for its implementation [9]. It provides a traceable relationship between components at the system analysis, design, and implementation stage, and helps users trace a component implementation in both forward and backward direction. We also call it a traceability feature.

In MetaEdit+, the metamodel level components are responsible for the methodology specification and construction. There is no implementation context between metamodel components. On the contrary, the model level components constitute the system development from the analysis stage to the implementation stage. Based on such a continuous process, we can define the component implementation context from its origins, through its development and specification, to its subsequent deployment and use, and through periods of on-going refinement and iteration in any of these phases. Such information provides a lifecycle of one component and helps users control the project as a whole, and finally improves the opportunity of reuse.

Summary. A component context is a complementary, but an important part that provides enriched contextual information including definitional dependency, reuse dependency, usage context and the implementation context. Without specifying the component context, the concept and reuse of components will remain ambiguous.

In MetaEdit+, Info Tools exist to represent definitional dependencies among components. Other contextual information may be represented in like manner. Moreover, we have hyperlink tools that represent the design rationale. The rationale provides basically understanding of why an artefact has been designed in a specific way, which may include information of e.g. requirements, assumptions, decisions, and alternative solutions [24]. Such hyperlink-based tools allow free hypertext linking of components. In the same way, we can define different types of contextual links to provide the access mechanism. By using the hyperlink functionality, component creators and users can easily to specify and navigate through the contextual information.

5   Conclusion

It is commonly accepted that components bring value to the information system development. In this paper, we have tried to extend component thinking to a metaCASE environment by defining components in MetaEdit+, a metaCASE environment. Accordingly, all types of design artefacts can be used as components after the necessary re-specialisation.

Component thinking brings several advantages to metaCASE tools. We identified three in particular. First, the definition of a hierarchical concept description makes components more comprehensible. The components have clearly defined interfaces based on predefined facet descriptors, which ease component search. Features of the project components can be shared across interfaces through a "SuperComp" facet, which avoids information loss and repetition. Second, the component context definition enhances component reuse. Different types of context represent conceptual relationships between the component and its environment, which makes it easy to capture the complementary status information in a project, its dependence on other components, and its reusability. Such descriptions enhance component reusability in a metaCASE environment. Finally, component-based thinking enhances the usefulness of a metaCASE environment. MetaEdit+ has diverse facilities to describe the contexts among components, and support reuse activities. However, none of them are organised and applied in a systematic manner. Introduction of components lets us rethink existing facilities, and improve them systematically.

Although recent wide-scale emergence of the component concept and the accompanying CBD has fostered increased attention to components in industry as well as in academia, CBD in metaCASE environments are new. Besides potential benefits, several problems abound when introducing components. Although we defined the interface for each component, the distinction between interface and content is sometimes ambiguous on the unit level components. The content of a component unit may be as simple as features represented in its interface. Meanwhile, although we have already planned to implement the component framework in MetaEdit+, systematic technique support forms a challenge. Components are not limited to chunks of source code and have versatile forms and characteristics. Therefore, we still need more studies on how to apply different types of components in the same environment.

References

1. Slootman, F.: A blueprint for component-base applications. Compuware Corporation URL: http://www.compuware.com/products/uniface/station/reading/ind_blue.htm (1999)
2. Softera: SoftModeler. Softera Ltd URL: http://www.softera.com/products.htm (1997)
3. GmbH: MicroTOOL - making IT better. microTOOL GmbH URL: http://www.microtool.de /e_index.htm (1999).
4. Garone, S. and A. Kehlenbeck: Rational Rose98: Another Major Step Toward Component-Based Development. Rational Software Corporation URL: http://www.rational.com/ products/rose/reviews/analysts/index.jtmpl (1998)
5. Short, K.: Component based development and object modeling. Sterling Software (1997)
6. Kelly, S., K. Lyytinen, and M. Rossi MetaEdit+: a Fully Configurable Multi-User and Multi-Tool CASE and CAME Environment. Proceedings of the 8th International Conference CAISE'96. Springer-Verlag (1996) 1 - 21
7. Tracz, W.: Implementation working group summary. Reuse in Practice Workshop Summary (1990) 10 - 19
8. Harmsen, A.F.: Situational Method Engineering. University of Twente (1997) p. 310.
9. Whittle, B.: Models and languages for component description and reuse. ACM SIGSOFT: 20(2) (1995) 76 - 87
10. Edwards, S.H.: Towards a model of reusable software sybsystems. Proc. of the 5th Annual Workshop on Software Reuse (1992)
11. Brinkkemper, S.: Method engineering: engineering of information systems development methods and tools. Information & Software Technology: 38(6) (1996) 275--280
12. Smolander, K.: GOPRR: a proposal for a meta level model. University of Jyväskylä: Finland (1993)
13. Lyytinen, K., et al.: MetaPHOR: Metamodelling, Principles, Hypertext, Objects and Repositories. Technical Report TR-7. University of Jyväskylä: Finland (1994)
14. Rossi, M.: Advanced Computer Support for Method Engineering: Implementation of CAME Environment in MetaEdit+. University of Jyväskylä: Finland (1998)

15. Tolvanen, J.-P.: Incremental Method Engineering with Modeling Tools: Theoretical principles and Empirical Evidence. University of Jyväskylä: Finland (1998)
16. Prieto-Díaz, R. and P. Freeman: Classifying Software for Reusability. IEEE Software: (1) (1987) 6 - 16.
17. Prieto-Díaz, R. and G. Arango (eds.): Domain Analysis and Software Systems Modeling. IEEE Computer Society Press: Los Alamitos, CA (1991)
18. Liao, H.-C. and F.-J. Wang: Software reuse based on a large object-oriented library. ACM SIGSOFT: Software Engineering Notes: 18(1) (1993) 74 - 80
19. Iivari, J.: Levels of abstraction as a conceptual framework for an information system. Information System Concepts: An In-depth Analysis, P.l. E. D. Falkenberg (ed.). Amsterdam North-Holland. (1989) 323 - 352
20. Olle, T.W., et al.: Information System Methodologies -- A Framework for Understanding. Addison-Wesley (1991)
21. Wand, Y.: Ontology as a Foundation for meta-modelling and Method Engineering. Information and Software Technology: 38(4) (1996) 281 - 287.
22. Isakowitz, T. and R.J. Kauffman: Supporting Search for Reusable Software Objects. IEEE Transactions on Software engineering: 22(6) (1996) 407 - 423
23. Castellani, X.: Overviews of Models Defined with Charts of Concepts. IFIP WG8.1 International Conference on Information System Concepts: An Integrated Discipline Emerging (1999)
24. Oinas-Kukkonen, H.: Debate Browser - a Design Rationale Tool for MetaEdit+ Environment. Working Paper Series B 40. Univ. of Oulu: Finland (1996)

Appendix: Component Facet Descriptors on the Project Level, the Graph Level, and the Component Unit Level

Project level. The facet descriptor of a project is defined as:

{Name, Application domain, Methodology, NoOfGraph}
Where Name: Project name
        Application Domain = {Method engineering, User interfaces, Communication and
                control system, Office management system, Real time
                system, Business application, ...}
        Methodology = {GOPRR, OMT, OOD, OOAD, UML, ...}
        NoOfGraph: the number of graph level components involved

Name provides a unique project name.
Application domain illustrates field(s) where a project operates and implies its services. If it is a metamodel level project to specialise and implement a methodology in MetaEdit+, its application domain belongs to method engineering. Otherwise, the model level project can be distinguished between the office management system, real time system, communication and control system, and so on. The value set of application domain can be augmented depending on projects involved.
Methodology represents the procedures, disciplines, rules and semantics that are applied in a project. A metamodel level project uses GOPRR metamodelling language as its methodology, while a model level project has more methodologies to choose. MetaEdit+ offers flexible method support, such as OMT (Rumbaugh et al.), OOD (Booch), OOAD (Coad/Yourdon), UML (Booch et al.), and the company's own methodologies that have been implemented in MetaEdit+.
NoOfGraphs presents the number of graph level components involved in a project. It indicates the scale and complexity of a project. Generally, the more graphs involved in one project, the more complicated the project will be.

Graph level. The facet descriptor of a graph is defined as:

{Name, SuperComp, Type, Abstraction aspect, Abstraction level, NoOfObject}
WhereName: Graph name
        SuperComp: Collection of names of the related project level component
        Type: The name of its metamodel (the name of the technique used)
        Abstraction aspect = {Structure, Function, Behaviour}
        Abstraction level = {Analysis, Design, Implementation, Maintenance}
        NoOfObject: the number of objects involved

Name provides a unique graph name. On the metamodel level, a graph is a specification of a method/technique; on the model level, a graph describes one aspect within a specific application domain, e.g. a state diagram, a class diagram, and so on.

SuperComp illustrates a collection of projects in which the graph is involved. It forms a necessary facet to trace the contextual relationship among the components that are in the same project, but on different granularity levels.

Type defines similar information for the methodology facet on the project level. It presents the method/technique a graph used. On the metamodel level, the type for a method definition is GOPRR, while on the model level, there a different types of graph depending on the methodology used. For example, if a project applies methodology UML as the development methodology, the types of its graph can be Class Diagram, Use Case Diagram, Statechart Diagram, Activity Diagram, Sequence Diagram, Collaboration Diagram, Component Diagram and Deployment Diagram.

Abstraction aspect represents different scopes of information system modelling. Generally, these scopes can be distinguished between the structure which specifies static objects and their relationships in information modelling, the function which indicates data input-output transformation, and the dynamic behaviour which describes aspects concerned with time and state changes [19-21].

Abstraction level specifies the development stage a graph belongs to. On the metamodel level, it indicates the development stage this method/technique supports; on the model level, it represents the development stages that a diagram represents.

NoOfObject presents the number of objects involved in a graph. In the same manner as NoOfGraph, it indicates the scale and complexity of a graph.

Component unit level. A component unit facet descriptor is defined as:

{Name, SuperComp, Type, Property, Behaviours}
WhereName: Component unit name
        SuperComp: collection of names of the related graph
        Type = {Object, Property, Relationship, Role, type name}
        Property: A collection of attributes of the component unit
        Behaviour: A collection of operations included in the component unit

Name provides a unique name of a component unit.

SuperComp illustrates a collection of graphs in which the component unit is involved. It forms a necessary facet to trace the contextual relationship among the components that are in the same project, but on different granularity levels.

Type represents a metamodel level component unit as an object, a property, a relationship, or a role. The name of the metamodel level component forms the type of its instances on the model level. For example, *State* is an object type component unit in a State diagram specification. *DialTone* is an instance of object *State*, and its type is state.

Property represents a collection of attributes that a component unit has.

Behaviour represents a collection of operations included in a component unit.

Tracing All Around

Gerald Ebner [1] and Hermann Kaindl [2]

[1] Significant Software, Zeltgasse 14/11, A-1080 Vienna, Austria
ebner@significantsoftware.com
[2] Siemens AG Österreich, Geusaugasse 17, A-1030 Vienna, Austria
hermann.kaindl@siemens.at

Abstract. Many information systems are reengineered and redeveloped in practice, since they are legacy software. Typically, no requirements and design specifications exist and, therefore, also no traceability information. While especially the long-term utility of such information is well known, an important question in reengineering is whether installing it can have immediate benefits in the course of the reengineering effort. Are there even special benefits of traceability for reengineering?

In this paper, we argue for completely tracing all around from code over specifications to code in the course of reverse engineering an existing software system and its subsequent redesign and redevelopment. Experience from a real-world project indicates that it can indeed be useful in practice to provide traceability all around also for the developers and in terms of short-term benefits already during the development. We found several cases where traceability provided benefits that appear to be specific for reengineering. As a consequence, we recommend special emphasis on traceability during reengineering legacy software.

1 Introduction

Given a legacy information system, a usual task in software development is to come up with a new system that can substitute the old one. Most legacy software in practice does not have its requirements or design documented. Consequently, no traceability information is available either.

First of all, the requirements and the design of the old information system are to be reverse-engineered [1], in order to understand what the new software should be all about. Is it also useful to spend the extra effort for installing traceability information from the old implementation to the reverse-engineered design and to the requirements? What could be gained from that already in the course of the redevelopment? Shall traceability information be installed also between the requirements and the new design and the new implementation?

The thesis of this paper is that it is indeed useful to trace "all around", i.e., to trace from existing code to design to requirements during reverse engineering, and from the modified requirements to the new design and the new code during development of

B. Wangler, L. Bergman (Eds.): CAiSE 2000, LNCS 1789, pp. 355-368, 2000
© Springer-Verlag Berlin Heidelberg 2000

the successor system. In effect, this means an integration of traceability during reverse engineering with (more standard) traceability during forward engineering. In addition, we argue for having design rationale integrated, where the old and the new design decisions can be traced as well.

In support of this thesis, we present a case study from a real-world project of reengineering a legacy information system in the context of stock trading. The experience from this case study suggests that in the course of developing new software based on the code of an existing predecessor system, it provides benefits for the developers even in the short term to establish traces "all around". We found several examples of such benefits from traceability that appear to be specific for reengineering.

This paper is organized in the following manner. First, we present both our high-level view and our realization of traceability in reengineering legacy software. Then we show several cases of how it was useful in the course of a real-world case study. Finally, we discuss our approach more generally and relate it to previous work on traceability.

2 Traceability in Reengineering Legacy Software

Since for legacy software little or no documentation exists on the requirements, design and design rationale, usually also no traceability information is available. This makes reengineering such software systems particularly hard. Because reengineering efforts under those conditions are common-place in the software industry, it is important to investigate how to improve them, e.g., by installing traceability in the course of reengineering.

Unfortunately, there are severe time and resource constraints in real-world projects, and establishing traceability takes time and may be costly (unless it can be automated). So, from a practitioner's perspective an important question is, whether and how traceability can immediately help in the course of such a reengineering effort. The trade-off between cost and *short-term* benefits of traceability seems not to be well understood yet. We argue in favor of the usefulness of traceability in the course of both reverse engineering the old software and developing the new software, since we found empirical evidence for short-term benefits.

2.1 High-Level View

Our high-level view of traceability in reengineering is illustrated in Fig. 1 in a UML (Unified Modeling Language) class diagram that is enhanced by arrows.[1] Tracing all around in reengineering means to trace from the implementation of the old system to design and to requirements during reverse engineering, and from the modified re-

---

[1] For the standardized specification of UML see http://www.omg.org.

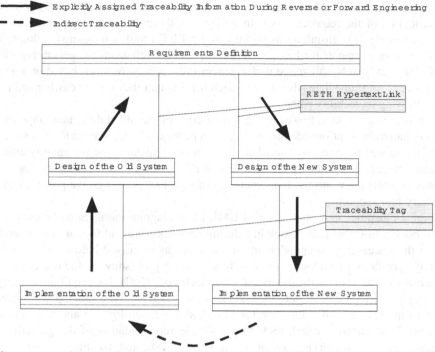

quirements to the new design and the implementation of the new system during development of the successor system.

Fig. 1. An illustration of tracing all around

Once traceability is explicitly established from the old to the new implementation via design and requirements specifications, it is indirectly available between those implementations, as illustrated by the arrow with the broken line. From a theoretical perspective, these relations are included in the transitive closure of explicitly represented traceability relations. In practice, this means that no explicit relation between the implementations needs to be represented, since it can be derived.

In our view, there is only one definition of the requirements necessary, if the old and the new software are supposed to satisfy more or less the same requirements. Reverse engineering projects in practice will typically have to deal with at least minor changes or additions to the requirements [1]. Still, there can be a single requirements specification in the course of the reengineering effort, defining both the old and the new requirements.

2.2 Our Realization

In the case study reported below, the tool RETH (Requirements Engineering Through Hypertext) was used (for the RETH method and its supporting tool see, e.g., [7]). It was not only used there for capturing the requirements, but also the software design (both old and new) and traces. Hyperlinks in the RETH tool served as a means for installing traceability information in our realization, linking various artifacts in the specification of the requirements with artifacts in the two software designs (also illustrated in Fig. 1). Installing hyperlinks in the RETH tool is inexpensive due to its semi-automatic support for link generation [9]. The mechanism for generating glossary links can also be utilized, e.g., for generating traceability links, based on textual references. An immediate advantage of such links is that they can be easily navigated for following traceability paths.

For technical reasons, however, the source code of the old and the new implementations had to be kept outside this tool. So, hyperlinks of that sort were infeasible to install, and we chose to use *traceability tags* in our realization of traceability among design artifacts and source code (see also Fig. 1). Installing traceability tags just means to insert a text string. For generating unique names of tags, we provided rudimentary tool support.

Fig. 2 illustrates in a more detailed UML class diagram the *metamodel* used, i.e., the model of how the models look like during reengineering and forward engineering. Since the traceability metamodels in the literature as discussed below are not sufficiently specific, we developed one ourselves. The top part (showing the object classes in white) is the previously published metamodel of RETH for requirements engineering [7, 8] (aggregated here by Requirements Definition). The other object classes (shown in grey) extend it for covering also design (shown lighter) and implementation artifacts (shown darker), including a simple representation of design rationale (Design Decision, which is part of Design). As indicated by Fig. 1 above, for reengineering those parts of the metamodel are instantiated twice: for the old and the new design and implementation.

Associations named Trace in the metamodel represent between which object classes traces are to be installed:

- between Requirements Definition and Design;[2]
- between several parts of Design and Implementation.

Especially for the latter, the granularity of traceability information is of practical importance. According to our experience, it should not be too coarse, e.g., to a source code module as a whole. But if it is too fine-grained, e.g., to each statement in the source code, then it becomes too expensive to install. As a balance, we chose to have a traceability tag assigned to each procedure of the source code as well as to each table definition, database trigger and stored procedure of the database script. This can be done with reasonable effort by the developers, and it can still be useful (see the experience from the case study reported below).

The representation of design rationale is also a practical compromise. Each Design Decision just describes the Design Chosen and the Alternatives Considered, since more elaborate structures like those in [12] would probably not have been maintained under the given time constraints of the given project. It was important, however, that the design decisions are traceable.

---

[2] In order not to clutter this diagram, we abstract here from the details of where exactly hyperlinks are installed.

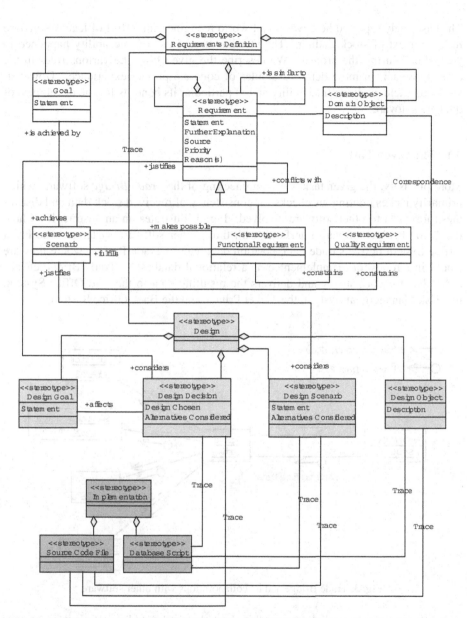

Fig. 2. The metamodel

3 A Case Study

The case study reported here was a real-world reengineering effort of legacy software in the context of stock trading. The installation and use of traceability happened in "real-time" during the project. We describe the given task, the various roles in the case study and, in more detail, examples of concrete project experience. However, we focus exclusively on traceability and in particular its benefits for the developers of the new software.

3.1 The Given Task

More precisely, the given task was reengineering of the *Trade Bridge* software, which primarily makes continuous checks for consistency of received stock data and distributes those data to other software involved. Fig. 3 illustrates on an abstract level how the Trade Bridge software interfaces with those other software systems. The Front Office System delivers trade data, position data, etc. to Trade Bridge, where they are stored in a repository (implemented as a relational database). Trade Bridge checks those data for consistency and delivers the resulting data to the Mid Office System, the Risk Management System, the Ticket Printer and the Back Office System.

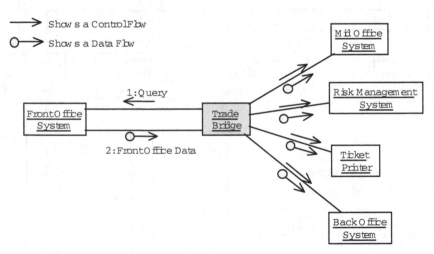

Fig. 3. Trade Bridge and its collaborations with other software

While for the other collaborations this short sketch should be sufficient in the context of this paper, we need to provide a few details of the collaboration between the Front Office System and Trade Bridge. As shown in the UML collaboration diagram in Fig. 3, the control flow happens from Trade Bridge to the Front Office System, while the data flow is the other way round. In fact, Trade Bridge is polling with queries for trade data, where both the queries and the data are transferred in ASCII text. The queries and the data transfer are asynchronous and, the response is on average in the order of minutes. It is also important to note, that transferring too much becomes a performance issue.

Fig. 4 illustrates the main part of the information model of the Trade Bridge software, i.e., an implementation-independent model of the data as viewed from outside the boundary of this software. The concrete data model is based on it, but optimized for its implementation in a relational database, that serves as a repository. The most important part of this model for the purpose of understanding the case study is the association between Trade Data and AdditionalTrade Data, where the former reference the latter. The Front Office System delivers those data asynchronously.

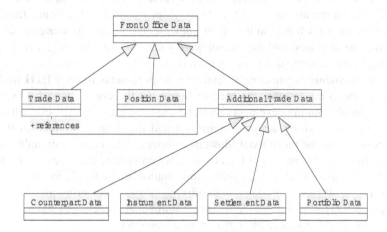

Fig. 4. Part of the Information Model of Trade Bridge

3.2 Various Roles in This Case Study

As usual in a software development project, several people participated in various roles. Since we describe our case study in terms of these roles, let us define them here:

- users:
  brokers and risk managers use the overall system, where Trade Bridge is an important part;
- developers of the old Trade Bridge software:
  they left the company and the project one month after its start;
- project leader for the reengineering effort:
  she was not involved in the development of the old Trade Bridge software;
- requirements engineer for the reengineering effort:
  the first author of this paper, who was also not involved originally;
- chief designer for the reengineering effort:
  same as the requirements engineer;

- developers of the new Trade Bridge software:
  including the first author of this paper; no single developer of the new software
  was involved in the development of the old Trade Bridge software.

3.3 Concrete Project Experience

In order to make the concrete project experience understandable, let us shortly sketch
first the major approach taken in the course of reengineering Trade Bridge. Immediately after the start of the project, the requirements engineer acquired information
about the requirements on the old software from its developers, rather than starting
with design recovery based on the given implementation (and its source code). However, after the developers of the old software were not available anymore, everything
(including requirements) had to be recovered.

The requirements engineer represented the requirements in the RETH tool and, in
his role as the chief designer, he tried to figure out the connection of those requirements acquired from the developers with the implementation of the old software. He
represented the resulting design information and the design rationale in the RETH
tool (according to the metamodel illustrated above). The design rationale was partly
acquired from the developers of the old software and partly hypothesized by the chief
designer. He also installed traceability information immediately in the form of hypertext links and traceability tags, both during reverse engineering and forward engineering. In the following, we demonstrate immediate benefits of having this traceability information available through concrete examples.

Traceability in the Context of Additional Requirements
First we present an example, where traceability helped in the context of additional
requirements. For the new Trade Bridge software, the users required additional functionality, which was captured, e.g., in the following requirement.

FunctionalRequirement *Synchronization of Referenced Counterpart Data:*

- Statement:
Trade Bridge shall transfer trade data to the Mid Office System only together with
the corresponding counterpart data as delivered from the Front Office System, i.e.,
Trade Bridge must synchronize those data delivered asynchronously from the
Front Office System.

As an immediate reaction to this additional requirement, the project leader thought
about a rather straight-forward solution, to request all those data in one query that
belong together. Instead of having to study this approach in detail, it was sufficient to
consider the design rationale that was already reverse-engineered before with the help
of the developers of the old software. In order to do so, however, it was necessary to
locate this information.

First of all, the existing functionality related to the additional one was located easily in the hierarchically ordered requirements on the old software:

Automatically Transferring Trades
  Transferring Referenced Additional Trade Data

Then, through the traceability links in the form of hyperlinks, it was easy and efficient to locate the related design information and design rationale:

Design Decision *Determine which Additional Trade Data to Request*:

• Design Chosen
- Triggers that fire after the insert of new trades into the Trade Bridge database fill special Get tables with the key information of the given data.
- After all trades have been stored in the database, the Trade Reader subsystem asks the Get tables which additional trade data it shall request from the Front Office System (the number of tries is configurable) and processes these transfers.
- The number of tries in the appropriate record of the corresponding Get table is incremented.
- The count of additional trade data items that will be requested from the Front Office System at once is configurable.
- When additional trade data is actually inserted in the Trade Bridge database, triggers delete the corresponding entries in the Get table.

• Alternatives Considered
1. Request trade data and all associated additional trade data at once from the Front Office System by using a join query:
(+) No inconsistent data of the Front Office System is ever stored in the Trade Bridge database.
(-) Inefficient: A given instrument or portfolio is referenced by many trades so that the same data will be requested from the Front Office System many times.
(-) Unreliable: During the day time (when the Front Office System suffers from heavy work load) it is likely that huge join queries cannot be processed by the Front Office System.
2. Request all trade data and all additional trade data that was altered or inserted in the Front Office System during a given time frame. A prerequisite is that first all „old" front office data must be stored in the Trade Bridge database.
(+) A consistent state of the Trade Bridge database can be easily maintained without any effort of maintaining Get tables.
(-) Too much data would be transferred to the Trade Bridge system because a lot of the instrument and portfolio data of the Front Office System is not of interest.
(-) The performance of the resulting queries that have to be executed by the Front Office System would be very poor (in the current installation of the Front Office System TOO poor) because the information of the update time of each record is not indexed in the database of the Front Office System.

In fact, the alternative 1 already stored here corresponds to the design solution in question. Due to its main disadvantage given here as well (poor performance), it was easily and quickly rejected, based on this rationale previously acquired from the developers of the old Trade Bridge software.

Still, another solution had to be found for the new software. Rethinking the chosen design of the old software as given here led to a change and enhancement of the design for the new software, fitting the additional requirement:

Design Decision *Synchronizing Counterpart Data:*

● Design Chosen
- Triggers that fire after the insert of new trades into the Trade Bridge database fill a special <u>Trade Sync Table</u> with the ID of the given trade and the counterpart synchronization flag set to „N".
- The needed counterpart data is retrieved from the Front Office System via the Get mechanism.
- When counterpart data is actually inserted into the Trade Bridge database, triggers set the counterpart synchronization flag of the Trade Sync Table of all trades referencing the given counterpart data to "Y".
- Trade Bridge applications that need synchronized counterpart data must query the Counterpart Sync Flag of the Trade Sync Table before using the data of a certain trade.

While in the RETH tool there are many similar links, we show here just an example. The underlined string "Trade Sync Table" is in the RETH tool the source of a hyperlink from such a description to a referenced design object:

Design Object *Trade Sync Table:*

● Description:
The Trade Sync Table contains synchronization flags for all kinds of additional trade data (i.e., a counterpart, an instrument, a portfolio and a settlement synchronization flag) while only the first of the four is actually used. Flags may contain "Y" (synchronized) or "N" (not synchronized). The primary key of the table is the trade ID field and it is also a foreign key on the trades table.

Finally, it was also easy to locate the related parts of the implementation with the help of the traceability tags.

Traceability for Improving Completeness
The next example highlights the utility of traceability for improving completeness in the sense, whether the new source code covers everything covered by the old code. The criterion for coverage of the old code was defined in such a way, that traceability tags must be installed at least according to the granularity described above. That is, there must be a traceability tag in each procedure of the source code as well as in each table definition, database trigger and stored procedure of the database script (containing some 20,000 lines of code).

After the reverse engineering effort, developers of the new software made a code inspection which revealed, e.g., that out of hundreds of database triggers, slightly more than a dozen did not yet have traceability tags attached. One of those (for filling a table of instrument data) was particularly important, since its absence in the new software could have lead to recommendations of the risk management based on wrong data.

In more detail, the requirement originally reverse-engineered from the incomplete view of the code was the following:

FunctionalRequirement *Transferring Referenced Additional Trade Data:*

* Statement:

Trade Bridge shall request Additional Trade Data from the Front Office System when Trade Data was captured from the Front Office System which references portfolios, instruments, etc. which are not yet stored in the Trade Bridge repository.

The over-generalized assumption was that for all kinds of additional trade data the data transfer from the Front Office System to Trade Bridge can be reduced, whenever data are already in the repository of Trade Bridge. For instrument data, however, the corresponding check was commented out in the code of the old software. This was found in the course of the focused code inspections of those database triggers that had not yet a traceability tag assigned. The rationale for this implementation was recovered from risk managers: during the period since the instrument data were stored in the Trade Bridge repository, they may have changed!

After the traceability tags have helped to find that out, the wrong requirement was corrected so that it takes this exception into account. So, also the design of the new software and its implementation take it into account and, a major error in the new Trade Bridge software was avoided.

Traceability for Diagnosing Errors

As a final example, let us illustrate the usefulness of traceability for diagnosing errors. While the granularity of installed traceability tags was useful in the above example, it turned out to be insufficient in another case.

After the implementation of the new software, tests revealed a performance problem. The Front Office System interfacing with it was unable to deliver the amount of data requested by the new Trade Bridge software. Why does that not happen with the old Trade Bridge software?

The traceability installed all around made it easy to answer that question quickly, since it allowed finding immediately the corresponding parts in the old and the new implementation. In order to avoid this performance problem, the old software requested only five data records each per request, which is well hidden in the code of the following old procedure:

```
function MakeInstrumentQuery(): string;
// determine which instrument data to request from the
// Front Office System and build the "where" part of
// the query string °41°
begin
   ...
   SqlExecute('select distinct ID into strID from
   Instrument_Get where tries < 10 order by tries');
   while SqlFetch() and (nLines < 5) do begin
```

```
    strQuery = strQuery + strID + ', ';
    nLines = nLines + 1;
  end;
  if (nLines > 0) then
    ...
end;
```

The critical condition is "and (nLines < 5)". This is clearly below the granularity of the tags, where "°41°" is the traceability tag for this procedure.

Still, finding the correct diagnosis for this problem making use of the traceability information was possible within one hour, while it might otherwise have taken days. So, while the granularity of traceability information was insufficient to guarantee sufficient completeness, this information was still very helpful to solve a problem caused by an incomplete re-implementation.

4 Discussion

So, there is a trade-off in the granularity of traceability information. It relates to the more general trade-off between cost of installing and maintaining traceability information vs. benefits from having it available. Common wisdom suggests that traceability should pay off at least in the long run, including maintenance.

Unfortunately, the success or failure of a software development or reengineering project is not usually determined in practice from whether it provides, e.g., traces in order to facilitate maintenance later. The budget often just covers the cost to deliver a running system and, cost arising later from missing traces are outside the scope. This looks very short-sighted and it is regrettable from a higher perspective. However, many software systems developed are never deployed for several reasons. So, the focus is on delivering a running system on time so that it will be deployed, rather than on preparing for an uncertain future where other people will have to take care of the cost during maintenance, if at all.

That is why we argue for a distinction between immediate and long-term benefits. While we cannot provide quantitative data from our case study that would show already that traceability paid off within the reengineering effort, we observed and described cases where it provided benefits already in its course. In fact, we found also additional cases where traceability was useful in the short term. These were particularly related to changes in the requirements and the software design. In all those cases, the developers got more or less immediate reward for their effort of installing traces. Due to this reward, the motivation of the developers was increased to do this „extra" work, and this may finally result also in long-term benefits during maintenance.

5 Related Work

Within the last years, there was increasing focus on pre-requirements traceability and extended requirements traceability, i.e., on where the requirements come from in the first place [5, 6]. While the RETH tool can also support this aspect of traceability through hypermedia, it was not a major focus in the course of this case study.

Traceability among requirements, primarily from higher level to lower level requirements, is considered already for a long time and much better supported by tools [4, 10]. The tracing tool TOOR presented in [10] shares with our approach that it treats requirements and relations among them as objects and, that it can be applied to any other artifacts produced in a software project as well.

In [11], a requirements traceability metamodel is presented that also covers design and implementation. It is more comprehensive than ours presented here, since it includes also stakeholders, etc. However, our metamodel as illustrated in Fig. 2 is more concrete in specifying specialized meta-classes and their relationships for the various artifacts used to represent requirements, design and implementation. For the case study presented in [11], installing all those traces according to their metamodel was reported to be very expensive. They did not report, however, on short-term benefits or specific utility of traceability in reengineering.

There is much literature available on design rationale (see, e.g., [11, 12]), that presents quite elaborate argumentation structures. While such structures could be easily represented using hypertext in the RETH tool, according to our experience it would be too expensive to maintain them under the conditions of this real-world project. So, we found a practical compromise with the inclusion of a simple representation for design rationale and its integration with the overall traceability supported.

Recently, a special section in CACM (edited by Jarke) included several articles dedicated to more advanced proposals for traceability. In [3], it is argued for project-specific trace definitions and guidance of stakeholders in trace capture and usage (including enforcement). Our tool support for installing traces through the automatic link-generation facility of the RETH tool is a small but important step towards making life easier for those who are supposed to install traces in practice. In [2], it is argued for improving requirements traceability beyond the systems facet to the group collaboration facet and to the organizational facet of information systems.

So, this sketch of important work shows many aspects and a rather comprehensive view of traceability. Still, we could not find much in the literature about the trade-off between cost and utility of traceability, and especially not about short-term benefits. In current practice, however, it is very important to show the developers certain rewards to be gained immediately from installing traces. Also, we found no mention of specific utility of tracing during reverse engineering or even of tracing all around.

6 Conclusion

We observed special benefits of traceability for reengineering that we could not find in the literature. Partly, those benefits require tracing all around. The major lesson learned from several examples in our real-world case study is, however, that such traceability information can already help the developers (of the new system) in the course of reengineering legacy software. Such short-term benefits for the developers from applying this form of traceability can motivate them to provide traces that may even result in further long-term benefits later.

Acknowledgments

Mario Hailing and Vahan Harput provided useful comments to an earlier draft of this paper. Finally, we acknowledge the cooperation by the project members in the course of this reengineering effort.

References

1. E.J. Chikofsky and J.H. Cross. Reverse engineering and design recovery: A taxonomy. *IEEE Software*, pages 13–17, January 1990.
2. G. De Michelis, E. Dubois, M. Jarke, F. Matthes, J. Mylopoulos, J.W. Schmidt, C. Woo, and E. Yu. A three-faceted view of information systems. *Communications of the ACM*, 41(12):64–70, December 1998.
3. R. Dömges and K. Pohl. Adapting traceability environments to project-specific needs. *Communications of the ACM*, 41(12):54–62, December 1998.
4. R.F. Flynn and M. Dorfman. The automated requirements traceability system (ARTS): An experience of eight years. In R.H. Thayer and M. Dorfman, editors, *System and Software Requirements Engineering*, pages 423–438. IEEE Computer Society Press, 1990.
5. O. Gotel and A. Finkelstein. Extended requirements traceability: Results of an industrial case study. In *Proceedings of the Third IEEE International Symposium on Requirements Engineering (RE'97)*, pages 169–178, Annapolis, MD, January 1997.
6. P. Haumer, P. Heymans, M. Jarke, and K. Pohl. Bridging the gap between past and future in RE: A scenario-based approach. In *Proceedings of the Fourth IEEE International Symposium on Requirements Engineering (RE'99)*, pages 66–73, Limerick, Ireland, June 1999.
7. H. Kaindl. A practical approach to combining requirements definition and object-oriented analysis. *Annals of Software Engineering*, 3:319–343, 1997.
8. H. Kaindl. Combining goals and functional requirements in a scenario-based design process. In *People and Computers XIII, Proc. Human Computer Interaction '98 (HCI '98)*, pages 101–121, Sheffield, UK, September 1998. Springer.
9. H. Kaindl, S. Kramer, and P.S.N. Diallo. Semiautomatic generation of glossary links: A practical solution. In *Proceedings of the Tenth ACM Conference on Hypertext and Hypermedia (Hypertext '99)*, pages 3–12, Darmstadt, Germany, February 1999.
10. F.A.C. Pinheiro and J.A. Goguen. An object-oriented tool for tracing requirements. *IEEE Software*, pages 52–64, March 1996.
11. B. Ramesh, C. Stubbs, T. Powers, and M. Edwards. Requirements traceability: Theory and practice. *Annals of Software Engineering*, 3:397–415, 1997.
12. B. Ramesh and V. Dhar. Supporting systems development by capturing deliberations during requirements engineering. *IEEE Transactions on Software Engineering*, 18(6):498–510, 1992.

A Framework for the Evolution of Temporal Conceptual Schemas of Information Systems

Juan-Ramón López[1,2] and Antoni Olivé[1]

[1]Universitat Politècnica de Catalunya,
Departament de Llenguatges i Sistemes Informàtics.
Barcelona - Catalonia.
`{jrlopez|olive}@lsi.upc.es`
[2]Universidade da Coruña,
Departamento de Computación

Abstract. This paper focuses on the problem of information systems evolution. Ideally, changes in the requirements of information systems should be defined and managed at the conceptual schema level, with an automatic propagation down to the logical database schema(s) and application programs. We propose here a framework for the evolution of temporal conceptual schemas of information systems. Our framework uses a reflective architecture with two levels: meta schema and schema, and two loosely coupled information processors, one for each level. We define a temporal minimal meta schema, and we show, using some examples, how to extend this minimal meta schema to support any usual conceptual modeling construct. We also show how the framework can be used to specify schema changes.

1 Introduction

This paper deals with the evolution of temporal conceptual schemas of information systems. We propose a general framework which allows defining schema evolutions and their effects. We illustrate the framework with a limited albeit representative number of widely used conceptual modeling constructs, define some evolution operations at the meta schema level, and analyze their impact on the conceptual schema and the information base.

In order to characterize our contribution, we find it useful to start with the abstract database evolution framework presented in [11], that we rephrase as follows: Assume that an information system satisfies requirements R0. The information system comprises a conceptual schema CS0, one (or more) database(s) with logical schema(s) LS0 and extension(s) E0, and several application programs P0. When requirements change to R1, the information system must evolve. In the general case, the evolution implies changes leading to a new conceptual schema CS1, new logical schema(s) LS1 and application programs P1. Moreover, the extension(s) E0 may not be valid, and need to be converted to E1.

Ideally, the evolution of information systems should follow the strategy of "forward information system maintenance" [11]: changes should be applied to the conceptual schema, and from here they should propagate automatically down to the

B. Wangler, L. Bergman (Eds.): CAiSE 2000, LNCS 1789, pp. 369-386, 2000
© Springer-Verlag Berlin Heidelberg 2000

logical schema(s) and application programs. If needed, the extension(s) should be also converted automatically.

In the context of the above framework, the aspect that has received more research effort is (logical) database schema evolution, including the propagation of changes to the extensional database. Data models that have been studied extensively include the relational and object-oriented models, both non-temporal and temporal. In several cases, research results have been incorporated into commercial or prototype database management systems (e.g., Orion [4], O_2 [27], F2 [1]). We refer to [19, 8, 24, 15] for extensive bibliographies and surveys.

We observe that the ideal strategy described above implies that the conceptual schema is the only description to be defined, and the basis for the specification of the evolution. This observation has led us to our framework, which we see as one step more towards that ideal strategy. Our framework is based on the commonly accepted approach that, from a conceptual point of view, an information system consists of a conceptual schema, an information base and an information processor. The conceptual schema defines all general domain knowledge relevant to the system, which includes entity and relationship types, all kind of integrity constraints and derivation rules, and the effects of external events. The information processor receives messages from the environment, reporting the occurrence of external events. In response to such events, the information processor changes the information base and/or issues messages making known the contents of the information base, in the way specified in the conceptual schema [12].

In this view, evolution can be accommodated elegantly by using the classical reflective architecture [18, 22], as shown in Figure 1. A distinction is made between an information system and a meta information system. The first consists of a conceptual schema, an information base (IB) and an information processor (IP). The second consists of a conceptual meta schema, a meta information base (MIB) and a meta information processor (MIP). In essence, the MIB of the meta information system describes the conceptual schema of the information system [12].

In our framework, possible changes in the conceptual schema are specified as meta external events in the conceptual meta schema. Occurrences of these events are reported to the MIP, which changes the MIB and indirectly the conceptual schema. In some cases, changes in the IB may be necessary too. These latter changes are not performed directly by the MIP. Instead of this, the MIP generates occurrences of external events, which are notified to the IP to perform the desired changes. In this way, the two processors are loosely coupled.

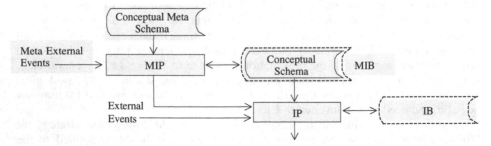

Fig. 1. Framework for the evolution of information systems

There is a lot of previous research and development work relevant to this framework. We can only give in the following a few comments relating a representative part of this work with our paper.

[14] describes SEA, Schema Evolution Assistant, a tool which allows the evolution of schemas in Chimera. Chimera is a rich data model that includes integrity constraints, derivation rules and triggers. SEA uses a reflective architecture [16], as we do. Initially, Chimera was non-temporal, but a temporal extension was published later [5]. SEA was developed for the non-temporal version.

[13] describes ConceptBase, a system based on the O-Telos language, a variant of Telos. O-Telos deals uniformly with objects at different levels of abstraction. O-Telos has a kernel, from which all other constructs can be bootstrapped. We have followed the same idea with our minimal meta schema. However, our framework allows that the information and the meta information processors be different. On the other hand, we deal with the temporal dimension and focus more on schema evolution.

Finally, we mention the work done in the context of the TIGUKAT temporal ODBMS [22, 23, 10]. The TIGUKAT schema objects include types, classes, behaviours, functions and collections. The model allows the representation of the temporal histories of real-world objects. We also adopt the temporal view, but conceptual schemas of information systems need to include other elements like integrity constraints, derivation rules, external events, etc. Evolution is performed by operations (add, drop and modify) on schema objects. These are similar to our meta external events, but we need many more to allow the evolution of other schema objects.

The remainder of this paper is organized as follows. In Section 2, we characterize temporal conceptual schemas and evolution at the temporal IB level. In Section 3 we do the same for the conceptual meta schema and MIB, and define the correspondence between the MIB and the conceptual schema. We also show how usual conceptual modeling constructs can be defined at the conceptual meta schema level. In Section 4 we then define the meta external events that perform schema evolution. Finally, Section 5 gives the conclusions and points out future work.

2 Temporal Conceptual Schema and Information Base

In this section, we briefly characterize the elements of a temporal conceptual schema (or, for short, schema). We wish our work to be of general applicability and language-independent. For this reason, we focus here on a set of minimal core elements of schemas. Any schema can be expressed in terms of these elements. They are entity types, relationship types, derivation rules, integrity constraints and external event types [3]. We represent them (and their instances in the IB) using the language of the first order logic (FOL), with some common extensions.

2.1 Temporal Conceptual Schema

The entities of a domain are instance of *entity types* at particular time points [7]. An entity may be instance of several entity types at the same time (multiple classification). On the other hand, an entity may change the entity types of which it is instance (dynamic classification).

In a temporal conceptual schema, entity types may be represented by binary predicates, whose first term is a symbol that denotes an entity in the domain, and the second a time point. In the IB, we represent by $E(e,t)$ the fact that entity e is instance of entity type E at time t.

We assume that time is discrete, linear and totally ordered. Time points are expressed in a common base time unit (or *chronon* [26]), such as second or day. We also assume that a schema includes a special unary predicate *Time*, whose instances are the time points (in the chosen unit) of the information system lifespan. In general, the set of entity types defined in a schema is time-varying. We denote by E_t the set of entity types defined in a schema at time t. An entity type may cease to exist in a schema and appear again later. We adopt here the usual *typing rule*, which in our case requires that, for all entity types E:

$$\forall e,t \ (E(e,t) \to E \in E_t) \ . \tag{1}$$

That is, we do not allow the IB to represent that e is instance of E at t, if E is not defined in the schema at t. For convenience, we assume that if an entity type E ceases to exist at time t, then all its instances at t-1 (if any) also cease to exist at t.

Entity types may be *lexical* or *non-lexical*. For the sake of uniformity we represent lexical entity types also by binary predicates, even if lexical entities are usually instance of their types during the whole lifespan of an information system.

The relationships of a domain are instance of *relationship types* at particular time points. In a temporal schema, a relationship type with n *participants* may be represented by a predicate of degree $n+1$, where the first n terms are symbols that denote the participant entities, and the $n+1$ term is a time point. In the IB, we represent by $R(e_1,...,e_n,t)$ the fact that entities $e_1,...,e_n$ participate in a relationship instance of relationship type R at time t. In general, the set of relationship types defined in a schema is time-varying, and we denote by R_t the set of relationship types defined in a schema at time t. The above typing rule also applies to relationship types.

Entity and relationship types may be *base* or *derived*. Instances of base types must be stated explicitly, as will be seen later, while those of derived types are defined by *derivation rules*. In a temporal schema, derivation rules must be considered also as time-varying. We denote by DR_t the set of derivation rules defined in a schema at time t. Our framework allows derivation rules to be written in the language understood by the IP. In the examples we use the FOL language.

Integrity constraints are conditions that the IB must satisfy. We consider them also as time-varying. We denote by IC_t the set of integrity constraints defined in a schema at time t. It is assumed that at any time t the IB satisfies all integrity constraints defined in IC_t.

Our framework could be extended by distinguishing, in the schema, several kinds of integrity constraints (and of derivation rules). However, in this paper we prefer not to make this distinction here, but we do it in the conceptual meta schema. The MIP will "generate" constraints in the language required by the IP.

The IB changes due to the occurrence of *external events*. As we did for entity types, we represent external event types in a schema by binary predicates, but now the first term denotes an event occurrence. In the IB we represent by $Ev(ev,t)$ the occurrence of event ev of type Ev at time t.

In general, the set of external event types defined in a schema is time-varying, and we denote by EE_t the set of external event types defined in a schema at time t. The above typing rule also applies to these types. External event types may be base or derived.

For each external event type, the schema includes the definition of its preconditions and effect rules (transactions). The *preconditions* are conditions that must be satisfied when an external event occurs. The *effect rules* define the changes produced in the IB by the event. Both preconditions and effect rules are formulas expressed in the language understood by the IP.

We find convenient to allow the possibility of defining, for each integrity constraint, a set of *compensating* effect rules. The IP adds these rules to the effect rules of an event type when an occurrence of this event type leads to a violation of the integrity constraint. This, however, does not mean that violations can be prevented in all cases by compensating rules.

2.2 Information Base Evolution

The effect rules of an external event type define the changes in the IB when an instance of that type occurs. We model possible changes in the IB as structural events, and we then say that an external event induces structural events, which, in turn, change the IB.

The *structural event types* are determined by the entity and relationship types defined in a conceptual schema and, thus, they are not defined by the designer. We represent structural event types by predicates, as follows:

- There is an insertion and a deletion event type for each non-lexical entity type E. We represent them by the binary predicates Ins_E and Del_E, respectively, where the first term is a symbol denoting an entity and the second a time point.
- There is an insertion and a deletion event type for each relationship type R. We represent them by the n+1-ary predicates Ins_R and Del_R, respectively, where the first n terms are symbols denoting entities and the n+1 term is a time point.

A structural event type is base (derived) if the corresponding entity or relationship type is base (derived). External events induce directly only base structural events, while derived ones are induced indirectly by the derivation rules. For example, if we have in a schema the derivation rule: $Young(p,t) \leftarrow Person(p,t) \land Age(p,a,t) \land a \leq 18$, then an increase of a person's age may induce a Del_Young event.

3 Temporal Conceptual Meta Schema and Information Base

All conceptual models have a conceptual meta schema (or, for short, meta schema). A meta schema is like an ordinary schema, except that its domain is a schema. The elements of a schema are seen as entities, which are instance of appropriate entity types defined in the meta schema. Similarly, relationships between the elements of a schema are seen as instances of relationship types of the meta schema. The MIB has a representation of the schema.

In this section, we first describe the minimal meta schema necessary to represent the core elements defined in the previous section. We then establish the correspondence rules between the MIB and the schema. In the last part of this section we describe how the meta schema can be enriched with other constructs.

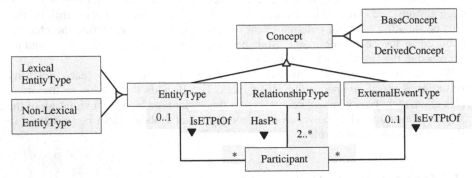

Fig. 2. Minimal conceptual meta schema (Part 1 of 2)

3.1 Minimal Meta Schema

Figures 2 and 3 illustrate, using the UML language [25], the minimal meta schema.[1] We now briefly define it in terms of the core elements explained in the previous section. For clarity, we call sometimes these elements meta elements, in order to distinguish them from schema elements.

- *Entity types.* The entity types are shown as rectangles in Figures 2 and 3. All entity types are non-lexical, except *Formula*, which is lexical. An instance of *Formula* is a formula in the language understood by the IP. For generality, we use here the FOL language. All entity types are base, except *Concept*, *EntityType* and *Rule*, which are derived. As we did in Section 2.1, in the MIB we represent by $E(e,t)$ the fact that e is instance of meta entity type E at time t. For example, *EntityType(Employee,T)*.

- *Relationship types.* The meta relationship types are shown as lines linking rectangles in Figures 2 and 3. All of them are binary and base. Note that a schema relationship type R may be of degree 2 or higher. R would be an instance of *RelationshipType* at T (Figure 2) and, if it has degree n, there would be n instances $HasPt(R,P_p,T)$ in the MIB.

- *Structural events.* Meta structural events are defined as we did in Section 2.2. For clarity, we will prefix them with $M\_$. For example, $M\_Del\_EntityType$, whose intended effect is that an entity type ceases to be instance of *EntityType* in the MIB.

- *Derivation rules.* There are three meta derivation rules, which define *Concept*, *EntityType* and *Rule*. We show here the one corresponding to *Concept*:

---

[1] Note that, in the figures, we use partitions and cardinality constraints. However, these constructs will be translated into core elements in what follows.

Concept(c,t)↔EntityType(c,t)∨RelationshipType(c,t)∨ExternalEventType(c,t)   **MDR1**

- *Integrity constraints.* A schema is a complex structure subject to a large number of integrity constraints. This implies that the meta schema must include many meta integrity constraints, usually called *invariants* in the schema evolution field [4]. We give bellow an example, that states that only existing rules and formulas can be related in *IsExpressedBy*. Other examples can be found in [17].

$$\text{IsExpressedBy}(r,f,t) \rightarrow \text{Rule}(r,t) \land \text{Formula}(f,t) \qquad \textbf{MIC1}$$

We define a compensating rule for MIC1, which states that when an rule is deleted so is the relationship, instance of *IsExpressedBy*, in which it participates:

$$\text{M\_Del\_IsExpressedBy}(r,f,t) \leftarrow \text{M\_Del\_Rule}(r,t) \land \text{IsExpressedBy}(r,f,t-1)$$

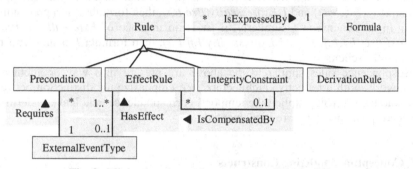

Fig. 3. Minimal conceptual meta schema (Part 2 of 2)

- *External event types.* The minimal meta schema includes meta event types that allow the insertion and deletion of the entity and relationship types shown in Figures 2 and 3. For example, there could be an external event type *NewIC*. Occurrences of *NewIC* would create an instance of *IntegrityConstraint* (Figure 3) and the associated instance of *IsExpressedBy*. We will discuss them in the next section.

3.2 Correspondence Rules

We can now define the correspondence rules in our framework between the MIB and the schema:

- *CR1.* There is a one-to-one correspondence between the instances at time t of *EntityType* in the MIB and the elements of E_t in the schema. If an instance of *EntityType* is also instance of *BaseConcept* (*DerivedConcept*) then it is base (resp., derived). If an instance of *EntityType* is also instance of *LexicalEntityType* (*Non-LexicalEntityType*) then it is lexical (resp., non-lexical).
- *CR2.* There is a one-to-one correspondence between the instances at time t of *RelationshipType* in the MIB and the elements of R_t in the schema. If an instance of *RelationshipType* is also instance of *BaseConcept* (*DerivedConcept*) then it is base

(resp., derived). If an instance R of *RelationshipType* is related (through *HasPt*) to n instances of *Participant*, then the degree of R in the schema is $n+1$.

- **CR3.** There is a one-to-one correspondence between the set of *Formula* in which *IsExpressedBy* the instances of *DerivationRule* at time t in the MIB and the elements of DR_t in the schema.
- **CR4.** There is a one-to-one correspondence between the set of *Formula* in which *IsExpressedBy* the instances of *IntegrityConstraint* at time t in the MIB and the elements of IC_t in the schema. If Ic is an instance of *IntegrityConstraint*, and *IsCompensatedBy(Ic,Eff,t)* and *IsExpressedBy(Eff,F,t)* then formula F is a compensating effect rule of Ic in the schema at t.
- **CR5.** There is a one-to-one correspondence between the instances at time t of *ExternalEventType* in the MIB and the elements of EE_t in the schema. If an instance of *ExternalEventType* is also instance of *BaseConcept* (*DerivedConcept*) then it is base (resp., derived). If Ev is an instance of *ExternalEventType*, and *Requires(Ev,Pre,t)* and *IsExpressedBy(Pre,F,t)*, then formula F is a precondition of Ev in the schema at t. Similarly, if Ev is an instance of *ExternalEventType*, and *HasEffect(Ev,Eff,t)* and *IsExpressedBy(Eff,F,t)*, then formula F is an effect rule of Ev in the schema at t.

Correspondence rules similar to the above are present in a way or another in all frameworks with a reflective architecture. We emphasize the distinction between the MIP and the IP, make explicit the temporal correspondence, and leave undefined how the correspondence rules are implemented.

3.3 Conceptual Modeling Constructs

The above minimal meta schema is hardly satisfactory because it does not take into account the important number of special constructs that have been developed in the conceptual modeling field. These constructs are useful because they ease the definition of the schema and, at the same time, allow the development of efficient implementations. In our framework, the modeling constructs are particular types in the meta schema. However, there is not a direct correspondence between the "instantiation" of these constructs and the schema, but an indirect one. The meta schema includes a set of derivation rules that "translate" the constructs into elements of the minimal meta schema. The above correspondence rules need not to be changed.

In what follows we explain how to extend the minimal meta schema to incorporate the constructs in our framework. Additional details can be found in [17]. The general idea is to partition *IntegrityConstraint* and *DerivationRule* (Figure 3) into two subtypes: a base and a derived one (Figure 4). The base subtypes will correspond to integrity constraints or derivation rules defined explicitly by the designer, while the derived ones are defined by derivation rules of the meta schema.

3.3.1 Cardinality Constraints. Figure 4 shows the conceptualization in the meta schema of the common cardinality constraints. In the MIB, these cardinalities are expressed as instances of relationship types *HasMinCard* and *HasMaxCard*. We will focus only on the minimum cardinality; the maximum one is similar. Each minimum cardinality constraint is an instance of *ICMinCard*, which is a specialization of

DerivedIntegrityContraint. A participant may not have minimum cardinality (i.e., zero) and then there is not a corresponding instance of *ICMinCard*. Entity type *ICMinCard* is derived. The corresponding derivation rule is:

$$\text{ICMinCard(s,t)} \leftarrow \text{HasMinCard(p,int,t)} \wedge s = \text{sym(ICMinCard,p)} \qquad \textbf{MDR2}$$

where *sym(ICMinCard,p)* is a function that denotes a time-independent symbol (*s*), distinct from any other used in the MIB. The MIP could, for example, create this symbol when symbol *p* is created.

Now, we need to define the *Formula* in which the constraint *IsExpressedBy*. We refine the base relationship type between *Rule* and *Formula* to a derived one between *ICMinCard* and *Formula*. The derivation rule is:

$$\text{IsExpressedBy(s,f,t)} \leftarrow \text{ICMinCard(s,t)} \wedge \text{ICMinFormula(s,f,t)} \qquad \textbf{MDR3}$$

In MDR3, *ICMinFormula(s,f,t)* is a predicate that gives in *f* the string representation of the corresponding formula. For a binary relationship type *R*, the general form of *f* for one of its participants (E_I) is "$E_1\ (e_1,t) \rightarrow min \leq |\{e_2 \mid R(e_1,e_2,t)\}|$", where E_I would be given by *IsETPtOf* (or *IsEvTPtOf*), *min* by *HasMinCard* and *R* by *HasPt*. We omit here the details of predicate *ICMinFormula* because they are a lengthy sequence of trivial string manipulation operations.

Note that, by MDR2 and MDR3, the MIB will have a relationship *IsExpressedBy(s,f,t)* during the period in which *p* exists as participant and has a non-zero minimum cardinality. By CR4, during this period $f \in IC_t$, that is, *f* will be a schema integrity constraint, to be enforced by the IP.

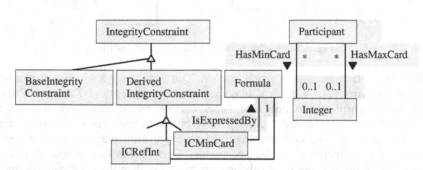

Fig. 4. Meta schema conceptualization of cardinality and referential integrity constraints

3.3.2 Referential Integrity Constraints. A referential integrity constraint must be defined for each participant of a base relationship type. We assume that for derived relationship types the corresponding derivation rule is correct and, therefore, also are the types of the participants in its instances. To represent these constraints, we define in the meta schema (see Figure 4) a derived subtype of *DerivedIntegrityConstraint*, called *ICRefInt*, with the following derivation rule:

$$\text{ICRefInt(s,t)} \leftarrow \text{HasPt(r,p,t)} \wedge \text{BaseConcept(r,t)} \wedge s=\text{sym(ICRefInt,p)} \qquad \textbf{MDR4}$$

where *sym* is again a function that gives us a time-independent symbol, that in this case denotes the referential integrity constraint related to a participant. We refine again *IsExpressedBy* to a derived type, in this case between *ICRefInt* and *Formula*:

$$\text{IsExpressedBy(s,f,t)} \leftarrow \text{ICRefInt(s,t)} \wedge \text{ICRefIntFormula(s,f,t)} \qquad \textbf{MDR5}$$

where *ICRefIntFormula* is a predicate that gives in *f* the string representation of the corresponding formula.[2] For a binary relationship type *R*, the general form of *f* for one of its participants (E_1) is „$R(e_1, e_2, t) \rightarrow E_1(e_1, t)$„, where *R* would be given by *HasPt*, and E_1 by *IsETPtOf* (or *IsEvTPtOf*).

3.3.3 Partitions.
Partitions are an important modeling construct in many conceptual models [20]. All generalizations and specializations can be transformed into partitions. We are going to see that partitions are represented in the core elements of a schema by zero or one derivation rule, and zero or more integrity constraints. Figure 5 shows the conceptualization of partitions in the meta schema.

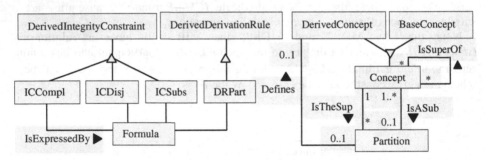

Fig. 5. Meta schema conceptualization of partitions

We allow the partition of any *Concept*. Thus, we deal also with partitions of relationship types [2]. A concept may be the superconcept (*IsTheSup*) of several partitions. A partition has only one superconcept, but it may have one or more subconcepts. We assume that a concept may be the subconcept (*IsASub*) of zero or only one partition. The concepts involved in a partition may be base or derived. Almost all combinations can be acceptable. One of the exceptions is when all concepts are base, because if all subconcepts are base, then the superconcept must be derived. For example, if P_1 is a partition with super *Person* and subs *Man* and *Woman*, and these are base, then *Person* must be derived, since it is the "union" of *Man* and *Woman*. In the meta schema, there is a relationship type (*Defines*) between *Partition* and *DerivedConcept*. An instance *Defines(P,C,T)*, where *C* must be a derived concept and the super of *P*, indicates that, at time *T*, concept *C* is derived as the union of the subconcepts of *P*. In the above example, we could have *Defines(P₁,Person,T)*. Entity type *Person* may be the super of another partition P_2 (for example, into the base entity

---

[2] This formula depends on the relationship type of the participant being *synchronous* or *asynchronous* (see [21] for more details), but for the sake of simplicity in this paper we are considering only synchronous relationship types.

types *Married* and *Unmarried*) but it is defined only by one of them, because the other definition would be redundant.

Partitions require several meta integrity constraints. See [17] for some of them.

In the schema, we define a *disjointness integrity constraint* for each concept that is a sub of a partition.[3] In the above example, a *Man* cannot be a *Woman*, and the inverse. These integrity constraints are modeled as instances of *ICDisj*. Entity type *ICDisj* is derived, with derivation rule:

$$\text{ICDisj}(s,t) \leftarrow \text{IsASub}(c,p,t) \wedge s = \text{sym}(\text{ICDisj},c) \wedge \text{IsASub}(c',p,t) \wedge c \neq c' \qquad \textbf{MDR6}$$

The *Formula* in which *ICDisj IsExpressedBy* is given by the derivation rule:

$$\text{IsExpressedBy}(s,f,t) \leftarrow \text{ICDisj}(s,t) \wedge \text{ICDisjFormula}(s,f,t) \qquad \textbf{MDR7}$$

where predicate *ICDisjFormula* gives in f the string representation of the formula. As an example, the general form of f for a base relationship type R_1 in a partition of a binary relationship type R into $R_1,..., R_n$ is "$R_1(e1,e2,t) \rightarrow \neg (R_2(e1,e2,t) \vee ... \vee R_n(e1,e2,t))$".

In the schema, we define also a *subset integrity constraint* for each subconcept, except when the partition defines a derived superconcept. For example, if *Person* is a derived concept, defined by the partition into *Man* and *Woman* and also partitioned into base concepts *Married* and *Unmarried*, then we must ensure that all instances of *Married* or *Unmarried* are also instances of *Person*. The general form of an integrity constraint for a base entity type E_1 in a partition of a derived entity type E into $E_1,...,$ E_n would be "$E_1(e,t) \rightarrow E(e,t)$". These integrity constraints are modeled as instances of the derived entity type *ICSubs* using two meta derivation rules similar to the preceding ones.

Finally, we also include in the schema a *completeness integrity constraint* for each partition, except when the partition defines a derived superconcept. In the above example, we must ensure that all instances of *Person* are also instance of *Married* or *Unmarried*. The general form of f for a base entity type E partitioned into $E_1,..., E_n$ would be "$E(e,t) \rightarrow (E_1(e,t) \vee ... \vee E_n(e,t))$". These integrity constraints are modeled as instances of the derived type *ICCompl*, using other two meta derivation rules.

Now, we describe the schema derivation rules implied by partitions. If a derived concept is defined by a partition, then the schema must include its derivation rule. We model it as an instance of *DRPart*, which is a derived entity type subtype of *DerivationRule* (Figure 5). Its derivation rule is:

$$\text{DRPart}(s,t) \leftarrow \text{Defines}(p,c,t) \wedge s = \text{sym}(\text{DRPart},c) \qquad \textbf{MDR8}$$

Note again the use of *sym(DRPart,c)*, which denotes a symbol we use to refer to the derivation rule. We refine the base relationship type *IsExpressedBy* between *Rule* and *Formula* to a derived one between *DRPart* and *Formula*. The derivation rule is:

$$\text{IsExpressedBy}(s,f,t) \leftarrow \text{DRPart}(s,t) \wedge \text{DRPartFormula}(s,f,t) \qquad \textbf{MDR9}$$

---

[3] For flexibility, we allow a partition with only one subtype (Figure 5). In this particular case, it is obvious that disjointness constraints would not apply.

where predicate *DRPartFormula* gives the string representation of *f*. The general form of *f* in a partition of a derived entity type *E* into $E_1,..., E_n$ is "$E(e,t) \leftarrow (E_1(e,t) \lor ... \lor E_n(e,t))$".

4 Schema Evolution

In our framework, schema evolution is performed by meta external events. When the designer wants to change a schema, she generates an instance of the appropriate meta external event type. The corresponding effect rules will induce meta structural events, which change the MIB. By the correspondence rules (Section 3.2), such changes imply changes to the schema.

The set of external event types included in the meta schema define the possible schema evolutions, either applied individually or by means of their composition. There is no other way to evolve a schema. Given that usually a schema may change in many different ways, it is necessary to include many external event types in the meta schema. For example, [1] defines 38 possible F2 schema changes. More are needed for richer schemas. We cannot show here the complete set of needed external event types. Rather, we are going to show how external event types and their effects can be defined in our framework.

Some meta external event types change only the schema, without affecting the IB. For example, *M_RemoveIntegrityConstraint* could have only the effect rule:

M_Del_BaseIntegrityConstraint(ic,t) ← M_RemoveIntegrityConstraint(rm,t) ∧ RemovesIC(rm,ic,t)

which, by CR4, would remove *ic* from the set of schema integrity constraints IC_t. Note that, in this case, the relationship *IsExpressedBy* between *ic* and its formula at *t* would be deleted by the compensating rule of MIC1 (Section 3.1).

Other meta external event types require changing the schema and the IB. We can distinguish two cases here: when the required changes to the IB are given by the typing rule (Section 2.1), and when they must be defined by explicit effect rules. An example of the former could be *M_RemoveRelType*, with appropriate preconditions and the effect rule:

M_Del_RelationshipType(r,t) ← M_RemoveRelType(rm,t) ∧ RemovesRT(rm,r,t)

which, by CR2, would remove *r* from the set of the schema relationship types R_t and, by the typing rule, would delete existing instances of *r* at *t* in the IB. We will show a more complete example of this case in Section 4.1 below.

In other cases, the changes implied by the typing rule are not enough. We need to define an appropriate external event type in the schema, generate an occurrence of it and notify the IP of this occurrence. We generate "on the fly" an instance *EvT* of *ExternalEventType*, without parameters, and then we notify the IP of an occurrence of *EvT*. We will use in the meta effect rules the notation "*EvT* ← to mean that the MIP notifies the IP of an occurrence of *EvT*. We will show a detailed example of this case in Section 4.2 below.

4.1 M_RemoveEntityType

We start with a rather simple external event type, *M_RemoveEntityType*. It has only one parameter, given by relationship type *Removes* between that type and *Non-LexicalEntityType*. A particular instance of *M_RemoveEntityType*, occurring at time *T* and removing *E*, represents the design decision that, from time *T*, *E* ceases to be instance of *EntityType* and, therefore, the IB must not record the instances of entity type *E*. However, *E* may be again instance of *EntityType* later. *E* may be base or derived. For illustration purposes, we only deal here with the simple case when *E* does not participate in any relationship type and is not involved in any partition.

Preconditions. We define first the preconditions. One of them is that E is a non-lexical entity type at time T-1. Formally,

M_RemoveEntityType(rm,t) $\wedge$ Removes(rm,e,t) $\rightarrow$ Non-LexicalEntityType(e,t-1)

The if-part of the rule serves only to declare that an instance of the event type has occurred and to give name to its parameters. We omit this part in the next rules. Then, the other preconditions are:

¬∃participant IsETPtOf(e,participant,t-1)
¬∃partition IsTheSup(e,partition,t-1)
¬∃partition IsASub(e,partition,t-1)

Effect rules. The first effect rule induces the meta structural event that deletes E from Non-LexicalEntityType:

M_Del_Non-LexicalEntityType(e,t)←M_RemoveEntityType(rm,t)∧Removes(rm,e,t)

As we did before, we omit the if-part of this rule in the next ones. Now, we must remove *E* from *BaseConcept* or from *DerivedConcept*:

M_Del_BaseConcept(e,t) $\leftarrow$ BaseConcept(e,t-1)
M_Del_DerivedConcept(e,t) $\leftarrow$ DerivedConcept(e,t-1)

Finally, if *E* is derived, we must delete its derivation rule:

M_Del_DerivationRule(s,t) $\leftarrow$ DerivedConcept(e,t-1) $\wedge$ s = sym(DerivationRule,e)

Induced effects on the MIB. The above effect rules are the only ones that need to be defined. We now reason (informally) about induced effects on the MIB:
– By the MDR's described in Section 3.1 (e.g. MDR1), *e* ceases to be instance of *Concept* and *EntityType*. The derived structural events *M_Del_Concept(e,t)* and *M_Del_EntityType(e,t)* are induced. Also, *M_Del_DerivationRule* induces *M_Del_Rule*. By the compensating rule of MIC1, *M_Del_IsExpressedBy(s,f,t)* is induced if *IsExpressedBy(s,f,t-1)*.

Induced effects on the schema and IB. We now reason about the induced effects on the schema and the IB:
– By CR1, *e* is not an entity type in the schema at *t* (that is, $e \notin E_t$)
– By the typing rule, all instances of *e* at *t-1* cease to be instances of *e* at *t*.

– By CR3, all instances of *DerivationRule* that have been deleted at *t* cease to exist in the schema at *t*.

Remarks. The removal of an entity type, or any other schema change, can affect indirectly to integrity constraints, derivation rules, or external event types defined explicitly in the schema by the designer. Some changes in those elements can be needed. The analysis of those changes results in a very complex task [15, 27], that is outside the scope of this paper.

4.2 M_ChangeParticipantToSET.

We now deal with a complex external event type, *M_ChangeParticipantToSET*. It has two parameters, given by relationship types *Changes*, with *Participant*, and *HasNewType*, with *EntityType*. An occurrence *M_ChangeParticipantToSET(CP,T)* of this event type, with *Changes(CP,P,T)* and *HasNewType(CP,NT,T)* represents the fact that, from time *T*, the participant *P* of a relationship type *R* changes its type to a supertype or a subtype,[4] the entity type *NT*. This means that, from *T*, instances of *R* are only valid if their corresponding participant is instance of *NT*.

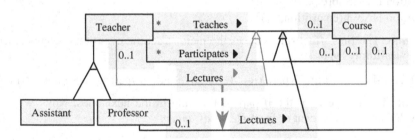

Fig. 6. An example of changing a participant in a relationship type

We consider the general case in which the relationship type has any degree, and is base or derived, subtype in zero or one partition, and super in any number of partitions. Changing a participant of a binary relationship type (attribute) has been studied extensively in the literature. However, we have not found the study of the change in our general settings.

If the relationship type is base, some of its instances may become invalid after the change. We have two possible strategies here: either to reject the change or to delete explicitly the invalid instances. The two possibilities must be offered to the designer. We could define a different external event type for each strategy, or add a new parameter to the event type, indicating the desired strategy [27]. In the following, we assume the existence of two different external event types, and present here the one that performs the strategy of deleting explicitly the invalid instances. In that case, if the relationship type is involved in a partition, deletion of some of its instances must be propagated through the partition hierarchy. For base types, the propagation must be

---

[4] *ToSET* stands for „*To a Super or a Sub Entity Type*„.

done explicitly. For derived types, the associated derivation rules might have to be corrected in the right way. On the other hand, if the relationship type changed is derived, the corresponding derivation rule needs to be changed too, so the invalid instances will be deleted implicitly.

This is a more complex change than the one exposed in Section 4.1, so for clarity we present here only an example. The complete formalization of the general case can be found in [17]. Assume a university information system (see Figure 6) with two base entity types, *Teacher* and *Course*, and also a base relationship type *Teaches* between *Teacher* and *Course*, partitioned into two subtypes, *Lectures* (base) and *Participates* (derived), with the same participants as the supertype. A teacher participates in a course if she teaches but does not lecture it. Any teacher can lecture courses or participate in them.

Assume now that the domain changes, and *Teacher* is transformed into a derived type, partitioned into *Professor* and *Assistant*. Now, among other changes, only a professor can be the lecturer of a course. That implies changing the participant of the relationship type *Lectures* from *Teacher* to *Professor*. The effects of this change, in our framework, would be the following:

The type of the participant must be explicitly changed in the MIB:

M_Del_IsETPtOf (Teacher, P, T)
M_Ins_IsETPtOf (Professor, P, T)

with P being the symbol representing the participant being changed, and T the time instant when the change is done.

As *Lectures* is base, P has a referential integrity constraint that must change. This change is performed automatically by MDR5, which induces:

M_Del_IsExpressedBy(S,'*Lectures(tch,c,t)* → *Teacher(tch,t)*', T)
M_Ins_IsExpressedBy(S,'*Lectures(tch,c,t)* → *Professor(tch,t)*', T)

with S=*sym(ICRefInt,P)*.

Some of the instances of *Lectures* may violate the above new integrity constraint. In that case, they must cease to exist. As *Lectures* is base, we must define a new external event type in the conceptual schema to explicitly eliminate its invalid instances; and also to eliminate them as instances of *Teaches*, since it is a base supertype of *Lectures*. We use the special function *newSymbol()* to obtain new symbols in the MIB, when needed. The explicitly defined effects in the MIB must be the following:

et=newSymbol()
M_Ins_ExternalEventType(et,T)

er_1=newSymbol()
M_Ins_EffectRule(er_1,T)
M_Ins_HasEffect(et,er_1,T)
M_Ins_IsExpressedBy(er_1,'*Del_Lectures(tch,c,t)* ← *Lectures(tch,c,t-1)*
        ∧ ¬*Professor(tch,t-1)*' ,T)
er_2=newSymbol()
M_Ins_EffectRule(er_2,T)
M_Ins_HasEffect(et,er_2,T)

M_Ins_IsExpressedBy(er$_2$,'*Del_Teaches(tch,c,t)* ← *Del_Lectures(tch,c,t)*',T)

Finally, we have to notify the IP of an occurrence of the external event type we have just defined:

et ←

Remarks. As pointed out at the beginning of this section, this event type can require the change of some derivation rules, corresponding to derived relationship types of the partition hierarchy. As we think that this kind of change must be modeled as an independent external event type, in this case would be needed the composition of instances of both event types to achieve the whole desired change.

5 Conclusions

We have presented a framework that allows the definition of the evolution of information systems, at the conceptual level. The framework is based on a reflective architecture, with two loosely coupled conceptual processors.

Our framework allows the definition of all conceptual modeling constructs in the meta schema. This has been illustrated with three representative constructs. On the other hand, our framework allows the definition of any evolution operation, and this has been illustrated also by two particular operations, which have been analyzed in detail.

Our work can be extended in at least five directions. First, we could define, in the meta schema, other modeling constructs (aggregation, materialization, etc.). Second, we could develop the complete (both at schema and instance-level [8]) set of meta external event types, for the minimal meta schema and for the considered constructs. Other complex external event types could be added to that set to facilitate the evolution to the designer [6]. Of course, this should be done on the basis of existing work. Third, a prototype implementation could be developed, preferably using two processors of different type. In view of practical applications, the two processors should be loosely coupled, as suggested by our framework. Fourth, that prototype could include a tool to assist and guide the designer in the definition and analysis of evolution operations [27, 9]. For instance, warning her about external event types possibly affected by a particular schema change. Finally, building on top of existing knowledge and experience, one could attempt the development of an industrial system, with several possible degrees of ambition.

Acknowledgments

The authors are indebted to Dolors Costal, Cristina Gómez, Camilo Ocampo and Toni Urpí, and to the anonymous referees, for their helpful comments. This work has been partially supported by CICYT program projects TIC99-1048-C02-1 and TEL99-0335-C04-02.

References

1. Al-Jadir, L., Léonard, M.: Multiobjects to Ease Schema Evolution in an OODBMS. In: Proc. ER'98, Singapore, LNCS 1507, Springer (1998) 316-333
2. Analyti, A., Spyratos, N., Constantopoulos, P.:Property Covering: A Powerful Construct for Schema Derivations. In: Proc. ER'97, LNCS 1331, Springer-Verlag (1997) 271-284
3. Boman, M., Bubenko jr., J.A., Johannesson, P., Wangler, B.: Conceptual Modelling. Prentice Hall (1997)
4. Banerjee, J., Chou, H-T., Garza, J.F., Kim, W., Woelk, D., Ballou, N.: Data Model Issues for Object-Oriented Applications. In: ACM TOIS Vol.5, No.1, January (1987) 3-26
5. Bertino, E., Ferrari, E., Guerrini, G.: T_Chimera: A Temporal Object-Oriented Data Model. TAPOS 3(2) (1997) 103-125
6. Brèche, P.: Advanced Primitives for Changing Schemas of Object Databases. 8Th. In: Intl. Conf. CAiSE'96, LNCS 1080, Springer (1996) 476-495
7. Bubenko jr., J.A.: The Temporal Dimension in Information Modelling. In: Architecture and Models in Data Base Management Systems, North-Holland (1977)
8. Casais, E.: Managing Class Evolution in Object-Oriented Systems, In: D.C. Tsichritzis (ed.): Object Management (1990) 133-195
9. Erwald, C.A., Orlowska, M.E.: A procedural approach to schema evolution. In: Proc. CAiSE'93, LNCS 685, Springer (1993) 22-38
10. Goralwalla, I., Szafron, D., Özsu, T., Peters, R.: A Temporal Approach to Managing Schema Evolution in Object Database Systems. In: Data&Knowledge Eng. 28(1), October (1998) 73-105
11. Hainaut, J-L., Englebert, V., Henrard, J., Hick, J-M., Roland, D.: Database Evolution: the DB-MAIN Approach. In: 13th. Intl. Conf. on the Entity-Relationship Approach - ER'94, LNCS 881, Springer-Verlag (1994) 112-131
12. ISO/TC97/SC5/WG3: Concepts and Terminology for the Conceptual Schema and Information Base. J.J. van Griethuysen (ed.), March (1982)
13. Jarke, M., Gallersdörfer, R., Jeusfeld, M.A., Staudt, M., Eherer, S.: ConceptBase - a deductive object base for meta data management. In: Journal of Intelligent Information Systems, 4(2) (1995) 167-192
14. Lemke, T., Manthey, R.: The Schema Evolution Assistant: Tool Description. IDEA.DE.22.O.004, University of Bonn (1995)
15. Lemke, T.:Schema Evolution in OODBMS: A Selective Overview of Problems and Solutions. IDEA.WP.22.O.002, University of Bonn (1994)
16. Lemke, T.: DDL = DML?. An Exercise in Reflective Schema Management for Chimera. IDEA.WP.22.O.003, University of Bonn (1995)
17. López, J.R., Olivé, A.: A Framework for the Evolution of Temporal Conceptual Schemas of Information Systems – Extended Version. LSI-00-14-R. Department of Software (LSI). Universitat Politècnica de Catalunya (2000)
18. Manthey, R.: Beyond Data Dictionaries: Towards a Reflective Architecture of Intelligent Database Systems. In: DOOD'93, Springer-Verlag (1993) 328-339
19. Nguyen, G.T., Rieu, D.: Schema evolution in object-oriented database systems. In: Data&Knowledge Eng. 4 (1989). 43-67
20. Olivé, A., Costal, D., Sancho, M.-R.: Entity Evolution in IsA Hierarchies. In: Proc. ER'99, LNCS 1728, Springer-Verlag (1999) 62-80
21. Olivé, A.: "Relationship Reification: A Temporal View". In: Proc. CAiSE'99, LNCS 1626, Springer (1999) 396-410
22. Peters, R.J., Özsu, T.: Reflection in a Uniform Behavioral Object Model. In: Proc. ER'93, Arlington, LNCS 823, Springer-Verlag. (1993) 34-45
23. Peters, R.J., Özsu, T.: An Axiomatic Model of Dynamic Schema Evolution in Objectbase Systems. In: ACM TODS Vol. 22, No. 1, March (1997) 75-114

24. Roddick, J.F.: Schema Evolution in DataBase Systems – An Updated Bibliography. In: ACM SIGMOD Rec., 21(4), May (1994) 35-40
25. Rumbaugh, J., Jacobson, I., Booch, G.: The Unified Modeling Language Reference Manual. Addison-Wesley (1999)
26. Tansel,A., Clifford,J., Gadia,S. et al.: Temporal Databases: Theory, Design and Implementation. Benjamin/Cummings (1993)
27. Zicari, R.: A Framework for Schema Updates in Object-Oriented Database System. In: Bancilhon,F.; Delobel,C.; Kanellakis, P. (eds.): Building an Object-Oriented Database System - The Story of O_2. Morgan Kaufmann Pub. (1992) 146-182

Distance Measures
for Information System Reengineering

Geert Poels, Stijn Viaene, and Guido Dedene

Management Information Systems Group
Department of Applied Economic Sciences
Katholieke Universiteit Leuven
Naamsestraat 69, B-3000 Leuven, Belgium
{geert.poels, stijn.viaene, guido.dedene}@econ.kuleuven.ac.be

Abstract. We present an approach to assess the magnitude and impact of information system reengineering caused by business process change. This approach is based on two concepts: object-oriented business modeling and distance measurement. The former concept is used to visualize changes in the business layer of an information system architecture. The latter concept is used to quantify these changes. The paper also describes the application of our approach in the context of front-office system design.

1 Introduction

There exists a wide spectrum of reasons for information system reengineering. The evolution of an information system over many years frequently leads to software that is unnecessarily complex and inflexible, making the maintenance and enhancement of the system more and more expensive [1]. Often, legacy systems are reengineered because of a desire to move to new generations of software technology, like component software [2]. Changes in the computer and network infrastructure may as well trigger reengineering efforts.

The focus of this paper is however on a different type of reengineering, i.e. information system reengineering because of changing business processes. Major strategic management decisions regarding business re-positioning and drastic business transformations (i.e. BPR as defined in [3], [4]) require the current business process(es) to be changed and the existing information system to be modified in order to further support the business operations. A characteristic of this type of information system reengineering is that it is fundamental. It affects the enterprise model, which is the core layer in an object-oriented information system architecture [5]. The enterprise model is an abstract image of business reality (either a single business process or a network of interrelated processes), capturing the relevant business entities, events and rules, their static relationships and dynamic interactions. In the implemented software system, the classes of the enterprise model are responsible for the business functionality that is offered by the information system.

Reengineering the information system is crucial for the overall success of a business process change. One aspect to consider is the reengineering cost. Promised benefits must be balanced against this cost, preferably before the actual change(s) take(s) place. In this paper we present an approach to assess the magnitude and

B. Wangler, L. Bergman (Eds.): CAiSE 2000, LNCS 1789, pp. 387-400, 2000
© Springer-Verlag Berlin Heidelberg 2000

impact of information system reengineering, more precisely the amount of changes in the enterprise model. An assessment of the effect of 'business process change'-driven reengineering on the core layer of an information system provides complementary quantitative information (apart from financial measures like ROI, etc.) to support strategic decision making with respect to business re-positioning and business transformation. Measurement allows assessing how 'big' the changes are, and thus provides an objective means to compare alternatives.

Our approach is based on two concepts: business modeling and distance measurement. First, a conceptual modeling method, called object-oriented business modeling by contract [6], is used to model the AS-IS enterprise model (i.e. the model before the business process change(s) take(s) place) and the TO-BE enterprise model (i.e. the model as it would look like after the business process change(s)). Comparing these models allows visualizing the changes that would be caused by reengineering. Next, the distance between the models is measured to quantify the magnitude of the changes. The basic assumption underlying our approach is that the larger the distance between the AS-IS and TO-BE models, the larger the amount of changes that must be handled, and thus the larger the impact and cost of information system reengineering.

This paper is organized as follows. Section 2 discusses previous work on distance measurement in the context of software reengineering. Section 3 presents the modeling and measurement aspects of our approach. In section 4 we discuss some experiences in using our approach in the context of front-office system design. Conclusions and topics for further research are presented in section 5.

2   Related Work

Distance measurement is of course not a new concept in the software reengineering field. Such measurements have been used to cluster components of a software system into subsystems or modules, for instance, to improve the modularity of the system [7], or to reverse engineer the system (i.e. design recovery) [8]. They have also been used to assess the cohesion of subsystems [9], again with the purpose of reengineering the system. In other software engineering related fields, distance measurement has been proposed as a technique for component reusability assessment [10] and component retrieval [11].

Generally, these approaches use distance measurement to assess the closeness between two software entities in terms of the properties they have in common and the properties that are unique to each of the entities. Most measures of 'closeness' take the form of a normalized similarity (or affinity) measure. Given a set of software entities E (e.g. classes in an object-oriented system), a set of properties P (e.g. the union of class methods in the system), and a function p mapping entities of E into subsets of P (e.g. all methods defined in a class or used by the class), the degree of similarity between $A \in E$ and $B \in E$ with respect to P is measured by

$$Sim(A,B) = \frac{|p(A) \cap p(B)|}{|p(A) \cup p(B)|} . \tag{1}$$

This measure returns the relative amount of common properties between A and B. The higher this value, the more similar A and B are with respect to P.

It is obvious that *Sim* works fine for purposes like cluster analysis and component matching. However, we need a measure for the distance (and not the closeness) between two software entities. In other words, we are not interested in the properties that A and B have in common, but in the properties in which they are different.

A measure that puts more emphasis on the difference between A and B is the dissimilarity measure *Dis* as proposed, for instance, in [9]

$$Dis(A,B) = \frac{|p(A) \cup p(B)| - |p(A) \cap p(B)|}{|p(A) \cup p(B)|} . \tag{2}$$

This measure however does not express the magnitude of the dissimilarity between A and B. The measure is normalized and thus implicitly accounts for the relative amount of common properties between A and B. For our research purpose we need to quantify the absolute amount of differences between entities A and B, regardless of how many properties they have in common.

An alternative measure is the distance measure *Dist*

$$Dist(A,B) = |p(A) \cup p(B)| - |p(A) \cap p(B)| = |p(A) - p(B)| + |p(B) - p(A)| . \tag{3}$$

This measure returns the cardinality of the symmetric difference between p(A) and p(B). It focuses upon the changes that are needed to turn entity A into entity B, and vice versa.

Our approach to distance measurement uses measures of the form *Dist*. The approach is different from previous research in the sense that distance measures satisfy the metric axioms [12]. Working with metrics offers the additional advantage that the measures can be formally validated within the framework of measurement theory, as required by software measurement scientists [13], [14], [15].

3   A Distance-Based Change Assessment Approach

We first present a brief introduction to object-oriented business modeling by contract. Next, a generic method to define distance measures for software entities is presented and illustrated for OO business models.

3.1   OO Business Modeling by Contract

Object orientation has proven an excellent paradigm to model business processes [16], [17]. Object-oriented enterprise models improve the communication between business professionals and software engineers. Moreover, many OOAD methods (see e.g. [18], [19]) develop information systems starting from such models. The enterprise model does not only describe the functioning of a business process; it is an integral part of the specifications of the information system that supports the business process. The object classes, identified during business modeling, take a prominent place amongst the classes in the OO information system, once it is implemented. Therefore, a comparison of the AS-IS and TO-BE enterprise models provides insight into business process changes as well as information system changes. Moreover, this insight is gained before the actual changes take place.

The object-oriented business modeling by contract method [6] places much emphasis on the concept of a 'business event', in so far as it has been classified as an event-driven method [20]. At the highest level of abstraction, a business process is seen as a sequence of occurrences of business events. The business entities affected by these occurrences are modeled as business objects. Business objects and events are further classified into types and subtypes (i.e. generalization / specialization).

Mathematically, each business object type is defined through the set of business event types it is involved in. Object life cycle models are used to specify sequence constraints on the participation of business objects into business events. They thus model an important class of business rules. The communication and synchronization between objects is modeled by means of common event participation (i.e. event broadcasting instead of message passing). This principle also allows modeling well-known structural relationships between business object types (e.g. categorization, aggregation, composition, association) in terms of existence dependency associations and/or contract object types.[1] The main advantage of the existence dependency concept is that the consistency between the static and dynamic aspects of the business model can be formally verified.[2]

At lower levels of abstraction, business object types are given a class definition, which can be gradually refined throughout the development process. Generalization / specialization relationships between business object types are specified by means of inheritance relationships between the corresponding classes. Existence dependency associations are implemented through the data abstraction mechanism (e.g. by means of attributes that are used as pointers to existence dependent and/or master classes). The end result is a fully (and formally) specified object-oriented model of the business process that acts at the same time as the kernel of a layered architecture for the information system [22].

As an illustration, part of the specification for a (simplified) library's loan circulation process is shown below. Fig. 1 presents the class diagram in UML notation [23]. Table 1 is an object-event association matrix, showing which business object types / classes are affected by the occurrence of business events. The symbols "C", "M", and "E" indicate respectively that the occurrence of the business event (of the type shown in the row header) creates, modifies or ends the life of a business object (of the type shown in the column header).

---

[1] A business object x is existence dependent on a business object y if x is during its life always associated to y (i.e. x cannot be created before y and it can no longer exist when the life of y has ended). In a library for instance, each LOAN object is always associated to a particular BOOK object. Therefore we say that the object type LOAN is existence dependent on the object type BOOK. For the existence dependent object type (e.g. LOAN), the association with the master object type (e.g. BOOK) is mandatory with a connectivity (cardinality, multiplicity) of one.

[2] The semantic integrity between the static business model (e.g. class diagram) and the dynamic business model (e.g. object-event association matrix) is guaranteed when the existence dependent object type is a subset of the master object type. Note that at this level of abstraction business object types are defined as sets of business event types. For a formal proof we refer to [21].

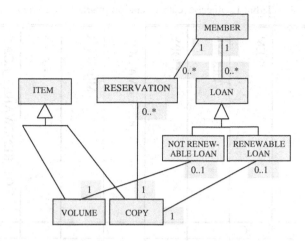

Fig. 1. Class diagram of a library

3.2   Distance Measures for OO Business Models

Our approach to define distance measures for software entities has been fully described elsewhere [24]. Here, we just present the basic principles.

Two software entities can be different in many aspects. For each aspect that is considered, a model or abstraction of the software entity is defined. The distance between software entities A and B with respect to aspect X is then measured by the count of elementary transformations (i.e. atomic changes of a given type) that are minimally needed to transform the model of A (for X) into the model of B (for X). The more elementary transformations that are needed, the larger the distance between A and B, with respect to aspect X.

As an example, the distance between business object types VOLUME and COPY can be expressed in terms of their involvement in business event types (cf. Table 1). The relevant model of an object type is here the set of event types it is involved in (i.e. all event types having their entries marked in the column for the object type in the object-event association matrix). Elementary transformations are of the type 'adding an event type' or 'removing an event type'. It can easily be seen that for VOLUME and COPY it takes minimally 12 such transformations. Hence, their distance with respect to business event type involvement is 12.

The measure thus defined is of the form *Dist* as presented in section 2. The aspect of distance X, i.e. business event type involvement, corresponds here to the set of properties P in the general definition of *Dist*. The function p referred to in this definition, maps the object types A and B into their mathematical definition. Hence, the sets p(A) - p(B) and p(B) - p(A) contain the business event types that have to be added or removed by means of elementary transformations. Consequently, the sum of the cardinalities of these sets equals the minimum number of elementary transformations that are needed to transform object type A into object type B, or vice versa.

Table 1. Object-event association matrix for a library

	ITEM	VOLUME	COPY	RESERVATION	MEMBER	LOAN	NOT_RENEWABLE_LOAN	RENEWABLE_LOAN
Acquire	C							
acq_vol.		C						
acq_cop.			C					
Catalogue	M	M	M					
Sell	E							
sell_vol.		E						
sell_cop.			E					
Reserve				M	C	M		
Cancel				M	E	M		
Fetch				M	E	M		C
Register					C			
Leave					E			
Borrow					M	C		
cr_nrloan		M			M		C	
cr_rloan			M		M			C
Return		M	M		M	E	E	E
Lose					M	E		
Lose_vol.		E			M		E	
Lose_cop			E		M			E
Renew				M		M		M

We have defined sets of elementary transformation types for different kinds of models like sets, multi-sets, matrices, state machines, etc. Similar notions for distance between trees, strings, clusters, etc. can be found in the literature [25], [26], [27]. An important result of our research is that this particular way of defining a distance measure results in a function that satisfies the metric axioms. The good news is that metric functions fit into the framework of measurement theory. According to [12], metrics are homomorphic mappings of proximity structures into metric spaces, i.e. they map an empirical notion of distance into a mathematical notion of distance. Another result from measurement theory is that metrics define ordinal scales of distance. They allow distance values to be ranked, which is useful when comparing alternatives.

In [28] we further showed that distance measures based on counts of elementary transformations represent a special type of proximity structure, i.e. segmentally additive proximity structures. Such a representation results in the definition of ratio scales of distance, which allows expressing distance values in ratios and percentages [12].

It should be noted that metrics focus on the difference between two entities, without regard to how much these entities have in common. We believe such a point of view is justified for the type of application described in this paper: to quantify the *amount of change* in the enterprise model due to business process changes.

4   Applying the Approach to a Reference Framework for Front-Office System Design

We applied our approach to a reference framework for front-office system design [29]. This framework concerns the organization of the front-office, i.e. the part of a service organization where the services required by a customer and offered by the service provider are agreed upon. The framework is based on the concept of service customization, as proposed by the management scientists Lampel and Mintzberg [30]. It distinguishes five types of front-office depending on the level of service customization: pure standardization, segmented standardization, customized standardization, tailored customization, and pure customization. Each type of front-office requires its own specific information system to support its specific information requirements. The framework proposes an object-oriented business model for each type of front-office. These models can be used as reference models for actual front-office system design.

The framework of de Vries is useful for companies wishing to introduce a front-office organization and its supporting information system. It is also useful as a strategic management instrument for changing the service specification process. Companies wishing to move to higher levels of service customization can use the framework to reengineer their front-office system. However, before such a move is decided on, companies must have an idea of the impact of the reengineering. This is a question that can be addressed by our distance-based change assessment approach.

In a first sub-section we present the generic front-office enterprise models of de Vries. The models in [29] were already specified using the object-oriented business modeling by contract method. For the sake of brevity, we only present here the static business models, i.e. class diagrams in UML notation. In the next sub-section we propose a distance measure for UML class diagrams. In a final sub-section the measurement results are presented and analyzed.

4.1   Generic Front-Office Object Models

Overall, the front-office needs product-information, process-information and information on the customer-relationship. Table 2 shows for each level of service customization and corresponding front-office type the type of information that is needed.

Table 2. Information model of front-office customer interaction of de Vries [29]

FRONT-OFFICE TYPE	DEGREE OF CUSTOMIZATION	RELATION-RELATED	PRODUCT-RELATED	PROCESS-RELATED
Counter	Pure standardization	Anonymous transactions	End products	Delivery times for products
One stop shop	Segmented standardization	Characteristics of market segments	Assortments	Delivery times for assortments
Field and inside service	Customized standardization	Customer profiles	Standard components	Available capacity
Control room	Tailored customization	Development of the relationship	Smallest replicating unit	Capacity assignment
Symbiosis	Pure customization	Opportunities for partnership	Design knowledge	Implementation and outsourcing opportunities

Fig. 2 presents the 'counter' model. The information needed for standardized service transactions can be encapsulated in the SUPPLIER, SERVICE and TRANSACTION classes in the diagram. For instance, descriptive attributes of the SERVICE class include the service functionality description, price and warranty conditions and service procedure descriptions. Transaction amounts and timestamps are descriptive attributes of the TRANSACTION class.

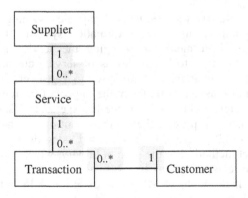

Fig. 2. The counter model

A 'one-stop-shop' offers a specific assortment of services to customers depending on the market segment to which they belong (Fig. 3). The essential front-office processes are the determination of market segments and assortments. Information like segmentation criteria, assortment discount rates, etc. can readily be encapsulated in the front-office enterprise classes.

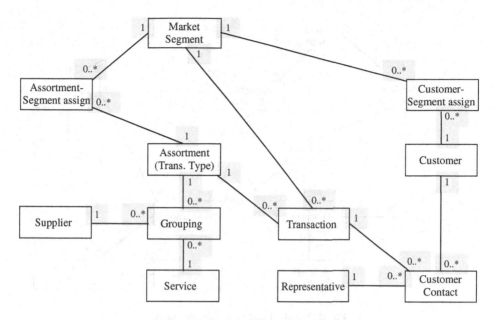

Fig. 3. The one-stop-shop model

According to de Vries *et al.* the 'one-stop-shop' model unfolds from the 'counter' model. The primary effects of customization are the concepts of segmentation and assortments.

The 'field and inside service' type of front-office is a clear extension of the 'one-stop-shop' (Fig. 4). To offer customized standardization the front-office is organized into a field service (e.g. sales people) that is supported by an inside service. The former is responsible for the customer relationships, whereas the latter is responsible for profiling, matching, and the bundling and offering of services.

Figs. 5 and 6 show the models of the 'control room' and 'symbiosis' types of front-office. The models clearly show that the emphasis shifts from product and process related information to the customer relation. The 'control room' front-office aims to establish a structural link with commercially attractive customers by means of tailored customization. Within the bounds of the standard service design and delivery process, the front-office representative and the customer specify the service to be provided. In the 'symbiosis' model the service provider and the customer collaborate completely in the various steps of designing, acquiring, and producing customized services.

4.2   A Distance Measure

A distance measure is needed for the UML class diagrams of Figs. 2 to 6. Note that these diagrams are built from only two types of elements: classes and existence dependency associations between classes. Note also that all associations are characterised by the same connectivity constraints (i.e. mandatory with a connectivity of 1 on one side and optional with a connectivity of many on the other side).

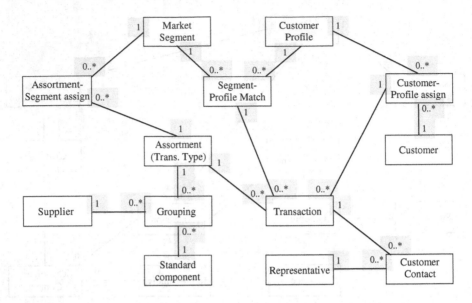

Fig. 4. The field and inside service model

A set of elementary transformation types that is sufficient to express all different types of atomic change in the UML class diagrams considered here, is the following:

t_1: remove a class from the diagram;
t_2: add a class to the diagram;
t_3: remove an association;
t_4: add an association.

The distance between any pair of front-office types, with respect to their static business models (i.e. the UML class diagrams of Figs. 2 to 6), is measured by the minimum number of elementary transformations of the types t_1 to t_4 that are needed to transform one model into the other.

The application of a distance measure for software entities may require syntactic, semantic and/or linguistic rules to decide on two entities being identical or not. We assume here that strict class labeling conventions have been followed, such that classes with the same name can be considered as identical. By convention, if part of the class name is between brackets, then only this part is used for matching classes. Associations are identical across models if the participating classes are also identical: if classes C and C' are associated in model M_i, and class C' is replaced by class C" in model M_j, without changing the connectivity constraints of the association with C, then we also consider this association to be the same in M_i and M_j. Generally however, removing a class implies that all the associations it is involved in are removed as well.

4.3   Analysis and Discussion of Measurement Results

Table 3 shows the distance measurements between all possible pairs of generic front-office object model. As an example, consider the distance between the 'control room' model (Fig. 5) and the 'symbiosis' model (Fig. 6). The table shows that 12 atomic changes are needed to transform one model into the other, or vice versa. Starting from the 'control room', the classes STANDARD COMPONENT, STANDARD SERVICE, TRANSACTION, REPRESENTATIVE and CUSTOMER CONTACT, and the associations STANDARD SERVICE - GROUPING, STANDARD SERVICE - TRANSACTION, TRANSACTION - CUSTOMER CONTACT and REPRESENTATIVE - CUSTOMER CONTACT are removed, whereas the classes RESOURCE and ACTION, and the association ACTION - GROUPING are added to obtain the 'symbiosis' front-office model.

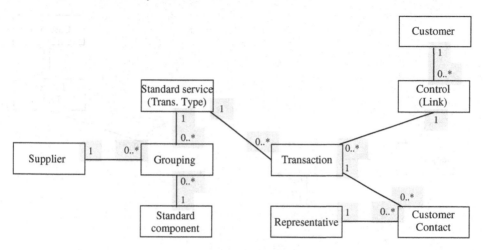

Fig. 5. The control room model

Table 3 can be used as a complementary evaluation instrument by companies wishing to reengineer their front-office and supporting front-office information system, in order to move to another level of service customization. Suppose for instance that a service organization with a 'counter' office wishes to offer customized services. The values of Table 3 suggest that a move towards segmented or customized standardization requires a far greater impact on the front-office enterprise model than a move towards the highest levels of service customization. The values also suggest that companies that gradually move towards the highest levels of service customization will face more changes in the beginning of this process than in the end. Note further the effect of the 'triangle inequality', i.e. one of the metric axioms. For instance, whereas the distance between the 'one stop shop' and the 'control room' is 14 and the distance between the 'control room' and the 'symbiosis' model is 12, the distance between the 'one stop shop' and the 'symbiosis' model is only 24, i.e. less than 14 + 12. The 'strict' triangle inequalities observed in Table 3 strongly suggest that it might be sub-optimal to move the level of service customization one step at a time. A more drastic reengineering of the current front-office may pay off in the long term.

The values in Table 3 must of course be interpreted with care. Moving to another level of service customization and re-organizing the front-office requires more than changing the front-office information system. Besides, the values only reflect the amount of change required for the enterprise model layer in the architecture of the front-office system. In the absence of further (empirical) studies, we can only assume that the impact on the other layers of the system architecture is proportional to the amount of enterprise model changes. The same remark holds for the reengineering costs. It is for instance assumed that each type of elementary transformation involves the same reengineering cost, which is of course only an approximation of reality. Finally, note that the generic object models of Figs. 2 to 6 are to be seen as domain models, that must be instantiated for individual companies. The actual front-office enterprise models might thus be different from the domain models proposed in the reference framework. As a consequence, the distance values might be different too.

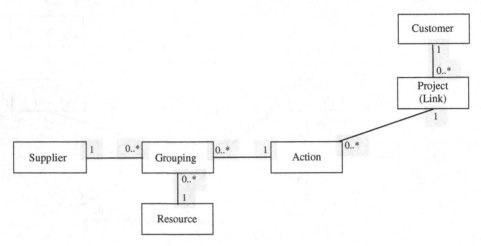

Fig. 6. The symbiosis model

Table 3. Distance values for the generic front-office object models in the reference framework of de Vries

	counter	one stop shop	field and inside service	control room	symbiosis
counter	0	22	28	18	14
one stop shop	22	0	16	14	24
field and inside service	28	16	0	16	28
control room	18	16	16	0	12
symbiosis	14	24	28	12	0

5   Conclusions and Further Research Topics

The approach presented in this paper provides information regarding the impact and magnitude of information system reengineering caused by business process change. Measuring the distance between the AS-IS and TO-BE models of a business process helps quantifying the amount of change that is needed to reengineer the supporting information system. We must note that further research, mainly empirical in nature, is needed to relate this modeled and measured amount of change to management variables like reengineering costs, migration costs, and risks (e.g. potential data loss).

We also acknowledge that measuring static enterprise models, as in section 4, gives only one view on the complex problem of 'business process change'-driven information system reengineering. A balanced approach requires measuring a whole array of static and dynamic product models, as well as process models, workflow models, etc.

Our distance-based modeling and measurement approach can be applied in other contexts too. In [24] a method is proposed to measure software attributes (e.g. coupling, cohesion, size) in terms of distances between software product models, that emphasize such attributes, and 'reference' models, that represent 'ideal' models for the attributes. In [31] this method has been used to measure the reuse of object-oriented business models. A topic of future research is to use distance measurement in object-oriented business models for the identification of reusable business (software) components [32]. In our opinion and experience, the concepts of distance and metric are both flexible and formal, allowing them to be used in a variety of software (re)engineering contexts.

Acknowledgements

Geert Poels is Postdoctoral Fellow of the Fund for Scientific Research - Flanders (Belgium)(F.W.O.). Stijn Viaene holds the KBC Insurance Research Chair in Management Information Systems at the Katholieke Universiteit Leuven. We wish to thank the anonymous referees for their valuable comments.

References

1. Ciupke, O.: Automatic Detection of Design Problems in Object-Oriented Reengineering. In: Proc. TOOLS'99. Santa Barbara, Calif. (1999) 18-32
2. Sahraoui, H.A., Melo, W., Lounis, H., Dumont, F.: Applying Concept Formation Methods to Object Identification in Procedural Code. In: Proc. 12th Int'l Automated Software Eng. Conf. (ASEC'97). Incline Village, Nev. (1997) 210-218
3. Davenport, T.H., Short, J.E.: The New Industrial Engineering: Information Technology and Business Process Redesign. Sloan Management Review. 31 (1990) 11-27
4. Hammer, M., Champy, J.: Reengineering the Corporation, A Manifesto for Business Revolution. Harper, New York (1993)
5. Zachman, J.A.: A framework for information architecture. IBM Systems J. 26 (1987) 276-292
6. Snoeck, M., Dedene, G., Verhelst, M., Depuydt, A.: Object-Oriented Enterprise Modelling with MERODE. University Press, Leuven (1999)
7. Brito e Abreu, F., Peirera, G., Sousa, P.: Reengineering the Modularity of Object-Oriented Systems. In: Proc. ECOOP'98, Workshop Reader, Workshop on Techniques, Tools and Formalisms for Capturing and Assessing the Architectural Quality in Object-Oriented Software. Brussels (1998) 62-63
8. Tzerpos, V., Holt, R.C.: Software Botryology: Automatic Clustering of Software Systems. In: Proc. Int'l Workshop on Large Scale Software Composition. Vienna (1998)
9. Simon, F., Löffler, S., Lewerentz, C.: Distance Based Cohesion Measuring. In: Proc. 2nd European Software Measurement Conf. Amsterdam (1999) 69-83
10.Castano, S., De Antonellis, V., Zonta, B.: Classifying and Reusing Conceptual Schemas. In: Proc. 11th Int'l Conf. on Conceptual Modelling (ER'92). Karlsruhe (1992) 121-138

11.Jilani, L.L., Mili, R., Mili, A.: Approximate Component Retrieval: An Academic Exercise or a Practical Concern? In: Proc. 8th Workshop on Institutionalising Software Reuse (WISR8). Columbus, Ohio (1997)

12.Suppes, P., Krantz, D.M., Luce, R.D., Tversky, A.: Foundations of Measurement: Geometrical, Threshold, and Probabilistic Representations. Academic Press, San Diego, Calif. (1989)

13.Briand, L., El Emam, K., Morasca, S.: Theoretical and Empirical Validation of Software Product Measures. Tech. rep. ISERN-95-03, International Software Engineering Network (1995)

14.Fenton, N., Pfleeger, S.L.,: Software Metrics: A Rigorous and Practical Approach. International Thomson Computer Press, London (1997)

15.Zuse, H.: A Framework for Software Measurement. Walter de Gruyter, Berlin (1998)

16.Wang, S.: OO Modeling of Business Processes: Object-Oriented Systems Analysis. Information Systems Management. (1994) 36-43

17.Dedene, G., Snoeck, M.: Generic Object Models and Business Process (Re)Design. Tech. rep. DTEW 9667, Catholic University of Leuven (1996)

18.Jacobson, I., et al.: Object-Oriented Software Engineering, A Use Case Driven Approach. Addison-Wesley, Reading, Mass. (1992)

19.D'Souza, D.F., Wills, A.C.: Objects, Components, and Frameworks with UML: The Catalysis Approach. Addison-Wesley, Reading, Mass. (1998)

20.Simons, A.J.H., Snoeck, M., Hung, K.S.Y.: Design Patterns as Litmus Paper to Test the Strength of Object-Oriented Methods. In: Proc 5th Int'l Conf. on Object Oriented Information Systems (OOIS'98). Paris (1998)

21.Snoeck, M., Dedene, G.: Existence Dependency: the key to semantic integrity between structural and behavioural aspects of object types. IEEE Trans. Software Eng. 24 (1998) 233-251

22.Poels, G.: Evaluating the Modularity of Model-Driven Object-Oriented Software Architectures, In: Proc. ECOOP'98, Workshop Reader, Workshop on Techniques, Tools and Formalisms for Capturing and Assessing the Architectural Quality in Object-Oriented Software. Brussels (1998) 52-53

23.Booch, G., Rumbaugh, J., Jacobson, I.: The Unified Modeling Language User Guide. Addison-Wesley, Reading, Mass. (1999)

24.Poels, G., Dedene, G.: Distance-based software measurement: necessary and sufficient properties for software measures. Information and Software Technology. 42 (2000) 35-46

25.Zhang, K., Shasha, D.: Simple fast algorithms for the editing distance between trees and related problems. Siam J. on Computing. 18 (1989) 1245-1262

26.Oommen, B.J., Zhang, K., Lee, W.: Numerical Similarity and Dissimilarity Measures Between Two Trees. IEEE Trans. on Computers, 45 (1996) 1426-1434

27.Tzerpos, V., Holt, R.C.: MoJo: A Distance Metric for Software Clusterings, In: Proc. 6th Working Conf. on Reverse Engineering (WCRE'99). Atlanta (1999)

28.Poels, G., Dedene, G.: Modelling and measuring object-oriented software attributes with proximity structures, In: Proc. 3rd Int'l Workshop on Quantitative Approaches in Object-Oriented Software Eng. Lisbon (1999) 1-22

29.de Vries, E.J., Maes, R., Dedene, G., Viaene, S., Poels, G., Snoeck, M.: Object Models for Customer Relations in the Front-Office. Tech. rep. PrimaVera 98-11, University of Amsterdam (1998)

30.Lampel, J., Mintzberg, H.: Customizing Customization, Sloan Management Review. 38 (1996)

31.Snoeck, M., Poels, G., Dedene, G.: Reusing Business Models. Tech. rep. DTEW 9934, Catholic University of Leuven (1999)

32.Poels, G., Dedene, G.: Moving from OOAD to COAD. In: Proc. 8th Object Technology Conf. (OT'2000). Oxford (2000)

StateLator - Behavioral Code Generation as an Instance of a Model Transformation

Thomas Behrens[1] and Simon Richards[2]

[1] Johann Wolfgang Goethe-Universität, Datenbanken und Informationssysteme,
Robert Mayer-Str.11-15, D-654 Frankfurt a.M., Germany
behrens@dbis.informatik.uni-frankfurt.de
[2] Alpheus Solutions Ltd.,
6, Lombard St., London, EC3V 9EA, England
simon.richards@alpheus.com

Abstract. A key issue in software engineering is the repeatable and rapid transition of software models into executable code. We have been faced with the specific problem to produce behavioral code from a UML State Diagram in the context of Enterprise Distributed Object Computing. Rather than associate code templates with the meta model elements of a StateMachine, we represent the StateMachine through a micro architecture based on design patterns represented as newly created model elements. The Object Constraint Language is used to specify these newly created model elements. From this specific solution (StateLator) we infer the generalized mechanism of a *Model Transformation* that algorithmically captures a transformation from a higher to a lower abstraction level in a software model and hence makes this process flexible and repeatable.

1 Introduction

Significant effort in software engineering is spent on the evolution of a software model into an executable implementation. Evolving a model is necessary because a large number of model constructs on the higher levels of abstraction do not map directly onto low level, programming language constructs. This problem can be addressed from two sides: Bottom-up, by extending programming environments through architectural layers [1], frameworks [2], or language extensions [3]. Top-down, by either elaborating or transforming the model until it can directly be mapped onto a programming language. The resulting effort has two primary causes. First, the large number of suitable solutions is embedded in an even larger number of unsuitable solutions. In practice, due to the large number of problem parameters, it is often difficult to predict in advance whether a solution is suitable or unsuitable. Second, similar evolution steps have to be applied for a large number of similar constructs. The significant part of this evolution is still of elaborational nature based on a "best-practices" approach, resulting in time consuming and error prone activities.

B. Wangler, L. Bergman (Eds.): CAiSE 2000, LNCS 1789, pp. 401–416, 2000

In this paper we present a mechanism that we refer to as Model Transformation to support the top-down approach.

This mechanism is derived from a solution to the particular problem in the domain of Enterprise Distributed Object Computing (EDOC), namely to generate behavioral code from a StateMachine in a UML model. Behavioral code generation demonstrates the strength of the Model Transformations mechanism in two ways. First, behavioral code generation is not well supported within current modeling tools, specifically not in EDOC. Secondly, the results of applying the transformation are clearly visible within the generated code. Generation of behavioral code is not, per se, the innovative aspect discussed here. Translations from a state diagram to executable code exist for various programming languages and target architectures. The main difference is that in contrast to directly creating a low level implementation target, the presented approach translates StateMachine related model constructs into a semantically equivalent micro architecture on the UML model level. The created model elements in turn can be directly mapped into a program language. This mapping can then be realized through the code generation function of any standard tool. This particular Model Transformation has been implemented as a prototype (StateLator), which allows us to discuss experience gained with this approach. A further aspect of our discussion is dedicated to the representation of the Model Transformation. As described, the result of applying the Model Transformation is a set of newly created model elements, or meta model instances. We show how the Object Constraint Language (OCL), which is part of the UML specification, can be used to specify these model elements.

The paper is organized as follows. In the remainder of the introduction, we define some terms and present related work. The main presentation is divided into two major parts. The first part presents StateLator, the specific instance of a Model Transformation, the second part the generalized mechanism. We believe that both abstraction levels are equally important. At the end we summarize our findings and look at future work. The discussion throughout the paper is restricted to UML[1] models. Given its evolution into the most widely practically applied modeling language since its acceptance through the OMG, this is not seen as a limitation. The prerequisite for the application of the concept in general, though, is accessibility to the underlying meta model.

We use the following terms throughout this paper in the meaning defined here. We refer to the process of creating a lower level abstraction from a higher level abstraction as *Evolution* or synonymously as *Transition*. These terms do not imply how this process is performed. *Elaboration* is then defined as a manual evolution and *Transformation*, or synonymously *Translation*, as an automated evolution, captured by an algorithm. The terms alone do not suggest any implementation technique. *Architecture* generally refers to the system level of design, addressing structural issues of component compositions and mechanisms [4]. We use the term though in the sense of a micro-architecture [5], as we feel that the term object-oriented design (see [6]) does not suffice to address the organization of structures at this level.

---

[1] in Version 1.1, where not explicitly stated otherwise.

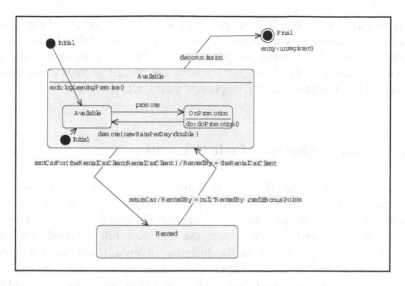

Fig. 1. The StateMachine represents the behavioral specification of the RentalCar class

The work on StateCharts [7] provides the basis for StateLator. We use some of the semantic ambiguities, [8] and [9], to show the flexibility of StateLator. The basic ideas for the application of pattern based program design can be recognized in the work of many other researchers and practitioners. The work of [1] can now be said to have entered mainstream software development [11]. In contrast to the manual evolution of such pattern architectures, we recommend the automated induction through the Model Transformation. [12] provides a description of an automated solution, that is based on design pattern transformation. The focus of this work is the maintenance cycle, it requires the code to be reverse engineered into a class diagram (our model level) in order to retrospectively apply automated primitive transformations. Where we recommend the use of OCL as a standardized language for syntax and semantics, a proprietary transformation language is used, in which only the syntax of the primitives is expressed. The Model Transformation approach allows for traceability, model consistency and integrity of different models, e.g. [13], describes how different software development artifacts can be linked and kept consistent. The need to address these requirements manifests itself in the software development practice and has triggered a number of practical recommendations, specific to UML, in [14] and [15]. In contrast to the latter procedural solutions, we present with the Model Transformation an algorithmic approach on the model level. In a number of places we refer to the work of Shlaer/Mellor [16], [17], [18]. Central to their object oriented approach is the method of Recursive Design. Recursive Design is focusing on an automated transition of an analysis model through a design (architecture) model into an implementation with strong emphasis on the autogeneration of the code as a final step. The automation is achieved through Transformation Rules, which transform the conceptual entities into instances of the architectural objects and further architectural entities into archetype code (instances of code templates).

A typographic note: Words with special meaning in the context of the presented examples are printed in capitalized one-word base font (DefinedClass). General multi-word technical terms are printed capitalized (Model Transformation). Where necessary, elements of the UML meta model are printed in capitalized one-word Courier font (StateMachine) to emphasize their UML semantics.

2 StateLator - Behavioral Code Generation

It is the authors' experience that very little behavioral (or dynamic) modeling takes place within most software development projects, especially in the area of EDOC. Powerful modeling techniques, such as StateChart Diagrams[2] as a visual representation of a StateMachine, are seldom used to their full potential. The authors believe that a principle reason is the inability of most CASE tools to generate behavioral code. Further, some software processes, such as the Rational Unified Process [19], indicate, incorrectly in our view, that most entity objects should not be modeled through State Diagrams, declaring them to dumb and data heavy objects. Based on our experience much more attention should be paid to State Diagrams in EDOC. This has been summarized by [2], page 287 concisely as "StateMachines are efficient, simple, adaptable and understandable". A StateMachine can be used to specify the dynamics of instances of classes, use cases, or the entire system. We restrict our approach to the dynamics of a class, which is probably the most common use [9]. In order to encourage this use in our projects, we were investigating flexible possibilities to integrate behavioral code generation with an existing tool. The result is StateLator, a utility that transforms a UML model to provide a low level design abstraction for a StateMachine.

In this part we introduce the specific problem that StateLator addresses through an example. This is followed by an explanation of the micro architecture we use to represent a StateMachine. We then show how OCL can be used to specify a Model Transformation followed by the description of the prototype implementation.

2.1 Example "Rental Car"

This section demonstrates with an example how a StateMachine can be represented on a lower abstraction level through a set of meta model instances, i.e. we present a possible micro architecture for the executability of a StateMachine.

Fig. 1 shows the State Diagram of the RentalCar class (DefinedClass[3]), which is shown in the context with a RentalCarClient in Fig. 2. It is the result of the entity specification of an analyst. This specification would normally be manually translated

---

[2] We abbreviate StateChart Diagrams as State Diagrams.
[3] DefinedClass in the sense that it is the class whose behavior is semantically defined by the State Diagram.

into the programming language of choice. StateLator transforms the RentalCar class and the underlying StateMachine into a set of new model elements.

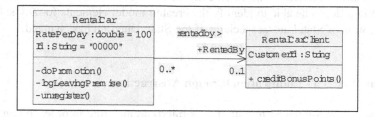

Fig. 2. A static specification for the RentalCar class

The output of the transformation is shown in Fig. 3 and Fig. 4. We use the StateMachine to derive the protocol, the Operations and the Methods. The latter will be possible, if the modeler has attached Actions and Events to Transitions. We restrict triggering Events to represent CallEvents, which allows us to specify Operations as shown in Fig. 3. We have chosen this approach as most programming languages support the concept of an operation natively. Operations with the Stereotype <<SMGenerated>>[4] are created by StateLator (e.g. decommission()). Fig. 4 shows the pattern based architecture for the execution model of the StateMachine. We chose to create the new classes within the scope of the RentalCar class and thereby achieved unobtrusiveness and also addressed potential namespace issues. Model elements created in this way are static and can be easily translated into a programming language. This translation (code generation) is provided by most tools.

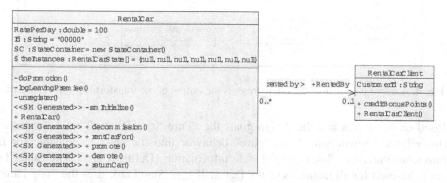

Fig. 3. StateLator transforms the static business specification and the StateMachine into an enriched static implementation specification

---

[4] The Stereotype is used here to indicate the Tagged Value of SMGenerated = true. It is actually not used in the implementation, but used here merely for ease of presentation.

The exception, in this case RentalCarStateException, is used to indicate a violation of the protocol, following the semantics that unexpected events are not tolerated [8]. The identification of the model elements that have been created by the Model Transformation is based on the UML concept of Tagged Values. The identification is required in order to be able to identify the created model elements for any subsequent re-application of StateLator, especially, if the State Diagram has changed.

2.2 State Pattern - Codification through Abstractions

We chose to employ the State Pattern as a micro architecture in order to compose the larger architecture of a StateMachine. This architecture is a UML abstraction of a StateMachine in a low level design target independent of a programming language. There are several derivations on the state pattern as presented in [21]. A very detailed description can be found in [22].

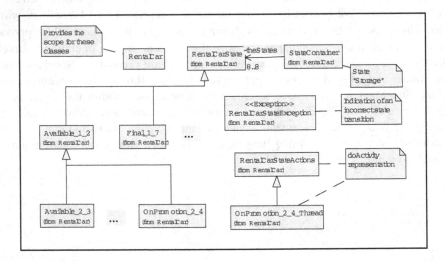

Fig. 4. A micro pattern architecture represents the output of the transformation for StateLator

Based on the forces and the design goals the "Pure State Pattern" has been chosen. This allows a separation of the "pure" behavior into the class responsible for the transition (PureStateClass) and the state information (DefinedClass). The StateClass can be re-used for all instances of the DefinedClass. StateLator uses the State Pattern as a proven architecture and applies this architecture recursively to composite states (StateMachines). This provides an architecture that is both resilient and adaptable. Consistency and standardization in the overall design follows through a wide spread application of this architecture in the overall system wide design.

2.3   Model Transformation Specification

In the previous sections we presented the "RentalCar" example and demonstrated the application of our chosen architecture. It now remains for us to define, how the new model elements relate to the existing elements. It is necessary to specify the Model Transformation, which will capture the creation of this architecture algorithmically. In this section we introduce the vocabulary and techniques that allow us to capture this specification. The focus is primarily the specification of the resulting meta model instances, the declarative aspect, not so much the programmatic aspect. We use OCL [23] as the specification language, and demonstrate its usage with an excerpt from StateLator. In section 3.2 we discuss the motivation for OCL as well as its limitations.

Any non-trivial transformation such as StateLator, cannot generally be presented as one single large specification. It becomes unmanageable. Hence, we show first, how this single specification can be split into smaller manageable specifications. This makes the overall approach scaleable and allows for the re-use of specifications. Therefore we represent the Model Transformation through sub-transformations.

A Model Transformation can be represented as a function:

$$f: uml \rightarrow uml. \tag{1}$$

where *uml* is an instance of a UML model represented by its meta model instances. We can choose to represent the Model Transformation by a sequence of functions:

$$f_{ReferenceName}: uml \rightarrow uml. \tag{2}$$

referred to as sub-functions. f can then be represented as:

$$f = f_{ReferenceName} \circ .. \circ f_{ReferenceName\,i}, \, i \in N. \tag{3}$$

We represent the UML model *uml* in a Model Transformation function f and $f_{ReferenceName}$ through a specific meta model element. This provides the context element for the related OCL expressions. However, this does not limit the accessibility to any other model elements[5], because of the defined associations in the UML meta model and the navigability along those associations. Only a coverage analysis of all individual Model Transformation functions would allow a statement about the subset of the UML model that is required to perform the transformation. For practical purposes this is an important analysis, as e.g. larger models are generally segregated for change management.

As indicated above, it is not our goal to present the complete specification for the Model Transformations for StateLator here. Instead Table 1 provides a high level overview of the main sub-functions, represented by their context element and the created model elements.

---

[5] In case of StateLator, the context element is a meta model instance of type Class. This Class does not necessarily contain all Classes that represent the type of an AssociationEnd in an Association with the context class, although they are required for the specification.

Table 1. Model Transformation Summary

Context Element	Transformation Result Elements
StateMachine	Exception (state exception)
	Class (storage container class)
	Attribute (storage space)
State	Class (abstract state pattern class)
Nested State	Class (state pattern class)
	Generalization (between parent state pattern class and nested state pattern class)
Transition / CallEvent	Operation (on the entity class)
History (nested PseudoState)	Attribute (storage space)
	Class (storage class)
do-ActionSequence	Class (thread execution class)
exit-ActionSequence	Operation (exit action)
entry-ActionSequence	Operation (entry action)

We present the OCL specification in table format. Table 2 presents a self-contained subset of the transformation function for the context element of a Nested State. The left hand side of the table shows the attributes and associations of model elements that will be added to the model with their attributes and associations as defined by the UML meta model. The right side shows the OCL expressions that specifies the value of the attribute or the association. The context for the OCL expressions is the context parameter of the transformation sub-function. A pre-condition at the top of the table indicates, if this function is applicable for a specific context instance. Multiple output elements of the same meta model type are unambiguously identified by a reference number (Ref.). In order to refer to an output meta model element of another transformation function, we use the following function:

$$mme(f_{ReferenceName}, metaModelElement, id). \tag{4}$$

where $f_{ReferenceName}$ is the referenced function, and id is the reference number assigned to the meta model element instance of type $metaModelElement$ in the transformation table of that function.

In order to simplify the presentation, the following OCL functions are defined for the presented example:

$$State.getLevel():Integer, \tag{5}$$
post: result = if parent->isEmpty() Then 1 Else parent.getLevel() + 1 endif.

$$State.getTopState():State, \tag{6}$$
post: result = if parent->isEmpty() Then self Else parent.getTopState() endif.

$$Integer.asString():String, \tag{7}$$
post: result = "returns the String representation of the Integer".

$$MTUtility.unique (context:String):Integer, \tag{8}$$
post: return = "unique number in the context *context*".

The following steps determine a basic algorithm for the Model Transformation, where the dependency is defined based on the usage of *mme*. First, resolve any cyclic dependencies between the sub-functions. Second, order the sub-functions based on the dependency relation to produce an execution order. Third, create the model elements that satisfy the OCL specifications for the sub-functions in that order by iterating over, potentially multiple, instances of the context elements associated with those OCL specifications.

Table 2. OCL specification for a context element of State

CONTEXT ELEMENT: STATE

$f_{NestedState}$(S: State)	pre-condition: not parent->isEmpty()
Class - Ref:	
Name	name.concat("_"). concat(getLevel().asString()).concat("_"). concat(MTUtility.unique("STATES").asString())
IsActive	False
isRoot	False
isLeaf	not oclIsTypeOf(CompositeState)
isAbstract	False
stereotype	"Singleton"
feature	feature->append(mme($f_{NestedState}$(self), Attribute,))
Attribute - Ref:	
name	"theParent"
changeable	#frozen
initialvalue	mme($f_{NestedState}$(self), Generalization,).supertype
multiplicity	"1..1"
type	mme(f_{State}(getTopState()), Class,)[6]
Generalization - Ref:	
discrimantor	""
supertype	mme($f_{NestedState}$(parent), Class,)
subtype	mme($f_{NestedState}$(self), Class,)

---

[6] This refers to the abstract state class that is created for the top state of the StateMachine.

2.4 StateLator Implementation

The Model Transformation that generates behavioral code from a State Diagram has been implemented for the target programming languages Java and C++ using Rational Rose. The translation of the OCL specification into Rose's proprietary scripting API was done manually.

We feel that StateLator provides sufficient functionality to carry out serious behavioral modeling that results in an executable implementation. In the light of the generalization in section 3 we point out the following observations that we made with the prototype.

Access to the specification of the transformation and ease of modification are essential. Based on this flexibility it is possible to provide different transformations with the most appropriate semantics, especially where the semantics are ambiguous, [9] and [8], new constructs need to be supported[7], or we experimented – beyond parameterization – with the existing architecture.

Various analysis entity classes have been modeled using State Diagrams. With StateLator it is possible to transform these classes quickly into a proven implementation pattern without individual elaboration. Making changes and reapplying the transformation is simple, quick and repeatable.

While moving towards a transformational approach we believe that the role of reverse and round-trip engineering will reduce in relevance, and probably disappear completely. Code regions or low level design patterns represent higher abstractions that cannot be easily derived without significant effort. In the case of StateLator, a reverse engineering tool would need to be able to re-create a State Diagram from the program code.

3 Model Transformation Mechanism

After some experimentation with StateLator, we believe that the mechanism of Model Transformation has general value for the software development process. A number of characteristics of Model Transformations allow us to speed up the development process by making it repeatable and quickly applicable. The first section enumerates and discusses these characteristics. The majority are demonstrated in the StateLator example. The section starts with a brief discussion of the current views about the evolution of models, illustrating two fundamental approaches. We discuss our findings in the context of each approach. In the second section we illustrate the benefits of using OCL as the specification language for the Model Transformation. Finally, we enumerate some other applications for the Model Transformation.

---

[7] We added doActivities that have been added in UML1.3 [0]. The implementation effort was ca. 2 man days. This is insignificant compared to the overhead individual developers require to add functionality through an "re-inventing the wheel" process.

3.1 Transformational Approach for Enterprise Distributed Object Computing

[25] summarizes a discussion of two inherently different approaches to evolve a model into executable code. Mellor/Lee present three different distinct abstraction levels (analysis - design/architecture - implementation) that exist independent of each other, and are related to each other through transformation rules, based on proprietary languages. Recursive Design is an instance of this approach. Martin/Booch on the other hand advocate a gradual transition from the highest to the lowest abstraction level through multiple models. These models are related to each other through standard object-oriented concepts.

We see the following problem with the former approach. Recursive Design makes the central assumption that 1% of the code is generated automatically from an object oriented model, that captures all semantics. Based on this assumption the conclusion that object-oriented analysis does *not* imply object-oriented design and implementation is possible. There are no maintenance requirements for the code (which is compared in [16], pg. 71, to maintaining the output of a compiler). Though we can believe that this holds true for embedded or real-time systems development, where Recursive Design originated, our experience is that the 1% - assumption does not hold true for EDOC. The issue is, that if the ratio is anything less than 1%, a programmer is required to navigate, modify and maintain the code. Object oriented concepts have supported this requirement well in the past. Components, such as frameworks or databases, are as well often integrated through an object model. Consequently, we come to the conclusion that the object-oriented paradigm as a concept should apply to all abstraction levels, leading us to support the latter approach for a gradual transition. This approach, though, does not make any statement, concerning how the transition is performed. The majority of the evolution of a model is carried out through elaboration, thereby limiting the rate of the process. The Model Transformation complements this approach with the transformational aspect of Recursive Design and accelerates a gradual process through the following characteristics.

Automated Repeatable Process. The Model Transformation represents an specification to evolve a model, respectively specific related meta model instances. This is a mechanistic task that can be executed automatically and can be applied to a large number of instances.

Highly Customizable and Adaptable. The Model Transformation is easily adjustable to accommodate new requirements in the system architecture, to experiment with different evolution paths or to fine tuning based on experience with the current implementation. Any changes can then be propagated quickly.

Increased Reliability. The reliability of the resulting lower level abstraction is improved because it is generated using an individually verifiable, well-testable pattern. The object oriented paradigm can be used consistently throughout different abstraction levels.

Capture Experience. Elaborational refinement of models can be captured and "replayed" through a Model Transformation. This leverages knowledge of experienced roles. Furthermore it makes it possible to control and maintain policies and standards.

Re-use. Re-use is fostered through the use of Model Transformations within projects and across and organizations. The re-use of Model Transformations makes it possible to automate "best practices" and to re-use proven architectures.

Addressing Complexity. The input and output of the Model Transformation is a model. This allows us to use the output of one Model Transformation as the input for another. Such a combination of Model Transformations makes it possible to break complex evolution steps apart and address them individually. On the other hand it is possible to aggregate and chain independent Model Transformations.

Model Traceability. Resulting model elements are on a lower abstraction level. All required information is already part of the existing model in a different representation. No further trace information, desirable to trace requirements and analyze change impact, is required in addition to the Model Transformation specification. The resulting elements can always be re-generated, if the input model and the algorithm are preserved.

In summary we propose a practical, gradual approach that automates part of the evolution of a model and can be applied incrementally and for subsets of the model *(Recursive Modeling)*. As the Model Transformation is applicable to all abstraction levels of the software development process, it extends the transformational design approach described in [26] to all development stages. New model elements can be created unobtrusively or temporary, as in the example of StateLator. This is suitable, if the Model Transformation results in completely generated executable code (in conjunction with other fully automated steps such as code generation and compilation). On the other hand it is possible to create new permanent and visible model elements. This is suitable, if the model elements need to be further processed through manual elaboration. Hence, the Model Transformation complements the elaborational approach in as far as both can coexist as part of the same process in any order. We point out though that the intertwined application of the elaborational and transformational approach requires the ability a) to identify automatically created model elements, b) to identify invalidated (i.e. inappropriately manually modified) elaborated model elements and c) to preserve elaborated elements, that are not invalidated.

3.2 Object Constraint Language as a Specification Language

OCL, which is part of the UML specification [23] is used to specify semantics as constraints that cannot (or cannot easily) be expressed visually through UML diagrams. The goal is to provide the various roles involved in the software development process, from analyst (to specify semantics) to programmer (to provide an implementation that fulfills the specified semantics), with a common language to define sufficiently precise semantics about the modeled domain [27].

We feel a natural approach to look at the output of a Model Transformation is as set of post conditions that need to be fulfilled by the resulting model. The primary aspect of the Model Transformation approach is the specification, i.e. the definition of the resulting model, and not the computation, i.e. the execution of the transformation. It is possible, as shown in Table 2 for a sub-function, to extend this "Design By

Contract" view to determine the applicability of a Model Transformation by a set of pre-conditions that must be fulfilled by the input model. From this specification viewpoint, OCL is well suited to describe the transformation. Further, OCL provides easy access and navigability along the model and meta model element associations. In addition, with its standardization as part of UML, it is becoming more widespread in the modeling community. This is important as the flexibility to experiment with different variations of a Model Transformation depends on the effort to modify the specifications. OCL is easy to learn and is established as a standard. It is used across the development process by various roles and therefore every role is able to define the specification for a Model Transformation.

Some limitations in the semantics of OCL have been identified [28]. Further, OCL is an expression and not a programming language. It is not possible to write program logic or flow control in OCL (see as well [29]). Although it is possible to represent some computational aspect in OCL, we find that there are more suitable imperative programming languages, which provide features such as iterations, selections, etc.. It would be possible to combine or embed the OCL specifications in such a language, comparable to the evolution of SQL. Further, we do not exclude that for very complex Model Transformations the pre and post conditions can be related to each other through more powerful techniques such as rule based engines. None of these considerations, though, eliminate the need for the specification aspect, hence our preferred usage of OCL. Some of the limitations and problems listed have already been addressed in [24]. Further [3],provides an approach to a formal meta model for OCL, resolving some of the semantic ambiguities. These probably will be reflected in revision 2. of the UML.

3.3 Further Examples for the Model Transformation

In addition to StateLator, we experimented with the Model Transformation approach in a number of areas. In general we inferred the applicability from the repeatable and mechanistic aspect of a process step. The following sections enumerate briefly other areas of application on different abstraction levels.

"Business Model" to "System Model" Transformation. [31] describes a simple algorithm to identify information system use cases from the business model. If the business model is captured in a UML model, we can use a Model Transformation to perform these steps automatically and create a first set of resulting system use cases from the business model.

"Use Case Realizations" Creation. [19], section "Tool Mentor", describes how to derives use case realizations, a representation of the design perspective of a use case, from a use case. The base part of this process is fairly mechanistic and lends itself to be captured in a Model Transformation.

Event Distribution Mechanism. Through defined stereotypes of a Dependency, <<publish>> and <<subscribe>>, we provide a set of base functionality to integrate with the protocol of a messaging service.

These examples should point out, that the applicability of Model Transformation is not limited to the abstractions of low level design and implementation. In addition its usage is not directly related to patterns as in the case of StateLator. Nevertheless, we recognize that the likelihood for applicability and effectiveness is related to the ability to carry out a large number of steps mechanically. This tends to be more often the case for lower abstraction levels.

4   Conclusions and Future Work

Models are created in the software development process as intermediate abstractions on different levels between the domain and the executing code as the final deliverable. The speed and the quality of the evolution relate directly to the software project turnaround. Any transformation, i.e. automation of the evolution, of models towards a lower level of abstraction contributes to those requirements. We have shown that the Model Transformation mechanism can be used to perform such a transformation. In contrast to other transformational approaches, it is gradual and can be applied on all abstraction levels captured by the UML. Individual instances of the Model Transformation can be combined to produce more complex ones. The last two characteristics result from the fact that the input and output of the Model Transformation is a UML model. In a UML model a Model Transformation waives the requirement for traceability as the trace information is represented by the specification of the transformation and the order of their application. However, we have no illusions, that our approach will eliminate procedural or tool supported consistency management, specifically where it is combined with elaboration. As long as elaboration of a model is required, the Model Transformation mechanism is able to coexist with it. We have indicated potential difficulties that need to be resolved. As a suitable specification language for a Model Transformation we have suggested OCL. The main aspect of the transformation is a specification that defines what the requirements for the resulting model are and not how it is created. OCL provides enough formalism to capture this specification unambiguously in addition to its ease of use and practical acceptance as part of the UML standard. We recommend, though, that it should be embedded into a base control flow language. With StateLator we have presented one instance of the Model Transformation in detail, including a prototype implementation. It provides a complete behavioral code generation in Java and C++ for a class, that is specified by a StateMachine. This allowed us to verify some of the general aspects of the Model Transformation approach. We further conclude that a translational approach in general requires powerful repository based modeling tools to capture detailed complex semantics.

For StateLator we are looking to complete missing aspects of the UML StateMachine, as tools start to support them and the integration of inheritance [31]. Further, we elaborate our examples for higher UML abstraction layers. With the advent of the XMI specification [33], a stream based model interchange format, which is based on the eXtensible Markup Language (XML), Model Transformation tools can share a standard exchange format with the modeling tools. As the first vendors start to support this format, we are currently looking to provide an implementation that is independent of a proprietary API, such as Rose, but instead is based on XMI. Direct support for OCL as a specification language for the Model Transformation is part of our target architecture, which is illustrated in Fig. 5.

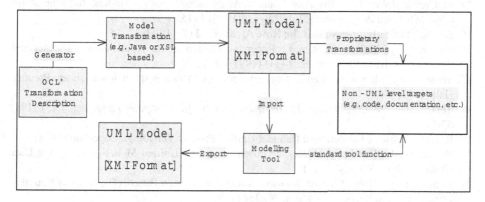

Fig. 5. A tool architecture that allows to integrate the Model Transformation into the standard development process

References

1. Object Management Group (ed.): CORBA Specification Version 2.3. Formal Specification formal/98-12-1, Framingham (1998)
2. ObjectSpace, Inc.: Voyager ORB Ver. 3.1 (1999)
3. Batory, Don; Dasari, Sankar; Geraci, Bart e.a.: The GenVoca Model of Software-System Generation. In: IEEE Software, 11 (5) (1994) 89–94
4. Shaw, Mary; Garlan, David: Software Architecture Perspectives On An Emerging Discipline. Prentice Hall (1996)
5. Booch, Grady: Object Solutions. Addison Wesley (1995)
6. Monroe, Robert T.; Kompanek, Andrew; Melton, Ralph; e.a.: Architectural Styles, Design Patterns, and Objects. In: IEEE Software, 14 (1) (1997) 43–52
7. Harel, David: Statecharts: A visual formalism for complex systems. In: Science of Computer Programming, 8 (1987) 231–274
8. Cook, Steve; Daniels, John: Designing Object Systems Object Oriented Modelling with Syntropy. Prentice Hall (1994)
9. Barbier, Franck; Briand, Henri; Dano, Benedicte e. a.: The Executability of Object–Oriented Finite State Machines. In: Journal for Object Oriented Programming, 11 (4), July/August (1998) 16–24
10. Gamma, Erich; Helm, Richard; Johnson, Ralph e. a.: Design Patterns: Abstraction and Reuse of Object-Oriented Design. In: ECOOP '93 - Object-Oriented Programming. Proceedings (1993) 46–421
11. Gamma, Erich; Beck, Kent: JUnit: A Cook's Tour. In: Java Report, 4 (5) (1999) 27–38

12. Tokuda, Lance; Bartory, Don: Automated Software Evolution via Design Pattern Transformations. In: Proceedings of the 3rd Int. Symposium on Applied Corporate Computing, Monterrey, Mexico (1995)
13. Grundy, John; Hosking, John; Mugridge, Warwick B.: Inconsistency Management for Multiple-View Software Development Environments. In: IEEE Transactions On Software Engineering, 24 (11) (1998) 961–981
14. McGregor, John: The Fifty-Foot Look at Analysis and Design Models. In: Journal for Object Oriented Programming, July/August (1998) 1–15
15. Schultz, Tom: Multiple Models. In: Rose Architect, 2 (1) (1999) 12–15
16. Shlaer, Sally; Mellor, Stephen J.: Recursive Design of an Application - Independent Architecture. In: IEEE Software, 14 (1) (1997) 61–72
17. Shlaer, Sally; Mellor, Stephen J.: Object Lifecycles Modeling the world in states. Prentice Hall (1992)
18. Shlaer, Sally; Mellor, Stephen J.: Recursive Design. In: Computer Language, 7 (3) (199) 53ff.
19. Rational Software Corporation: Rational Unified Process Version 5.. Cupertino (1998)
20. Booch, Grady; Rumbaugh, James; Jacobsen, Ivar: The Unified Modeling Language User Guide. Addison Wesley (1999)
21. Gamma, Erich; Helm, Richard; Johnson, Ralph e. a.: Design Patterns Elements of Reusable Object-Oriented Software. Addison Wesley (1994)
22. Martin, Robert C.; Riehle, Dirk; Buschmann, Frank (eds.): Pattern Languages Of Program Design 3. Addison Wesley (1998)
23. Object Management Group, Rational; Microsoft; HP; Oracle e.a. (eds.): UML Semantics Version 1.1. (1997)
24. Object Management Group, UML Revision Task Force (ed.): UML Semantics Version 1.3. (1999)
25. Fraser, Steven; Martin, Robert C.; Mellor, Stephen J. e.a.: Translation: Myth or Reality?, Summary of the Panel / Debate Session. In: Proceedings of OOPSALA '96 (1996) 441–443
26. Gossain, Sanjiv: Object Modeling and Design Strategies Tip and Techniques. SIGS Publications (1997)
27. Warmer, Jos; Kleppe, Anneke: The Object Constraint Language - Precise Modeling With UML. Addison Wesley (1999)
28. Richters, Mark; Gogolla, Martin: On Formalizing the UML Object Constraint Language OCL. In: Conceptual Modeling - ER'98, Proceedings, Springer Verlag (1998) 449–464
29. Mandel, Luis; Cengarle, Victoria: On the Expressive Power of OCL. In: FM'99 - Formal Methods, Proceedings, Springer Verlag (1999) 854–874
30. Richters, Mark; Gogolla, Martin: A Metamodel for OCL. In: UML'99 - The Unified Modeling Language, Proceedings, Springer Verlag (1999)
31. Jacobsen, Ivar; Ericson, Maria; Jacobsen, Agneta: The Object Advantage, Business Process Reengineering with Object Technology. Addison Wesley (1995)
32. Harel, David; Kupferman, Orna: On the Inheritance of State-Based Object Behavior. The Weizmann Institute of Science, Rehovot Israel, Department of Computer Science and Applied Mathematics, Internal Report, MCS99-12 (1999)
33. Object Management Group, Fujitsu, IBM, Oracle, Recerca Informatica, Unisys e.a. (eds.): XMI Specification. (1998)

An Overview of RoZ :
A Tool for Integrating UML and Z Specifications

Sophie Dupuy, Yves Ledru, and Monique Chabre-Peccoud

BP72 –38402 Saint-Martin d'Hères Cedex – France
Sophie.Dupuy@imag.fr

Abstract. This paper presents an approach and a tool to increase specification quality by using a combination of UML and formal languages. Our approach is based on the expression of the UML class diagram and its annotations into a Z formal specification. Our tool called RoZ supports this approach by making the transition between the UML world and the Z world : from an annotated class diagram, it automatically generates a complete Z specification, the specifications of some elementary operations and some proof obligations to validate the model constraints.

1 Introduction

Analysis and design methods for information systems propose graphical representations in order to express the structural, dynamic and functional aspects of a system. These aspects are described using models, each model representing a view of the studied domain. Graphical models facilitate communication with users by presenting a synthetic view of the system. But they are imprecise and incomplete. First their semantics can be ambiguous. This is for instance the case for composition in object-oriented modelling [1]. Moreover all the constraints compelling a system cannot be described graphically. So a model is generally complemented by constraints expressed in natural language. This prevents from consistency checking between the model and its constraints.

Recently, the Unified Modelling Language, UML [2], has been standardised by the OMG (Object Management Group). Like previous object-oriented notations, UML does not enable to express all integrity constraints. Thus some complementary proposals have been done to better integrate constraint expressions in UML. The first one [3] proposes to extend the meta-model adding to each class a part where constraints are written. The second one, the Object Constraint Language (OCL [4]) adds constraints expressed in first order logic to the diagrams. This language makes it possible to express constraints precisely and without ambiguity. Unfortunately, current OCL tools do not exploit this preciseness. Therefore we propose to take advantage of formal method tools to help verify the constraints of such annotated diagrams. Formal languages have precise notations based on mathematical concepts which enable to do proofs on specifications. Their use can help to increase information system quality by providing more precise and consistent models. But as writing formal specifications seems often difficult and tedious, we propose an

B. Wangler, L. Bergman (Eds.): CAiSE 2000, LNCS 1789, pp. 417-430, 2000
© Springer-Verlag Berlin Heidelberg 2000

approach and a tool generating automatically from an annotated UML diagram formal specifications in Z [5] and proof obligations.

Our tool, called RoZ, is integrated in the Rational Rose environment. It allows the integration of data specifications expressed in UML with formal annotations in the Z language. Starting from an annotated specification, the tool automatically produces a formal specification by translating the UML constructs and merging them with the annotations expressing predicates not included in the graphical design.

RoZ can also complete the UML class diagram by automatically generating in the UML environment Z specifications of elementary operations on the classes (attributes modifications, adding and deleting objects of the class). The tool also allows to record a guard for each operation and can generate corresponding proof obligations to show that guards are consistent with the actual pre-conditions of these operations. The Z-EVES prover [6] (from ORA) can be used to discharge these proof obligations.

The remainder of the paper is organised as follows. In section 2, an overview of our approach and the principles of our tool RoZ is presented. Section 3 proposes a guided tour of our tool. Section 4 introduces related work. Finally, section 5 draws the conclusions and perspectives of this work.

2   RoZ

2.1 Overview of the Approach

The proposed approach (Fig. 1) uses the complementarity of UML diagrams and the constraints annotating these diagrams to produce a formal specification :

1. From the initial problem, a UML specification is developed. The UML class diagram is edited as usual in the Rational Rose tool ([7, 8]) and complemented with annotations that state several constraints on the data and operation specifications. The annotations must be written in a formalism using first order logic and set theory in order to be expressible in Z. Actually they could be written in OCL.

2. This diagram is the starting point of a translation process which produces a formal specification skeleton. This translation gives a Z semantics for the UML diagram. Many translations from object-oriented notations into formal notations ([9, 10, 11, 12]) have already been proposed. But using a tool guarantees the strict correspondence between the UML model and the Z skeleton. In this paper, we will present the RoZ tool which automatically produces Z specification skeletons based on the translation rules for the main concepts (class, operation, association, inheritance, aggregation and composition) of class diagrams presented in [13].

3. The formal skeleton is completed with the annotations. This can also be done automatically by RoZ thanks to a classification of annotations presented in [14].

4. The formal specification is used to realise consistency checks with a Z prover, Z-EVES. First, the mutual consistency of the constraints can be checked. Secondly, operation guards can be designed to verify that operations do not violate constraints ([15]). The theorems to prove the validity of operations guards can be automatically generated by RoZ. Thanks to the translation process, this reasoning done on the formal specification can be reported to the UML diagram and to its annotations.

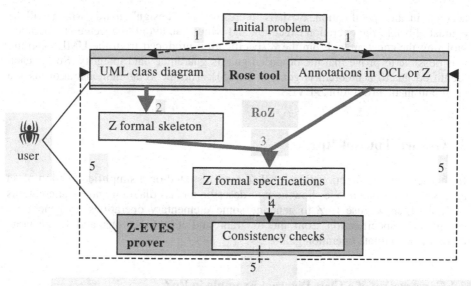

Fig. 1. the proposed approach

2.2 RoZ Principle

RoZ is an extension of the Rational Rose tool to integrate UML and Z notations. The Rose environment is used to build the UML models which are completed by formal annotations in Z. The annotations are expressed into forms. A form should contain all the information mandatory to complete Z skeletons. So each form corresponds to a kind of annotation. It is attached to the class diagram element that it complements. In the Rose environment, a pre-defined form is associated to each element of a diagram. We would like to modify these forms in order to add the fields needed to complete formal specifications. But this being impossible in Rose 4.0, we use the standard Rose forms.

From a class diagram and the information contained in its forms, RoZ uses Rose scripts to :

- *generate Z specifications*

From a UML class diagram and its annotations, a complete Z specification can be generated in a file. We choose to express Z specifications in the Latex style in order to be able to use Z tools such as Z-EVES.

- *generate elementary operations*

The main idea is that for some concepts, there are operations which always exist. For instance, a class has always operations to modify its attributes. Moreover if the class is concrete, there are also operations to add or remove an instance to or from the class instances. So for concrete classes, the specification of these operations can be generated automatically.

- *generate theorems to validate operation guards*

From a UML class diagram, elementary operations and a Z formal specification can be generated automatically. Data must often respect constraints which are not taken into account by the code generated automatically and only implicitly taken into account in the specification. So it is interesting to ``design'' guards which will be evaluated before the operation execution and which can avoid to execute an operation violating the constraints. From the Z specification produced from the UML diagram, it is possible to prove that the proposed guards guarantee data integrity. So for each identified guard, a theorem is generated ([15]). The theorems demonstration uses a semi-automatic proof tool Z-EVES.

3   Guided Tour of RoZ

In this section, the functionalities of RoZ are illustrated on a simplified version of an access control system. We show how to describe a class diagram and its annotations in RoZ. Then we use RoZ to generate some elementary operations, to generate a complete Z specification from the diagram and its annotations and to generate theorems to validate operation guards.

3.1 Construction of a Class Diagram Example in RoZ

To illustrate the use of RoZ, we describe a simplified version of the access control system presented in [16]. This model (Fig. 2) features two classes : "PERSON" and "GROUP". Each person has four attributes: his last and first names, the set of his telephone numbers and the number of his magnetic card. Each group is characterised by a name (e.g. "Accounting Department") and a code (e.g. "AccD"). One can note that the types of the attributes are expressed in the Z style. For instance, the "tel" attribute is multi-valued i.e. it corresponds to a set of telephone numbers (\finset tel).

The PersonGroupRel association links each person to one group.

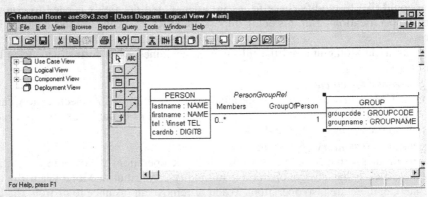

Fig. 2. Rose interface - the access control class diagram

This class diagram does not express the full specification of the application data. Three additional constraints complement this diagram :
1. Every person has at least one telephone number.

2. The card number is a key of persons.

3. The telephone numbers of the members of a given group have the same prefix.

The UML class diagram of the access control system is built in a class diagram window of the Rose environment. This diagram can be complemented by the expression of the constraints. The constraints are expressed in the Z Latex syntax in the "Documentation" field of the forms.

The first constraint (every person has at least one telephone number) holds on the attribute "tel". So it is written in the field "Documentation" of the attribute "tel" (Fig. 3). It is expressed in Z that the set of telephone numbers cannot be empty :

```
tel ≠∅
```

This is expressed in the Z Latex style:

```
tel \neq \empty
```

The second constraint (the card number is a key of persons) means that two different persons have distinct card numbers. It is a comparison between existing objects of the class, so it is in the field documentation of the class "PERSON" (Fig. 3) :

$$\forall p1, p2 : \text{Person} \mid p1 \neq p2 \bullet p1.\text{cardnb} \neq p2.\text{cardnb}$$

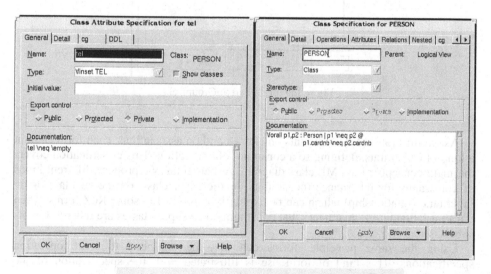

Fig. 3. the forms for "tel" and "Person"

Finally we have to express the third constraint (the telephone numbers of the members of a given group have the same prefix.). This constraint is related to the relationship between "PERSON" and "GROUP", so it is expressed in the "Documentation" field of "PersonGroupRel" (Fig. 4). Let us consider that we have defined a "prefix" function which gives the prefix of a telephone number. The constraint states that for two persons which belong to the same group, each telephone number of their sets of telephone numbers have the same prefix :

$$\forall p1, p2 : \text{Person} \mid$$
$$\text{GroupOfPerson}(p1) = \text{GroupOfPerson}(p2) \bullet$$
$$\forall t1 : p1.tel \bullet \forall t2 : p2.tel \bullet$$
$$\text{prefix}(t1) = \text{prefix}(t2)$$

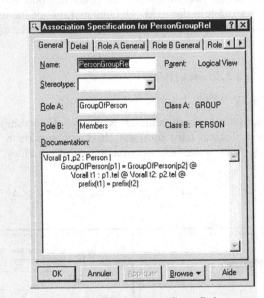

Fig. 4. the form «PersonGroupRel»

As we illustrate it for constraints on classes and on associations, each form contain a kind of constraints, defining so a constraint classification. This classification covers the main concepts of a UML class diagram. In particular, we propose different kinds of constraints for inheritance (constraints on the super-class, on the subclass or on inheritance relationship) which can be explicitly expressed in some RoZ forms. Then our translation into Z guarantees that constraints on a super-classes are inherited by its subclasses.

Using the same principle, forms can also be exploited to write operation specifications. This kind of form use is illustrated with the specification of the "ChangeLastname" operation in the next subsection.

This annotated UML diagram will be the basis for the generation of a specification (sect. 3.3).

3.2 Generation of Elementary Operations

In information systems, some operations associated to classes or associations are very often used. They enable to create or delete an object or a link, or to modify an attribute value. Their systematic generation has been studied in [17, 18].

RoZ uses the same principle to generate the specification of all the elementary operations of the diagram classes : for each attribute of a given class, a modification operation is generated. Moreover if the class is concrete, the specification of operations adding or deleting an object to/from the class objects are added.

The generation of elementary operations does not take into account the eventual constraints on a diagram. In order to check that an operation is consistent with the constraints, we must validate its guard by proving a theorem generated by RoZ (see 3.4)

For example, for the class "PERSON", the operations "ChangeLastname", "ChangeFirstname", "ChangeTel", "ChangeCardnb", "AddPerson" and "RemovePerson" are generated automatically by RoZ (Fig. 5). The specification of these operations is contained in their form.

For instance, let us consider "ChangeLastname" which modifies the last name of a person. In the operation part of "PERSON", one can see the operation signature : "ChangeLastname" has an argument "newlastname" which is the input parameter of the operation. In the "PostConditions" (Fig. 5) tab of the "ChangeLastname" operation, the post condition of the operation is written as a Z Latex style : it means that the new value of the attribute "lastname" is the argument of the operation "newlastname" and that the others attributes of "PERSON" are unchanged by the operation. RoZ also fills the "Semantics" tab with the key-word *intension operation* which signifies that "ChangeLastname" is an operation on the attributes of the class.

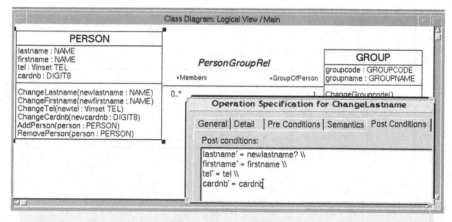

Fig. 5. Post-condition for «ChangeLastname»

3.3 Generation of a Z Specification

RoZ automatically generates the Z schema skeletons corresponding to a UML class diagram. The Z skeletons are produced by translation of the concepts (class, association, inheritance...) of the diagram. In order to complete these specification skeletons, you must add information like the definition of the types of the attributes and the constraints on the class diagram. In sections 3.1 and 3.2, we have shown how constraints and operation specifications can be included in the RoZ environment.

On the contrary, we did not find a place global to the model to express type definitions in the Rose standard forms. So type are not defined in the RoZ environment, but in a file containing them. In the example of access control system, we have to define the types NAME, TEL, DIGIT8, GROUPCODE and GROUPNAME. Moreover the third constraint (the telephone numbers of the members of a given group have the same prefix.) requires the declaration of the prefix function.

So from the class diagram and the annotations, RoZ generates a complete Z specification. For example, from the class "PERSON" and its annotations, RoZ generates two Z schemas ("PERSON" and "PersonExt"). A Z schema is a data specification structure composed of two parts: the declarations which constitute the local variable lexicon and the predicates expressing constraints on these variables. The "PERSON" schema defines the attributes of the class and the "PersonExt" one describes the set of existing persons. These schemas include the constraints expressed in the "Documentation" fields of "PERSON" and "tel". The constraint on the telephone numbers (constraint 1) is expressed in the Z schema defining attributes, while the key constraint (constraint 2) is defined in the Z schema representing the existing objects of "PERSON".

$$
\begin{array}{|l}
\hline
\_PERSON _____ \\
lastname : NAME \\
firstname : NAME \\
tel : \mathbb{F}\ TEL \\
cardnb : DIGIT8 \\
\hline
tel \neq \varnothing \\
\hline
\end{array}
$$

$$
\begin{array}{|l}
\hline
\_PersonExt _____ \\
Person : \mathbb{F}\ PERSON \\
\hline
\forall\, p1, p2 : Person \mid p1 \neq p2 \bullet p1.cardnb \neq p2.cardnb \\
\hline
\end{array}
$$

3.4 Theorems Generation

At this point, we have produced a Z specification and we can start to investigate the properties of our model. Let us consider the operation "ChangeTel" which changes the value of the "tel" attribute and corresponds to the following instruction :

```
tel := newtel?
```

The automatically generated specification for this operation is :

```
┌─ PERSONChangeTel ────────────────────────────────
│ ΔPERSON
│ newtel? : 𝔽 TEL
├──────────────────────────────────────────────────
│ lastname' = lastname
│ firstname' = firstname
│ tel' = newtel?
│ cardnb' = cardnb
└──────────────────────────────────────────────────
```

In this specification, newtel? is the input parameter. The last predicate constraints the new value of the "tel" attribute (denoted by tel') to be equal to the input parameter. The remaining predicate expresses that the other attributes keep their initial value. The first line of the declaration part ΔPERSON expresses that the effects of this operation are limited to change an object of type "PERSON".

Its actual pre-condition can be computed from the text of the specification and the constraints listed in the included schemas. When specifications get complex, it is good software engineering practice to state these pre-conditions more explicitly. For the "PERSONChangeTel" operation, we identify the pre-condition

```
newtel? ≠ ∅
```

This pre-condition depends only on the constraint concerning the "tel" attribute because the "PERSONChangeTel" operation only changes an object of type "PERSON" and is not promoted at the level of existing objects of "PERSON". So we do not have to take into account constraints on the existing objects of "PERSON" or on the association with "GROUP". These constraints will be considered for alternate versions of this operation which promote "PERSONChangeTel" at the level of the existing persons and for the operations on the "PersonGroupRel" association. For these alternate versions, the precondition become more complex in order to consider the key of " PERSON" and the telephone number prefix constraint.

We guess that the pre-condition (newtel? ≠ ∅) is strong enough to imply the actual pre-condition of the operation. This predicate states that the new set of telephone numbers must not be empty. We add it to the field "Pre Conditions" of the operation "ChangeTel":

```
newtel? \neq \empty
```

Then RoZ is used to generate a theorem to validate proposed pre-conditions for each operation. It uses the information given in the operation form to generate the following proof obligation for "ChangeTel" (Fig. 6):

```
\begin{theorem}{ PERSONChangeTel \_Pre}
        \forall PERSON ;newtel? : \finset TEL |
            newtel? \neq \empty @
                \pre PERSONChangeTel
\end{theorem}
```

It means that the proposed pre-condition (newtel? ☐ ☐) is stronger than the computed pre-condition (pre PERSONChangeTel).

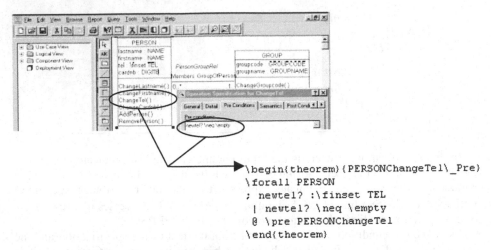

```
\begin{theorem}{PERSONChangeTel\_Pre}
\forall PERSON
; newtel? :\finset TEL
| newtel? \neq \empty
@ \pre PERSONChangeTel
\end{theorem}
```

Fig. 6. Generation of theorems

If you want to prove the theorems generated, you can use any Z standard prover. We use the Z-EVES theorem prover because it offers a high level of proof automation. For instance, the pre-condition theorem for "ChangeTel" is proved automatically using the following commands :

```
try lemma PERSONChangeTel\_Pre;
```

```
prove by reduce;
```

which demonstrates that the proposed pre-condition is correct.

4 Related Work

Two kinds of environments have been proposed to couple different kinds of notations. In the first one [19], the various specifications are developed independently and some consistency rules are defined to check the consistency between them. These tools have the advantage of being formalism-independent. But the consistency rules do not guarantee that the specifications are semantically equivalent. So if you use such tools to couple UML and formal specifications, you cannot be sure that the formal specifications are equivalent to the UML ones. The reasoning done on the formal specifications cannot be reported to the UML ones. The other kind of tools are based on some translation from a formalism to another one so as to have equivalent versions of the specifications. As this is the approach we have chosen, the following paragraphs develop the characteristics of such tools and a comparison with ours.

Some tools are based on meta-CASE such as GraphTalk ([20, 21, 18]). A meta-CASE is a tool intended to build other tools. Others, like ours, propose to extend existing environments. In particular, the Rational Rose tool is used to make the link between UML and VDM++ ([22]) and UML and Z ([23]). Using a meta-CASE enables to build exactly the desired environment. But its development is much longer than the extension of an existing tool and rarely reaches the standard of dedicated environments. Moreover, using a "standard" environment enables to keep close to the practice of conceptual modellers.

Another criterion of comparison is the way of coupling the different kinds of specifications. [21] and [23] propose multi-modelling environments in which the different kinds of specifications are available in the same modelling tool. Graphical and formal specifications are thus developed in parallel. In this approach, the different formalisms used must be mastered to be able to add constraints to formal specifications or to specify operations.

Another approach consists in automatically generating the formal specifications into a file. The main advantage is to have a file that can be used by the tools for formal notations. That is what is proposed in [24]. But [24] does not specify how the formal skeleton generated in the file can be complemented and how the model is updated taking into account the code added to the skeleton.

Our proposal goes on a little further by proposing to perform all the modelling work (diagrams and annotations) in the UML environment. Only the strictly necessary formal specifications are seen to permit their exploitation. This one depends on the level of mastery of the formal language. It is not necessary to know the details of the formal language to have a documentation with formal specification. But the verification of the formal specifications by proving operation pre-conditions for instance, requires a higher degree of expertise.

Moreover, tools like [22, 23] allow modifications of the model from both the UML and the formal method environments. We have chosen to use Rose as the only interface to the model which means that any update of the Z specifications should be done by modifying the corresponding model or annotations.

5 Conclusion and Perspectives

In this article, we present RoZ, an automate tool for specification and illustrate its use on a simple example. The RoZ tool aims at increasing system quality by adding precision to the system specification. It exploits the standard Rose environment to make UML notations and formal annotations live together: the class diagram provides the structure of Z formal skeleton while details are expressed in forms attached to the diagram. RoZ offers the following possibilities:

- automatic generation of Z formal specifications from an annotated UML class diagram,
- generation in Rose of the specifications of elementary operations on classes,
- generation of proof obligations to validate operation guards.

5.1 Advantages

An important characteristics of RoZ is that all the modelling work (diagrams and annotations) is realised in Rose to be as close as possible to the usual practitioner working environment. So the environment is employed as usual and some information can complement the diagrams when necessary. Our ambition is that it does not require to have a deep understanding of Z to be able to have complete Z specification. In particular, we expect that many constraints can be expressed be adapting similar ones from other RoZ diagrams (see 3.2).

The main advantage of RoZ is that it automatically realises some tedious work. First, it generates formal specifications from annotated UML diagrams. Secondly, it creates elementary operations on classes. Finally, it generates proof obligations. This automation limits human efforts of designers to write precise specifications and to check them.

Moreover RoZ offers guidance to know where to express each kind of annotation. In particular, the definition of the tool gives rise to a classification of integrity constraints on class diagrams. So each kind of constraints is expressed in a specific form. This helps the user to know where to write constraints and how to complement a class diagram.

Finally, it is important to have synchronised evolutions of the UML and Z specifications. Our tool allows to always have equivalent versions of the UML and the Z specifications. As all the modelling work is made in the UML environment, a specification change is made in this environment, and   the corresponding Z specification is generated again accordingly. The consistency of the constraints may be checked against this new version and corrected.

The classification of annotations and the synchronised versions of UML and Z specifications facilitate specification evolutions by providing a clear framework about where changes must be made.

5.2 Future Work

Currently, RoZ only considers static constraints. It does not enable to express dynamic constraints. This is due to the fact that Z is intended to express invariant constraints. In order to take into account other constraints, RoZ must be extended to translate dynamic aspects of UML diagrams into other formal languages such as Lustre [25], more appropriate for dynamic aspects.

Moreover annotations written in the prototype are currently in the Z Latex style which is not intuitive. But all annotations expressed in a formalism close to first order logic could be easily integrated into Z specifications. Particularly using OCL can be a way to get closer to practitioner uses. As OCL and Z are close formalisms, annotations could be written in OCL and automatically translated into Z before their integration in the Z skeletons. So RoZ can be an easily usable tool for people knowing UML and its constraints language, OCL.

We can also imagine to simplify the writing of constraints by developing an interface which would propose a list of "standard" constraints. For instance, one could choose in the list, the key constraint. Then one would just have to give the name of the key attribute(s) and the corresponding constraint would be automatically written in Z. This knowledge would enable to produce more relevant elementary operations, by avoiding for instance to generate operations modifying a key attribute. This could also be avoided by extending Rose to express more characteristics about attributes such as the modification permission defined in [26].

Another way of improving the generation of elementary operation could be to consider elementary operations of other concepts. As we do it for classes, we can generate the elementary operations of associations. This would enable to consider dependencies between classes related to association cardinalities. For example, if the cardinality of the association between the A and B classes is 1, this means that if you create (res. delete) an object, a, of A, you must create (res. delete) an object of B linked to a.

Finally, proof is a very important task, even if it is a difficult one, since it can reveal errors or unsuspected problems. Currently RoZ generates proof obligations, but it does not provide any help in order to prove them. This help can be to increase proof automation by using domain knowledge. We are currently working on the definition of proof patterns for elementary operations in order to help the designer to validate the system.

Although RoZ is only at its initial development step, we hope that it can bring a useful help in the improvement of specifications quality.

Acknowledgments

We are grateful to the SIGMA and the PFL research teams at Grenoble, in particular to Olivier Maury for his comments on the RoZ use. Thanks are also due to José-Celso Freire from UNESP (São Paulo, Brasil) for his useful suggestions on the documentation and the distribution of RoZ. Finally we would like to thank the anonymous reviewers for their positive and detailed comments and feedback.

References

1.   J. Brunet. An enhanced definition of composition and its use for abstraction. The 5th international conference on Object Oriented Information Systems, Paris, September 1998.
2.   Rational Software Corporation. UNIFIED MODELING LANGUAGE – notation guide version 1.1. September1997.
3.   Y. Ou. On Using UML Class Diagram for Object-Oriented Database Design – Specification of Integrity Constraints. Proc „ UML „'98 Beyong the Notation, Mulhouse, France, June 1998.
4.   J. Warmer and A. Kleppe. The Object Constraints Language. Addison-Wesley, 1998.
5.   J.M. Spivey. The Z notation – a reference manual (second edition). Prentice-Hall International, 1992.
6.   M. Saaltink. The Z/EVES system. In j. Bowen, M. Hinchey and D. Till editors, Proc. 10th Int. Conf. On the Z formal method (ZUM), volume 1212 of Lecture Notes in Computer Science, pages 72-88, Reading, UK, April 1997.
7.   Rational Software Corporation. Rational Rose – Using Rational Rose 4.0. 1996.
8.   Rational Software Corporation. Rational Rose – Using Rational Rose 98. 1998.
9.   R. France and JM. Bruel and M. Larrondo-Petrie and M. Shroff. Exploring the Semantics of UML type structures with Z. Proc. 2nd IFIP Workshop on Formal Methods for Open Object-Based Distributed Systems (FMOODS), 1997.
10. M. Shroff and R.B. France. Towards a Formalization of UML class structures in Z. COMPSAC'97, 1997.
11. K. Lano, H. Houghton, P. Wheeler. Integrating Formal and Structured Methods in Object-Oriented System Development. In Formal Methods and Object technology, Chapter 7, Springer, 1996.

12. P. Facon, R. Laleau Laleau and H.P. Nguyen. Mapping Object Diagrams into B Specifications. Proc of the Method Integration Workshop, Springer-Verlag, Leeds, March 1996.
13. S. Dupuy, Y.Ledru and M. Chabre-Peccoud. Vers une intégration utile de notations semi-formelles et formelles : un expérience en UML et Z. revue l'Objet, numéro spécial sur les méthodes formelles pour les systèmes à objets, 2000, to appear.
14. S. Dupuy. RoZ version 0.3 an environment for the integration of UML and Z. technical report Laboratoire LSR-IMAG, 1999.
    http://www-lsr.imag.fr/Les.Groupes/PFL/RoZ/index.html
15. Y.Ledru. Identifying pre-conditions with the Z/EVES theorem prover. Proc Int. IEEE Conference on Automated Software Engineering'98, IEEE Computer Society Press, October 1998.
16. Y. Ledru. Complementing semi-formal specifications with Z. KBSE'96, IEEE Computer Society Press, 1996.
17. N. Hadj-Rabia and H. Habrias. Formal specification from NIAM model : a Bottom-Up Approach. ISCIS XI (11th int. Symposium on Computer and Information Sciences), Antalya, Turkey, November 1996.
18. H.P. Nguyen. Dérivation de Spécifications Formelles B à Partir de Spécifications Semi-Formelles. PhD thesis, CNAM, December 1998.
19. B. Nuseibeh and A. Finkelstein. ViewPoints : a vehicle for method and tool integration. IEEE Proc. Of the 5th Int. Workshop on CASE (CASE'92), p50-60, Montreal, Canada, July 1992.
20. R. Laleau, N. Nadj-Rabia. Génération automatique de spécifications VDM à partir d'un schéma conceptuel de données. Dans Actes du 13ème congrès INFORSID, Grenoble, France, June 1995.
21. J.C. Freire Junior, M. Chabre-Peccoud, A. Front and J.-P. Giraudin. A CASE Tool for modeling of methods and information systems. OOIS'98, Int. Conference on Object-Oriented Information Systems, Springer, Paris, France, September 1998.
22. IFAD. the Rose-VDM++ Link.
    http://www.ifad.dk/Products/rose-vdmpp.htm
23. Headway Software. RoZeLink 1.0.
    http://www.calgary.shaw.wave.ca./headway/index.htm
24. R.B. France, J.-M. Bruel, M.M. Larrondo-Petrie. An Integrated Object-Oriented and Formal Modeling Environment. Journal of Object Oriented Programming, November/December 1997.
25. P. Caspi, N. Halbwachs, D. Pilaud and J. Plaice. LUSTRE, a declarative language for programming synchronous systems. In 14th Symposium on Principles of Programming Languages (POPL'87), ACM, p 178-188, Munich, 1987.
26. G. Booch, I. Jacobson and J. Rumbaugh. The Unified Modeling Language- User Guide. Addison-Wesley, 1998.

On Structured Workflow Modelling*

Bartek Kiepuszewski[1], Arthur Harry Maria ter Hofstede[2],
and Christoph J. Bussler[3]

[1] Mincom Limited, GPO Box 1397, Brisbane, Qld 4001, Australia,
bartek@mincom.com
[2] Cooperative Information Systems Research Centre, Queensland University of
Technology, GPO Box 2434, Brisbane, Qld 4001, Australia, arthur@icis.qut.edu.au
[3] Netfish Technologies Inc., 2350 Mission College Blvd., Santa Clara, CA 95054,
USA, cbussler@netfish.com

Abstract. While there are many similarities between the languages of
the various workflow management systems, there are also significant differences. One particular area of differences is caused by the fact that
different systems impose different syntactic restrictions. In such cases,
business analysts have to choose between either conforming to the language in their specifications or transforming these specifications afterwards. The latter option is preferable as this allows for a separation of
concerns. In this paper we investigate to what extent such transformations are possible in the context of various syntactical restrictions (the
most restrictive of which will be referred to as *structured workflows*). We
also provide a deep insight into the consequences, particularly in terms
of expressive power, of imposing such restrictions.

1 Introduction

Despite the interest in workflow management, both from academia and industry,
there is still little consensus about its conceptual and formal foundations (see
e.g. [7]). While there are similarities between the languages of various commercially available workflow management systems, there are also many differences.
However, it is often not clear whether these differences are fundamental in nature. For example, as different systems impose different syntactic restrictions,
one may wonder whether this affects the expressive power of the resulting languages. In addition to that, such variations result in business analysts being
confronted with the question as to whether to conform to the target language
right away when they specify their workflows, or to transform their specifications
in a later stage.

In this paper focus is on syntactic variations in workflow specification languages. Different workflow management systems impose different syntactical restrictions. The most restrictive types of workflows will be referred to as *structured*

---

* This research is supported by an ARC SPIRT grant "Component System Architecture for an Open Distributed Enterprise Management System with Configurable
Workflow Support" between QUT and Mincom.

B. Wangler, L. Bergman (Eds.): CAiSE 2000, LNCS 1789, pp. 431–445, 2000.

workflows. Systems such as SAP R/3 and Filenet Visual Workflo allow for the specification of structured workflows only. While enforcing restrictions may have certain benefits (e.g. verification and implementation become easier), the price that may have to be paid is that the resulting language is more difficult to use and has less expressive power.

In this paper, it will be shown that some syntactic restrictions will lead to a reduction of expressive power of the language involved, while other restrictions are of a less serious nature and can be overcome by the introduction of equivalence preserving transformation rules. It will be also shown that even though for certain workflow models it is possible to transform them to equivalent structured forms, the resulting models are less suitable than the original ones. Nevertheless, the automation of such rules could potentially lead to tools giving business analysts greater freedom in workflow specification without compromising their realisability in terms of commercially available (and preferred) workflow management systems.

2   Structured Workflows: Definitions

In this section the notion of a structured workflow is formally defined and some elementary properties stated. Workflows as used in this paper will employ concepts used in most commercial workflow management systems. Although the graphical notation used for representing workflows is irrelevant in terms of the results presented in this paper, we have to agree on one in order to provide examples to illustrate our arguments. Process elements will be represented by large circles; or-joins and or-splits will correspond to small, white circles, while and-joins and and-splits will correspond to small, shaded circles (the indegree and outdegree will always make it clear whether we are dealing with a join or a split). There are many examples of languages that support the specification of arbitrary workflows, e.g. Staffware (www.staffware.com), Forte Conductor (www.forte.com) and Verve WorkFlow (www.verveinc.com).

A structured workflow is a workflow that is syntactically restricted in a number of ways. Intuitively a structured workflow is a workflow where each or-split has a corresponding or-join and each and-split has a corresponding and-join. These restrictions will guarantee certain important properties shown later in the paper and in some cases correspond to restrictions imposed by commercial workflow management systems.

Definition 1. *A structured workflow model (SWM) is inductively defined as follows.*

1. *A workflow consisting of a single activity is a SWM. This activity is both initial and final.*
2. *Let X and Y be SWMs. The concatenation of these workflows, where the final activity of X has a transition to the initial activity of Y, then also is a SWM. The initial activity of this SWM is the initial activity of X and its final activity is the final activity of Y.*

3. Let $X_1, \ldots, X_n$ be SWMs and let j be an or-join and s an or-split. The workflow with as initial activity s and final activity j and transitions between s and the initial activities of X_i, and between the final activities of X_i and j, is then also a SWM. Predicates can be assigned to the outgoing transitions of s. The initial activity of this SWM is s and its final activity is j.

4. Let $X_1, \ldots, X_n$ be SWMs and let j be an and-join and s an and-split. The workflow with as initial activity s and final activity j and transitions between s and the initial activities of X_i, and between the final activities of X_i and j, is then also a SWM. The initial activity of this SWM is s and its final activity is j.

5. Let X and Y be SWMs and let j be an or-join and s an or-split. The workflow with as initial activity j and as final activity s and with transitions between j and the initial activity of X, between the final activity of X and s, between s and the initial activity of Y, and between the final activity of Y and j, is then also a SWM. The initial activity of this SWM is j and its final activity is s.

All commercial WfMSs known to the authors allow for the specification of workflow models that are equivalent to structured models as defined in definition 1. Some of these WfMSs do not allow for the specification of arbitrary models though and they impose certain levels of structuredness by means of syntactical restrictions typically implemented in the graphical process designer.

The most restricted workflow modelling languages known to the authors with respect to imposing structuredness are the languages of FileNet's Visual Work-Flo (www.filenet.com) (VW) and SAP R/3 Workflow. In both languages it is possible to design structured models only. These models resemble the definition provided earlier very closely with some minor exceptions such as that in VW the loops can only be of the form "WHILE p DO X". In SAP R/3 Workflow no loops are allowed to be modelled in a direct way. An example of syntactical restrictions in the more general area of data and process modelling can be found in UML's activity diagrams where business modellers are forced to exclusively specify structured models.

The definition of SWMs guarantees these types of workflows to have certain properties. Specifically, by the use of structural induction it can easily be shown that SWMs do not deadlock (see [5]). In addition to that, in SWMs it is not possible to have multiple instances of the same activity active at the same time. This situation is easily modelled in an arbitrary workflow if an and-split is followed by an or-join construct. Similarly, an arbitrary workflow will deadlock if an or-split is followed by an and-join.

Since in the following sections we will regularly pay attention to arbitrary workflow models that do not deadlock and do not result in multiple instances, for terminological convenience we introduce the notion of *well-behaved* workflows.

Definition 2. *A workflow model is* well-behaved *if it can never lead to deadlock nor can it result in multiple active instances of the same activity.*

Corollary 1. *Every structured workflow model is well-behaved.*

Instead of requiring workflows to be structured, it is more common for workflow languages to impose restrictions on loops only. For example IBM MQSeries/Workflow (www.ibm.com/software) and InConcert (www.inconcert.com) do not allow the explicit modelling of loops. Instead they have to be modelled by the use of decomposition. This is equivalent to using a "REPEAT X UNTIL p" loop. In case of MQSeries/Workflow, predicate p is specified as the *Exit Condition* of the decomposition. Hence, in between arbitrary workflow models and structured workflow models, we recognise a third class of workflow models, referred to as *restricted loop models*.

Definition 3. *A restricted loop workflow model (RLWFM) is inductively defined as follows:*

1. *An arbitrary workflow model without cycles is an RLWFM.*
2. *Let X and Y be RLWFMs with each one initial and one final node. Let j be an or-join and s an or-split. The workflow with as initial activity j and as final activity s and with transitions between j and the initial activity of X, between the final activity of X and s, between s and the initial activity of Y, and between the final activity of Y and j, is then also a RLWFM.*

Note that languages that support loops through decomposition are a subset of the class defined by the above definition (in those cases, essentially, Y corresponds to the empty workflow). Naturally, every SWF is an RLWFM and every RLWFM is an arbitrary workflow model.

3   Equivalence in the Context of Control Flow

As there exist workflow languages that do not allow for the specification of arbitrary workflows, business analysts are confronted with the option to either restrict their specifications such that they conform to the tool that is used or specify their workflows freely and transform them to the required language in a later stage. From the point of view of separation of concerns, the latter option is preferable. To support such a way of working it would be best to have a set of transformations that could be applied to a workflow specification in order to transform it to a structured workflow in the sense of the previous section. Naturally, these transformations should not alter the semantics of the workflows

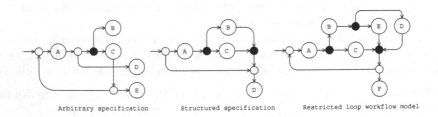

Arbitrary specification   Structured specification   Restricted loop workflow model

Fig. 1. Illustration of the three different workflow model classes

to which they are applied, they should be *equivalence preserving*. However, this immediately raises the question as to what notion of process equivalence is the most applicable in the context of workflows (for an overview of different notions of process equivalence the reader is referred to [4]).

One of the most commonly used equivalence notions is that of bisimulation. The formal definition of bisimulation between two different workflow systems, given the fact that they would most likely use different syntax and semantics, would have to be defined using some common formalism that can be applied to both systems. One of the most convenient ways to do it is to define bisimulation formally in terms of their Petri-net representation. That immediately leads to the conclusion that *weak bisimulation* has to be considered since Petri-net representations of workflow models may use many, internal, non-labelled places.

In the context of workflow processes with parallelism, the notion of basic weak bisimulation is not strong enough. Bisimulation is defined in terms of execution sequences, i.e. in terms of arbitrary interleaving. As such, however, bisimulation cannot distinguish between a concurrent system and its sequential simulation. For that reason a stronger equivalence notion is needed. Such a notion is provided in [3] where it is referred to as *fully concurrent bisimulation*. Given the fact that the formal definition is relatively complex and the details are not particularly useful for the purpose of this paper, we will present fully concurrent bisimulation in the context of workflow specification in terms of the *bisimulation game* (adapted from [8]):

1. There are two players, Player A and Player B, each of which having a workflow model specification (Workflow A and Workflow B).
2. Player A starts the initial activities in his workflow model specification. Player B responds by starting the initial activities in his workflow model specification (which should exactly correspond to those of player A).
3. Player A may choose to finish any of its activities and start a corresponding subsequent activity. Player B responds accordingly by finishing and starting an activity with the same label (possibly performing some internal, non-labeled, steps first).
4. If Player B cannot imitate the move of Player A, he looses. By imitating we mean that at any point in time the same set of activities in workflow B should be completed and started as in workflow A. Player B wins if he can terminate his workflow once Player A has terminated his workflow. Similarly Player B wins if he can deadlock his workflow once Player A has deadlocked his workflow. The case of an infinite run of the game is considered to be successful for Player B too.

If there is a strategy for defending player (Player B) to always prevent Player A from winning then we say that workflow B can simulate workflow A. If the reverse applies as well (workflow A can simulate workflow B) then we consider the two workflow specifications to be equivalent.

4 From Arbitrary Workflow Models to SWMs

In this section transformations from arbitrary workflow models to SWMs are studied and to what extent such transformations are possible. All transformations presented in this section assume that the workflow patterns they operate on do not contain data dependencies between decisions, in other words for all intents and purposes all decisions can be treated as nondeterministic. This assumption allows us to assume that all possible executions permitted by the control flow specification are possible.

4.1 Simple Workflows without Parallelism

Workflows that do not contain parallelism are simple models indeed. Their semantics is very similar to elementary flow charts that are commonly used for procedural program specification. The or-split corresponds to selection (if-then-else statement) while the activity corresponds to an instruction in the flow chart. It is well known that any unstructured flow chart can be transformed to a structured one. In this section we will revisit these transformation techniques and present and analyse them in the context of workflow models.

Following [11] we will say that the process of *reducing* a workflow model consists of replacing each occurrence of a base model. within the workflow model by a single activity box. This is repeated until no further replacement is possible. A process that can be reduced to a single activity box represents a structured workflow model. Each transformation of an irreducible workflow model should allow us to reduce the model further and in effect reduce the number of activities in the model.

The strong similarity of simple workflow models and flow diagrams suggests that if we do not consider parallelism, there are only four basic causes of unstructuredness (see e.g. [11,9]): 1) Entry into a decision structure, 2) Exit from a decision structure, 3) Entry into a loop structure, and 4) Exit from a loop structure. Entry to any structure is modelled in a workflow environment by an or-join construct. Similarly, an exit is modelled by an or-split. Once parallelism is introduced we will also consider synchronised entry and parallel exit modelled by and-join and and-split constructs respectively.

The first transformation (all transformations in this section are based on [9]), depicted in figure 2, can be performed when transforming a diagram containing an exit from a decision structure. It is important to observe that variable Φ is needed since activity D can potentially change the value of β or, if β is a complex expression, it could change the value of one of its components. This transformation is achieved through the use of auxiliary variables.

The transformations as depicted in figure 3 are used when a workflow model contains an entry to a decision structure. Here workflow $B2$ is a transformation of $B1$ achieved through *node duplication*, whereas workflow $B3$ is a transformation of $B1$ achieved through the use of auxiliary variables. The following two diagrams, depicted in figures 4 and 5, capture transformations to be used when

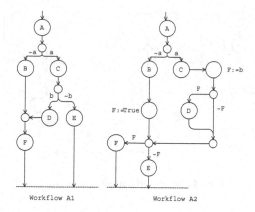

Fig. 2. Exit from a decision structure

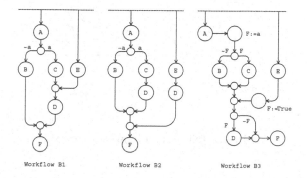

Fig. 3. Entry into a decision structure

a model contains an entry to, or an exit from a loop structure, respectively. Repeated application of the transformations discussed in this section can remove all forms of unstructuredness from a workflow. Hence the following theorem.

Theorem 1. *All unstructured workflows without parallelism have an equivalent structured form.*

Finally, it should be remarked that in some cases we have presented alternative transformations (not using auxiliary variables) and in some cases we have not. In later sections, we will show that this has a reason: in the cases where no extra transformations (not using auxiliary variables) are presented, such transformations turn out not to exist.

4.2 Workflows with Parallelism but without Loops

Addition of parallelism immediately introduces problems related to deadlock and multiple instances. As noted in section 2, structured workflow models never

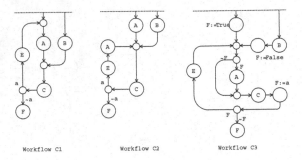

Workflow C1   Workflow C2   Workflow C3

Fig. 4. Entry into a loop structure

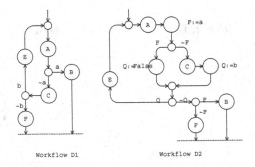

Workflow D1   Workflow D2

Fig. 5. Exit from a loop structure

result in deadlock nor multiple instances of the same activity at the same time. Hence, structured workflow models are less expressive than arbitrary workflow models. This immediately raises the question as to whether well-behaved workflow models can be transformed to structured workflow models. As the next theorem shows, the answer to this question is negative.

Theorem 2. *There are arbitrary, well-behaved, workflow models that cannot be modelled as structured workflow models.*

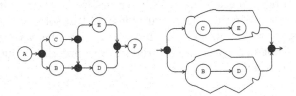

Fig. 6. Arbitrary workflow and illustration of its essential causal dependencies

Proof. Consider the workflow fragment in figure 6. The first observation is that as activities B and C are causally independent (that is, they can be executed concurrently) they have to be in different branches of some parallel structure in a corresponding structured workflow. As activities C and E are causally dependent (E is always performed after C) there must be a path from C to some activity named E. This activity has to be in the same branch as C as it cannot be outside the parallel structure as that would make it causally dependent on B. By applying similar reasoning, an activity named D has to be in the same branch of a parallel structure as B. Now we have that as C and D are in different branches of a parallel structure they are causally independent. However, in the original model they are causally dependent. Contradiction. No corresponding structured workflow exists.   □

To find out which workflow models can be effectively transformed into SWMs, let us concentrate on the causes of unstructuredness that can occur when parallelism is added. If loops are not taken into account, these causes are: 1) Entry to a decision structure, 2) Exit from a decision structure, 3) Entry to a parallel structure, 4) Exit from a parallel structure, 5) Synchronised entry to a decision structure, 6) Parallel exit from a decision structure, 7) Synchronised entry to a parallel structure, and 8) Parallel exit from a parallel structure. In the remainder of this section we will concentrate on which of these structures can be transformed to a structure model.

Entries and exits from decision structures are dealt with in section 4.1 and can obviously be transformed to a structured model.

As a synchronised entry to a decision structure and an exit from a parallel structure leads to a potential deadlock (i.e. there are instances of the model that will deadlock), it follows that if the original workflow contains any of these patterns, it cannot be transformed into a SWM.

Parallel exits and synchronised entries to a parallel structure are dealt with in theorem 2. The reasoning of this theorem can be applied to any model that contains these patterns. Hence such models, even though they may be well-behaved, cannot be transformed into SWMs.

Before analysing the two remaining structures let us define a syntactical structure called an *overlapping structure*. This structure has been previously introduced in the context of workflow reduction for verification purposes in [10]. A specific instance of it is shown in figure 7. An overlapping structure consists of an or-split followed by i instances of and-splits, followed by j instances of or-joins and finally by an and-join. The structure of figure 7 has both i and j degrees equal to two. The overlapping structure contains both an entry to a parallel structure and a parallel exit from a decision structure and it never results in a deadlock. It is possible to transform an overlapping structure into a SWM as shown in figure 7.

A thorough analysis of the causes of deadlock and multiple instances in workflow models (see e.g. [10]) leads to the conclusion that workflow models containing a parallel exit from a decision or an entry to a parallel structure will cause a potential deadlock unless they form a part of an overlapping structure or the

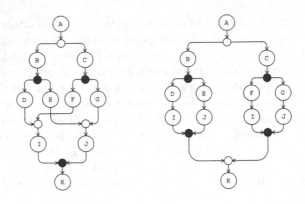

Fig. 7. Overlapping structure

exit path from the decision does not join the main execution path. Hence we conclude:

- An entry to a parallel structure can cause a potential deadlock unless it is part of an overlapping structure (in which case it can be transformed as shown).
- Similarly, a parallel exit from a decision structure can cause a potential deadlock and cannot be transformed into a SWM unless it is part of an overlapping structure or if the exit path does not join the main path (figure 8 illustrates the second case and the corresponding transformation).

The observations in this section have led us to the following conjecture:

Conjecture 1. Any arbitrary well-behaved workflow model that does not have loops, when reduced, does not have a parallel exit from a parallel structure, and, when reduced, does not have a synchronised entry into a parallel structure, can be translated to a SWM.

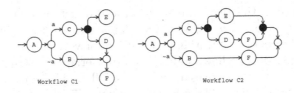

Fig. 8. Exit path not joining main path in parallel exit from decision structure

4.3   Workflows with Parallelism and Loops

Finding out whether a workflow can deadlock or not in the context of loops is much more complex and conjecture 1 cannot be automatically applied. To expose

potential difficulties let us concentrate on what kind of loops we can encounter
in a workflow model once and-join and and-split constructs are used. Every cycle
in a graph has an entry point that can be either an or-join or an and-join and an
exit point that can be either an and-split or an or-split. Cycles without an entry
point cannot start and cycles without an exit point cannot terminate. The latter
case can be represented by a cycle with an exit point where the exit condition
on the or-split is set to false.

Most cycles will have an or-joins and or-splits as entry and exit points respectively (note that there may be many exit and entry points in the cycle)
provided that the workflow is well-behaved. The transformation of such cycles
is straightforward using transformations as presented earlier in this section.

If the cycle has an and-join as an entry point, the workflow will most likely
deadlock. Examples of two workflows containing cycles with and-join as an entry-
point that do not deadlock are shown in figure 9.

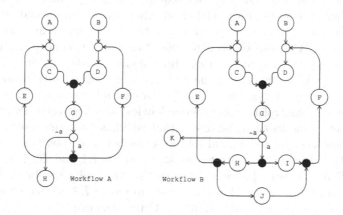

Fig. 9. Two workflow models with arbitrary loops

Conversely, most workflows that have an and-split as an exit point will most
likely result in multiple instances. Our previous observation that any workflow
resulting in deadlock or multiple instances cannot be modelled as a structured
workflow certainly holds whether or not the workflow has loops. The major
impact of introducing loops though is that finding out if the workflow deadlocks
or results in multiple instances becomes a non-trivial task [6].

In rare cases when a cycle has an and-join as entry and an and-split as
exit point and the workflow involved does not deadlock nor result in multiple
instances, theorem 2 is helpful when determining if such a workflow can be
remodelled as a structured workflow. In figure 9 for example, workflow A can be
remodelled as a structured workflow whereas workflow B cannot. The equivalent
workflow to workflow A is shown in figure 10.

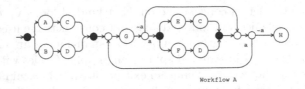

Fig. 10. Structured version of leftmost workflow of figure 9

4.4   Suitability of Transformations

The transformations presented earlier in this section are using two major techniques: 1) node duplication and 2) use of auxiliary variables to control conditions. In this section we will comment on the suitability of these solutions.

Suitability in general refers to the relation between concepts offered in the specification technique and concepts required by the problem domain. There are a number of aspects in a workflow specification, e.g. data and control flow, and there are a number of ways in which the same underlying model can be presented, e.g. data flow and control flow "view". Yet, conceptual models, in general, are required to convey a certain amount of information which should not be split up, if the model is to be effective (this corresponds to the *Cognitive Sufficiency Principle* promulgated by [2]). For example we believe that the model that conveys all control flow interdependencies between activities in a control view is a better model than the model that requires both the control flow view and data flow view to understand relationships between activities. Consider for example the three models from figure 3. In models $B1$ and $B2$ it is clear that activities B and D are exclusive in the sense that they will never be both executed in any process instance. On the other hand, in model $B3$, it seems that activity D can follow the execution of activity B. Only close inspection of the or-splits' predicates as well as implicit knowledge that activity B does not change the value of variable Φ can lead to the conclusion that activities B and D are indeed exclusive.

To retain the suitability of a certain workflow model, transformations should avoid using auxiliary variables to control or-splits through predicates. Unfortunately, this is not always possible.

Theorem 3. *There are forms of unstructuredness that cannot be transformed without the use of auxiliary variables.*

Proof. Consider the workflow model of figure 5. This workflow model contains multiple exits from a loop and as such is unstructured. Now consider another workflow model equivalent to this model, which is structured. The first observation is that as workflow representations are finite, this structured workflow model needs to contain at least one loop as the associated language is infinite. On one such loop there has to be an occurrence of both activities A and C. Activities B and F should be outside any loop (as we cannot use predicates anymore to prevent paths containing these activities to be chosen if they are included in the body of the loop). Playing the bisimulation game yields that after each instance of activity A one should be able to choose to perform either C or B. Since B is outside any loop, there has to be an exit point from the loop sometime after activity A (but before activity C, as one cannot use predicates that guarantee that activity C will be skipped after the decision has been made to exit the loop). Similarly, after each instance of activity C one should be able to choose to perform either activity E or activity F. As F is outside any loop, we also have an exit point from this loop after activity C (but before activity E). Hence, the loop under consideration has at least two exit points and the workflow cannot be structured. Contradiction. Hence a structured workflow equivalent, not using auxiliary variables, to the workflow of figure 5 does not exist.   □

An alternative technique to transform arbitrary models into a structured form requires node duplication. As has been proved earlier, it cannot be used for every model, but even when it can be used, it is not without associated problems. Consider once again the model in figure 3. If activity D in the left model is followed by a large workflow specification, the transformation presented in the right model would need to duplicate the whole workflow specification following activity D. The resulting workflow will be almost twice as big as the original and will therefore be more difficult to comprehend.

5   Restricted Loops

In this section we will focus on languages that impose restrictions on loops only. Examples of such languages are MQSeries/Workflow and InConcert. The main reason these languages impose restrictions on loops is that the introduction of cycles in their workflow specifications would result in an immediate deadlock because of their evaluation strategy. MQSeries/Workflow for example propagates true and false tokens and its synchronizing or-join expects tokens from every incoming branch before execution can resume; this results in deadlock if one of these branches is dependent on execution of the or-join itself. Note that the semantics of the synchronising or-join is different from the semantics of the or-join as presented earlier in this paper, but that does not compromise the obtained results. The approach chosen in MQSeries/Workflow and InConcert guarantees that their specifications are well-behaved (for MQSeries/Workflow this is formally proven in [5]).

Even though one may ask the question whether any arbitrary workflow specification can be translated to a specification that uses restricted loops only, the more practical question would be to ask whether any well-behaved arbitrary specification can be translated to a specification using restricted loops only. As the next theorem shows, the answer to this question is negative.

Theorem 4. *There are well-behaved arbitrary workflow specifications that cannot be expressed as RLWFMs.*

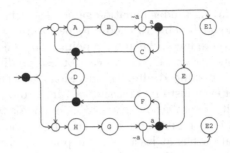

Fig. 11. Well-behaved arbitrary workflow

Proof. By showing that the workflow from figure 11 cannot be modelled as an RLWFM. Observe that after completion of the initial activity and as long as α evaluates to true, there will be at least two tokens in the corresponding Petri-net. That means that in an equivalent workflow specification that has restricted loops only, there have to be two concurrent restricted loops running in parallel (if there was only one loop, the moment the exit condition was evaluated there would be only one token in the corresponding Petri-net). One of the restricted loops would have to contain activities A, B, C, and E, and the other loop would have to contain activities D, F, G, and H. In the original workflow specification A is causally dependent on D. That means that there must be a path between A and D but that is impossible if A belongs to a different restricted loop than D according to the definition of a restricted loop.   □

The careful reader may have noticed that in the workflow model of figure 11 data is used to make sure that both loops are exited at the same time (otherwise dead-lock would occur). It is an open question as to whether there exist well-behaved arbitrary workflow specifications that do not contain decision dependencies and that can not be transformed into an RLWFM.

6   Conclusions

The transformation of arbitrary workflow models to workflows in a structured form is a necessity typically faced by either an application programmer who has to implement a non-structured workflow specification in an environment sup-porting structured specifications only (e.g. SAP R/3 workflow or Filenet Visual Workflo), or by a business analyst who is trying to capture real-world require-ments in a structured workflow specification technique (e.g. UML's activity di-agrams). In this paper we have shown that even simple transformations require the use of auxiliary variables which results in the introduction of dependencies between decisions in a workflow graph. As a result the transformed workflow specification is typically more difficult to understand for end-users. Moreover, some arbitrary specifications cannot be transformed at all to a structured form. Hence in general, structured models are less expressive and less suitable than arbitrary models. For these reasons it is our contention that any high-end work-flow management system should support the execution of arbitrary workflow specifications. To some, this might seem to contrast with the common consensus of avoiding GOTO statements (and using WHILE loops instead) in procedural programming languages, but, as shown throughout this paper, the presence of parallelism as well as the nature of workflow specifications provide the essential difference. As a consequence, the good workflow modelling environment should be supported by a powerful verification engine that would help process modellers detect syntactical problems such as potential deadlock or unwanted multiple instances. Using sophisticated verification tools for these purposes (incorporating techniques from state-of-the-art Petri-net theory) seems feasible from a practical perspective (see [1]).

References

1. W.M.P. van der Aalst and A.H.M. ter Hofstede. Verification of Workflow Task Structures: A Petri-net-based Approach. *Information Systems*, 2000. (to appear).
2. A.P. Barros and A.H.M. ter Hofstede. Towards the construction of workflow-suitable conceptual modelling techniques. *Information Systems Journal*, 8(4):313–337, October 1998.
3. E. Best, R. Devillers, A. Kiehn, and L. Pomello. Concurrent bisimulations in Petri nets. *Acta Informatica*, 28:231–254, 1991.
4. R.J. van Glabbeek. The linear time-branching time spectrum. In J.C.M. Baeten and J.W. Klop, editors, *Proceedings of CONCUR'90. Theories of Concurrency: Unification and Extension*, pages 278–297, Berlin, Germany, 1990. Springer-Verlag.
5. A.H.M. ter Hofstede and B. Kiepuszewski. Formal Analysis of Deadlock Behaviour in Workflows. Technical report, Queensland University of Technology/Mincom, Brisbane, Australia, April 1999. (submitted for publication).
6. A.H.M. ter Hofstede and M.E. Orlowska. On the Complexity of Some Verification Problems in Process Control Specifications. *Computer Journal*, 42(5):349–359, 1999.
7. S. Jablonski and C. Bussler. *Workflow Management: Modeling Concepts, Architecture, and Implementation*. International Thomson Computer Press, London, United Kingdom, 1996.
8. P. Jančar. Decidability Questions for Bismilarity of Petri Nets and Some Related Problems. In P. Enjalbert, E.W. Mayr, and K.W. Wagner, editors, *STACS 94, 11th Annual Symposium on Theoretical Aspects of Computer Science*, volume 775 of *Lecture Notes in Computer Science*, pages 581–592, Caen, France, February 1994. Springer-Verlag.
9. G. Oulsnam. Unravelling Unstructured Programs. *Computer Journal*, 25(3):379–387, 1982.
10. W. Sadiq and M.E. Orlowska. Applying Graph Reduction Techniques for Identifying Structural Conflicts in Process Models. In *Proceedings of the 11th Conf on Advanced Information Systems Engineering (CAiSE'99)*, pages 195–209, Hildeberg, Germany, June 1999.
11. M. H. Williams. Generating structured flow diagrams: the nature of unstructuredness. *Computer Journal*, 20(1):45–50, 1977.

A Model for Data Warehouse Operational Processes

Panos Vassiliadis[1], Christoph Quix[2], Yannis Vassiliou[1], and Matthias Jarke[2,3]

[1] National Technical University of Athens, Dept. of Electrical and Computer Eng.,
Computer Science Division, Iroon Polytechniou 9, 157 73, Athens, Greece
{pvassil,yv}@dbnet.ece.ntua.gr
[2] Informatik V (Information Systems), RWTH Aachen, 52056 Aachen, Germany
{quix,jarke}@informatik.rwth-aachen.de
[3] GMD-FIT, 53754 Sankt Augustin, Germany

Abstract. Previous research has provided metadata models that enable the capturing of the static components of a Data Warehouse (DW) architecture, along with information on different quality factors over these components. This paper complements this work with the modeling of the dynamic parts of the DW, i.e., with a metamodel for DW operational processes. The proposed metamodel is capable of modeling complex activities, their interrelationships, and the relationship of activities with data sources and execution details. Finally, the metamodel complements proposed architecture and quality models in a coherent fashion, resulting in a full framework for DW metamodeling, capable of supporting the design, administration and evolution of a DW. We have implemented this metamodel using the language Telos and the metadata repository system ConceptBase.

1   Introduction

Data Warehouses (DW) are complex and data-intensive systems that integrate data from multiple heterogeneous information sources and ultimately transform them into a multidimensional representation, which is useful for decision support applications. Apart from a complex architecture, involving *data sources,* the *operational data store (ODS),* the *global data warehouse,* the *client data marts,* etc., a DW is also characterized by a complex lifecycle. The DW involves a permanent *design phase*, where the designer has to produce various modeling constructs accompanied by a detailed physical design for efficiency reasons. The designer must also deal with the DW processes, which are complex in structure, large in number and hard to code at the same time. Viewing the DW as a set of layered, materialized views is thus a very simplistic view. For example, the DW refreshment process can already consist of many different subprocesses like *data cleaning, archiving, transformations, aggregations* interconnected through a complex schedule [2]. The *administration* of the DW is also a complex task, where deadlines must be met for the population of the DW and contingency actions taken in the case of errors. Finally, we must add the *evolution* phase, which is a combination of design and administration: as time passes,

B. Wangler, L. Bergman (Eds.): CAiSE 2000, LNCS 1789, pp. 446-461, 2000
© Springer-Verlag Berlin Heidelberg 2000

new data are requested by the end users, new sources of information become available, and the DW architecture must evolve to meet these challenges.

All the data warehouse components, processes and data are – or at least should be – tracked and administered from a metadata repository. The metadata repository controls the data warehouse components and is therefore the essential starting point for design and operational optimization. Moreover, the schema of the metadata repository, expressed as the *DW architecture model* should also be powerful enough to capture the semantics and structure of the data warehouse processes (design, refreshment, cleaning, etc.). Expressiveness and ease of use of the metadata schema are crucial for data warehouse quality.

In [12], we have presented a metadata modeling approach which enables the capturing of the *static* parts of the architecture of a data warehouse, along with information over different quality dimensions of these components. The linkage of the architecture model to quality parameters (quality model) and its implementation in ConceptBase have been formally described in [13]. [27] presents a methodology for the actual exploitation of the information found in the metadata repository and the quality-oriented evolution of a data warehouse based on the architecture and quality model. In this paper, we complement these approaches with the metamodeling for the *dynamic* part of the data warehouse environment: the *processes*.

As we will show in this paper, this kind of meta-information can be used to support the design and the evolution of the DW. In these phases of the DW lifecycle, the designers of a DW need information about processes: what are they supposed to do, why are they necessary, how are they implemented and how they affect other processes in the DW. We have identified several requirements for a DW process model. Specifically, the requirements involve: (i) the coverage of the *complexity of the structure* of DW processes, in terms of tasks executed within a single process, execution coherence, contingency treatment, etc.; (ii) the capturing of the *relationship of processes with involved data*; (iii) the *tracking of specific executed processes*, so that people can relate the DW objects to decisions, tools and the facts which have happened in the real world [10]; (iv) a *clear separation of perspectives*: *what* components a process consists of (logical perspective), *how* they perform (physical perspective) and *why* these components exist (conceptual perspective); and finally (v) the representation of the *linkage of the modeled processes to concrete quality factors* which measure the quality of the DW.

The contribution of this paper is towards the fulfillment of all the aforementioned requirements. We do not claim that our approach is suitable for any kind of process, but rather we focus our attention to the internals of DW systems. Our model has been implemented in the metadata repository ConceptBase [11]. Its usefulness is demonstrated by the fact that the proposed model enables DW management, design and evolution, as we will show in section 5. Our model supports the following steps in the DW lifecycle: (i) the design of the DW is supported by extended use of consistency checks, to ensure the correctness of the representation; (ii) the model facilitates the administration of the DW, by enabling the measurement of quality of DW processes and the spotting of inefficiencies; (iii) a specific task of DW administration, namely evolution, is supported by the exploitation of the information on the interdependencies of DW components, to forecast any possible impact by the change of any of these components. To facilitate these tasks, we derive the description of the DW materialized views from the process definitions used for their population, instead of treating the DW as a set of layers of materialized views.

This paper is organized as follows: in section 2, we discuss briefly related work. Section 3 describes the process metamodel, and in section 4, we present its linkage to the quality model. In section 5, we present how the metadata repository can be exploited, when enriched with this kind of information. Finally, in section 6 we conclude our results and present issues for future research. For lack of space, many issues are not thoroughly presented here. We refer the interested reader to [28] for more examples and explanations.

2   Related Work

Our approach is build around the Workflow Reference Model, presented in [29] by the Workflow Management Coalition (WfMC). We have adapted this model to the specific requirements in DW systems.

We found the Workflow Reference Model too abstract for the purpose of a repository serving DW operational processes. First, the relationship of an activity with the data it involves is not really covered, although this would provide extensive information of the data flow in the DW. Second, the separation of perspectives is not clear, since the WfMC proposal focuses only on the structure of the workflows. To compensate this shortcoming, we employ the basic idea of the Actor-Dependency model [31] (and its latest version, the Strategic Dependency model [30]) to add a conceptual perspective to the definition of a process, capturing the reasons behind its structure. In [31], three different ways to view a process are identified: *what* steps it consists of, *how* they are to be performed and *why* these steps exist. This separation is also represented in a software process data model to support software information systems [10]. The model captures the representation of design objects ("what"), design decisions ("why") and design tools ("how").

The idea of mapping the conceptual representation of a workflow to its execution is presented in [3]. The proposed model captures the mapping from workflow specification to workflow execution (in particular concerning exception handling). Importance is paid to the inter-task interaction, the relationship of workflows to external agents and the access to databases.

An approach to validate workflow models is presented in [24,16]. The algorithms uses a set of graph reduction rules to identify structural conflicts in a control flow specification, and to check the consistency of workflow temporal constraints.

3   Metamodel for Data Warehouse Operational Processes

In [12] a basic metamodel for data warehouse architecture and quality has been presented (Fig. 1). The framework describes a data warehouse in three *perspectives*: a *conceptual*, a *logical* and a *physical* perspective. Each perspective is partitioned into the three traditional data warehouse *levels*: *source, data warehouse* and *client* level.

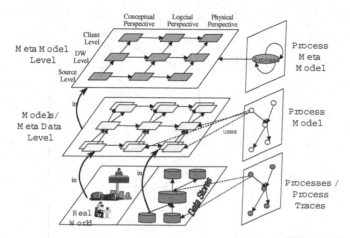

Fig. 1. Framework for Data Warehouse Architecture [12]

On the *metamodel* layer, the framework gives a notation for data warehouse architectures by specifying meta classes for the usual data warehouse objects like data store, relation, view, etc. On the *metadata* layer, the metamodel is instantiated with the concrete architecture of a data warehouse, involving its schema definition, indexes, tablespaces, etc. The lowest layer in Fig. 1 represents the real world where the actual processes and data reside.

The *static* description of the architecture parts of the DW (left part of Fig. 1) is complemented in this paper with a metamodel of the *dynamic* parts of the DW, i.e. the DW operational processes. As one can notice on the right side of Fig. 1, we follow again a three level instantiation: a *Process Metamodel* deals with generic entities involved in all DW processes (operating on entities found at the DW metamodel level), the *Process Model* covers the processes of a specific DW by employing instances of the metamodel entities and the *Process Traces* capture the execution of the actual DW processes happening in the real world.

Our process model (cf. Fig. 2.) has also different perspectives covering distinct aspects of a process: the *conceptual, logical* and *physical* perspective. The categorization fits naturally with the architecture model, since the perspectives of the process model operate on objects of the respective perspective of the architecture model. As mentioned in [31] there are different ways to view a process: *what* steps it consists of (logical perspective), *how* they are to be performed (physical perspective) and *why* these steps exist (conceptual perspective). Thus, we view a DW process from three perspectives: a central *logical* part of the model, which captures the basic structure of a process, its *physical* counterpart which provides specific details over the actual components that execute the activity and the *conceptual* perspective which abstractly represents the basic interrelationships between DW stakeholders and processes in a formal way. In the following subsections, we will elaborate on each of the three perspectives, starting from the logical one.

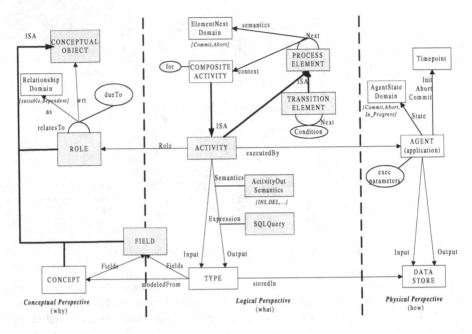

Fig. 2. The DW Operational Process Metamodel

3.1   Complexity of the Process Structure

Following [29], the main entity of the logical perspective is an *Activity*. An activity represents an amount of "work which is processed by a combination of resource and computer applications". Activities are rather complex in nature and this complexity is captured by the specialization of *Activity*, namely *CompositeActivity*. We follow here the lessons coming both from repository and workflow management: there must be the possibility of zooming in and out the repository. Composite activities are composed of *ProcessElements* which is a generalization of the entities *Activity* and *TransitionElement*. A transition element is the "bridge" between two activities: it is employed for the interconnection of activities participating in a complex activity. The attribute *Next* of the process elements captures the sequence of events.

Formally, a *Process Element* is characterized by the following attributes:

- *Next*: a *ProcessElement* which is next in the sequence of a composite activity. The attribute *Next* has itself two attributes, that characterize it:
  - *Context*: Since two activities can be interrelated in more than one complex DW processes, the context is captured by a *CompositeActivity* instance.

- *Semantics*: This attribute denotes whether the next activity in a schedule happens on successful termination of the previous activity (*COMMIT*) or in the case where a contingency action is required (*ABORT*).

A *TransitionElement* inherits the attributes of *ProcessElement*, but most important, is used to add more information on the control flow in a composite activity. This is captured by two mechanisms. First, we enrich the *Next* link with more meaning, by adding a *Condition* attribute to it. A *Condition* is a logical expression in Telos denoting that the firing of the next activity is performed when the *Condition* is met.

Second, we specialize the class *Transition Element* to four prominent subclasses, capturing the basic connectives of activities, as suggested by [29]: *Split_AND*, *Split_XOR, Join_AND, Join_XOR*. Their semantics are obviously the same with the ones of the WfMC proposal. The proposed model supports two other constructs of the WfMC proposal, namely the *dummy activities* (modeled as simple Transition Elements) and the *LOOP activities*, captured as instances of *CompositeActivity*, with the extra attribute *for*, expressed as a string.

3.2   Relationship with Data

We introduce the entity *Type* to capture the logical representation of a data store. A *Type* denotes the schema for all kinds of data stores. Formally, a *Type* is defined as a specialization of *LogicalObject* with the following attributes:

- *Fields*: a multi-value attribute. In other words, each *Type* has a name and a set of *Fields*, exactly like a relation in the relational model.
- *Stored*: a *DataStore*, i.e., a physical object representing any application used to manipulate stored data (e.g., a DBMS, cf. section 3.3).

Any kind of physical data store (multidimensional arrays, COBOL files, etc.) can be represented by a Type in the logical perspective. For example, the schema of multidimensional cubes is of the form $[D_1,...,D_n,M_1,...,M_m]$ where the D_i represent dimensions (forming the primary key of the cube) and the M_j measures [26].

Each activity in a DW environment is linked to a set of incoming types as well as to a set of outcoming types. The DW activities are of data intensive nature, in their attempt to push data from the data sources to the DW materialized views or client data marts. We capture the outcome of a DW process as a function over the inputs. These semantics are captured through SQL queries, extended with functions wherever richer semantics than SQL are required.

Therefore, an *Activity* is formally characterized by the following attributes:

- *Next*: inherited by *Process Element*.
- *Input*: represents all data stores used by the activity to acquire data.
- *Output*: represents all data stores or reports, where the activity outputs data. The *Output* attribute is further explained by two attributes:
  - *Semantics*: a single value belonging to the set {*Insert, Update, Delete, Select*}. A process can either add (i.e., append), or delete, or update the data in a data store. Also it can output some messages to the user (captured by using a "Message" Type and Select semantics).

- *Expression*: an   SQL query (extended with functions) to denote the relationship of the output and the input types.
- *ExecutedBy*: a physical *Agent* (i.e., an application program) executing the Activity. More information on agents will be provided in the sequel.
- *Role*: a conceptual description of the activity. This attribute will be properly explained in the description of the conceptual perspective.

To motivate the discussion, we will use a part of a case study, enriched with extra requirements, to capture the complexity of the model that we want to express. The discussed organization has to collect various data about the yearly activities of all the hospitals of a particular region. The system relies on operational data from COBOL files. The source of data is a COBOL file, dealing with the annual information by class of beds and hospital (here we use only three classes, namely A, B and C). The COBOL file yields a specific attribute for each class of beds. Each year, the COBOL file is transferred from the production system to the data warehouse and stored in a "buffer" table of the data warehouse, acting as mirror of the file inside the DBMS. Then, the tuples of the buffer table are used by computation procedures to further populate a "fact" table inside the data warehouse. Several materialized views are then populated with aggregate information and used by client tools for querying.

We assume the following four *Types*: *CBL, Buffer, Class_info* and *V1*. The schemata of these types are depicted in Fig. 3. There are four *Activities* in the DW: *Loading, Cleaning, Computation* and *Aggregation*. The *Loading* activity simply copies the data from the *CBL* Cobol file to the *Buffer* type. *H_ID* is an identifier for the hospital and the three last attributes hold the number of beds per class. The *Cleaning* activity deletes all the entries violating the primary key constraint. The *Computation* activity transforms the imported data into a different schema. The date is converted from American to European format and the rest of the attributes are converted to a combination (*Class_id, #Beds*). The *Aggregation* activity simply produces the sum of beds by hospital and year. The expressions and semantics for each activity are listed in Fig. 4. All activities are appending data to the involved types, so they have *INS* semantics, except for the cleaning process, which deletes data, and thus has *DEL* semantics.

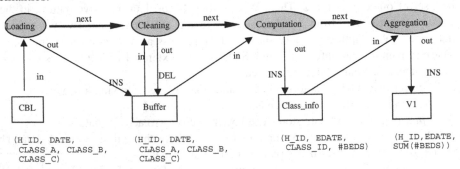

Fig. 3. Motivating Example

Attribute name	Expression	Semantics
Loading.Out:	`SELECT * FROM CBL`	INS

Cleaning.Out:	`SELECT * FROM BUFFER B1`
	`WHERE EXISTS (SELECT B2.H_ID, B2.DATE FROM`
	`        BUFFER B2 WHERE B1.H_ID = B2.H_ID AND`
	`        B1.DATE = B2.DATE GROUP BY H_ID,DATE`
	`        HAVING COUNT(*) > 1)`
		DEL

Computation.
 	
Out:
	`SELECT H_ID, EUROPEAN(DATE) AS EDATE, 'A',`
	`        CLASS_A AS #BEDS`
	`FROM BUFFER WHERE CLASS_A <> 0`
	`UNION`
	`SELECT H_ID, EUROPEAN(DATE) AS EDATE, 'B',`
	`        CLASS_B AS #BEDS`
	`FROM BUFFER WHERE CLASS_B <> 0`
	`UNION`
	`SELECT H_ID, EUROPEAN(DATE) AS EDATE, 'C',`
	`        CLASS_C AS #BEDS`
	`FROM BUFFER WHERE CLASS_C <> 0`
		INS

Aggregation.
Out:
	`SELECT H_ID, EDATE, SUM(#BEDS) AS SUM_BEDS`
	`FROM CLASS_INFO`
	`GROUP BY H_ID, EDATE`
		INS

Fig. 4. Expressions and semantics for the motivating example

3.3 The Physical Perspective

Whereas the logical perspective covers the structure of a process ("what" in [31] terminology), the *physical perspective* covers the details of its execution ("how"). Each process is executed by an *Agent* (i.e. an application program). Each *Type* is physically stored by a *DataStore* (providing information for issues like tablespaces, indexes, etc.). An *Agent* can be formalized as follows:

- *State*: a value of *AgentStateDomain* = {*In_Progress, Commit, Abort*}.
- *Init_time, Abort_time, Commit_time*: timestamps.
- *Execution_parameters*: represent any information about the execution of an agent.
- *In, Out*: physical *DataStores* communicating with the *Agent*. The types used by the respective logical activity must be stored within these data stores.

The information of the physical perspective can be used to trace and monitor the execution of the processes. The relationship between the logical and the physical perspective is done by linking each activity to a specific application program.

3.4 The Conceptual Perspective

A major purpose behind the introduction of the conceptual perspective is to help the interested stakeholder to understand the reasoning behind any decisions on the architecture and characteristics of the DW processes. First of all, each *Type* (i.e. *Relation, Cube*, etc.) in the logical perspective is a representation of a *Concept* in the conceptual perspective. A concept is an abstract entity representing a real world class of objects, in terms of a conceptual metamodel, e.g., the ER model. Both *Types* and

Concepts are constructed from *Fields* (representing their attributes), through the attribute *fields*.

The central entity in the conceptual perspective is the *Role*, which is the conceptual counterpart both of activities and concepts. The *Role* is basically used to express the interdependencies of these entities, through the attribute *RelatesTo*. Formally, a *Role* is defined as follows:

– *RelatesTo*: another Role.
  – *As*: a value of the *RelationshipDomain* = {*suitable, dependent*}.
  – *Wrt*: a multi-value attribute including instances of class *ConceptualObject*.
  – *dueTo:* a string documenting any extra information on the relationship.

A role represents any program or data store participating in the environment of a process, charged with a specific task and/or responsibility. The interrelationship between roles is modeled through the *RelatesTo* relationship. Since both data and processes can be characterized by SQL statements, their interrelationship can be traced in terms of attributes (Fig. 5). An instance of this relationship is a statement about the interrelationship of two roles in the real world, such as 'View V1 *relates to* table Class_Info *with respect to* the attributes Id, Date and number of beds *as* dependent *due to* data loading reasons'.

Attribute	Example 1	Example 2
Role 1	Buffer	Aggregation
Role 2	CBL	Class_Info
As	Dependent	Dependent
Wrt	CBL.*	H_ID, Edate, #Beds

Fig. 5. Examples of role interrelationships for the motivating example

The conceptual perspective is influenced by the Actor-Dependency model [31]. In this model, the actors *depend* on each other for the accomplishment of goals and the delivery of products. The *dependency* notion is powerful enough to capture the relationship of processes where the outcome of the preceding process in the input for the following one. Still, our approach is more powerful since it can capture *suitability,* too (e.g., in the case where more than one concept can apply for the population of an aggregation, one concept is suitable to replace the other).

In the process of understanding errors or design decisions over the architecture of a DW, the conceptual perspective can be used as a reasoning aid, to discover the interdependencies of the actors (possibly in a transitive fashion) and the possible alternatives for different solutions, through a set of *suitable* candidates. Moreover, the provided links to the logical perspective can enable the user to pass from the abstract relationships of roles to the structure of the system. Finally, DW evolution can be designed and influenced by the interdependencies tracked by the *Role* entities. It can be shown that these interdependencies do not have to be directly stored, in all the cases, but can also be computed due to the transitivity of their nature [28].

4   Issues on Process Quality

We adopt the metamodel for the relationship between architecture objects and quality factors presented in [13], which is based on the Goal-Question-Metric approach (GQM) described in [21]. Each object in a DW architecture is linked to a set of quality goals and a set of quality factors (Fig. 6). A *quality goal* is an abstract requirement, defined on DW objects, and documented by a purpose and the stakeholder interested in it. *Quality dimensions* are used to classify quality goals and factors into different categories. A *Quality Factor* represents a quantitative assessment of particular aspect of a DW object, i.e. it relates quality aspects both to actual measurements and expected ranges for these quality values.

The bridge between the abstract, subjective quality goals and the specific, objective quality factors is determined through a set of *quality queries* (or questions), to which quality factor values are provided as possible answers. Quality questions are the outcome of the methodological approach described in [27]. The methodology offers "template" quality factors and dimensions, defined at the metadata level and instantiates them, for the specific DW architecture under examination. As a result of the goal evaluation process, a set of improvements (e.g. design decisions) can be proposed, in order to achieve the expected quality. An extensive list of such "templates" can be found in [12].

Quality goals describe *intentions* or *plans* of the DW users with respect to the status of the DW. In contrast, our process model presented in section 3 describes *facts* about the current status of the DW and what activities are performed in the DW. However, the reason behind the execution of a process is a quality goal which should be achieved or improved by this process. For example, a data cleaning process is executed on the ODS in order to improve the accuracy of the DW. We have represented this dependency between processes and quality goals by extending the relationship between roles and DW objects in the conceptual perspective of the process model (relationship *Expressed For*). This is shown in the upper part of Fig. 6.

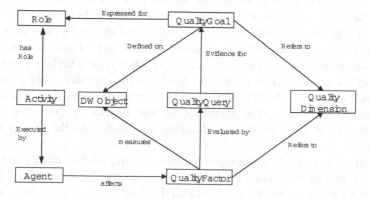

Fig. 6. Relationships between processes and quality

The lower part of Fig. 6 represents the relationship between processes and quality on a more operational level. The operation of an agent in the DW will have an impact on quality factors of DW objects. The relationship *affects* represents both the measured and expected effect of a DW process on DW quality. The effect of a DW process must always be confirmed by new measurements of the quality factors. Unexpected effects of DW processes can be detected by comparing the measurements with the expected behavior of the process.

The vocabulary / domain of the quality questions, with respect to the process model is anticipated to be the set of DW activities, which can of course be mapped to reasons (roles) and conditions (of agents) for a specific situation. Thus, the discrimination of logical, conceptual and physical perspectives is verified once more, in the quality management of the DW: the quality goals can express "why" things have happened (or should happen) in the DW, the quality questions try to discover "what" actually happens and finally, the quality factors express "how" this reality is measured.

We define a set of generic quality dimensions to classify quality goals and factors of DW processes. It is influenced mainly from the quality criteria for workflows defined in [7] and the quality dimensions for software evaluation presented in [9]: (i) *Correctness*: a specification exists, describing the conditions under which the process has achieved its aim; (ii) *Functionality*: the process satisfies specific needs of data warehouse stakeholders; (iii) *Efficiency*: the process has a good balance between level of performance and amount of used resources; (iv) *Maintainability*: the degree of easiness with which the process can be modified.

5   Exploitation of the Metadata Repository

We exploit the metadata repository in all the phases of the DW lifecycle. During the *design* phase, the user can check the consistency of his/her design, to determine any violations of the business logic of the DW, or the respect of simple rules over the structure of the DW schema. During the *administration* phase (i.e., in the everyday usage of the DW) we can use the repository to discover quality problems. A particular task in the DW lifecycle, *DW evolution*, is supported by the repository, in order to determine possible impacts, when the schema of a particular object changes.

The consistency of the metadata repository should be checked to ensure the validity of the representation of the real world in the repository. For example, the repository can check if the type definitions of activities, agents and data stores are consistent with each other. The repository can also be used by external programs to support the execution of consistency checking algorithms like the ones proposed in [24, 16].

In addition, the quality information stored in the repository may be used to find deficiencies in data warehouse. For example, we can search the repository for all the data cleaning activities which have decreased the availability of a data store according to the stored measurements. The significance of such a query is that it can show that the implementation of the data cleaning process has become inefficient.

We do not elaborate these two issues and proceed to deal with the problem of DW evolution. We refer the interested reader to [28] for a complete discussion.

Algorithm Extract_Type_Definitions
Input: a list of processes **P**= [P₁, P₂, …, Pₙ], a set of types **T**={ T₁, T₂, …, Tₘ}. Each process P[i] has a type P[i].out, belonging to **T**, and an expression P[i].expr. Each type of **T**, say t, has an SQL expression t.expr comprised of a set of "inserted data" (t.i_expr) and "deleted" data (t.d_expr). Also there is a subset of **T**, **S**, with the source types.
Output: A set of SQL definitions for each type of **T**.

```
Begin
    Initialize all the expressions of T-S to {}.
    For i := 1 to n
        Case
            P[i].semantics = 'INS'
                P[i].out.i_expr := P[i].out.i_expr UNION
                    Reduce(P[i].expr)
            P[i].semantics = 'DEL'
                P[i].out.d_expr := P[i].out.d_expr UNION
                    Reduce(P[i].expr)
        End_case
        P[i].out.expr := P[i].out.i_expr MINUS P[i].out.d_expr
    End_for
End
```

Where *Reduce(expr)*:
1. Use the technique of [17] to represent SQL queries; if self-references exist (e.g. in the case of DEL statements) discriminate between multiple occurrences of the same table.
2. Use the reduction techniques of [22,14,15] wherever applicable to reduce the query definition to a compact form.

Fig. 7. Algorithm for extracting the definition of a type in the repository

5.1   Interdependencies of Types, Processes and Roles

We suppose that there is a set of types belonging to the set *SourceSchema*, denoting all the types found in the data sources. We treat the types of *SourceSchema* as source nodes of a graph: we do not consider any processes affecting them. For the rest of the types, we can derive an SQL expression by using existing view reduction algorithms. Several complementary proposals exist such as [14], corrected with the results of [5, 18, 19] (to which we will collectively refer to as [14] in the sequel) as well as [15, 17, 22]. The proposed algorithm is applicable to graphs of activities that do not involve updates. In most cases, an update operation can be considered as the combination of insertions and deletions or as the application of the appropriate function to the relevant attributes.

5.2   Repository Support for Data Warehouse Evolution

The problem that arises is to keep all the DW objects and processes consistent to each other, in the presence of changes. For example, suppose that the definition of a materialized view in the DW changes. This change triggers a chain reaction in the DW: the update process must evolve (both at the refreshment and the cleaning steps), and the old, historical data must be migrated to the new schema (possibly with respect to the new selection conditions, too). All the data stores of the DW and client level which are populated from this particular view must be examined with respect to their schema, content and population processes.

In our approach, we distinguish two kinds of impact:

- *Direct impact*: the change in the DW object imposes that some action must be taken against an affected object, e.g., an attribute is deleted from a materialized view, then the activity which populates it must also be changed accordingly.
- *Implicit impact:* the change in the DW object might change the semantics of another object, without obligatorily changing the structure of the latter.

Our model enables us to construct a partially ordered graph (which can be produced by proper queries in Telos): for each *Type* instance, say t, there is a set of types and activities, used for the population of t ("before" t), denoted as $\mathbf{B}(t)$. Also, there is another set of objects using t for their population ("after" t), denoted as $\mathbf{A}(t)$.

In Fig. 7, we showed how we could derive an SQL definition for each type in the repository. Suppose that a type t is characterized by an expression e which is supported by a set of auxiliary SQL expressions producing, thus the set $\mathbf{e}=\{e_1,e_2,\ldots,e\}$. Obviously some of the expressions belonging to $\mathbf{e}$ belong also to $\mathbf{B}(t)$. Thus, we extend $\mathbf{B}(t)$ as $\mathbf{B}(t)\cup\mathbf{e}$ (with set semantics). Suppose, then, that the final SQL expression of a type t, say e, changes into e'. Following the spirit of [8], we can use the following rules for schema evolution in a DW environment (we consider that the changes abide by the SQL syntax and the new expression is valid):

- If the *select clause* of e' has an extra attribute from e, then propagate the extra attribute down the line to the base relations: there must be at least one path from one type belonging to a *SourceSchema* to an activity whose out expression involves the extra attribute. If we delete an attribute from the select clause of a Type, it must not appear in the select clause of the processes that directly populate the respective type, as well as in the following Types and the processes that use this particular Type. In the case of addition of an attribute, the impact is direct for the previous objects $\mathbf{B}(t)$ and implicit for the successor objects $\mathbf{A}(t)$. In the case of deletion the impact is direct for both categories.
- If the *where clause* of e' is more strict than the one of e, then the *where clause* of at least one process belonging to $\mathbf{B}(t)$ must change identically. If this is not possible, a new process can be added just before t simply deleting the respective tuples through the expression $e'-e$. If the *where clause* of e' is less strict than the one of e, then we can use well known subsumption techniques [20, 25] to determine which types can be (re)used to calculate the new expression e' of t. The *having clause* is treated in the same fashion. The impact is direct for the previous and implicit for the successor objects.

– If an attribute is deleted from the *group by clause* of *e*, then at least the last activity performing a *group-by* query should be adjusted accordingly. All the consequent activities in the population chain of *t* must change too (as if an attribute has been deleted). If this is not feasible we can add an aggregating process performing this task exactly before *t*. If an extra attribute is added to the *group by clause* of *e*, then at least the last activity performing a *group -by* query should be adjusted accordingly. The check is performed recursively for the types populating this particular type, too. If this fails, the subsumption techniques mentioned for the *where-clause* can be used for the same purpose again. The impact is direct both for previous and successor objects. Only in the case of attribute addition it is implicit for the successor objects.

We do not claim that we provide a concrete algorithmic solution to the problem. Rather, we sketch a methodological set of steps, in the form of suggested actions to perform this kind of evolution. Similar algorithms for the evolution of views in DW's can be found in [1,8]. A tool could easily visualize this evolution plan and allow the user to react to it.

6   Conclusions

This paper describes a metamodel for DW operational processes. This metamodel enables DW management, design and evolution based on a high level conceptual perspective, which can be linked to the actual structural and physical aspects of the DW architecture. The proposed metamodel is also capable of modeling complex activities, their interrelationships, the relationship of activities with data sources and execution details. Finally, the metamodel complements existing architecture and quality models in a coherent fashion, resulting in a full framework for DW metamodeling. We have implemented this metamodel using the language Telos and the metadata repository system ConceptBase.

In this paper, we have used the *global-as-view* approach for the DW definition, i.e., we reduce the definition of the DW materialized views to the data sources. We plan to investigate the possibility of using the *local-as-view* approach (which means reducing both the view definitions and the data sources to a global enterprise model), as it appears to provide several benefits over the global-as-view approach [4].

Acknowledgments

This research is sponsored in part by the European Esprit Projects "DWQ: Foundations of Data Warehouse Quality", No. 22469, and "MEMO: Mediating and Monitoring Electronic Commerce", No. 26895, and by the Deutsche Forschungsgemeinsschaft (DFG) under the Collaborative Research Center IMPROVE (SFB 476). We would like to thank all our DWQ partners who contributed to the progress of this work, and especially Professors Timos Sellis, Mokrane Bouzeghoub, Manfred Jeusfeld and Maurizio Lenzerini.

References

1. Z. Bellahsène. Structural View Maintenance in Data Warehousing Systems. Journées Bases de Données Avancées (BDA '98), Tunis, October 1998.
2. M. Bouzeghoub, F. Fabret, M. Matulovic. Modeling Data Warehouse Refreshment Process as a Workflow Application. Workshop on Design and Management of Data Warehouses (DMDW'99), Heidelberg, Germany, 1999.
3. F. Casati, S. Ceri, B. Pernici, G. Pozzi. Conceptual Modeling of Workflows. Conf. On Object-Oriented and Entity-Relationship Modelling (OOER'95), Australia, 1995.
4. D. Calvanese, G. De Giacomo, M. Lenzerini, D. Nardi, R. Rosati. A principled approach to data integration and reconciliation in data warehousing. Workshop on Design and Management of Data Warehouses (DMDW'99), Heidelberg, 1999.
5. Richard A. Ganski, Harry K. T. Wong. Optimization of Nested SQL Queries Revisited. In Proc. of ACM SIGMOD Conference, San Francisco, pp. 23-33, 1987
6. D. Georgakopoulos, M. Hornick, A. Sheth. An overview of workflow management: From process modeling to workflow automation infrastructure. Distributed and parallel databases, 3(2):119-153, 1995.
7. D. Georgakopoulos, M. Rusinkiewicz. Workflow management: From business process automation to inter-organizational collaboration. Tutorials of the 23rd International Conference on Very Large Data Bases, Athens, Greece, 1997.
8. A. Gupta, I. Mumick, K. Ross. Adapting Materialized Views after Redefinitions. In Proc. of ACM SIGMOD Conference, San Jose, CA, pp. 211-222, 1995.
9. ISO/IEC 9126 International Standard. Intl. Organization for Standardization. 1991
10. M. Jarke, M.A. Jeusfeld, T. Rose. A software process data model for knowledge engineering in information systems. Information Systems, 15(1):85-116, 1990.
11. M. Jarke, R. Gallersdörfer, M.A. Jeusfeld, M. Staudt, S. Eherer. ConceptBase - a deductive objectbase for meta data management. J. Intelligent Information Systems, 4(2):167-192, 1995.
12. M. Jarke, M.A.Jeusfeld, C. Quix, P. Vassiliadis: Architecture and quality in data warehouses: An extended repository approach. Information Systems, 24(3):229-253, 1999. (a previous version appeared in CAiSE '98, Pisa, Italy, 1998)
13. M.A. Jeusfeld, C. Quix, M. Jarke. Design and Analysis of Quality Information for Data Warehouses. 17th Conf. Entity Relationship Approach (ER'98), Singapore, pp. 349-262, 1998.
14. W. Kim. On Optimizing an SQL-like Nested Query. ACM TODS 7(3):443-469, 1982.
15. A. Levy, I. Mumick, Y. Sagiv. Query Optimization by Predicate Move-Around. In Proc. of 20th VLDB Conference, Chile, pp. 96-107, 1994.
16. O. Marjanovic, M. Orlowska. On Modeling and Verification of Temporal Constraints in Production Workflows. Knowledge and Information Systems, 1(2):157-192, 1999.
17. I. Mumick, S. Finkelstein, H. Pirahesh, R. Ramakrishnan. Magic is Relevant. In Proc. of ACM SIGMOD Conference, Atlantic City, NJ, pp. 247-258, 1990.
18. M. Muralikrishna. Optimization and Dataflow Algorithms for Nested Tree Queries. In Proc. of 15th VLDB Conference, Amsterdam, The Netherlands, pp. 77-85, 1989.
19. M. Muralikrishna. Improved Unnesting Algorithms for Join Aggregate SQL Queries. In Proc. of 18th VLDB Conference, Vancouver, Canada, pp. 91-102, 1992.
20. W. Nutt, Y. Sagiv, S. Shurin. Deciding Equivalences among Aggregate Queries. In Proc. of 17th Symposium on the Principles of Databases (PODS'98), Seattle, pp. 214-223, 1998.
21. M. Oivo, V. Basili. Representing software engineering models: the TAME goal-oriented approach. IEEE Trans .Software Engineering, 18(10):886-898, 1992.

22. H. Pirahesh, J. Hellerstein, W. Hasan. Extensible/Rule Based Query Rewrite Optimization in Starburst. In Proc. of ACM SIGMOD Conference, San Diego, CA, pp. 39-48, 1992.
23. B. Ramesh, V. Dhar. Supporting systems development by capturing deliberations during requirements engineering. IEEE Trans. Software Eng., 18(6):498-510, 1992.
24. W. Sadiq, M. Orlowska. Applying Graph Reduction Techniques for Identifying Structural Conflicts in Process Models. In Proc. of 11th Intl. Conf. Advanced Information Systems Engineering, (CAiSE'99), Heidelberg, Germany, pp. 195-209, 1999.
25. D. Srivastava, S. Dar, H.V. Jagadish, A.Y. Levy. Answering Queries with Aggregation Using Views. In Proc. of 22nd VLDB Conference, Bombay, India, pp. 318-329, 1996.
26. P. Vassiliadis. Modeling Multidimensional Databases, Cubes and Cube Operations. In Proc. of 10th SSDBM Conference, Capri, Italy, pp. 53-62, 1998.
27. P. Vassiliadis, M. Bouzeghoub, C. Quix. Towards Quality-Oriented Data Warehouse Usage and Evolution. In Proc. of 11th Conference of Advanced Information Systems Engineering (CAiSE '99), Heidelberg, Germany, pp. 164-179, 1999.
28. P. Vassiliadis, C. Quix, Y. Vassiliou, M. Jarke. A Model for Data Warehouse Operational Processes (long version). Available at http://www.dblab.ece.ntua.gr/~pvassil/publications/process-model00.gz
29. Workflow Management Coalition. Interface 1: Process Definition Interchange Process Model. Doc. No. WfMC TC-1016-P, 1998. (http://www.wfmc.org)
30. E. Yu. Strategic Modelling for Enterprise Integration. In Proc. 14th World Congress of Int. Federation of Automatic Control, China 1999.
31. E. Yu, J. Mylopoulos. Understanding 'Why' in Software Process Modelling, Analysis and Design. In Proc. of 16th Intl. Conference Software Engineering, Sorrento, Italy, pp. 159-168, 1994.

Temporally Faithful Execution
of Business Transactions

Werner Obermair[1] and Michael Schrefl[2]

[1] Institut für Wirtschaftsinformatik
Universität Linz, Austria
obermair@dke.uni-linz.ac.at
[2] School of Computer and Information Science
University of South Australia, Australia
schrefl@cs.unisa.edu.au

Abstract. Serializability is a prominent correctness criterion for an interleaved execution of concurrent transactions. Serializability guarantees that the interleaved execution of concurrent transactions corresponds to *some* serial execution of the same transactions. Many important business applications, however, require the system to impose a partial serialization order between transactions pinned to a specific point in time and conventional transactions that attempt to commit before, at, or after that point i n time. This paper introduces *temporal faithfulness* as a new correctness criterion for such cases. Temporal faithfulness does not require real-time capabilities but ensures that the serialization order of a set of business transactions is not in conflict with precedence requirements between them. The paper also shows how a temporally faithful transaction scheduler can be built by extending proven scheduling techniques.

1 Introduction

Transaction processing as it is discussed widely in literature and as it is supported in many commercial systems follows a prominent principle: Concurrent transactions are executed in an interleaved manner and serializability is used as the correctness criterion for the interleaving. This means that an interleaved execution of concurrent transactions is considered correct if it produces the same output and has the same effect on the database state as *some* serial execution of the same transactions. O f course, not all serial executions produce the same output and have the same effect.

Important business applications are not supported appropriately if transaction processing follows this principle. Consider the following scenario: In a trading system, a trader intends to adjust the selling price of a product at 12:00 noon. The trader intuitively expects that sales transactions performed before 12:00 noon should be performed on the old selling price, and that sales transactions performed after 12:00 noon should be performed on the new selling price. In deciding whether a sales transaction i s performed before or after 12:00 noon, the trader considers relevant the point in time when the customer commits to

B. Wangler, L. Bergman (Eds.): CAiSE 2000, LNCS 1789, pp. 462–481, 2000.
© Springer-Verlag Berlin Heidelberg 2000

a sale, i.e., when the customer decides to buy. This point in time corresponds to the "handshake" between the seller and buyer in a traditional sales transaction; in a computer-based trading sytem, this point in time corresponds to the attempt to commit the sales transaction. If the attempt to commit the sales transaction is placed before 12:00 noon, the sales transaction has to be performed on the old selling price and, therefore, serialized before the adjusting transaction. If the attempt to commit the sales transcation is placed after 12:00 noon, the sales transaction has to be performed on the new selling price and, therefore, serialized after the adjusting transaction.

We refer to transactions as contained in the described scenario as *business transactions*. Business transactions require a combination of concepts that is not yet appropriately provided by current transaction execution models. From a user's perspective, the required concepts are:

First, business transactions behave as if executed instantaneously. Although they may be actually executed over some time period, the end user will assume that each business transaction is performed at a particular point in time.

Second, business transactions can be linked to wall-clock time. This point in time indicates when the transaction is performed from the perspective of the end user, regardless when it is actually executed internally.

Third, two types of business transactions can be distinguished. Those which are performed (from the user's point of view) at a specific wall-clock time and those which are performed at the wall-clock time of the "handshake", i.e., at the request to commit the business transaction.

Fourth, real-time capabilities are not required. It is sufficient that the effect of the execution of a set of business transactions is the same as if each transaction had been executed instanteneously at its specified wall-clock time.

How can this desired semantics of business transactions be achieved in a system that guarantees only that the interleaved execution of concurrent transactions corresponds to some serial execution? In our scenario, starting the adjusting transaction at 12:00 noon is not sufficient. The transaction execution may be delayed due to concurreny conflicts, and there may be sales transactions reading the old price but attempting to commit after 12:00 noon. A solution for this particular case would be to incorporate the price of a product as a time-stamped attribute (perhaps in a historical database). The price change could have been recorded proactively, and sales transactions could read the current selling price just before they attempt to commit. This solution, however, is not general since it may not be applied in cases in which the time critical update relies on a complex computation. For example, consider the case that the new product price should be determined through an analysis of the market as it is at 12:00 noon. The market at 12:00 noon cannot be anticipated and, thus, no proactive price change can be recorded. Also using some form of multi-version concurrency control will not be sufficient as such, since multi-version concurrency control is typically based on internal processing time rather than on real-world time. Business transactions are better supported by a system that provides a general mechanism for influencing the order in which transactions are serialized.

In this paper, we present such a general mechanism. Its key advantage is that it is based on standard concurrency control techniques and applicable to conventional database systems. As such it does neither rely on sophisticated, special concurrency control mechanisms (such as multi-version concurrency control) nor does it require specialized database systems (such as temporal or real-time).

We introduce a new category of transactions, so-called *pinned transactions*. A user who submits a pinned transaction gives the transaction an explicit timestamp. If a pinned transaction needs to be aborted internally during its processing (e.g., because of a deadlock), the transaction is automatically restarted with the same timestamp. In our example scenario, the transaction adjusting the selling price would be a pinned transaction with timestamp 12:00 noon. Also conventional transactions, we refer to them as *unpinned transactions*, receive timestamps. The timestamp of an unpinned transaction is not given by a user, but is the current reading of the system clock when the transaction attempts to commit. If an unpinned transaction needs to be aborted internally during its processing, it is the user who decides whether to restart or to dismiss the transaction. A user who decides to commit an unpinned transaction relies on the database state as it is at the attempt to commit. It cannot be assumed t hat the user decides to issue the attempt to commit again if the database state has changed after a restart. In our example scenario, sales transactions would be unpinned transactions receiving as timestamps the reading of the system clock when they attempt to commit.

The timestamps associated with transactions do not mean that the transactions are executed real-time at the indicated points in time. A less stringent criterion than real-time execution is sufficient for many business applications: *temporal faithfulness*. Timestamps are interpreted as precedence requirements and temporal faithfulness means that the serialization of transactions follows these precedence requirements. Although possibly laging behind real time, a system that behaves in a temporally faithf ul manner guarantees the expected serialization order. Reconsider the transaction adjusting the selling price of a product upon an analysis of the market as it is at 12:00 noon: If this pinned transaction is still running after 12:00 noon, unpinned sales transaction carrying a later time stamp but incorrectly relying on the old selling price are prevented from committing. Moreover, if such an uncommitted sales transaction keeps the adjusting transaction from committing (e.g., because of a lock conflict), th e sales transaction is aborted.

We first encountered the need for a temporally faithful execution of transactions when we developed an execution model for *rules on business policies* in [9]. Rules on business policies express how an external observer, e.g., a swift clerk, could monitor calendar time and the database state to recognize predefined situations and to react to them accordingly in order to meet a company's business policy. They are formulated according to the event-condition-action structure of rules in acti ve database systems [4] and can be classified into two categories, (1) rules that are executed asynchronously to user transactions and (2) rules that are executed "immediately" upon temporal events. The second rule category is not supported appropriately by the execution models of existing active database systems. Existing active database systems allow to react upon temporal events only by starting independent transactions without any possibility to predict when the reaction will actually be committed to the database. A rule of the second category, however, relies on a temporally faithful execution of transactions where the execution of the rule is reflected by a pinned transaction. For details on rules on business policies and their execution semantics see [9].

The remainder of this paper is organized as follows: Section 2 introduces the concept of temporal faithfulness. Section 3 establishes a theory for a concurrent and temporally faithful execution of transactions. Section 4 outlines a scheduler that provides for a temporally faithful execution of transactions and that is based on strict two-phase locking. Section 5 concludes the paper by summarizing its main achievements and by outlining future work .

2   Temporal Faithfulness

In this section, we introduce the concept of temporal faithfulness. Section 2.1 starts with the presentation of the time model underlying our timestamping mechanism. Section 2.2 discusses the precedence requirements imposed by the timestamps assigned to transactions. Section 2.3 relates temporal faithfulness with concepts presented in the diverse literature.

2.1   Time Model

The timestamps assigned to pinned transactions bear application semantics. Timestamps have to be meaningful for users. Time as it is perceived by users may be of a coarser granularity than it is supported in some database system. In other words, the temporal unit that is not further decomposable from a user's perspective can often be of a coarser granularity than the temporal unit defined by two successive clock ticks of an internal clock of some target system. E.g., timestamps showing only minutes but not seconds are sufficient for many business applications. We consider time as a finite sequence of chronons. A chronon is the smallest temporal unit that is not further decomposable from a user's perspective. The timestamps that are assigned to transactions—either explicitly in the case of pinned transactions, or upon their attempt to commit in the case of unpinned transactions—are of the same granularity as chronons. This means that several transactions will share a common timestamp.

2.2   Precedence Requirements

Timestamps that are associated with transactions impose precedence requirements that induce a partial execution order. For the sake of simplicity, we assume an execution model in which transactions are executed serially. We will relax this assumption in Sect. 3.

If a transaction t has a lower timestamp than another transaction t', temporal faithfulness requires that t has to be executed before t'. Irrespective of chronon length, there may be several transactions that share a common timestamp. Even if chronons are extremely short, the timestamp given to a pinned transaction by an external user may coincide with the point in time at which an unpinned transaction requests to commit. Several pinned transactions with the same timestamp cannot be further distingu ished and, therefore, no precedence requirements can be identified among them. Correspondingly, also several unpinned transactions with the same timestamp can be executed in an arbitrary order. Pinned and unpinned transactions sharing a common timestamp, however, may be related in different ways:

1. *Head policy:* All pinned transactions are performed before all unpinned transactions. In this policy, the unpinned transactions are performed on a database state that reflects the updates of the pinned transactions. Scenarios can be drawn in which this execution semantics is favourable.

   Example 1. Consider a pinned transaction that updates selling prices at 12:00 noon upon market analysis. This pinned transaction is expected to be performed before any unpinned sales transaction attempting to commit during the chronon from 12:00 to 12:01 noon. The sales transactions should be performed on the new price.

2. *Tail policy:* All pinned transactions are performed after all unpinned transactions. In this policy, the pinned transactions are performed on a database state that reflects the updates of all unpinned transactions. Favourable scenarios can be drawn, too.

   Example 2. Consider a transaction pinned to 11:59 a.m. that publishes the selling prices and computes the morning sales figures. This pinned transaction is expected to be performed after all unpinned sales transactions attempting to commit during the chronon from 11:59 a.m. to 12:00 noon. The sales performed during the last chronon of the morning should be reflected in the sales figures.

3. *Don't care policy:* Pinned transactions and unpinned transactions are executed in arbitrary order. If a pinned transaction precedes some unpinned transactions with the same timestamp and succeeds some others, it is not predictable on which database states transactions are executed. We did not encounter any realistic application scenario that is best supported by the *don't care policy* and believe that this case is probably not relevant in practice.

We support the *head policy* and the *tail policy* by introducing two kinds of pinned transactions: transactions that are pinned to the begin of a chronon (*head transactions*) and transactions that are pinned to the end of a chronon (*tail transactions*). One may argue that a tail transaction t pinned to the end of chronon i (case 1) could be replaced by a head transaction t' pinned to the begin of chronon $i + 1$ (case 2). This is not true for the following reason: In the first case, all head transactions pinned to the begin of chronon $i + 1$ work on a database state that reflects the changes performed by t, in the second case, there may be some head transactions pinned to the begin of chronon $i + 1$ that are executed before t' since transactions of the same kind sharing a common timestamp are performed in any order.

From the view point of a chronon i—lasting from clock-tick i to clock-tick $i+1$—there are transactions pinned to the begin of chronon i (head-transactions, H^i), unpinned transactions attempting to commit during i (body-transactions, B^i), and transactions pinned to the end of chronon i (tail-transactions, T^i).

2.3   Related Work

Timestamps that are associated with transactions have a long tradition in transaction processing: They are employed in timestamp ordering as a concurrency control mechanism or in deadlock prevention without risking livelocks. The commit time of transactions is often used as transaction time in rollback or bitemporal databases. Commit-time timestamping guarantees transaction-consistent pictures of past states of a database ([11]). In all those cases, however, the timestamps assigned to tra nsactions are generated by the database system and do not bear application semantics.

Georgakopoulos et al. [7] introduce transaction timestamps that bear application semantics. They call their timestamps "value-dates". By means of value-dates, Georgakopoulos et al. specify "succession dependencies". Like precedence requirements in our model, succession dependencies do not impose real-time constraints on the execution of transactions, but they influence the ordering of transactions. If a succession dependency is specified between two transactions, the two transacti ons are serialized in the requested order irrespective whether they conflict in their operations or not. This is an important difference to temporal faithfulness where a precedence requirement influences only the ordering of conflicting transactions. Disregarding other transactions, two transactions that do not conflict in their operations can be serialized in an arbitrary order in a temporally faithful setting. We will discuss this in detail in Sect. 3.

Finger and McBrien [6] introduce "perceivedly instantaneous transactions" for valid-time databases. For a perceivedly instantaneous transaction it is guaranteed that "current time" (usually referred to as now) remains constant during its execution. The point in time at which a transaction is submitted is taken as the transaction's value of now. Transactions that conflict in their operations are serialized according to their values of now, i.e., according to their subm ission points. Contrary to our approach, timestamps assigned to transactions do not bear application semantics in the approach of Finger and McBrien. Further, all transactions are timestamped in the same way. This is an important difference to our approach where usually a high number of unpinned transactions is serialized around a few pinned transactions.

The specification of temporal transaction dependencies has been discussed in the literature also without using timestamps. For example: Ngu [10] builds precedence graphs that reflect temporal dependencies. Dayal et al. [5] use rules as they are provided by active database systems to specify the ordering of transactions. They do this by specifying rules that are triggered by transaction events and by exploiting the capabilities of coupling modes (cf. [3]). The bas ic limitation of these approaches is that all related transactions must be known in advance. Our model is by far more modular and general: A transaction can be pinned to a point in time without the need to consider all the transactions that potentially may be executed around the critical point in time.

3 Theory of Concurrent and Temporally Faithful Histories

A theory to analyze the concurrent temporally faithful execution of transactions can be formulated similarly to the classical serializability theory (cf. [1]). We will establish our theory through the following steps: First, we will define the conditions under which a serial history is temporally faithful. Then, we will recall the conditions under which two histories are equivalent, and we will define a history to be temporally faithfully serializable—and thus correct—if it is equivalent to a temporally faithful serial history. Finally, we will show how it can be tested whether a history is temporally faithfully serializable.

A history covers a set of chronons C and a set of transactions T where T contains all committed transactions $t_1, t_2, \ldots, t_n$ that are time-stamped with a chronon in C. History h indicates the order in which the operations of $t_1, t_2, \ldots, t_n$ are executed. T can be subdivided into disjoint subsets according to two dimensions: (1) For every chronon c ($c \in C$) there is a subset T_c containing the transactions time-stamped with c. (2) According to the transactio n categories, T can be subdivided into a set of head-transactions T^h, body-transactions T^b, and tail-transactions T^t. Combining the two dimensions, for every chronon c ($c \in C$) there is a set T_c^h containing the head-transactions that are pinned to the begin of c, a set T_c^b embracing the body-transactions that attempt to commit during c, and a set T_c^t containing the tail-transactions that are pinned to the end of c.

Definition 1. *A history is* temporally faithfully serial *if it is serial, if it observes timestamps, and if it observes priorities:*

1. *A history is* serial *if, for every two transactions t_i and t_j, either all operations of t_i are executed before all operations of t_j or vice versa. Thus, a serial history represents an execution in which there is no interleaving of the operations of different transactions.*
2. *A history observes* timestamps *if, for every two transactions $t_i \in T_{c_k}$ and $t_j \in T_{c_l}$ where $c_k < c_l$, t_i is executed before t_j. Thus, timestamp observation requires that transactions with different timestamps are executed in timestamp order.*
3. *A history observes* priorities *if (1) for every two transactions $t_i \in T_{c_k}^h$ and $t_j \in T_{c_k}^b \cup T_{c_k}^t$, t_i is executed before t_j and if (2) for every two transactions $t_i \in T_{c_k}^b$ and $t_j \in T_{c_k}^t$, t_i is executed before t_j. Thus, priority observation*

requires that head-transactions are executed before body- and tail-transactions and that body-transactions are executed before tail-transactions if they have the same timestamp.

Example 3. We examine histories over the set of chronons $C = \{c_1, c_2\}$ and the set of transactions $T = \{t_1, t_2, t_3, t_4, t_5\}$ with[1]

$$t_1 = r_1[x] \to w_1[x]$$
$$t_2 = r_2[z] \to w_2[z]$$
$$t_3 = r_3[y] \to r_3[x] \to w_3[y]$$
$$t_4 = r_4[z] \to r_4[x] \to w_4[z]$$
$$t_5 = r_5[y] \to w_5[y]$$

where $T_{c_1}^h = \{\}$, $T_{c_1}^b = \{t_1\}$, $T_{c_1}^t = \{\}$, $T_{c_2}^h = \{t_2\}$, $T_{c_2}^b = \{t_3, t_4\}$, and $T_{c_2}^t = \{t_5\}$.

Different timestamps and different priorities impose precedence requirements on the transactions contained in T. Figure 1 shows the imposed precedence requirements graphically. A circle depicts a transaction, an arrow from a transaction t_i to a transaction t_j indicates that t_i has to be performed before t_j. In our example: Timestamp observation requires for a temporally faithfully serial history that transaction t_1 is executed before transactions t_2, t_3, t_4, and t_5. Priority observation requires that head-transaction t_2 is executed before body-transactions t_3 and t_4 and before tail-transaction t_5 and that body-transactions t_3 and t_4 are executed before tail-transaction t_5.

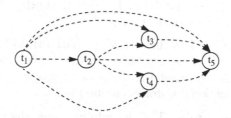

Fig. 1. Precedence requirements imposed by timestamps and priorities

Definition 2. *Two histories h and h' are equivalent if (1) they cover the same set of transactions performing the same operations, and if (2) they order conflicting operations in the same way. The second condition requires that for any conflicting operations o_i belonging to transaction t_i and o_j belonging to transaction t_j, their execution order in h corresponds with their execution order in h'. (This definition follows the basic serializability theory, cf. [1]).*

Definition 3. *A history is* temporally faithfully serializable *(TFSR) if it is equivalent to a temporally faithfully serial history.*

---

[1] We denote the ordering of operations within a transaction or history by means of arrows ($\to$).

Whether a history is temporally faithfully serializable can be determined by checking an extended form of a serialization graph (SG), a so-called *temporally faithful serialization graph (TFSG)*, for cycles. Like an SG, a TFSG is a directed graph whose nodes are the transactions covered by the analyzed history. The edges of a TFSG, however, do not represent only precedence requirements imposed by conflicts, but also precedence requirements imposed by different time-stamps and priorities. Throughout the rest of this paper, we refer to precedence requirements imposed by different timestamps or different priorities as *temporal precedence requirements*.

A TFSG is built in two steps:

1. An SG is built by introducing edges that represent precedence requirements imposed by conflicts. An SG for a history h contains an edge from transaction t_i to transaction t_j $(i \neq j)$ if t_i issues an operation o_i that conflicts with an operation o_j of t_j and if o_i precedes o_j in h. An edge from t_i to t_j expresses that t_i has to precede t_j in a serial history equivalent to h. According to the classical Serializability Theorem, an equivalent serial history can be found—and thus a history is serializable—iff its serialization graph is acyclic (for the Serializability Theorem and a proof see [1]). An acyclic SG means that the precedence requirements imposed by conflicts do not contradict each other.

   Example 4. We continue the above example. Consider the histories:

   $$h_1 = r_5[y] \to w_5[y] \to r_2[z] \to r_3[y] \to r_3[x] \to w_2[z] \to r_4[z] \to w_3[y] \to$$
   $$r_1[x] \to r_4[x] \to w_1[x] \to w_4[z]$$
   $$h_2 = r_1[x] \to r_2[z] \to w_1[x] \to r_3[y] \to w_2[z] \to r_4[z] \to r_3[x] \to r_4[x] \to$$
   $$w_4[z] \to w_3[y] \to r_5[y] \to w_5[y]$$

   Figure 2 shows the SG for history h_1 in part (a) and the SG for history h_2 in part (b). The edges representing precedence requirements imposed by conflicts are shown as solid lines. Both graphs are acyclic, i.e., for both histories equivalent serial histories can be found.

2. The SG is extended to a TFSG by adding edges that represent temporal precedence requirements. Since a cyclic SG implies a cyclic TFSG, this second step is applied only if the SG of a history is acyclic, i.e., if the history is serializable. To capture different timestamps, for every pair of transactions (t_i, t_j) with $t_i \in T_{c_k}$, $t_j \in T_{c_l}$ and $c_k < c_l$, there is an edge from t_i to t_j. To capture different priorities, for every pair of transactions (t_i, t_j) with (1) $t_i \in T_{c_k}^h$ and $t_j \in T_{c_k}^b \cup T_{c_k}^t$, or with (2) $t_i \in T_{c_k}^b$ and $t_j \in T_{c_k}^t$, there is an edge from t_i to t_j. If a TFSG is built according to these rules, the TFSG contains also all edges implied by transitivity: If there is an edge from t_j to t_k and an edge from t_k to t_l, there is necessarily an edge from t_j to t_l. We draw edges implied by transitivity since they allow to efficiently decide whether a TFSG is acyclic (see below).

   Example 5. We continue the above examples: Figure 2 (c) shows the TFSG for h_1 and Fig. 2 (d) shows the TFSG for h_2. The edges representing temporal precedence requirements are shown as dashed lines.

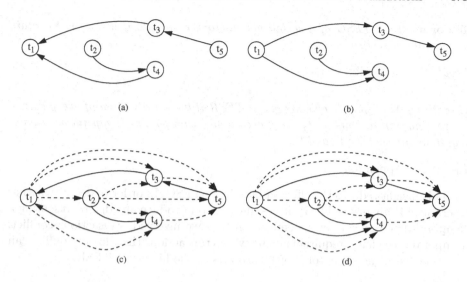

Fig.2. Building TFSGs (example)

A history is TFSR if there are no contradicting precedence requirements. Precedence requirements contradict, for example, if conflicts require transaction t_i to be executed before transaction t_j in a serial execution whereas timestamp observation requires t_j to be executed before t_i. Contradicting precedence requirements become visible in TFSGs as cycles. This can be summarized in a theorem closely related with the classical Serializability Theorem:

Theorem 1. *A history is TFSR iff its TFSG is acyclic.*

Proof. See Appendix.

Example 6. We continue the above examples: Figure 2 shows that the TFSG of h_1 contains cycles. History h_1 is not TFSR since the precedence requirements imposed by timestamps and priorities contradict the precedence requirements imposed by conflicts. The TFSG of h_2, however, is acyclic. History h_2 is TFSR since the precedence requirements imposed by timestamps and priorities do not contradict the precedence requirements imposed by conflicts.

Cycles can be detected efficiently in a TFSG if their characteristics are exploited:

Lemma 1. *Every cycle in a TFSG contains at least one edge representing a precendence requirement imposed by a conflict.*

Proof. See Appendix.

Cycles that can be detected efficiently are cycles of length two. In fact, it can be shown that the existence of a cycle of an arbitrary length in a TFSG of a serializable history implies the existence of a cycle of length two. This is captured by the following theorem:

Theorem 2. *A TFSG of a serializable history is acyclic if it does not contain a cycle of length two.*

Proof. See Appendix.

Corollary 1. *A serializable history is TFSR if the serialization of every pair of conflicting transactions (t_i, t_j) is in accordance with possible temporal precedence requirements between t_i and t_j.*

Proof. See Appendix.

This insight reduces the effort of building a TFSG. In order to decide whether a serializable history is TFSR, it is sufficient to introduce an edge representing a temporal precedence requirement only if the two involved transactions conflict. Temporal precedence requirements between transactions that do not conflict can be neglected. If no cycle (of length two) arises, the history is TFSR.

4   A Temporally Faithful Scheduler

This section presents a scheduler that provides a temporally faithful and of course serializable execution of concurrent transactions. First, we select strict two-phase locking as the basis for discussing a temporally faithful scheduler. Then, we present a temporally faithful scheduler built on strict two-phase locking. Finally, we sketch possible enhancements to the presented scheduler.

4.1   Rationale

Similar as serialization-graph testing (SG-testing) can be used in conventional systems to ensure serializability, TFSG-testing could be used to ensure temporal faithfulness. SG-testing is rarely used in conventional systems. It suffers from the considerable overhead of maintaining a graph and checking for cycles. Since TFSG-testing implies SG-testing, TFSG-testing suffers from the same problems and does not seem promising. One of the most prominent scheduling techniques, implemented by many commercial data base systems, is *strict two-phase locking* (strict 2PL). We select strict 2PL as the basis for our considerations since we want to discuss temporally faithful scheduling on a broad and well known basis.

Strict 2PL guarantees serializability of a produced history. An add-on is necessary to achieve temporal faithfulness. The add-on has to ensure that the serialization order imposed by the underlying 2PL scheduler does not contradict the temporal precedence requirements. As we have shown in Corollary 1, a serializable history is TFSR if the serialization of every pair of conflicting transactions (t_i, t_j) is in accordance with possible temporal precedence requirements between t_i and t_j. Thus, the add-on has to check only the serialization order of pairs of conflicting transactions.

In strict 2PL, conflicts occur only between two transactions that run concurrently. Only then, a lock conflict arises if the two transactions try to perform conflicting operations. When a conventional strict 2PL scheduler encounters a lock conflict, the scheduler forces the requesting transaction (requester) to wait until the holding transaction (holder) releases its locks, which temporally coincides with the commit of the holding transaction. The scheduler serializes the requester after the holder. In a te mporally faithful setting, this may contradict the temporal precedence requirements between the involved transactions. A temporally faithful scheduler has to behave according to the principle *"abort holder if younger"*. If the holder of a lock has a higher timestamp or the same timestamp but a lower priority than the requester of an incompatible lock, the holder has to be aborted. Otherwise, the requester has to be blocked.

If two transactions do not run concurrently, an existing conflict between them does not become visible. A way to avoid that conflicts are missed is to delay the commit of transactions. A temporally faithful scheduler built on strict 2PL cannot grant the commit of a transaction t before it is sure that no lock conflict can arise upon which t would have to be aborted. No such lock conflict can arise after all transactions that have a lower timestamp than t or that have the same timestamp as t but a hi gher priority are committed.

Example 7. Consider a tail-transaction with timestamp 11:59 a.m. that publishes the selling prices and computes the morning sales figures. Further, consider a head-transaction with timestamp 12:00 noon that adjusts the selling prices of all items according to market analysis. Obviously, the two transactions conflict, and the tail-transaction has to be serialized before the head-transaction. Assume that the head-transaction attempts to commit already at 11:58 a.m. since it has been pre-scheduled (see below). If the c ommit is granted and the locks are removed, conflicts between the transactions do not become visible. The commit of the head-transaction has to be delayed until all transactions with a lower timestamp and all transactions with the same timestamp but a higher priority are committed. Only then, a lock conflict arises and the head-transaction can be aborted (and restarted).

In a system where a commit is not granted immediately, the point in time when the execution of a pinned transaction is started influences the system's behavior significantly. The start time determines whether a pinned transaction may have to wait for its commit rather long or whether other transactions may have to wait for the commit of the pinned transaction. Two extreme approaches in starting pinned transactions are:

1. *Full pre-scheduling:* A pinned transaction is started immediately when it is submitted. This approach may be inefficient if the transaction is submitted pro-actively long before its timestamp. Then, the transaction has to wait rather long for its commit and has to be aborted every time it runs into a lock conflict with a transaction carrying a lower timestamp.
2. *No pre-scheduling:* A pinned transaction is started only after all transactions that have to precede it are committed (i.e., the transaction is not "pre-scheduled"). This approach may be inefficient if the transaction performs

time-consuming operations. Then, other transactions will have to wait rather long for the commit of the pinned transaction.

Both approaches are not satisfactory for all application scenarios. Different application scenarios need different start times for pinned transactions. Therefore, we assume that the user who submits a pinned transaction specifies the point in time when the transaction has to be started. Depending on the nature of a transaction, the user may use the submission time, the timestamp of the transaction, or any time in between as the start time.

By forcing a transaction to wait upon its attempt to commit, some form of *two-phase commit* is introduced. In the first phase, the scheduler receives a commit request from a transaction that is ready to commit and registers the request for future handling. In the second phase, the scheduler actually grants the commit request and waits for the commit to be performed.

4.2   The TFSR Scheduler

For our presentation, we need a common understanding how transaction processing is done in a database system. Similar to Bernstein et al. [1], we suppose a modularized architecture in which a transaction manager, a scheduler, and a data manager contribute to transaction processing: The transaction manager (TM) performs any required preprocessing of transaction operations it receives from applications. It uses the services of the scheduler to schedule transaction operations and to commit or abort transactions. The scheduler provides its functionality by utilizing the services of a data manager (DM), which is responsible for recovery and cache management. In the following, we restrict our discussion to the scheduler, in particular, to those scheduling services in which a temporally faithful scheduler differs from a conventional strict 2PL scheduler. We do not further elaborate on the TM and the DM in the scope of this paper.

Like a conventional scheduler, the TFSR scheduler concurrently provides services for scheduling operations, for handling commit requests, and for handling abort requests. In handling abort requests, the TFSR scheduler does not differ from a conventional scheduler. In scheduling operations and in handling commit requests, however, the scheduler deviates from standard strategies. The scheduler cannot grant commit requests immediately and has to deal with lock conflicts in the realm of temporal precedence requirements. Further, the scheduler requires a new transaction to be registered before its operations can be scheduled. A transaction's timestamp has to be accepted. The TFSR scheduler does not act only upon invocation of one of its services but also as time proceeds. The scheduler steps forward from chronon to chronon and grants pending and arriving commit requests of transactions.

In the following, we discuss how the TFSR scheduler registers transactions, how it schedules operations, how it handles commit requests, and how it grants the commit of transactions:

Registering Transactions. Before the scheduler may schedule any operation of a transaction, the transaction has to be registered with the scheduler. In the case of a pinned transaction, the scheduler has to check the transaction's timestamp. A pinned transaction could theoretically be time-stamped with c at every time. Then, however, a temporally faithful scheduler could never grant the commit of a transaction with a timestamp higher than c. It would never hold that all transactions with tim estamp c had been committed. We therefore allow pinned transactions to be scheduled only pro-actively. We refer to the current reading of the wall-clock time reduced to chronon granularity as *WCT*. In particular, the timestamp assigned to a head-transaction must be greater than the WCT and the timestamp assigned to a tail-transaction must be greater than or equal to the WCT.

Scheduling Operations. As motivated above, the TFSR scheduler acts according to the principle *"abort holder if younger"* if a lock conflict arises. The strategy of aborting and blocking transactions relies on transaction timestamps: The timestamp of a pinned transaction is known immediately when the transaction is registered. The timestamp of a body-transaction, however, is unknown before the transaction's commit request. The timestamp of a body-transaction that has not yet requested to commit is resolved dynamically to the WCT, i.e., to the lowest timestamp potentially assigned to the transaction.

Alternatively, it would be possible to block a requesting body-transaction irrespective of the WCT. The produced serialization order would still remain valid since the timestamp of the blocked body-transaction would increase as time proceeds. Such a blocking, however, usually cannot be accepted.

Example 8. Assume a head-transaction with timestamp 12:00 noon that adjusts selling prices. Further assume that the transaction has been pre-scheduled and is waiting for its commit. Let the WCT be 11:55 a.m. If now a sales transaction (body-transaction) runs into a lock conflict with the head-transaction, it cannot be accepted that the sales transaction is delayed for such a long time. Rather, the timestamp of the sales transaction is resolved to 11:55 a.m., the two timestamps are compared, and the head-transaction is aborted and automatically restarted.

When the timestamp of a body-transaction is resolved dynamically, a decision to force a pinned transaction to wait until a body-transaction has committed may become invalid as time proceeds. This means that lock tables and queues of blocked transactions have to be reconsidered as time proceeds (and the WCT changes).

Example 9. We continue the above example. Assume that the customer hesitates to commit the sales transaction. Let the WCT be 11:58 a.m. in the meantime. If now the restarted head-transaction runs into a lock conflict with the sales transaction again, the head-transaction is forced to wait. If the WCT increases to 12:00 noon, however, the decision to block the head-transaction becomes invalid. The sales transaction has to be aborted, and lock tables and queues have to be adjusted accordingly.

The presented strategy for resolving precedence requirements is only a supplement to existing strategies for detecting and dealing with deadlocks. Conventional deadlocks are outside the scope of our paper, they may still occur for transactions among which no temporal precedence requirements are defined (i.e., among transactions sharing a common timestamp and priority).

If a head- or tail-transaction needs to be aborted, the transaction is restarted automatically with the same timestamp. The transaction manager re-submits the transaction's operations for scheduling. If a body-transaction needs to be aborted, the transaction is *not* restarted automatically. It is the user who decides whether to restart or dismiss an aborted body-transaction.

Handling Commit Requests. When a transaction requests to commit, the transaction is not committed immediately, but is marked ready-to-commit. In the case of a body-transaction, the transaction additionally is time-stamped with the WCT. Transactions that are marked ready-to-commit are actually committed when the scheduler considers the corresponding chronon (see below).

Granting Commits. The scheduler continuously steps forward from chronon to chronon and grants pending and arriving commit requests of transactions. We refer to the chronon the scheduler currently considers as the scheduler's *current processing time (CPT)*. The scheduler's CPT may lag behind the WCT (CPT $\leq$ WCT). Figure 3 depicts the scheduler's state "granting commits" as a UML statechart diagram (cf. [2]). After its creation, the scheduler resides in this substate concurrently to other substates in which it registers transactions, schedules operations, and registers commit/abort requests. The diagram shows the steps the scheduler runs through after changing its CPT to chronon c_i:

1. *Grant commit requests of head-transactions:* In this state (named "head"), the assertion holds for a head-transaction t with timestamp c_i that all transactions that have to precede t have been committed. First, the scheduler commits head-transactions with timestamp c_i that have been marked ready-to-commit in the past. Then, the scheduler waits until all head-transactions with timestamp c_i have been committed. If a head-transaction with timestamp c_i is marked ready-to-c ommit in this phase, the commit is granted immediately.

2. *Grant commit requests of body-transactions:* In this state (named "body"), the assertion holds for a body-transaction t with timestamp c_i that all transactions that have to precede t have been committed. First, the scheduler commits body-transactions with timestamp c_i that have been marked ready-to-commit in the past. As long as the WCT corresponds to c_i, the scheduler commits a body-transaction that is marked ready-to-commit. After the WCT increases beyond c_i, no further body-transaction is time-stamped with c_i (but with a higher timestamp).

3. *Grant commit requests of tail-transactions:* In this state (named "tail"), the assertion holds for a tail-transaction t with timestamp c_i that all transactions that have to precede t have been committed. First, the scheduler commits

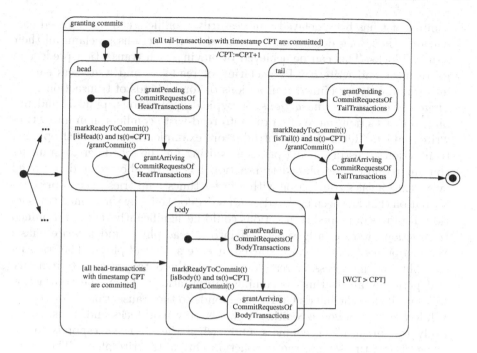

Fig.3. Granting commits (a substate of the scheduler)

tail-transactions with timestamp c_i that have been marked ready-to-commit in the past. Then, the scheduler waits until all tail-transactions with timestamp c_i have been committed. If a tail-transaction with timestamp c_i is marked ready-to-c ommit in this phase, the commit is granted immediately.

After running through these states, the scheduler has finished processing of chronon c_i and changes its CPT to c_{i+1}.

4.3   Advanced Scheduling Techniques

The performance of a temporally faithful scheduler can be increased if it has more knowledge at hand about what is going to be scheduled. In the following, we sketch advanced scheduling techniques that employ information on predeclared read-sets and write-sets of transactions, on the structure of pinned transactions, or on the expected durations of body-transactions.

– *Predeclared read-sets and write-sets of transactions:* The commit of a transaction can be granted if there is no conflicting transaction that has to be executed before. Without additional knowledge, every transaction has to be treated as a potentially conflicting one. All conflicts between a transaction t waiting for its commit and a transaction t' that has to be executed before t have become visible only after t' has committed. If no conflict arises, the commit of t has been delayed unnecessarily. Conflicts can be detected earlier and, thus, long delays can be avoided if transactions preclaim all their required locks. This can be achieved by having each transaction predeclare its read-set and write-set. Predeclaring of read-sets and write-sets can be introduced only for pinned transactions or for all kinds of transactions.

- *Structure of pinned transactions:* In typical applications, pinned- and unpinned transactions more often run into read-write conflicts than into write-write conflicts. Remember the introductory example: Assume that the pinned transaction adjusting selling prices is waiting for the scheduler to grant its commit request. The pinned transaction has to be aborted and restarted every time a sales transaction with a lower timestamp tries to read price information that has been updated—and write-loc ked—by the pinned transaction. Restarts of pinned transactions could be significantly reduced if pinned transactions were clearly separated into a read-phase and a write-phase: When a pinned transaction is started, it enters its read-phase. The transaction obtains the necessary read-locks, reads the database objects it needs, and performs all its time-consuming computations. Then, the transaction waits until the scheduler's CPT corresponds to the transaction's timestamp. While the transaction is waiting, it holds only read-locks and, thus, is less likely to run into lock conflicts. Only when the CPT corresponds to the transaction's timestamp, the transaction enters its write-phase. The transaction obtains the necessary write-locks (or upgrades some of its read-locks) and actually performs write operations.

- *Duration of body-transactions:* The timestamp of a body-transaction is resolved dynamically to the WCT during its execution. If a body-transaction is long, its associated timestamp increases continuously. If the timestamp of a body-transaction increases beyond the timestamp of a blocked transaction, the body-transaction has to be aborted and the lock tables and the queues of blocked transactions have to be updated. This represents an overhead that can be reduced by associating with every body-t ransaction an estimation how long the execution of the transaction will probably take. In the presence of such an estimation, the timestamps assigned to body-transactions would be more realistic and would reduce overhead.

5   Conclusion

In this paper, we have presented an approach to execute business transactions in a temporally faithful manner. The main characteristics of our approach are:

- The approach is general. It relieves the designer from inventing a case-specific solution every time a particular precedence order should be enforced on the execution of transactions.
- The approach is modular. By means of pinned transactions, precedence requirements can be imposed without the need to consider all the unpinned transactions that potentially may be executed around the critical point in time.

- The approach is simple. A temporally faithful scheduler can be implemented by extending proven scheduling techniques in conventional database systems. It does neither rely on special concurrency control mechanisms nor does it require specialized database systems.

Currently, a prototype of a temporally faithful scheduler is being implemented within a master thesis. The prototype is built on top of the active object-oriented database system TriGS [8]. The reason to select an active object-oriented database system is that we consider active rules a well-suited concept for enhancing system capabilities without the need to introduce special-purpose mechanisms.

Appendix

Proof (Theorem 1). First, we prove that a history is TFSR if its TFSG is acyclic: We suppose that the TFSG of a history h is acyclic. An acyclic TFSG may be topologically sorted. Consider $t_1, t_2, \ldots, t_m$ as a topological sort of the TFSG of h, and let h_s be the history $t_1 \rightarrow t_2 \rightarrow \ldots \rightarrow t_m$. History h_s is temporally faithfully serial since (1) it is serial, (2) it observes timestamps, and (3) it observes priorities (cf. Definition 1). Now we show that h is equivalent to h_s. If a transaction t_i performs an operation o_i and another transaction t_j performs a conflicting operation o_j where o_i precedes o_j in h, this is reflected by an edge from t_i to t_j in the TFSG of h. In any topological sort of the TFSG of h, t_i must appear before t_j. Since a history h_s is serial, all operations of t_i appear before any operation of t_j in h_s. Thus, we have proved that any two conflicting operatio ns are ordered in h in the same way as they are ordered in h_s (and that h and h_s are equivalent).

Second, we prove that a history is TFSR only if its TFSG is acyclic. We do this by showing that no cyclic TFSG can exist for a history that is TFSR: We suppose a history h that is TFSR. Since h is TFSR, there is a temporally faithfully serial history equivalent to h. We refer to this history as h_s. Now we suppose a cycle in the TFSG of h and let the cycle be $t_1 \rightarrow t_2 \rightarrow \ldots \rightarrow t_k \rightarrow t_1$. An edge from t_i to t_j exists in the TFSG of h (1) if t_i performs an operation o_i and t_j performs a conflicting operation o_j where o_i precedes o_j in h, (2) if t_i has a lower timestamp than t_j, or (3) if t_i has the same timestamp as t_j but a higher priority. Since h_s is serial, an edge from t_i to t_j in the TFSG of h requires that t_i appears before t_j in h_s. The existence of the cycle implies that each of $t_1, t_2, \ldots, t_k$ appears before itself in h_s, w hich is a contradiction. So, no cycle can exist for a history that is TFSR.

Proof (Lemma 1). In our setting, time is linear. Transaction timestamps impose a linear order on transactions with different timestamps, while priorities impose a linear order on transactions with the same timestamp. Thus, timestamp observation and priority observation impose acyclic precedence requirements. At least one edge representing a precedence requirement imposed by a conflict is necessary to form a cycle in a TFSG.

Proof (Theorem 2). We prove that the existence of a cycle in a TFSG of a serializable history implies the existence of a cycle of length two. We use the following notational conventions: With $t_i \rightarrow t_j$ we denote an edge from t_i to t_j representing a precedence requirement imposed by a conflict. With $t_i \Rightarrow t_j$ we denote an edge from t_i to t_j representing a temporal precedence requirement. With $t_i \gg t_j$ we denote an arbitrary edge from t_i to t_j.

We assume a cycle involving the transactions $t_1, t_2, \ldots, t_n$ ($n > 2$). The cycle contains at least one edge representing a temporal precedence requirement. This is true since the TFSG of a serializable history is built on an acyclic SG, and thus at least one edge representing a temporal precedence requirement is necessary to form a cycle. We refer to one of these edges as $t_n \Rightarrow t_1$ and let the cycle be $t_n \Rightarrow t_1 \gg t_2 \gg \ldots \gg t_{n-1} \gg t_n$.

Now, we analyze the precedence requirements among the nodes contained in the cycle. We consider the triple (t_n, t_i, t_{i+1}), where i initially is 1 and increases with each iteration by 1. Before the i-th iteration, $t_n \Rightarrow t_i$ holds. After the i-th iteration, either we have shown the existence of $t_n \Rightarrow t_{i+1}$ in the TFSG or we have detected a cycle of length two and stop analyzing. Depending on the kind of precedence requirement between t_i and t_{i+1}, the pr ecedence requirements among the triple of transactions may follow only one of two alternative patterns:

1. $t_n \Rightarrow t_i \Rightarrow t_{i+1}$: In this case, also edge $t_n \Rightarrow t_{i+1}$ exists in the TFSG.
2. $t_n \Rightarrow t_i \rightarrow t_{i+1}$: In this case, edge $t_n \Rightarrow t_i$ indicates that t_n either has a lower timestamp than t_i or the same timestamp but a higher priority. This means that t_{i+1} cannot be temporally independent from both, t_n and t_i. One of the following temporal precedence requirements must hold:

   (a) t_{i+1} succeeds t_i: Then, edges $t_i \Rightarrow t_{i+1}$ and $t_n \Rightarrow t_{i+1}$ exist in the TFSG.
   (b) t_{i+1} succeeds t_n and is temporally independent from t_i: Then, edge $t_n \Rightarrow t_{i+1}$ exists in the TFSG.
   (c) t_{i+1} succeeds t_n and precedes t_i: Then, edge $t_{i+1} \Rightarrow t_i$ exists in the TFSG, and we detect the cycle of length two $t_{i+1} \Rightarrow t_i \rightarrow t_{i+1}$.
   (d) t_{i+1} precedes t_i and is temporally independent from t_n: Then, edge $t_{i+1} \Rightarrow t_i$ exists in the TFSG, and we detect the cycle of length two $t_{i+1} \Rightarrow t_i \rightarrow t_{i+1}$.
   (e) t_{i+1} precedes t_n: Then, edges $t_{i+1} \Rightarrow t_n$ and $t_{i+1} \Rightarrow t_i$ exist in the TFSG and we detect the cycle of length two $t_{i+1} \Rightarrow t_i \rightarrow t_{i+1}$.

We show that we necessarily detect a cycle of length two after at most $n - 1$ iterations: The analyzed cycle contains at least one edge representing a precedence requirement imposed by a conflict (see Lemma 1). This means that we find pattern 2 at least once. Now suppose that condition (a) or (b) would hold every time we find pattern 2. Then, after $n - 1$ iterations, the TFSG would contain an edge $t_n \Rightarrow t_n$, which is clearly never the case. Thus, condition (c), (d), or (e) must hold at least o nce when we find pattern 2. But then, we detect a cycle of length two. We have shown that if a cycle exists in a TFSG built on an acyclic SG, then there is also a cycle of length two.

Proof (Corollary 1). Every cycle of length two contains an edge representing a precedence requirement imposed by a conflict (cf. Lemma 1). Thus, when a TFSG is checked for cycles, only pairs of conflicting transactions have to be considered. A history is TFSR and its TFSG is acyclic if no pair of conflicting transactions (t_i, t_j) can be found where conflicts require t_i to precede t_j while at the same time different timestamps or priorities require t_j to precede t_i.

References

1. P.A. Bernstein, V. Hadzilacos, and N. Goodman. *Concurrency Control and Recovery in Database Systems.* Addison-Wesley, 1987.
2. G. Booch, J. Rumbaugh, and I. Jacobson. *The Unified Modeling Language—User Guide.* Addison Wesley, 1999.
3. A.P. Buchmann, J. Zimmermann, J.A. Blakeley, and D.L. Wells. Building an Integrated Active OODBMS: Requirements, Architecture, and Design Decisions. In *Proc. of the 11th Intl. Conf. on Data Engineering (ICDE)*, 1995.
4. U. Dayal. Active Database Management Systems. In *Proc. of the 3rd Intl. Conf. on Data and Knowledge Bases*, pages 150–167, June 1988.
5. U. Dayal, U. Hsu, and R. Ladin. Organizing Long-running Activities with Triggers and Transactions. In *Proc. of the ACM SIGMOD Conf. on Management of Data*, 1990.
6. M. Finger and P. McBrien. Concurrency Control for Perceivedly Instantaneous Transactions in Valid-Time Databases. In *Proc. of the 4th Intl. Workshop on Temporal Representation and Reasoning.* IEEE Comp. Soc. Press, 1997.
7. D. Georgakopoulos, M. Rusinkiewicz, and W. Litwin. Chronological Scheduling of Transactions with Temporal Dependencies. *VLDB Journal*, 3(3), 1994.
8. G. Kappel, S. Rausch-Schott, and W. Retschitzegger. A Tour on the TriGS Active Database System—Architecture and Implementation. In *Proc. of the ACM Symposium on Applied Computing, Atlanta, Georgia*, 1998.
9. P. Lang, W. Obermair, and M. Schrefl. Modeling Business Rules with Situation/Activation Diagrams. In A. Gray and P. Larson, editors, *Proc. of the 13th Intl. Conf. on Data Engineering (ICDE)*, pages 455–464. IEEE Computer Society Press, April 1997.
10. A.H.H. Ngu. Specification and Verification of Temporal Relationships in Transaction Modeling. *Information Systems*, 15(2):5–42, March 1990.
11. B. Salzberg. Timestamping After Commit. In *Proc. of the 3rd Intl. Conf. on Parallel and Distributed Information Systems, Austin, Texas*, 1994.

Modelling and Optimisation Issues for Multidimensional Databases[1]

Panos Vassiliadis and Spiros Skiadopoulos

National Technical University of Athens
Department of Electrical and Computer Engineering
Computer Science Division
Knowledge and Database Systems Laboratory
Zografou 15773, Athens, Greece
{pvassil,spiros}@dbnet.ece.ntua.gr

Abstract. It is commonly agreed that multidimensional data cubes form the basic logical data model for OLAP applications. Still, there seems to be no agreement on a common model for cubes. In this paper we propose a logical model for cubes based on the key observation that a cube is not a self-existing entity, but rather a view over an underlying data set. We accompany our model with syntactic characterisations for the problem of cube usability. To this end, we have developed algorithms to check whether (a) the marginal conditions of two cubes are appropriate for a rewriting, in the presence of aggregation hierarchies and (b) an implication exists between two selection conditions that involve different levels of aggregation of the same dimension hierarchy. Finally, we present a rewriting algorithm for the cube usability problem.

1 Introduction

On-Line Analytical Processing (OLAP) is a trend in database technology based on the multidimensional view of data. Although multidimensional data cubes form the basic logical data model for OLAP applications, up to now, no common agreement has been obtained on the elements of a cube model. Several industrial standards already exist [13,14,15,16], yet, apart for the last one, none of them seems to propose a well-founded model for OLAP databases. In academia, several proposals on the modelling of cubes also exist [1,2,9,10,11,21]. Despite all these efforts, we feel that several key characteristics of a cube model have not been stressed, neither by the academia nor the industry (see [19] for a complete discussion). To this end, we present a *logical* model for cubes. This model extends the proposal of [21] in a more formal and systematic way. It deals with all the commonly encountered entities of a multidimensional model (dimension hierarchies, data cubes and cube operations)

[1] This research is sponsored by the European Esprit Project "DWQ: Foundations of Data Warehouse Quality", No. 22469. We also wish to thank Prof. Timos Sellis and Dr. Dimitri Theodoratos for useful discussions on the topic.

B. Wangler, L. Bergman (Eds.): CAiSE 2000, LNCS 1789, pp. 482-497, 2000

without being restricted from their physical implementation (e.g., ROLAP or MOLAP architectures). One of our key observations is that *a cube is not a self-existing entity, but rather a view* (materialised or not) *over an underlying data set*. This property allows us to develop complex operations, not dealt by other models so far (e.g., the drill-down operation and the change of aggregation function).

To our knowledge, existing OLAP tools behave in an "extensional" fashion. Cubes are treated simply as sets of tuples, ignoring the fact that they are produced as queries over an underlying detailed data set (e.g., the fact table of a data warehouse). Our framework, instead, suggests a different strategy: we keep the "history" of performed selections and thus, we are able to compute a new cube taking into account its "intentional" description. Therefore, we can define more complex operations (such as drill-down) and sequences of operations, which are not covered by other models. Our model is accompanied by an algebra powerful enough to capture the usual OLAP operations such as (a) *selection* over a cube, (b) *roll-up*, which means aggregation over a cube to coarser granularities of information and (c) *drill-down*, which involves de-aggregation of a specific cube and presentation of more detailed information.

The contribution of this paper lies not only in terms of expressiveness, but also we present results on optimisation issues for multidimensional databases. We investigate the *cube usability problem*, a variant of the relational view usability problem, for multidimensional cubes. We accompany our framework with optimisation techniques for the cube usability problem that enable the exploitation of existing cubes in order to compute new cubes. To handle the cube usability problem, we extend well-known techniques already found in the relational context on the containment of selection conditions [17]. We have observed that although quite a lot of work has been performed in the field of query containment and view usability in the context of relational databases [4,5,8], there exist no results to exploit the information about dimension hierarchies in the context of multidimensional databases. We present results on two major topics. First, we tackle the problem of containment of two selections, taking into account their marginal conditions in the presence of dimension hierarchies. Secondly, we come up with a set of axioms to characterise containment for expressions involving functionally dependent attributes. Although several results already exist to characterise query containment between expressions involving one domain [17], to our knowledge, no results exist for expressions involving different functionally dependent levels. For lack of space, all the proofs, as well as further explanations, are found in [20].

This paper is organised as follows. In Section 2 we present the logical cube model. Section 3 presents optimisation issues. Finally, in Section 4 we discuss our results and present future work.

2   Cubes for Multidimensional Databases

In this section we present the basic entities and operations of our model. Entities involve dimensions, data sets and cubes. Operations involve selections and change in the granularity of data. This model extents previous proposals of [2,10,21].

One of the main characteristics of OLAP applications is the *multidimensional view of data* in the perception of the user, which considers that information is stored in a *multidimensional array*, called *Cube* or *HyperCube*. Thus, a *Cube* is a group of data cells. Each cell is uniquely defined by the corresponding values of the dimensions of the cube. The contents of the cell are named *measures* and represent the measured values of the real world. Measures are functionally dependent, in the relational sense, on the dimensions of the cube.

A *dimension* is defined in [15] as "a structural attribute of a cube that is a list of members, all of which are of a similar type in the user's perception of the data". Informally, a dimension models all the possible ways in which the user can group the detailed information stored in the multidimensional database with respect to a specific context. Each dimension has an associated *hierarchy of levels* of aggregated data i.e., it can be viewed from different levels of detail. Formally, a *dimension* D is a lattice $(L, \square)$: $L = (L_1, ..., L_n, ALL)$. We require that the upper bound of the lattice is always the level ALL, so that we can group all the values of the dimension into the single value 'all'. The lower bound of the lattice is called the *detailed level* of the dimension. For instance, let us consider the dimension Date of Fig. 2. Levels of dimension Date are Day, Week, Month, Year and ALL. Day is the most detailed level. Level ALL is the most coarse level for all the dimensions. Aggregating to the level ALL of a dimension ignores the respective dimension in the grouping (i.e., practically groups the data with respect to all the other dimensions of the cube, except for this particular one).

The relationship between the values of the dimension levels is achieved through the use of the set of anc^{L_2, L_1} functions. A function anc^{L_2, L_1} assigns a value of the domain of L_2 to a value of the domain of L_1. For instance $anc^{Year}_{Month}(Feb-97) = 1997$.

The major multidimensional operations are *selection* and *navigation*. Selection is used whereby a criterion is evaluated against the data or levels of a dimension in order to restrict the set of retrieved data. Navigation is a term used to describe the processes employed by users to explore a cube interactively by changing the granularity of the multidimensionally viewed data [15]. Possible navigation operations, which can be applied to a cube, are: (a) *Roll-up* which corresponds to the aggregation of data from a lower to a higher level of granularity within a dimension's hierarchy, (b) *Drill-Down* which is the inverse of roll-up and allows the de-aggregation of information moving from higher to lower levels of granularity and (c) *Slice* which corresponds to the grouping of data with respect to a subset of the dimensions of a cube. For instance, let us consider the dimension Date; aggregating from Month to Year is a roll-up operation and de-aggregating from Month to Day is a drill-down operation. In our model, the slice operation is modelled as a roll-up to level ALL.

We denote sets of tuples under a specific schema by the term *data set*. Moreover, we assume the existence of a *detailed data set*, i.e., a data set that is defined at the finest levels of granularity for all its dimensions. This detailed data set is the central source of data, which will populate any cubes produced during an OLAP session (e.g., a fact table in a data warehouse).

One of our key observations is that a *cube* is not a self-existing entity (as commonly encountered in the literature), but rather a view over an underlying detailed data set. As usual, a view (and thus a cube) can be either materialised or not. Therefore, a cube can be seen either as a data set or simply a query. In our model, we retain this dual nature formally; a cube is not only a set of tuples, but also has a definition. This definition is a query that reduces the computation of the cube to a set of operations over the initial materialised detailed data set.

Formally, a *cube* c over the schema $[L_1, \ldots, L_n, M_1, \ldots, M_m]$, is an expression of the form: $c = (DS^0, \varphi, [L_1, \ldots, L_n, M_1, \ldots, M_m], [agg_1(M^{0,1}), \ldots, agg_m(M^{0,m})])$, where DS^0 is a detailed data set over the schema $S = [L^{0,1}, \ldots, L^{0,n}, M^{0,1}, \ldots, M^{0,k}]$, $m \leq k$, φ is a detailed selection condition, $M^{0,1}, \ldots, M^{0,m}$ are detailed measures, $M_1, \ldots, M_m$ are aggregated measures, $L^{0,i}$ and L_i are levels such that $L^{0,i} \sqsubseteq L_i$, $1 \leq i \leq n$ and agg_i, $1 \leq i \leq m$ are aggregated functions from the set $\{sum, min, max, count\}$.

Intuitively, to compute a cube, first we apply the selection condition to the detailed data set. Then, we replace the values of the levels for the tuples of the result, with their respective ancestor values at the levels of the schema of the cube and group them into a single value for each measure, through the application of the appropriate aggregate function. Note that a detailed data set can be trivially expressed as a cube, having a `true` selection condition and an arbitrary aggregation function. For instance, the cube of the detailed data set DS^0 of Fig. 1 is expressed as: $c^0 = (DS^0, true, [day, day, item, salesman, city, sales], sum(sales))$.

This approach introduces a powerful expression mechanism, able to directly capture operations like drill-down and change of aggregate function and thus, aimed towards the modelling of sequences of operations, as normally encountered in OLAP systems. To our knowledge, no other model can capture these operations directly. The reduction of a cube's definition to a normalised form seems to be the only alternative that directly achieves this kind of functionality.

Formally, the model consists of the following elements:

- Each *dimension* D is a lattice $(L, \sqsubseteq)$ such that: $L = (L_1, \ldots, L_n, ALL)$ is a finite subset of *levels* and $\sqsubseteq$ is a partial order defined among the levels of L, such that $L_i \sqsubseteq L_i \sqsubseteq ALL$ for every $1 \leq i \leq n$.

- A family of functions anc^{L_2, L_1} satisfying the following conditions (extending [2]):
  1. For each pair of levels L_1 and L_2 such that $L_1 \sqsubseteq L_2$ the function anc^{L_2, L_1} maps each element of $dom(L_1)$ to an element of $dom(L_2)$.
  2. Given levels L_1, L_2 and L_3 such that $L_1 \sqsubseteq L_2 \sqsubseteq L_3$, the function anc^{L_3, L_1} equals to the composition $anc^{L_2, L_1} \circ anc^{L_3, L_2}$.
  3. For each pair of levels L_1 and L_2 such that $L_1 \sqsubseteq L_2$ the function anc^{L_2, L_1} is monotone, i.e., $\forall x, y \in dom(L_1), L_1 \sqsubseteq L_2 : x < y \Rightarrow anc^{L_2, L_1}(x) \leq anc^{L_2, L_1}(y)$.
  4. For each pair of levels L_1 and L_2 the anc^{L_2, L_1} function determines a set of finite equivalence classes X_i such that: $\forall x, y \in dom(L_1), L_1 \sqsubseteq L_2 : anc^{L_2, L_1}(x) = anc^{L_2, L_1}(y) \Rightarrow x, y$ belongs to the same X_i.

5. The relationship desc^{L_2,L_1} is the inverse of the anc^{L_2,L_1} function -i.e., desc^{L_2,L_1}

$(1) = \{x \in \text{dom}(L) : \text{anc}^{L_2,L_1}(x) = 1\}$.

- Each *data set* DS over a schema $S = [L_1, ..., L_n, M_1, ..., M_m]$ is a finite set of tuples over S such that the set $[L_1, ..., L_n]$ comprises a primary key (in the usual sense).
- Each *selection condition* φ is a formula in disjunctive normal form. An *atom* of a selection condition is true, false or an expression of the form $x \; \theta \; y$, where θ is an operator from the set $(>, <, =, \geq, \leq, \neq)$ and each of x and y can be one of the following: (a) a level L, (b) a value 1, (c) an expression of the form $\text{anc}^{L_2,L_1}(L_1)$ where $L_1 \square L_2$ and (d) an expression of the form $\text{anc}^{L_2,L_1}(1)$ where $L_1 \square L_2$ and $1 \in \text{dom}(L_1)$. The *detailed equivalent of* φ, denoted by φ^0, is a selection condition obtained through the following procedure: for each occurrence of a level name L in φ, we substitute it with the equivalent expression $\text{anc}^L_{L^0}(L^0)$, where L^0 is the detailed level of the dimension to which L belongs. Note that the detailed equivalent of a selection condition is directly applicable to a detailed data set.
- Each *cube* c over the schema $[L_1, ..., L_n, M_1, ..., M_m]$, is an expression of the form: $c = (DS^0, \varphi, [L_1, ..., L_n, M_1, ..., M_m], [\text{agg}_1(M^{0,1}), ..., \text{agg}_m(M^{0,m})])$, where DS^0 is a detailed data set over the schema $S = [L^{0,1}, ..., L^{0,n}, M^{0,1}, ..., M^{0,k}]$, $m \leq k$, φ is a detailed selection condition, $M^{0,1}, ..., M^{0,m}$ are detailed measures, $M_1, ..., M_m$ are aggregated measures, $L^{0,i}$ and L_i are levels such that $L^{0,i} \square L_i$, $1 \leq i \leq n$ and agg_i, $1 \leq i \leq m$ are aggregated functions from the set $\{\text{sum}, \text{min}, \text{max}, \text{count}\}$. The expression characterising a cube has the following formal semantics:

$c = \{x \in \text{Tup}(L_1, ..., L_n, M_1, ..., M_m) \mid \exists y \in \varphi(DS^0), x[L_i] = \text{anc}^{L_i}_{L^{0,i}}(y[L^{0,i}]), 1 \leq i \leq n,$

$x[M_j] = \text{agg}_j(\{q \mid \exists z \in \varphi(DS^0), x[L_i] = \text{anc}^{L_i}_{L^{0,i}}(z[L^{0,i}]),$

$1 \leq i \leq n, q = z[M^{0,j}]\}), 1 \leq j \leq m\}$.

- The *Cube Algebra* (CA) is composed of three operations (consider a cube $c^a = (DS^0, \varphi^a, [L^{a,1}, ..., L^{a,n}, M^{a,1}, ..., M^{a,m}], [\text{agg}^{a,1}(M^{0,1}), ..., \text{agg}^{a,m}(M^{0,m})])$ over which the operations are applied):

   1. *Navigate*: Let $S = [L_1, ..., L_n, M_1, ..., M_m]$ be a schema and $\text{agg}_1, ..., \text{agg}_m$ be aggregate functions. If $L^{a,i}$ and L_i belong to the same dimension D_i and $\text{agg}_i \in \{\text{sum}, \text{min}, \text{max}, \text{count}\}$ then, navigation is defined as follows:

   $\text{nav}(c^a, S, \text{agg}_1, ..., \text{agg}_m) = (DS^0, \varphi^a, S, [\text{agg}_1(M^{0,1}), ..., \text{agg}_m(M^{0,m})])$.

   2. *Selection*: Let φ be a selection condition applicable to c^a. Then, we define the *selection* operation as:

   $\sigma_\varphi(c^a) = (DS^0, \varphi^a \wedge \varphi^0, [L^{a,1}, ..., L^{a,n}, M^{a,1}, ..., M^{a,m}], [\text{agg}^{a,1}(M^{0,1}), ..., \text{agg}^{a,m}(M^{0,m})])$

   where φ^0 is the detailed equivalent of the selection condition φ.

   3. *Split measure*: Let M be a measure of the schema of the cube c. Without loss of generality, let us assume that M is M_m. Then *split measure* is defined as follows:

   $\pi_{M_m}(c^a) = (DS^0, \varphi^a, [L^{a,1}, ..., L^{a,n}, M^{a,1}, ..., M^a_{m-1}], [\text{agg}^{a,1}(M^{0,1}), ..., \text{agg}^a_{m-1}(M^0_{m-1})])$.

Day	Title	Salesman	Store	Sales
6-Feb-97	Symposium	Netz	Paris	7
18-Feb-97	Karamazof brothers	Netz	Seattle	5
11-May-97	Ace of Spades	Netz	Los Angeles	20
3-Sep-97	Zarathustra	Netz	Nagasaki	50
3-Sep-97	Report to El Greco	Netz	Nagasaki	30
1-Jul-97	Ace of Spades	Venk	Athens	13
1-Jul-97	Piece of Mind	Venk	Athens	34

Fig. 1. Detailed Data Set DS^0.

Theorem 1. The Cube Algebra CA is *sound* (i.e., the result of all the operations is always a cube) and *complete* (i.e., any valid cube can be computed as the combination of a finite set of CA operations). ∎

Example 1. To motivate the discussion we customise the example presented in [14] to an international publishing company with travelling salesmen selling books and CD's to stores all over the world. The database (Fig. 1) stores information about the sales of a title that a salesman achieved on a particular date and city. The dimensions of our example are Person, Location, Product and Date (Fig. 2). Measure Sales is functionally dependent on dimensions Date, Product, Person and Location. ∎

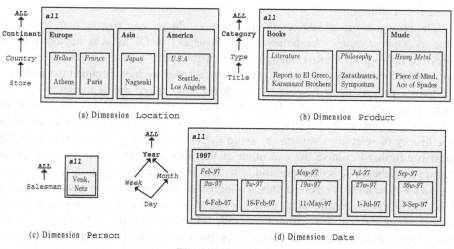

(a) Dimension Location   (b) Dimension Product

(c) Dimension Person   (d) Dimension Date

Fig. 2. Dimensions

The organisation of information in different levels of aggregation (i.e., dimensions) is in hand because OLAP users are unlikely to directly ask questions about the detailed data that are stored in the database. Instead, they are more interested in aggregated information according to the categorisation groupings.

Following, we present three queries and the respective algebraic representation that could have been a typical sequence of operations during an OLAP session.

Query 1. Find the maximum sales by month, category of item, salesman and country.

```
c¹=nav(DS⁰,[Month,Category,Salesman,Country,Max_val],max(sales))
=(DS⁰,true,[Month,Category,Salesman,Country,Max_val],max(sales))
```

Query 2. Find the maximum sales outside the American continent by month, category of item, salesman and country.

$$c^2 = \sigma_{anc_{country}^{continent}(country) \neq 'America'}(c^1) = (DS^0, anc_{city}^{continent}(City) \neq 'America',$$

[Month,Category,Salesman,Country,Max_val],max(sales)).

Query 3. Find the summary of sales outside the continent of America by month, type of title and country of store.

$$c^3 = nav(c^2, [Month,Type,All,Country,Sum\_val],sum(Sales)) =$$
$$(DS^0, anc_{city}^{continent}(City) \neq 'America', [Month,Type,All,Country,Sum\_val],$$

sum(sales)).

During this particular OLAP session the user has performed (a) a roll-up from the detailed data set, (b) a selection and (c) a slicing (of dimension Person), a drill down (from Category to Type level) and a change in the aggregation function (from max to sum).

In the first operation, one can notice that the semantics of the navigation operation allow us to use an arbitrary name (e.g., Max_val) for the measure that computes the maximum value per group of aggregation. In the second operation, notice that the expression $anc_{country}^{continent}$ (Country) which is directly applicable to the schema (and data) of the cube c^1 is transformed to its equivalent $anc_{city}^{continent}$ (City), that directly applies to the detailed data set DS^0, through the use of the definition of the detailed selection condition.

The presented model stresses the fact that *a cube we can treated both as a query and as a set of tuples*. We believe that this aspect of OLAP was neglected in the previous approaches. In this example, the contribution of treating cubes as views over the detailed data set is eminent. Actually, the fact that we have retained the history of selections permits us to be able to drill-down and change the aggregation function. Otherwise, to perform the drill-down operations we should employ a join operation of c^2 with DS^0. The same also holds for the change in the aggregation function. Using the history of selections we can (a) avoid to perform a costly join operation and (b) possibly further optimise the execution of the operation through the use of already computed cubes. The second possibility will be investigated in Section 3.

As we have already stressed, this is a *logical* model for cubes. We do not advocate that the *physical* computation of the results of an operation should actually be computed all the way back from the detailed data set. Actually, although drill-down and change of aggregation function can be performed directly, only through the use of the semantics of our model, can the selection and roll-up operations be performed over the original cube, without referring to the detailed data set. In the case of selection, it suffices to simply pass all the tuples of the cube from the filter of the applied selection condition. In the case of roll-up to coarser levels of granularity, it also suffices to group the tuples of the cube and apply the appropriate aggregate function. These simple optimisation strategies are generalised in Section 3 with a more powerful approach, capable of detecting whether any cube can be computed from the data of another cube, simply by comparing their definitions.

3   The Cube Usability Problem

Problem description. There are several cases where there is the need to decide whether a view can be recomputed from another view. In the case of OLAP, the problem can be stated as follows: the OLAP user selects some data and performs an operation over them. The result of the new query can be computed, of course, from the detailed data. Nevertheless, it is possible that previously computed and cached results, or existing materialised views, could also allow the computation of the requested information. As a general statement, we could say that the problem lies in whether the computation of a new cube can be performed from an intermediate level of aggregation, than from the detailed data set.

Formally, let DS^0 be a detailed data set. Let also c^{old} and c^{new} be two cubes defined over DS^0. By definition, cubes c^{old} and c^{new} can be calculated from DS^0. The *cube usability problem* lies on determining whether the tuples of c^{old} can be used to compute cube c^{new}. It is clear that the cube usability problem is a variant of the *view subsumption* problem, already investigated in the field of relational databases [18].

Shortcomings of current approaches. Too much effort has been spent, in the past, to tackle the problem of view subsumption and query rewriting in the presence of views [4,5,8,22]. Nevertheless, the previous approaches are relational-oriented and lack to deal with specific characteristics of the multidimensional modelling. We will use two examples to demonstrate these shortcomings.

Example 2. Intuitively, someone would expect, that in order to solve the cube usability problem, the new cube c^{new} should:

1. be defined over the same dimensions with c^{old} and at a higher or equal level;
2. be defined over the same measure of DS^0. Moreover, the aggregation functions agg^{new} and agg^{old} should be the same;
3. have a more restrictive selection condition than c^{old}, i.e., φ^{new} is contained in φ^{old} in the usual relational sense.

Checking conditions 1 and 2 is an easy task. To perform the comparison of Condition 3, we need to transform the selection conditions of the two cubes in order to treat them as conjunctive queries [17]. One could argue that existing relational techniques are adequate to handle this problem. Unfortunately, as we will show, there are cases where those techniques are not sufficient.

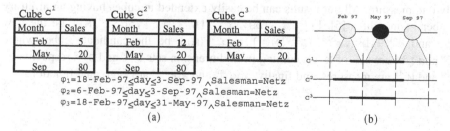

$\varphi_1 = 18\text{-Feb-97} \leq day \leq 3\text{-Sep-97} \wedge Salesman=Netz$
$\varphi_2 = 6\text{-Feb-97} \leq day \leq 3\text{-Sep-97} \wedge Salesman=Netz$
$\varphi_3 = 18\text{-Feb-97} \leq day \leq 31\text{-May-97} \wedge Salesman=Netz$

(a)   (b)

Fig. 3. Cube usability problems with marginal conditions.

Let us consider the detailed data set DS^0 of Fig. 1. Let c^i, $1 \leq i \leq 3$ be cubes defined as $c^i = [DS^0, \varphi_i, [Month, ALL, ALL, ALL, ALL, ALL, ALL, Sales], sum(sales)]$. Fig. 3a presents the Month level, the Sales measure and the selection conditions for each of the cubes. The problem is whether a new cube c^3 can be computed using the tuples of one of the existing cubes c^1 and c^2. Since Conditions 1, 2 and 3 hold, one could argue that this is feasible. Yet, as we can see in Fig. 3a, only c^1 can be used to compute c^3. The intuitive explanation of the problem is depicted in Fig. 3b. There are three horizontal axes defined at the day level, each for one of the cubes c^1, c^2 and c^3. Each bold line denotes the set of days participating in the computation of the respective cube. All cubes are defined at the month level; consequently, we partition the three axes with respect to the function anc_{day}^{month}. As we can see, we have three partitions: Feb'97, May'97 and Sep'97. Cube c^3 can be computed from c^1 because for all the partitions of c^3 (i.e., Feb'97, May'97), cubes c^1 and c^3 cover exactly the same days. This does not hold for c^1 and c^2. ∎

Example 3. Suppose the case, where a cube c^1 has a selection condition $\varphi_1 = arr.year < dep.year$ (where arr denotes dimension arrival date and dep denotes the dimension departure date). Suppose also that a cube c^2 is defined at the month level and has a selection condition $\varphi_2 = arr.month < dep.month$. We can see that cube c^1 can be computed from c^2. This means that if c^2 is materialised we can use its tuples to compute c^1. We are able to perform this kind of reasoning because we take advantage of the relationship between months and years, expressed through the dimension hierarchies, and the family of anc functions. To our knowledge, there is no effort in the view subsumption literature that uses this kind of knowledge. ∎

Contribution. In this section, we will show that the cube usability problem is reduced to simple tests and operations. Different tests apply for different classes of queries. We explore the selection conditions of two categories: (a) selection conditions with atoms involving values (i.e., of the form $L\theta l$, $L\theta anc^{L_2, L_1}(l)$, etc.) and (b) selection conditions with atoms involving only levels (i.e., of the form $L_1\theta L_2$, $L\theta anc^{L_2, L_1}(L_1)$, etc.). We will examine the optimisation issues for the former in Section 3.1 and for the latter in Section 3.2. Finally, Section 3.3 presents a theorem with sufficient criteria and the corresponding rewriting algorithm for both cases of the cube usability problem under consideration.

In the rest of the paper, for reasons of simplicity, we will deal with cubes having only one measure. All our results can be easily extended to cubes having an arbitrary number of measures [5]. Let $c^{new} = (DS^0, \varphi^{new}, [L^{new}, M^{new}], agg^{new}(M))$ be the new cube and $c^{old} = (DS^0, \varphi^{old}, [L^{old}, M^{old}], agg^{old}(M))$ be the candidate cube, where L^{new} and L^{old} are sets of levels coming from dimension sets D^{new} and D^{old} respectively, M^{new} and M^{old} are measures, and finally, agg^{new} and agg^{old} are aggregate functions.

3.1   Equivalent Transformations for Atoms Involving Values

Suppose two levels L^{old} and L^{new}, such that $L^{old} \sqsubseteq L^{new}$. Function $anc^{L^{new},L^{old}}$ defines a partition over the values of L^{old} with respect to the values of L^{new} (e.g., the partition of year to month). Suppose now, two atoms a_1 and a_2 over L^{old}, as in the case of Fig. 3. To perform an aggregation to L^{new}, the two atoms must hold the same ranges of values for each and every partition that L^{new} defines over L^{old}. Generalising this observation, in the case where two selection conditions involve a larger conjunction of atoms, we must:

1. transform the selection conditions to concrete ranges for each dimension;
2. reduce the atoms to the same level, using appropriate transformations (so that they can be compared);
3. check whether the broader selection condition is defined identically for the marginal constraints of the other selection condition.

The following auxiliary definition introduces the notion of *dimension interval*, which is a concrete range over the domain of a certain dimension level.

Definition 1: A *dimension interval* (DI) is one of the following (a) $true$, (b) $false$ and (c) an expression of the form $l_1 \leq L \leq l_2$, where L is a variable ranging over the level of a dimension and l_1 and l_2 are values. ∎

Atom	Dimension Interval
true	True
false	False
$anc_L^{L'}(L)=1$	$min(desc_L^{L'}(1)) \leq L \leq max(desc_L^{L'}(1))$
$anc_L^{L'}(L)<1$	$-\infty < L \leq max(desc_L^{L'}(prev(1)))$
$1 < anc_L^{L'}(L)$	$min(desc_L^{L'}(next(1))) \leq L < +\infty$
$anc_L^{L'}(L) \leq 1$	$-\infty < L \leq max(desc_L^{L'}(1))$
$1 \leq anc_L^{L'}(L)$	$min(desc_L^{L'}(1)) \leq L < +\infty$

Fig. 4. Transformation from atoms to dimension intervals

Fig. 4 shows how single atoms can be transformed to DI's. Values $-\infty$ and $+\infty$ have the obvious semantics. Moreover, functions $prev$ and $next$ result in the previous and the following value of 1 in the domain of L respectively.

In general, to determine whether a cube c^{old} can be used for the computation of c^{new}, we need to partition the detailed level of each dimension according to the respective level of c^{new}. If for each partition of c^{new}, there exists an identical partition of c^{old}, then c^{old} can be used to compute c^{new}. We formalise this relationship between two cubes, through Definition 2.

Definition 2. L-containment: Let D be a set of dimensions and φ^{old}, φ^{new} be two selection conditions involving levels only from D. Let L be a set of levels, each belonging to a different dimension of D. Let also the two cubes $c^{new} = (DS^0, \varphi^{new}, [L,M], agg(M))$ and $c^{old} = (DS^0, \varphi^{old}, [L,M], agg(M))$, defined over an arbitrary detailed data set DS^0. Selection condition φ^{new} is L-*contained* in φ^{old} (denoted by $\varphi^{new} \sqsubseteq_L \varphi^{old}$) if $c^{new} \sqsubseteq c^{old}$ for any data set DS^0. ∎

To tackle the problem of cube usability between cubes of different aggregation granularities, we introduce Algorithm `Check_Atoms_Usability` that is checking the containment of conjunctions of atoms that involve values. Notice that our analysis does not include $\neq$. This case will be handled in Section 3.3.

Algorithm `Check_Atoms_Usability`.

Input: Two conjunctions of atoms **a** and **b** involving only values, and a set of levels **L'**.

Output: true if $a \subseteq_{L'} b$, false otherwise.

1. Write all atoms of **a** and **b** as DI's using the transformations of Fig. 4 (where the level L is the detailed level of each dimension).
2. Group all DI's of **a** and **b** by dimension level and produce for every set a single DI' having the most restrictive boundaries. Let **a'** and **b'** be the result, respectively.
3. If there exists a DI `false` in **a'** Then <u>Return</u> true.
4. If there exists a DI `false` in **b'** Then <u>Return</u> false.
5. <u>For</u> every DI a of **a'**
6.   <u>If</u> a is defined over dimension level D_i. L^0 that does not exist in any DI of **b'** <u>Then</u>
7.   Introduce DI $-\infty \leq D_i$. $L^0 \leq \infty$ to **b'**.
8. <u>EndFor</u>
9. If **b'** has more DI's than **a'** <u>Then</u> <u>Return</u> false.
10. <u>For</u> every DI a= (A_s, A_e) of **a'**
11.   Let the DI b= (B_s, B_e) of **b'** involving the same dimension with a. Let also L' be the respective level in **L'**.
12.   <u>Case</u> $A_s < B_s$ or $B_e < A_e$ or b=false
13.   <u>Return</u> false
14.   <u>Case</u> $A_s \neq \min(\text{desc}^{L',L^0}(\text{anc}^{L',L^0}(A_s)))$ and $A_s \neq B_s$
15.   <u>Return</u> false
16.   <u>Case</u> $A_e \neq \max(\text{desc}^{L',L^0}(\text{anc}^{L',L^0}(A_e)))$ and $A_e \neq B_e$
17.   <u>Return</u> false
18. <u>EndFor</u>
19. <u>Return</u> true

Fig. 5. Algorithm `Check_Atoms_Usability`

For Example 1, Algorithm `Check_Atoms_Usability` deduces that φ_1 L-contains φ_3 (with respect to level `Month`), while φ_2 does not. Moreover, it is interesting to see that if one considers the `year` level, neither φ_1 nor φ_2 L-contains φ_3.

3.2   Equivalent Transformations for Atoms Involving only Levels

Following [17], we assume the existence of two infinite, totally ordered domains, **L** and **L'** isomorphic to the integers. Let also f be a total, monotone function over **L**, mapping the values of domain **L** to the values of domain **L'**. The family of `anc` functions fulfils these requirements.

We assume that we are given a collection of inequalities of the form X<Y, X≤Y, X≠Y, f(X)<f(Y), f(X)≤f(Y), f(X)≠f(Y) and equalities of the form f(X)=f(Y). We do not allow equalities of the form X=Y. If such a subgoal is found in a query, we

substitute every occurrence of X with Y. We also eliminate any pair of inequalities $f(X) \leq f(Y)$ and $f(Y) \leq f(X)$, where X,Y are distinct variables, with $f(X) = f(Y)$.

We will use the following set of axioms for these inequalities:

A1 $X \leq X$

A2 $X < Y$ implies $X \leq Y$

A3 $X < Y$ implies $X \neq Y$

A4 $X \leq Y$ and $X \neq Y$ imply $X < Y$

A5 $X \neq Y$ implies $Y \neq X$

A6 $X < Y$ and $Y < Z$ imply $X < Z$

A7 $X \leq Y$ and $Y \leq Z$ imply $X \leq Z$

A8 $X \leq Z$, $Z \leq Y$, $X \leq W$, $W \leq Y$ and $W \neq Z$ imply $X \neq Y$

A9 $X \leq Y$ implies $f(X) \leq f(Y)$

A10 $f(X) < f(Y)$ implies $X < Y$

A11 $f(X) \neq f(Y)$ implies $X \neq Y$

A12 $f(X) \leq f(Y)$ and $f(Y) \leq f(X)$ implies $f(X) = f(Y)$

A13 $f(X) = f(Y)$ and $f(Y) \leq f(Z)$ implies $f(X) \leq f(Z)$

A14 $f(X) = f(Y)$ and $f(Y) \neq f(Z)$ implies $f(X) \neq f(Z)$

A15 $f(X) = f(Y)$ implies $f(X) \leq f(Y)$

Fig. 6. Axioms for L-containment checking.

We assume that our models are assignments of integers to variables. Expressions of the form $f(X)$ are also treated as variables. For variables of the form X we apply axioms A1 to A9 and for variables of the form $f(X)$ we apply axioms A1 to A15.

Theorem 2. The axioms A1-A15 are sound and complete. ∎

In order to check whether one set of inequalities T follows from another set of inequalities S we compute the closure S^+ by applying the axioms A1-A15 until they no longer generate any new inequalities. Then, we check whether T is a subset of S^+.

3.3   Testing Cube Usability

In this section, we combine the results of Sections 3.1 and 3.2 to provide a test for several cases of cube usability. One can transform any kind of formula using logical transformations [6] to an equivalent formula consisting of disjunctions of conjunctions which do not involve $\neq$ and $\neg$. Theorem 3 provides sufficient criteria for a cube c^{old} to be used for the computation of another cube c^{new}. Algorithm Cube_Usability describes the specific steps to be followed for this computation.

Theorem 3. Suppose a detailed data set $DS^0 = [L^{0,1}, ..., L^{0,n}, M^0]$ and two cubes $c^{old} = (DS^0, \varphi_{old}, [L_1^{old}, ..., L_n^{old}, M_{old}], agg_{old}(M^0))$ and $c^{new} = (DS^0, \varphi_{new}, [L_1^{new}, ..., L_n^{new}, M_{new}], agg_{new}(M^0))$. If

1. $agg_{old} = agg_{new}$,

2. $L_i^{old} \sqsubseteq L_i^{new}$, $1 \leq i \leq n$, and

3. one of the following two cases holds for φ_{old} and φ_{new}:
   - φ_{old} and φ_{new} involve conjunctions of atoms only of the form $L_i \theta L_j$, all the levels L_i, L_j are higher from the respective levels of the schema of c^{old} (i.e. $L^{old,i;j} \sqsubseteq L_{i,j}$) and φ_{old} belongs to the closure of φ_{new}, or,
   - φ_{old} and φ_{new} involve conjunctions of atoms of the form $L \theta l$ and $\varphi_{new} \subseteq_{[L_1^{new}, ..., L_n^{new}]} \varphi_{old}$,

then Algorithm Cube_Usability correctly computes c^{new} from the tuples of c^{old}.

Theorem 3 tests for usability, pairs of cubes involving conjunctive selection conditions which do not involve $\neq$ and $\neg$. Cubes involving disjunctive selection conditions can be treated in the usual way [17].

Example 4. Let c^{new} and c^{old} be the cubes over DS^0 of Fig. 1 defined as follows.

$$c^{old}=(DS^0,\varphi_{old},[\text{Month},\text{Country},\text{Type},\text{Salesman},\text{Sum\_old}],\text{sum}(\text{Sales}))$$

and

$$c^{new}=(DS^0,\varphi_{new},[\text{Month},\text{Country},\text{Category},\text{Salesman},\text{Sum\_new}],$$
$$\text{sum}(\text{Sales}))$$

where $\varphi_{old}=18\text{-Feb-97}\leq\text{day} \wedge \text{day}\leq3\text{-Sep-97} \wedge \text{anc}_{\text{Item}}^{\text{Category}}(\text{Item})=\text{"Books"}$

and $\varphi_{new}=1\text{-Mar-97}\leq\text{day} \wedge \text{day}\leq3\text{-Sep-97} \wedge \text{"Literature"}\leq\text{anc}^{\text{Type},\text{Item}}$

$(\text{Item}) \wedge \text{anc}^{\text{Type},\text{Item}}(\text{Item})\leq\text{"Philosophy"}$.

Algorithm Cube_Usability.

Input: A detailed data set $DS^0=[L^{0,1},...,L^{0,n},M^0]$ and two cubes $c^{old}=(DS^0,\varphi_{old},[L_1^{old}$
$,...,\quad L_n^{old},M_{old}],\text{agg}_{old}(M^0))$ and $c^{new}=(DS^0,\varphi_{new},[L_1^{new},...,L_n^{new}$
$,M_{new}],\text{agg}_{new}(M^0))$ such that φ_{old} and φ_{new} involve either (a) conjunctions of atoms of the form $L\theta1$ or (b) conjunctions of atoms of the form $L\theta L'1$ where L and L' are levels and 1 is a value.

Output: A rewriting that calculates cube c^{new} from the tuples of c^{old}.

1. If all atoms of φ_{old} and φ_{new} involve conjunctions of atoms of the form $L\theta1$ <u>Then</u>
2. For every atom $a=\text{anc}_{L^0}^L(L^0)\theta1$ in φ_{new} (or equivalent to this form)
3. If L^{old} is the respective level in the schema of c^{old} and $L^{old}\sqsupseteq L$ <u>Then</u>
4. Transform a to $\text{anc}_{L^{old}}^L(L^{old})\theta1$
5. EndIf
6. <u>ElseIf</u> L^{old} is the respective level in the schema of c^{old} and $L\sqsupseteq L^{old}$ <u>Then</u>
7. Transform a to $L^{old}\theta_i\text{anc}_L^{L^{old}}(1)$ where $\theta_i=\theta$ except for two cases:
    (a) $a=\text{anc}_{L^0}^L(L^0)<1$ and $1\neq\min(\text{desc}_L^{L^{old}}(\text{anc}_L^{L^{old}}(1)))$ where $\theta_i=\leq$,
    (b) $a=\text{anc}_{L^0}^L(L^0)>1$ and $1\neq\max(\text{desc}_L^{L^{old}}(\text{anc}_L^{L^{old}}(1)))$ where $\theta_i=\geq$
8. EndIf
9. EndFor
10. EndIf
11. If all atoms of φ_{old} and φ_{new} involve conjunctions of atoms of the form $a=\text{anc}_{L^0}^L$
    $(L^0)\theta\text{anc}_{L^0}^{L'}(L^0)$ (or equivalent to this form), where both L and L' are higher than the respective levels of c^{old} <u>Then</u>
12. For every atom $a=\text{anc}_{L^0}^L(L^0)\theta\text{anc}_{L^0}^{L'}(L^0)$ in φ_{new}
15. Transform a to $\text{anc}_{L^{old}}^L(L^{old})\theta\text{anc}_{L^{old}}^{L'}(L^{old'})$
16. EndFor
17. EndIf
18. Apply the transformed selection condition to c^{old} and derive a new data set DS^1.
19. Replace all the values of DS^1 with their ancestor values at the levels of c^{new}, resulting in a new data set DS^2.
20. Aggregate ("group by" in the relational semantics) on the tuples of DS^2, so that we produce c^{new}.

Fig. 7. Algorithm Cube_Usability

Month	Type	Salesman	Country	Sum_old
Feb-97	Literature	Netz	USA	5
Sep-97	Philosophy	Netz	Japan	50
Sep-97	Literature	Netz	Japan	30

(a)

Month	Type	Salesman	Country	Sum_1
Sep-97	Philosophy	Netz	Japan	50
Sep-97	Literature	Netz	Japan	30

(b)

Month	Category	Salesman	Country	Sum_2
Sep-97	Book	Netz	Japan	50
Sep-97	Book	Netz	Japan	30

(c)

Month	Category	Salesman	Country	Sum_new
Sep-97	Book	Netz	Japan	80

(d)

Fig. 8. Calculating c^{new} from c^{old}

To check whether c^{new} can be computed from c^{old} we apply Theorem 3. The schemata and aggregation functions of the two cubes are compatible (conditions (a), (b) of Theorem 3). Moreover, φ_{new} is **L**-contained from φ_{old} with respect to the levels of c^{new}. Following, Lines 2-10 of Algorithm Cube_Usability, we transform φ_{new} so that it can be applied to the schema of cube c^{old}. The transformations of Lines 3-8 result in

$\varphi_{n@o}$=Mar-97≤Month ∧ Month≤Sep-97 ∧ "Literature"≤Type ∧ Type≤"Philosophy".

We apply the transformed selection condition to c^{old} (depicted in Fig. 8a) and derive a new data set DS^1 (depicted in Fig. 8b). Then, we replace all the values of DS^1 with their ancestor values at the levels of c^{new} (Line 19), resulting in a new data set DS^2 (depicted in Fig. 8c). Finally, we aggregate the tuples of DS^2 and we produce c^{new} (depicted in Fig. 8d). ∎

4   Discussion and Future Work

We have presented a *logical* model for cubes based on the key observation that a cube is not a self-existing entity, but rather a view over an underlying data set. The proposed model is powerful enough to capture all the commonly encountered OLAP operations such as selection, roll-up and drill-down, through a sound and complete algebra. We have showed how this model can be used as the basis for processing cube operations and have provided syntactic characterisations for the problems of cube usability. Theorem 3, which provides these syntactic characterisations, is very important for the usual operations of the model. Two of the most eminent cases are: (a) navigation from a certain cube c to a cube having all its levels higher (or equal) than the respective levels of c and (b) selection over a certain cube c where all the levels acting as variables are higher (or equal) than the levels of c.

Of course, the applicability of Theorem 3 is not restricted in these two simple cases. Normally, an OLAP screen contains more than one cubes [14]. Thus, an interactive OLAP session produces many cubes which possibly overlap. Computing a new set of cubes can possibly be achieved by using already computed and cached cubes (provided that they fulfil the criteria of Theorem 3). Consequently, the results on the problem of cube usability can be used both for the query optimisation and the caching processes. The cube usability results can also be applied in the problem of data warehouse design, where the optimal set of views (with respect to query and maintenance cost) has to be derived. Testing for cube usability can avoid redundancy in the final data warehouse schema and improve the run-time of the design algorithm [12].

As future work, we plan to incorporate our results in a system under construction in NTUA. The modelling parts could be extended to take into account aspects of the hierarchy structure (partial ancestor functions, hierarchies that are not well captured as lattices, etc.). The theoretical results over query processing can be extended to handle optimisation issues for a broader set of selection conditions, partial rewritings and optimisation of the physical execution for cube operations. Finally, a challenging issue is how to devise smarter algorithms for the cube usability problems.

References

1.   R. Agrawal, A. Gupta, and S. Sarawagi. Modelling multidimensional databases. Technical report, IBM Almaden Research Center, San Jose, California, 1995.

2.   L. Cabbibo and R. Torlone. Querying Multidimesional Databases. *6th International Workshop on Database Programming Languages (DBPL6)*, 1997.

3.   S. Chaudhuri, K. Shim. Optimizing Queries with Aggregate Views. In *Proceedings of the 5th International Conference on Extending Database Technology (EDBT-96)*, Avignon, France, March 25-29, 1996.

4.   S. Chaudhuri, S. Krishnamurthy, S. Potamianos, and K. Shim. Optimizing queries with materialized views. In *Proceedings of the 11th International Conference on Data Engineering (ICDE)*, IEEE Computer Society, pp. 190-200, Taipei, March 1995.

5.   S. Cohen, W. Nutt, A. Serebrenik. Rewriting Aggregate Queries Using Views. *Proceedings of the 18th ACM SIGACT-SIGMOD-SIGART Symposium on Principles of Database Systems (PODS)*, Philadelphia, Pennsylvania. ACM Press, 1999.

6.   H.B. Enderton, A Mathematical Introduction to Logic. Academic Press, 1972.

7.   M. Gebhardt, M. Jarke and S. Jacobs. A toolkit for negotiation support on multi-dimensional data. In *Proceedings of ACM SIGMOD International Conference on Management of Data.* Tucson, Arizona, 1997.

8.   A. Gupta, V. Harinarayan, and D. Quass. Aggregate query processing in data warehouses. In *Proceedings of the 21st International Conference on Very Large Data Bases (VLDB)*, Zurich, Switzerland, Morgan Kaufmann Publishers, August 1995.

9.   M. Gyssens, L.V.S. Lakshmanan. A Foundation for Multi-Dimensional Databases. In *Proceedings of the 23rd International Conference on Very Large Databases (VLDB)*, Athens, August 1997.

10.   W. Lehner. Modeling Large Scale OLAP Scenarios. In *Proceedings of the 6th International Conference of Extending Database Technology (EDBT-98)*, 1998.

11.   C. Li, X. Sean Wang. A Data Model for Supporting On-Line Analytical Processing. In *Proceedings of the International Conference on Information and Knowledge Management (CIKM)*, 1996.

12. S. Ligoudistianos, T. Sellis, D. Theodoratos, and Y. Vassiliou. Heuristic Algorithms for Designing the Data Warehouse with SPJ Views. In *Proceedings of the First International Conference on Data Warehousing and Knowledge Discovery, (DaWaK),* Lecture Notes in Computer Science, Vol. 1676, Springer, 1999.

13. Metadata Coalition. Metadata Interchange Specification (MDIS v. 1.1). http://www.metadata.org/standards/toc.html 1997.

14. Microsoft Corp. OLEDB for OLAP February 1998. Available at http://www.microsoft.com/data/oledb/olap/

15. OLAP Council. The APB-1 Benchmark. 1997. Available at http://www.olapcouncil.org/research/bmarkly.htm

16. TPC. TPC Benchmark H and TPC Benchmark R. Transaction Processing Council. June 1999. Available at http://www.tpc.org/

17. J. Ullman. Principles of Database and Knowledge-Base Systems. Volume II: The New Technologies. Computer Science Press. 1989.

18. J.D. Ullman. Information integration using logical views. *Proceedings of the 6th International Conference on Database Theory (ICDT-97),* Lecture Notes in Computer Science, pp. 19-40. Springer-Verlag, 1997.

19. P. Vassiliadis, T. Sellis. A Survey on Logical Models for OLAP Databases. *SIGMOD Record,* vol. 28, no. 4, December 1999.

20. P. Vassiliadis, S. Skiadopoulos. (Not) Yet Another Model for Multidimensional Databases (Extended version). Technical Report, KDBSL 1999. Available at http://www.dblab.ece.ntua.gr/~pvassil/publications/cube99.ps.gz

21. P. Vassiliadis. Modeling Multidimensional Databases, Cubes and Cube Operations. In *Proceedings of 10th International Conference on Scientific and Statistical Database Management (SSDBM),* Capri, Italy, July 1998.

22. P. Larson, H. Z. Yang. Computing Queries from Derived Relations. In *Proceedings of the 11th International Conference on Very Large Data Bases (VLDB),* Stockholm, Sweden, Morgan Kaufmann Publishers, August 1985.

Managing the Software Process in the Middle of Rapid Growth: A Metrics Based Experiment Report from Nokia

Tapani Kilpi

Nokia
Elektroniikkatie 3, 90570 Oulu, Finland
tapani.kilpi@nokia.com

Abstract. Software Process Improvement is a well known approach in software organisations these days. Process assessments or audits have been experienced in one form or another by 'almost everybody' in the business. What are the benefits that have been reached through these efforts? An assessment or an audit is often planned and carried out by people who are outsiders in the organisation and the result of these approaches is normally an improvement plan or a set of process improvement ideas. What happens after an assessment? Who takes the responsibility to take care that the improvement plan is really implemented in an organisation? More and more organisations take this challenge seriously and have allocated a remarkable amount of resources to develop their process improvement a continuous activity. This paper presents one approach for organising process management activity in an organisation and also practical experiences collected in using the approach.

1 Introduction

Process management and improvement are concepts that have become to everebody's consciousness in software business during the past decade. The aim of these approaches is to teach organisations to carry out their daily routines in a correct and careful way. The quality must not be sacrificed even under the threat of tight deadlines. In an ideal situation the software projects can be planned in a way that resource usage and schedules are in balance and at the same time the quality of the products is on satisying level. This provides good facilities for keeping the customer satisfaction high. All these observations are often heard as arguments when process improvement is offered as a mean of increasing the overall effectiveness and quality in an organisation. Do these ideas work in practice then? Certainly, if you manage to to implement them succesfully in an organisation.

Several process improvement methods use assessments as their main source of information in collecting data of a target organisation: ISO/IEC 9000 standards [5, 6], CMM [2, 3, 4, 11], Bootstrap [1], ISO/IEC 15504 [7], etc. However, in order to make an improvement approach a continuous and fundamental activity in an organisation

B. Wangler, L. Bergman (Eds.): CAiSE 2000, LNCS 1789, pp. 498-508, 2000
© Springer-Verlag Berlin Heidelberg 2000

there is a need to create a capable process management activity. In a large organisation this normally means a separate process management organisation with several full-time process developers belonging to it. How to build this type of sub-organisation then? How to plan its activities? How to create effective communication mechanism between the process management activity and the rest of the organisation? These are just few of the questions that need to be solved in an organisation that aims to make a severe attempt to start a process management activity as a part of its daily routines.

Fixed Switching Research & Development (FSG R&D) unit of Nokia produces software for the DX200-product line of phone switches. As a separate Nokia unit its history started in the year 1995 and today it has approximately 600 employees. The volume of production has together with the number of employees grown rapidly in FSG R&D ever since the beginning. All these attributes make FSG R&D an interesting environment from the point of view of Software Process Improvement. This paper presents the experiences got in FSG R&D in developing a process management activity in it a systematic way.

2 FSG R&D

FSG R&D (Fixed Switching Research and Development) unit of Nokia produces software for the DX200-product line of phone switches. DX200 development was started in early 70's as a research project and the first customer delivery took place in 1980. Currently the third generation of DX200 is in production and the applications of it cover all the main areas of switching business. There are over 15 million source lines of code in the DX200 program library and more than 2000 engineers are committed to carry out the DX200 development work. Unofficially DX200 is the largest software project in Finland. FSG R&D produces Fixed Applications on DX200 System Platform, presented in figure 1.

Another important type of applications being developed on DX200 platform is the GSM applications. The phone switches applications typically have common core part on the top of which a customer specific part is built for building the separate customer deliveries.

From the point of view of FSG R&D the DX200 environment means the following challenges to cope with:
• large and complex software,
• large and growing software and
• a multisite environment.

Ever since year 1995 the number of customer deliveries and projects has strongly grown each year in FSG. Figure 2. presents the trend of increase in the number of projects in FSG R&D from year 1996 to year 1999. Today the number of customer delivery projects is four times as big as it was in year 1996. This fact, together with the increased number of employees, have led FSG R&D to a situation where it has had to develop a high standard Process Management activity to be able to cope with the increased demands. High standard processes make it possible on the one hand to create capable facilities for the new employees to be trained to their tasks and on the other hand to coordinate increased numbers of people and projects – without sacrifying the quality.

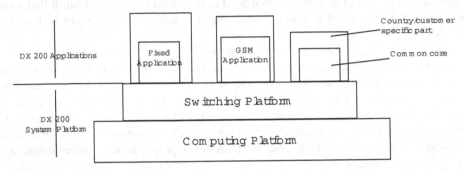

Fig. 1. DX200 Applications and System Platform [9]

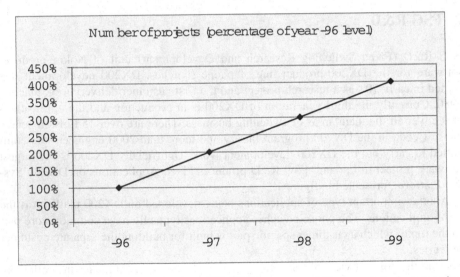

Fig. 2. The relative trend of the number of FSG R&D customer delivery projects in comparison to year –96 level.

3 Process Management Activity of FSG R&D

In front of the challenges presented in the previous chapter FSG R&D has already from the beginning clearly realised that high standard processes and efficient process improvement have a vital role in the organisation. FSG R&D allocates remarkable effort on reaching these goals, i.e. there are fourteen full-time process developers in the organisation and more than 60 part time process developers on the different organisational levels. The common objective of all these process developers is taking care of continuous improvement of FSG R&D processes, methods and tools.

The process improvement activity of FSG R&D, illustrated in figure 3, is steered by the FSG R&D Management Team. The processes of FSG R&D have been divided to five separate process areas: *Release-, Design-, Testing-, Maintenance-* and *Quality Assurance Processes.* All these process areas are managed by the Process Teams each of which are responsible of one specific area. Each process team is headed by a Process Development Manager who is a full-time process developer. The rest members of the teams are part-time process developers, i.e. their primary role in FSG R&D is sw development, testing, etc. The Management Team defines the long-term process improvement Road Maps and Action Plans and also accepts and gives resource commitment to the process improvement projects proposed by the Process

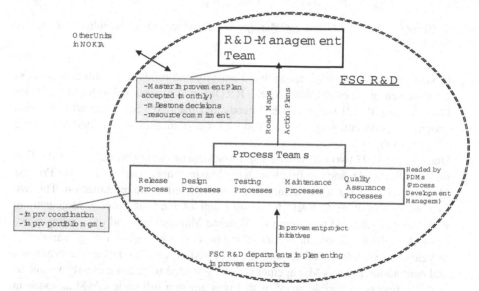

Fig. 3. The Steering Structure of FSG R&D Process Improvement Activity [9]

Teams. All process improvement projects are carried out the same way like the software projects in FSG R&D and their progress and resource usage are followed and compared to the project plan. FSG was originally separated from another Nokia unit to a unit of its own in year 1995. It inherited the key process models for itself partly from its Nokia mother unit and partly from the general process models of Nokia. The inherited models were based on ISO 9000 standard and the general project milestone model of Nokia and offered a firm base for starting productive work in FSG. However, it was obvious already in the beginning that the business of FSG will grow rapidly during the following years. The need for tailoring and improving the process models further to satisfy the FSG specific needs became urgent. The most important process improvement activities carried out in FSG R&D from year 1996 to 1999, illustrated in figure 4, are:

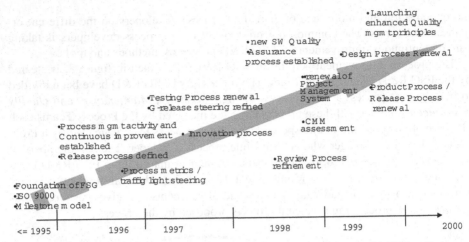

Fig. 4. History of FSG R&D Process Management Development: the highlights from year 1996 to 1999 [9].

1. In year 1996, the Process Management activity and model for continuos process improvement were established in FSG R&D. It was also started to build a Metrics Programme [10, 12] for FSG R&D needs and the first FSG R&D wide Metrics Programme concentrating on the Product Process metrics was started at the end of year 1996.

2. During year 1997 two CMM based self assessments were carried out for the first time in FSG R&D, and the first long term Master Improvement Plans for Process Management process were defined and implemented in the organisation. The two first main aims in FSG R&D from the point of view of Process Management were reorganising and redefining the Release Management and the Testing processes. Also the development of Innovation process was started during year 1997.

3. In year 1998 the effects of as well the renewed process models as the organised and continuous Process Management activity started to become clearly visible as practical results. A visible proof of this was got in a full scale CMM assessment held at the end of year 1998 in which FSG R&D reached a high maturity level. The most important process improvement approaches started in FSG R&D during 1998 were the redefinitions of the SQA-, Review- and Project-management processes. The renewed SQA included capable facilities for the use of metrics throughout the organisation.

4. Finally, during year 1999, the most important process improvement approaches have been the implementation of a company wide Quality Management system and renewals of as well the Design- and the Product-processes.

Overall conclusion of the status of the FSG R&D software process is that it is educated, well-organised and effectively established through the organistion. However, FSG R&D has gone through a challenging path during the past four years. Despite the fact that the whole Process Management approach seems to have turned to a success story in FSG R&D, there has also been many difficulties that have been encountered and that have had to be overcome before reaching the recent status. The next section will present some metrics based findings and analyse the details of the effect of systematic Process Management improvement of FSG R&D from the beginning of year 1996 to the end of year 1999.

4 Metrics Based Findings from FSG R&D

The aim of the first Metrics Programme of FSG R&D (see the previous section) was defined to measure the status of the Product Process. The programme was based on a set of metrics each of which were followed four times a year. The programme has been going on for four years now and some trends that show progress of the FSG processes can be seen. Earlier in this paper, in figure 2, the remarkable increase in the number of customer delivery projects in FSG R&D was presented. This number shows strongly increasing trend from year 1996 to 1999. In the middle of this type of rapid growth any organisation has to allocate remarkable amount of resources for developing its processes in order to prevent the accuracy of the projects and the quality of the products to decrease. In the following presentation the progress of four metrics included to the Product Process metrics programme of FSG R&D are presented as trend curves from year 1996 to 1999 (the Measuring Period).

Figure 5. shows the relative trend curve of the delayed projects in FSG R&D during the Measuring Period. This chart is based on the *Release Accuracy* metric of FSG R&D. *Release Accuracy* metric measures the absolute number of days of delay in the projects. A project is classified to be delayed if the delay exceeds the predefined number of days when checked against the original schedule. The trend of the number of delayed customer delivery projects shows slightly decreasing trend during the

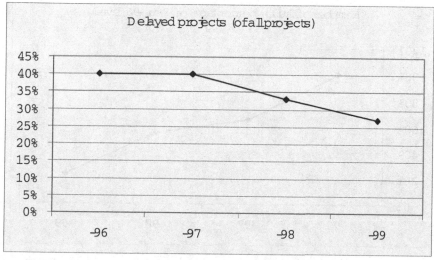

Fig. 5. Relative trend curve of delayed projects in FSG R&D from 1996 to 1999.

Measuring Period. This finding shows that keeping of the project schedules is today on a slightly better level than it was in year 1996. During this period the number of customer delivery projects has grown 400 % in FSG R&D.

Figure 6. shows the relative trend curve of the number of faults in FSG R&D during the Measuring Period. This chart is based on the *Release Maturity* metric of FSG R&D. *Release Maturity* metric measures the sum of internally found and customer found faults at major milestones of a project. FSG R&D uses several severity classes for the faults. The faults of the two most severe fault classes, the critical and the important, are counted in to the *Release Maturity* metric value. The curve in figure 6. shows a relative trend of the one year averages of the absolute numbers of faults in FSG R&D projects during the Measuring Period. The trend of the number of faults is showing a remarkable decrease. This finding implies that the average number of faults in FSG R&D projects has strongly decreased during the Measuring Period. The most important factors that have made it possible to reach this result in the middle of the growth have been the renewed Testing and Review processes (mentioned in section 3 of this paper).

Figure 7. shows the relative trend curve of the *Fault Fixing Coverage* metrics in FSG R&D during the Measuring Period. Fault Fixing Coverage measures the ratio of the fixed faults in comparison to the total number of faults in a project. The curve in figure 7. shows a relative trend of the one year averages of the fault fixing coverage percentages in FSG R&D projects during the Measuring Period. The trend of the fault fixing coverage is showing slight decrease from year 1996 to 1997. From year 1997 to 1999 the trend is showing steady increase. It can be concluded that at the same time when the number of faults has decreased in average the effectiveness of fixing the faults has increased. These two findings together show that the quality of software and handling of the faults have improved greatly during the Measurement Period in FSG R&D.

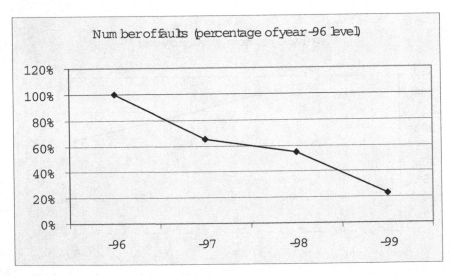

Fig. 6. Relative trend curve of number of fault in FSG R&D from 1996 to 1999.

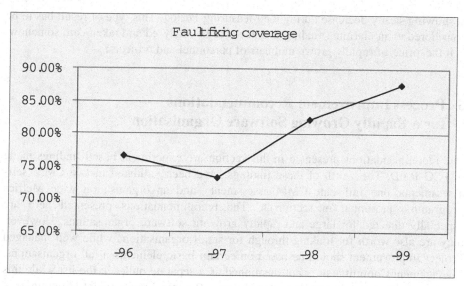

Fig. 7. Relative trend curve of fault fixing coverage in FSG R&D from 1996 to 1999.

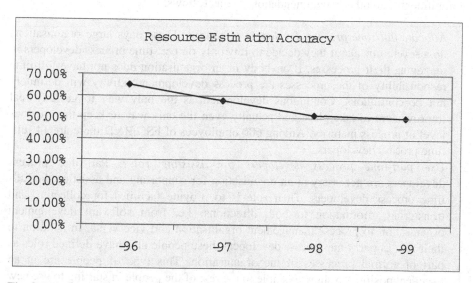

Fig. 8. Relative trend curve of Resource Estimation Accuracy in FSG R&D from 1996 to 1999.

Figure 8. shows the relative trend curve of the *Resource Estimation Accuracy* metrics in FSG R&D during the Measuring Period. The *Resource Estimation Accuracy* metric measures the deviation between the planned use of resources in a project in comparison to the realised amount of resources. The metric value shows the corresponding coverage percentage. The curve of figure 8. shows a relative trend of the one year averages of the Resource Estimation Accuracy percentages in FSG R&D projects during the Measuring Period. The trend of the Resource Estimation Accuracy is showing steady decrease during the Measuring Period. This type of result has to be considered as an alarming finding that needs to be analysed and taken care somehow. Is it the 'price' of rapidly grown numbers of personnel and projects?

5 Process Improvement Recommendations for a Rapidly Growing Software Organisation

The recommendations presented in this section are experiment based findings made in FSG R&D. The worth of these findings have been validated in two CMM self-assessments, one full-scale CMM assessment and an organisation wide Metrics Programme presented in section 4. The recommendations presented here are especially directed for large and rapidly growing software organisations. However, they are also worth for looking through for small organisations while well managed Project Improvement should be based on certain basic elements in all organisations. Management Commitment is not mentioned as a separate bullet in the list while this subject is an underlying requirement for any Process Improvement Programme – there is no process improvement without active and continuous Management Commitment. The other recommendations are as follows:

1. *Allocate full time process developers in charge.* These days large organisations do a severe mistake if they decide to rely only on part-time process developers in managing their processes. If anybody in an organisation does not have full-time responsibility of the processes the process development activity will definitely not be continuous. Continuous development is the only way to get any real improvement to take place and actually even the only way to keep the previous level of process maturity. Among 600 employees of FSG R&D there are 14 full-time process developers.

2. *Use part-time process developers for assisting roles.* Part-time process developers are necessary in an organisation for supporting and assisting the full-time process developers. Their role is to provide facilities for collecting and transfering information to both directions, i.e. from software development organisation to process management organisation and vice versa. In addition to their role as part-time process developers these people also have defined roles as part of normal processes of the organisation. This type of people are in an excellent position to show example to the rest of the people in starting to use new models, tools, etc. FSG R&D has approximatly 60 part-time process developers who participate process management monthly.

3. *Plan process improvement approaches as projects.* Project improvement approaches should be planned and followed as projects, i.e. they should be treated the same way like the product development projects. This is the only way to ensure that they get the resources they need and that they are fullfilled in the defined schedule. Process improvement is not something that somebody does on his/her 'own' time.

4. *Get resource commitment of all the necessary groups in organisation.* Process improvement activities can not be implemented by 'external forces' alone in an organisation. Unavoidably these approaches bind also a certain extent of product or software development resources. In practice this means that people who are expected to follow the processes are also required to participate in planning of them. The commitment for allocating these resources for process improvement projects should be given by the organisation resource owners the same way it is given for product development or software projects. Otherwise it is likely that the planned resources will not be available.

5. *Define clear milestones for process improvement projects.* Process improvement projects need the same type of follow up as the 'normal' projects. Plans, resource allocations, schedules, etc. are all necessary also in process improvement projects. Clear milestones with defined set of exit criteria are vital part of the follw-up.

6. *Test new models and ideas by piloting.* Costs of spreading a new process or a practice to a large organisation are normally high. Number of people need to be trained, number of installations need to be done, and so on. A good idea is to select a part of organisation for piloting the new practice there at first. By this way the errors found must be fixed only for the people in the scope of the pilot. The rest of the organisation then get the fixed delivery of the practice already at the first hand.

7. *Plan the roll out of new processes and practices carefully[8].* A new process model or a practice will propably not be popular in an organisation if the roll-out of it is not planned carefully. Things to be noticed in planning the roll-out are for example: target group, technical questions, technical support, training channel, training events, training material, usage support, information for interest groups, etc.

8. *Use metrics for follow-up and planning of continuous improvement.* Comparable and valid long-term follow-up results can not be collected without proper set of metrics. Definition of the metrics is a wide task that is recomendable to carry out as a Metrics Programme. In FSG R&D there are several Metrics Programmes going on continuously.

6 Conclusions

A well planned and carefully implemented Process Management Organisation is a vital part of any large software organisation these days. The existing Process Maturity models and assessments based on them offer a good base to get started in arranging an effective Process Management activity in an organisation. However, a process assessment is only a start – the practical process improvement efforts need to be planned and carried out after it. In many organisations these days it is not realised clearly enough that reaching good results in process improvement requires capable resources. This is understandable while the pressure of product development and software projects is hard and demands often 'all possible resources'. However, resources spent on process improvement efforts will bring the money spent on them back if the efforts are planned well.

A long term plan for process improvement is required in order on the one hand to coordinate and fit together the separate process improvement activities in an organisation and on the other hand to evaluate the progress made through years. Learning from the history is a vital part of process improvement. It is also important to regard the process improvement approaches as 'normal projects' with proper follow up, clear milestones and capable resource allocations. Othervise there will not be any remarkable results. Also things like piloting the big improvement approaches first in smaller groups and carefull planning of the roll-out of new models and tools are worthwhile to notice. Finally, the definition and implementation of well focused metrics give a firm base for evaluating the quality of the processes and the products and offer an effective way to inform the employees of the strategical goals.

References

1. Bicego, A. & Khurana, M. & Kuvaja, P. 1998. Bootstrap 3.0 – Software Process Assessment Methodology. In Proceedings of SQM'98,.
2. Curtis, B. & Hefley, W. E. & Miller, S. 1995. People capability maturity model (P-CMM), CMU/SEI-95-MM-02, Software Engineering Institute.
3. Humphrey, W. S. 1989. Managing the Software Process, Addison-Wesley Publishing Company. Pp. 299-359.
4. Humphrey, W. S. 1995. A Discipline for Software Engineering", Addison-Wesley Publishing Company. Pp. 271 – 306.
5. ISO 9000-3. 1991. Guidelines for the application of ISO9001 to the development, supply and maintenance of software: Quality Management and Quality Assurance Standards – Part 3", International Organisation for Standardisation.
6. ISO 90001. 1994. Quality Systems – Model for quality assurance in design/development, production, installation and servicing. International Organisation for Standardisation.
7. ISO/IEC. 1998. Information Technology: Software Process Assessment. ISO/IEC Tech. Rep. 15504 Type 2, ISO (Ed.), Geneva, Switzerland.
8. Kiiskilä, J. 1999. Piloting as a Part of Process Improvement of Reviews – a Case Study at Nokia Telecommunications. In the Proceedings of the International Conference on Product Focused Software Process Improvement (PROFES'99), June 22-24, 1999, Oulu, Finland. Technical Research Centre of Finland, Espoo .
9. Marjakangas, H. 1999. Process Management in FSG R&D. Presentations in Finesse Seminar in Technical Research Centre of Oulu, Finland April 13th 1999 and in Nokia Quality Conference Helsinki, Finland June 8th-9th 1999.
10. NASA (National Aerobautics and Space Administration). 1995. Software Measurement Guidebook, Revision 1, June. Goddard Space Flight Center, Greenbelt, Maryland 20771.
11. Paulk, M. C. & Curtis, B. & Chrissis, M. B. & Weber, C. V. 1993. "Capability Maturity Model, Version 1.1", IEEE Software. Volume 10, Number 4, July.
12. Solingen, R. & Berghout, E. 1999. „The Goal/Question/Metric Method A practical Guide for Quality Improvement of Software Improvement. Great Britain, Gambridge: McGraw-Hill. 199 pages.

The Impacts of Electronic Commerce in the Automobile Industry: An Empirical Study in Western Australia

Peter Marshall, Roger Sor, and Judy McKay

School of Management Information Systems
Edith Cowan University
Perth, Australia

Abstract. While the hype surrounding the promise of electronic commerce seems all pervasive currently, as academics there is a need to conduct empirical studies to establish balanced and credible reviews of the impacts of the Internet and associated technologies on business practice and performance. Also, while the USA is clearly a leader in the uptake of such technologies, it is a moot point as to whether industry trends identified there translate into forecasts for similar industries in different countries and regions. This paper reports findings of a qualitative study of car retailing in Western Australia, aimed at finding out about the impacts of the Internet and electronic commerce from the perspective of senior executives in car retail outlets. Generally speaking, the executives interviewed are experiencing great uncertainty with respect to electronic commerce and its effect on their businesses: they are uncertain about its likely impacts long term (although not much is currently happening), they are uncertain about the ultimate magnitude of electronic commerce in their industry, they are uncertain about the costs and benefits of electronic commerce investments, but they are unwilling not to be involved at all. There appear to be few articulated and carefully thought-out business strategies driving their electronic commerce activities at this stage, nor is there much evidence of internal business processes being reengineered to accommodate the requirements of an electronic commerce presence.

1   Introduction

Electronic commerce is said to have the potential to alter industry structures and affect the way businesses compete for markets [1]. These effects are already apparent in some industries and specific business organisations in the USA particularly [16], and are just now becoming visible in Australia (see [8]). Arguably therefore, there is a need for Australian-based empirical research particularly at the industry and supply chain level to identify and validate early trends in electronic commerce, and to evaluate and further refine strategies being adopted by business in response to the e-commerce phenomenon. This paper focuses particularly on the anticipated impacts and trends of electronic commerce with respect to the business practices and behaviours, and decision making of car dealers. All the car dealers involved in the study to date are well aware of the Internet, are somewhat aware of the trends in the USA, and the potential of electronic commerce and the Internet to transform their business and to have an immense impact on the way they operate as a business. They

B. Wangler, L. Bergman (Eds.): CAiSE 2000, LNCS 1789, pp. 509-521, 2000
© Springer-Verlag Berlin Heidelberg 2000

are all represented in Web sites of various types, or are in advanced stages of preparation of a web presence. But while the promises and the potential are vaguely understood, there appears to be comparatively little direct activity, comparatively little evidence of businesses being engineered to support web-based customer interactions of various types, and a pervasive attitude of *"This could suddenly go up like a rocket so we can't ignore it"*. The paper which follows will describe the research project and explore some of these themes more fully.

2   The Impacts of Electronic Commerce

While electronic commerce has been subjected to a wide range of definitions in its comparatively short history, for the purposes of this paper it will be regarded as involving the buying and selling of goods and services over the Internet, and related information provision and gathering [20], [21]. Thus defined, electronic commerce would include business-to-business, and business-to-end consumer transactions and information provision over the Internet.

Many pundits have forecast enormous impacts from electronic commerce in most industry sectors, predicting momentous changes in the world of commerce as we know it today. The interconnectivity and pervasiveness of the Internet do open new possibilities for the organisation of work, for the management of the supply chain and formation of dynamic trading networks [18], and for entrepreneurs to meet the needs and demands of ever-better informed consumers [4]. These trends clearly impact the retail sector. While some authors go as far as to predict the demise of bricks and mortar, 'High Street' shopping [3], others forecast a rapid growth in Internet shopping but still anticipate healthy activity in High Street shops, arguing that such shopping in fact meets important social, cultural and psychological needs [9],[16]. The extent of the impacts of electronic commerce in retailing remains somewhat difficult to predict with accuracy: conservative estimates suggest that Internet shopping may ultimately account for 10 – 15% of the retail sector [15].

Arguably as a particular categories' on-line sales surpass 10% of total sales, retailers will be forced to change their business models and practices, and take account of these trends towards electronic commerce [16], [17]. Of particular interest for this paper are trends in car sales, with obvious interest placed in the changes to existing High St car yard business practices and models.

3   Impacts of Electronic Commerce on the Car Retail Industry

As there is to date no known published information on the effects of electronic commerce on car retailing in Australia, discussion at this stage must be limited to a consideration of trends and forecasts in the USA. Sales of cars in the USA, both new and used, have not escaped the impacts of electronic commerce. By 1998, for example, it was argued that more than 10% of sales of new and used cars were influenced by the Internet. Thus, 2 million purchases of new cars and 4.2 million purchases of used cars were reliant to some extent on electronic commerce [14]. The exact role of the Internet perhaps need to be clarified however. In some retail categories, the Internet plays an important role in most, if not all, phases of the business transaction. Thus, information provision, purchase request, financial transaction, and possibly delivery of the good are all facilitated by the Internet, for example. Typically, this is not the case in the car industry, nor is it predicted to be [13].

Currently, some car purchasers are using the Internet to research vehicle types and features, and to identify and locate vehicles potentially of interest. Having made a decision about the make and model of car(s) in which they are interested, typically these consumers then go about transacting the rest of their car purchase in the more traditional manner. Of the 2.8 million Internet-influenced sales of new cars in 1998, approximately 2 million of these used the Internet for exactly this purpose [11]. Most of the remaining Internet-influenced purchasers used the Internet to locate a dealer stocking the particular type of vehicle they are interested in. At the moment, almost no complete sales are made over the Internet, nor are additional arrangements such as finance, insurance and additional warranty options generally made over the Internet. Both these areas however, are anticipated to become available by 2000, and to grow substantially by 2003 [12].

Thus, in America at the moment, comparatively few new car sales are made directly by the car manufacturer to the end consumer. Occupying a far more important role in both the new and used car marketplace are various intermediaries, who each list many dealers and offer the consumer the ability to search on various parameters, such as car type, price range, geographic location, and so on, in order to locate a smaller cohort of potentially suitable cars within reach of their homes or offices to facilitate further personal enquiry. In total, it is estimated that more than 4 million used cars will be listed on these on-line buying services in 1999, some 10% of the used cars that will be purchased this year. These intermediaries offer car dealers a substantial number of referrals each month: the larger and more successful sites may be referring more than 100,000 clients to dealers each month [11].

It could be argued that the US experience with electronic commerce seems several years in advance of Australia with respect to its acceptance and adoption of on-line retailing, and given reasonable similarities in business trends and culture between the USA and Australia, it could provide a useful model for local businesses to consider in order that they can prepare for the future. However, it could also be asserted that there are important differences in the Australian business environment, thus rendering the data and trends from the USA unreliable as predictors of trends in Australia.

4   The Research Project

The research project was designed to consist of a series of qualitative, semi-structured, research interviews with senior executives (managers and/or owners) of a variety of car dealerships in the capital city of Western Australia. Each interview was based on a set of interview questions, based on the trends in electronic commerce in the retailing sector, and specifically, in the car industry, and also on the authors' knowledge of electronic commerce trends in Australia. Some flexibility in approach was adopted to accommodate and be responsive to the varied responses received from interviewees. The interviews conducted lasted between 1.5 and 3 hours, and were crafted to encourage the senior executives interviewed to describe their understandings of electronic commerce, and to articulate their beliefs about the impacts of electronic commerce and the Internet on their business activities and practices in the future. The interest of the researchers was thus to arrive at an understanding of the impacts of electronic commerce from the CEOs'/owners' perspectives and to reveal their feelings and beliefs about electronic commerce, indicating that the qualitative research interview was an appropriate vehicle for the conduct of this research [6].

Each of the interviews was transcribed and subject to qualitative content analysis. The specific approach used is detailed elsewhere (see [10]), but involved categorisation of responses into certain themes, some of which were inherent in the interview questions, and some of which emerged through the interviewees' responses to questions posed. Some nine interviews have been conducted to date. In citing from these transcribed interviews, the convention CY1-CY9 has been adopted (Car Yards 1 – 9) in order to conceal the identity of any specific dealer.

5   Findings of the Research

A number of themes or issues have emerged as a result of the interviews conducted to date. Each of these will be briefly described and discussed below. However, generally speaking, it seems fair to say that the Internet is causing both interest and uncertainty amongst the car dealers. Already, there are some impacts of electronic commerce being felt, such as the reengineering of the industry supply chain (discussed below). However, few of the car dealers feel certain as to how large the impacts of electronic commerce might ultimately be, and few of the businesses seem to be adopting quite deliberate and explicit strategies with respect to electronic commerce. There was generally little evidence of internal changes being made in response to opportunities offered by electronic commerce initiatives.

5.1   Impacts of Electronic Commerce on the Car Industry Supply Chain

The car industry has traditionally relied on a fairly uncomplicated supply chain. Car manufacturers (typically fairly large, prominent organisations) draw raw materials and other component parts from a number of suppliers. Finished new cars are then distributed to a network of car dealers, for on-selling to the end consumer. End consumers may sell used cars back to dealers (perhaps as a trade-in on another car, although not necessarily), or alternatively, may privately organise sales of used cars direct to other end consumers. Figure 1 illustrates these relationships.

Proponents of electronic commerce might argue that, amongst other things, the advent of the Internet in the car industry supply chain may result in disintermediation [2], [7]. Long term this may occur, with new car buyers specifying requirements and purchasing direct from manufacturers. However, current industry activity with respect to electronic commerce does not indicate that this is occurring to any great extent as yet. Rather, Figure 2 portrays the changes occurring in the industry.

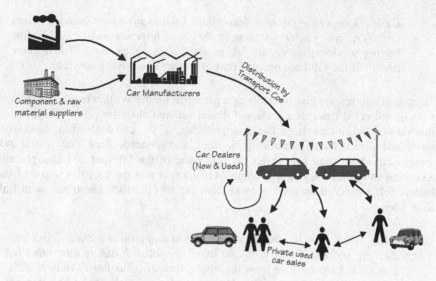

Fig. 1. Traditional Car Industry Supply Chain

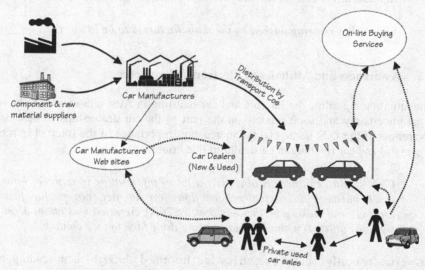

Fig. 2. The Effects of Electronic Commerce in the Car Industry

Already in the Australian car retailing industry, electronic commerce has seen the advent of on-line listing and buying services, acting as a conduit of information, referrals and expressions of interest between end consumers and new and used car dealers. Thus dealers register with these on-line buying services, regularly providing updates on the range and features of vehicles they have available for sale. In exchange, the on-line service providers facilitate placing interested customers in touch with the relevant dealer. Some of the dealers interviewed believed it was necessary to be represented on at least one of these electronic marketplaces.

> *CY4: "I mean the job of a dealership, I believe is to get customers into the door, once you've got them in the door, hopefully, sales...it [on-line buying services] is very useful, so soon some of us, we will lose some deals"* (if they did not become part of the on-line buying service).

Car manufacturers are also developing a presence on the Web, whereby interested end users are directed towards a preferred dealer located close-by [19]. While the CEOs interviewed did not envisage the disappearance of the car dealerships as consumers purchased direct from manufacturers, they did concede that they could not be complacent about their role given the influence of the Internet and changes already occurring in the industry supply chain. Of interest was the fact that some of the car dealers felt pressured by the car manufacturers to establish a web site with links to other sites.

> *CY3: "Our name's already on all the manufacturer's sites. And our address and email address...and when we finish building our web site, you'll click down to us from the manufacturer...Further to that, there's pressure on us from the manufacturer to have a web site...*(And then in response to a question whether the pressure came from a particular manufacturer) *Yes. From all of them. From the manufacturers."*

> *CY5: "We're being pushed by the manufacturers to be in there."*

5.2   Awareness and Attitudes to Electronic Commerce

The situation regarding the Internet and car retailing in Australia seemed to be one of great uncertainty and some anxiety on the part of the car dealerships. There is some awareness of the U.S. scene and the increasing importance of the Internet in retailing in general and car retailing in particular in that country.

> *CY4:   "But, eh, there is obviously a lot of information in terms of how much business has actually been done on the net, not people just looking, and making predictions that by 2000, America was about 35% signing contracts without actually being done face to face contact."*

However, typically, senior executives are informed through their reading of the popular press and through television reports, but none of those interviewed to date have undertaken serious research into electronic commerce. Very few persons in the car retailing industry in Australia are willing to forecast the future role and importance of the Internet in car retailing in Australia, although they generally suspect that it will be significant.

> *CY8: "We really are nowhere yet with the Internet other than we know it's going to work and it's in the infancy stages. It's already showing positive signs, and we will move towards it pretty quickly. Should be interesting to see in 12 months time reflect and see."*

However most of the larger car dealerships, particularly those with annual revenues of greater than $10 million per year, have an Internet presence now or plan to have one in the near future. The smaller players in the industry are also either established on the Web, or are planning to become so in the foreseeable future. The web presence is usually accomplished through the electronic malls or marketplaces which were briefly outlined previously when discussing changes to the car retail industry supply chain.

Overall there is a moderate amount of skepticism about the Internet and its importance in new and used car retailing in Western Australia. Little has happened yet, and there is some feeling that despite some journalistic stories and government reports heralding great changes, little will happen, at least in the short term future.

> *CY4: "What is happening is that we are getting some initial interest-only enquiries over the Internet...but so far is so small relative to the opening of the site."*

But there is great uncertainty also. Interviewees generally acknowledged that electronic commerce and the Internet could become enormously important to their businesses, although they were uncertain as to exactly what impacts it might have, how dramatic these impacts would be, and on how these changes might be realised in their specific businesses. Despite the skepticism, none of the interviewees were willing to completely ignore electronic commerce at the moment: there was always the concern that it might suddenly become very significant, and they did not want to risk being 'left behind'.

> *CY7: "No, no we suspect that we'd better be there."*

> *CY5: "So the whole email thing and Internet is a wild card. This one's from our point of view, but we don't know where the hell it's going."*

> *CY1: "Obviously our business has to be competitive, and we have to keep up with the latest marketing trends...I am only at this stage paying a token gesture I think towards the Internet, we haven't really done it properly."*

Also, it must be said that many of the dealers wanted to use the Internet to arouse interest, but actually wanted then to handle the transaction face-to-face.

> *CY2: "What is happening is that people are searching for products from the Internet...I don't know whether, or how many people would buy from the Internet, if you're talking about a commodity like a motor car, I still believe people still want to touch it."*
>
> *CY9: "I don't think anyone would spend their money firstly without being able to touch it, see it, and I don't think we want that way either, because that person is important..."*

> *CY4: "The point I was getting to, I don't think anybody would want to buy used cars without touching it and seeing it."*

> *CY8: "I'm certainly not trying to encourage people to buy a motor car on the Internet. I'm trying to initialise enquiries as a result of finding a car on the Internet...The Internet is very useful to provide interesting useful information...I require enquiries from the Internet, I want then to get face-to-face."*

It could hardly be asserted that the car dealerships had articulated a clear vision of electronic commerce for their organisation, which they were now pursuing through appropriate strategies. Rather, the articulated strategy was 'We have to be on the Web, because otherwise we might miss out'.

> *CY3: "Jeez, we've got to have a bloody web site now before everybody else out there does it."*

> *CY4: "I am computer illiterate, emm...effectively the only decision that I had was to keep it simple. By me bringing the vehicle into stock, my car system automatically goes to the system [the on-line buying service] and then links it straight to the Internet."*

> *CY8: "It has been said time enough that the worst thing you could do is wait until the Internet gets big...it would be so much behind...We might as well get in at an early stage."*

In terms of the electronic commerce maturity model developed by the Nolan Norton Institute for KPMG, these car dealerships were at the Experimentation Stage or Stage 1 in their adoption and use of electronic commerce (see Figure 3 below) [5]. If they are to migrate to more mature stages, then according to this model, considerable changes will be required. To achieve Stage 2, they will need to develop policies and have more of a deliberate business focus to their web-based activities. Comparatively few of the dealers interviewed seemed to believe that the car industry would ever achieve Stage 3, where transactions are completed on-line, although some thought that the Internet would over time become more and more integrated with their normal business operations.

5.3   Effect on Business

All of those interviewed said that there was little effect of the Internet on sales to date and they felt that this would remain the case for the short-term future.

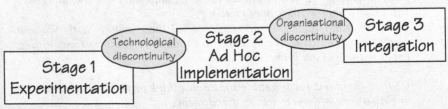

Fig. 3. Electronic Commerce Maturity Model [5:11]

> *CY4:   "New car enquiries...zero June, zero July, zero August, zero September, October to November 7 [enquiries], December zero, January 1 [enquiry]...So its zero, zero, zero..."*

The Internet, they felt, would not be a medium over which actual sales would take place, but might be a medium which would influence buyers in terms of which car dealerships that they approached. The actual selling of cars, or at least the end sub-process of selling cars, would thus remain in the hands of the car dealerships' sales persons, but the flow of customers to car dealerships might well in the future be affected by the Internet. Their sentiments very much echoed the trends that were discussed earlier in this paper with respect to the impact of electronic commerce on the American car industry.

> *CY1:* (reporting on a story he had heard about a customer) *"...I would never buy a car that way* [over the Internet]*...I want to smell it!...Computers can not open and shut the doors, I can't smell the trunk, and I can't smell the car..*(Responding to a question about whether salespeople would disappear because of the Internet) *"I don't see that happening for a long, long time in Australia."* (Responding to whether customers decision making would be informed by the Internet) *"Yeh, yeh, sure, sure I think in time it will be...I think it will be."*

However, a particular point which moderates the comments above needs to made at this juncture. None of the car yards involved in the interviews to date appeared to have any mechanism to detect whether a customer walking in did so as a result of newspaper advertising, Internet on-line buying services, referral by a satisfied customer, quite serendipitously, and the like. Thus, it appeared that none of these businesses had made any effort to find out whether their customers had conducted an initial search over the Web, and whose approach to the company was thus motivated by information obtained over the Internet.

5.4   Impact on Business Processes

Despite each of the car dealerships having web sites, the business processes of each dealership were not well integrated with the web site. It was not always clear in each dealership just how Internet based enquiries were to be dealt with nor exactly who would deal with them. All the car yards had well-established mechanisms for handling new 'walk/phone-in' customer enquiries, but they were somewhat concerned about how equitably, efficiently and effectively to deal with e-mails generated from on-line buying services. It is one thing to enable e-mail links to the organization: it is quite another to design internal business processes to ensure the e-mail is responded to appropriately. Neither did it appear the dealerships were geared up to keep good commercial records of web activity, nor ready to measure important statistics such as look-to-buy ratios. Generally speaking, they had not carefully thought out appropriate business processes to handle Internet enquiries.

> *CY1:   "Can I tell you something that would probably surprise you? I don't know."*

> *CY4:   "You've got a job to link the Internet activities to your sales people, something that changes the business a bit, with a lot of stuff made through the Internet…How do you monitor your salespeople, and then reward it?"*

5.5   Drivers and Inhibitors of Electronic Commerce

By far the major driver of developing a presence of some sort on the Internet was the fear of being left behind by competitors when (and if) 'something happened'. These business people seemed very concerned not to miss out on a business opportunity should one present itself!

> *CY8:   "It's paramount. Anyone who doesn't get into it [electronic commerce] is bloody mad!"*

The presence of competitor car dealerships on the Internet is not the only factor driving car dealerships to consider a web presence in some form. The dealerships that sell new as well as used cars are under pressure from the automobile manufacturers to have a web-site. This leads to listings of car dealerships on manufacturer's sites. These listings often include some web pages with advertisements for used cars from the dealership. However these alternative web sites are not always linked to the electronic marketplace presence of the dealer, thus illustrating that it is early days yet in the utilisation of the Internet and a well planned coordinated approach to the web has not occurred yet.

By contrast, others expressed suspicion of the concept of on-line buying and Internet-influenced sales, particularly given the fact that the electronic malls or marketplaces that were being establishing were such that each dealer was there as one among a crowd, his/her cars part of a larger pool to be searched by customers. The car dealers interviewed were clearly accustomed to regarding fellow dealers as competitors, and many seemed decidedly uncomfortable at participating in the same on-line buying service as their major rivals. However, they also had enough business acumen to realise that from a customer's perspective, such on-line buying services facilitating cross-dealer searches were an attractive proposition.

> *CY1:   "So, so, I am anti-the Internet because of its over-information in this particular instance of the car business…I don't want anything to do with other Ford dealers or Mitsubishi dealers…I mean…they are my enemy!"*

> *CY9:   "I have heard that in the USA, you can find the price that new cars are sold to dealers by the manufacturers on the Internet…I think that's obscene!"*

The other major inhibitor to electronic commerce seemed to stem from the difficulty that the senior executives interviewed seemed to be experiencing in evaluating their investment in electronic commerce. Most of these executives were looking for some sort of cost / benefit with respect to their Web and associated investments. However, at this stage, they generally felt that there were few tangible benefits to speak of other than comparatively low-cost advertising, and typically, they struggled to appreciate the 'worth' of so-called intangible benefits. This issue certainly contributed to a feeling of uncertainty about the value and impact of the Internet. Nevertheless, none of the dealers interviewed was prepared not to remain totally uninvolved until someone else (one of their competitors!) demonstrated the value of electronic commerce investments by deriving considerable business benefits from the Internet.

> CY8: "The cost of advertising is bloody expensive. And at the moment, the majority of used car advertising is in real life...predominantly newspaper...One of the big advantages with the Internet for you is the low cost of actually advertising."

5.6   Web Site Design and Management

Most of the dealers had an ad hoc approach to their web sites. Many talked about feeling pressurised by IT consultants into developing web sites without too much consideration of a planned business initiative to move into electronic commerce. The care and maintenance of the web site was not, in general, professionally planned and managed. In one case, for example, the finance manager had somewhat reluctantly inherited the task of maintaining the web site, without having any apparent great interest or expertise in the area.

> CY8: "We've been interviewed by enough web site manufacturers to sink a ship. It's a bit like "You need to get involved in our web site." But once you see the sites, you know...there's room there for someone to say "Give us $700 and we'll come back next week with your web site." Yeah, Ok. There are con-merchants, yes. There are con-merchants."

It was not always clear what policies and standards had been set for presenting individual cars and the dealership in general on the web. Sometimes a number of cars in the dealership stocks did not appear on the web site. Of those that did appear some had photographs of the car concerned and others did not. There appeared neither rhyme nor reason to these and other aspects of the web advertisements. There seemed to be a much more professional attitude and practice in dealing with conventional media such as newspapers and radio.

6   Conclusion

The car industry in Western Australia thus remains only superficially affected by the technology and presence of the Internet. Each of the major car dealerships interviewed for this study have web sites, albeit on electronic malls which seem very much like the forerunners of the powerful Internet buying services of the USA. Some, again like their US counterparts, have web sites connected to manufacturers' sites. However, their Internet site, detached from the energetic, everyday business of selling cars and making money, is the beginning and end of Internet-based commerce for the car dealerships. Cars are not selling over the Internet, and apparently in the eyes of the car dealers, people's buying behaviour is not being influenced by the Internet.

Thus, after a small burst of activity in establishing a web site so as to be prepared for electronic commerce, all has gone quiet. CEOs and senior managers are back to the main job of selling cars as usual. They are, however, quietly anxious about what might happen next week, in the next year or so, or next decade on the Internet in their industry.

What is needed is some reflective thinking and some action planning with respect to electronic commerce. If the US experience is a guide as to what will happen in Australia, then it would seem timely to plan and enact the reengineering of business processes such that the Internet and associated internal systems are well integrated with the selling processes integral to the business. Included in this will be careful monitoring of web site activity and the establishment of procedures to measure Internet-based referrals and Internet-influenced sales. For example, dealers may need to become familiar with electronic commerce metrics such as look-to-buy ratios, and so on. The new position of the car dealerships to the Internet buying service companies must be thought through as should the other new relationships in the industry supply chain. A time of moderate to significant change is approaching and some strategy formulation together with some IT and electronic commerce supporting strategy formulation would be helpful in charting an appropriate path to the future.

References

1. Applegate, L.M., Holsapple, C.W., Kalakota, R., Radermacher, F., and Whinston, A.B. (1996) Electronic commerce: building blocks of new business opportunity. *Journal of Organizational Computing and Electronic Commerce*, 6(1): 1-10.
2. Choi, S.Y., Stahl, D. and Whinston, A.B. (1998) Intermediation, contracts and micropayments in electronic commerce. *Electronic Markets*, 8(1): 20-22.
3. Davidow, W.H. and Malone, M.S. (1992) *The Virtual Corporation*. HarperCollins, NewYork.
4. Hoffman, D., Novak, T.P., and Chatterjee, P. (1999) Commercial scenarios for the web: opportunities and challenges. *Journal of Computer Mediated Communications*, 1(3) URL http://www.ascusc.org/jcmc/vol1/issue3/hoffman.htm
5. KPMG (1999) *Electronic Commerce: The Future is Here!* URL www.kpmg.com.au
6. Kvale, S. (1996) *InterViews: an Introduction to Qualitative Research Interviewing*. Sage, Thousand Oaks.
7. Laudon, K.C. and Laudon, J.P. (1999) *Management Information Systems: Organization and technology in the Networked Enterprise*. 6th ed. Prentice Hall, New Jersey.
8. Lawrence, E., Corbitt, B., Tidwell, A., Fisher, J. and Lawrence, J.R. (1998) *Internet Commerce: Digital Models for Business*. Wiley, Bridbane.
9. Maruca, R.F. (1999) Retailing: confronting the challenges that face bricks-and-mortar stores. *Harvard Business Review*, 77(4): 159-168.

10.McKay, J. (1999) *The Application of soft Management Science / Operational Research to Information requirements Analysis: a Study using Cognitive Mapping and the SODA Methodology.* Unpublished PhD thesis (under preparation), Edith Cowan University.
11.McQuivey, J.L. (1999) Used Car Buying Builds Steam, *The Forrester Brief*, March 1999, URL http://www.Forrester.com
12.McQuivey, J.L., Delhagen, K. and Ardito, C. (1999) New-Car Buying Races On-line, *The Forrester Report*, 1(10), January 1999, URL http://www.Forrester.com
13.McQuivey, J.L., Delhagen, K., Levin, K. and LaTour Kadison, M. (1998) Retail's Growth Spiral, *The Forrester Report*, 1(8), November 1998, URL http://www.Forrester.com
14.Ohlson, K. 40% of new-car shoppers use net for research. *Computerworld Online News*, 08/23/99.
15.Reynolds, J. (1987) The Internet as a strategic resource: evidence from the European retail sector. In L. Willcocks et al. (eds.) *Managing IT as a Strategic Resource.* McGraw Hill, London.
16.Robinson, K.G. (1999) E-commerce: sales and demand suppression. *Telecommunications Reports Journal*, 3(1): 17-20.
17.Salnoske, K. (1999) E-commerce in 1999: what to look for. *Telecommunications Reports Journal*, 3(1): 45-49.
18.Scharl, A. and Brandtweiner, R. (1998) A conceptual research framework for analyzing the evolution of electronic markets. *Electronic Markets*, 8(2): 39-42.
19.Stair, R.M. and Reynolds, G.W. (1999) *Principles of Information Systems*, 4th ed. Course Technology, Cambridge, MA.
20.Von Versen, K. (1999) The three commercial functions of the internet. In B. Buchet et al (eds.) EC in the Insurance Industry, *Electronic Markets*, 8(4):02/99.
21.Whiteley, D. (1999) Internet commerce – hot cakes and dead ducks. In F. Sudweeks and C.T. Romm (eds.) *Doing Business on the Internet: Opportunities and Pitfalls.* Springer, London.

Author Index